THE BIRDWATCHER
and
DIARY 20ʋ4

Designed and published by
Hilary Cromack

Edited by
David Cromack

BUCKINGHAM PRESS

in association with

Published in 2003 by:
Buckingham Press
55 Thorpe Park Road, Peterborough
Cambridgeshire PE3 6LJ
United Kingdom

01733 561739
e-mail: admin@buckinghampress.com

ISBN 0 9533840 71
ISSN 0144-364 X

Cover image: Puffins, a watercolour by Peter Partington.
Peter has written three books in the HarperCollins *Learn to Draw* series, *Farm Animals, Wildlife* and *Birds*. He prefers to paint in watercolour, followed by oils and also produces etchings. He travels widely and has many one-man shows. His work is widely collected and commissions are welcome.
Address: The Hall, Kettlebaston, Suffolk, IP7 7QA; 01449 741538; (Fax)01449 744286. e-mail: peter.partington@ kettlebaston.co.uk
www.peter-partington.fsnet.co.uk

Printed and bound in Great Britain by:
Biddles Ltd Book Manufacturers, Guildford, Surrey.

CONTENTS

CONTENTS

CONTENTS

PREFACE

COMPILING *THE YEARBBOOK* every 12 months is a mammoth undertaking for publisher Hilary Cromack each year. To update the entries, she must communicate with hundreds of individuals from all parts of the ornithological community and then spend long, long hours in front of her computer inputting and checking the new data, revising the county bird site maps, designing and laying out the features as well as undertaking all the administrative tasks needed to keep Buckingham Press functioning.

The reward comes in the form of letters, e-mails and phone calls praising the usefulness of *The Birdwatchers' Yearbook & Diary*, together with suggestions on how the next Edition might be developed. We are always grateful for this encouragement and for the sponsorship support from Swarovski UK which has enabled us to introduce colour to the Reserves and Observatories section of the book.

In 2003 two things happened to introduce *The Yearbook* to a wider audience. Swarovski used the book as part of a nationwide promotional campaign for the company's binoculars and telescopes, while Buckingham Press were able to offer copies to subscribers of the new quarterly magazine, *Birds Illustrated* before it launched in August 2003 at the British Birdwatching Fair.

Together, these two promotions put copies of *The Yearbook* into the hands of nearly a thousand non-regular readers. We trust they will find the publication is both accurate and useful and that they, along with our traditional supporters, will recommend it to their birdwatching friends.

2003 will go down as a year of great significance for Buckingham Press. One of the stalwart supporters of *The Yearbook*, Chris Mead died early in the year and we will greatly miss his enthusiastic contributions. For the past two Editions Chris had trawled the world's ornithological publications for interesting titbits of scientific discovery to compile a digest for our readers. This innovation proved very popular and this year we have secured the services of Richard Facey to provide the same service.

Tributes to Chris and his contribution to ornithology were legion and I was particularly pleased to be able to attend the Memorial Day in his honour staged in May at the Thetford headquarters of his beloved British Trust for Ornithology. We heard many tales - usually very humourous - of Chris' exploits as a bird ringer and latterly the important role he performed in publicising BTO activities via the national press. However the aspect of his life that came through most strongly was his own personal enthusiasm for birds and bird study and his ability to pass on that passion to other people.

I will not be alone in missing Chris for many years to come and I hope I can encourage readers of *The Yearbook* who have not already done so to make a contribution to the Chris Mead Memorial Appeal. The proceeds will be used by the BTO to develop the library at The Nunnery headquarters into a permanent and useful memorial to an inspirational man. Cheques, made payable to BTO, can be sent to: British Trust for Ornithology, The Nunnery, Thetford, Norfolk IP24 2PU.

Last year also saw the passing of two other eminent ornithologists, Guy Mountfort and Max Nicholson, within two days of each other in April. Both men took part in an expedition to Spain's Coto Donana national park in 1956 and Max's resulting book *Portrait of a Wilderness* played a leading part in inspiring a whole generation of young men to take up birdwatching as a prime activity. Guy went on to help create national parks in several countries and together with Roger Tory Peterson and Phil Hollom he co-authored the ground-breaking and influential *A Field Guide to the Birds of Britain and Europe* in 1954.

Trying to summarise the life and achievements of Max Nicholson is equally difficult. He was a founding member of the Wildfowl Trust, helped establish the BTO, World Wildlife Fund, IUCN (the World Conservation Organisation) and Earthwatch. He was the Director General of English Nature for 14 years and co-editor of the landmark nine-volume *Birds of the Western Palearctic*.

On a more cheerful note, 2003 saw the relaunch of *Birds Illustrated*. Originally published in the early 1990s by Emap, this high-quality A4 quarterly magazine built a circulation of around 11,000. While this established the title as the second largest seller after *Bird Watching*, sales weres not high enough to cover the overheads of a national magazine group and it was closed after two and half years. As I had conceived the magazine, I always dreamed it might make a reappearance and this year I was successful in persuading Emap to allow Buckingham Press to publish the magazine under licence.

Though *Birds Illustrated* will shortly be available for sale at Wildfowl & Wetland Trust centres and selected RSPB reserves, it will primarily be a subscription-only magazine. Advertising within it will be strictly limited so that authors have the space to develop essay-length articles on a wide range of bird-related topics. As the name suggests, there is a heavy emphasis on bird art and photography and our overall goal is to create the world's most beautiful bird magazine. Cover price is £5, but we are happy to make sample copies available to Buckingham Press customers at £4 (including postage and packing). Alternatively the introductory subscription offer of four copies for just £15.80 is still available - contact Buckingham Press on 01733 561 739.

Also making its debut at the British Birdwatching Fair was our latest county-based guide *Best Birdwatching Sites in Sussex*, written by two enthusiastic birdwatchers Adrian Thomas and Peter Francis. This book follows the format of the acclaimed *Best Birdwatching Sites in Norfolk* (Neil Glenn) which broke new ground in several ways. Both titles assess each site for disabled access and public transport provision and provocatively offer readers a percentage rating of how likely they are to see specific key species at each site. All these features have been greatly appreciated by purchasers of the Norfolk guide and we anticipate that the Sussex book will meet with high levels of approval, too. In spring 2004 Buckingham Press intends to publish *Best Birdwatching Sites in the Highlands of Scotland* by Gordon Hamlett.

Finally, I would like to draw your attention to the black and white line illustrations that grace this issue. For the past two Editions we have published work from the *British Birds* Illustrator of the Year competition, but as this was not run in 2003 we approached competitors from previous years to submit work. We are grateful for their support and Buckingham Press is giving active consideration to organising an artwork competition in 2004 to encourage more artists to continue with pen and ink and scraperboard illustration. The competition is likely to be promoted in *Birds Illustrated* and *Bird Watching* magazines.

David Cromack EDITOR

Key contributors in this Edition

BO BEOLENS is the founder of the Fatbirder website and the Disabled Birders Association. The latter organisation is open to all people interested in campaigning for better birdwatching facilities and trasport infra structure.

RICHARD FACEY is interested in all wildlife, although birds are definitely his favourite and were part of the reason for taking a degree in zoology. He is a keen birder and photographer and his main interests are bird behaviour and evolution. He has worked for the RSPB doing upland bird surveys in the Scottish Borders.

GORDON HAMLETT, a freelance writer, is a regular contributor to *Bird Watching* magazine, both as a reviewer of books and computer software and also as sub-editor of the UK Bird Sightings section. Gordon is an incorrigable net surfer and once again he has valiantly trawled the internet for our Annual Website Survey.

PETER PARTINGTON has written three books in the HarperCollins *Learn to Draw* series, *Farm Animals, Wildlife* and *Birds*. He prefers to paint in watercolour, followed by oils and also produces etchings. He travels widely and has many one man-shows.

RON TOFT is a professional freelance journalist interested in wildlife topics. He has previously written articles for *Bird Watching* magazine.

MIKE UNWIN is not only a talented illustrator, winning the Bird Illustrator of the Year award in 2001, but also divides his time between editing natural history books, writing and photography. His latest book published by Bradt, is *Southern African Wildlife - A Visitor's Guide* and features many of his own pieces of artwork.

OUR SPECIAL THANKS go to Chris Hamlett, Cherry Hadley, Alex Williams and Derek Toomer for their help with putting this edition of the *Yearbook* together. We would also like to thank all of our contacts in the various bird groups and clubs, bird reserves and national organisations as it would be impossible to produce this book without their continued support and assistance.

FEATURES

Slavonian Grebes by Thelma Sykes

SCIENTIFIC DISCOVERIES IN 2003

(A REVIEW OF THE YEAR'S LITERATURE)

Keeping abreast of the world's ornithological publications is an almost impossible task. To ensure you don't miss anything interesting, we are pleased to present this digest of reports compiled by Richard Facey. Illustrations are by Mike Unwin.

Population trends of upland species

UPLAND HABITATS, which account for a third of the UK's landscape, provide an important environment for a variety of birds, including several species of conservation concern. Unfortunately, modest amounts of long term monitoring means researchers know little of the population trends of many upland birds.

An attempt to remedy this, the RSPB, in collaboration with the Countryside Council for Wales, English Nature and DEFRA, re-surveyed upland sites in 2002 last visited between 1977 and 1991.

Though population trends for any particular species varied from site to site, general trends were gleaned. Between surveys the populations of species such as Wren, Stonechat and Raven have increased, while the populations of other have declined.

The Ring Ouzel was among species such as the Lapwing, Curlew and Dunlin which showed declining populations. The Ring Ouzel is one of our least known species, but has shown a worrying 58% decline within the UK. Two RSPB studies have helped to fill the gap in our knowledge.

Looking into the Ring Ouzel's ecology, the first study revealed that while the species' home range contains a wide variety of habitats, the birds were found to prefer grassland as foraging sites, but favoured heather for nesting, especially on steeper slopes.

The second study, looking at what factors correlated with the decline in numbers, revealed that the declines were greatest in less steep areas, and greatest at the extremes of the species' altitudinal range. Further more the Ring Ouzel's population was found to have declined more in areas with a greater covering of conifer plantations.

Following the Flamingo

BENT BILLS, pink plumage and lanky legs, make flamingos unmistakable birds. With a history dating back at least 30 million years, the five species alive today represent the remnants of an old family, yet little is known about certain aspects of their lives.

A project headed by the Wildfowl and Wetlands Trust (WWT) hopes to change this. By tagging several Lesser Flamingos, WWT hopes to uncover some of the mystery surrounding the movements of this species.

Satelite tracking may uncover some surprises in terms of Lesser Flamingo movements.

The Lesser Flamingo (*Phoeniconaias minor*), smallest of the five species, outnumbers the combined populations of the other species, but it is considered 'near threatened' due to its reliance on a small number of breeding sites. Successful breeding has only been recorded in three areas in the past 30 years, with 90% of the breeding population being found on Lake Natron in Tanzania.

Lesser Flamingos are a nomadic species, with birds moving from lake to lake. Small, lightweight transmitters have been attached to three birds to allow their movements to be monitored. The units weigh around 35g, are solar powered and each sends out a unique identification code that is picked up by satellites. The satellites then relay this information to a ground station where the birds' positions can be triangulated.

By tracking the movements of the three birds, named Safari, Imara, and Bahati, the WWT hopes to identify if the birds have 'home lakes' and which areas are used most frequently. This information will go a long way to protecting the Lesser Flamingo's wetland habitats, which are under threat from Man's activities. Furthermore it is hoped that this study will reveal whether there is a link between the east African and southern African populations. In the past these have been considered separate, but recently evidence has come to light that suggests that there may be significant movement of birds between the two populations.

Already the Flamingo Tracking Project has proved its worth. On July 1, scientist working on the project spotted one bird which is believed to have been ringed while nesting in 1962, making it the oldest known wild flamingo known, at 40 years of age.

News species discovered

THE WORLD of birds is dynamic, especially when it comes to new species. Taxonomic reviews often result in a species split here and new taxa there,. Though this boosts the global species list, the 'new' species are already wellknown to birdwatchers and scientists. however from time to time the list is swelled by the discovery of new species previously unknown to science. In the last 12 months Brazil has provided two bombshells.

While birdwatching in Caxiuanã, Brazil, Andrew Whittaker heard the call of an unfamiliar Forest-falcon and on seeing the bird, he became convinced he had found a new species. Though the bird resembled the Lined Forest-falcon (*Micrastur gilvicollis*), subtle plumage differences prompted the ornithologist to examine specimens held by the Museu Paraenese Emílio Goeldi. He found that 23 of these were a dead match for the bird he had seen in the field.

The new species, aptly named the Cryptic Forest-Falcon (*M. mintoni*), has a slightly longer tail, more contrasting nape and crown, and a more orange breast. The future for the Cryptic Forest-falcon looks reasonably good in certain parts of its range, but the future of Brazil's newest owl is not so good.

After comparing specimens collected from the Pernambuco state, Brazil, scientists realised they had discovered a new species of Pygmy owl. Though it has taken 23 years to be recognised, the newly described Pernambuco Pygmy-owl (*Gucidium mooreorum*), has already been put forward for classification as 'critically endangered'. The Atlantic Forests it calls home is one of the most endangered habitats on the planet, with less than 10% of its original cover remaining. It is ironic that just as we gain a new species we are in immediate danger of losing it.

Slump in the Sub-continent

DENTIFYING the causes of decline in bird species can be tricky. Scientists from the Institute of Zoology, RSPB and the Bombay Natural History Society, are still mystified about drastic declines in three of India's vulture species, the Indian White-rumped (*Gyps bengalenis*), the Long-billed (*G. indicus*) and the Slender-billed Vultures (*G.tenuirostris)*.

The ornithologists found that the populations of the three species had declined by more than 90% since the early 1990s, but causes have been hard to pinpoint.

There has been no decline in food sources, and as the decline has occurred in protected and unprotected areas, persecution is not likely. Disease seems to be the most likely cause and if this is the case then this could become a global problem for the Gyps genus. Griffon Vulture (*G.fulvus*) and Himalayan Vulture (*G.himalayensis*) have both breeding and wintering populations within India and have been seen feeding alongside the sub-continent's other Gyps species. These species, through association, could transfer this problem from India into the wider world.

This situation raises some interesting questions. With many of our raptor species enjoying a wide distribution, with close relatives, across much of

White-rumped and Slender-billed Vultures at a carcass.

Europe and the Northern Hemisphere, what would be the effect of an infectious disease on them? How or could we contain its effects?

Future research will explore the role of the anti-inflammatory drug, diclofenac, which has been implicated in the deaths of Gyps vultures in Pakistan. The vultures are exposed to the drug, now used extensively in veterinary medicine since being banned for humans, as a result of scavenging from livestock carcasses. At this point it is uncertain if the drug is connected to vulture deaths in India.

Flying for food

THE MODERN farming landscape is a patchwork mosaic of varying habitats, meaning that seed-eating birds now have to travel to find an adequate supply of food during the winter months. But exactly how far are they required to travel?

A pilot study undertaken by the Tay Ringing Group and BTO Scotland set out to answer this very question. Using a combination of mark and recapture, and radio tracking at four ringing sites, the team monitored the movements of three granivorous bird species, Tree Sparrow (*Passer montanus*), Chaffinch (F*ringilla coelebs*) and Yellowhammer (*Emberiza citrinella*).

The three species had very different patterns of movement. Tree Sparrows were by far the most mobile, moving to sites up to 3km apart in a four week period, while Chaffinches were the least mobile. Yellowhammers showed movements between the two.

The patterns shown by the different species reflects the variety of habitats they utilise in order to find food. Tree Sparrows were found in a restricted range of habitats, only using certain stubble fields. Yellowhammers also used pasture and scrub. Chaffinches, by comparison, made the most of a wide range of habitats, allowing them to stay in a more restricted range than the more specialist Tree Sparrows.

Hungry Harriers

DELIBERATE PERSECUTION, agri-chemical use and habitat loss are often cited for the demise of raptors such as Hen Harrier Circus cyaneus), but recent research on the Scottish island of Orkney indicates lack of food as the probable cause of decline. Numbers have been falling since the late 1970s when an average of 69 breeding females were recorded. By the late 1990s only 25 were present. A team of scientists postulated that the decline was due to a shortage of available prey.

In a three year study, scientists looked at how the ability of male Hen Harriers on Orkney to provide food for incubating females affected their breeding performance. It then compared them to males from a stable population in Langholm, southern Scotland

Both before laying and during incubation, female harriers rely on the male to provide them with food. Females that do not receive enough food usually fail to breed, either because they are not in good enough condition to lay, or have to desert the nest to hunt, leaving it prone to predation or exposure.

When the scientists compared the two populations they found that the males from Langholm were better at providing food and had a better breeding success. It was estimated that almost half the females and a quarter of the male harriers on Orkney, did not breed.

The researchers believe that changes in land use have decreased the availability of prey for Hen Harriers. Between 1960 and 1998 the amount of land under pasture increased from 36% to more than 50%. This, coupled with increased stock densities, resulted in a significant loss of rough grassland, the harriers' favoured hunting terrain.

On the wave of a crest

IT APPEARS that at least in the Shag (*Phalacrocorax aristotelis*), an answer has been found to the long standing question 'does size matter?'.

New research provides a clear link between breeding success and the size of a Shag's crest.

At the start of the breeding season, prior to pair formation, both male and female Shags grow a crest of feathers as sexual ornamentation. Research into the part these play in partner selection has been directed mainly at males, but more recently ornithologists have been examining both sexes.

The group took pictures of both male and female Shags once they had developed their crests and used a group of volunteers to grade the size of the crests displayed by each bird from one (small) to five (large).

Using this data the team then looked at how crest size related to the birds' breeding success. This led to some very interesting discoveries, which were published in *Ibis* in 2003.

The study was carried out on the Isle of May, Scotland, in 1999, which proved to be a bad breeding year for this particular colony. Failed breeders, both male and female birds, were all ranked as having the smallest crests. Out of the birds that did breed those with the largest crests bred earlier than their less well endowed counterparts. Furthermore, the males with the most prominent crests mated with bigger crested females.

The team believe that crest size acts as a signal to birds of both sexes, telling potential partners about an individual's nutritional state or their ability to obtain resources such as food or a nest site. (*Ibis* 145, pages 54-60)

Mordern Farming Makes Doves Suffer

BRITISH FARMLAND has become so unfriendly to Turtle Doves, they are incapable of raising the traditional three broods a year and BTO surveys have shown that the population has declined by 75% while its range has been reduced by a quarter.

Now a group of scientists from the Game Conservancy Trust has reported results from a five year study in the March-April edition of *BTO News*. Using a variety of techniques, including radio tracking and faecal analysis, data from on-going BTO surveys such as the Common Bird Census and Nest Record Scheme, the scientists examined how the breeding ecology of the Turtle Dove has changed as farming practices have developed.

The species historically relied on weed seeds, but has now switched its diet to nutritionally inferior cultivated seeds; a change probably linked to an increase in herbicide use. Cultivated seeds are only available to the birds once they have been harvested, usually when the bird's breeding season is coming to a close, and represent a source variable in both space and time. This affects both the bird's ranging behaviour and home range size. One bird was tracked flying more than ten kilometres to feed!

Turtle Doves were recorded making long flights to find enough food to survive.

The bird's favoured nesting site - thorny, overgrown hedges – have also become fewer in the modern intensified agricultural landscape. Such hedges are usually kept in check and are not allowed to develop fully, resulting in potentially fewer nest sites.

The team also studied data from bird observatories, and found that the Turtle Dove's breeding season has become almost two weeks shorter, with birds arriving later and leaving earlier. All this seems to have combined to reduce the breeding output of the Turtle Dove. In the 1960s, pairs laid about three clutches of eggs and successfully fledged approximately two young. These figures have fallen to roughly two and one respectively.

The researchers point out that other factors such as shooting on migration and degradation of over-wintering habitat have also contributed to Turtle Dove population decline.

YOUR GUIDE TO WEBSITES COVERING OVERSEAS BIRDS AND BIRDING LOCATIONS

Let Gordon Hamlett be your guide to some of the most useful websites when it comes to investigating birdwatching locations outside Britain and researching birds in all parts of the globe.

PLANNING for a birdwatching trip can be one of the great joys in life and really serves to heighten the sense of anticipation. What birds will I see? Which reserves can I get to? How should I plan my itinerary? How many species can I expect to see?

The Internet now makes this research relatively straightforward. There are plenty of trip reports so you can whet your appetite by reading the experiences of those who have gone before. There are links to reserves, site guides and places where you can tap into local knowledge. With luck, someone on the net may even offer to show you around, saving you any amount of time and frustration.

One of the best sources of information is to sign up to the local mailing list for your chosen area. Post a letter saying that you are heading for a particular destination, looking for any information on the best places to go etc. Not only will you get information on birds, but also suggestions for places to stay, the best restaurants and so on. Who knows? You might even strike up a life-long friendship.

This year's selection of websites looks at birding outside of the UK. Paradoxically, though there are many more sites to look at, the final selection is shorter than in recent years for a variety of reasons. As it would be easy to include more than 100 pages about Texas alone, for instance, it was decided to confine this survey by and large to sites that cover an entire country or geographical area. Most of these have links to the various states or regions within that country and details about individual reserves.

Much of the information on birding abroad comes from tour companies, advertising their various products as they attempt to sell you holidays. These are a great source of information and you would do well to explore them, though, for the purposes of this book, commercial sites have been omitted.

I've included pages only where much of the content is written in English. This again automatically excludes thousands of pages. If you are lucky enough to be fluent in another language, then you will find plenty more sites to visit.

There is a lot of local information available on wildlife that never turns up on birding mega-links sites. For example, hotels' websites often have sections on nearby attractions and these often include wildlife.

ANNUAL WEBSITE SURVEY

Try putting ' < name of the place in which you are interested > and either 'wildlife' or 'bird*' into your favourite search engine and see what comes back (I recommend www.google.com) If you have not come across the use of an '*' in searching before, it acts as a wild card so that 'bird*' finds all references to bird, birds, birding, birdwatching etc.

I am always happy to hear about your favourite sites. Please email any suggestions to me at gordon.hamlett@btinternet.com

HOW TO USE THIS GUIDE

Many of the listed websites are so wide-ranging it is almost impossible to categorise them simply. However, to try to help you find the most pertinent sites first we have divided the list into the following categories:

GENERAL

Bird-orientated websites
Books and maps
Broad-based sites to aid trip planning
Location-orientated websites
Trip reports

CONTINENT-BY-CONTINENT

Africa
America, Central and South
America, North
Antarctica and Australasia
Asia
Europe

GENERAL

BIRD-ORIENTATED SITES

http://www.birdlife.net/
From a simple looking home page, there is a wealth of information available on the BirdLife International site, which is devoted to threatened species and habitats across the world. Particularly impressive is the data zone where you can find out the current status and threats for any given site or species.

http://www.bsc-eoc.org/avibase/avibase.jsp
Wow! All the birds of the world – including subspecies – in one massive database of one million records. There are taxonomic details and distribution maps. One nice touch is that searches are already set up so that you click on buttons for Google text and image searches. If you want to research any given species of bird, then start here.

http://members.aol.com/sbsp/index.html
Though this is a commercial site for a bird recording program for your PC, the company is prepared to send you a free checklist for anywhere in the world. All you have to do is send them an email. Could be ideal for that holiday of a lifetime.

http://www.ornitaxa.com/SM/New/NewSpecies.html
If you must keep bang up to date with the latest discoveries in the ornithological world, then this site has information and references on 75 new or recently discovered species. Or not, as the case may be, given the current state of taxonomic flux. There are a few photographs and links where available.

http://www.printablebirdchecklists.homestead.com/index.html
If you are looking for a checklist to take with you on holiday, try this site. Not every country is covered yet, but it tends to be only the obscure ones that are missing. The main problem is that there is only one tick box per species. It would be nice to have 15 or so to allow for different days/trips to be recorded.

http://www.zoonomen.net/
If you want a detailed checklist of all the birds in the world, then here it is. The bad news is that it is scientific names only. There are biographies of all the key players eg Linnaeus and a full range of appropriate citations but this is probably one for the hardcore taxonomy buff.

BOOKS AND MAPS

http://www.nhbs.com
http://www.wildlifebooks.com/
http://www.wildsounds.co.uk/
Choosing the right field guide to accompany your trip is obviously very important. The three companies listed above all specialise in natural history books and which one you choose to use regularly is a matter of personal taste. It is worth checking them all periodically though as they have assorted special offers throughout the year.

Remember to check too for multimedia items such as videos, tapes, CDs and CD-ROMs. Wildsounds is the best for telling you about forthcoming titles, though NHBS will send you a monthly email of new titles.

http://www.abebooks.co.uk/
One of my all-time favourite sites, this is the number one place to try to find secondhand books. Even if the book you want is still in print, given the huge price of buying new, you may well be able to find a cheaper copy here. The site works by linking thousands of secondhand dealers across the world and forming one giant database of about 40 million titles.

http://www.birdbooksdirect.com/index.htm
Another specialist site, though this time something of a hybrid in so much as it offers new and secondhand titles. There was a major site development taking place at the time of writing so the final website may differ from the above description.

http://www.bookbrain.co.uk/
This site will find the cheapest online price for you but, and it is a big but, it will only search 14 mainstream sites so there is a chance that you will not be able to find a specialist title and have to resort to trying one of the sites listed above.

http://www.stanfords.co.uk/
If you are planning your own trip, you are going to need maps. This is a commercial site but it specialises in maps, charts and travel guides for the whole world and you should be able to find just what you want before you go. They have a selection of bird books too, though you will find a wider choice at a specialist bird book retailer.

BROAD-BASED SITES TO AID TRIP PLANNING

http://www.birdforum.net/
If all your other researches have turned up a blank, you can always ask other birders for help. Bird Forum is growing all the time with about 2,800 members posting 300 messages/day at the time of writing. The discussion group is subdivided: identification, books, trip reports, digiscoping, recent sightings etc. so it easy to just check the bits which will interest most. One other advantage is that it is all moderated so you get none of the personal abuse that mars other groups.

http://www.birdingpal.org/
A fantastic idea. Birders all round the world submit their details so that other birders can contact them for local information and/or guided trips. While you are at it, why not sign up and offer your expertise to others?

http://www.bsc-eoc.org/links/links.jsp
You simply can't have enough mega-links sites bookmarked; they all have their strengths and weaknesses. This one – Bird Links to the World – currently boasts more than 16,000 links. Again, you can click on a map of the world to zoom in on the area in which you are particularly interested.

http://dir.groups.yahoo.com/dir/Recreation___Sports/Outdoors/Birding
Another directory of assorted mailing lists covering all matters birding. At my last visit, there were 446 such groups listed and described. Many of the groups have open archives so you can see the sorts of things discussed before you sign up.

http://www.camacdonald.com/birding/birding.htm
This is the site I always start with when researching a country for the first time. Pick your continent and then country and you are presented with a whole list of useful links, trip reports, checklists etc. First class.

http://www.expedia.co.uk
So, you've read all the trip reports and planned your itinerary down to the last bit of marsh. All you need to do now is book your plane tickets. Expedia isn't necessarily the cheapest option but it is pretty competitive and gives you an excellent choice of just what's on offer at any given time. Choose your destination and date of travel and it tells you what's available, sorted by price. You can book online.

http://www.fatbirder.com/
Another mega-links site and another mandatory inclusion in your favourites list. There are plenty of other sections too, not just foreign birding, so this should help you find most of your Internet birding needs. As with all portals like this, there are a few broken links and a tendency to try to include everything regardless of quality.

http://www.fatbirder.com/links/signpost_and_discussion/mailing_lists.html
There are any number of discussion groups from all round the world, talking about birds in various countries and regions, specific groups of birds, scientific studies. This is an excellent guide to many of the mailing lists available, together with clear instructions for joining.

www.fco.gov.uk
Before you travel abroad, it is always worth checking the current state of play of your destination country with the Foreign Office. From the main page, head to the travel section then pick your country for advice of health, travel, visas, crime, local customs etc.

http://www.guidedbirding.com/
Try this site if you are looking to hire a guide to take you out birding; there are contacts worldwide. Alternatively, if you are a guide, you can pay for an entry on the website. Still being developed, the largely good layout really needs many more contacts. The scrolling 'late news' box is a waste of space. If it's worth writing down, then do it properly.

LOCATION-ORIENTATED WEBSITES

http://www.odci.gov/cia/publications/factbook/index.html
If you want to do any background research on the country you plan to visit, the chances are, the CIA (yes, that CIA) already knows the answer. What is more, those nice friendly spies have decided to share that information with you. There is absolutely nothing about birds as far as I can tell, but this is a huge resource for just about everything else.

http://proaction.tripod.com/
Proact is a non-political organisation co-ordinating campaigns and lobbying governments about their concerns for the environment, particularly where birds are concerned. Some campaigns such as the problems with Malta are well known but others, while mostly Eurocentric, spread as far as Siberia.

http://www.skof.se/lank/andra/fagelstation.htm
There are links here to bird observatories and ringing stations around the world. Being Scandinavian in origin, they are at their strongest in that part of the world though they helpfully tell you if a site has English text. There are plenty of other birding links too.

http://www.unep-wcmc.org/protected_areas/
If you are interested in researching protected areas worldwide, then the United Nations Environment Programme site has plenty of information available, both via the site itself or through assorted links. The higgledy-piggledy layout is totally non-intuitive and a sense of frustration soon sets in. A good site for casual browsers who don't care where they end up!

TRIP REPORTS

http://www3.ns.sympatico.ca/maybank/main.htm
Don't be put off by the basic design. Once you work your way through the menus,

there are hundreds of reports covering North and South America – there were more than 50 listed for Alaska alone.

http://www.birdtours.co.uk/
Currently featuring more than 500 trip reports from more than 100 countries and including an estimated 8,500 species. Site navigation could be improved, as there are currently tiny links to the different countries. They seem to get in the way of the adverts!

http://www.camacdonald.com/birding/tripreports/TripReports.html
An excellent selection of reports, mainly from the old world. No new reports are being accepted, so the information won't be bang up to date.

http://www.eurobirding.com/tripreports/
This site went online just as I was finishing this article and pretty impressive it looks, too. It aims to be a portal to all trip reports online and currently has access to 2,800. Filters that allow you to select reports according to area, time of year, author and language further help the blissfully uncluttered interface.

http://johnbirding.wolweb.nl/
This is only a small site but it is well presented and there are some excellent reports here, biased towards Central and Southern America. The reports include sketch maps, colour photos and sound samples.

www.surfbirds.com
Another site with a good selection of up-to-date reports from around the world. Reports vary in length from a couple of pages to some truly monumental efforts. With more and more birders using digital cameras, an increasing number are illustrated.

http://www.ukbishosting.co.uk/FBRIS/index.htm
With so many trip reports available for free on the net, it is difficult to imagine why anyone would want to pay for them. But, if you can't find what you want elsewhere, have a look here for another 1,800 reports. No prices are given online, you have to write off for a quote.

http://worldtwitch.virtualave.net
Aimed at 'Finding rare birds around the world', this is more for the traveller prepared to venture deep into the rain forest or jungle in search of that elusive tick. Somewhat confused style and plenty of incredibly annoying pop-up adverts. Good selection of foreign links.

CONTINENT-BY-CONTINENT

AFRICA & THE MIDDLE EAST

http://www.africanbirdclub.org/
As the name suggests, this club is interested in all matters African and there are selected articles and features as well as a downloadable checklist. The main problem is that there seems to be no-one in the club interested in maintaining the website – the latest bit of 'news' was 18 months old when I last checked.

East & West Africa

http://www.gambiabirding.org/
A useful basic introduction to birding in Gambia, one of the most popular African destinations. There is a basic site guide, travel information, tips and suggestions for hiring a guide, conservation news and a page of recent sightings.

http://www.kenyabirds.org.uk/
Don't be put off by the fairly basic page design. There is a phenomenal amount of information here on Kenya, one of Africa's most popular birding destinations. Trip reports, articles, lists, pictures of all the species, up to date sightings, site guides, it's all here.

North Africa and the Middle East

http://www.arabianwildlife.com/main.htm
Though it doesn't appear to have been updated since 2001, there is a lot of

information here about Arabian wildlife, including all the articles from their magazine. There are some basic articles on birding and an annotated list of species though this is in alphabetic rather than systematic order. The flashing screen will be a distraction to some users.

http://www.birds.org.il
This is a must-see site for anyone interested in migration. Click on the 'English' button in the top right (unless you are fluent in Hebrew) and then enjoy assorted radar maps of birds moving through Israel. You can also follow the fortunes of assorted satellite-tracked storks and pelicans etc.

http://www.birdingegypt.com/
Though there is plenty going on here, with nearly 20 main sections, I came away feeling that the good-looking Birding Egypt site was just lacking a little in depth; there was only the odd paragraph where you were crying out for half a page or so of information or more photos etc. Then I looked at the 'latest sightings', which were two years out of date. Even so, there is some good information here with the potential to make it outstanding if someone puts in the time and effort.

http://www.birdingisrael.com/index.html
Details of recent sightings and migration news, plenty of colour photos, checklists, where-to-watch guide and plenty of trip reports. The only problem was that there was so much information, I kept getting lost in the navigations. All in all, an excellent introduction to the area.

http://www.birdlifemed.org/index.html
BirdLife International has identified nearly 400 sites as important bird areas in the Middle East. At the moment, there is only a broad overview of these sites. If their other websites are anything to go by though, presumably full details of the sites and their importance will be published in one large, searchable database.

http://www.ifrance.com/Go-South/
Everything you wanted to know about Morocco but were afraid to ask. Plenty of trip reports, systematic list and basic site guide etc. you can e-mail the authors for more detailed site information but the information will be in French. A good but very annoying site with too many pop-up adverts and a 'force to front' system which makes it impossible to work on other documents at the same time.

http://www.osme.org/index.html
For anyone with a major interest in the area, the pages of OSME (Ornithological Society of the Middle East) will make for essential reading. As well as selected articles from their journal, there is a comprehensive selection of trip reports and an impressive selection of links to other sites in the area.

Southern Africa

http://www.sabirding.co.za/birdspot/index.htm
This site covers some of the birding hotspots across the whole of Southern Africa, though with a decided bias towards South Africa itself. Some of the other sections of the website, including, strangely, the home page are being revamped and didn't work at the time of writing. One annoying feature is that the links to individual species only work if you have purchased the appropriate CD-ROM. Very naughty.

http://www.zestforbirds.co.za/
Largely, though not exclusively, concerned with pelagic birding out of South Africa, this site has an excellent series of statistics, photographs, trip reports etc though it could do with a more recent update as far as the 'news' is concerned. Well worth visiting if only for the gruesome pictures of a squid eating a skua - from the inside!

AMERICA, CENTRAL AND SOUTH

http://www.neotropicalbirdclub.org
The main aim of this site is to persuade you to join the Neotropical Bird Club. There is not a lot of information available for casual browsers, just the odd article and news story taken from the club magazine – *Cotinga*. Just think how a photo gallery, trip reports, tourist information and checklists could improve interest in the area.

Central America and the Caribbean

http://www.belizebirds.com/
This is another website still in a fairly embryonic state but prospects look good. Already, there is a printable checklist, trip reports, and database of relevant bird literature. Hundreds of photos are promised in the near future. Someone is taking this site very seriously.

http://www.cubanbirds.com/home.htm
With Cuba becoming an increasingly popular destination, not least because of its good list of endemic species, this site provides a good introduction to birding on the island. There are photographs, videos, sounds and checklists, showing what you can expect to see as well as a page of useful tourist information. A good introduction rather than detailed specifics.

http://www.quetzalcam.org/
Quetzals and hummingbirds on webcams are the highlights here though there is a lot of other information on cloudforests, albeit at a level more likely to appeal to younger members of the family. Navigation of this Costa Rican site is not wonderful, but the information is there – somewhere.

South America

http://www.imarpe.gob.pe/aves/homepage.html
You would think that with twice as many birds as the whole of North America, Peruvian ornithologists would find something really exotic to keep them happy. But no, like mad birders the world over, they get drawn first and foremost to seabirds. This site details the latest knowledge, threats and research. Some nice photos but awful wallpaper impairs the readability.

http://www.museum.lsu.edu/~Remsen/SACCBaseline.html
Like it or loathe it, taxonomic studies of birds and where each species fits into the grand scheme of things, are quite important as far as scientists are concerned. This site offers a heavily annotated list of all the South American species, including hypothetical inclusions and hybrids.

http://www.natureserve.org/infonatura/index.html
This site is a searchable database of more than 5,500 species, giving information on their conservation status. You can search by common or scientific name as well as in Spanish and Portuguese. Large, clear maps show the countries where the birds occur though not their actual distribution. Mammals are also included.

http://www.tc.umn.edu/~mulho005/plain.html
This personal site has downloadable checklists for Ecuador and Peru as well as several trip reports. You can also print off assorted indices for various field guides. If you like style as well as substance, there is a link to a snazzier version of the site that requires you to have Flash installed.

http://www.venezuelavoyage.com/birdvenezuela/index.htm
Like birding in Venezuela, this site is still in its infancy though the author claims big developments by 2004. At the moment, there are a few basic details including the top ten birding sites, a couple of reviews, a few basic articles and a useful series of links to other Venezuelan sites.

AMERICA, NORTH

Canada

http://www.birdinfo.com/index.html
Centred on British Columbia, the North American Bird Information Site is still being developed. Already though, there is a nice selection of photos, database of species, recent sightings and site guide. One section is devoted to tricky gull identification. Worth keeping an eye on if development continues.

http://www.web-nat.com/bic/
Plenty of information about birding all over Canada and particularly strong on Ontario. When you decide where you are going, you will probably want to drop down to sites on a more provincial level for extra details.

United States of America

http://www.abcbirds.org
'Environmental concerns' and 'Americans' aren't always comfortable bedfellows so it is good to see the American Bird Conservancy trying to spread the message. There are details of all the globally important bird areas in the US, plus campaigns on educating cat owners etc. You can sign up for free newsletters by email.

http://www.americanbirding.org
Given the excellence of their magazines, I had high hopes of the American Birding Association's site but it is a huge disappointment. Certainly it is slick if you want to join, or buy anything or know anything about the organisation, but there is nothing about birds or birding to generate any excitement. A classic case of producing something for management rather than users.

http://www.audubon.org/
The American equivalent of the RSPB, the Audubon Society's site has plenty of information about the society, its work and current conservation projects. One unusual aspect is the digitised images of all John James Audubon's paintings, more than 500 in all.

http://www.birdingamerica.com
A cracking little personal site that just bubbles with enthusiasm, it is produced by a lone woman and her camera birding across America, recording the birds and reserves she sees en route. There are nearly 200 locations ranging from back gardens, through major reserves to pelagic trips. As you read the notes and look at the pictures, you continually feel 'I want to be there.'

http://www.birdphotography.com/index.html
Though intended as a commercial site, there are up four photographs for some 347 species (and increasing all the time), which you can browse freely. Though the resolution is low, it is more than adequate for screen viewing. The standard of the pictures is pretty high.

http://www.birdzilla.com
I didn't particularly like most of this site, but it does have links to more than 8,000 pages of information on around 900 North American species taken from Bent's *Life Histories*, together with photographs and some songs.

http://www.enature.com
Among the various commercial bits, there are 13 different photographic field guides, covering everything from birds through trees and plants to butterflies and shoreline creatures. There's a separate section on birding and garden wildlife.

http://www.partnersinflight.org/
Partners in Flight was originally set up to monitor endangered land birds not covered by other treaties or conservation programmes. Since then, it has spread somewhat. Though this is a heavy-duty site, it is well laid out and the database – which is being added to all the time, has lot of information on Neotropical and Hawaiian birds that is difficult to find elsewhere.

ANTARCTICA AND AUSTRALASIA

http://www.70south.com/resources/animals
With sections on penguins, other birds, seals, whales and other marine animals, this is a great place to start for a trip to Antarctica. Coverage is mixed - some species get audio and video clips, others need even a photo. There is plenty of other information too, ranging from current research projects to stuff for sale.

http://www.ausbird.com/
No doubt about it, if you plan to visit Australia, then you must start here. There is information on books and mailing lists and any number of links to other Australian birding sites. If you can't find what you want here, it probably doesn't exist.

http://www.birdsaustralia.com.au
If you have a serious interest in Australian birds, then you might want to consider joining Birds Australia, a sort of antipodean equivalent of the BTO. This site has plenty of information on threatened species as well as details on assorted reserves and observatories.

http://www.nzbirds.com
This site from New Zealand has a very homely feel to it with plenty of personal anecdotes and Maori mythology as well as suggested B&B accommodation. There are illustrated pages on all the country's birds as well as a few sample bird songs.

http://www.pacificbirds.com/index.html
Covering some of the Pacific Islands including Niue, Samoa, Tonga, Tokelau, Wallis & Futuna, Tuvalu and Fiji, there are a few trip reports, checklists for all the various islands and reviews of the field guides currently available. Some of the lists have formatting problems but otherwise, you would be hard pressed to find this information elsewhere.

http://users.bigpond.net.au/palliser/pelagic/index.html
This site will excite anyone who loves seabirds and is into pelagic trips, here running out of Sydney and Wollongong. Not only is there detailed statistical analysis showing what species you can expect to see in which month, but also a series of mind-blowing close-up photographs of some of the species. The main problem is finding the page you want in a very poorly designed internal navigation system.

ASIA

http://asianbird.zo.ntu.edu.tw/checklist.htm
This simple site provides a checklist of all the breeding landbirds in East Asia. You can opt for non-passerines, passerines of the full list, which amounts to 2,408 species. The list was last updated in 2001 so won't show the very latest additions.

http://www.orientalbirdclub.org/index.html
As well as being able join the Oriental Bird Club, you can also read a couple of articles online from all their recent bulletins. There is also a photographic library of more than 1,400 images for you to browse, though navigating backwards and forwards through these is cumbersome.

http://www.rdb.or.id/index.html
The Red Data Book concerns itself with threatened species and this site contains the latest information for every such species in Asia. Well laid out, you can browse by content, country or species and in turn, the species can be sorted by scientific name, common name or taxonomic order. This is just what the Internet should be about. Information can be easily updated and it saves you having to buy a 3,000-page book.

Asian islands

http://www5b.biglobe.ne.jp/~raptor/index.htm
The Asian Raptor Migration Page is a fairly recent site and has records going back to autumn 1999. All records are welcome. There is a gallery of photographs and a good section of links for anyone interested in raptors.

http://cjvlang.info/Birds/
Another dictionary site, this one covering Chinese, Japanese and Vietnamese as well as English. Transliteration and literal translation of the oriental characters is given so you get, for example, 'wear headdress', 'eight-heads' and 'axed-head' for Hoopoe. A variety of Chinese dialect names are also given.

http://members.tripod.co.jp/bluebonnet/japanesee.htm
How can you fail to be seduced by the birds of Japan when you see a picture of a stunning Narcissus Flycatcher on the front page? Even though the author tries to match as many of the bird's hues with his choice of background colours, there is quite a lot of good, basic information here.

Mainland Asia

http://birds.krasu.ru/eng/index.shtml
Eastern vagrants have always held a fascination for British birders, so this site on the Birds of Central Siberia is bound to be of interest. There is an annotated checklist and, currently, 45 pages of photos but frustratingly, no search facility. This site is still being heavily

developed so expect many additions. Very much second-language English.

http://www.hkbws.org.hk/frame.html
The Hong Kong Birdwatching Society site has plenty of news, photos and bird songs. The where-to-watch guide is a little disappointing though. I was hoping for a little bit more on the internationally famous Mai Po Marshes than 'What you see depends on the time of year and water level.'

http://martinwilliams.tripod.com/beidaihe/beidaihebirding.html
Think of birding in China and the chances are, you will probably think of Beidaihe. It seems a strange choice; there are only about 14 resident species after all. It is however a migration hotspot par excellence. This article, dating back to 1995, captures the excitement of watching birds on the move. There is also a checklist of birds seen.

http://www.wbkenglish.com/
Until recently, Korea's bird life was largely unknown outside the country itself. This lack of knowledge has hampered conservation measures and internationally important habitats were being lost. This fine site gives an impressive overview of the birds in Korea and the problems facing them.

EUROPE

http://www.aerc.be/index.html
The Association of European Rarities Committees is attempting to produce a standard set of guidelines across the continent as well as producing a definitive European list. As well as all the relevant contact addresses and details of all their recent meetings, there are a few galleries of pictures of difficult-to-identify species.

http://digilander.libero.it/avifauna/w_palearctic/home.htm
Distribution maps are the name of the game here with the intention to eventually cover every Western Palearctic species. At present the list only goes as far as Terns. There are checklists too, in a variety of different orders, though the design of the pages here are less than wonderful.

http://www.eurobirding.co.uk/index.html
This site is unusual in that it works two ways. You can look up a specific country and get details of some of the top reserves and the birds to be found there. Or you can do it in reverse, and look up a specific species and get a list of reserves across Europe where the bird can be seen.

http://www.megabytedata.com/online.htm
Do you need to know the Lapp name for a Dotterel, or the Gaelic for a Terek Sandpiper? These dictionaries will do all the translations for you. There are 26 North European languages, including English folk names, covering a total of 23,000 names. There are also dictionaries for mammals and flora.

http://home.planetinternet.be/~pin02658/index.htm
If you find a bird with coloured rings on its legs, wing-tags or neck-collars, this is the site to visit in order to discover more about the appropriate scheme. Contact details are provided so you can inform the co-ordinator of the project about your sighting. It is not the easiest site to use as it is written by someone for whom English is not the first language.

http://www.ramsar.org
This is a massive, somewhat formal, site detailing all the wetland areas of the world afforded special protection under the Ramsar Convention. Check out the 'Ramsar a la carte' link if you want quick access to the country of your choice.

http://www.wpbirds.com/Index.htm
This site is in the process of detailing the status and occurrence of every species recorded in the Western Palearctic. Dates and locations of vagrants are given. It is a massive undertaking and still in a fairly embryonic state but it will be a major resource once completed.

Iceland and northern Europe

http://www.arcticbirds.ru/
Here you can find details of the various bird research projects undertaken in the Arctic

Circle. Data is currently provided for the last four years of study with details given for breeding success, rodent populations and weather. Full reports can be downloaded, though you will need to have Acrobat installed (free download available)

http://hem.fyristorg.com/vera/index.html
A small, personal site, there are plenty of links here to birding in Scandinavia, Holland and, something that is hard to track down elsewhere, the Arctic. The author is a Dutch woman living in Sweden so those two countries are covered particularly well. Not all the linked pages are in English but there is enough here to get you started.

http://www.hi.is/~yannk/index-eng.html
An excellent section on the status of vagrants, including distribution maps and month and year histograms is the highlight of this first class site about birds in Iceland. There are summaries of migrant arrival dates. Recent sightings are updated daily and a there is plethora of mouth-watering photos.

Mediterranean region

http://www.ebnitalia.it/
Written in a mixture of English and Italian, this site provides a useful selection of information for anyone interested in birding in Italy including regional checklists (in Italian though with scientific names too), trip reports, photos and a few recent sightings. It's just a pity it all takes so long to download each page.

http://northcyprusbirds.iecnc.org/default.htm
Not just the birds of North Cyprus are discussed here, but also butterflies, dragonflies and turtles. The birding sections include pages on some of the top sites, recent sightings and tips on when and where to find the local specialities. There is a downloadable checklist and recent ringing details.

http://www.ornithologiki.gr/en/enmain.htm
The Hellenic Ornithological Society is busy translating most of its pages from Greek into English. A lot of the pages are about the club itself but there is a large database of protected bird areas and a variety of articles. Strangely, there was very little about birding in Lesvos. Given the huge popularity of birding on this island, there is probably information on the net about this one small island than all the rest of Greece put together.

http://welcome.to/spainbirding
This is a fairly basic introduction to birding in Spain but there is enough here – if you can read the small print – to give you a fair idea of what's on offer in the different regions. As well as ten trip reports, there are links to other birding sites, regional tourist boards etc.

Western Europe

http://www.bavarianbirds.de/index_e.html
As well as recent news and where to watch guides, this impressive site has plenty of quizzes and a 'Babelbird' feature which translates names into German, French and Spanish.

http://www.chew.demon.co.uk/lpo.htm
The Ligue pour la Protection des Oiseaux is the French equivalent of the RSPB and this is the English version of their web site. This page is fairly basic and the 'news' was four months old when I last checked, but if you can speak French, there are links to the parent web site.

http://www.xs4all.nl/~sbpoley/nl/index.html
Designed to be of most use to visiting Brits, this well-designed, simple site has a few suggestions for birding in the Netherlands. The main birding areas are discussed, together with status details and rough location details of the 30 most sought-after specialities. Eight sites are dealt with in greater detail, though there are no maps.

BIRD OBSERVATORIES GEAR UP FOR THE 21st CENTURY

Freelance journalist Ron Toft examines how the Bird Observatories Council aims to raise the network's profile and attract a new generation of volunteer enthusiasts.

FOR MANY BIRDWATCHERS, visiting a bird observatory, especially at the height of spring or autumn migration, is an unforgettable experience. The highlight could be watching wave after wave of passing seabirds, seeing mist-netted birds being weighed, measured and ringed, trying to identify a bush full of similar-looking warblers, or being the first to spot a rarity.

However, in recent times the availability of cheap overseas holidays and the thrills of twitching have meant that fewer and fewer birdwatchers have been sampling the unique experience afforded by establishments affiliated to the Bird Observatories Council (BOC). So how bright is the future for the observatory network?

The main aim of bird observatories in the 21st Century, according to the BOC, is 'to conduct long-term monitoring of bird populations and migration'. Census and other observations are logged daily. Ringing, which is conducted under the auspices of The British Trust for Ornithology (BTO), is also an integral part of observatory work and provides invaluable data for statutory conservation bodies, including English Nature, Scottish Natural Heritage and the Countryside Council for Wales.

Observatories encourage volunteers to take part in bird and environmental studies, the results of which, along with other information, are freely made available to researchers and members of the public who are welcome to visit these establishments.

A survey of the year-round highlights of the 17 observatories currently in the network quickly demonstrates that the pontential for birding excitement remains as high as ever. "A trip to Fair Isle in May could coincide with an arrival of Bluethroats and Red-backed Shrikes," reports licensed bird ringer Peter Howlett, who acts as honorary secretary of BOC. "You would also see the massive seabird colonies at their busiest, with the cliffs on the west side of the island teeming with Fulmars, Kittiwakes and auks."

The challenge at both North Ronaldsay and Bardsey on overcast nights at the height of migration might be trying to identify nocturnal migrants attracted by the lighthouse beams. Special lamps installed on Bardsey in 1978 safely divert some birds away from the lighthouse itself and into nearby gorse bushes where up to 3,000 migrants have roosted in a single night.

Late May and early June is a good time for rarities at North Ronaldsay, notable ones in recent years having been White-throated Sparrow, Rustic and Pine Buntings, Red-necked Stint, Red-throated Pipit and Collared Flycatcher.

Autumn, says Peter, is probably the best time to visit the east coast observatories - Isle of May, Filey, Spurn, Gibraltar Point, Holme and Landguard. "There is always the possibility of large movement of common migrants, as well as the added spice of possible eastern vagrants, though the Isle of May can expect similar arrivals to Fair Isle and North Ronaldsay during spring."

Spectacular movements of migratory birds been observed at Gibraltar Point, such as the one on September 9, 1995 involving 30,000 Swallows. Just a few days later 481 Redstarts were counted.

At Portland Bird Observatory in Dorset, there is virtually a never-ending stream of migrants from early March, when the first Northern Wheatears begin arriving, until mid-June. "There's only a five or six-week period in the middle of summer when there isn't a great deal coming through," warden Martin Cade told me.

Portland's commonest spring migrants are Willow Warblers. "Sub-rarities at this time of the year include Bee-eaters, Woodchat Shrikes and Hoopoes, all of which are over-shooting. You expect them annually and if you miss one or other of them, you are really disappointed!"

Autumn migration kicks off in late July with Sedge and Willow Warblers and continues until the end of November. "It's a season when you can get vagrants from virtually anywhere in the Northern Hemisphere. Among those in recent years have been Hume's Yellow-browed Warbler from Russia, Blyth's Reed Warbler from Scandinavia and Northern Waterthrush from America."

From early March onwards, Portland sees a constant stream of incoming migrants.

In February 2002, Portland made birding headlines when it identified an exhausted vagrant picked up by a member of the public as an Allen's Gallinule – only the second record for Britain (the first being in 1902).

"Sandwich Bay, Dungeness and Portland Observatories on the south coast can have good days in both spring and autumn, although spring arrivals tend to move through very quickly," said Peter. You can literally see birds making their way north up through the hedges at Portland in spring. Seawatching can be good in spring and autumn. Even in winter at Dungeness there are large movements and plenty of activity at The Patch – the outlet for the water used in cooling the nearby power station."

Manx Shearwater and other seabird colonies and Britain's densest breeding population per square mile of Choughs are the ornithological claims to fame of the tiny islet off the Isle of Man where the Calf of Man Bird Observatory is situated.

Vagrants from all over the world have been recorded at Cape Clear Bird Observatory on Cape Clear Island – the most southerly tip of Ireland apart from Fastnet Rock. "Seabirds also pass the island in impressive numbers with varieties and views rarely witnessed elsewhere," says its web site. Among the breeding gems are Black Guillemot and Chough. The observatory building was completely refurbished and extended in 2000.

"A visit to Cape Clear in August could well produce huge movements of Manx Shearwaters, Storm Petrels and Gannets, along with the excitement of Great Shearwaters and Cory's Shearwaters, plus several species of large whale and dolphin," said Peter.

Landguard Nature Reserve and Bird Observatory in Suffolk is particularly good for Bluethroat, Ortolan Bunting, Wryneck, Icterine Warbler, Barred Warbler and Firecrest. Mouth-watering rarities have included Thrush Nightingale, Paddyfield Warbler, Dusky Warbler, Yellow-browed Warbler, Yellow-billed Cuckoo, Sabine's Gull, Red-rumped Swallow, Desert Wheatear and Little Bunting. Up to 10,000 birds are ringed annually at Languard.

Valuable data-gathering

"Recent work suggests that the daily census information collected by each observatory could be a valuable tool in the long-term monitoring of bird populations," said Peter.

Analysis of the daily counts for eight species – Sparrowhawk, Turtle Dove, Song Thrush, Common Whitethroat, Willow Warbler, Spotted Flycatcher, Goldfinch and Reed Bunting – from 1990 onwards has revealed similar trends to the population changes tracked by the Common Bird Census, Waterway Bird Census and other surveys.

"This makes the data of real value as the daily census goes back much further than any other comparable data sets. The observatory data would also provide a handle on species not covered by other current methods, such as Northern Wheatear, Ring Ouzel, Whinchat and others with a westerly, non-farmland distribution."

The realisation of the importance of the daily census data means there is now a drive to make it readily available for wider scientific study and analysis – and to try to attract more birdwatchers and researchers to observatories. It is already known from observatory records that summer migrants are arriving slightly earlier than in the past. Swallow counts are even being used by the Government as one of its 'Health Of The Nation' indicators.

BOC's aim is to obtain between £120,000 and £150,000 of Heritage Lottery Fund cash to pay for the computerisation of observatory records. "It will be no mean feat, for altogether there is something like 750 years of data to input! Computerisation is essential, however, if the value of these records is to be fully realised."

Peter hopes that individual observatories will try to obtain grant aid or other local funding should lottery cash not be forthcoming. "North Ronaldsay, which is one of the newer observatories, has all of its data computerised. The Isle of May has also computerised a lot of its records, thanks to a local grant, and Bardsey has been computerised for the past four or five years.

"It's already happening and will probably continue to happen on a piecemeal basis, but it would nice to obtain a lump sum from the Heritage Lottery Fund so that the entire backlog could be computerised within a reasonably short period of time and then be available to anyone at the touch of a few keys."

Added Peter: "To many people, the heyday of bird observatories was in the 1950s and 1960s. Certainly the growth of mobile birding, with people waiting to find out what was being seen before deciding where to go at weekends, had a serious impact on observatories in the 1980s and 1990s, and many observatories have experienced financial concerns in recent years. Though rarity chasing still has a huge following, it would appear there is renewed interest in bird counting.

"I believe that the increasing computerisation and, therefore, accessibility of observatory records will give the whole network a much-needed boost and result in observatories being seen in a new and increasingly valuable light."

Origins of the BOC

In February 1946, four people - WB Alexander, EJM Buxton, RM Lockley and G Waterston - gathered at a private house in Long Crendon, Buckinghamshire and, after due deliberation, defined a bird observatory as 'a field station cooperatively manned for the purposes of making continuous observations on migrant birds and for catching, examining and marking them'.

These birding stalwarts, along with Miss E P Leach and HFD Elder, who were not present, were the first members of the Bird Observatories Sub-Committee. Set up in December of the previous year by the Advisory Scientific Committee of the Oxford University Committee for Ornithology, the Sub-Committee later became The Bird Observatories Council (BOC), which coordinates and promotes the work of a growing chain of accredited coastal bird observatories throughout Britain and Ireland.

"In those early days, there were only a handful of bird observatories, such as Fair Isle and the Isle of May," said BOC honorary secretary Peter Howlett, curator of vertebrates in the BioSyB department of The National Museums & Galleries of Wales, Cardiff.

"Others, like Lundy, came and went over the years. Today we have 17, the latest addition to the network being Flamborough Head whose application was accepted in January 2001."

BRITISH OBSERVATORIES

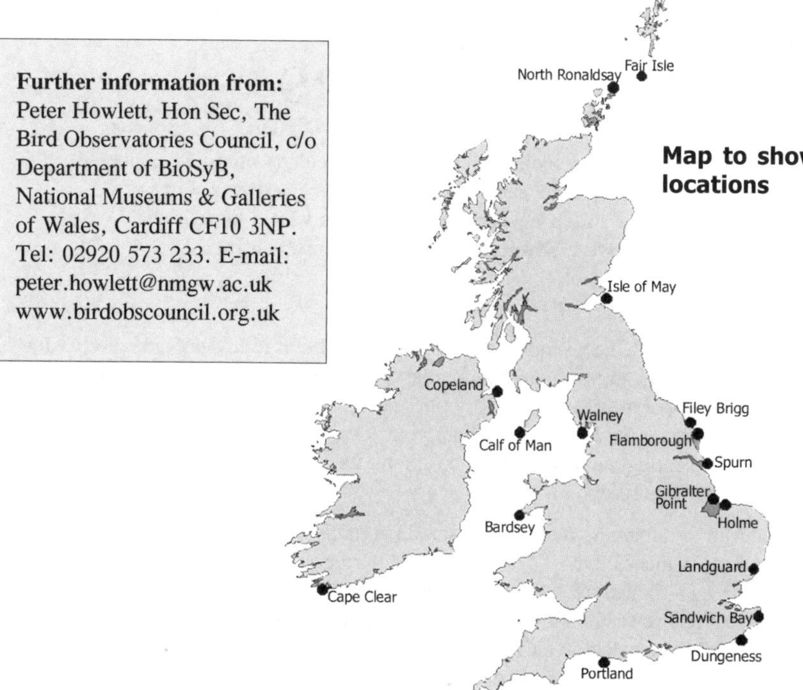

Further information from:
Peter Howlett, Hon Sec, The Bird Observatories Council, c/o Department of BioSyB, National Museums & Galleries of Wales, Cardiff CF10 3NP. Tel: 02920 573 233. E-mail: peter.howlett@nmgw.ac.uk www.birdobscouncil.org.uk

The 17 BOC-accredited observatories

Bardsey	steve@bbfo.freeserve.co.uk
Calf of Man	07624 462858.
Cape Clear	info@birdwatchireland.org
Copeland	talisker.lodge@btopenworld.com
Dungeness	dungeness.obs@tinyonline.co.uk
Fair Isle	fairisle.birdobs@zetnet.co.uk
Filey	pjdunn@fbog.co.uk
Flamborough Head	trog@outerhead.freeserve.co.uk
Gibraltar Point	lincstrust@gibpoint.freeserve.co.uk
Holme	jedandrews@shrike4.freeserve.co.uk
Isle of May	MargaretThorne@woodland-trust.org.uk
Landguard	sPiotrowski@anglianwater.co.uk
North Ronaldsay	alison@nrbo.prestel.co.uk
Portland	obs@btinternet.com
Sandwich Bay	crosske@globalnet.co.uk
Spurn	ian.walker@homeoffice.gsi.gov.uk
Walney	keith.parkes@furness.ac.uk

BRINGING DOWN THE BARRIERS

Disabled Birding Association founder Bo Beolens might be expected to be a campaigner for easier access at nature reserves, but he argues that the much-needed improvements would benefit the majority of active birdwatchers, not just those confined to wheelchairs.

BARRIER-FREE ACCESS – not a concept that is difficult to understand, surely? Just like it says on the tin, to misquote the popular TV commercial, it means access is easy if there are no barriers in the way. So why does such a simple idea prove to be a mystery to so many service providers? Think about your local reserve and I'm sure you'll have no difficulty accepting that access must be among the very last things considered by those who own or manage reserves.

Consider this – at any moment only a small percentage of the population are fit, taller than five feet six inches, have 20-20 vision and perfect hearing and are able to walk a kilometre along a rugged track carrying a telescope, binoculars, fieldguide and flask without needing a rest. For the rest of us, and I include those who've ever sprained an ankle, worn glasses or had to carry toddlers or those simply getting on in years, we are not part of that elite capable to using most of the facilities currently on offer.

I started the Disabled Birders Association (DBA) in April 2000 because I was fed up with the lack of response and sensitivity at nature reserves. Paths were too steep, narrow or sticky for wheelchairs, car parks were miles from hides with no benches to rest on, signs were too small to read and hides with flights of steps seem to be the norm.

When concessions were made they were inadequate, because wheelchair-friendly paths often led to hides with steps, upward-opening viewing slots and fixed seating, or lay beyond impassable kissing-gates. Sadly many reserve providers, like most of the world, have seen 'disabled' to be synonymous with 'wheelchair user' and they've failed to make provision for other disabilities.

Benefiting the majority

In the last three years things have begun to change but the majority of providers still do not embrace the concept fully. So, for their, and your, benefit, this is how it goes.

If you take away all the barriers to access *everyone* benefits. We all age and most of us find walking harder the older we get. All of us have been children and have had to struggle with out-of-scale facilities. Cyclists and pram pushers cannot cope with cattle grids.

There are, according to most sources, between seven and ten million people in the UK with some form of disability; there are many millions of people over retirement age and many millions who are not fully grown – none of us are average. Basing all facilities on the needs of fit and able young men (which most reserve wardens happen to be) is like selling nothing but size ten boots – no size five slippers or size six stilettos – would people put up with that? Clearly not, so why should birders with sensory or mobility restrictions put up with this lack of respect and arrogance?

Most of the problems that exist do so because of lack of thought or poor design and not because what is needed costs more than what is provided. A simple wooden bench [virtually cost-free when put together by volunteers out of re-cycled materials] every 150 yards along a trail could double the number of people who make it all the way round – in woodland reserves a fallen tree would make a natural alternative.

Movable benches, lower viewing slots, downward opening slot covers and ramps to doors would make hides accessible and usable by children, the infirm elderly, etc. not just to those who have to use wheelchairs. Firm, flat and wide paths and large print notices make it easier for everyone. Improvements made for people with mobility or sensory restrictions will not have a detrimental effect on able-bodied visitors, nor compromise the needs of the birds the reserves are created to protect.

So I am calling on all birding facility providers to think about access. Call in the DBA or a local disability group at the planning stage of any development. Better still, ask for comments on what exists now, as many annual maintenance tasks could be done in a way which starts the barrier-free ball rolling.

In my home county of Kent the County Wildlife Trust, the RSPB, the Sandwich Bay Bird Observatory and the like regularly consult the DBA. Wardens at Northward Hill and Cliffe, Elmley, Dungeness, Sandwich Bay Bird Observatory, Oare Marshes and so forth are fully committed to improving matters and see every disaster (like a rotten hide collapsing) as an opportunity to make access better for all. Their colleagues nationwide could easily copy what they are doing.

When new reserves are planned, human access should be on the agenda right after the needs of the birds – if a reserve is open to the public it must be accessible by all, not just fit birders in the prime of life.

There are only two choices, either the facility should be closed to the public or it must be usable by everyone – anything else is elitist and unacceptable. This is not a minority issue needing action by the sufferers or on their behalf by worthy citizens. It's high time that all birders championed this cause – out of selfishness; you may not need special provision today but someone you know does and one day you probably will, too!

For further information about the Disabled Birders Association, please see their entry in the National Directory.

ENGLISH-LANGUAGE BIRD MAGAZINES

RECOGNISING that birdwatchers in Great Britain increasingly want information about birds and birding opportunities overseas, we have compiled this Directory of English language magazines (a mix of commercial and society-based titles) that we know of personally. We welcome further reader recommendations for future Editions of *The Yearbook*.

GREAT BRITAIN

Birding World

A subscription-only title produced by the Bird Information Service team that runs the national Birdline telephone news service. The magazine caters for serious birders with a keen interest in UK rarities and overseas travel. Each monthly issue details the most significant bird sightings in Britain and the remainder of the Western Palearctic. Other regulars include first-person accounts of the finding of rare birds in the UK and accounts of overseas birding trips.

Editor: Steve Gantlett

Contact details: Birding World, Sea Lawn, Coast Road, Cley-next-the-Sea, Holt, Norfolk NR25 7RZ. Tel: 01263 740 913.
E-mail: Steve@birdingworld.co.uk
Web-site: www.birdingworld.co.uk

Birds

The quarterly members-only magazine issued by the Royal Society for the Protection of Birds is a full-colour super-A4 magazine that promotes the organisation's work in conservation and education. In addition to an extensive general news section, the magazine carries features on RSPB reserves, international initiatives with partner organisations, tips on developing birdwatching skills, members' letters and book reviews. *Birds* is available on tape for visually-impaired members.

Editor: Rob Hume

Contact details: Birds magazine, The Lodge, Sandy, Bedfordshire SG19 2DL. Tel: 01767 680 551. Web-site: www.rspb.org.uk

Birds Illustrated

Available on subscription and from WWT Centres and selected RSPB reserves, *Birds Illustrated* was launched in August 2003. Its focus is on the aesthetic appreciation of wild birds anywhere in the world.

Editor: David Cromack.

Contact details: Buckingham Press, 55 Thorpe Park Road, Peterborough PE3 6LJ. 01733 561739.
E-mail: editor@ buckinghampress.com

Birdwatch

A monthly full-colour A4 magazine available on subscription and from main newsagents in Britain. Contains a range of features on identification, UK and foreign birding areas and taxonomic issues designed to appeal to experienced birders. Also contains news, readers' letters, product reviews and summaries of British bird sightings.

Editor: Dominic Mitchell

Contact details: Solo Publishing Ltd, 3D/F Leroy House, 436 Essex Road, Islington, London N1 3QP. Tel: 020 7704 9495.
Web-site: www.birdwatch.co.uk

Bird Watching

Britain's best-selling monthly bird magazine available from all leading newsagents and on subscription. This A4 full-colour title caters for all active birdwatchers with articles to help beginners as well as the more experienced.
Every issue contains

articles on garden birds and identification, plus news, readers' letters, leading columnists such as John Gooders and Ian Wallace, and the *Go Birding* pull-out guide to bird walks and reserves. The UK Bird Sightings section is the world's largest monthly round-up of bird news. Individual product reviews, plus surveys of leading optical products. The annual travel supplement *Destinations* appears with the November issue.
Editor: David Cromack
Contact details: Emap Active Ltd, Bretton Court, Peterborough PE3 8DZ. Tel: 01733 282 601. E-mail: david.cromack@emap.com

British Birds

A long-established subscription-only journal of record that aims to publish material on behaviour, conservation, distribution, ecology, identification, status and taxonomy for birders throughout the Western Palearctic. Organises the *BB Bird Photograph of the Year* competition. Publishes the annual report of the British Birds Rarities Committee.
Editor: Roger Riddington
Contact details: BB 2000 Ltd, Chapel Cottage, Dunrossness, Shetland ZE2 9JH.
Tel: 01950 460 080.
E-mail: editor@britishbirds.co.uk

BTO News

A bi-monthly A4 cloour magazine sent to all members of the British Trust for Ornithology. Features include articles about the full range of BTO research projects, plus the status of various species, book reviews and an events guide.
Editor: Derek Toomer
Contact details: BTO, The Nunnery, Thetford, Norfolk IP24 2PU.
Tel; 01842 750050
E-mail: btonews@bto.org www.bto.org

World Birdwatch

This is the long-established quarterly subscription-only magazine from BirdLife International that seeks to promote its global conservation activities. An extensive round-up of world bird-related news is supported with features such as Sites To Save and Country Fact File, plus articles on education, habitat protection and events.
Editor: Richard Thomas
Contact details: BirdLife International, Wellbrook Court, Girton Road, Cambridge CB3 0NA. E-mail: birdlife@birdlife.org.uk

FINLAND

Alula

Started in 1995, *Alula* is an independent journal for people interested in birds and bird identification. Regular topics include ID papers by field experts, articles about birding sites, tests of optical equipment, literature reviews, competitions and current birding issues. In order to widen its sales appeal, this high-quality quarterly A4 magazine is now available in an English-language edition as well as Finnish.
Editor: Antero Topp
Contact details: Alula Oy, Eestinkalliontie 16D, FIN-02280 Espoo, Finland.
E-mail: antero.topp@alula.fi
Web-site: www.alula.fi

HOLLAND

Dutch Birding

Many of the articles in this long-established monthly journal that caters for serious birders and twitchers are published in English, and the Dutch pieces generally have an English summary. Regular topics include ID papers by field experts, extensive coverage of scarcer birds in Holland and the Western Paearctic generally, literature reviews, competitions and current birding issues.
Editor: Arnoud van den Berg,
E-mail: arnoud.van.den.berg@dutchbirding.nl
www.dutchbirding.nl

SOUTH AFRICA

Africa Birds & Birding

This award-winning glossy A4 bi-monthly colour magazine enjoys support from BirdLife South Africa but remains totally independent. It strives to foster an awareness of the continent's birdlife and encourages birdwatching as a pastime and for its ecotourism potential. High quality photographic features are included along with articles on sites, book and product reviews, news and letters.

Editor-in-Chief/Publisher: Peter Borchert

Contact details: Black Eagle Publishing, PO Box 44223, Claremont 7735, Cape Town, South Africa.
E-mail: wildmags@blackeaglemedia.co.za
Web-site: www.africa-geographic.com

USA

Birder's World

A popular title for American birdwatchers of all experience levels, this A4 all-colour monthly magazine carries features on garden birds, profiles of individual bird species, guides to top birding locations in the US, conservation issues, bird behaviour, book and optics reviews. In addition to readers' letters, there is usually a section devoted to answering reader questions and a photo-quiz. Copies can be found in larger branches of leading British newsagents.

Editor: Charles J Hagner.

Contact details: Klambach Publishing Co, Birder's World editorial dept, PO Box 1612, Waukesha, WI 53187-1612, USA.
E-mail: mail@birder'sworld.com

Birding

Issued exclusively to members six times a year by the American Birders Association, a not-for-profit organisation that aims to help field birders develop their knowledge, skills and enjoyment of wild birds. The organisation (membership open to all birdwatchers) also encourages the conservation of birds and their habitats. In practice this means the magazine carries full-colour features on bird-finding in the USA and Canada, in-depth ID articles, book and product reviews, photo quizzes, fieldcraft, taxonomy and conservation articles.

Editor: Paul J Baicich

Contact details: American Birding Association, 720 W Monument Street, Colorado Springs, Colorado 80904-3624, USA.
Web-site: www.americanbirding.org

Birdwatcher's Digest

This pocket-sized full-colour bi-monthly magazine is unashamedly populist in its approach and features a high proportion of articles about backyard birding and readers' birding tales as well as helpful advice on ID and fieldcraft. Top birding areas in the USA are spotlighted and Book Notes covers the latest publications.

Editor: William H Thompson.

Contact details: Birdwatcher's Digest, PO Box 110, Marietta, Ohio 45750, USA.
E-mail: editor@birdwatchersdigest.com
Web-site: www.birdwatchersdigest.com

EVENTS DIARY 2004

JANUARY

24-25th Big Garden Birdwatch contact Richard Bashford, RSPB. e-mail: richard.bashford@rspb.org.uk

11-17th Jonathan Pomroy Exhibition
WWT, Slimbridge.
Beautiful water-colours of birds and landscapes.

FEBRUARY

5-6th GM Crops and Birds
A BOU Two-Day Scientific Meeting. The Royal Society, London, UK.

7-8th The Great West Bird Fair
WWT, Slimbridge, Glos.
01453 890333.

14-15th Lee Valley Bird Fair. 10am – 4pm
Lee Valley Park Farms, nr Fishers Green, Essex.
01992 702200.
www.leavalleypark.org.uk

Feb 22nd–April 6th Richard Smith Exhibition
WWT, Slimbridge.
A countryman who uses colour superbly in all his work.

28th North East Ringers' Conference.
Durham. Contact Chris Spray, email: chris.spray@nwl.co.uk or Dawn Balmer at BTO HQ, email: dawn.balmer@bto.org

MARCH

7th–13th Birdlife International Conference
Waterbirds Around the World.
Edinburgh, Scotland.
Contact Birdlife International, 01223 277318.

13th BTO South West Regional Conference
Contact John Tully, 6 Falcondale Walk, Westbury-On-Trym, Bristol, Avon, BS9 3JG, email: johntully4@aol.com or Dawn Balmer at BTO HQ, email: dawn.balmer@bto.org

26-28th Ecology and Conservation of Lowland Farmland and Birds
BOU Annual Conference and AGM, University of Leicester.

27th East of England Regional Ringing Conference.
Wicken Fen. Contact Dawn Balmer at BTO HQ,
email: dawn.balmer@bto.org

APRIL

April 11th-May 11th Sean Connell Exhibition
WWT, Slimbridge.
Exquisite bronze sculptures, mainly on bird studies.

16-18th RSPB members weekend in York
Contact Christine McDowell, RSPB.

MAY

8-9th Leighton Moss Bird Fair
Contact Leighton Moss RSPB Reserve, 01524 701601.

May 16th-June 15th Owen Williams Exhibition
WWT, Slimbridge.
A Welshman producing beautiful atmospheric pieces.

SE Bird Fair
(date to be confirmed)
WWT, Arundel.
01903 883355.

JUNE

5-6th Wildlife Photo and Bird Fair
Brandon Marsh Nature Reserve, Warwickshire. Contact Alan Richards, 0152 785 2357.
www.birder.co.uk

June 20th-July 20th Mike Read, Colin Wolfe and Paul Kedwards joint Exhibition
WWT, Slimbridge.
Great wildlife photography, sculpture and original art work.

National Exhibition of Wildlife Art
Date to be confirmed.
Gordale Garden Centre, The Wirral. Contact NEWA, 11 Dibbins Hey, Poulton Lancelyn, Bebington, Wirral. CH63 9JU; www.newa.cwc.net

JULY

July 25th-Aug 31st Terence Lambert Exhibition
WWT, Slimbridge. Stunning oil painting from an established master

AUGUST

20-27th The British Birdwatching Fair
Rutland Water.
www.birdfair.org.uk

SEPTEMBER

Sept 5th- Oct 5th Chris Rose Exhibition
WWT, Slimbridge. A bird watcher and conservationist, is widely collected.

22nd–3rd October SWLA annual exhibition.
Mall Galleries, London.
Contact SWLA.

OCTOBER

2nd RSPB AGM
Queen Elizabeth II Conference Centre, London,
Contact Christine McDowell, RSPB.

Oct 10th- Nov 9th David Cook Exhibition
WWT, Slimbridge.
Vibrant designs in chromacolour and beautiful papercuts.

NOVEMBER

12-14th NW Bird Fair
WWT, Martin Mere
01704 895181.

DECEMBER

3-5th The BTO's Annual Conference.
Hayes Conference Centre, Swanwick, Derbyshire.
Contact Sue Starling, BTO.

Full contact details for the clubs and organisations listed here can be found under their entries in the County, National and International directories.

DIARY - JANUARY 2004

1	Thu	*New Year's Day*
2	Fri	*Holiday (Scotland)*
3	Sat	
4	Sun	
5	Mon	
6	Tue	
7	Wed	
8	Thu	
9	Fri	
10	Sat	
11	Sun	
12	Mon	
13	Tue	
14	Wed	
15	Thu	
16	Fri	
17	Sat	
18	Sun	
19	Mon	
20	Tue	
21	Wed	
22	Thu	
23	Fri	
24	Sat	
25	Sun	
26	Mon	
27	Tue	
28	Wed	
29	Thu	
30	Fri	
31	Sat	

BIRD NOTES - JANUARY 2004

DIARY - FEBRUARY 2004

1 Sun

2 Mon

3 Tue

4 Wed

5 Thu

6 Fri

7 Sat

8 Sun

9 Mon

10 Tue

11 Wed

12 Thu

13 Fri

14 Sat

15 Sun

16 Mon

17 Tue

18 Wed

19 Thu

20 Fri

22 Sat

22 Sun

23 Mon

24 Tue

25 Wed

26 Thu

27 Fri

28 Sat

29 Sun

BIRD NOTES - FEBRUARY 2004

DIARY - MARCH 2004

1 Mon	
2 Tue	
3 Wed	
4 Thu	
5 Fri	
6 Sat	
7 Sun	
8 Mon	
9 Tue	
10 Wed	
11 Thu	
12 Fri	
15 Sat	
16 Sun	
15 Mon	
16 Tue	
17 Wed	
18 Thu	
19 Fri	
20 Sat	
21 Sun	*Mothering Sunday*
22 Mon	
23 Tue	
24 Wed	
25 Thu	
26 Fri	
27 Sat	
28 Sun	*British Summertime begins*
29 Mon	
30 Tue	
31 Wed	

DIARY - APRIL 2004

1 Thu	
2 Fri	
3 Sat	
4 Sun	
5 Mon	
6 Tue	
7 Wed	
8 Thu	
9 Fri	*Good Friday*
10 Sat	
11 Sun	*Easter Day*
12 Mon	*Easter Monday*
13 Tue	
14 Wed	
15 Thu	
16 Fri	
17 Sat	
18 Sun	
19 Mon	
20 Tue	
21 Wed	
22 Thu	
23 Fri	
26 Sat	
27 Sun	
26 Mon	
27 Tue	
28 Wed	
29 Thu	
30 Fri	

BIRD NOTES - APRIL 2004

DIARY - MAY 2004

1 Sat	
2 Sun	
3 Mon	*May Day*
4 Tue	
5 Wed	
6 Thu	
7 Fri	
8 Sat	
9 Sun	
10 Mon	
11 Tue	
12 Wed	
13 Thu	
14 Fri	
15 Sat	
16 Sun	
17 Mon	
18 Tue	
19 Wed	
20 Thu	
21 Fri	
22 Sat	
23 Sun	
24 Mon	
25 Tue	
26 Wed	
27 Thu	
28 Fri	
29 Sat	
30 Sun	
31 Mon	*Spring Bank Holiday*

DIARY - JUNE 2004

1 Tue	
2 Wed	
3 Thu	
4 Fri	
5 Sat	
6 Sun	
7 Mon	
8 Tue	
9 Wed	
10 Thu	
11 Fri	
12 Sat	
13 Sun	
14 Mon	
15 Tue	
16 Wed	
17 Thu	
18 Fri	
19 Sat	
20 Sun	
21 Mon	
22 Tue	
23 Wed	
24 Thu	
25 Fri	
26 Sat	
27 Sun	
28 Mon	
29 Tue	
30 Wed	

DIARY - JULY 2004

1	Thu
2	Fri
3	Sat
4	Sun
5	Mon
6	Tue
7	Wed
8	Thu
9	Fri
10	Sat
11	Sun
12	Mon
13	Tue
14	Wed
15	Thu
16	Fri
17	Sat
28	Sun
19	Mon
20	Tue
21	Wed
22	Thu
23	Fri
24	Sat
25	Sun
26	Mon
27	Tue
28	Wed
29	Thu
30	Fri
31	Sat

BIRD NOTES -JULY 2004

DIARY - AUGUST 2004

1 Sun	
2 Mon	
3 Tue	
4 Wed	
5 Thu	
6 Fri	
7 Sat	
8 Sun	
9 Mon	
10 Tue	
11 Wed	
12 Thu	
13 Fri	
14 Sat	
15 Sun	
16 Mon	
17 Tue	
18 Wed	
19 Thu	
20 Fri	
21 Sat	
22 Sun	
23 Mon	
24 Tue	
25 Wed	
26 Thu	
27 Fri	
28 Sat	
29 Sun	
30 Mon	*Late Summer Holiday*
31 Tue	

BIRD NOTES AUGUST 2004

DIARY - SEPTEMBER 2004

1	Wed
2	Thu
3	Fri
4	Sat
5	Sun
6	Mon
7	Tue
8	Wed
9	Thu
10	Fri
11	Sat
12	Sun
13	Mon
14	Tue
15	Wed
16	Thu
17	Fri
18	Sat
19	Sun
20	Mon
21	Tue
22	Wed
23	Thu
24	Fri
25	Sat
26	Sun
27	Mon
28	Tue
29	Wed
30	Thu

BIRD NOTES -SEPTEMBER 2004

DIARY - OCTOBER 2004

1 Fri	
2 Sat	
3 Sun	
4 Mon	
5 Tue	
6 Wed	
7 Thu	
8 Fri	
9 Sat	
10 Sun	
11 Mon	
12 Tue	
13 Wed	
14 Thu	
15 Fri	
16 Sat	
17 Sun	
18 Mon	
19 Tue	
20 Wed	
21 Thu	
22 Fri	
23 Sat	
24 Sun	
25 Mon	
26 Tue	
27 Wed	
28 Thu	
29 Fri	
30 Sat	
31 Sun	*British Summertime ends*

DIARY - NOVEMBER 2004

1 Mon	
2 Tue	
3 Wed	
4 Thu	
5 Fri	
6 Sat	
7 Sun	
8 Mon	
9 Tue	
10 Wed	
11 Thu	
12 Fri	
13 Sat	
14 Sun	*Rememberance Sunday*
15 Mon	
16 Tue	
17 Wed	
18 Thu	
19 Fri	
20 Sat	
21 Sun	
22 Mon	
23 Tue	
24 Wed	
25 Thu	
26 Fri	
27 Sat	
28 Sun	
29 Mon	
30 Tue	

BIRD NOTES - NOVEMBER 2004

DIARY - DECEMBER 2004

1	Wed	
2	Thu	
3	Fri	
4	Sat	
5	Sun	
6	Mon	
7	Tue	
8	Wed	
9	Thu	
10	Fri	
11	Sat	
12	Sun	
13	Mon	
14	Tue	
15	Wed	
16	Thu	
17	Fri	
18	Sat	
19	Sun	
20	Mon	
21	Tue	
22	Wed	
23	Thu	
24	Fri	
25	Sat	*Christmas Day*
26	Sun	*Boxing Day*
27	Mon	*Bank Holiday*
28	Tue	*Bank Holiday*
29	Wed	
30	Thu	
31	Fri	

YEAR PLANNER 2005

January
February
March
April
May
June
July
August
September
October
November
December

LOG CHARTS

Ruddy Ducks by David Thelwell

LOG CHARTS

NEW ORDER OF THE BRITISH LIST
an explanation

NEWCOMERS to birdwatching are sometimes baffled when they examine their first fieldguide as it is not immediately clear why the birds are arranged the way they are. The simple answer is the order is meant to reflect the evolution of the included species. If one were to draw an evolutionary tree of birds, those families that branch off earliest (i.e are the most ancient) should be listed first.

Previously the British List was based on Voous Order (BOU 1977), the work of an eminent Dutch taxonomist. However, more than 26 phylogenetic studies, many using DNA analysis, have been published in recent years that together form a large body of evidence showing that the order of birds in the British List did not properly reflect their evolution. A change in order was required.

The British Ornithologists' Union's Records Committee (BOURC) is responsible for maintaining the British List and it relies on its Taxonomic Sub-Committee (BOURC-TSC) to advise on taxonomic issues relating to the species that form the British List. This advice usually takes the form of recommendations relating to the status of a species or sub-species which sometimes results in 'splitting' (creating two or more species from a single species) and 'lumping' (creating a single species from two or more).

At the end of 2002, BOURC-TSC recommended that the order of species on the British List be changed as it accepted the most likely hypotheses for bird evolution stemmed from the following key characters:

1. That the deepest branch point in the evolutionary tree of birds splits them into the Palaeognathae (tinamous and 'ratites') and the Neognathae (all other birds).
2. That within the Neognathae, the deepest branch-point splits them into Galloanserae (composed of two 'sister' groups – Anseriformes (waterfowl) and Galliformes (turkeys, guineafowl, megapodes, grouse, pheasants etc) and Neoaves (all remaining birds).
3. The World list would therefore start with Palaeognathae, but because only Neognathae occur in Britain, the new British List starts with the Galloanserae, as the deepest split from all other birds (Neoaves).

Within the Galloanserae there are fewer species of Anseriformes than Galliformes, therefore Anseriformes are listed first in accordance with normal custom. The orders of families within these groups remains unchanged, so the British List now starts with Anatidae (swans, ducks, geese), followed by Tetraonidae and Phasianidae (grouse, pheasants, quail and partridges), followed by all remaining families as in the old order (divers, grebes etc).

These recommendations have been accepted by the British Ornithologists' Union who have advised all book, magazine and bird report editors and publishers to begin using the new order as soon as possible and preferably no later than the publication of reports covering the year 2003.

Martin Collinson & Steve Dudley - British Ornithologists' Union

SPECIES, CATEGORIES, CODES AND GUIDE TO USE

Species list
The charts include all species on the British List and is based on the 1992 *BOU Checklist of Birds of Britain and Ireland* and the various BOURC reports published up to September 2002, when a major revision of taxonomic order was announced by the BOU.

The current list is augmented by birds which breed or occur regularly in Europe - almost 600 species altogether. Vagrants which are not on the British List, but which may have occurred in other parts of the British Isles, are not included. Readers who wish to record such species may use the extra rows provided on the last page. In this connection it should be noted that separate lists exist for Northern Ireland (kept by the Northern Ireland Birdwatchers' Association) and the Isle of Man (kept by the Manx Ornithological Society), and that Irish records are assessed by the Irish Rare Birds Committee.

Taxonomic changes introduced last year mean there is a new order of species (as outlined on the previous page). The species names are those most widely used in the current field guides (with some proposed changes shown in parentheses); each is followed by its scientific name, printed in italics.

Species categories
The following categories are those assigned by the British Ornithologists' Union.

A Species which have been recorded in an apparently natural state at least once since January 1, 1950.

B Species which would otherwise be in Category A but have not been recorded since December 31, 1949.

C Species that, although originally introduced by man, either deliberately or accidentally, have established breeding populations derived from introduced stock that maintain themselves without necessary recourse to further introduction. (This category has been subdivided to differentiate between various groups of naturalised species, but these subdivisions are outside the purpose of the log charts).

D Species that would otherwise appear in Categories A or B except that there is reasonable doubt that they have ever occurred in a natural state. (Species in this category are included in the log charts, though they do not qualify for inclusion in the British List, which comprises species in Categories A, B and C only. One of the objects of Category D is to note records of species which are not yet full additions, so that they are not overlooked if acceptable records subsequently occur. Bird report editors are encouraged to include records of species in Category D as appendices to their systematic lists).

E Species that have been recorded as introductions, transportees or escapees from captivity, and whose populations (if any) are thought not to be self-sustaining. They do not form part of the British List and are not included in the log charts.

EU Species not on the British List, or in Category D, but which either breed or occur regularly elsewhere in Europe.

Life list
Ticks made in the 'Life List' column suffice for keeping a running personal total of species. However, added benefit can be obtained by replacing ticks with a note of the year of first occurrence. To take an example: one's first-ever Marsh Sandpiper, seen on April 14, 2004, would be logged with '04' in the Life List and '14' in the April column (as well as a tick in the 2004 column). As Life List entries are carried forward annually, in years to come it would be a simple matter to relocate this record.

First and last dates of migrants
Arrivals of migrants can be recorded by inserting dates instead of ticks in the relevant month columns. For example, a Common Sandpiper on March 11 would be recorded by inserting '11' against Common Sandpiper in the March column. The same applies to departures, though dates of last sightings can only be entered at the end of the year after checking one's field notebook.

Unheaded columns
The three unheaded columns at the right hand end of each chart are for special (personal) use. This may be, for example, a, second holiday, a particular county or a 'local patch'. Another use could be to indicate species on, for example, the Northern Ireland List or the Isle of Man List.

BTO species codes
British Trust for Ornithology two-letter species codes are shown in brackets in the fourth column from the right. They exist for many species, races and hybrids recorded in recent surveys. Readers should refer to the BTO if more codes are needed. In addition to those given in the charts, the following are available for some well-marked races or forms - Whistling Swan (WZ), European White-fronted Goose (EW), Greenland White-fronted Goose (NW), dark-bellied Brent Goose (DB), pale-bellied Brent Goose (PB), Black Brant (BB), domestic goose (ZL), Green-winged Teal (TA), domestic duck (ZF), Yellow-legged Gull (YG), Kumlien's Gull (KG), Feral Pigeon (FP), White Wagtail (WB), Black-bellied Dipper (DJ), Hooded Crow (HC), intermediate crow (HB).

Rarities
Rarities are indicated by a capital letter 'R' immediately preceding the 'Euring No.' column.

EURING species numbers
EURING species numbers are given in the last column. As they are taken from the full Holarctic bird list there are many apparent gaps. It is important that these are not filled arbitrarily by observers wishing to record species not listed in the charts, as this would compromise the integrity of the scheme. Similarly, the addition of a further digit to indicate sub-species is to be avoided, since EURING has already assigned numbers for this purpose. The numbering follows the Voous order of species.

Rare breeding birds
Species monitored by the Rare Breeding Birds Panel (see National Directory) comprise all those on Schedule 1 of the Wildlife and Countryside Act 1981 (see Quick Reference) together with all escaped or introduced species breeding in small numbers. The following annotations in the charts (third column from the right) reflect the RBBP's categories:

(b)^A Rare species. All breeding details requested.
(b)^B Less scarce species. Totals requested from counties with more than 10 pairs or localities; elsewhere all details requested.
(b)^C Less scarce species (specifically Barn Owl, Kingfisher, Crossbill). County summaries requested.
(b)^D Escaped or introduced species. Treated as less scarce species.

	SWANS, GEESE, DUCKS		Life list	2004 list	24 hr	Garden	Holiday	Jan	Feb	Mar	Apr	May	Jun	Jul	Aug	Sep	Oct	Nov	Dec				BTO	RBBP	Bou	EU No
A C	**Mute Swan**	*Cygnus olor*																					MS			0152
A	**Bewick's Tundra Swan**	*C. columbianus*																					BS			0153
A	**Whooper Swan**	*C. cygnus*																					WS	b^{AD}		0154
A	**Bean Goose**	*Anser fabalis*																					BE	b^{D}		0157
A	**Pink-footed Goose**	*A. brachyrhynchus*																					PG	b^{AD}		0158
A	**White-fronted Goose**	*A. albifrons*																					WG	b^{D}		0159
A	**Lesser White-fr Goose**	*A. erythropus*																					LC	b^{B}	R	0160
A C	**Greylag Goose**	*A. anser*																					GJ			0161
A	**Snow Goose**	*A. caerulescens*																					SJ	b^{D}		0163
A C	**Canada Goose**	*Branta canadensis*																					CG			0166
A	**Barnacle Goose**	*B. leucopsis*																					BY	b^{D}		0167
A	**Brent Goose**	*B. bernicla*																					BG	b^{D}		0168
A	**Red-breasted Goose**	*B. ruficollis*																					EB	b^{B}	R	0169
C	**Egyptian Goose**	*Alopochen aegyptiacus*																					EG	b^{D}		0170
B	**Ruddy Shelduck**	*Tadorna ferruginea*																					UD	b^{D}		0171
A	**Shelduck**	*T. tadorna*																					SU			0173
C	**Mandarin Duck**	*Aix galericulata*																					MN			0178
A	**Wigeon**	*Anas penelope*																					WN	b^{B}		0179
A	**American Wigeon**	*A. americana*																					AW		R	0180
D	**Falcated Duck**	*A. falcata*																					FT		R	0181
A C	**Gadwall**	*A. strepera*																					GA	b^{B}		0182
D	**Baikal Teal**	*A. formosa*																					IK		R	0183
A	**Eurasian Teal**	*A. crecca*																					T			0184
A	**Green-winged Teal**	*A. carolinensis*																								
	Sub-total																									

	DUCKS continued		Life list	2004 list	24 hr	Garden	Holiday	Jan	Feb	Mar	Apr	May	Jun	Jul	Aug	Sep	Oct	Nov	Dec				BTO	RBBP	Bou	EU No
A C	**Mallard**	*A. platyrhynchos*																					MA			0186
A	**American Black Duck**	*A. rubripes*																					BD		R	0187
A	**Pintail**	*A. acuta*																					PT	b^{A}		0189
A	**Garganey**	*A. querquedula*																					GY	b^{A}		0191
A	**Blue-winged Teal**	*A. discors*																					TB	b^{B}	R	0192
A	**Shoveler**	*A. clypeata*																					SV			0194
D	**Marbled Duck**	*Marmaronetta angustirostris*																							R	0195
A	**Red-crested Pochard**	*Netta rufina*																					RQ	b^{D}		0196
A	**Canvasback**	*Aythya valisineria*																							R	0197
A	**Pochard**	*A. ferina*																					PO	b^{B}		0198
A	**Redhead**	*A. americana*																					AZ		R	0199
A	**Ring-necked Duck**	*A. collaris*																					NG			0200
A	**Ferruginous Duck**	*A. nyroca*																					FD			0202
A	**Tufted Duck**	*A. fuligula*																					TU			0203
A	**Scaup**	*A. marila*																					SP	b^{A}		0204
A	**Lesser Scaup**	*A. affinis*																					AY		R	0205
A	**Eider**	*Somateria mollissima*																					E			0206
A	**King Eider**	*S. spectabilis*																					KE		R	0207
A	**Steller's Eider**	*Polysticta stelleri*																					ES		R	0209
A	**Harlequin**	*Histrionicus histrionicus*																					HQ		R	0211
A	**Long-tailed Duck**	*Clangula hyemalis*																					LN	b^{A}		0212
A	**Common Scoter**	*Melanitta nigra*																					CX	b^{A}		0213
A	**Surf Scoter**	*M. perspicillata*																					FS			0214
A	**Velvet Scoter**	*M. fusca*																					VS			0215
	Sub-total																									

	DUCKS, GAMEBIRDS, DIVERS		Life list	2004 list	24 hr	Garden	Holiday	Jan	Feb	Mar	Apr	May	Jun	Jul	Aug	Sep	Oct	Nov	Dec				BTO	RBBP	Bou	EU No
A	**Bufflehead**	*Bucephala albeola*																					VH		R	0216
A	**Barrow's Goldeneye**	*B. islandica*																							R	0217
A	**Goldeneye**	*B. clangula*																					GN	b^{AD}		0218
A	**Smew**	*Mergellus albellus*																					SY			0220
A	**Red-breasted Merganser**	*Mergus serrator*																					RM			0221
A	**Goosander**	*M. merganser*																					GD			0223
c	**Ruddy Duck**	*Oxyura jamaicensis*																					RY			0225
E U	**White-headed Duck**	*0. Leucocephala*																					WQ			0226
E U	**Hazel Grouse**	*Bonasa bonasia*																								0326
A	**Red Willow Grouse**	*Lagopus lagopus*																					RG			0329
A	**Ptarmigan**	*L. mutus*																					PM			0330
A	**Black Grouse**	*Tetrao tetrix*																					BK			0332
B C	**Capercaillie**	*T. urogallus*																					CP			0335
E U	**Rock Partridge**	*Alectoris graeca*																								0357
C	**Red-legged Partridge**	*A. rufa*																					RL			0358
E U	**Barbary Partridge**	*A. barbara*																								0359
A C	**Grey Partridge**	*Perdix perdix*																					P			0367
A	**Quail**	*Coturnix coturnix*																					Q	b^{B}		0370
C	**Pheasant**	*Phasianus colchicus*																					PH			0394
C	**Golden Pheasant**	*Chrysolophus pictus*																					GF	b^{D}		0396
C	**Lady Amherst's Pheasant**	*C. amherstiae*																					LM	b^{D}		0397
A	**Red-throated Diver**	*Gavia stellata*																					RH	b^{B}		0002
A	**Black-throated Diver**	*G. arctica*																					BV	b^{A}		0003
A	**Great Northern Diver**	*G. immer*																					ND			0004
	Sub-total																									

	DIVERS, GREBES, ALBATROSS, FULMAR, PETRELS		Life list	2004 list	24 hr	Garden	Holiday	Jan	Feb	Mar	Apr	May	Jun	Jul	Aug	Sep	Oct	Nov	Dec				BTO	RBBP	Bou	EU No
A	**White- Yellow billed Diver**	*G. adamsii*																					WV		R	0005
A	**Pied-billed Grebe**	*Podilymbus podiceps*																					PJ		R	0006
A	**Little Grebe**	*Tachybaptus ruficollis*																					LG			0007
A	**Great Crested Grebe**	*Podiceps cristatus*																					GG			0009
A	**Red-necked Grebe**	*P. grisegena*																					RX	b[A]		0010
A	**Slavonian Grebe**	*P. auritus*																					SZ	b[A]		0011
A	**Black-necked Grebe**	*P. nigricollis*																					BN	b[A]		0012
A	**Black-browed Albatross**	*Thalassarche melanophris*																					AA		R	0014
A	**Fulmar**	*Fulmarus glacialis*																					F			0020
A	***'Soft-plumaged Petrel**	*'Pterodroma mollis/madeira/feae*																							R	0026
B	**Capped Petrel**	*Pterodroma hasitata*																							R	0029
B	**Bulwer's Petrel**	*Bulweria bulwerii*																							R	0034
A	**Cory's Shearwater**	*Calonectris diomedea*																					CQ			0036
A	**Great Shearwater**	*Puffinus gravis*																					GQ			0040
A	**Sooty Shearwater**	*P. griseus*																					OT			0043
A	**Manx Shearwater**	*P. Puffinus*																					MX			0046
A	**Mediterranean Shearwater**	*P. mauretanicus*																								0046
A	**Little Shearwater**	*P. assimilis*																							R	0048
A	**Wilson's Petrel**	*Oceanites oceanicus*																							R	0050
B	**White-faced Petrel**	*Pelagodroma marina*																							R	0051
A	**Storm Petrel**	*Hydrobates pelagicus*																					TM			0052
A	**Leach's Petrel**	*Oceanodroma leucorhoa*																					TL	b[B]		0055
A	**Swinhoe's Petrel**	*O. monorhis*																							R	0056
B	**Madeiran Petrel**	*O. castro*																							R	0058
	Sub-total																									

*Alternative sub-species

	TROPICBIRD, CORMORANTS, PELICANS, HERONS, STORKS, SPOONBILL		Life list	2004 list	24 hr	Garden	Holiday	Jan	Feb	Mar	Apr	May	Jun	Jul	Aug	Sep	Oct	Nov	Dec				BTO	RBBP	Bou	EU No
A	**Red-billed Tropicbird**	*Phaethon aethereus*																								
A	**Gannet**	*Morus bassanus*																					GX			0071
A	**Cormorant**	*Phalacrocorax carbo*																					CA			0072
A	**Double-crested Cormorant**	*P. auritus*																							R	0078
A	**Shag**	*P. aristotelis*																					SA			0080
E U	**Pygmy Cormorant**	*P. pygmeus*																								0082
D	**Great White Pelican**	*Pelecanus onocrotalus*																					YP		R	0088
E U	**Dalmatian Pelican**	*P. crispus*																								0089
A	**Ascension Frigatebird**	*Fregata aquila*																							R	
A	**Bittern**	*Botaurus stellaris*																					BI	b[A]		0095
A	**American Bittern**	*B. lentiginosus*																					AM		R	0096
A	**Little Bittern**	*Ixobrychus minutus*																					LL		R	0098
A	**Night Heron**	*Nycticorax nycticorax*																					NT	b[AD]	R	0104
A	**Green Heron**	*Butorides virescens*																					HR		R	0107
A	**Squacco Heron**	*Ardeola ralloides*																					QH		R	0108
A	**Cattle Egret**	*Bubulcus ibis*																					EC		R	0111
A	**Little Egret**	*Egretta garzetta*																					ET	b[A]		0119
A	**Great White Egret**	*Ardea alba*																					HW		R	0121
A	**Grey Heron**	*A. cinerea*																					H			0122
A	**Purple Heron**	*A. purpurea*																					UR			0124
A	**Black Stork**	*Ciconia nigra*																					OS		R	0131
A	**White Stork**	*C. ciconia*																					OR			0134
A	**Glossy Ibis**	*Plegadis falcinellus*																					IB			0136
A	**Spoonbill**	*Platalea leucorodia*																					NB	b[A]		0144
	Sub-total																									

FLAMINGO, RAPTORS			Life list	2004 list	24 hr	Garden	Holiday	Jan	Feb	Mar	Apr	May	Jun	Jul	Aug	Sep	Oct	Nov	Dec				BTO	RBBP	Bou	EU No
D	**Greater Flamingo**	*Phoenicopterus roseus*																					FL		R	0147
A	**Honey Buzzard**	*Pernis apivorus*																					HZ	b^A		0231
E U	**Black-winged Kite**	*Elanus caeruleus*																								0235
A	**Black Kite**	*Milvus migrans*																					KB		R	0238
A C	**Red Kite**	*M. milvus*																					KT	b^A		0239
A	**White-tailed Eagle**	*Haliaeetus albicilla*																					WE	b^A		0243
D	**Bald Eagle**	*H. leucocephalus*																							R	0244
E U	**Lammergeier**	*Gypaetus barbatus*																								0246
B D	**Egyptian Vulture**	*Neophron percnopterus*																							R	0247
D	**Black Monk Vulture**	*Aegypius monachus*																							R	0255
A	**Short-toed Eagle**	*Circaetus gallicus*																								0256
A	**Marsh Harrier**	*Circus aeruginosus*																					MR	b^A		0260
A	**Hen Harrier**	*C. cyaneus*																					HH	b^B		0261
A	**Pallid Harrier**	*C. macrourus*																							R	0262
A	**Montagu's Harrier**	*C. pygargus*																					MO	b^A		0263
A C	**Goshawk**	*Accipiter gentilis*																					GI	b^B		0267
A	**Sparrowhawk**	*A. nisus*																					SH			0269
E U	**Levant Sparrowhawk**	*A. brevipes*																								0273
A	**Buzzard**	*Buteo buteo*																					BZ			0287
E U	**Long-legged Buzzard**	*B. rufinus*																								0288
A	**Rough-legged Buzzard**	*B. lagopus*																					RF			0290
E U	**Lesser Spotted Eagle**	*Aquila pomarina*																								0292
B	**Greater Spotted Eagle**	*A. clanga*																							R	0293
E U	**Imperial Eagle**	*A. heliaca*																								0295
	Sub-total																									

	RAPTORS continued RAILS, CRAKES, GALLINULES		Life list	2004 list	24 hr	Garden	Holiday	Jan	Feb	Mar	Apr	May	Jun	Jul	Aug	Sep	Oct	Nov	Dec				BTO	RBBP	Bou	EU No
A	**Golden Eagle**	*A. chrysaetos*																					EA	b^B		0296
E U	**Booted Eagle**	*Hieraaetus pennatus*																								0298
E U	**Bonelli's Eagle**	*H. fasciatus*																								0299
A	**Osprey**	*Pandion haliaetus*																					OP	b^A		0301
A	**Lesser Kestrel**	*Falco naumanni*																							R	0303
A	**Kestrel**	*F. tinnunculus*																					K			0304
A	**American Kestrel**	*F. sparverius*																							R	0305
A	**Red-footed Falcon**	*F. vespertinus*																					FV		R	0307
A	**Merlin**	*F. columbarius*																					ML	b^B		0309
A	**Hobby**	*F. subbuteo*																					HY	b^B		0310
A	**Eleonora's Falcon**	*F. eleonorae*																							R	0311
E U	**Lanner**	*F. biarmicus*																					FB			0314
D	**Saker**	*F. cherrug*																					JF		R	0316
A	**Gyrfalcon**	*F. rusticolus*																					YF		R	0318
A	**Peregrine**	*F. peregrinus*																					PE	b^B		0320
E U	**Andalusian Hemipode**	*Turnix sylvatica*																								0400
A	**Water Rail**	*Rallus aquaticus*																					WA			0407
A	**Spotted Crake**	*Porzana porzana*																					AK	b^A		0408
A	**Sora**	*P. carolina*																							R	0409
A	**Little Crake**	*P. parva*																					JC		R	0410
A	**Baillon's Crake**	*P. pusilla*																					VC		R	0411
A	**Corncrake**	*Crex crex*																					CE	b^A		0421
A	**Moorhen**	*Gallinula chloropus*																					MH			0424
B	**Allen's Gallinule**	*Porphyrula alleni*																							R	0425
	Sub-total																									

	GALLINULES cont. COOTS, CRANES, BUSTARDS, WADERS		Life list	2004 list	24 hr	Garden	Holiday	Jan	Feb	Mar	Apr	May	Jun	Jul	Aug	Sep	Oct	Nov	Dec				BTO	RBBP	Bou	EU No
A	**American Purple Gallinule**	*P. martinica*																							R	0426
E U	**Purple Swamp-hen Gallinule**	*Porphyrio porphyrio*																								0427
A	**Coot**	*Fulica atra*																					CO			0429
A	**American Coot**	*F. americana*																							R	0430
EL	**Crested Coot**	*F. cristata*																								0431
A	**Crane**	*Grus grus*																					AN	b^A		0433
A	**Sandhill Crane**	*G. canadensis*																							R	0436
A	**Little Bustard**	*Tetrax tetrax*																							R	0442
C	**Houbara Bustard**	*Chlamydotis undulata*																							R	0444
B	**Macqueen's Bustard**	*Chlamydotis macqueenii*																							R	0444
A	**Great Bustard**	*Otis tarda*																					OC		R	0446
A	**Oystercatcher**	*Haematopus ostralegus*																					OC			0450
A	**Black-winged Stilt**	*Himantopus himantopus*																					IT		R	0455
A	**Avocet**	*Recurvirostra avosetta*																					AV	b^A		0456
A	**Stone Curlew**	*Burhinus oedicnemus*																					TN	b^A		0459
A	**Cream-coloured Courser**	*Cursorius cursor*																							R	0464
A	**Collared Pratincole**	*Glareola pratincola*																							R	0465
A	**Oriental Pratincole**	*G. maldivarum*																					GM		R	0466
A	**Black-winged Pratincole**	*G. nordmanni*																					KW		R	0467
A	**Little Ringed Plover**	*Charadrius dubius*																					LP	b^B		0469
A	**Ringed Plover**	*C. hiaticula*																					RP			0470
A	**Semipalmated Plover**	*C. semipalmatus*																					TV		R	0471
A	**Killdeer**	*C. vociferus*																					KL		R	0474
A	**Kentish Plover**	*C. alexandrinus*																					KP			0477
	Sub-total																									

	WADERS continued		Life list	2004 list	24 hr	Garden	Holiday	Jan	Feb	Mar	Apr	May	Jun	Jul	Aug	Sep	Oct	Nov	Dec				BTO	RBBP	Bou	EU No
A	**Lesser Sand Plover**	*C. mongolus*																							R	0478
F A	**Greater Sand Plover**	*C. leschenaultii*																					DP		R	0479
A	**Caspian Plover**	*C. asiaticus*																							R	0480
A	**Dotterel**	*C. morinellus*																					DO	b^B		0482
A	**American Golden Plover**	*Pluvialis dominica*																					ID		R	0484
A	**Pacific Golden Plover**	*P. fulva*																					IF		R	0484
A	**Golden Plover**	*P. apricaria*																					GP			0485
A	**Grey Plover**	*P. squatarola*																					GV			0486
E U	**Spur-winged Plover**	*Hoplopterus spinosus*																					UW			0487
A	**Sociable Lapwing**	*Vanellus gregarius*																					IP		R	0491
A	**White-tailed Lapwing**	*V. leucurus*																							R	0492
A	**Lapwing**	*V. vanellus*																					L			0493
A	**Great Knot**	*Calidris tenuirostris*																					KO		R	0495
A	**Knot**	*C. canutus*																					KN			0496
A	**Sanderling**	*C. alba*																					SS			0497
A	**Semipalmated Sandpiper**	*C. pusilla*																					PZ		R	0498
A	**Western Sandpiper**	*C. mauri*																					ER		R	0499
A	**Red-necked Stint**	*C. ruficollis*																							R	0500
A	**Little Stint**	*C. minuta*																					LX			0501
A	**Temminck's Stint**	*C. temminckii*																					TK	b^A		0502
A	**Long-toed Stint**	*C. subminuta*																							R	0503
A	**Least Sandpiper**	*C. minutilla*																					EP		R	0504
A	**White-rumped Sandpiper**	*C. fuscicollis*																					WU		R	0505
A	**Baird's Sandpiper**	*C. bairdii*																					BP		R	0506
	Sub-total																									

	WADERS continued		Life list	2004 list	24 hr	Garden	Holiday	Jan	Feb	Mar	Apr	May	Jun	Jul	Aug	Sep	Oct	Nov	Dec				BTO	RBBP	Bou	EU No
A	**Pectoral Sandpiper**	*C. melanotos*																					PP			0507
A	**Sharp-tailed Sandpiper**	*C. acuminata*																					VV		R	0508
A	**Curlew Sandpiper**	*C. ferruginea*																					CV			0509
A	**Purple Sandpiper**	*C. maritima*																					PS	b^A		0510
A	**Dunlin**	*C. alpina*																					DN			0512
A	**Broad-billed Sandpiper**	*Limicola falcinellus*																					OA		R	0514
A	**Stilt Sandpiper**	*Micropalama himantopus*																					MI		R	0515
A	**Buff-breasted Sandpiper**	*Tryngites subruficollis*																					BQ			0516
A	**Ruff**	*Philomachus pugnax*																					RU	b^A		0517
A	**Jack Snipe**	*Lymnocryptes minimus*																					JS			0518
A	**Snipe**	*Gallinago gallinago*																					SN			0519
A	**Great Snipe**	*G. media*																					DS		R	0520
A	**Short-billed Dowitcher**	*Limnodromus griseus*																								
A	**Long-billed Dowitcher**	*L. scolopaceus*																					LD		R	0527
A	**Woodcock**	*Scolopax rusticola*																					WK			0529
A	**Black-tailed Godwit**	*Limosa limosa*																					BW	b^A		0532
A	**Hudsonian Godwit**	*L. haemastica*																					HU		R	0533
A	**Bar-tailed Godwit**	*L. lapponica*																					BA			0534
A	**Little Whimbrel Curlew**	*N. minutus*																							R	0536
B	**Eskimo Curlew**	*N. borealis*																							R	0537
A	**Whimbrel**	*N. phaeopus*																					WM	b^A		0538
A	**Curlew**	*N. arquata*																					CU			0541
A	**Upland Sandpiper**	*Bartramia longicauda*																					UP		R	0544
A	**Spotted Redshank**	*T. erythropus*																					DR			0545
	Sub-total																									

	WADERS continued, GULLS		Life list	2004 list	24 hr	Garden	Holiday	Jan	Feb	Mar	Apr	May	Jun	Jul	Aug	Sep	Oct	Nov	Dec			BTO	RBBP	Bou	EU No
A	**Redshank**	*T. totanus*																				RK			0546
A	**Marsh Sandpiper**	*T. stagnatilis*																				MD		R	0547
A	**Greenshank**	*T. nebularia*																				GK	b^B		0548
A	**Greater Yellowlegs**	*T. melanoleuca*																				LZ		R	0550
A	**Lesser Yellowlegs**	*T. flavipes*																				LY		R	0551
A	**Solitary Sandpiper**	*T. solitaria*																				I		R	0552
A	**Green Sandpiper**	*T. ochropus*																				GE			0553
A	**Wood Sandpiper**	*T. glareola*																				OD	b^A		0554
A	**Terek Sandpiper**	*Xenus cinereus*																				TR		R	0555
A	**Common Sandpiper**	*Actitis hypoleucos*																				CS			0556
A	**Spotted Sandpiper**	*A. macularia*																				PQ		R	0557
A	**Grey-tailed Tattler**	*Heteroscelus brevipes*																				YT		R	0558
A	**Turnstone**	*Arenaria interpres*																				TT			0561
A	**Wilson's Phalarope**	*Phalaropus tricolor*																				WF		R	0563
A	**Red-necked Phalarope**	*P. lobatus*																				NK	b^A		0564
A	**Grey Phalarope**	*P. fulicarius*																				PL			0565
A	**Pomarine Skua**	*Stercorarius pomarinus*																				PK			0566
A	**Arctic Skua**	*S. parasiticus*																				AC			0567
A	**Long-tailed Skua**	*S. longicaudus*																				OG			0568
A	**Great Skua**	*Catharacta skua*																				NX			0569
B	**Great Black-headed Pallas's Gull**	*L. ichthyaetus*																						R	0573
A	**Mediterranean Gull**	*L. melanocephalus*																				MU	b^A		0575
A	**Laughing Gull**	*L. atricilla*																				LF		R	0576
A	**Franklin's Gull**	*L. pipixcan*																				FG		R	0577
	Sub-total																								

	GULLS continued, TERNS		Life list	2004 list	24 hr	Garden	Holiday	Jan	Feb	Mar	Apr	May	Jun	Jul	Aug	Sep	Oct	Nov	Dec				BTO	RBBP	Bou	EU No
A	**Little Gull**	*L. minutus*																					LU			0578
A	**Sabine's Gull**	*L. sabini*																					AB			0579
A	**Bonaparte's Gull**	*L. philadelphia*																					ON		R	0581
A	**Black-headed Gull**	*L. ridibundus*																					BH			0582
A	**Slender-billed Gull**	*L. genei*																					EI			0585
F U	**Audouin's Gull**	*L. audouinii*																								0588
A	**Ring-billed Gull**	*L. delawarensis*																					IN			0589
A	**Common Mew Gull**	*L. canus*																					CM			0590
A	**Lesser Black-backed Gull**	*L. fuscus*																					LB			0591
A	**Herring Gull**	*L. argentatus*																					HG			0592
A	**Iceland Gull**	*L. glaucoides*																					IG			0598
A	**Glaucous Gull**	*L. hyperboreus*																					GZ			0599
A	**Great Black-backed Gull**	*L. marinus*																					GB			0600
A	**Ross's Gull**	*Rhodostethia rosea*																					QG		R	0601
A	**Kittiwake**	*Rissa tridactyla*																					KI			0602
A	**Ivory Gull**	*Pagophila eburnea*																					IV		R	0604
A	**Gull-billed Tern**	*S.nilotica*																					TG		R	0605
A	**Caspian Tern**	*S.caspia*																					CJ		R	0606
A	**Royal Tern**	*S.maxima*																					QT		R	0607
A	**Lesser Crested Tern**	*S.bengalensis*																					TF	b^{A}	R	0609
A	**Sandwich Tern**	*S.sandvicensis*																					TE			0611
A	**Roseate Tern**	*S.dougallii*																					RS	b^{A}		0614
A	**Common Tern**	*S.hirundo*																					CN			0615
A	**Arctic Tern**	*S.paradisaea*																					AE			0616
	Sub-total																									

TERNS cont. AUKS, SANDGROUSE, DOVES/PIGEONS			Life list	2004 list	24 hr	Garden	Holiday	Jan	Feb	Mar	Apr	May	Jun	Jul	Aug	Sep	Oct	Nov	Dec				BTO	RBBP	Bou	EU No
A	**Aleutian Tern**	*S.aleutica*																							R	0617
A	**Forster's Tern**	*S.forsteri*																					FO		R	0618
A	**Bridled Tern**	*S.anaethetus*																							R	0622
A	**Sooty Tern**	*S.fuscata*																							R	0623
A	**Little Tern**	*S.albifrons*																					AF	b^B		0624
A	**Whiskered Tern**	*Chlidonias hybrida*																					WD		R	0626
A	**Black Tern**	*C. niger*																					BJ			0627
A	**White-winged Black Tern**	*C. leucopterus*																					WJ		R	0628
A	**Guillemot**	*Uria aalge*																					GU			0634
A	**Brünnich's Guillemot**	*U. lomvia*																					TZ		R	0635
A	**Razorbill**	*Alca torda*																					RA			0636
A	**Black Guillemot**	*Cepphus grylle*																					TY			0638
A	**Ancient Murrelet**	*Synthliboramphus antiquus*																							R	0645
A	**Little Auk**	*Alle alle*																					LK			0647
A	**Puffin**	*Fratercula arctica*																					PU			0654
E U	**Black-bellied Sandgrouse**	*Pterocles orientalis*																								0661
E U	**Pin-tailed Sandgrouse**	*P. alchata*																								0662
A	**Pallas's Sandgrouse**	*Syrrhaptes paradoxus*																							R	0663
A C	**Rock Dove**	*Columba livia*																					DV			0665
A	**Stock Dove**	*C. oenas*																					SD			0668
A	**Woodpigeon**	*C. palumbus*																					WP			0670
A	**Collared Dove**	*Streptopelia decaocto*																					CD			0684
A	**Turtle Dove**	*S. turtur*																					TD			0687
A	**Rufous Oriental Turtle Dove**	*S. orientalis*																							R	0689
	Sub-total																									

DOVES continued, CUCKOOS, OWLS, NIGHTJARS, SWIFTS			Life list	2004 list	24 hr	Garden	Holiday	Jan	Feb	Mar	Apr	May	Jun	Jul	Aug	Sep	Oct	Nov	Dec				BTO	RBBP	Bou	EU No
A	**Mourning Dove**	*Zenaida macroura*																							R	0695
C	**Rose-ringed Parakeet**	*Psittacula krameri*																					RI	b^{D}		0712
A	**Great Spotted Cuckoo**	*Clamator glandarius*																					UK		R	0716
A	**Cuckoo**	*Cuculus canorus*																					CK			0724
A	**Black-billed Cuckoo**	*Coccyzus erythrophthalmus*																							R	0727
A	**Yellow-billed Cuckoo**	*C. americanus*																							R	0728
A	**Barn Owl**	*Tyto alba*																					BO	b^{C}		0735
A	**Scops Owl**	*Otus scops*																							R	0739
E U	**Eagle Owl**	*Bubo bubo*																					EO	b^{D}		0744
A	**Snowy Owl**	*Nyctea scandiaca*																					SO	b^{A}	R	0749
A	**Hawk Owl**	*Surnia ulula*																							R	0750
E U	**Pygmy Owl**	*Glaucidium passerinum*																								0751
c	**Little Owl**	*Athene noctua*																					LO			0757
A	**Tawny Owl**	*Strix aluco*																					TO			0761
E U	**Ural Owl**	*S. uralensis*																								0765
E U	**Great Grey Owl**	*S. nebulosa*																								0766
A	**Long-eared Owl**	*Asio otus*																					LE			0767
A	**Short-eared Owl**	*A. flammeus*																					SE			0768
A	**Tengmalm's Owl**	*Aegolius funereus*																							R	0770
A	**Nightjar**	*Caprimulgus europaeus*																					NJ			0778
B	**Red-necked Nightjar**	*C. ruficollis*																							R	0779
A	**Egyptian Nightjar**	*C. aegyptius*																							R	0781
A	**Common Nighthawk**	*Chordeiles minor*																							R	0786
A	**Chimney Swift**	*Chaetura pelagica*																							R	0790
	Sub-total																									

	SWIFTS etc. KINGFISHERS, BEE-EATERS, ROLLER, HOOPOE, WOODPECKERS		Life list	2004 list	24 hr	Garden	Holiday	Jan	Feb	Mar	Apr	May	Jun	Jul	Aug	Sep	Oct	Nov	Dec			BTO	RBBP	Bou	EU No
A	**White-throated Needletail**	*Hirundapus caudacutus*																				NI		R	0792
A	**Swift**	*Apus apus*																				SI			0795
A	**Pallid Swift**	*A. pallidus*																						R	0796
A	**Pacific Swift**	*A. pallidus*																						R	0797
A	**Alpine Swift**	*A. pacificus*																				AI		R	0798
EL	**White-rumped Swift**	*A. melba*																							0799
A	**Little Swift**	*A. affinis*																						R	0800
A	**Kingfisher**	*Alcedo atthis*																				KF	b[C]		0831
A	**Belted Kingfisher**	*Ceryle alcyon*																						R	0834
A	**Blue-checked Bee-eater**	*Merops superciliosus*																						R	0839
A	**Bee-eater**	*M. apiaster*																				MZ			0840
A	**Roller**	*Coracias garrulus*																						R	0841
A	**Hoopoe**	*Upupa epops*																				HP			0846
A	**Wryneck**	*Jynx torquilla*																				WY	b[A]		0848
E U	**Grey-headed Woodpecker**	*Picus canus*																							0855
A	**Green Woodpecker**	*P. viridis*																				G			0856
E U	**Black Woodpecker**	*Dryocopus martius*																							0863
A	**Yellow-bellied Sapsucker**	*Sphyrapicus varius*																						R	0872
A	**Great Spotted Woodpecker**	*Dendrocopos major*																				GS			0876
E U	**Syrian Woodpecker**	*D. syriacus*																							0878
E U	**Middle Spotted Woodpecker**	*D. medius*																							0883
E U	**White-backed Woodpecker**	*D. leucotos*																							0884
A	**Lesser Spotted Woodpecker**	*D. minor*																				LS			0887
E U	**Three-toed Woodpecker**	*Picoides tridactylus*																							0898
	Sub-total																								

	PHOEBE, LARKS, MARTINS, SWALLOWS, PIPITS		Life list	2004 list	24 hr	Garden	Holiday	Jan	Feb	Mar	Apr	May	Jun	Jul	Aug	Sep	Oct	Nov	Dec			BTO	RBBP	Bou	EU No
A	**Eastern Phoebe**	*Sayornis phoebe*																						R	0909
E U	**Dupont's Lark**	*Chersophilus duponti*																							0959
A	**Calandra Lark**	*Melanocorypha calandra*																						R	0961
A	**Bimaculated Lark**	*M. bimaculata*																						R	0962
A	**White-winged Lark**	*M. leucoptera*																						R	0965
A	**Short-toed Lark**	*Calandrella brachydactyla*																				VL			0968
A	**Lesser Short-toed Lark**	*C. rufescens*																						R	0970
A	**Crested Lark**	*Galerida cristata*																						R	0972
E U	**Thekla Lark**	*G. theklae*																							0973
A	**Wood Lark**	*Lullula arborea*																				WL	b[B]		0974
A	**Sky Lark**	*Alauda arvensis*																				S			0976
A	**Shore Horned Lark**	*Eremophila alpestris*																				SX			0978
A	**Sand Martin**	*Riparia riparia*																				SM			0981
A	**Tree Swallow**	*Tachycineta bicolor*																						R	0983
A	**Crag Martin**	*Ptyonoprogne rupestris*																						R	0991
A	**Swallow**	*Hirundo rustica*																				SL			0992
A	**Red-rumped Swallow**	*H. daurica*																				VR		R	0995
A	**Cliff Swallow**	*H. pyrrhonota*																						R	0998
A	**House Martin**	*Delichon urbica*																				HM			1001
A	**Richard's Pipit**	*Anthus novaeseelandiae*																				PR			1002
A	**Blyth's Pipit**	*A. godlewskii*																						R	1004
A	**Tawny Pipit**	*A. campestris*																				TI			1005
A	**Olive-backed Pipit**	*A. hodgsoni*																				OV		R	1008
A	**Tree Pipit**	*A. trivialis*																				TP			1009
	Sub-total																								

	PIPITS cont. WAGTAILS, WAXWINGS, DIPPER, WREN, ACCENTORS, ROBINS		Life list	2004 list	24 hr	Garden	Holiday	Jan	Feb	Mar	Apr	May	Jun	Jul	Aug	Sep	Oct	Nov	Dec				BTO	RBBP	Bou	EU No
A	**Pechora Pipit**	*A. gustavi*																							R	1010
A	**Meadow Pipit**	*A. pratensis*																					MP			1011
A	**Red-throated Pipit**	*A. cervinus*																					VP		R	1012
A	**Rock Pipit**	*A. petrosus*																					RC			1014
A	**Water Pipit**	*A. spinoletta*																					WI			1014
A	**Buff-bellied Pipit**	*A. rubescens*																							R	1014
A	**Yellow Wagtail**	*Motacilla flava*																					YW			1017
A	**Citrine Wagtail**	*M. citreola*																							R	1018
A	**Grey Wagtail**	*M. cinerea*																					GL			1019
A	**Pied White Wagtail**	*M. alba*																					PW			1020
A	**Cedar Waxing**	*Bombycilla cedrorum*																							R	1046
A	**Bohemian Waxwing**	*Bombycilla garrulus*																					WX			1048
A	**Dipper**	*Cinclus cinclus*																					DI			1050
A	**Wren**	*Troglodytes troglodytes*																					WR			1066
A	**Northern Mockingbird**	*Mimus polyglottos*																							R	1067
A	**Brown Thrasher**	*Toxostoma rufum*																							R	1069
A	**Gray Catbird**	*Dumetella carolinensis*																								
A	**Dunnock**	*Prunella modularis*																					D			1084
A	**Alpine Accentor**	*P. collaris*																							R	1094
A	**Rufous-tailed Scrub Robin**	*Cercotrichas galactotes*																							R	1095
A	**Robin**	*Erithacus rubecula*																					R			1099
A	**Thrush Nightingale**	*Luscinia luscinia*																					FN		R	1103
A	**Nightingale**	*L. megarhynchos*																					N			1104
A	**Siberian Rubythroat**	*L. calliope*																							R	1105
	Sub-total																									

	REDSTARTS, CHATS, WHEATEARS, THRUSHES		Life list	2004 list	24 hr	Garden	Holiday	Jan	Feb	Mar	Apr	May	Jun	Jul	Aug	Sep	Oct	Nov	Dec				BTO	RBBP	Bou	EU No
A	**Bluethroat**	*L. svecica*																					BU			1106
A	**Siberian Blue Robin**	*L. cyane*																								
A	**Red-flanked Bluetail**	*Tarsiger cyanurus*																							R	1113
A	**White-throated Robin**	*Irania gutturalis*																							R	1117
A	**Black Redstart**	*Phoenicurus ochruros*																					BX	b[A]		1121
A	**Redstart**	*P. phoenicurus*																					RT			1122
A	**Moussier's Redstart**	*P. moussieri*																							R	1127
A	**Whinchat**	*Saxicola rubetra*																					WC			1137
A	**Stonechat**	*S. torquata*																					SC			1139
A	**Isabelline Wheatear**	*Oenanthe isabellina*																							R	1144
A	**Wheatear**	*O. O.*																					W			1146
A	**Pied Wheatear**	*O. pleschanka*																					PI		R	1147
A	**Black-eared Wheatear**	*O. hispanica*																							R	1148
A	**Desert Wheatear**	*O. deserti*																							R	1149
A	**White-crowned -tailed Black Wheatear**	*O. leucopyga*																								1157
E U	**Black Wheatear**	*0. Leucura*																							R	1158
A	**Rock Thrush**	*Monticola saxatilis*																					OH		R	1162
A	**Blue Rock Thrush**	*M. solitarius*																							R	1166
A	**White's Thrush**	*Zoothera dauma*																							R	1170
A	**Siberian Thrush**	*Z. sibirica*																							R	1171
A	**Varied Thrush**	*Z. naevia*																					VT		R	1172
A	**Wood Thrush**	*Hylocichla mustelina*																							R	1175
A	**Hermit Thrush**	*Catharus guttatus*																							R	1176
A	**Swainson's Thrush**	*C. ustulatus*																							R	1177
	Sub-total																									

	THRUSHES continued, WARBLERS		Life list	2004 list	24 hr	Garden	Holiday	Jan	Feb	Mar	Apr	May	Jun	Jul	Aug	Sep	Oct	Nov	Dec				BTO	RBBP	Bou	EU No
A	**Grey-cheeked Thrush**	*C. minimus*																							R	1178
A	**Veery**	*C. fuscescens*																							R	1179
A	**Ring Ouzel**	*Turdus torquatus*																					RZ			1186
A	**Blackbird**	*T. merula*																					B			1187
I A	**Eyebrowed Thrush**	*T. obscurus*																							R	1195
A	**Dusky Thrush**	*T. naumanni*																							R	1196
A	**Dark-throated Thrush**	*T. ruficollis*																					XC		R	1197
A	**Fieldfare**	*T. pilaris*																					FF	b^A		1198
A	**Song Thrush**	*T. philomelos*																					ST			1200
A	**Redwing**	*T. iliacus*																					RE	b^A		1201
A	**Mistle Thrush**	*T. viscivorus*																					M			1202
A	**American Robin**	*T. migratorius*																					AR		R	1203
A	**Cetti's Warbler**	*Cettia cetti*																					CW	b^A		1220
A	**Zitting Cisticola Fan-tailed Warbler**	*Cisticola juncidis*																							R	1226
A	**Pallas's Grasshopper Warbler**	*Locustella certhiola*																							R	1233
A	**Lanceolated Warbler**	*L.lanceolata*																							R	1235
A	**Grasshopper Warbler**	*L.naevia*																					GH			1236
A	**River Warbler**	*L.fluviatilis*																					VW		R	1237
A	**Savi's Warbler**	*L.luscinioides*																					VI	b^A	R	1238
A	**Moustached Warbler**	*Acrocephalus melanopogon*																							R	1241
A	**Aquatic Warbler**	*A. paludicola*																					AQ			1242
A	**Sedge Warbler**	*A. schoenobaenus*																					SW			1243
A	**Paddyfield Warbler**	*A. agricola*																					PY		R	1247
A	**Blyth's Reed Warbler**	*A. dumetorum*																							R	1248
	Sub-total																									

	WARBLERS continued		Life list	2004 list	24 hr	Garden	Holiday	Jan	Feb	Mar	Apr	May	Jun	Jul	Aug	Sep	Oct	Nov	Dec				BTO	RBBP	Bou	EU No
A	**Marsh Warbler**	*A. palustris*																					MW	b[A]		1250
A	**Reed Warbler**	*A. scirpaceus*																					RW			1251
A	**Great Reed Warbler**	*A. arundinaceus*																					QW		R	1253
A	**Thick-billed Warbler**	*A. aedon*																							R	1254
A	**Eastern Olivaceous Warbler**	*Hippolais pallida*																							R	1255
A	**Western Olivaceous Warbler**	*Hippolais opaca*																							R	
A	**Booted Warbler**	*H. caligata*																								1256
A	**Syke's Warbler**	*H. rama*																								
EU	**Olive-tree Warbler**	*H. olivetorum*																								1258
A	**Icterine Warbler**	*H. icterina*																					IC			1259
A	**Melodious Warbler**	*H. polyglotta*																					ME			1260
A	**Marmora's Warbler**	*Sylvia sarda*																					MM			1261
A	**Dartford Warbler**	*S. undata*																					DW	b[B]		1262
A	**Spectacled Warbler**	*S. conspicillata*																								1264
A	**Subalpine Warbler**	*S. cantillans*																								1265
A	**Sardinian Warbler**	*S. melanocephala*																								1267
EU	**Cyprus Warbler**	*S. melanothorax*																								1268
A	**Rüppell's Warbler**	*S. rueppelli*																								1269
A	**Desert Warbler**	*S. nana*																								1270
A	**Orphean Warbler**	*S. hortensis*																								1272
A	**Barred Warbler**	*S. nisoria*																					RR			1273
A	**Lesser Whitethroat**	*S. curruca*																					LW			1274
A	**Whitethroat**	*S. communis*																					WH			1275
A	**Garden Warbler**	*S. borin*																					GW			1276
	Sub-total																									

WARBLERS continued, ‘CRESTS’, FLYCATCHERS, TITS			Life list	2004 list	24 hr	Garden	Holiday	Jan	Feb	Mar	Apr	May	Jun	Jul	Aug	Sep	Oct	Nov	Dec				BTO	RBBP	Bou	EU No
A	**Blackcap**	*S. atricapilla*																					BC			1277
A	**Greenish Warbler**	*Phylloscopus trochiloides*																					NP			1293
A	**Arctic Warbler**	*P. borealis*																					AP			1295
A	**Pallas’s Warbler**	*P. proregulus*																					PA			1298
A	**Yellow-browed Warbler**	*P. inornatus*																					YB			1300
A	**Hume’s Leaf Warbler**	*P. humei*																								1300
A	**Radde’s Warbler**	*P. schwarzi*																								1301
A	**Dusky Warbler,**	*P. fuscatus*																					UY		R	1303
A	**Western Bonelli’s Warbler**	*P. bonelli*																					IW		R	1307
A	**Eastern Bonelli’s Warbler**	*P. orientalis*																							R	1307
A	**Wood Warbler**	*P. sibilatrix*																					WO			1308
A	**Common Chiffchaff**	*P. collybita*																					CC			1311
A	**Iberian Chiffchaff**	*P. ibericus*																							R	1311
A	**Willow Warbler**	*P. trochilus*																					WW			1312
A	**Goldcrest**	*Regulus regulus*																					GC			1314
A	**Firecrest**	*R. ignicapilla*																					FC	b[A]		1315
D	**Asian Brown Flycatcher**	*Muscicapa dauurica*																								1335
A	**Spotted Flycatcher**	*Muscicapa striata*																					SF			1335
A	**Red-breasted Flycatcher**	*Ficedula parva*																					FY			1343
D	**Mugimaki Flycatcher**	*F. mugimaki*																							R	1344
E U	**Semi-collared Flycatcher**	*F. semitorquata*																								1347
A	**Collared Flycatcher**	*F. albicollis*																							R	1348
A	**Pied Flycatcher**	*F. hypoleuca*																					PF			1349
A	**Bearded Tit**	*Panurus biarmicus*																					BR	b[B]		1364
	Sub-total																									

TITS continued, NUTHATCHES, TREECREEPERS, ORIOLE, SHRIKES			Life list	2004 list	24 hr	Garden	Holiday	Jan	Feb	Mar	Apr	May	Jun	Jul	Aug	Sep	Oct	Nov	Dec				BTO	RBBP	Bou	EU No
A	**Long-tailed Tit**	*Aegithalos caudatus*																					LT			1437
A	**Marsh Tit**	*Parus palustris*																					MT			1440
E U	**Sombre Tit**	*P. lugubris*																								1441
A	**Willow Tit**	*P. montanus*																					WT			1442
E U	**Siberian Tit**	*P. cinctus*																								1448
A	**Crested Tit**	*P.cristatus*																					CI	b^B		1454
A	**Coal Tit**	*P. ater*																					CT			1461
A	**Blue Tit**	*P. caeruleus*																					BT			1462
A	**Great Tit**	*P. major*																					GT			1464
E U	**Krüper's Nuthatch**	*Sitta krueperi*																								1469
E U	**Corsican Nuthatch**	*S. whiteheadi*																								1470
A	**Red-breasted Nuthatch**	*S. canadensis*																							R	1472
A	**Nuthatch**	*S. europaea*																					NH			1479
E U	**Rock Nuthatch**	*S. neumayer*																								1481
A	**Wallcreeper**	*Tichodroma muraria*																							R	1482
A	**Treecreeper**	*Certhia familiaris*																					TC			1486
A	**Short-toed Treecreeper**	*C. brachydactyla*																					TH		R	1487
A	**Penduline Tit**	*Remiz pendulinus*																					DT		R	1490
A	**Golden Oriole**	*Oriolus oriolus*																					OL	b^A		1508
A	**Brown Shrike**	*Lanius cristatus*																							R	1513
A	**Isabelline Shrike**	*L. isabellinus*																					IL		R	1514
A	**Red-backed Shrike**	*L. collurio*																					ED	b^A		1515
A	**Lesser Grey Shrike**	*L. minor*																							R	1519
A	**Great Grey Shrike**	*L. excubitor*																					SR			1520
	Sub-total																									

	SHRIKES continued, CROWS, STARLINGS, SPARROWS, FINCHES		Life list	2004 list	24 hr	Garden	Holiday	Jan	Feb	Mar	Apr	May	Jun	Jul	Aug	Sep	Oct	Nov	Dec				BTO	RBBP	Bou	EU No
A	**Southern Grey Shrike**	*L. meridionalis*																							R	1520
A	**Woodchat Shrike**	*L. senator*																					OO			1523
E U	**Masked Shrike**	*L. nubicus*																								1524
A	**Jay**	*Garrulus glandarius*																					J			1539
E U	**Siberian Jay**	*Perisoreus infaustus*																								1543
E U	**Azure-winged Magpie**	*Cyanopica cyana*																								1547
A	**Magpie**	*Pica pica*																					MG			1549
A	**Nutcracker**	*Nucifraga caryocatactes*																					NC		R	1557
E U	**Alpine Chough**	*Pyrrhocorax graculus*																								1558
A	**Chough**	*P. pyrrhocorax*																					CF	b[B]		1559
A	**Jackdaw**	*Corvus monedula*																					JD			1560
A	**Rook**	*C. frugilegus*																					RO			1563
A	**Carrion Hooded Crow**	*C. corone*																					C			1567
A	**Hooded Crow**	*C. cornix*																								
A	**Raven**	*C. corax*																					RN			1572
D	**Daurian Starling**	*Sturnus sturninus*																							R	1579
A	**Starling**	*S. vulgaris*																					SG			1582
E U	**Spotless Starling**	*S. unicolor*																								1583
A	**Rose-coloured Rosy Starling**	*Sturnus roseus*																					OE		R	1594
A	**House Sparrow**	*Passer domesticus*																					HS			1591
A	**Spanish Sparrow**	*P. hispaniolensis*																							R	1592
A	**Tree Sparrow**	*P.r montanus*																					TS			1598
A	**Rock Sparrow**	*Petronia petronia*																							R	1604
D	**Snow Finch**	*Montifringilla nivalis*																							R	1611
	Sub-total																									

	FINCHES continued		Life list	2004 list	24 hr	Garden	Holiday	Jan	Feb	Mar	Apr	May	Jun	Jul	Aug	Sep	Oct	Nov	Dec				BTO	RBBP	Bou	EU No
A	**Yellow-throated Vireo**	*Vireo flavifrons*																							R	1628
A	**Philadelphia Vireo**	*V. philadelphicus*																							R	1631
A	**Red-eyed Vireo**	*V.olivaceus*																					EV		R	1633
A	**Chaffinch**	*Fringilla coelebs*																					CH			1636
A	**Brambling**	*F. montifringilla*																					BL	b^A		1638
A	**Serin**	*Serinus serinus*																					NS	b^A		1640
A	**Greenfinch**	*Carduelis chloris*																					GR			1649
A	**Goldfinch**	*C carduelis*																					GO			1653
A	**Siskin**	*C. spinus*																					SK			1654
A	**Linnet**	*C. cannabina*																					LI			1660
A	**Twite**	*C. flavirostris*																					TW			1662
	Lesser Redpoll	*C. cabaret*																								
A	**Mealy Redpoll**	*C. flammea*																					LR			1663
A	**Arctic Redpoll**	*C. hornemanni*																					AL		R	1664
A	**Two-barred Crossbill**	*Loxia leucoptera*																					PD		R	1665
A	**Crossbill**	*L. curvirostra*																					CR	b^C		1666
A	**Scottish Crossbill**	*L. scotica*																					CY	b^B		1667
A	**Parrot Crossbill**	*L. pytyopsittacus*																					PC	b^A	R	1668
A	**Trumpeter Finch**	*Bucanetes githagineus*																							R	1676
A	**Common Rosefinch**	*Carpodacus erythrinus*																					SQ	b^A		1679
A	**Pine Grosbeak**	*Pinicola enucleator*																							R	1699
A	**Bullfinch**	*Pyrrhula pyrrhula*																					BF			1710
A	**Hawfinch**	*Coccothraustes coccothraustes*																					HF			1717
A	**Evening Grosbeak**	*Hesperiphona vespertina*																							R	1718
	Sub-total																									

	NORTH AMERICAN WARBLERS, NEW WORLD SPARROWS		Life list	2004 list	24 hr	Garden	Holiday	Jan	Feb	Mar	Apr	May	Jun	Jul	Aug	Sep	Oct	Nov	Dec				BTO	RBBP	Bou	EU No
A	**Black-and-white Warbler**	*Mniotilta varia*																							R	1720
A	**Golden-winged Warbler**	*Vermivora chrysoptera*																							R	1722
A	**Tennessee Warbler**	*V. peregrina*																							R	1724
A	**Northern Parula**	*Parula americana*																							R	1732
A	**Yellow Warbler**	*Dendroica petechia*																							R	1733
A	**Chestnut-sided Warbler**	*D. pensylvanica*																							R	1734
A	**Blackburnian Warbler**	*D. fusca*																							R	1747
A	**Cape May Warbler**	*D. tigrina*																							R	1749
A	**Magnolia Warbler**	*D. magnolia*																							R	1750
A	**Yellow-rumped Warbler**	*D. coronata*																							R	1751
D	**Palm Warbler**	*D. palmarum*																							R	1752
A	**Blackpoll Warbler**	*D. striata*																							R	1753
A	**Bay-breasted Warbler**	*D. castanea*																							R	1754
A	**American Redstart**	*Setophaga ruticilla*																					AD		R	1755
A	**Ovenbird**	*Seiurus aurocapilla*																							R	1756
A	**Northern Waterthrush**	*S. noveboracensis*																							R	1757
A	**Yellowthroat**	*Geothlypis trichas*																							R	1762
A	**Hooded Warbler**	*Wilsonia citrina*																							R	1771
A	**Wilson's Warbler**	*Wilsonia pusilla*																							R	1772
A	**Summer Tanager**	*Piranga rubra*																							R	1786
A	**Scarlet Tanager**	*P. olivacea*																							R	1788
A	**Eastern Towhee**	*Pipilo erythrophthalmus*																							R	1798
A	**Lark Sparrow**	*Chondestes grammacus*																							R	1824
A	**Savannah Sparrow**	*Passerculus sandwichensis*																							R	1826
	Sub-total																									

	SPARROWS continued BUNTINGS		Life list	2004 list	24 hr	Garden	Holiday	Jan	Feb	Mar	Apr	May	Jun	Jul	Aug	Sep	Oct	Nov	Dec				BTO	RBBP	Bou	EU No
A	**Song Sparrow**	*Melospiza melodia*																							R	1835
A	**White-crowned Sparrow**	*Zonotrichia leucophrys*																							R	1839
A	**White-throated Sparrow**	*Z. albicollis*																							R	1840
A	**Dark-eyed Junco**	*Junco hyemalis*																					JU		R	1842
A	**Lapland Bunting**	*Calcarius lapponicus*																					LA			1847
A	**Snow Bunting**	*Plectrophenax nivalis*																					SB	b^A		1850
A	**Black-faced Bunting**	*Emberiza spodocephala*																							R	1853
A	**Pine Bunting**	*E. leucocephalos*																					EL		R	1856
A	**Yellowhammer**	*E. citrinella*																					Y			1857
A	**Cirl Bunting**	*E. cirlus*																					CL	b^A		1958
A	**Rock Bunting**	*E. cia*																							R	1860
E U	**Cinereous Bunting**	*E. cineracea*																								1865
A	**Ortolan Bunting**	*E. hortulana*																					OB			1866
A	**Cretzschmar's Bunting**	*E. caesia*																							R	1868
A	**Yellow-browed Bunting**	*E. chrysophrys*																							R	1871
A	**Rustic Bunting**	*E. rustica*																							R	1873
A	**Little Bunting**	*E. pusilla*																					LJ			1874
D	**Chestnut Bunting**	*E. rutila*																							R	1875
A	**Yellow-breasted Bunting**	*E. aureola*																							R	1876
A	**Reed Bunting**	*E. schoeniclus*																					RB			1877
A	**Pallas's Bunting**	*E. pallasi*																							R	1878
D	**Red-headed Bunting**	*E. bruniceps*																								1880
A	**Black-headed Bunting**	*E. melanocephala*																							R	1881
A	**Corn Bunting**	*Miliaria calandra*																					CB			1882
	Sub-total																									

	NORTH AMERICAN GROSBEAKS, PREVIOUSLY UNLISTED SPECIES		Life list	2004 list	24 hr	Garden	Holiday	Jan	Feb	Mar	Apr	May	Jun	Jul	Aug	Sep	Oct	Nov	Dec				BTO	RBBP	Bou	EU No
A	**Rose-breasted Grosbeak**	*Pheucticus ludovicianus*																							R	1887
D	**Blue Grosbeak**	*Guiraca caerulea*																							R	1891
A	**Indigo Bunting**	*Passerina cyanea*																							R	1892
A	**Bobolink**	*Dolichonyx oryzivorus*																							R	1897
A	**Brown-headed Cowbird**	*Molothrus ater*																							R	1899
A	**Baltimore Oriole**	*Icterus galbula*																							R	1918
	Sub-total																									

DIRECTORY OF ART, PHOTOGRAPHY AND LECTURERS

Common Eider with King Eider by Thelma Sykes

DIRECTORY OF WILDLIFE ART GALLERIES

THE KITTIWAKE GALLERY AT ST ABBS HEAD

Frederick J Watson, on-going display of work from Mar-Nov.
Opening times: Mar and Oct-Dec 11am-5pm (weekends only or by appointment on 01890 771 588), Apr-Sept 11am-5pm daily (closed Tuesdays).
Address: The Kittiwake Gallery at St Abbs Head, St Abbs, Eymouth, TD14 5QF. 018907 71588(home), 018907 71504(work).
e-mail: derickwatson@ btopenworld.com

NATURE IN ART MUSEUM AND ART GALLERY

World's first museum dedicated to art inspired by nature. Picasso to David Shepherd, Flemish Masters to contemporary crafts. Permanent collection plus regular special exhibitions and 70 artists in residence each year. Look on our website.
Opening times: Tues-Sun (10am-5pm) and Bank holidays. Closed Dec 24-26.
Address: Wallsworth Hall, A38, Twigworth, Gloucester, GL2 9PA; 01452 731422; (Fax)01452 730937. e-mail: ninart@globalnet.co.uk www.nature-in-art.org.uk

OLD BREWERY STUDIOS

Changing exhibitions of work the whole year through. Various painting and drawing courses available.
Opening times: Variable, best to telephone first.
Address; The Manor House, Kings Cliffe, Peterborough, PE8 6XB; 01780 470247; (Fax)01780 470334.
www.oldbrewerystudios.co.uk

DIRECTORY OF WILDLIFE ARTISTS

BENINGTON, Michael

Original paintings of mainly Western Palearctic wildlife, in natural settings, from field sketches. Illustrations for many books, including *Breeding Birds of the Algarve* and for own articles in birding press. Commissions a specialty.
Exhibitions for 2004: Artists for Nature Foundation Algarve exhibitions and related book, *Living Paintings*, Island Arts Centre, Lisburn Apr 28 - May 22. www.lisburn.gov.uk.
Address: Eyrie Studio, 3 The Courtyard, Tollymore Road, Newcastle, Northern Ireland, BT33 0TE:028 4372 5224.

BINNS, David SWLA, NDD, Doctor of Letters

Watercolours of British wildlife. Published work includes book illustrations, jigsaw designs for RSPB, RSNC, designs for Country Artists Ltd, Medici Society and in-house designs and limited edition prints for the Brent Gallery, run with wife Molly at 60a Keighley Rd, Cowling, BD22 0BH. Award-winning member of the SWLA. Commissions usually accepted.
Exhibitions for 2004: NEWA (Liverpool), SWLA (London), Brent Gallery (Cowling, W.Yorks), Milnethorpe (Silverdale).
Address: Holmestead, 9 Boundary Avenue, Sutton-in-Craven, Nr Keighley, Yorkshire, BD20 8BL; (Tel/ Fax)01535 632774.

BURTON, Philip

Acrylics on canvas; current enthusiasm seabirds. Many book illustrations e.g. in recent *Raptors of the World*. Founder member of Society of Wildlife Artists.
Exhibitions for 2004: Some works at SWLA, London, annually.
Address: High Kelton, Doctors Commons Road,

Key: BBF = British Birdwatching Fair. NEWA = National Exhibition of Wildlife Art. SWLA = Society of Wildlife Artists.

Berkhamsted, Herts, HP4 3DW; 01442 865020. e-mail: pjkburton@aol.com

BUSBY, John SWLA

Illustrator of natural history books and articles, especially bird and animal behaviour. Lifelong field experience. More than 30 books illustrated, including nine Poyser titles. Also oil and watercolour landscapes. See website for examples. Studio visits by appointment.
Exhibitions for 2004: The Wildlife Art Gallery, Lavenham. Sept.
Address: Easter Haining, Ormiston Hall, Tranent, E.Lothian, EH35 5NJ; (Fax)01875 341011. e-mail: jj.busby@lineone.net www.johnbusby-artist.com

CALE, Steve

Steve is a keen naturalist and specialises in painting in acrylics. His paintings have gone as far afield as Hong Kong and New Zealand. Undertaking work for The Mareeba Wetland Foundation in Australia and for Pensthorpe, Norfolk. Has just completed a mural for the RSPB at Titchwell.
Address: Bramble Cottage, Westwood Lane, Gt Rysburgh, Fakenham, Norfolk, NR21 7AP; 01328 829589.

COOK, David

Sponsor of PJC Drawing Award via SWLA. Original paintings, drawings, paper cuts and paper sculptures of wildlife, especially waterfowl. Book, videos, WWT greetings cards, open & limited edition prints available through www.wwt.org.uk/shop. Annual residency each September, Nature in Art, Gloucestershire.
Exhibitions for 2004: Cheng Kim-Loke Wildlife Gallery, WWT Slimbridge Oct 10 (private view) - Nov 10. Will be in residence during exhibition.
Address: Holly House, 3 Lynn Road, South Runcton, King's Lynn, Norfolk, PE33 0EW; 01553 811980.

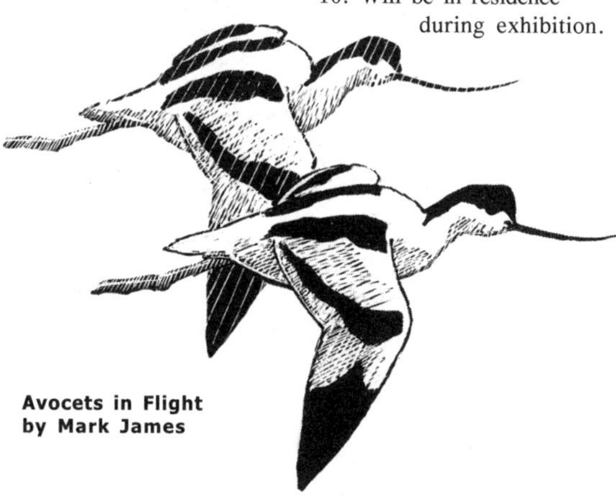

Avocets in Flight by Mark James

DAVIS, John SWLA

Diverse natural history subjects and landscapes. Happiest scribbling in the field, also more finished work in watercolour, oils and acrylics. Published work including *Birds of the Western Palearctic, 'Downland Wildlife'*, cover picture for *Best Birdwatching Sites in Sussex*, *British Wildlife* magazine, work for the RSPB etc. Won black and white section of *Birdwatch* Artist of The Year 2002. Commissions accepted.
Exhibitions for 2004: WWT Arundel July - Sept.
Address: 6 Redmoor, Birdham, Chichester, West Sussex, PO20 7HS; 01243 512351.

GREENHALF, Robert

Watercolours, oils, woodcuts and drypoints of birds in landscape. Book *Towards the Sea* published 1999 by Pica Press/A&C Black contains many examples. Commissions accepted.
Exhibitions for 2004: Regular exhibitor at Wildlife Art Gallery, Lavenham, Suffolk and Bircham Gallery, Holt, Norfolk.
Address: Romney House, Saltbarn Lane, Playden, Rye, East Sussex, TN31 7PH; 01797 222381.

JONES, Chris

Original paintings, primarily in oils, of British, exotic and domestic species. Animal and bird portraiture a specialism. Recent work includes reconstruction of the appearance of the Dodo. International Young Artist of the Year 1998. Illustration work and commissions accepted.
Exhibitions for 2004: Falconry Fair, Shropshire, Marwell Zoo, Hants, Barnes WWT reserve, London Sept-Oct.
Address: 47 Church Lane, North Bradley, Trowbridge, Wilts, BA14 0TE; 01225 769717. e-mail: chrisjones@eco-art.freeserve.co.uk www.chrisjoneswildlifeart.com

KOSTER, David

Original prints - etchings, woodcuts, linocuts, lithographs - of birds, fish, flowers, insects etc. Watercolours, oils. Commisions accepted. Published work includes wood engravings for *Down to Earth* by John Stewart Collis, ink drawings for *Fellow Mortals*, anthology of animal poetry.
Exhibitions for 2004: SWLA London (Sept).
Address: 5 East Cliff Gardens, Folkestone, Kent, CT19 6AR; 01303 240544.

MACKAY, Andrew

Colour and line artwork of birds and insects.
Illustrations in *Concise Birds of the Western Palearctic, RSPB Birds of Britain and Europe, Birds of South-east Asia* etc. Commissions for paintings and illustrations welcome.
Address: 68 Leicester Road, Markfield, Leicester, LE67 9RE:01530 243770. e-mail: AndrewjMackay@aol.com www.ajm-wildlife-art.co.uk

PAIGE, John SWLA, PAIGE, Jane Leycester FSBA

Wildlife and wild flowers in their natural surroundings. Watercolour, oil, acrylic, collage, mono, screen and lino prints.
Annual exhibitions of the SWLA and The society of Botanical Artists.
Address: The Manor House, Kings Cliffe, Peterborough, PE8 6XB; 01780 470247; (Fax)01780 470334. www.oldbrewerystudios.co.uk

PARTINGTON, Peter

Beloved medium is watercolour, followed by oils and etching. Happiest in the field with sketchbook - favourite habitat East Anglian shoreline and marshland. Travels widely. Many one man shows, work widely collected. Commissions welcome. Three books; HarperCollins *Learn to Draw* series, *Farm Animals, Wildlife* and *Birds*.
Exhibitions for 2004: WWT Arundel Jan 15 - Feb 17. One-man show.
Address: The Hall, Kettlebaston, Suffolk, IP7 7QA; 01449 741538; (Fax)01449 744286. e-mail: peter.partington@kettlebaston.co.uk www.peter-partington.fsnet.co.uk

PEARSON. Bruce

Working in oils, watercolour and mixed media, paintings are completed either directly in the field or re-evaluated and reworked in the studio to express the natural rhythm, elemental energy and sheer excitement of 'being there'.
Exhibitions for 2004: SWLA, Sept
Address: The Old Plough, Caxton Road, Great Gransden, Sandy, Beds, SG19 3BE; 01767 677558. e-mail: bep@openstudio.evesham.net www.brucepearson.info

RIDLEY, Martin

Artist specialising in British wildlife. Original oils and watercolours of birds and animals in their natural habitat. Prints, cards and commissions. RSPB 2002 calendar, cover of 2002 *Birdwatcher's Yearbook*. Extensive website.
Address: Rossal, The Ross, Comrie, PH6 2JU; (Fax) by arrangement. e-mail: art@martinridley.com www.martinridley.com

ROSE, Chris

Originals in oils and acrylics of birds and animals in landscapes. Particularly interested in painting water and its myriad effects. Limited edition prints available. Illustrated many books including *Grebes of the World* (publ. end 2002), *Handbook to The Birds of The World* and *Robins and Chats of the World* (in progress).

Exhibitions for 2004: One-man show at the Cheng-Kim Loke Gallery, WWT Slimbridge, Sept 5 - Oct 5; SWLA, Mall Galleries, London, Sept; British Birdwatching Fair, Rutland, Aug. **Address:** Maple Cottage, Holydean, Bowden, Melrose, Scotland, TD6 9HT; (Tel/Fax)01835 822547. e-mail: chrisroseswla@onetel.net.uk

SNOW, Philip

Original paintings, sketches and illustrations of wildlife, mainly birds in landscape. Has illustrated or contributed to over 50 books, magazines etc. including *Collins Guide to Character of Birds*, 2003 and *Hebridean Wildlife and Landscape Sketch Book*, 2003.
Exhibitions for 2004: Tegfryn Gallery, Menai Bridge, Anglesey; Pensychnant Nature Centre, Conwy, N.Wales; NEWA, Liverpool.
Address: 2 Beach Cottages, Malltraeth, Anglesey, North Wales,LL62 5AT; (Tel/ Fax)01407 840512.
e-mail: creationwitness@ tiscali.co.uk

SYKES, Thelma K SWLA

Artist printmaker: (haunts coastal marsh and estuaries). Original linocuts, woodcuts of British birds. Publications include BTO Atlases, *Birdwatcher's Yearbooks* 1986 to 1996, RSPB greetings cards, including Christmas 2003. Exhibits SWLA, Society of Wood Engravers. Artist in residence, Nature in Art, Gloucester.
Exhibitions for 2004: Inspired by Nature, Nature in Art, Gloucester, Nov 11 - Dec 7 2003. SWLA London, Sept. SWE UK touring exhibition, NEWA Cheshire.
Address: Blue Neb Studios, 18 Newcroft, Saughall, Chester, CH1 6EL; 01244 880209. e-mail: thelmasykes@tiscali.co.uk

WALLACE, D.Ian.M.

Gouache paintings, pencil and ink drawings; "paints birds like birdwatchers see them", supplies roughs free for commissions. Many published illustrations in own/other books. Illustrates own column in *Bird Watching* magazine.
Exhibitions for 2004: SWLA London, Sept. **Address:** Mount Pleasant Farm, Main Road, Anslow, Burton-on-Trent, Staffs, DE13 9QE; 01283 812364.

WATSON, Derick

Wildlife/bird paintings in watercolour, acrylic. Digitally generated 'original' limited edition prints. Illustrations in scraperboard/ pen and ink. Has been featured in various publications in the UK and USA including *Artists's Magazine* (USA), Leigh Yawkey Woodson *Birds in Art Catalogues* and several bird atlases and annual bird reports.
Address: The Kittiwake Gallery at St Abbs Head, St Abbs, Eyemouth, TD14 5QF; (H)018907 71588, (W)018907 71504.
e-mail: derickwatson@ btopenworld.com

WARREN, Michael

Original watercolour paintings of birds, all based on field observations. Books, calendars, cards and commissions.
Exhibitions for 2004: Town

Adult Male and Female Smew by Graham Brittain

Hall, Newark. Feb 11 - Mar 3; WWT Arundel, Eye of the Wind Wildife Art Gallery, Apr 30 - June 8; British Birdwatching Fair, Rutland, Aug; SWLA, London, Sept.
Address: The Laurels, The Green, Winthorpe, Nottinghamshire, NG24 2NR; 01636 673554; (Fax)01636 611569. e-mail: mike.warren.birdart@care4free.net
www.mikewarren.co.uk

WILCZUR, Jan

Original gouache/ watercolours of birds and landscapes. Published illustrations for *Handbook of Birds of the World*, *Concise Birds of the Western Palearctic* and other fieldguides. Commissions accepted.
Exhibitions: WWT London Wetland Centre, Barnes, Sept 28 - Nov 11 2003.
Address: 74 Huntingfield Road, London, SW15 5EU; 0208 878 8925.
www.birdillustrators.com

WILLIAMSON-BELL, James, SWLA, HC (Paris)

Any wildlife subject, in watercolour and acrylics. Also limited edition original prints. Chinese watercolours and woodblock prints a speciality. Illustrated details available. Commisions welcome.
Exhibitions for 2004: SWLA, London.
Address: 2 Pauline Gardens, Newcastle-upon-Tyne, NE15 7TD; (Tel/Fax)0191 274 6594. e-mail: autumnleaves@supanet.com

WOODHEAD, Darren MA(RCA), SWLA

Original watercolours and woodcuts of birds, butterflies, mammals and other wildlife subjects, as well as landscapes and cloudscapes. All subjects painted direct in the field. Commissions undertaken.
Exhibitions for 2004: SWLA, London, Sept.
Address: 44F(2F3), Millhill, Musselburgh, East Lothian, EH21 7RN; 0131 665 6802. e-mail: darren.woodhead@virgin.net

WOOLF, Colin

Beautiful original watercolour paintings. The atmosphere of a landscape and the character of his subject are his hallmark, also the pure watercolour technique that imparts a softness to the natural subjects he paints. Owls, birds of prey and ducks are specialities. Wide range of limited editions, reproductions and greetings cards. Special commissions also accepted.
Exhibitions for 2004: British Birdwatching Fair, August.
Address: Tremallt, Penmachno, Betws y Coed, Conwy, LL24 0YL; +44 (0) 1690 760 308.
e-mail: colin@wildart.co.uk
www.wildart.co.uk

DIRECTORY OF WILDLIFE PHOTOGRAPHERS

BASTON, Bill
Photographer
Subjects: East Anglian rarities and common birds, Mediterranean birds and landscapes, UK wildlife and landscapes, Florida birds and landscapes.
Formats: Prints, slides, digital, mounted/ unmounted.
Address: 86 George Street, Hadleigh, Ipswich, IP7 5BU; 01473 827062.
e-mail: bill.baston@bt.com

BATES,Tony
Photographer and lecturer.
Subjects: Mainly British wildlife, landscapes and astro landscapes.
Formats: 35mm, prints (loose, mounted or framed), original handmade photo greetings cards.
Address: 22 Fir Avenue, Bourne, Lincs, PE10 9RY; 01778 425137. e-mail: mtr@masher.f9.co.uk

BORG, Les
Photographer, course leader.
Subjects: Mostly British wildlife, with some from Florida, Jamaica and elsewhere.
Formats: Mounted, unmounted or framed, inkjet prints or Ilfochromes if required.
Address: 17 Harwood Close, Tewin, Welwyn, Herts, AL6 0LF; 01438 717841, (Fax)01438 840459.
e-mail: les@les-borg-photography.co.uk www. les-borg-photography.co.uk

BROADBENT, David
Professional photographer.
Subjects: UK birds and wild places.
Formats: 35mm, 6x7, CD-Roms, scans.
Address: Rose Cottage, Bream Road, Whitepool, St Briavels, Lydney, GL15 6TL; 01594 531381; (M)07771 664973. e-mail: info@davidbroadbent.com www.davidbroadbent.com

BROOKS, Richard
Wildlife photographer, writer, lecturer.
Subjects: Owls (Barn especially), raptors, Kingfisher and a variety of European birds (Lesvos especially) and landscapes.
Formats: Mounted and unmounted computer prints (6x4 - A3+ size), framed pictures, A5 greetings cards, surplus slides for sale.
Address: 24 Croxton Hamlet, Fulmodeston, Fakenham, Norfolk, NR21 0NP; 01328 878632.
e-mail: email@richard-brooks.co.uk www.richard-brooks.co.uk

CANIS, Robert
Professional photographer, tour leader.
Subjects: British flora and fauna, landscapes and environment of southern England, also Finland and Poland.
Formats: 35mm transparencies. Digital and conventional mounted/ unmounted prints available.
Address: 26 Park Avenue, Sittingbourne, Kent, ME10 1QY; 07939 117570.
e-mail: rmcanis@msn.com

CHAPMAN, David
Natural history photographer, writer, speaker and workshop leader.
Subjects: British natural history (esp.birds) and farm animal images.
Formats: 35mm slides, mounted &/or framed photos, photo cards.
Address: 41 Bosence Road, Townshend, Cornwall, TR27 6AL; (Tel/fax) 01736 850 287. e-mail: David@ Ruralimages.freeserve.co.uk www. Ruralimages.freeserve.co.uk

CONWAY, Wendy PSA4. AFIAP
Award-winning wildlife photographer.
Subjects: Birds, mammals, landscapes : UK, USA, Lesvos and Africa.
Formats: 35mm and medium format. Prints matted and unmatted, greetings cards.
Address: 4 Meriden Close, Winyates Green, Redditch, B98 0QN; 01527 457793.
e-mail: wendy@terry-wall.com

COOK, Garry
Photographer, birder.
Subjects: UK rarities and miscellaneous bird photographs.
Formats: Unmounted prints.
Address: Herons Flight, New Road, Blakeney, Nr Holt, Norfolk, NR25 7PA; 01263 741614.

DENNING, Paul
Wildlife photographer, lecturer.
Subjects: Birds, mammals, reptiles, butterflies and plants from UK, Europe, North and Central America.
Formats: 35mm transparencies and prints.
Address: 17 Maes Maelwg, Beddau, Pontypridd, CF38 2LD; (H)01443 202607; (W)02920 673243. e-mail: pgdenning.naturepics@virgin.net

DOODY, Dee
Professional wildlife cameraman, TV presenter, film-maker, writer and artist. (Also voice-overs).
Subjects: All UK wildlife (plus Gambia, Iceland and Europe).
Formats: Images on digital video (all broadcast quality).
Address: 2 Fan Terrace, Fan, Llanidloes, Powys, SY18 6NW: 01686 413819.

GARBUTT, Nick
Author, photographer, artist, tour leader.
Subjects: Madagascar (Ground rollers, Vangas, Couas, Mesites etc), East/ Southern Africa, Indian subcontinent, Borneo.
Formats: Mounted 35mm and 70mm transparencies, cibachrome prints to order.
Address: Fell Side Cottage, 3 Lime Street, Shap, Penrith, Cumbria CA10 3PQ; 07900 811140.
e-mail: nick@nickgarbutt.com
www.nickgarbutt.com

HARROP, Hugh
Professional wildlife guide, photographer and author.
Subjects: European birds, cetaceans, wild flowers, butterflies and dragonflies. I specialise in all Shetland subjects.
Formats: 35mm transparency. Digital images on CD or via modem. Commercial enquiries only please.
Address: Longhill, Maywick, Shetland, ZE2 9JF; 01950 422483; (Fax)01950422430.
e-mail: hugh@hughharrop.com
www.hughharrop.com

KNELL, Steve
Wildlife photographer and lecturer.
Subjects: Birds, mammals, butterflies, dragon flies etc. Mostly British, Lesvos, Florida, Spain and Tanzania.
Formats: 35mm slides mounted/unmounted and high class prints. Slides for lectures for sale/hire. Wildlife calendar 2004 - £2.
Address: 49 Lower Gate, Paddock, Huddersfield, Yorks, HD3 4ER; 01484 322251; (M)07798 828576.

LANE, Mike
Wildlife photographer.
Subjects: Birds and wildlife from around the world also landscapes and the environment.
Formats: 35mm, medium format and digital.
Address: 36 Berkeley Road, Shirley, Solihull, West Midlands, B90 2HS; 0121 744 7988. www. nature-photography.co.uk
e-mail: mikelane@nature-photography.co.uk

LANGSBURY, Gordon FRPS
Professional wildlife photographer, lecturer, author and tour leader.
Subjects: Birds and mammals from UK, Europe, Scandinavia, N America, Gambia, Kenya, Tanzania, Morocco and Falklands.
Formats: 35mm transparencies for publication, lectures and prints.
Address: Sanderlings, 80 Shepherds Close, Hurley, Maidenhead, Berkshire, SL6 5LZ; (Tel/fax)01628 824252.
e-mail: gordonlangsbury@birdphoto.org.uk

McKAVETT, Mike
Wildlife photographer and lecturer.
Subjects: Birds and mammals from India, Kenya, The Gambia, Lesvos, N.America and UK.
Formats: 35mm transparencies for publication and commercial use, prints and lectures.
Address: 34 Rectory Road,

Churchtown, Southport, PR9 7PU; 01704 231358.

MOCKLER, Mike

Safari guide, tour leader, writer and photographer.
Subjects: Birds and wildlife of Britain, Europe, Central and South America, India and several African countries.
Formats: 35mm transparencies.
Address: Gulliver's Cottage, Chapel Rise, Avon Castle, Ringwood, Hampshire, BH24 2BL; 01425 478103. e-mail: mikemockler@lineone.net

OFFORD, Keith

Photographer, writer, tour leader, conservationist.
Subjects: Raptors, UK wildlife and scenery, birds and other wildlife of USA, Africa, Spain, Australia, India.
Formats: Conventional prints, greetings cards, framed pictures.
Address: Yew Tree Farmhouse, Craignant, Selattyn, Nr Oswestry, Shropshire, SY10 7NP; 01691 718740. e-mail: keith.offord@virgin.net www.keithofford.co.uk

Tawny Owl
by Richard Whittlestone

PARKER, Susan and Allan ARPS

Professional photographers (ASPphoto - images of nature) lecturers and tutors.
Subjects: Birds plus other flora and fauna from the UK, Spain, Lesvos, Cyprus, Florida and Texas.
Formats: 35mm and 645 medium format, slides, mounted digital prints, greetings cards and digital images on CD for reproduction (high quality scans up to A3+).
Address: Ashtree House, 51 Kiveton Lane, Todwick, Sheffield, South Yorkshire, S26 1HJ; 01909 770238. e-mail: aspaspphoto@clara.co.uk

PIKE, David

Photographer, presenter and writer
Subjects: Wildlife, including birds from Japan, N America and Africa.
Formats: 35mm mounted. Conventional prints and digital.
Address: Uffington Manor, Main Road, Uffington, Lincs, PE9 4SN; 01780 751944;(W)01780 767711; (Fax)01780 489218. e-mail: david.pike@ukphotographics.co.uk www.ukphotographics.co.uk.com

POWER, John FRPS

Bird photographer.
Subjects: British birds, dragonflies, wild flowers.
Formats: Mounted, unmounted or framed prints. Cibachrome or computer prints if required.
Address: 15 Brynmor Road, Mossley Hill, Liverpool, L18 4RW; 0151 724 5004, (W)0151 729 0094, (fax)0151 724 3667.

READ, Mike

Photographer (wildlife and landscapes), tour leader, writer.
Subjects: Birds, mammals, plants, landscapes, and some insects. UK, France, USA, Ecuador (including Galapagos).
Formats: 35mm.
Address: Claremont, Redwood Close, Ringwood, Hampshire, BH24 1PR; 01425 475008, (Fax)01425 473160. e-mail: mike@mikeread.co.uk www.mikeread.co.uk

SIMPSON, Geoff

Professional natural history and landscape photographer.
Subjects: Specialises in evocative images of Britain's wildlife and landscape.
Formats: 35mm and panoramic. Slides and CD.
Address: Camberwell, 1 Buxton Road, New Mills, High Peak, Derbyshire, SK22 3JS; 01633 743089.

e-mail:
info@geoffsimpson.co.uk
www.geoffsimpson.co.uk

SWASH, Andy

Photographer, author, tour leader.
Subjects: Birds, habitats/ landscapes and general wildlife from all continents; photographic library currently 1,600 bird species.
Formats: Slides for publication and duplicates for lectures. High resolution scans on CD-Rom. Conventional and digital prints, unmounted, mounted or framed.
Address: Stretton Lodge, 9 Birch Grove, West Hill, Ottery St Mary, Devon, EX11 1XP; (H&fax)01404 815383, (W)01392 822901. e-mail: andy_swash@ wildguides.co.uk
www.wildguides.co.uk

TIPLING, David

Wildlife and landscape photographer, photographic tour leader, author, with a passion for birds.
Subjects: Worldwide wildlife and landscapes. Specialist areas include; UK, Antarctic, Finland and Arctic Norway, N India, Amazon, Alaska, China, Namibia.
Formats: 35mm to 6x17 panoramas available as transparencies for commercial use only. Greetings cards and glicée limited edition prints for sale. Prints are truly archival, using the finest printing techniques and papers.
Address: 99 Noah's Ark, Kemsing, Sevenoaks, Kent, TN15 6PD; 01732 763486.
e-mail: dt@ windrushphotos.demon.co.uk
www.windrushphotos.co.uk

WALL, Terry ARPS EFIAP PPSA

Wildlife photographer.
Subjects: Birds, mammals, landscapes from UK, USA, Lesvos, Africa and Galapagos.
Formats: 35mm/medium. Prints matted/unmatted, greetings cards. 35mm scanning service and restoration and retouching service. Quality printing service. *One-to-One Photoshop Tuition* book and individual lessons.
Address: 4 Meriden Close, Winyates Green, Redditch, B98 0QN; 01527 457793.
e-mail: wildimages@ terry-wall.com
www.terry-wall.com

WARD, Chris

Photographer.
Subjects: Birds and landscapes, plus some other wildlife. UK (mostly commoner species, some rarities), W.Palearctic, S.Africa, Florida, California, Venezuela, Argentina, Australia.
Formats: Prints and framed pictures, slide copies for lectures.
Address: 276 Bideford Green, Linslade, Leighton Buzzard, Beds, LU7 7TU; 01525 375528.
e-mail: chris@ chriswardphotography.co.uk

WILKES, Mike FRPS

Professional wildlife photographer, tour leader.
Subjects: African, European and British birds.
Address: 43 Feckenham Road, Headless Cross, Redditch, Worcestershire, B97 5AS; 01527 550686.
e-mail:
wilkes@photoshot.com

WILLIAMS, Nick

Photographer, lecturer, author, tour leader.
Subjects: W.Palearctic including Cape Verde Islands and Falkland Islands.
Formats: Duplicate slides, some originals, prints also available.
Address: Owl Cottage, Station Road, Rippingale, Lincs, PE10 0TA; (Tel/ Fax)01778 440500.
e-mail: birdmanandbird@ hotmail.com

WILMSHURST, Roger

Wildlife photographer, particularly birds.
Subjects: All aspects of wildlife, particularly British and European birds, butterflies, plants, mammals etc.
Formats: 35mm, 6x6, 6x7, 645. Digital, mounted and framed pictures.
Address: Sandhill Farmhouse, Sandhill Lane, Washington, Pulborough, West Sussex, RH20 4TD; 01903 892210, (fax)01903 893376. e-mail: roger@ naturepics.freeserve.co.uk
www.nature-pictures.co.uk

DIRECTORY OF LECTURERS

Lecturers who have indicated that they are willing to travel to all parts of Britain are listed first. For the remainder we have grouped them geographically in the following regions: England, Eastern; North-eastern; North-western; South-eastern; South-western; West Midlands and Wales; Scotland.

To ensure this valuable section continues strongly in the future, we would be grateful if you would mention the *Yearbook* when contacting any of the listed lecturers.

If your group has enjoyed a talk from anyone not listed here, we would appreciate receiving contact details so they might be included in the 2005 edition.

NO LIMITS

BATES,Tony
Photographer and lecturer.
Subjects: Mainly British wildlife, landscapes and astro landscapes.
Fees: £65 plus travel.
Limits: None. **Times:** To suit.
Address: 22 Fir Avenue, Bourne, Lincs, PE10 9RY; 01778 425137. e-mail: mtr@masher.f9.co.uk

BELL, Graham
Cruise lecturer worldwide, photographer, author.
Subjects: Arctic, Antarctic, America, Siberia, Australia, Canada, Iceland, Seychelles, UK - identification, behaviour, seabirds, entertaining bird imitations etc.
Fees: £35 plus travel.
Limits: None. **Times:** Any.
Address: Ros View, South Yearle, Wooler, Northumberland, NE71 6RB; (Tel/fax)01668 281310. e-mail: seabirdsdgb@hotmail.com

BOND, Terry
Bank director, photographer, group field leader, conference speaker worldwide.
Subjects: 8 talks (including Scilly Isles, Southern Europe, USA - shorebirds and inland birds, Birdwatching Identification - a new approach).
Fees: By arrangement (usually only expenses).
Limits: Most of UK.
Times: Evenings.
Address: 3 Lapwing Crescent, Chippenham, Wiltshire, SN14 6YF; 01249 462674.
e-mail: terryebond@btopenworld.com

BROOKS, Richard
Wildlife photographer, writer, lecturer.
Subjects: 12 talks (including Lesvos, Ebros Delta, Israel, Canaries, E.Anglia, Scotland, Wales, Oman).
Fees: £65 plus petrol.
Limits: None if accom provided. **Times:** Any.
Address: 24 Croxton Hamlet, Fulmodeston, Fakenham, Norfolk, NR21 0NP; 01328 878632.
e-mail: email@richard-brooks.co.uk
www.richard-brooks.co.uk

BUCKINGHAM, John
Lecturer, photographer, tour leader.
Subjects: 60+ titles covering birds, wildlife, botany, ecology and habitats in UK, Europe, Africa, Australia, India and the Americas.
Fees: £58 plus expenses.
Limits: None. **Times:** Any.
Address: 3 Cardinal Close, Tonbridge, Kent, TN9 2EN; (Tel/fax) 01732 354970.

BURROWS, Ian
Tour leader.
Subjects: Papua New Guinea, Cape Clear Island

and 'Food from the Wild'.
Fees: £70 plus mileage over 100.
Limits: Anything considered.
Times: Evenings preferable but other times considered.
Address: Well Cottage, 38 Creake Road, Sculthorpe, Fakenham, Norfolk, NR21 9NQ; 01328 856925; (Fax) 01328 862014. e-mail: Ian@sicklebill.demon.co.uk www.sicklebill.com

CANIS, Robert
Professional photographer, tour leader.
Subjects: Illustrated talks (including British and Finnish wildlife).
Fees: £45 plus petrol.
Limits: None. **Times:** Oct-Mar.
Address: 26 Park Avenue, Sittingbourne, Kent, ME10 1QY; 07939 117570.
e-mail: rmcanis@msn.com

CARRIER, Michael
Lifelong interest in natural history.
Subjects: 1) 'Birds in Cumbria', 2) 'The Solway and its Birds' and 3)'The Isle of May'.
Fees: £20. **Limits:** None but rail connection essential.
Times: Sept-March, afternoons or evenings.
Address: Lismore Cottage, 1 Front Street, Armathwaite, Carlisle, Cumbria, CA4 9PB; 01697 472218.

CHAPMAN, David
Writer, natural history photographer, speaker and workshop leader.
Subjects: British natural history, birds, photography, small holding wildlife.
Fees: £30 plus travel.
Limits: Negotiable. **Times:** Negotiable.
Address: 41 Bosence Road, Townshend, Cornwall, TR27 6AL; (Tel/fax) 01736 850 287. e-mail: David@Ruralimages.freeserve.co.uk www.Ruralimages.freeserve.co.uk

CHARTERS, Roger
Experienced wildlife sound recordist and one-time professional photographer.
Subjects: 'Are Sounds more Important than Notes?', 'Scandinavia including the Arctic', 'Ukraine', 'Spain', 'The Australian Outback'. Each talk lasts about one hour with extensive use of sound recordings and visual sequences.
Fees: £30 made payable to Warwickshire Wildlife Trust, plus 25p per mile.
Limits: None.
Address: 11 Eastnor Grove, Leamington Spa, Warwickshire CV31 1LD: 01926 882583.
e-mail: Roger.Charters@btinternet.com

CLARKE, Roger
Author of books on harriers, Phd in raptor feeding ecology.
Subjects: Harriers (overview and feeding ecology), other raptors if pressed.
Fees: £60 plus petrol.
Limits: Negotiable.
Times: Flexible.
Address: New Hythe House, Reach, Cambridge, CB5 0JQ; 01638 742447.

CROUCHER, Roy
Wildlife tour leader, former local authority ecologist.
Subjects: Four talks (Northern France, Montenegro, Managing Britain's Habitats, Bird song).
Fees: £50 plus petrol from Birmingham. **Limits:** Mainland Britain. **Times:** November and December.
Address: Place de L'Eglise, 53700, Averton, Mayenne, France; 00 33 243 00 6969.
e-mail: roy_croucher@lineone.net

DOODY, Dee
Ornithologist, wildlife cameraman, wildlife artist, television presenter (wildlife) and voice-overs.
Subjects: Dee can offer an evening of wildife films taken from his recent TV series. Subjects are; The Coast, Rivers, Moorland, Woodland, Estuaries, Urban, Lakes and Reservoirs, Farmland, Welsh Bird Reserves, The Red Kite, The Goshawk. All are 23 mins long, any combination available plus talk, art display and questions.
Fees: £250 + £50 travel and accom. **Limits:** None.
Times: Any (birdwatching fairs), Autumn and Winter preferred (groups).
Address: 2 Fan Terrace, Fan, Llanidloes, Powys, SY18 6NW: 01686 413819.

DUGGAN, Glenn
Ex-Commander Royal Navy, tour leader, researcher.
Subjects: Ten talks

including, birds of paradise and bower birds, history of bird art (caveman to present day), famous Victorian bird artists (John Gould, the Birdman and John James Andubohon.
Fees: £50 plus expenses.
Limits: none with o.n accom. **Times:** Any.
Address: 25 Hampton Grove, Fareham, Hampshire, PO15 5NL; 01329 845976, (M)07771 605320. e-mail: glenn.m.duggan@ntlworld.com

EYRE, John
Author, photographer, conservationist and chairman Hampshire Ornithological Society.
Subjects: World birding (Europe, Africa, Australasia and the Americas), plus special Hampshire subjects (eg. Gilbert White's birds and heathland birds).
Fees: £55 plus travel.
Limits: Any location negotiable. **Times:** Any.
Address: 3 Dunmow Hill, Fleet, Hampshire, GU51 3AN; 01252 677850. e-mail: JohnEyre@compuserve.com

GALLOP, Brian
Speaker, photographer, tour leader.
Subjects: 25 plus talks covering UK, Africa, India, Galapagos and Europe - all natural history subjects.
Fees: £45 plus 20p per ml.
Limits: None - o.n acc. if over 100 mls. **Times:** Any.
Address: 13 Orchard Drive, Tonbridge, Kent, TN10 4LT; 01732 361892.

GARBUTT, Nick
Author, photographer, artist, tour leader.
Subjects: Madagascar, (mammals, birds, reptiles, frogs), India, Borneo, East and Southern Africa.
Fees: £150 plus expenses.
Limits: None. **Times:** Any.
Address: Fell Side Cottage, 3 Lime Street, Shap, Penrith, Cumbria CA10 3PQ; 07900 811140. e-mail: nick@nickgarbutt.com www.nickgarbutt.com

GARNER, David
Wildlife photographer.
Subjects: 17 live talks and audio-visual shows on all aspects of wildlife in UK and some parts of Europe - list available.
Fees: £35 plus 20p per ml.
Limits: None. **Times:** Any.
Address: 73 Needingworth Road, St Ives, Cambs, PE27 5JY; (H)01480 463194; (W)01480 463194.

GIBSON, Chris
Conservation professional, tour leader, photographer, writer, broadcaster.
Subjects: Include the wildlife, lepidoptera, botany and conservation of Essex, East Anglia and the Mediterranean.
Fees: £50 plus expenses in Essex and Suffolk, £100 plus expenses elsewhere.
Limits: None.
Times: Evenings.
Address: 1 Dove House Cottage, Oakley Road, Dovercourt, Essex, CO12 5DR; 01255 502960. e-mail: gibson@dovehc.freeserve.co.uk

GUNTON, Trevor
Ex.RSPB Staff, recruitment advisor, lecturer.
Subjects: Eight talks - Birds and Pits, Yorkshire, NT Reserves, membership recruitment workshops a speciality, UK Bird Islands, Geese, Shetland, Garden Birds, 'I know an Island', 'Wildlife and Vikings - UK and beyond', European Conservation.
Fees: Variable (basic £55 plus expenses). **Limits:** None. **Times:** Anytime, anywhere.
Address: 15 St James Road, Little Paxton, St Neots, Cambs, PE19 6QW; (tel/fax)01480 473562. e-mail: trevor.gunton@tesco.net

HARROP, Hugh
Professional wildlife guide, photographer and author.
Subjects: 15 talks including Shetland wildlife, Shetland birds, polar bears, whales and dolphins, Galapagos, seals and sea lions, Alaska, Iceland, general wildlife photography.
Fees: £125 plus accom at cost and return flight from Shetland. **Limits:** UK only.
Times: November to March.
Address: Longhill, Maywick, Shetland, ZE2 9JF; 01950 422483; (Fax)01950422430. e-mail: hugh@hughharrop.com www.hughharrop.com

KNYSTAUTAS, Algirdas
Ornithologist, photographer, writer, tour leader.
Subjects: Birds and natural history of Russia, Baltic States, S America,

Indonesia, Birding the Silk Route (seven talks).
Fees: £1 per person. £70 minimum plus £20 travelling. **Limits:** None - in UK, o.n accom needed.
Times: Oct and Nov.
Address: 7 Holders Hill Gardens, London, NW4 1NP; 020 8203 4317.
e-mail ibisbill@talk21.com

LANE, Mike
Wildlife photographer.
Subjects: Seven talks from the UK and worldwide, mostly on birds.
Fees: Varies. **Limits:** None.
Times: None.
Address: 36 Berkeley Road, Shirley, Solihull, West Midlands, B90 2HS; 0121 744 7988. www.nature-photography.co.uk
e-mail: mikelane@nature-photography.co.uk

LANGSBURY, Gordon FRPS
Professional wildlife photographer, lecturer, author and tour leader.
Subjects: 20 talks - Africa, Europe, USA, Falklands and UK. Full list provided.
Fees: £80 plus travel expenses. **Limits:** None.
Times: Any.
Address: Sanderlings, 80 Shepherds Close, Hurley, Maidenhead, Berkshire, SL6 5LZ; (Tel/fax)01628 824252.
e-mail: gordonlangsbury@birdphoto.org.uk

McKAVETT, Mike
Photographer.
Subjects: Five talks, Birds and Wildlife of India, North and Western Kenya and the Gambia, Bird Migration in North America.
Fees: £30 plus expenses.
Limits: None. **Times:** Any.
Address: 34 Rectory Road, Churchtown, Southport, PR9 7PU; 01704 231358.

MOCKLER, Mike
Safari guide, tour leader, writer and photographer.
Subjects: Birds and other wildlife of: Botswana, Kenya, Tanzania, Spain, Finland and Norway, Costa Rica, India and Brazil.
Fees: negotiable. **Limits:** None. **Times:** evenings.
Address: Gulliver's Cottage, Chapel Rise, Avon Castle, Ringwood, Hampshire, BH24 2BL; 01425 478103.
e-mail: mikemockler@lineone.net

MOIR, Geoffrey DFC, FRGS, FRPSL
Ret. Schoolmaster, lecturer, writer, philatelist, lived in Falkland Islands.
Subjects: Fully illustrated talks on subjects including: 'Falklands 2000', 'The Island of South Georgia and its Wildlife', 'The Flora of the Falkland Islands', 'Falkland Wildlife'.
Fees: £20. **Limits:** None.
Times: Any. **Address:** 37 Kingscote Road, Croydon, Surrey, CR0 7DP; (Tel/fax) 020 8654 9463.

OFFORD, Keith
Photographer, writer, tour leader, conservationist.
Subjects: 14 talks covering raptors, uplands, gardens, migration, woodland wildlife, Australia, Southern USA, Tanzania, Gambia, Spain, SW.Africa.
Fees: £90 plus travel.
Limits: none.
Times: Sept - April.
Address: Yew Tree Farmhouse, Craignant, Selattyn, Nr Oswestry, Shropshire, SY10 7NP; 01691 718740. e-mail: keith.offord@virgin.net
www.keithofford.co.uk

PICKFORD, Terry
Co-ordinator NW Raptor Protection Group, advisory member to the government's raptor forum committee. Advisory member of the Lancashire Access Forum.
Subjects: 1)Raptor conservation/persecution NW England; 2)Home Life of the Golden Eagle in Scotland; 3)Wildlife of the Czech Republic.
Fees: £70 plus 15p per ml.
Limits: None. **Times:** Any.
Address: Plane Tree House, 114 Pilling Lane, Preesall, Lancs,FY6 0HG; 01253 810620, (M)07977 890116.
e-mail: conservation@raptor.uk.com

POWER, John FRPS
Bird photographer.
Subjects: British birds - four talks (slides) plus photographic workshop (equipment/prints).
Fees: Negotiable. **Limits:** To be discussed. **Times:** Evenings (days poss).
Address: 15 Brynmor Road, Mossley Hill, Liverpool, L18 4RW; 0151 724 5004, (W)0151 729 0094, (Fax)0151 724 3667.

ROBINSON, Peter
Consultant ornithologist and former Scilly resident.
Subjects: Various talks on sea and landbirds of Scilly and life in an island environment; Song Thrushes, Storm Petrels and Kittiwakes.
Fees: £45 plus Petrol.
Limits: None. **Times:** Any.
Address: 19 Pine Park Road, Honiton, Devon, EX14 2HR; 01404 549873.
e-mail: pjrobinson2@ compuserve.com

RUMLEY-DAWSON, Ian
Photographer, course leader.
Subjects: 96 talks using twin dissolving projectors. Birds, mammals, insects, plants, habitats, ethology. Arctic, Antartic, Falklands, N and S America, N.Z, Seychelles. albatrosses, penguins, Snowy Owls, polar bears etc.
Fees: £50 plus expenses.
Limits: None. **Times:** Any.
Address: Oakhurst, Whatlington Road, Battle, East Sussex, TN33 0JN; 01424 772673.

SCOTT, Ann and Bob
Ex-RSPB staff, tour leaders, writers, lecturers, tutors, trainers.
Subjects: 16 plus talks (including nature reserves, RSPB, tours, gardening, Europe, Africa, S America, after dinner talks etc).
Fees: £60 plus travel over 50 mls. **Limits:** None (by arrangement). **Times:** Any.
Address: 8 Woodlands, St Neots, Cambridgeshire, PE19 1UE; 01480 214904; (fax)01480 473009.
e-mail: abscott@tiscali.co.uk

SIMPSON, Geoff
Professional natural history and landscape photographer.
Subjects: 1)'A Nature Photographer's Diary', 2)'Wild Britain', 3)'The Flora and Fauna of the Peak District'.
Fees: £100 plus petrol.
Limits: Anywhere in the UK. **Times:** Any.
Address: Camberwell, 1 Buxton Road, New Mills, High Peak, Derbyshire, SK22 3JS; 01633 743089.
e-mail:
info@geoffsimpson.co.uk
www.geoffsimpson.co.uk

SWASH, Andy
Photographer, author, tour leader.
Subjects: Various talks (birds and general wildlife: Brazil, Argentina, Galapagos, Antarctica, Namibia, South Africa, Kenya, Australia, China, USA, Costa Rica, Venezuela).
Fees: £85 plus petrol.
Limits: None.
Times: Evenings.
Address: Stretton Lodge, 9 Birch Grove, West Hill, Ottery St Mary, Devon, EX11 1XP; (H&fax)01404 815383, (W)01392 822901.
e-mail: andy_swash@ wildguides.co.uk
www.wildguides.co.uk

TAYLOR, Mick
Co-ordinator South Peak Raptor Group, photographer, ornithologist, writer.
Subjects: Several talks including (Merlins, Raptors, Peak District birds, Alaskan wildlife, Spanish Birds).
Fees: £50 plus petrol.
Limits: Negotiable. **Times:** Evenings preferred.
Address: 76 Hawksley Avenue, Chesterfield, Derbyshire, S40 4TL; 01246 277749.

TODD, Ralph
Tour leader.
Subjects: Six talks incl. Galapagos Wildlife, Antarctica, Pyrenees, Iceland, Osprey wardening at Loch Garten, Wintering in Africa, On the Trail of the Crane, Where Ole meets Yeha, Polar Odyssey.
Fees: £60 plus expenses.
Limits: None, neg over 120 mls. **Times:** Any - also short notice.
Address: 9 Horsham Road, Bexleyheath, Kent, DA6 7HU; (Tel/fax)01322 528335. e-mail: rbtodd@todds9.fsnet.co.uk

WALLACE, D.Ian.M.
Field ornithologist, writer, artist.
Subjects: Early birdwatching (1930s-1960s) and other subjects.
Fees: Negotiable plus travel.
Limits: None, overnight accom over 150 mls.
Times: Any.
Address: Mount Pleasant Farm, Main Road, Anslow, Burton on Trent, Staffordshire, DE13 9QE; 01283 812364.

WATTS, Nicholas
Farmer, conservationist,

ornithologist, photographer. **Subjects:** Farming and Wildlife', 'Birds on my Farm'.
Fees: £40 within 40 miles. **Limits:** None. Over 40 miles, larger fee. **Times:** Evenings, not Jun-Sep.
Address: Vine House Farm, Deeping St Nicholas, Spalding, PE11 3DG; 01775 630208. e-mail: p.n.watts@farming.co.uk

WILKES, Mike FRPS
Professional wildlife photographer, tour leader.
Subjects: 13 talks - natural history - Africa, America, South America, Europe, Gt Britain.
Fees: According to distance on request. **Limits:** None. **Times:** Any.
Address: 43 Feckenham Road, Headless Cross, Redditch, Worcestershire, B97 5AS; 01527 550686. e-mail: wilkes@photoshot.com

WILLIAMS, Nick
Photographer, lecturer, author, tour leader.
Subjects: Several audio visual shows (including Spain, Camargue, Turkey, Canaries and Cape Verde Islands, Falklands) and birds of prey.
Fee: £80-£99 depending on group size and distance.
Limits: None. **Times:** Any.
Address: Owl Cottage, Station Road, Rippingale, Lincs, PE10 0TA; (Tel/ Fax)01778 440500. e-mail: birdmanandbird@ hotmail.com

WREN, Graham ARPS
Wildlife photographer, lecturer, tour guide.
Subjects: 17 talks, birds - UK and Scandinavia, the environment - recent habitat changes and effect on bird populations, wildlife - Ohio and Kenya.
Fees: £50-70 plus petrol.
Limits: None. **Times:** Any.
Address: The Kiln House, Great Doward, Whitchurch, Ross-on-Wye, Herts, HR9 6DU; 01600 890488, (Fax)01600 890294. e-mail: grahamjwren@aol.com

WYATT, John
Tour leader, photographer, writer, co-author of *Teach Yourself Bird Sounds* cassette series.
Subjects: Over 40 talks (including birds and other wildlife of Africa, Central America, Europe and of specific habitats within these areas, bird identification by sight and sound), general natural history topics.
Fees: £55 plus travel.
Limits: England and Wales only. **Times:** Any.
Address: Little Okeford, Christchurch Road, Tring, Hertfordshire, HP23 4EF; 01442 823356. e-mail: wyatt@waxwing.u-net.com

EASTERN

APPLETON, Tim
Reserve Manager, Rutland Water
Subjects: Rutland Water, British Birdwatching Fair, Return of Ospreys to England, Trips and birds of Spain, Australia, Papua New Guinea, various African countries, Argentina and more.
Fees: Negotiable. **Limits:** Preferably within 2hrs of Rutland. **Times:** Winter preferred but can be flexible.
Address: Fishponds Cottage, Stamford Road, Oakham, Rutland, LE15 8AB; (H)01572 724101, (W)01572 770651: (Fax) 01572 755931.

BROOKS, David
Freelance naturalist.
Subjects: Various talks on wildlife, principally birds, in UK and overseas.
Fees: £50 plus petrol.
Limits: 50 mls without o.n. accom 100 mls otherwise.
Times: Any.
Address: 2 Malthouse Court, Green Lane, Thornham, Norfolk, PE36 6NW; 01485 512548. e-mail: david.g.brooks@tesco.net

COOK, Tony MBE
35 years employed by WWT. Travelled in Europe, Africa and N. America.
Subjects: 22 talks from Birds of The Wash, garden birds to travelogues of Kenya, E and W North America, Europe (Med to North Cape).
Fees: £35 plus 20p per ml.
Limits: 100 mls.
Times: Any.
Address: 11 Carnoustie Court, Sutton Bridge, Spalding, Lincs, PE12; 01406 350069.

COURT, John
Enthusiastic amateur naturalist and photographer. **Subjects:** Seven talks (including general wildlife, butterflies, dragonflies and birdwatching). **Fees:** £32 plus 20p per mile. **Limits:** 100 mls. **Times:** Any (not July or August), also short notice. **Address:** Cedars, Hulletts Lane, Pilgrims Hatch, Brentwood, Essex, CM15 9RX; 01277 372217.

CROMACK, David
Editor of *Bird Watching* and *Birds Illustrated* magazines, author, bird tour leader. **Subjects:** 1) 'Bird Magazines and the Art of Bird Photography' and 2) 'Birds of Arizona and California'. **Fees:** 1) No fee - expenses only, 2) £50 plus expenses. **Limits:** 175 mls. **Times:** Jan/ Feb. **Address:** c/o *Bird Watching* Magazine, Bretton Court, Peterborough, PE3 8DZ. e-mail: david.cromack@emap.com

JOHNSTONE, Leslie
Photographer. **Subjects:** Several (St Kilda, Hebrides and Shetland and offbeat view of bird photography). **Fees:** £45 or 45p per ml (whichever greater). **Limits:** 70 mls without o.n. accom, 200 mls otherwise. **Times:** Any. **Address:** 3 Muirfield Way, Woodhall-Spa, Lincs, LN10 6WB; 01526 354696.

PIKE, David
Photographer, presenter and writer **Subjects:** Winter Birds of Japan'. **Fees:** £50. **Address:** Uffington Manor, Main Road, Uffington, Lincs, PE9 4SN; 01780 751944; (W)01780 767711; (Fax) 01780 489218. www. ukphotographics.co.uk.com e-mail: david.pike@ ukphotographics.co.uk

SHERWIN, Andrew
Interests in natural history and photography. **Subjects:** Ten talks including Kenya, Gambia, Israel, California, Canada, India, Lesvos, Pyrenees. **Fees:** £45. **Limits:** 50 mls. **Times:** Evenings only. **Address:** 26 Rockingham Close, Ashgate, Chesterfield, Derbyshire, S40 1JE; 01246 221070. e-mail: andrew.sherwin @btinternet.com

NORTH-EASTERN

DOHERTY, Paul
Video Maker/photographer. **Subjects:** Five talks (Birds of Prey, Waders, Wetlands, Israel and California). **Fees:** £60 plus petrol. **Limits:** 100 mls. **Times:** Any. **Address:** 28 Carousel Walk, Sherburn in Elmet, North Yorkshire, LS25 6LP; (Tel/ fax)01977 684666. e-mail: paul@birdvideodvd.com

KNELL, Steve
Wildlife photographer and lecturer. **Subjects:** Scotland, Shetland, Yorkshire, Derbyshire, Florida, Lesvos, Tanzania, British wildlife, wetland wildlife. **Fees:** £50 plus travel. **Limits:** 150 miles. **Times:** Sept-Apr inclusive. **Address:** 49 Lower Gate, Paddock, Huddersfield, Yorks, HD3 4ER; 01484 322251;(M)07798 828576.

MATHER, John Robert
Ornithologist, writer, tour guide, lecturer. **Subjects:** Birds and wildlife of; Kenya, Tanzania, Uganda, Costa Rica, Romania/Bulgaria, India, Nepal, S.Africa. 'Bird on the Bench'. **Fees:** £65 plus 20p per ml. **Limits:** 100 mls. **Times:** Evenings. **Address:** Eagle Lodge, 44 Aspin Lane, Knaresborough, North Yorkshire, HG5 8EP; 01423 862775.

PARKER, Susan and Allan ARPS
Professional photographers, (ASPphoto - Images of Nature), lecturers and tutors. **Subjects:** Talks on birds and natural history, natural history photography - countries include UK, USA (Texas, Florida), Spain, Greece, Cyprus. **Fees:** On application. **Limits:** Up to 120 mls without o.n accom. **Times:** Any. **Address:** Ashtree House, 51 Kiveton Lane, Todwick, Sheffield, South Yorkshire, S26 1HJ; 01909 770238. e-mail: aspaspphoto@clara.co.uk

NORTH-WESTERN

MELLOR GREENHALGH, Pauline

Photographer, writer, countryside ranger.
Subjects: Hebridean Wildlife - birds, flora, insects, fauna.
Fees: £50 plus petrol.
Limits: 100 mls from Leigh.
Times: Evenings.
Address: 2 Suffolk Grove, Leigh, Lancashire, WN7 4TA; (H)01942 606576, (W)01695 625338. e-mail: pauline@mellor-greenhalgh.fsnet.co.uk

SOUTH-EASTERN

BEVAN, David

Conservation officer, photographer, writer.
Subjects: Nature conservation, natural history of the garden, butterflies, wild flowers. SAE for full details.
Fees: £70 plus petrol.
Limits: 50 miles without o.n. accom 150 mls otherwise. **Times:** Evenings, days poss.
Address: 3 Queens Road, Bounds Green, London, N11 2QJ; (H)020 8889 6375, (W)020 8348 6005, Fax 020 8342 8754. e-mail: conserving.bevan@virgin.net

BORG, Les

Photographer, course leader.
Subjects: Florida (mostly birds), nature photography (parts I, II and III), cetaceans of the Azores, images of 2001.
Fees: Negotiable. **Limits:** 150 mls without o.n accom.
Times: Any.
Address: 17 Harwood Close, Tewin, Welwyn, Herts, AL6 0LF; 01438 717841. e-mail: les@les-borg-photography.co.uk www.les-borg-photography.co.uk

BRITTEN, John

Former leader of local RSPB group.
Subjects: Birding trips to Antarctica, Caribbean, Galapagos, Australia, New Zealand (full list available).
Fees: No fee (donation to RSPB requested), petrol costs. **Limits:** About an hour from Watford. **Times:** Any.
Address: Harlestone, 98 Sheepcot Lane, Garston, Hertfordshire, WD25 0EB; 01923 673205. e-mail; john.britten@btinternet.com

CLEAVE, Andrew MBE

Head of environmental education centre, author, tour leader.
Subjects: 30 talks (including Galapagos, Arctic, Mediterranean and Indian birds, dormice, woodlands). List available.
Fees: £60 plus petrol.
Limits: 60 mls without o.n accom. **Times:** Evenings, not school holidays.
Address: 31 Petersfield Close, Chineham, Basingstoke, Hampshire, RG24 8WP; (H)01256 320050, (W)01256 882094, (Fax)01256 880174. e-mail: andrew@bramleyfirth.co.uk

COOMBER, Richard

Tour leader, photographer, writer.
Subjects: Alaska, Australia, Botswana, Namibia, Seychelles, Falklands, Galapagos, S America, USA, seabirds.
Fees: £60 plus petrol.
Limits: 50 mls without o.n. accom 150 mls otherwise.
Times: Afternoons or evenings.
Address: 1 Haglane Copse, Lymington, Hampshire, SO41 8DT; 01590 674471. e-mail: richard@coomber1.fsbusiness.co.uk

FURNELL, Dennis

Natural history writer, radio and television broadcaster, artist and wildlife sound recordist.
Subjects: British and European wildlife, France, (*The Nature of France*). Wildlife sound recording, wildlife and disability access issues.
Fees: £100. **Limits:** 50 miles, further with o.n. accom. **Times:** Afternoons or evenings according to commitments.
Address: 19 Manscroft Road, Gadebridge, Hemel Hempstead, Hertfordshire, HP1 3HU; 01442 242915, (Fax)01442 242032. e-mail; dennis.furnell@btinternet.com www.natureman.co.uk

HAMMOND, Nicholas

Writer, Wildlife Trust director.
Subjects: Nine talks (including Modern Wildlife Painting, In Search of Tigers, Wildlife Artists in Extremadura, Wildlife Trusts, John James Audubon, Carl Linnaeus).
Fees: £70 plus petrol.

Limits: 50 mls without o.n. accom. **Times:** Evenings/ weekends.
Address: 30 Ivel Road, Sandy, Bedfordshire, SG19 1BA; (H)01767 680504, (W)01223 712406. e-mail: n.hammond4@ ntlworld.com

HASSELL, David
Birdwatcher and photographer.
Subjects: Five talks (including Seabirds, Shetland Birds, British Birds, USA Birds, including Texas, California, Florida etc.).
Fees: £40 plus petrol.
Limits: 100 mls. **Times:** Evenings.
Address: 15 Grafton Road, Enfield, Middlesex, EN2 7EY; (H)020 8367 0308, (W)020 7587 4500. e-mail: david@ hassell99.freeserve.co.uk www.davidhassell.co.uk

MASON, Barrie
Wildlife photographer, RSPB group leader.
Subjects: The Brilliant Kingfisher', 'The Birds of Strawberry Hill Farm', Grassholm and Skokholm, Wildlife of Scotland, trips by lorry in Peru and Africa.
Fees: £30 plus petrol.
Limits: 100 mls. **Times:** Evening.
Address: 6 Landseer Walk, Bedford, MK41 7LZ; (H)01234 262280.

NOBBS, Brian
Amateur birdwatcher and photographer.
Subjects: Wildlife of the Wild West, Israel, Mediterranean, Florida, wildlife gardening.
Fees: £30 plus 25p per ml.
Limits: Kent, Surrey, Sussex. **Times:** Evenings.
Address: The Grebes, 36 Main Road, Sundridge, Sevenoaks, Kent, TN14 6EP; 01959 563530. e-mail: Brian.nobbs@tiscali.co.uk

READ, Mike
Photographer, tour leader, writer.
Subjects: 12 talks featuring British and foreign subjects (list available on receipt of sae).
Fees: £70 plus travel.
Limits: 175 mls. **Times:** Any.
Address: Claremont, Redwood Close, Ringwood, Hampshire, BH24 1PR; 01425 475008, (Fax)01425 473160. e-mail: mike@mikeread.co.uk www.mikeread.co.uk

TREVIS, Barry
Nature reserve warden, birdringer, widely travelled birdwatcher.
Subjects: Birding in Peru; Birds of Churchill, Manitoba; Tanzania - birds, parks and Kilimanjaro; Birding 'Down-under'; Lemford Springs Nature Reserve.
Fees: £75. **Limits:** Up to 20mls, travel costs otherwise. **Times:** Any.
Address: 11 Lemsford Village, Welwyn Garden City, Hertfordshire, AL8 7TN; (H)01707 335517. e-mail: trevis@unisonfree.net

WARD, Chris
Photographer.
Subjects: 16 talks on UK and worldwide topics (W.Palearctic, Americas, Africa, Australia) - primarily birds, some other wildlife.
Fees: £35 plus petrol.
Limits: 100 mls. **Times:** Evenings, afternoons poss.
Address: 276 Bideford Green, Leighton Buzzard, Bedfordshire, LU7 7TU; 01525 375528; e-mail: chris@ chriswardphotography.co.uk

WRIGHT, Barry
Biomedical scientist, widely travelled abroad.
Subjects: Various South American countries and West Indies. 'A Year Abroad!', 'Journey across South America', 'Travels in Tibet', 'Travels in Uganda' - all talks based on birding trips.
Fees: £50 plus petrol.
Limits: 60 mls without o.n accom. **Times:** Evenings.
Address: 18 Chestnut Grove, Wilmington, Kent, DA2 7PG; (H)01322 527345, (W)01322 428100 (4895). e-mail: barry@ birding98.fsnet.co.uk

COOMBER, Richard
Tour leader, photographer, writer.
Subjects: Alaska, Australia, Botswana, Namibia, Seychelles, Falklands, Galapagos, S America, USA, seabirds.
Fees: £60 plus petrol.
Limits: 50 mls without o.n. accom 150 mls otherwise.
Times: Afternoons or evenings.

Address: 1 Haglane Copse, Lymington, Hampshire, SO41 8DT; 01590 674471. e-mail: richard@ coomber1.fsbusiness.co.uk

SOUTH-WESTERN

COUZENS, Dominic

Full-time birdwatcher, tour leader (UK and overseas), writer and lecturer.
Subjects: The Secret Habits of Garden Birds', 'Birds Behaving Badly - the trials and tribulations of birds through the year', 'Bird Sounds - As You've Never Heard Them Before'.
Fees: £50 plus travel.
Limits: London and south.
Times: Any.
Address: 3 Clifton Gardens, Ferndown, Dorset, BH22 9BE; (Tel/fax) 01202 874330. e-mail: Dominic@birdwords.co.uk www.birdwords.co.uk

GREEN, DR George

Author, birdguide and tour leader.
Subjects: Nine talks including Dorset birds, African wildlife safari, wildlife of the Picos Mountains, birds of Northern India, Costa Rica, Florida, Gambia, N.Africa and Middle East.
Fees: £50 plus petrol.
Limits: 200 mls. **Times:** Afternoons and evenings.
Address: 20 Paget Close, Wimborne, Dorset, BH21 2SW; (H)01202 886885, (W)01258 483414.

WEST MIDLANDS AND WALES

CONWAY, Wendy PSA4. AFIAP

Award-winning wildlife photographer.
Subjects: Several talks, birds, mammals, landscapes from UK, USA, Lesvos and Africa.
Fees: £45 plus petrol.
Limits: Over 50mls please contact. **Times:** Any.
Address: 4 Meriden Close, Winyates Green, Redditch, B98 0QN; 01527 457793. e-mail: wendy@ terry-wall.com

BROADBENT, David

Photographer.
Subjects: UK birds and wild places. In praise of natural places.
Fees: £70 plus travel.
Limits: 50mls without o.n accom Anywhere otherwise.
Times: Any.
Address: Rose Cottage, Bream Road, Whitepool, St Briavels, Lydney, GL15 6TL. 01594 531381; (M)07771 664973; e-mail: info@davidbroadbent.com www.davidbroadbent.com

DENNING, Paul

Wildlife photographer, lecturer.
Subjects: 15 talks, (birds, mammals, reptiles, butterflies etc, UK, western and eastern Europe, north and central America, Canaries).
Fees: £30 plus petrol.
Limits: 80 mls. **Times:** Evenings, weekends.
Address: 17 Maes Maelwg, Beddau, Pontypridd, CF38 2LD; (H)01443 202607; (W)02920 673243. e-mail: pgdenning.naturepics@ virgin.net

WALL, Terry ARPS EFIAP PPSA

Wildlife photographer.
Subjects: Several (birds, mammals, landscapes - USA, UK, Lesvos, Africa and Galapagos).
Fees: £45 plus petrol.
Limits: Over 50 mls please contact. **Times:** Any.
Address: 4 Meriden Close, Winyates Green, Redditch, B98 0QN; 01527 457793. e-mail: wildimages@ terry-wall.com www.terry-wall.com

SCOTLAND

WATSON, Derick

Wildlife artist and gallery owner
Subjects: Painting demonstrations with commentary. Slide talks: Birding with a Sketchbook, the Art of Birding, Seabirds of the North Sea, Citizens of the Bass, California etc.
Fees: £75 plus petrol.
Limits: 250 mls. **Times:** All year, autumn/winter preferred.
Address: The Kittiwake Gallery at St Abbs Head, St Abbs, Eyemouth, TD14 5QF; (H)018907 71588, (W)018907 71504. e-mail: derickwatson@ btopenworld.com

TRADE DIRECTORY

Lesser Spotted Woodpeckers by Norman McCanch

BIRD GARDEN SUPPLIERS

BAMFORDS TOP FLIGHT

Company ethos: Family-owned manufacturing company providing good quality bird foods via a network of UK stockists or mail order. RSPB Corporate Member, BTO Business Ally, Petcare Trust Member.
Key product lines: A range of wild bird mixtures containing the revolutionary new 'Pro-tec Health Aid', developed by Bamfords, to protect and promote the welfare of wild birds. Vast array of other foods and seeds for birds.
Other services: Trade suppliers of bulk and pre-packed bird and petfoods. Custom packing/own label if required.
Opening times: Mon-Fri 8am-5.30pm; Sat 8am–12 noon; (Sunday 10am–12 noon, Mill Shop only).
Address; Globe Mill, Midge Hall, Leyland, Lancashire, PR26 6TN:01772 456300;(Fax) 01772 456302. email: sales@bamfords.co.uk www.bamfords.co.uk

Goldfinch by Richard Whittlestone

CJ WILDBIRD FOODS LTD

Company ethos: High quality products, no-quibble guarantee, friendly, professional service.
Key product lines: Complete range of RSPB Birdcare feeders, food, nest boxes, bird tables and accessories, alongside a collection of other wildlife related products.
Other services: Mail order company, online ordering, 24hr delivery service. Free handbook.
Opening times: Mon-Fri (9am-5pm).
Address; The Rea, Upton Magna, Shrewsbury, Shropshire, SY4 4UR; 0800 731 2820; Fax; 01743 709504. e-mail: enquiries@birdfood.co.uk www.birdfood.co.uk

ERNEST CHARLES

Company ethos: Member of Birdcare Standards Assoc. ISO 9002 registered. Offering quality bird foods/ wildlife products through a friendly mail-order service.
Key product lines: Bird foods, feeders, nest boxes and other wildlife products.
Other services: Own label work for other companies considered and trade enquiries.
Opening times: Mon to Fri (8am-5pm).
Contact: Stuart Christophers, Copplestone Mills, Crediton, Devon EX17 5NF; 01363 84842; (Fax)01363 84147. e-mail: stuart@ernest-charles.com www.ernest-charles.com

JACOBI JAYNE & CO.

Company ethos: To supply products of proven conservation worth and highest quality. To offer expertise and special prices to wildlife groups, schools and colleges.
Key product lines: Birdfeeders, birdfoods, nest boxes & accessories. UK distributor of Schwegler woodcrete nest boxes, Droll Yankees feeders and Jacobi Jayne wildlife foods.
Other services: *Wild Bird News* mail-order catalogue.
Opening times: 24hrs (use websites or answering service when office is closed).
Contact: Graham Evans/ Sally Haynes, Jacobi Jayne & Co, Wealden Forest Park, Canterbury, Kent, CT6 7LQ; 0800 072 0130; (Fax)01227 719235. e-mail: enquiries@jacobijayne.com www.jacobijayne.com www.birdon.com www.wildbirdnews.com

JAMIE WOOD LTD

Company ethos: Quality hand-made products at competitive prices as supplied to the RSPB,

universities, film units, householders. Thirty years experience.
Key products: Hides, photographic electronics, nest boxes, feeders, bird tables, patio stands.
Other services: Mail order, delivery ex-stock, within seven days.
Opening times: Telesales, Mon to Fri (9am-9pm), Sat to Sun (10am-4pm).
Contact: Keith, Karen or Ron, Jamie Wood Ltd, Dept BYD, 1 Green Street, Old Town, Eastbourne, Sussex, BN21 1QN; Tel/Fax; 01323 727291. e-mail: Jamiewood@birdtables.com www.birdtables.com

www.thebirdtable.co.uk

Company ethos: A family business that supplies an extensive range of quality products combined with superb service. Supporters of The Essex Wildlife Trust.
Key product lines: Bird tables, bird feeders, nest boxes, bird baths and a variety of mixes and feeds for wild birds and other wildlife.
Other services: Courier service, 48 hour delivery.
Contact: Browse our website for our extensive range of products, advice, drawings and photographs; 01268 413109; (Fax)01268 419258. e-mail: enquiries@thebirdtable.co.uk www.thebirdtable.co.uk

VINE HOUSE FARM BIRD FOODS

Company ethos: Growing and selling black sunflowers and other bird seed direct from the farm.
Key product lines: Full range of bird food plus feeders and other accessories.
Other services: Open days in the winter to view all the finches and buntings feeding at our farm. Farm walks in the summer.
Opening times: Mon to Sat(8am-5pm).
Contact: Nicholas Watts, Vine House Farm, Deeping St Nicholas, Spalding, PE11 3DG; 01775 630208; (Fax) 01775 630244. e-mail p.n.watts@farming.co.uk

BOOK PUBLISHERS

BRITISH ORNITHOLOGISTS' UNION

Single imprint specialising in the highly acclaimed Checklists Series providing detailed avifaunas for poorly known cuontries, regions and islands around the world.
Address: The Natural History Museum, Tring, Herts, HP23 6AP; 01 442 890 080; (Fax)020 7942 6150. www.bou.org.uk e-mail: sales@bou.org.uk

BUCKINGHAM PRESS

Imprints: Single imprint company - publishers of *The Birdwatcher's Yearbook* since 1980, *Who's Who in Ornithology* (1997), *Best Birdwatching Sites in Norfolk.*
New for 2004: *Birds Illustrated,* a new quarterly magazine, *Best Birdwatching sites in Sussex* by Adrian Thomas and Peter Francis, *Best Birdwatching Sites in the Highlands of Scotland* by Gordon Hamlett.
Address: 55 Thorpe Park Road, Peterborough, PE3 6LJ. 01733 561739. e-mail: admin@buckinghampress.com

CHRISTOPHER HELM PUBLISHERS

Imprints: An imprint of A & C Black Publishers Ltd, incorporating Pica Press (acquired Oct 2000) and T&AD Poyser (acquired June 2002).
New for 2004: *The Migration Atlas, Birds of the Mediterranean, Birds of Venezuela, 'Howard & Moore'* complete checklist of the *Birds of the World* (3rd edition). *Secret Lives of Garden Birds, Birds of Africa Vol VII, Birds of Belize, Mammals of the World: A Checklist.*
Address: 37 Soho Square, London, W1D 3QZ; 020 7758 0200; (Fax)020 7758 0222. e-mail: ornithology@acblack.com www.acblack.com

HARPER COLLINS PUBLISHERS

Imprints: Collins Natural History — the leading publisher of fieldguides to the natural world.
Collins New Naturalist Series, the encyclopaedic reference for all areas of British natural history.
HarperCollins, publisher of

the best illustrated books.
New for 2004: *New Naturalist British Bats* by John Altringham; *Collins Birds by Behaviour* by Dominic Couzens, illustrated by Philip Snow, Anthony Disley, Richard Jarvis, Michael Webb and Dave Nurney; *Field Guide to Warbler Songs and Calls* by Geoff Sample; *Nature Safari: 100 Things to do in the Wild* by Geoff Sample.
Address: 77-85 Fulham Palace Rd, Hammersmith, London, W6 8JB; 020 8307 4998; (Fax)020 8307 4037. e-mail: isabel.sheehy@harpercollins.co.uk www.fireandwater.com www.collins.co.uk

NEW HOLLAND PUBLISHERS (UK) LTD

Imprints; New Holland, illustrated bird books, general wildlife and personality-led natural history.
New for 2004: Please contact New Holland for further information.
Address: Garfield House, 86-88 Edgware Road, London, W2 2EA; 020 7724 7773; (Fax)020 7258 1293. www.newhollandpublishers.com e-mail: jo@nhpub.co.uk

WILD*Guides* LTD

Imprints; WILD*Guides* — definitive natural history fieldguides. Hardback and flexicover.
OCEAN*Guides* — definitive identification guides to marine wildlife. Flexicover.
Your Countryside Guides — regional heritage guides for walkers. Hardback and flexicover.
WILD eARTh — lavishly illustrated celebrations of wildlife and natural places. Hardback.
New for 2004: *Marine Mammals of the North American Pacific, Britain's Bumblebees, Britain's Wild Orchids, Wildilfe Walks in The Thames Valley.*
Address: Parr House, 63 Hatch Lane, Old Basing, Hants, RG24 7EB; 01256 478309; (Fax)01256 818039. e-mail: info@wildguides.co.uk www.wildguides.co.uk

BOOK SELLERS

ATROPOS/ATROPOS BOOKSHOP

Company ethos: All the latest information about butterflies, moths and dragonflies published in a lively and entertaining journal.
Key subjects: Journal suited to birdwatchers interested in butterflies, moths and dragonflies. Field guides and key books supplied.
Other services: Insectline: 09068 700250 (calls 60p per minute), recorded message gives news of latest sightings. Hotline to report your sightings 01326 291218.
Address: Mark Tunmore, 36 Tinker Lane, Meltham, Holmfirth, West Yorkshire, HD9 4EX; 01326 290287. e-mail: atropos@atroposed.freeserve.co.uk www.atropos.info

BOOKS FOR BIRDERS/ BIRDING WORLD SALES

Company ethos: Friendly and informative staff, providing a fast delivery service.
Key subjects: Ornithology, (fieldguides, site guides and monographs).
Other services: *Birding World* magazine. Mail-order.
Opening times: Mon-Fri (9am-5pm), answerphone outside office hours.
Address; Stonerunner, Coast Road, Cley, Norfolk, NR25 7RZ; 01263 741139. e-mail: sales@birdingworld.co.uk

NHBS MAIL ORDER BOOKSTORE

Company ethos: A unique natural history, conservation and environmental bookstore.
Key subjects: Natural history, conservation, environmental science, zoology, habitats and ecosystems, botany, marine biology.
Other services: NHBS.com offers a searchable and browsable web catalogue with more than 85,000 titles.
Opening times: Mon-Fri (9am-5pm). Mail-order, viewing by appointment only.
Address; 2-3 Wills Road, Totnes, Devon, TQ9 5XN; 01803 865913; (Fax)01803 865280. www.nhbs.com e-mail: nhbs@nhbs.co.uk

ORNITHOLIDAYS *BOOK STOP*

Company ethos: Friendly and helpful staff on hand to assist in the purchase of ornithological and natural history books.
Key subjects: Ornithology and natural history books by mail order.
Other services; We are primarily a tour operator sending birdwatching and natural history tours worldwide, including cruises to Antarctica, Kamchatka and Galapagos. Since 2000 we have complemented our business by successfully supplying a wide range of books published by the leading companies at a 10% discount with free postage and packing within the UK.
Opening times: Mail order only. Mon-Fri (9am-5pm).
Address: 29 Straight Mile, Romsey, Hampshire SO51 9BB; 01794 523500; (Fax)01794 523544. e-mail: ornitholidays@compuserve.com www.ornitholidays.co.uk

PORTLAND OBSERVATORY BOOK SHOP

Company ethos: To meet the needs of amateur and professional naturalists.
Key subjects: Ornithology, general natural history, topography, art and local history. New and secondhand.
Other services: Mail order, discount on new books, increased discount for observatory members.
Opening times: Wed, Thur, Fri and Sunday; (10am to 4pm). Other times on request.
Address; Bird Observatory, Old Lower Light, Portland Bill, Dorset, DT5 2JT; 01305 820553. e-mail: petermonday@tiscali.co.uk www.portlandbirdobs.btinternet.co.uk

SECOND NATURE

Company ethos: Buying and selling out-of-print/secondhand/antiquarian books on natural history, topography and travel.
Key subjects: Birds, mammals and travel with a natural history interest. Very large specialist stock.
Other services; Occasional catalogues issued. Often exhibiting at bird/natural history fairs.
Opening times: Mail order only.
Address; Knapton Book Barn, Back Lane, Knapton, York, YO26 6QJ; (Tel/fax) 01904 339493. e-mail: SecondnatureYork@aol.com

SUBBUTEO BOOKS

Company ethos: Specialist knowledge on all aspects of natural history, friendly service.
Key subjects: Wildlife, natural history and travel books.
Other services: Source any natural history book from around the world. Online ordering, free catalogue.
Opening times: Mon-Fri (9am-5pm).
Address: The Rea, Upton Magna, Shrewsbury, Shropshire, SY4 4UR; 0870 010 9700; (Fax)0870 010 9699. e-mail: info@wildlifebooks.com www.wildlifebooks.com

WAXWINGS NATURAL HISTORY BOOKS

Company ethos: Friendly, helpful and personal service promoting customer satisfaction. Catering for all levels of interest from beginner to professional.
Key subjects: Ornithology, avian science reference, all aspects of natural history and countryside management. Free catalogue.
Other services: Freelance ornithological research, bird survey and monitoring, education and environmental assessment provided by qualified staff through Waxwings Ornithology Ecological Consultants).
Opening times: Mail order only, orders or enquiries at any reasonable time.
Address: Sunnybank Cottage, Ruston Parva, Driffield, East Yorkshire YO25 4DG. +44(UK) (0)1377 254775; e-mail: dmp.waxwings@btinternet.com

WILDSOUNDS

Company ethos: Donates a significant portion of profit to bird conservation, committed to sound environmental practices, official bookseller to African Bird Club and Oriental Bird Club.
Key product lines: Mail order, post-free books and multi-media guides i.e. the award winning *Bird Songs &*

Calls of Britain and Europe on four CDS. Field recording equipment.
New for 2004: New 2004 catalogue.
Address: Cross Street, Salthouse, Norfolk, NR25 7XH; (Tel/fax) +44(UK) (0)1263 741100. e-mail: duncan@wildsounds.com www.wildsounds.com

CLOTHING SUPPLIERS

COUNTRY INNOVATION

Company ethos: Friendly advice by well-trained staff.
Key product lines: Full range of outdoor wear: Jackets, fleeces, trousers, walking boots, poles, lightweight clothing, hats, gloves, bags and pouches. Ladies fit available. Good range of children's outerwear.
Other services: Mail order.
Opening times; Mon-Fri (9am-5pm). Sat (10-4)
Address: No 1 Broad Street, Congresbury, North Somerset BS49 5DG; 01934 877333; (Fax)01934 877999. e-mail: sales@ countryinnovation.com

EQUIPMENT and SERVICES

BIRDGUIDES LTD

Company ethos: Top quality products and services especially using new technologies such as CD-ROM, DVD, websites, plus one-stop on-line shop for books, bird food etc.
Key product lines: CD-ROM, DVD, video guides to British, European and American birds. Rare bird news services via e-mail, website and SMS.
New for 2004: BWPi - an interactive version (on one DVD-ROM disk) of the *Handbook of the Birds of the Western Palearctic* combining text, maps and illustrations from BWP, Concise BWP and BWP Update with even more video clips and sound recordings than are currently in BirdGuides' CD-ROM *'All the Birds of Europe'*.
Address: Dave Gosney, Jack House, Ewden, Sheffield, S36 4ZA; 0114 2831002; order line (freephone) 0800 919391. e-mail: birdguides@birdfood.co.uk www.birdguides.com

BIRD IMAGES

Company ethos: High quality products at affordable prices.
Key product lines: Bird videos and DVDs.
New for 2004: A new line-up of DVDs plus *British Bird Songs* video.
Address: 28 Carousel Walk, Sherburn in Elmet, North Yorkshinre LS25 6LP; 01799 684666. www.birdvideodvd.com

EagleEye OpticZooms

Company ethos: Innovative design, quality manufacturing, custom products, comprehensive and expert advice on all aspects of digital photography and digiscoping.
Key product lines: Telephoto lenses for fixed lense digital cameras/ camcorders, digiscoping adapters and accessories, custom digital camera accessories.
New for 2004: Digiscoping eyepiece.
Opening times: Mon-Fri (9am-6pm).
Address: Carlo Bonacci, Wentshaw Lodge, Fairseat, Sevenoaks, Kent, TN15 7LR; Tel/(Fax)01474 871219. e-mail: info@eagleeyeuk.com www.eagleeyeuk.com

WILDLIFE WATCHING SUPPLIES

Company ethos: To bring together a comprehensive range of materials, clothing and equipment to make it easier and more comfortable for you to blend in with the environment. Quick and friendly service.
Key product lines: Hides, camouflage, bean bags, lens and camera covers, clothing etc. Free CD of website available.
New for 2004: Wider range of hides and equipment.
Opening times: Mon to Fri (9am-5pm), Mail order. Visitors by appointment.
Address: Town Living Farmhouse, Puddington, Tiverton, Devon, EX16 8LW; 01884 860692(24hr); (Fax)01884 860994. e-mail: enquiries@wildlife watchingsupplies.co.uk www.wildlifewatching supplies.co.uk

HOLIDAY COMPANIES

AVIAN ADVENTURES

Company ethos: Quality tours, escorted by friendly, expert leaders at a relaxed pace. ATOL no 3367.
Types of tours: Birdwatching, birds and wildlife photography and wildlife safaris. Suitable for both the first-time and the more experienced traveller.
Destinations: 70 tours to Europe, Africa, Asia & Australasia, North & South America.
New for 2004: Thailand, Jamaica, Sri Lanka, Ghana, Oman, Shetland and Fair Isle. Also birdwatching and art theme tours with Steve Cale.
Brochure from: 49 Sandy Road, Norton, Stourbridge, DY8 3AJ; 01384 372013; (Fax)01384 441340. e-mail: aviantours@argonet.co.uk www.avianadventures.co.uk

BIRDFINDERS

Company ethos: Top-value birding tours to see all specialities/endemics of a country/area, using top UK and local guides.
Types of tours: Birdwatching tours for all abilities.
Destinations: 44 tours in Europe, Africa, Asia, Australasia, North and South America and Antarctica.
New for 2004: Ghana, Iceland, Peninsular Thailand, Canary Islands (re-introduced).
Brochure from: Vaughan Ashby, Westbank, Cheselbourne, Dorset, DT2 7NW.(Tel/fax)01258 839066. e-mail: birdfinders@compuserve.com www.birdfinders.co.uk
Our office is open seven days a week.

BIRD HOLIDAYS

Company ethos: Relaxed pace, professional leaders, small groups, exciting itineraries.
Types of tours: Birdwatching for all levels, beginners to advanced.
Destinations: Worldwide (40 tours, 5 continents).
New for 2004: Canary Islands, Tigers in India, Classical Greece, Falsterbo, Fontainebleau and the Loire, Spitsbergen, Peru, Catalonia.
Brochure from: 10 Ivegate, Yeadon, Leeds, LS19 7RE; (Tel/fax)0113 3910 510. e-mail: pjw.birdholidays@care4free.net www. birdholidays.fsnet.co.uk

BIRDSEEKERS

Company ethos: Best value-for-money birdwatching tours, with an enviable success at finding the most sought-after species.
Types of tours: High standard birdwatching tours with an emphasis on seeing the birds and other wildlife well!
Destinations: Britain, Europe and worldwide.
New for 2004: Peru, Uganda, Madagascar, Malaysia, Trinidad and Tobago, Nepal (trek), California, Romania.
Brochure from: 19 Crabtree Close, Marshmills, Plymouth, Devon, PL3 6EL; 01752 342001; (Fax)01752 342001. e-mail: Bird@birdseekers.freeserve.co.uk www.birdseekers.co.uk

CARPATHIAN WILDLIFE SOCIETY

Company ethos: A non-profit organisation bringing together people with a shared interest in conservation of large mammals and birds.
Types of tours: Wildlife tours for everyone contributing to research. Tracking of wolves, bears and lynx. Enjoyable birdwatching holidays.
Destinations: Slovakia: National parks, primeval forests and wetlands.
New for 2004: Top birding site, Senne wetland and Polana Wildlife Reserve.
Brochure from: Driftwood, The Marrams, Sea Palling, Norfolk NR12 0UN; 01692 598135;(Fax)01692 598141. www.cws.szm.sk e-mail: cws@szm.sk

CLASSIC JOURNEYS

Company ethos: Professional and friendly company, providing well organised and enjoyable birdwatching holidays.
Types of tours: General birdwatching and wildlife holidays on the Indian sub-continent.
Destinations: Nepal, India, Bhutan, Sri Lanka.
New for 2004: South India

Brochure from: 33 High Street, Tibshelf, Alfreton, Derbyshire, DE55 5NX; 01773 873497; (Fax)01773 590243. e-mail: birds@classicjourneys.co.uk www.classicjourneys.co.uk

FSC OVERSEAS

Company ethos: A selection of study tours aiming to increase environmental understanding and awareness, led by experienced tutors and open to anyone.
Types of tours: Birdwatching, natural history, photography, botany, insects, geology, mammals, ecology, art.
Destinations: Around 40 locations in all continents.
Brochure from: Montford Bridge, Shrewsbury, Shropshire, SY4 1HW; 01743 852150; (Fax)01743 852155.
e-mail: fsc.overseas@ukonline.co.uk
www.fscOverseas.org.uk

GREAT GLEN WILDLIFE

Company ethos: Quality wildlife watching experience at a relaxed pace.
Types of tours: General wildlife watching, predominantly birds and mammals, also butterflies and wild flowers. Small groups (eight participants), high standards of accommodation.
Destinations: Full range of Scottish Highland and Island destinations, also Belarus, France, Sweden, Spain, Greece, Norway.
New for 2004: Norway (Northern lights), Hardanger area, Spain (Pyrenees and Ebro Delta), Sweden (Central mountains), N.America (Mississipi to Great Lakes).
Brochure from: Sherren, Harray, Orkney, KW17 2JU; (Tel/fax)01856 761604. e-mail: davidkent@onetel.net.uk

GULLIVERS NATURAL HISTORY HOLIDAYS

Company ethos: "The small company that takes care of you", while fulfilling your holiday dreams. ATOL 4256.
Types of tours: Friendly, expertly guided tours enjoying birds, flowers and wildlife in an informal, considerate atmosphere. Also hassle-free quotes for group trips (leader can travel free).
Destinations: Worldwide.
New for 2004: Gullivers' tenth anniversary competition - win Swarovski EL binoculars!
Brochure from: Bob Gulliver, Oak Farm (H), Stoke Hammond, Milton Keynes, MK17 9DB; 01525 270100; (Fax)01525 270777.

HEATHERLEA

Company ethos: Exciting holidays to see all the birds of Scotland. Experienced guides and comfortable award-winning hotel to give great customer service.
Types of tours: Birdwatching and other wildlife watching tours in the beautiful Scottish Highlands.
Destinations: Scottish Highlands, including holidays from our base in Nethybridge, plus Outer Hebrides, Orkney, Shetlands and more.
New for 2004: Majorca and other overseas destinations.
Brochure from: The Mountview Hotel, Nethybridge, Inverness-shire, PH25 3EB; 01479 821248; (Fax)01479 821515.
e-mail: hleabirds@aol.com
www.heatherlea.co.uk

HONEYGUIDE WILDLIFE HOLIDAYS

Company ethos: Relaxed natural history holidays with wildlife close to home. Quality accommodation, expert leaders, beginners welcome.
Types of tours: Birds, flowers and butterflies, with a varied mix depending on the location.
Destinations: Europe, including Extremadura, Spanish Pyrenees, Crete, Lesvos, Menorca, Camargue, French Pyranees, Dordogne and Danube Delta.
New for 2004: Eastern Greece.
Brochure from: 36 Thunder Lane, Thorpe St Andrew, Norwich, Norfolk, NR7 0PX; 01603 300552 (Evenings). e-mail: honeyguide@tesco.net
www.honeyguide.co.uk

HOSKING TOURS LTD

Company ethos: The best in wildlife photographic holidays.
Types of tours: Wildlife photography for all levels of

experience.
Destinations: Africa, America, Europe.
New for 2004: French Alps and Colorado.
Brochure from: Pages Green House, Wetheringsett, Stowmarket, Suffolk, IP14 5QA; 01728 861113; (Fax)01728 860222. www.hosking-tours.co.uk

IBIS EXCURSIONS

Company ethos: Providing you with the "holiday of a lifetime".
Types of tours: Tailor-made specialist: Anywhere you want to go, whenever you want. Also 'your favourite' catalogue tours.
Destinations: Tailor-made - you choose! - anywhere in the world. Catalogue tours Finland, Norway, Sweden, Denmark (Scandinavia specialist), Spain, Spitsbergen.
New for 2004: Heligoland, Orkney, Nepal.
Brochure from: Ganloseparken 46, 3660 Stenlose, Denmark.(UK no)01327 831225, (DK no)0045 48195940; (Fax)0045 48195945. e-mail: jeffprice@ibis-excursions.dk www.ibis-excursions.dk

ISLAND HOLIDAYS

Company ethos: Relaxed holidays with conservation and responsibility to the environment paramount.
Types of tours: Relaxed birding and natural history tours. We like to enjoy all aspects of the islands we visit, not just the birds.
Destinations: More than 20 island destinations in the UK and worldwide.
New for 2004: Borneo, Ireland, Donana (Spain).
Brochure from: Drummond Street, Comrie, Perthshire, PH6 2DS; 01764 670107; (Fax)01764 670958. e-mail: enquiries@islandholidays.net www.islandholidays.net

LIMOSA HOLIDAYS

Company ethos: The very best in birdwatching and wildlife holidays - expertly led, fun, friendly and full of birds. AITO member. ATOL 2950.
Types of tours: Birdwatching tours, plus birds and butterflies, bears and whales.
Destinations: More than 70 holidays worldwide.
New for 2004: Argentina, Jamaica, Taiwan and Hong Kong, Venezuela, plus six special tours in support of the Wildfowl and Wetlands Trust.
Brochure from: Suffield House, Northrepps, Norfolk, NR27 0LZ; 01263 578143; (Fax)01263 579251. e-mail: limosaholidays@compuserve.com

NATURETREK

Company ethos: Friendly, gentle-paced, birdwatching holidays with broad-brush approach. Sympathetic to other wildlife interests, history and local culture. ATOL no 2962.
Types of tours: Escorted birdwatching, botanical and natural history holidays worldwide.
Destinations: Worldwide - see brochure.
New for 2004: Belarus, Estonia, Japan, Kamchatka, Mexico.
Brochure from: Cheriton Mill, Cheriton, Alresford, Hampshire, SO24 0NG; 01962 733051; (Fax)01962 736426. e-mail: info@naturetrek.co.uk www.naturetrek.co.uk

NORTHERN FRANCE WILDLIFE TOURS

Company ethos: Friendly personal attention. Normally a maximum of five in a group. Totally flexible.
Types of tours: Mini-bus trips catering for all, from beginners to experienced birders. Local birds include Bluethroat, Black Woodpecker, Melodious Warbler.
Destinations: Brittany, Normandy and Pays de la Loire.
Brochure from: Place de L'Eglise, 53700, Averton, Mayenne, France; 0033 243 006 969; (fax)00 33 243 00 8060) www. northernfrancewildlifetours.com e-mail: nfwt@online.fr

NORTH WEST BIRDS

Company ethos: Friendly, relaxed and unhurried, but targetted to scarce local birds.
Types of tours: Very small groups (up to four) based on large family home in South Lakes with good home cooking. Short breaks with birding in local area. Butterflies in season.

Destinations: Local to Northwest England. Lancashire, Morecambe Bay and Lake District.
Brochure from: Mike Robinson, Barn Close, Beetham, Cumbria, LA7 7AL; (Tel/fax)015395 63191. e-mail: mike@nwbirds.co.uk www.nwbirds.co.uk

ORNITHOLIDAYS AND CRUISES FOR NATURE

Company ethos: Full-time tour leaders and a company with more than 35 years experience. ABTA member. ATOL no 0743.
Types of tours: Birdwatching and natural history tours as well as cruises to Antarctica and Galapagos.
Destinations: 80 tours to all seven continents.
New for 2004: Mexico, Malawi and Zambia and Estonia in the autumn.
Brochure from: 29 Straight Mile, Romsey, Hampshire, SO51 9BB; 01794 519445; (Fax)01794 523544. e-mail: ornitholidays@compuserve.com www.ornitholidays.co.uk

SHETLAND WILDLIFE

Company ethos: Award-winning small group travel with the very best naturalist guides.
Types of tours: A unique blend of itineraries to bring you the very best of Shetland. Week-long or three-day holidays dedicated to wildlife, photography, walking and archaeology.
Destinations: All corners of Shetland including Fair Isle.
New for 2004: Orkney, 'Hands on Shetland' - new recording weeks.
Brochure from: Longhill, Maywick, Shetland, ZE2 9JF; 01950 422483; (Fax)01950 422430. e-mail; info@shetlandwildlife.co.uk www.shetlandwildlife.co.uk

SICKLEBILL SAFARIS LTD

Company ethos: Qualified and very experienced, genial leader, to show you the real natural world. Under ATOL 4002.
Types of tours: A range of birdwatching and general natural history tours including mammals, insects, higher plants and macrofungi.
Destinations: East Anglia, Ireland, Papua New Guinea and other South Pacific countries we have lived in.
New for 2004: Irian Jaya and Burma.
Brochure from: Well Cottage, 38 Creake Road, Sculthorpe, Fakenham, Norfolk, NR21 9NQ;01328 856925; (Fax) 01328 862014. e-mail: Ian@sicklebill.demon.co.uk www.sicklebill.com

SPEYSIDE WILDLIFE

Company ethos: Expert leaders, personal attention and a sense of fun - it's your holiday. ATOL no 4259.
Types of tours: Experts in Scotland and leaders worldwide - birdwatching, mammals and whale watching.
Destinations: Speyside and the Scottish Islands, Scandinavia, the Arctic, Europe, Middle East, N America.
New for 2004: New Zealand, Antarctica, The Maldives, Namibia, The Azores.
Brochure from: Garden Office, Inverdruie House, Inverdruie, Aviemore, Inverness-shire, PH22 1QH; (Tel/fax)01479 812498. e-mail: enquiries@speysidewildlife.co.uk www.speysidewildlife.co.uk

SUNBIRD

Company ethos: Enjoyable birdwatching tours lead by full-time professional leaders. ATOL no 3003
Types of tours: General birdwatching, birds & music, birds & history, birds & butterflies, Sunbirder events.
Destinations: Worldwide.
Brochure from: PO Box 76, Sandy, Bedfordshire, SG19 1DF; 01767 682969; (Fax)01767 692481. e-mail: sunbird@sunbirdtours.co.uk www.sunbirdtours.co.uk

THE BIRD ID COMPANY

Company ethos: Expert tour guides teaching bird watchers of all levels bird identification and field craft skills.
Types of tours: Daily guided tours £25. Weekend breaks, five day migration tours, rare breeding bird tours to see Golden Oriole, Montagu's Harrier and Honey Buzzard. Personalised and customised tours UK and abroad.
Destinations: Norfolk, Britain, Europe, America, Middle East.

New for 2004: Northern France, Dorset, Kent.
Brochure from: Paul Laurie, 37 Westgate, Warham Road, Binham, Norfolk, NR21 0DQ; 01328 830617. e-mail: Paul.seethebird@virgin.net www.birdtour.co.uk

THE TRAVELLING NATURALIST

Company ethos: Friendly, easy-going, expertly-led birdwatching and wildlife tours. ATOL no 3435.
Types of tours: Tours include birds and history, birds and bears, whale-watching, birds and flowers.
Destinations: Worldwide.
New for 2004: Arctic Canada, Garrotxa (Spain), Kos, Malawi, Zambia, Switzerland, Great Auk pilgimage to Iceland.
Brochure from: PO Box 3141, Dorchester, Dorset, DT1 2XD; 01305 267994; (Fax)01305 265506. e-mail: jamie@naturalist.co.uk www.naturalist.co.uk

THE ULTIMATE TRAVEL COMPANY - WILDLIFE JOURNEYS

Company ethos: Shared enjoyment of the natural world.
Types of tours: Relaxed wildlife and birdwatching holidays with friendly groups and Britain's most experienced leaders.
Destinations: 21 locations in Africa, Antartica, Central and South America, India, Indian Ocean, South-east Asia and Europe.
New for 2004: Peru and the Czech Repblic
Brochure from: The Ultimate Travel Company, 27 Vanston Place, London, SW6 1AZ; 020 7386 4676; (Fax)020 7381 0836. e-mail: enquiry@theultimatetravelcompany.co.uk

WILD INSIGHTS

Company ethos: Our goal is to enable clients to savour, understand and enjoy birds and wildlife fully, rather than simply build large tick lists. ATOL no 5429 (in association with Wildwings)
Types of tour: Relaxed breaks in UK and overseas, plus three Reader Breaks for *Bird Watching* magazine and skills-building UK courses.
Destinations: Various UK locations, plus Florida, Texas, Pyrenees, Namibia, Andalucia, Southern Morocco.
New for 2004: This is the first year Keith and Linda Offord are running holidays under the Wild Insights banner.
Brochure from: Yew Tree Farmhouse, Craignant, Selattyn, Oswestry, Salop SY10 7NP. (Tel/fax)01691 718 7401; e-mail: keith.offord@virgin.net www.keith.offord.co.uk

WILDWINGS

Company ethos: Superb value holidays led by expert guides.
Types of tours: General birdwatching holidays, whale and dolphin watching holidays, wildlife cruises, ecovolunteers.
Destinations: Europe, Arctic, Asia, The Americas, Antarctica, Africa, Trinidad and Tobago.
New for 2004: Jamaica, Wild Insights - birdwatching holidays led by Keith Offord.
Brochure from:
Address: 577-579 Fishponds Road, Fishponds, Bristol, BS16 3AF; e-mail: wildinfo@wildwings.co.uk

OPTICAL MANUFACTURERS & IMPORTERS

ACE OPTICS

Company ethos: To be the best - service, price and stock.
Product lines: Importers of Optolyth, Ace Avian, Questar and other products.
Address: 16 Green Street, Bath, BA1 2JZ; 01225 466364; (fax)01225 469761.
e-mail: aceoptics@balzjz.freeserve.co.uk

CARL ZEISS LTD

Company ethos: World renowned, high quality performance and innovative optical products.
Product lines: Product ranges of stabilised, Victory, Dialyt, compacts and binoculars and Diascope telescopes.
Address: PO Box 78, Woodfield Road, Welwyn Garden City, Hertfordshire, AL7 1LU;

01707 871350; (Fax)01707 871287.
e-mail: binos@zeiss.co.uk
www.zeiss.co.uk

INTRO 2020 LTD
Company ethos: Experienced importer of photo and optical products.
Product lines: Summit (binoculars and scopes), Velbon (tripods), Kenko (range of scopes), Slik (tripods), Hoya and Cokin (filters), Oyster and Crumpler (bags).
Address: Unit 1, Priors Way, Maidenhead, Berkshire, SL6 2HR; 01628 674411; (Fax)01628 771055. e-mail: sales@intro2020.co.uk
www.intro2020.co.uk

LEICA CAMERA LTD
Company ethos: Professional advice from Leica factory-trained staff.
Product lines: Duovid the world's first dual magnification binocular. Trinovid and new Ultravid full-size binoculars, Trinovid compacts. Televid 62 and 77 spotting scopes with angled or straight view with a choice of five eyepieces, a photo-adapter and a digiscope adaptor for the Leica Digilux 1 digital camera.
Address: Leica Camera Limited, Davy Avenue, Knowlhill, Milton Keynes, MK5 8LB; 01908 256400;(Fax)01908 671316. e-mail: info@leica-camera.co.uk
www.leica-camera.com

CT DISTRIBUTION
Company ethos: Distributor of Manfrotto tripods and accessories for the wildlife and birding specialist. National dealer network.
Product lines: Manfrotto tripods, heads and accessories. Available as separates or kits, suitable for video, scope and camera use.
Address: PO Box 3128, Tilbrook, Milton Keynes, MK7 8JB; 01908 646444; (Fax)01908 646434. e-mail: sales@ctdistribution.com

MARCHWOOD
Company ethos: Quality European optics offering outstanding value for money.
Product lines: Kahles binoculars from Austria, Meopta telescopes from the Czech Republic and Eschenbach Optik binoculars from Germany. Dowling and Rowe optics for the discerning observer.
Address: Unit 308, Cannock Chase Enterprise Park, Hednesford, Staffordshire, WS15 5QU; 01543 424255; (Fax01543 422082.
e-mail: john@ lancashirej.freeserve.co.uk

OPTICRON
Company ethos: To provide the highest quality, value-for-money optics for today's birdwatcher.
Product lines: Official importers of Opticron binoculars and telescopes, plus mounting systems and accessories.
Address: PO Box 370, Unit 21, Titan Court, Laporte Way, Luton, LU4 8YR; 01582 726522: (Fax)01582 273559.
e-mail: info@opticron.co.uk

SWAROVSKI UK
Company ethos: Constantly improving on what is good in terms of products and committed to conservation world-wide.
Product lines: ATS 65 spotting scope and EL 8x32 and 10x32 binoculars, the latest additions to a market-leading range of telescopes and binoculars. Swarovski tripods also available.
Address: Perrywood Business Park, Salfords, surrey, RH1 5JQ; 01737 856812: (Fax)01737 856885. e-mail: christine.percy@swarovski.com
www.swarovskibirding.com

VICKERS SPORTS OPTICS
Company ethos: Importers of world renowned products from American companies Bausch & Lomb and Bushnell.
Product lines: High performance Bausch & Lomb binoculars (including compacts) and telescopes. The extensive Bushnell list includes market-leading Natureview range and Legacy compacts.
Address: Unit 9, 35 Revenge Road, Lordswood, Kent, ME5 8DW; 01634 201284: (Fax)01634 201286.
e-mail: info@jjvickers.co.uk
www.jjvickers.co.uk

OPTICAL DEALERS

EAST MIDLANDS AND EAST ANGLIA

BIRDNET OPTICS LTD

Company ethos: To provide the birdwatcher with the best value for money on optics, books and outdoor clothing.
Viewing facilities: Clear views to distant hills for comparison of optics at long range and wide variety of textures and edges for clarity and resolution comparison.
Optical stock: Most leading binocular and telescope ranges stocked. If we do not have it in stock we will endeavour to get it for you.
Non-optical stock: Books incl. New Naturalist Series and Poysers, videos, CDs, audio tapes, tripods, hide clamps, accessories and clothing.
Opening times: Mon-Sat (9:30am-5:30pm). Sundays by appointment only.
Address: 5 London Road, Buxton, Derbyshire, SK17 9PA;01298 71844; (Fax)01298 73052. e-mail: paulflint@birdnet.co.uk www.birdnet.co.uk

In focus

Company ethos: The binocular and telescope specialists, offering customers informed advice at birdwatching venues throughout the country. Main sponsor of the British Birdwatchng Fair.
Viewing facilities: Available at all shops (contact your local outlet), or at field events (10am-4pm) at bird reserves (see *Bird Watching* magazine or website www.at-infocus.co.uk for calendar)
Optical stock: Many leading makes of binoculars and telescopes, plus own-brand Delta range of binoculars and tripods.
Non-optical stock: Wide range of tripods, clamps and other accessories. Repair service available.
Opening times: Vary - please contact local shop or website before travelling.
NORFOLK; Main Street, Titchwell, Nr King's Lynn, Norfolk, PE31 8BB; 01485 210101.
RUTLAND; Anglian Water Birdwatching Centre, Egleton Reserve, Rutland Water, Rutland, LE15 8BT; 01572 770656.

LONDON CAMERA EXCHANGE

Company ethos: To supply good quality optical equipment at a competitive price, helped by knowlegeable staff.
Viewing facilities: In shop and at local shows. Contact local branch.
Optical stock: All leading makes of binoculars and scopes.
Non-optical stock: All main brands of photo, digital and video equipment.
Opening times: Mon-Sat (9am-5.30pm).
CHESTERFIELD: 1A South Street, Chesterfield, Derbyshire, S40 1QZ; 01246 211891; (Fax)01246 211563; e-mail: chesterfield@lcegroup.co.uk
DERBY: 17 Sadler Gate, Derby, Derbyshire, DE1 3NH; 01332 348644; (Fax)01332 369136; e-mail: derby@lcegroup.co.uk
LINCOLN; 6 Silver Street, Lincoln, LN2 1DY; 01522 514131; (Fax)01522 537480; e-mail: lincoln@lcegroup.co.uk
NOTTINGHAM: 7 Pelham Street, Nottingham, NG1 2EH; 0115 941 7486; (Fax)0115 952 0547; e-mail: nottingham@lcegroup.co.uk

WAREHOUSE EXPRESS

Company ethos: Mail order and website.
Viewing facilities: By appointment only.
Optical stock: All major brands including, Leica, Swarvoski, Opticron, Kowa, Zeiss, Nikon, Bushnell, Canon, Minolta etc.
Non-optical stock: All related accessories including hides, tripods and window mounts etc.
Opening times: Mon-Fri (9am-5.30pm).
Address: PO Box 659, Norwich, Norfolk, NR2 1UJ; 01603 626222; (Fax)01603 626446. www.warehouseexpress.com

NORTHERN ENGLAND

FOCALPOINT

Company ethos: Friendly advice by well-trained staff. Competitive prices, no 'grey imports'.
Viewing facilities: Fantastic open countryside for superb viewing from the shop, plenty of wildlife. Parking for up to 20 cars.
Optical stock: All leading brands of binoculars and telescopes from stock, plus many pre-owned binoculars and telescopes available.
Non-optical stock: Bird books, outdoor clothing, boots, tripods plus full range of Skua products etc. available from stock.
Opening times: Mon-Sat (9:30am-5pm).
Address: Marbury House Farm, Bentleys Farm Lane, Higher Whitley, Warrington, Cheshire, WA4 4QW; 01925 730399; (Fax)01925 730368.
e-mail: focalpoint@dial.pipex.com
www.fpoint.co.uk

In focus

(see entry in Eastern England).
LANCASHIRE: WWT Martin Mere, Burscough, Ormskirk, Lancs, L40 0TA: 01704 897020.
WEST YORKSHIRE: Westleigh House Office Est. Wakefield Road, Denby Dale, West Yorks, HD8 8QJ: 01484 864729.

LONDON CAMERA EXCHANGE

(See entry in Eastern England).
CHESTER: 9 Bridge Street Row, CH1 1NW; 01244 326531.
MANCHESTER: 37 Parker Street, Picadilly, M1 4AJ; 0161 236 5819.

SOUTH EAST ENGLAND

FORESIGHT OPTICAL

Company ethos: Personal service is our pleasure. Quality optical products - no 'grey imports'.
Viewing facilities: Showroom with viewing facilities.
Optical stock: Wide range of binoculars and telescopes, most popular brands stocked. New, secondhand and ex-demonstration stock for sale. Part exchange undertaken. Mail order available, credit cards accepted and credit facilities.
Non-optical stock: Night vision equipment, magnifiers, microscopes, tripods and accessories.
Opening times: Mon-Fri (8:30am-5:30pm).
Address: 13 New Road, Banbury, Oxon, OX16 9PN; 01295 264365.

In focus

(see entry in Eastern England).
ST ALBANS; Bowmans Farm, London Colney, St Albans, Herts, AL2 1BB: 01727 827799: (Fax)01727 827766.
SOUTH WEST LONDON: WWT The Wetland Centre, Queen Elizabeth Walk, Barnes, London, SW13 9WT: 020 8409 4433.

KAY OPTICAL

Company ethos: Unrivalled expertise, experience and service, since 1962.
Viewing facilities: At Morden. Also field-days every weekend at reserves in South.
Optical stock: All leading makes of binoculars and telescopes stocked. Also giant binoculars and astronomical.
Non-optical stock: Tripods, clamps etc.
Opening times: Mon-Sat (9am-5pm) closed (1-2pm).
Address: 89(B) London Road, Morden, Surrey, SM4 5HP: 020 8648 8822; (Fax)020 8687 2021.
e-mail: info@kayoptical.co.uk
www.kayoptical.co.uk and www.bigbinoculars.co.uk

LONDON CAMERA EXCHANGE

(See entry in Eastern England).
FAREHAM: 135 West Street, Fareham, Hampshire, PO16 0DU; 01329 236441; (Fax)01329 823294; e-mail: fareham@lcegroup.co.uk
PORTSMOUTH: 40 Kingswell Path, Cascados, Portsmouth, PO1 4RR; 023 9283 9933; (Fax)023 9283 9955; e-mail: portsmouth@lcegroup.co.uk

GUILDFORD: 8/9 Tunsgate, Guildford, Surrey, GU1 2DH; 01483 504040; (Fax)01483 538216; e-mail: guildford@lcegroup.co.uk
READING: 7 Station Road, Reading, Berkshire, RG1 1LG; 0118 959 2149; (Fax)0118 959 2197; e-mail: reading@lcegroup.co.uk
SOUTHAMPTON: 10 High Street, Southampton, Hampshire, SO14 2DH; 023 8022 1597; (Fax)023 8023 3838; e-mail: southampton@lcegroup.co.uk
STRAND, LONDON: 98 The Strand, London, WC2R 0AG; 020 7379 0200; (Fax)020 7379 6991; e-mail: strand@lcegroup.co.uk
WINCHESTER: 15 The Square, Winchester, Hampshire, SO23 9ES; 01962 866203; (Fax)01962 840978; e-mail: winchester@lcegroup.co.uk

SOUTH WEST ENGLAND

ACE OPTICS

Company ethos: To be the best - service, price and stock.
Viewing facilities: Bird of prey at 100 yds, Leica test card to check quality.
Optical stock: All the top brands, including Questar. Official importer for Optolyth products.
Non-optical stock: All the best tripods and an array of optical related accessories.
Opening times: Mon-Sat (8:45am-6pm).
Address: 16 Green Street, Bath, BA1 2JZ; 01225 466364; (fax)01225 469761. e-mail: aceoptics@balzjz.freeserve.co.uk

LONDON CAMERA EXCHANGE

(See entry in Eastern England).
BATH: 13 Cheap Street, Bath, Avon, BA1 1NB; 01225 462234; (Fax)01225 480334. e-mail: bath@lcegroup,co.uk
BOURNEMOUTH: 95 Old Christchurch Road, Bournemouth, Dorset, BH1 1EP; 01202 556549; (Fax)01202 293288; e-mail: bournemouth@lcegroup.co.uk
BRISTOL: 53 The Horsefair, Bristol, BS1 3JP; 0117 927 6185; (Fax)0117 925 8716; e-mail: bristol.horsefair@lcegroup.co.uk
EXETER: 174 Fore Street, Exeter, Devon, EX4 3AX;01392 279024/438167; (Fax)01392 426988. e-mail: exeter@lcegroup.co.uk
PAIGNTON: 71 Hyde Road, Paingnton, Devon, TQ4 5BP;01803 553077; (Fax)01803664081. e-mail: paignton@lcegroup.co.uk
PLYMOUTH: 10 Frankfort Gate, Plymouth, Devon, PL1 1QD; 01752 668894; (Fax) 01752 604248. e-mail: plymouth@lcegroup.co.uk
SALISBURY: 6 Queen Street, Salisbury, Wiltshire, SP1 1EY; 01722 335436; (Fax)01722 411670; e-mail: salisbury@lcegroup.co.uk
TAUNTON: 6 North Street, Taunton, Somerset, TA1 1LH; 01823 259955; (Fax)01823 338001. e-mail: taunton@lcegroup.co.uk

WESTERN ENGLAND

FOCUS OPTICS

Company ethos: Friendly, expert service. Top quality instruments. No ‘grey imports’.
Viewing facilities: Our own pool and nature reserve with feeding stations.
Optical stock: Full range of leading makes of binoculars and telescopes.
Non-optical stock: Waterproof clothing, fleeces, walking boots and shoes, bird food and feeders. Books, videos, walking poles.
Opening times: Mon-Sat (9am-5pm). Some Bank-holidays.
Address: Church Lane, Corley, Coventry, CV7 8BA; 01676 540501/542476; (Fax) 01676 540930.
e-mail: focopt1@aol.com
www.focusoptics.co.uk

In focus

(see entry in Eastern England).
GLOUCESTERSHIRE: WWT Slimbridge, Gloucestershire, GL2 7BT: 01453 890978.

LONDON CAMERA EXCHANGE
(see entry in Eastern England).
CHELTENHAM: 10-12 The Promenade, Cheltenham, Gloucestershire, GL50 1LR; 01242 519851; (Fax)01242 576771; e-mail: cheltenham@lcegroup.co.uk
GLOUCESTER: 12 Southgate Street, Gloucester, GL1 2DH; 01452 304513; (Fax)01452 387309; e-mail: gloucester@lcegroup.co.uk
LEAMINGTON: Clarendon Avenue, Leamington, Warwickshire, CV32 5PP; 01926 886166; (Fax)01926 887611; e-mail: leamington@lcegroup.co.uk
WORCESTER: 8 Pump Street, Worcester, WR1 2QT; 01905 22314; (Fax)01905 724585; e-mail: worcester@lcegroup.co.uk

BIRD RESERVES AND OBSERVATORIES

Capercaillie by David Thelwell

PLEASE NOTE:
It is our intention to update this section annually, adding new reserves where we can. This means that space becomes limited and some reserves that have not changed for some time are now shown with contact details and a location on the county map. These sites have been shown in full in previous editions of *The Yearbook* and will do so again in future ones. However, if you require more information on a particular site that is not shown in full, please contact Buckingham Press and we will do our best to provide you with more complete information.

Bedfordshire

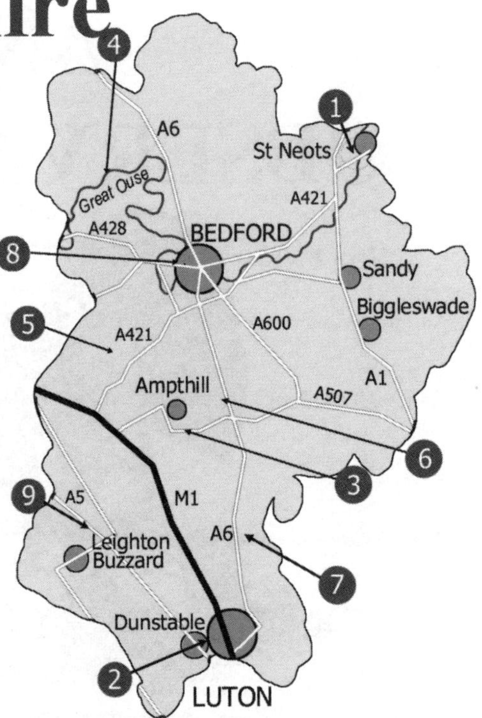

1. BEGWARY BROOK

The Wildlife Trust for Beds, Cambs, Northants & Peterborough. **Contact:** Trust HQ, 01223 712400.

2. BLOW'S DOWNS

The Wildlife Trust for Beds, Cambs, Northants & Peterborough.
Location: TL 033 216. On the outskirts of Dunstable, W of Luton. Parking is at Skimpot roundabout, off Hatters Way on A505 and in Half Moon Lane, Dunstable.
Access: Open all year.
Facilities: None.
Public transport: None.
Habitat: Chalk downland, scrub and grassland, that is a traditional resting place for incoming spring migrants.
Key birds: *Spring/summer*: Hobby, Turtle Dove, Grasshopper Warbler, Lesser Whitethroat, Cuckoo, Spotted Flycatcher, Golden Plover. *Winter*: Buzzard, winter thrushes, possible Brambling. *Passage*: Ring Ouzel, Wheatear, Redstart. *All year*: Marsh and Willow Tits, Bullfinch, Sparrowhawk.
Contact: Trust HQ, 3B Langford Arch, London Road, Sawtry, Cambridge, CB2 4EE, 01223 712400. e-mail: cambswt@cix.co.uk www.wildlifetrust.org.uk/bcnp

3. FLITWICK MOOR

Wildlife Trust for Beds, Cambs, Northants and Peterborough.
Location: TL 046 354. SE of Ampthill. From Flitwick town centre, take the road towards Greenfield. After approx 0.8km turn L into Maulden Road. Head N to Folly Farm (approx 0.8km), opposite an industrial estate. Turn R at the farm and follow road to car park.
Access: Open all year.
Facilities: Car park. Please stick to public paths.
Habitat: SSSI, valley fen, woodland, sedge, reed.
Key birds: *Spring/summer*: Turtle Dove, possible Grasshopper Warbler, Chiffchaff, Cuckoo, warblers. *Winter*: Teal, Lapwing, Woodcock, Siskin. *All year*: Water Rail, Little Owl, Great Spotted and Lesser Spotted Woodpeckers, possible Willow and Marsh Tits, Jay.
Contact: Trust HQ.

4. HARROLD ODELL COUNTRY PARK

Harrold Odell Country Park.
Location: SP 960 570. 10 miles NW of Bedford off the Harrold to Carlton road.
Access: Open at all times.
Facilities: Visitor centre. Cafe open 9am-5.30pm every day. Hide.
Public transport: United Counties bus service, 124, 125 and 126 stop at entrance.
Habitat: Lakes (one with island), lagoons, osier beds, meadows adjacent River Great Ouse, woodland.
Key birds: *Summer*: Breeding Reed and Sedge Warblers, Lesser Whitethroat. Passage waders, Common and Black Terns, late summer Hobby. *Winter*: Wildfowl, Water Rail.
Contact: Bill Thwaites, Country Park, Carlton Road, Harrold, Bedford MK43 7DS. 01234 720016. e-mail: billthwaites@bedscc.gov.uk www.ivelandouse.co.uk

5. MARSTON VALE

Marston Vale Trust
Contact: Forest Centre, 01234 767037. e-mail: info@marstonvale.org www.marstonvale.org

6. MAULDEN WOODS

Forestry Commission.
Location: TL 070 390. E of Ampthill. 1.5km N of Clophill W of A6. Car parking is in a lay-by.
Access: Open all year. **Facilities:** Nature trail.
Public transport: None.
Habitat: Plantation.
Key birds: *Spring/summer*: Cuckoo, Turtle Dove, Tree Pipit, Nightingale, Grasshopper Warbler, Garden Warbler, Spotted Flycatcher, Whitethroat. *Winter:* Crossbill. *All year*: Woodcock, all three woodpeckers, possible Willow Tit, Marsh Tit.
Contact: Forestry Commission, Upper Icknield Way, Aston Clinton, Aylesbury, Buckinghamshire HP22 5NF.

7. PEGSDON HILL RESERVE

Wildlife Trust for Beds, Cambs, Northants and Peterborough.
Location: N of Luton, between Hitchin and Barton-le-Clay, S of the B655 at Pegsdon. Look for the Live and Let Live pub.
Access: Open all year. **Facilities:** None.
Public transport: Bus: from Barton (Mon-Sat), Hitchin (Thu).
Habitat: Rough grassland, scrub, woodland.
Key birds: *Spring/summer*: Warblers, Turtle Dove, Hobby, Grasshopper Warbler, Tree Pipit. *All year*: Meadow Pipit, partridges, Corn Bunting.
Contact: Trust HQ.

8. PRIORY MARINA COUNTRY PARK

Bedford Borough Council.
Contact: Errol Newman, 01234 211182.

9. STOCKGROVE COUNTRY PARK

Greensand Trust on behalf of Bedfordshire and Buckinghamshire Councils.
Location: SP 920 293. From Leighton Buzzard take the Woburn Road N. Turn W at sign into Brickhill Road. Alternatively, from Flying Fox roundabout on A5 head S to Heath and Reach for 0.5 miles following signs for country park.
Access: Park by Visitor Centre (£1 contribution) or along lane if full. Footpath round the lake is suitable for wheelchair users.
Facilities: Visitor Centre has disabled toilets, sightings boards and new restaurant.
Public transport: Arriva bus from Leighton Buzzard stops in Woburn Road, a five-minute walk from the park. Tel: 08706 082 608.
Habitat: Mixed woodland, lake, heathland.
Key birds: *Spring*: Mandarin Duck, Goshawk, Buzzard, Tawny Owl, Lesser Spotted Woodpecker, Wood Lark, Marsh Tit, Nuthatch, Siskin, Redpoll, Crossbill. *Summer*: Woodcock, Hobby, Turtle Dove, Cuckoo, Spotted Flycatcher, Tree Pipit, warblers, Linnet, Yellowhammer.
Contact: The Site Manager, Brickhill Road, Heath and Reach, Leighton Buzzard, Beds, LU7 0BA, 01525 237760. e-mail: rangers@stockgrove.co.uk

Berkshire

1. BAYNES AND BOWDOWN RESERVE

Berks, Bucks & Oxon Wildlife Trust.
Contact: Trust HQ, 01865 775476.
e-mail: bbowt@cix.co.uk
www.wildlifetrust.org.uk/berksbucksoxon

2. DINTON PASTURES CP

Wokingham District Council.
Location: SU 784 718. Country Park E of Reading off B3030 between Hurst and Winnersh.
Access: Open all year, dawn to dusk.
Facilities: Hides, information centre, car park, café, toilets. Suitable for wheelchairs.
Public transport: Information not available.
Habitat: Gravel pits and banks of River Loddon.
Key birds: Kingfisher, Water Rail, Little Ringed Plover, Common Tern, Nightingale. *Winter*: Wildfowl (inc. Goldeneye, Wigeon, Teal, Gadwall).
Contact: Dave Webster, Ranger, Dinton Pastures Country Park, Davis Street, Hurst, Berks. 0118 934 2016.

3. HUNGERFORD MARSH

Berks, Bucks & Oxon Wildlife Trust.
Location: SU 333 687. On W side of Hungerford, beside the Kennet and Avon Canal. From town centre, go along Church Street past the town hall. Turn R under the railway. Follow public footpath over swing bridge on the canal near the church. The reserve is separated from Freeman's Marsh by a line of willows and bushes.

Berkshire

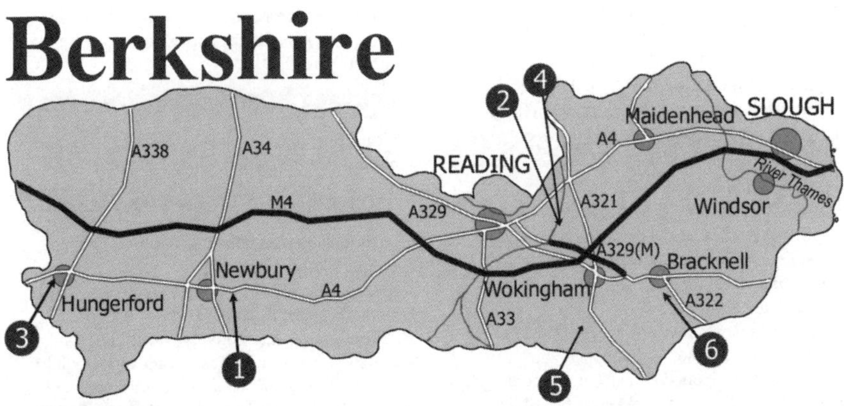

Access: Open all year.
Please keep to the footpath. Dogs on leads please.
Facilities: Car park.
Public transport: None.
Habitat: Unimproved rough grazing and reedbed.
Key birds: *Spring/summer*: Reed Warbler. *Winter*: Siskin. *All year*: Mute Swan, Mallard. Birds seen in the last ten years include Kingfisher, Yellow Wagtail, Water Rail and Grasshopper Warbler.
Contact: Trust HQ, 01865 775476.

4. LAVELL'S LAKE

Wokingham District Council.
Location: SU 781 729. Via Sandford Lane off B3030 between Hurst and Winnersh, E of Reading.
Access: Dawn to dusk. No permit required.
Facilities: Hides.
Public transport: Information not available.
Habitat: Gravel pits, two wader scapes, although one congested with *crassula helmsii*, rough grassland, marshy area,between River Loddon, Emm Brook. To N of Lavell's Lake, gravel pits are being restored and attact birds. A lake is viewable walking N along River Lodden from Lovell's Lake over small green bridge. The lake is in a field immediately on R but is only viewable through hedge. No access is permitted.
Key birds: Sparrowhawk. *Summer*: Garganey, Common Tern, Redshank, Lapwing, Hobby, Red Kite, Peregrine, Buzzard. Passage waders. *Winter*: Green Sandpiper, ducks (inc. Smew), Bittern.
Contact: Dave Webster, Ranger, Dinton Pastures CP, Davis Street, Hurst, Berks. 0118 934 2016.

5. MOOR GREEN LAKES

Blackwater Valley Countryside Service.
Location: SU 805 628. Main access and parking off Lower Sandhurst Road, Finchampstead. Alternatively, Rambler's car park, Mill Lane, Sandhurst (SU 820 619).
Access: Car parks open dawn-dusk. Two bird hides open to members of the Moor Green Lakes Group (contact them for details). Dogs on leads. Site can be used by people in wheelchairs though surface not particularly suitable.
Facilities: Two bird hides, footpaths around site, Blackwater Valley Long-distance Path passes through site.
Public transport: Nearest bus stop, Finchampstead (approx 1.5 miles from main entrance). Local bus companies – Stagecoach Hants & Surrey, tel. 01256 464501, First Beeline & Londonlink, tel. 01344 424938.
Habitat: Thirty-six hectares (90 acres) in total. Three lakes with gravel islands, beaches and scrapes. River Blackwater, grassland, surrounded by willow, ash, hazel and thorn hedgerows.
Key birds: *Spring/summer*: Redshank, Little Ringed Plover, Sand Martin, Willow Warbler, and of particular interest, a flock of Goosander. Also Whitethroat, Sedge Warbler, Common Sandpiper, Common Tern, Dunlin and Black Terns. Lapwings breed on site and several sightings of Red Kite. *Winter*: Ruddy Duck, Wigeon, Teal, Gadwall.
Contact: Blackwater Valley Countryside Service, Ash Lock Cottage, Government Road, Aldershot, Hants GU11 2PS. 01276 686615.
e-mail: blackwater.valley@hants.gov.uk
www.blackwater-valley.org.uk

6. WILDMOOR HEATH

Berks, Bucks & Oxon Wildlife Trust.
Location: SU 842 627. Between Bracknell and Sandhurst. From Sandhurst shopping area, take the

A321 NW towards Wokingham. Turn E at the mini-roundabout on to Crowthorne Road. Continue for about one mile through one set of traffic lights. Car park is on the R at the bottom of the hill.
Access: Open all year. No access to woodland N of Rackstraw Road at Broadmoor Bottom. Please keep dogs on a lead.
Facilities: Car park.
Public transport: None.
Habitat: Wet and dry lowland heath, bog, mixed woodland and mature Scots pine plantation.
Key birds: *Spring/summer*: Wood Lark, Nightjar, Dartford Warbler, Stonechat. Good for dragonflies.
Contact: Trust HQ, 1 Armstrong Road, Littlemore, Oxford, OX4 4XT, 01865 775476. e-mail: bbowt@cix.co.uk
www.wildlifetrust.org.uk/berksbucksoxon

Buckinghamshire

1. BURNHAM BEECHES NNR

Corporation of London.
Location: SU 950 850. N of Slough and on W side of A355, running between J2 of the M40 and J6 of M4. There are several entrances from A355. Also entrances from Hawthorn Lane and Pumpkin Hill to S and Park Lane to W. Small network of metalled roads . Several meet at Victory Cross.
Access: Open all year. Main Lord Mayor's Drive open from 8am-dusk.
Facilities: Car parks, toilets, café, seasonal refreshment book.
Public transport: Train: nearest station Slough on the main line from Paddington.
Habitat: Ancient woodland, streams, pools, heathland, grassland, scrub.
Key birds: *Spring/summer*: Whitethroat, Cuckoo, possible Turtle Dove and Mandarin. *Winter*: Siskin, Redpoll, occasional Brambling and Crossbill. Possible Woodcock, Mandarin. *All year*: all three woodpeckers, Sparrowhawk, Marsh Tit, possible Willow Tit.
Contact: Corporation of London, Open Spaces Department, PO Box 270, Guildhall, London EC2P 2EJ. 020 7332 3514.

2. CHURCH WOOD RSPB RESERVE

RSPB Central England Office.
Location: SU 972 872. Reserve lies 3 miles from J2 of M40 in Hedgerley Village. Park in village, walk down small track beside village pond for approx 200m. Reserve entrance is on L.
Access: Open all year.
Facilities: Two marked paths.
Public transport: None.
Habitat: Mixed woodland.
Key birds: *Spring/summer*: Blackcap, Garden Warbler, Spotted Flycatcher, Swallow. *Winter*: Redpoll, Siskin. *All year*: Marsh Tit, Willow Tit, Nuthatch, all three woodpeckers.
Contact: RSPB Central England Office, 46 The Green, South Bar, Banbury, Oxfordshire, OX16 9AB, 01295 253330.
www.rspb.org.uk/wildlife/reserves

3. COLLEGE LAKE WILDLIFE CENTRE

Berks, Bucks & Oxon Wildlife Trust with Castle Cement (Pitstone) Ltd.
Location: SP 935 139. On B488 Tring/Ivinghoe road at Bulbourne.
Access: Open daily 10am-5pm. Permits available on site or from Trust HQ.
Facilities: Hides, nature trails, visitor centre, toilets. **Public transport:** None.
Habitat: Marsh area, lake, islands, shingle.
Key birds: *Spring/summer*: Breeding Lapwing, Redshank, Little Ringed Plover. Hobby. Passage waders inc. Green Sandpiper.
Contact: Graham Atkins, College Lake Wildlife Centre, Upper Icknield Way, Bulbourne, Tring, Herts HP23 5QG. H: 01296 662890.

4. FOXCOTE AND HYDELANE WATERS

Berks, Bucks & Oxon Wildlife Trust.
Location: SP 715 364 and SP 725 348. Foxcote Reservoir is one mile NE of Buckingham, off A422 on a lane between Maids Moreton and Leckhampstead. Hydelane Lake is S of A422 opposite the entrance to Home Farm.
Access: Open all year. The hides are for BBOWT members only. View from road or follow public footpath to Foxcote Wood that runs parallel to E bank for views over the water.
Facilities: Hides. **Public transport:** None.
Habitat: Open water.
Key birds: *Spring*: Common Tern, Hobby,

Buckinghamshire

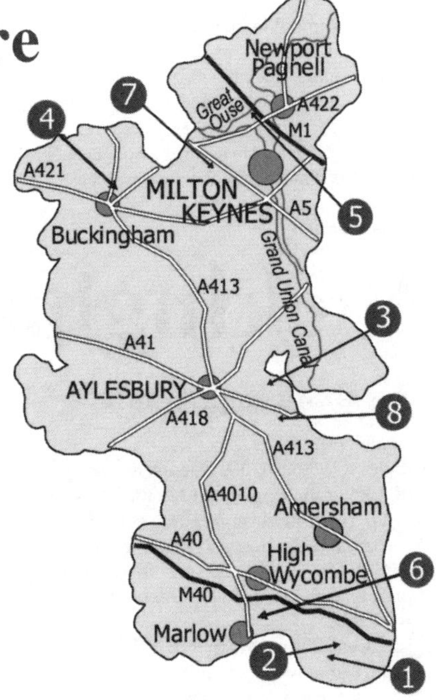

Common Sandpiper, Corn Bunting. *Summer*: Spotted Flycatcher at Hydelane, warblers, Common Tern, ducks, Great Crested and Little Grebes. *Winter*: Water Rail, duck, inc. Wigeon and Goldeneye, Goosander. Possible, Smew, Slavonian Grebe, winter thrushes, wild swans at Hydelane. *All year*: Sparrowhawk, Kingfisher, Little and Tawny Owls, Grey Wagtail, Green and Great Spotted Woodpeckers, Marsh Tit, Jay.
Contact: Trust HQ, The Lodge, 1 Armstrong Road, Littlemore, Oxford, OX4 4XT, 01865 775476. e-mail: bbowt@cix.co.uk

5. HANSON ENVIRONMENTAL STUDY CENTRE

Milton Keynes Council.
Location: SP 842 429. Two miles N of central Milton Keynes. Entrance almost opposite Proud Perch public house on A422 Wolverton to Newport Pagnell road.
Access: Open daily dawn-dusk. Day or annual permit from warden - no access without permission. No dogs. Please ring in advance.
Facilities: Three hides for keyholders.
Public transport: None.
Habitat: Lake (with islands), lagoons, meadows, woodland, ponds.
Key birds: *Spring/summer*: Breeding warblers, wildfowl and waders, terns, hirundines, heronry, Hobby, Barn Owl. *Winter*: Wildfowl, Cormorant, Water Rail, Long-eared Owl (occasional), Siskin.
Contact: Andrew Stevenson, Hanson Environmental Study Centre, Wolverton Road, Great Linford, Milton Keynes, Bucks MK14 5AH. 01908 604810.

6. LITTLE MARLOW GRAVEL PITS

Lefarge Redland Aggregates.
Location: SU 880 880. NE of Marlow from J4 of M40. Permissive path from Coldmoorholm Lane to Little Marlow village. Follow path over wooden bridge to N end of lake. Permissive path ends just past the cottages where it joins a concrete road to sewage treatment works.
Access: All year. Please do not enter gravel works.
Facilities: Paths.
Public transport: None.
Habitat: Gravel pit, lake, scrub.
Key birds: *Spring*: Passage migrants, Sand Martin, Garganey, Hobby. *Summer*: Reed Warblers, Kingfisher, wildfowl. *Autumn*: Passage migrants. *Winter*: Wildfowl, possible Smew, Goldeneye, Yellow-legged Gull, Lapwing, Snipe.

7. STONY STRATFORD WILDLIFE CONSERVATION AREA

Berks, Bucks & Oxon Wildlife Trust.
Contact: Trust HQ, 01223 712400.

8. WESTON TURVILLE

Berks, Bucks & Oxon Wildlife Trust.
Location: SP 859 095. SE of Aylesbury. From Wendover take A413 north; turn right after one mile opp Marquis of Granby pub; park in lay-by after 600 yards and reserve is on right.
Access: Public access on perimeter path.
Facilities: Hide.
Public transport: None.
Habitat: Reservoir, large reed fen.
Key birds: Water Rail. *Summer*; Breeding wablers. *Winter*: Wildfowl and gulls.
Contact: Trust HQ, 01223 712400.
www.wildlifetrust.org.uk/berksbucksoxon

Cambridgeshire

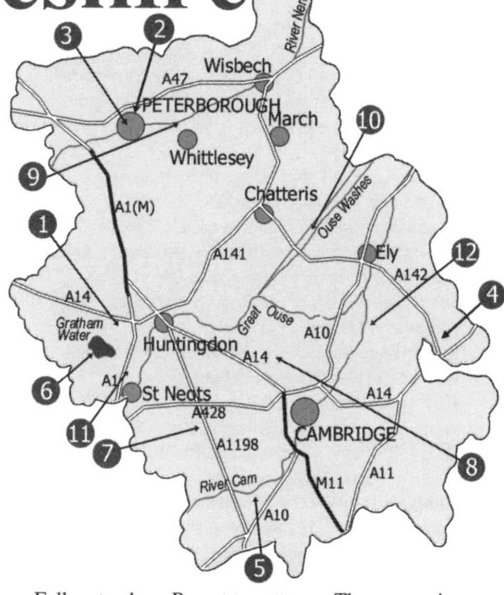

1. BRAMPTON WOOD

Wildlife Trust for Beds, Cambs, Northants & Peterborough. 01223 712400. www.wildlifetrust.org.uk/bcnp

2. DOGSTHORPE STAR PIT SSSI

Wildlife Trust for Beds, Cambs, Northants & Peterborough.
Location: TF 213 025. On NE edge of Peterborough. From A47 turn into White Post Road on Eye by-pass. No parking at reserve. Entrance is via the Green Wheel cycle track in the disused Welland Road behind Star Pit.
Access: Open all year.
Facilities: None.
Public transport: None.
Habitat: Brackish water, scrub.
Key birds: *Winter*: large numbers of gulls, attracted to nearby rubbish tip inc. Mediterranean, Glaucous and Yellow-legged. *Passage*: Occasional waders, inc Green Sandpiper. *All year*: Common water fowl, Kingfisher, Green Woodpecker. *Summer*: Common warblers.
Contact: Trust HQ, 3B Langford Arch, London Road, Sawston, Cambridge, CB2 4EE, 01223 712400. e-mail: cambswt@cix.co.uk

3. FERRY MEADOWS COUNTRY PARK

Nene Park Trust.
Location: TL 145 975. Three miles W of Peterborough town centre signed off A605.
Access: Open all year. **Facilities:** Car park (fee at weekends), visitor centre, toilets, café, hide.
Public transport: Tel. 01733 453540.
Habitat: Lakes, meadows, scrub, woodland and small nature reserve.
Key birds: *Spring*: Common and Arctic Terns, waders, Yellow Wagtail. *Winter*: Siskin, Redpoll, Water Rail, occasional Hawfinch. *All year*: Good selection of woodland and water birds, Kingfisher.
Contact: Nene Park Trust, Ham Farm House, Orton, Peterborough, PE2 5UU, 01733 234443.

4. FORDHAM WOODS SSSI

English Nature (Beds & Cambs Team).
Location: TL 633 701. Take the A142 from Newmarket to Soham. Turn R down River Lane, cross the River Snail and park at the roadside. Follow track on R next to cottages. The reserve is on R at end of track.
Access: All year. **Facilities:** Car park, paths.
Public transport: None.
Habitat: Damp valley woodland, alder carr, reed.
Key birds: *Spring/summer*: Nightingale, warblers. *All year*: All three woodpeckers, Kingfisher, possible Marsh and Willow Tits.
Contact: English Nature (Bedfordshire & Cambridgeshire Team), Ham Lane House, Ham Lane, Nene Park, Orton Waterville, Peterborough PE2 5UR. 01733 405850 (Fax)01733 394093. e-mail: beds.cambs@english-nature.org.uk

5. FOWLMERE

RSPB (East Anglia Office).
Location: TL 407 461. Turn off A10 Cambridge to Royston road by Shepreth and follow sign.
Access: Access at all times along marked trail.
Facilities: Four hides, portable toilets.
Public transport: Shepreth railway station 3km away.
Habitat: Reedbeds, meres, woodland, scrub.
Key birds: *Summer*: Nine breeding warblers. *All Year:* Water Rail, Kingfisher. *Winter*: Snipe, raptors. Corn Bunting roost.
Contact: Doug Radford, RSPB, Manor Farm, High Street, Fowlmere, Royston, Herts SG8 7SH. Tel/fax 01763 208978.

6. GRAFHAM WATER

Wildlife Trust for Beds, Cambs, Northants & Peterborough.
Location: TL 143 671. Follow signs for Grafham Water from A1 at Buckden or A14 at Ellington. Nature Reserve entrance is from Mander car park, W of Perry village.
Access: Open all year. Dogs barred in wildlife garden only, on leads elsewhere.
Facilities: Five bird hides in nature reserve. Two in wildlife garden accessible to wheelchairs. Cycle track through reserve also accessible to wheelchairs. Visitor centre with restaurant, shop and toilets. Disabled parking.
Public transport: None. **Habitat:** Open water, ancient and plantation woodland, grassland.
Key birds: *Winter*: Wildfowl, gulls. *Spring/ summer*: Breeding Nightingale, Reed, Willow and Sedge Warblers, Common and Black Terns. *Autumn*: Passage waders.
Contact: The Warden, Grafham Water Nature Reserve, c/o The Lodge, West Perry, Huntingdon, Cambs PE28 0BX. 01480 811075. e-mail: grafham@cix.co.uk www.wildlifetrust.org.uk/bcnp

7. HAYLEY WOOD

Wildlife Trust for Beds, Cambs, Northants & Peterborough. 01223 712400.

8. MARE FEN

English Nature (Beds & Cambs Team).
Location: TL 366 698. From A14 take Swavesey exit between Huntingdon and Cambridge, continue through village towards Over. Reserve is just past level crossing. Park on road verge and enter over stile.
Access: All year. **Facilities:** Car park.
Public transport: None.
Habitat: Flood storage for surrounding drains.
Key birds: *Spring/summer*: Wildfowl. *Winter*: Swans, geese, duck.
Contact: English Nature, 01733 405850. e-mail: beds.cambs@english-nature.org.uk

9. NENE WASHES

RSPB (East Anglia Office).
Contact: Charlie Kitchin, RSPB Nene Washes, 01733 205140.

10. OUSE WASHES

RSPB (East Anglia Office).
Contact: Cliff Carson, (Site Manager), 01354 680212. e-mail: cliff.carson@rspb.org.uk www.rspb.org.uk

11. PAXTON PITS

Huntingdonshire District Council.
Location: TL 197 629. Access from A1 at Little Paxton, two miles N of St Neots.
Access: District Council site – no charge. Open 24 hours. Visitor centre manned at weekends. Dogs allowed under control. Heron trail suitable for wheelchairs during summer.
Facilities: Toilets available most days 9am-5pm (including disabled), two bird hides (always open), marked nature trails.
Public transport: Stagecoach X46. Runs between Huntingdon-Bedford. Tel 0870 608 2608.
Habitat: Grassland, scrub, lakes.
Key birds: *Spring/summer*: Nightingale, Kingfisher, Common Tern, Sparrowhawk, Hobby, Grasshopper, Sedge and Reed Warblers, Lesser Whitethroat. *Winter*: Smew, Goldeneye, other ducks.
Contact: Head Ranger, The Visitor Centre, High Street, Little Paxton, St Neots, Cambs PE19 6ET. 01480 406795. e-mail: tony@howfreeserve.co.uk www.paxton-pits.org.uk

12. WICKEN FEN

The National Trust. **Contact:** Martin Lester,01353 720274. e-mail: martin.lester@natinaltrust.org.uk www.wicken.org.uk

Cheshire

1. ALDERLEY WOODS

National Trust.
Location: SJ 860 773. Woods are on B5087 Alderley Edge-Macclesfield road nearly 1 mile from Alderley.
Access: Open all year. Please keep to the paths.
Facilities: Car parks, paths.
Public transport: None.
Habitat: Woodland, mainly oak.
Key birds: *Spring/summer*: Redstart, flycatchers, Woodcock, warblers. *Winter*: finches, woodpeckers, Redpoll, Siskin, Brambling.
Contact: National Trust.

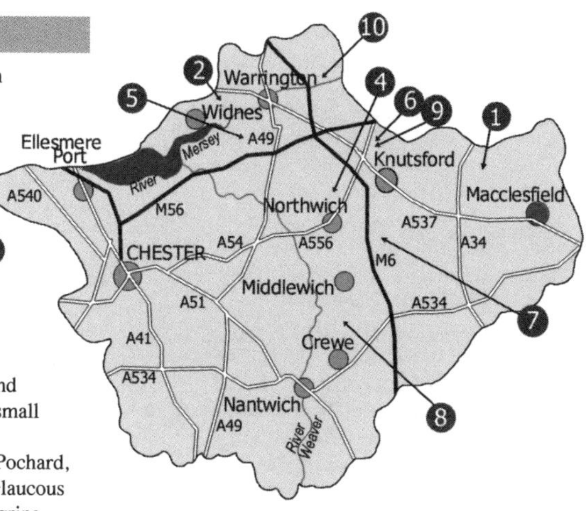

2. FIDDLERS FERRY

Location: SJ 552 853. Off A562 between Warrington and Widnes.
Access: Parking at main gate of power station. Summer (8am-8pm); winter (8am-5pm). For free permit; apply in advance with sae to Manager, Fiddlers Ferry Power Station, Warrington WA5 2UT.
Facilities: Hide, nature trail.
Public transport: Arriva bus 110 every 20 minutes.
Habitat: Ash and water lagoons, tidal and non-tidal marshes with phragmites and great reedmace, meadow grassland with small woods.
Key birds: *Summer*: Breeding Gadwall, Pochard, Buzzard, Peregrine and Raven. *Winter:* Glaucous and Iceland Gulls, Short-eared Owl, Peregrine, Jack Snipe and Twite. Recent rarities: Little Egret, Marsh Harrier, Hobby, Caspian Gull, Mediterranean Gull, Kumlien's Gull and Chiffchaff (*abietinus*).
Contact: Keith Massey, 4 Hall Terrace, Great Sankey, Warrington WA5 3EZ. 01925 721382.

3. GAYTON SANDS

RSPB (North West England Office).
Location: SJ 275 785. On W side of Wirral, S of Birkenhead. View high tide activity from the Old Baths car park near the Boathouse pub, Parkgate.
Access: Open at all times. Viewing from public footpaths and car parks. Please do not walk on the saltmarsh, the tides are dangerous.
Facilities: Car park, picnic area, group bookings, guided walks, special events, wheelchair access. Toilets at Parkgate village opposite the Square.
Public transport: Bus - Parkgate every hour. Rail - Neston, two miles.
Habitat: Estuary - saltmarsh, pools, mud, sand.
Key birds: *Spring/summer/autumn*: Greenshank, Spotted Redshank, Curlew Sandpiper. *Winter*: Shelduck, Teal, Wigeon, Pintail, Oystercatcher, Black-tailed Godwit, Curlew, Redshank, Merlin, Peregrine, Water Rail, Short-eared Owl.
Contact: Colin E Wells, Burton Point Farm, Station Rd, Burton, Nr Neston, Cheshire CH64 5SB. 0151 3367681.
e-mail: Colin.wells@rspb.org.uk

4. MARBURY REEDBED

Cheshire Wildlife Trust. 01270 610180.

5. MOORE NATURE RESERVE

Waste Recycling Group.
Location: SJ 577 854. Located SW of Warrington. Take A56 towards Chester. At Higher Walton follow signs for Moore village into Moore Lane. Cross swing bridge and park beyond crossroads.
Access: Open all year. Not suitable for disabled.
Facilities: Hides, nature trails.
Public transport: None.
Habitat: Wetland, woodland, grasslands.
Key birds: *Spring/summer*: Breeding wildfowl and waders (including Little Ringer Plover). *Winter*: Wigeon, Gadwall, Goldeneye and waders (including Snipe, Jack Snipe and Green Sandpiper). Excellent for gulls (including Glaucous, Iceland and Mediterranean) and Bittern in winter.
Contact: Paul Cassidy, c/o Arpley Landfill Site, Forest Way, Sankey Bridge, Warrington WA4 6YZ. 01925 444 689.
e-mail: paul.cassidy@wrg.co.uk

6. ROSTHERNE MERE

English Nature.
Location: SJ 744 843. Lies N of Knutsford and S of M56 (junction 8).
Access: View from Rostherne churchyard and lanes; no public access, except to A W Boyd Observatory (permits from D A Clarke, 1 Hart Avenue, Sale M33 2JY, tel 0161 973 7122).
Facilities: None. **Public transport:** None.
Habitat: Deep lake, woodland, willow bed, pasture.
Key birds: *Winter*: Good range of duck (inc

Ruddy Duck and Pintail), gull roost (inc. occasional Iceland and Glaucous). Passage Black Terns.
Contact: Tim Coleshaw, Site Manager. English Nature, Attingham Park, Shrewsbury SY4 4TW. 01743 282000; fax 01743 709303; e-mail: tim.coleshaw@english-nature.org.uk.

7. RUDHEATH WOODS NR

Cheshire Wildlife Trust. 01270 610180. www.wildlifetrust.org.uk/cheshire

8. SANDBACH FLASHES

Management Committee. **Contact:** Patrick Whalley, 3 Barracks Lane, Ravensmoor, Nantwich, Cheshire CW5 8PR (please enclose SAE if writing). 01270 624420.

9. TATTON PARK

National Trust/Cheshire County Council. 01270 610180. e-mail: cheshirewt@cix.co.uk www.wildlifetrust.org.uk/cheshire/

10. WOOLSTON EYES

Woolston Eyes Conservation Group.
Location: SJ 654 888. E of Warrington between the River Mersey and Manchester Ship Canal. Off Manchester Road down Weir Lane or from Latchford to end of Thelwall Lane.
Access: Open all year. Permits required from Chairman, £6 each, £12 per family (see address below).
Facilities: Good hides, some elevated.
Public transport: Buses along A57 nearest stop to Weir Lane.
Habitat: Wetland, marsh, scrubland, wildflower meadow areas.
Key birds: Breeding Black-necked Grebe, warblers, all raptors (Merlin, Peregrine, Marsh Harrier). SSSI for wintering wildfowl, many duck species breed.
Contact: B R Ankers, Chairman, 9 Lynton Gardens, Appleton, Cheshire WA4 5ED01925 267355. www.woolstoneyes.co.uk

Cornwall

1. BRENEY COMMON

Cornwall Wildlife Trust.
Location: SX 054 610. Three miles S of Bodmin. Take minor road off A390 one mile W of Lostwithiel to Lowertown.
Access: Open at all times but please keep to paths. Disabled access.
Facilities: Wilderness trail.
Public transport: None.
Habitat: Wetland, heath and scrub.
Key birds: Willow Tit, Nightjar, Tree Pipit, Sparrowhawk, Lesser Whitethroat, Curlew.
Contact: Eric Higgs, Crift Farm, Lanlivery, Bodmin PL30 5DE. 01208 872702.

2. BUDE MARSHES

North Cornwall District Council.
Location: SS 208 057. By public footpath beside Bude Canal.
Access: Keep to paths. Public hide.
Facilities: Level walk along edge of flood plain, with several viewing points.
Public transport: None.
Habitat: Reedbed, grassland and pools. Now extended by a flood plain adjoining the marshes.
Key birds: *Summer*: Breeding Reed, Sedge and Cetti's Warblers. *Winter*: Wildfowl (inc. Shoveler, Teal, Goosander), Snipe and occasional Bittern. *Late summer/autumn*: Little Egret.
Contact: R Braund, 36 Killerton Road, Bude, Cornwall EX23 8EN. 01288 353906.

3. CROWDY RESERVOIR

South West Water.
Location: Follow signs from A39 at Camelford to Davidstow Airfield and pick up signs to reservoir. On edge of forestry plantation, park in pull-in spot near a cattle grid. A track leads to a hide via stiles.
Access: Open all year.
Facilities: Hide. A key and permit is required to use the hide.
Public transport: None.
Habitat: Reservoir, bog, moorland, forestry.
Key birds: *Spring:* Passage migrants, inc Wheatear, Whimbrel, Ruff. *Summer*: Black-headed Gull, Reed and Sedge Warblers, returning waders. *Autumn*: waders, raptors possible inc Peregrine, Goshawk, Merlin. *Winter*: Wild swans, wildfowl, possible Smew. Golden Plover, Woodcock, Fieldfare, Redwing.
Contact: Leisure Services Dept, South West Water,

Higher Coombe Park, Lewdown, Okehampton EX20 4QT. 01837 871565.

4. DRIFT RESERVOIR

South West Lakes Trust/Cornwall BWPS.
Location: Two miles W of Penzance on A30 (signposted).
Access: CBWPS members only (not suitable for disabled).
Facilities: Walk round W side of reserve to the unlocked hide for CBWPS members only.
Public transport: Bus service passes through Drift on route to Lands End.
Habitat: Reservoir, fresh water with muddy margins.
Key birds: *Autumn*: Gulls, ducks, waders plus regular rarities.
Contact: Graham Hobin, Lower Drift Farmhouse, Buryas Bridge, Drift, Penzance, 01736 362206.

5. GOLITHA NNR

Cornwall Wildlife Trust.
Location: SX 227 690. Golitha is three miles NW of Liskeard in E Cornwall. Take minor roads N for 2.5 miles from Dobwalls on A38.
Access: Various paths from 0.5 mile to four miles. Can be muddy after rain. Limited disabled access.
Facilities: Toilets. **Public transport:** None.
Habitat: Ancient woodland, deep granite gorge.
Key birds: *All year*: Sparrowhawk, Buzzard, Kingfisher, all three woodpeckers, Jay, Grey Wagtail, Dipper, Marsh Tit, Treecreeper, Nuthatch. *Summer:* Redstart, Wood Warbler, Pied Flycatcher.
Contact: Trust HQ, Five Acres, Allet, Truro, Cornwall, TR4 9DJ. 01872 273939.
e-mail: cornwt@cix.co.uk
www.wildlifetrust.org.uk/cornwall

6. HAYLE ESTUARY

RSPB (South West England Office).
Location: SW 550 370. In town of Hayle. Follow signs to Hayle from A30.
Access: Open at all times. No permits required. No admission charges. Dogs on leads please.
Facilities: Eric Grace Memorial Hide at Ryan's Field has disabled parking and viewing. Nearest disabled toilets at Wyevale Garden centre, Lelant, 600 yards W just off the roundabout. No visitor centre but information board at hide.
Public transport: Buses and trains at Hayle.
Habitat: Intertidal mudflats, saltmarsh, lagoon and islands, sandy beaches and sand dunes.
Key birds: *Winter*: Wildfowl, gulls, Kingfisher, Ring-billed Gull, Great Northern Diver. *Spring/ summer*: Migrant waders, breeding Shelduck. *Autumn*: Rare waders, often from N America! Terns, gulls.
Contact: Dave Flumm, RSPB, The Manor Office, Marazion, Cornwall TR17 0EF. Tel/fax; 01736 711682.

7. KIT HILL COUNTRY PARK

Location: SX 382 714. On the A390 Liskeard-Tavistock road. From Liskeard, head E on A390 for eight miles. Turn R at Hingston Down to Monkscross. Turn L at crossroads and park on R.
Access: Open all year. **Facilities:** Car park. Paths can be muddy. Not suitable for those with walking disabilities. Please close all gates.
Public transport: Train: ring 08457 484 950 for details. Bus: ring 0870 6082 608 for details.
Habitat: Old mining site, heath, pasture.
Key birds: *Spring/summer*: Possible Black Redstart. Dartford Warbler, Stonechat, Linnet. *Winter*: Brambling, Little Bunting possible. *All year*: Buzzard, finch flocks inc Linnet, Goldfinch, Raven.
Contact: Kit Hill Country Park, Callington, Cornwall, 01579 370030.

8. LOVENY RESERVE - COLLIFORD RESERVOIR

Cornwall Birdwatching & Preservation Society.
Location: SS 208 075. View from private road next to Maer Lodge Hotel, heading N.
Access: Keep to road. **Facilities:** None.
Public transport: Not known.
Habitat: Wetland meadows.
Key birds: Wildfowl and waders (inc. rarities eg. Temminck's Stint, Wilson's Phalarope).

9. MARAZION MARSH

RSPB (South West England Office).
Location: SW 510 315. Reserve is one mile E of Penzance, 500 yards W of Marazion. Entrance off seafront road near Marazion.
Access: Open at all times. No permits required. No admission charges. Dogs on leads please.
Facilities: One hide. No toilets. No visitor centre. Nearest toilets in Marazion and seafront car park.
Public transport: Bus from Penzance.
Habitat: Wet reedbed, willow carr.
Key birds: *Winter*: Wildfowl, Snipe, occasional Bittern. *Spring/summer*: Breeding Reed, Sedge and Cetti's Warblers, herons, swans. *Autumn*: Occasional Aquatic Warbler, Spotted Crake. Large roost of swallows and martins in reedbeds, migrant warblers and waders.
Contact: Dave Flumm, RSPB, The Manor Office, Marazion, Cornwall TR17 0EF. Tel/fax; 01736 711682.

10. NANSMELLYN MARSH

Cornwall Wildlife Trust.01827 273939.
e-mail stuart@cornwt.demon.co.uk

11. NARE HEAD

National Trust.
Location: Approx ten miles SE of Truro. from A390 head S on A307 to two miles S of Tregony just past the garage. Follow signs to Veryan then L signposted to Carne. Go straight over at crossroad, following Carne and Pendower. Turn L on a bend following NT signs for Nare Head. From the garage, Nare Head is about four miles.
Access: Open all year. **Facilities:** Car park.
Public transport: None.
Habitat: Headland.
Key birds: *Spring/summer*: Razorbill, Guillemot, Sandwich, Common and Arctic Terns, possible Whimbrel, Fulmar. *Winter*: Black-throated and Great Northern Divers. Red-throated Diver possible, Scoter, Velvet Scoter, Slavonian, Black-necked and Red-necked Grebes.
Contact: National Trust, Lanhydrock House, Lanhydrock, Cornwall, PL30 4DE, 01208 432691.

12. PENDARVES WOOD

Cornwall Wildlife Trust. **Contact:** Malcolm Perry, 7 Relistian Park, Reawla, Gwinear, Hayle TR27 5HF. 01736 850612.

13. STITHIANS RESERVOIR

Cornwall Birdwatching & Preservation Society.
Location: SS 715 365. From B3297 S of Redruth.
Access: Good viewing from causeway. Hides accessible to members only.
Facilities: None. **Public transport:** None.
Habitat: Open water, marshland.
Key birds: Wildfowl and waders (inc. rarities, eg. Pectoral and Semipalmated Sandpipers, Lesser Yellowlegs).

14. TAMAR ESTUARY

Cornwall Wildlife Trust.
Location: SX 434 631. (Northern Boundary). SX 421 604 (Southern Boundary). From Plymouth head W on A38. Access parking at Cargreen and Landulph from minor roads off A388.
Access: Open at all times.
Facilities: Information boards at Cargreen and Landulph. **Public transport:** None.
Habitat: Tidal mudflat with some saltmarsh. 404 hectares.
Key birds: *Winter*: Avocet, Snipe, Black-tailed Godwit, Redshank, Dunlin, Curlew, Whimbrel, Spotted Redshank, Green Sandpiper, Golden Plover, Kingfisher.
Contact: Stuart Hutchings, 5 Acres, Allet, Cornwall TR4 9DJ. 01827 273939.
e-mail: stuart@cornwt.demon.co.uk

15. TAMAR LAKES

Tamar Lakes Country Park.
Location: SS 295 115. Leave A39 at Kilkhampton. Take minor road E to Thardon, car park off minor road running between upper and lower lakes.
Access: Open all year.
Facilities: Hide open all year round. New centre on lower Tamar. Cafe, toilets (Apr-Sep).
Habitat: Two large bodies of water.
Key birds: Migrant waders (inc. North American vagrants). *Spring*: Black Tern. *Winter*: Wildfowl (inc. Goldeneye, Wigeon, Pochard).
Contact: Ranger,Tamar Lakes Water Park, Kilkhampton, N Cornwall, 01288 321262.

Cumbria

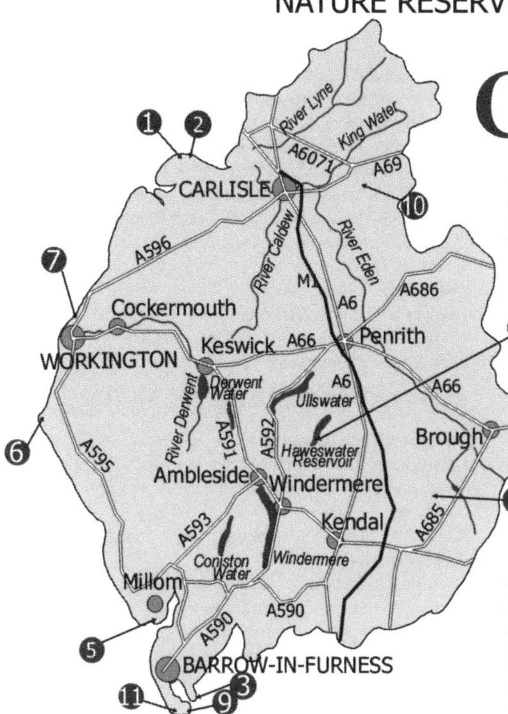

1. CAMPFIELD MARSH

RSPB (North of England Office).
Location: NY 207 620. On S shore of Solway estuary, W of Bowness-on-Solway. Follow signs from B5307 from Carlisle.
Access: Open at all times, no charge. View high-tide roosts from lay-bys (suitable for disabled).
Facilities: Viewing screens overlooking wetland areas, along nature trail (1.5 miles). No toilets or visitor centre.
Public transport: Nearest railway station – Carlisle (13 miles). Infrequent bus service.
Habitat: Saltmarsh/intertidal areas, open water, peat bog, wet grassland.
Key birds: *Winter*: Waders and wildfowl include Barnacle Goose, Shoveler, Scaup, Grey Plover. *Spring/summer*: Breeding Lapwing, Redshank, Snipe, Tree Sparrow and warblers. *Autumn*: Passage waders.
Contact: Norman Holton, North Plain Farm, Bowness-on-Solway, Wigton, Cumbria CA7 5AG.
e-mail: norman.holton@rspb.org.uk
www.rspb.org.uk

2. DRUMBURGH MOSS NNR

Cumbria Wildlife Trust. 01539 816300. e-mail: mail@ cumbriawildlifetrust.org.uk
www.cumbriawildlifetrust.org.uk

3. FOULNEY ISLAND

Cumbria Wildlife Trust.
Location: SD 246 640. Three miles SE of Barrow town centre on the A5087 from Barrow or Ulverston. At a roundabout 2.5 miles S of Barrow take a minor road through Rampside to Roa Island. Turn L into reserve car park. Walk to main island along stone causeway.
Access: Open all year. Access restricted to designated paths during bird breeding season. Slitch Ridge is closed at this time. No dogs allowed during bird breeding season.
Facilities: None.
Public transport: Bus: regular service from Barrow to Roa Island.
Habitat: Shingle, sand, grassland.
Key birds: *Summer*: Arctic and Little Terns, Oystercatcher, Ringed Plover, Eider Duck. *Winter*: Brent Goose, Redshank, Dunlin, Sanderling.
Contact: Trust HQ, Plumgarths, Crook Road, Kendal LA8 8LX.
e-mail: mail@cumbriawildlifetrust.org.uk

4. HAWESWATER

RSPB and United Utilities.
Contact: Bill Kenmir, 7 Naddlegate, Burn Banks, Penrith, Cumbria CA10 2RL.

5. HODBARROW

RSPB (North of England Office).
Location: SD 174 791. Lying beside Duddon Estuary on the outskirts of Millom. Follow signs via Mainsgate Road.
Access: Open at all times, no charge.
Facilities: One hide overlooking island. Public toilets in Millom (two miles). Nature trail around the lagoon.
Public transport: Nearest trains at Millom (two miles).
Habitat: Brackish coastal lagoon bordered by limestone scrub and grassland.
Key birds: *Winter*: Waders and wildfowl includes

Redshank, Dunlin, Goldeneye, Red-breasted Merganser. *Spring/summer*: Breeding gulls and terns, Eider, grebes. *Autumn*: Passage waders.
Contact: Norman Holton, (Site Manager), North Plain Farm, Bowness-on-Solway, Wigton, Cumbria CA7 5AG. www.rspb.org.uk
e-mail: norman.holton@rspb.org.uk

6. ST BEES HEAD

RSPB (North of England Office).
Location: NX 962 118. S of Whitehaven via the B5345 road to St Bees village.
Access: Open at all times, no charge. Access via coast to coast footpath. The walk to the viewpoints is long and steep in parts.
Facilities: Three viewpoints overlooking seabird colony. Public toilets in St Bee's beach car park at entrance to reserve.
Public transport: Nearest station St Bees (0.5 mile).
Habitat: Three miles of cliffs up to 300 ft high.
Key birds: *Summer*: Largest seabird colony on W coast of England: Guillemot, Razorbill, Puffin, Kittiwake, Fulmar and England's only breeding Black Guillemot.
Contact: Norman Holton, (see Hodbarrow).

7. SIDDICK POND

Allerdale Borough Council/EN/Cumbria WT.
Contact: Patrick Joyce, Technical Officer Leisure Services, Allerdale BC, Allerdale House, Workington, Cumbria CA14 3YJ. 01900 326324; (fax) 01900 326346.

8. SMARDALE GILL NNR

Cumbria Wildlife Trust.01539 48280.
e-mail: mail@cumbriawildlifetrust.org.uk

9. SOUTH WALNEY

Cumbria Wildlife Trust.
Location: SD 215 620. Six miles S of Barrow-in-Furness. From Barrow, cross Jubilee Bridge onto Walney Island, turn L at lights. Continue through Biggar village to South End Caravan Park. Follow unsurfaced road for 1 mile to reserve.
Access: Open daily (10am-5pm) plus Bank Holidays. No dogs except assistance dogs. Small charge for day permits (£2 adults, 80p children). Cumbria Wildlife Trust members free.
Facilities: Toilets, nature trails, eight hides (two with wheelchair accessible), 200m boardwalk, cottage available to rent.
Public transport: Bus service as far as Biggar.
Habitat: Shingle, lagoon, sand dune, saltmarsh.
Key birds: *Spring/autumn*: Passage migrants. *Summer*: Breeding Eider, Herring, Greater and Lesser Black-backed Gulls, Shelduck. *Winter*: Teal, Wigeon, Goldeneye, Redshank, Greenshank, Curlew, Oystercatcher, Knot, Dunlin, Twite.
Contact: The Warden, No 1 Coastguard Cottages, South Walney Nature Reserve, Walney Island, Barrow-in-Furness, Cumbria LA14 3YQ. 01229 471066. www.cumbriawildlifetrust.org.uk
e-mail: mail@cumbriawildlifetrust.org.uk

10. TALKIN TARN COUNTRY PARK

Cumbria County Council.
Location: NY544 591. Twelve miles E of Carlisle. From A69 E at Brampton, head S on B6413 for two miles.
Access: All year. Wheelchair access restricted by ten kissing gates.
Facilities: Toilets and restaurant open all year (11am-4pm Easter-Oct, limited opening times in winter). Dogs allowed around Tarn.
Public transport: Bus: infrequent. Tel: 0870 608 2608. Train: nearest station is Brampton Junction. Tel: 0845 748 4950. Footpath from Brampton.
Habitat: Natural tarn, mature woodland.
Key birds: *Spring/summer*: Pied Flycatcher, Spotted Flycatcher, Redstart, Chiffchaff, Wood Warbler. *Winter*: Grebes, Smew, Long-tailed Duck, Goosander, Gadwall.
Contact: Talkin Tarn Country Park, Brampton, Cumbria, CA8 1HN. 01697 741050. e-mail: ccs@cumbriacc.gov.uk www.ccs-cumbria.com

11. WALNEY BIRD OBSERVATORY

Location: S tip of Walney Island, Barrow-in-Furness.
Access: Open daily.
Facilities: Monitoring and ringing of breeding and migrant birds. Cottage accommodation plus facilities for qualified ringers. For bookings write to Walney Bird Observatory, South End, Walney Island, Barrow-in-Furness, Cumbria LA14 3YQ.
Public transport: None.
Habitat: Mud flats, sandy beaches and dunes, pools.
Key birds: Uncommon and rare species on spring and autumn migration.
Contact: As South Walney.

Derbyshire

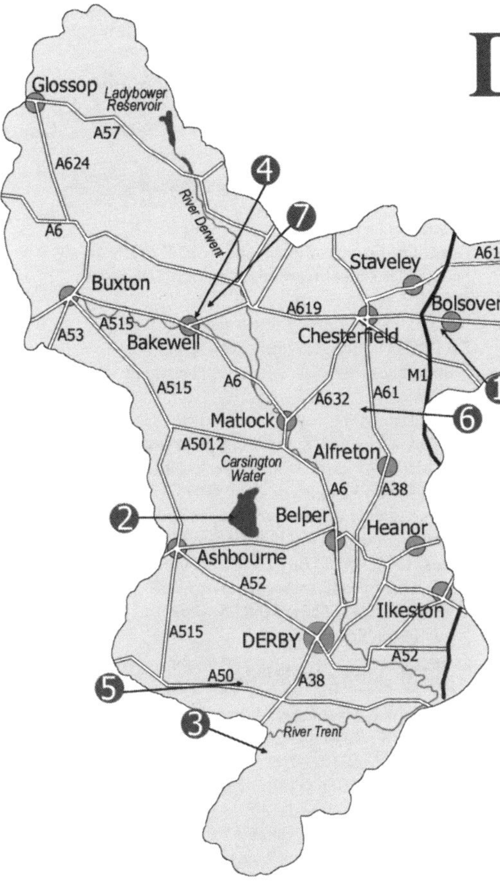

1. CARR VALE NATURE RESERVE

Derbyshire Wildlife Trust.
Location: SK 45 70. Approach Bolsover on the A632 from Chesterfield. Continue over roundabout. Take first R onto Villas Road at crossroads. At a very sharp L bend, carry straight on to a rough track. Follow this to R. Small parking area next to old railway embankment. Alternatively, turn R at roundabout to car park at end of road. Reserve is reached via a footpath over the reclaimed colliery tip.
Access: Open all year.
Facilities: Car park, good disabled access, paths, viewing platform.
Public transport: Various Stagecoach services from Chesterfield (Stephenson Place) all pass close to the reserve: Mon to Sat - 83 serves Villas Road, 81, 82, 82A and 83 serve the roundabout on the A632. Sun - 81A, 82A serve the roundabout on the A632.
Habitat: Lakes, wader flashes, sewage farm, scrub, arable fields.
Key birds: *Spring/summer*: Warblers, waders.
Contact: Derbyshire Wildlife Trust, East Mill, Bridgefoot, Belper, Derbyshire DE56 1XH. 01773 881188. e-mail: derbywt@cix.co.uk www.derbyshirewildlifetrust.org.uk

2. CARSINGTON RESERVOIR

Severn Trent Water.
Location: SK 24 51. Follow B5035 from either Ashbourne or B5036, then B5035 from Cromford. There are various access points.
Access: Open all year except 25 Dec, 7am to sunset. Track is very steep in places and can be slippery in winter.
Facilities: Car parks (charge made) visitor centre, toilets, restaurant, hides.
Public transport: D&G Coach & Bus 111 (Sun and BH Mon) from Derby. D&G Coach & Bus (daily) Matlock-Ashbourne via Wirksworth. D&G Coach & Bus (Wed only) from Derby. Some D&G Coach & Bus 109 journeys from Derby are extended to Carsington Water Sun & BH Mon.
Habitat: Reservoir, woodland.
Key birds: *Spring/summer*: Gulls. *Winter*: Usual woodland species, gulls.
Contact: Severn Trent Water, Sherbourne House, 87 St Martin's Road, Finham, Coventry CV3 6SD. e-mail: customer.relations@severntrent.co.uk

3. DRAKELOW WILDFOWL RESERVE

Powergen PLC.
Location: SK 22 72 07. Drakelow Power Station, one mile NE of Walton-on-Trent.
Access: Permit by post from Drakelow Power Station, Burton-on-Trent. Open daily 9:30am-dusk (closed to 11am for wildfowl count on Sun once a month. Date in hide). Closed June. No dogs. Unsuitable in parts for disabled. Parties by special arrangement, limit ten.

Facilities: Seven hides, no other facilities.
Public transport: None.
Habitat: Disused flooded gravel pits with wooded islands and reedbeds.
Key birds: *Summer*: Breeding Reed and Sedge Warblers. Water Rail, Hobby. *Winter*: Wildfowl (Goldeneye, Gadwall, Smew), Merlin. Regular sightings of Peregrine in Station area. Recent rarities include Little Egret, Cetti's Warbler and Golden Oriole, Bittern and Spotted Crake. Excellent for dragonflies and butterflies.
Contact: Tom Cockburn, Hon, Warden 1 Dickens Drive, Swadlincote, Derbys DE11 0DX. 01283 217146.

4. GREAT LONGSTONE

Location: SK 205 731. N of Bakewell. From A623 go S near Houseley/Foolow, signposted to Cavendish Mill and follow signs for Longstone Edge.
Access: Open all year. Public footpaths. No dogs allowed across farmland. Not suitable for disabled.
Facilities: None. Watch out for vehicles on tracks.
Public transport: Bus: From Bakewell catch the No 4 or 173 to Great Longstone or No 175 to Stoney Middleton. Tel: 01246 582 246.
Habitat: Moorland, farmland, mud lagoons, copse, scrub, patchy gorse.
Key birds: *Spring/summer*: Redstart, migrants, passage waders, Wheatear.

5. HILTON GRAVEL PITS

Derbyshire Wildlife Trust.
Location: SK 24 31. From Derby, take A516 from Mickleover W past Etwall. Follow this to A50 junction at Hilton. Turn R at first island onto Willow Pit Lane. Turn L onto old road next to a large white house. Park next to gate. Follow track along the S side of pools. Alternatively, take A516 into Hilton. Take first R at crossroads opposite pub. Follow road to Sutton-on-the-Hill over A50. Take first R onto old road and park at end of road.
Access: Open all year.
Facilities: Tracks. Please observe the footpath restrictions along the side of the lakes.
Public transport: None.
Habitat: Ponds, scrub, wood.
Key birds: *Spring/summer*: Canada Geese, possible Common Tern, warblers. *Winter*: Siskin, Goldcrest. *All year*: all three Woodpeckers, Kingfisher, tits inc possible Willow Tit, Tawny Owl, Bullfinch.
Contact: Derbyshire Wildlife Trust, East Mill, Bridgefoot, Belper, Derbyshire DE56 1XH. 01773 881188. e-mail: derbywt@cix.co.uk www.derbyshirewildlifetrust.org.uk

6. OGSTON RESERVOIR

Severn Trent Water Plc.
Location: From Matlock, take A615 E to B6014. From Chesterfield take A61 S of Clay Cross onto B6014.
Access: View from roads, car parks or hides
Facilities: Four hides (three for Ogston BC members, one public), toilets. Information pack on request.
Public transport: None.
Habitat: Open water, pasture, mixed woodland.
Key birds: All three woodpeckers, Little and Tawny Owls, Kingfisher, Grey Wagtail, warblers. Passage raptors (inc. Osprey), terns and waders. *Winter*: Gull roost, wildfowl, tit and finch flocks.
Contact: Malcolm Hill, Treasurer, Ogston Bird Club, c/o 2 Sycamore Avenue, Glapwell, Chesterfield, S44 5LH. 01623 812159. www.ogstonbirdclub.co.uk

7. PADLEY GORGE SSSI

The National Trust (East Midlands).
Location: From Sheffield, take A625. After eight miles, turn L on B6521 to Nether Padley. Grindleford Station is just off B6521 (NW of Nether Padley), one mile NE of Grindleford.
Access: All year. Not suitable for disabled or those unused to steep climbs. Some of the paths are rocky. No dogs allowed.
Facilities: Café and toilets at Grindleford Station.
Public transport: Bus: from Sheffield to Bakewell stops at Grindleford/Nether Padley. Tel: 01709 566 000. Train: from Sheffield to Manchester Piccadilly stops at Grindleford Station. Tel: 0161 228 2141.
Habitat: A steep-sided valley containing the largest area of sessile oak woodland in the south Pennines.
Key birds: *Summer*: Pied Flycatcher, Spotted Flycatcher, Redstart, Wheatear, Whinchat, Wood Warbler, Tree Pipit.
Contact: The National Trust. 01433 670368. www.nationaltrust.org.uk

Devon

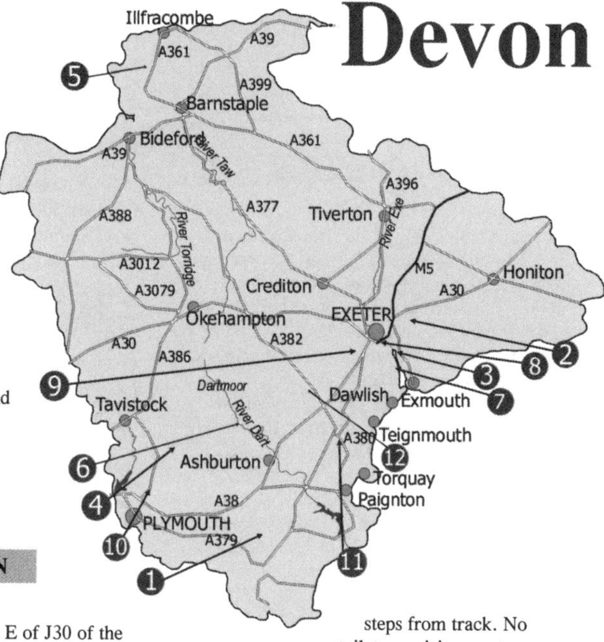

1. ANDREW'S WOOD

Devon Wildlife Trust.
Location: SX 707 515. SW of Ivybridge near Loddiswell, off B3196.
Access: All year.
Facilities: Car park, two circular way-marked trails, boardwalks. Path is extremely muddy.
Public transport: None.
Habitat: Woodland, grassland, scrub.
Key birds: *Spring/summer*: Warblers. *All year*: Usual woodland species.
Contact: Devon Wildlife Trust, Shirehampton House, 35-37 St David's Hill, Exeter, Devon EX4 4DA. 01392 279 244.

2. AYLESBEARE COMMON

RSPB (South West Office).
Location: SY 058 897. Five miles E of J30 of the M5 at Exeter, 0.5 miles past the Halfway Inn on the B3052. Turn R to Hawkerland, car park is on L. The reserve is on opposite side of main road.
Access: Open all year. One track suitable for wheelchairs and pushchairs.
Facilities: Car park, picnic area, group bookings, guided walks and special events. Disabled access via metalled track to private farm
Public transport: Bus, Exeter to Sidmouth, 53, 52a, 52b. Request stop at Joynes Grass (reserve entrance).
Habitat: Heathland, wood fringes, streams and ponds.
Key birds: *Spring/summer*: Nightjar, Stonechat. *All year*: Dartford Warbler, Buzzard. *Winter*: Possible Hen Harrier.
Contact: Toby Taylor, Hawkerland Brake Barn, Exmouth Road, Aylesbeare, Nr Exeter, Devon, Nr Exeter, Devon EX5 2JS. 01395 233655.

3. BOWLING GREEN MARSH

RSPB (South West England Office).
Location: SX 972 876. On E side of River Exe, four miles SE of Exeter, 0.5 miles SE of Topsham.
Access: Open at all times. Please park at public car parks in Topsham, not in the lane by reserve.
Facilities: One hide suitable for wheelchair access. Viewing platform overlooking estuary reached by steps from track. No toilets or visitor centre.
Public transport: Exeter to Exmouth railway service every 30 mins to Topsham station (half a mile from reserve). Stagecoach Devon – T bus has frequent service (every 10-20 mins) from Exeter to Topsham.
Habitat: Coastal grassland, open water/marsh, hedgerows.
Key birds: *Winter*: Wigeon, Shoveler, Teal, Black-tailed Godwit, Curlew, Golden Plover. *Spring*: Shelduck, passage waders – Whimbrel, passage Garganey and Yellow Wagtail. *Summer*: Gull/tern roosts, high tide wader roosts contain many passage birds. *Autumn*: Wildfowl, Peregrine, wader roosts.
Contact: RSPB, Unit 3, Lions Rest Estate, Station Road, Exminster, Exeter EX6 8DZ. 01392 824614. www.rspb.org.uk

4. BURRATOR RESERVOIR

South West Lakes Trust.
Contact: South West Lakes Trust, Higher Coombe Park, Lewdown, Okehampton, Devon, EX20 4QT. 01837 871565. www.swlakestrust.org.uk

5. CHAPEL WOOD

RSPB (South West England Office).
01392 432691.

6. DART VALLEY

Devon Wildlife Trust. 01392 279244.
e-mail: devonwt@cix.co.uk
www.devonwildlifetrust.org

7. DAWLISH WARREN NNR

Teignbridge District Council.
Location: SX 983 788. At Dawlish Warren on S side of Exe estuary mouth. Turn off A379 at sign to Warren Golf Club, between Cockwood and Dawlish. Turn into car park adjacent to Lea Cliff Holiday Park. Pass under tunnel and turn left away from amusements. Park at far end of car park and pass through two pedestrian gates.
Access: Open public access but avoid mudflats. Also avoid beach beyond groyne nine around high tide due to roosting birds. Parking charges apply. Restricted access for dogs so please contact the wardens for more information.
Facilities: Visitor centre (tel 01626 863980) open most weekends all year (10.30am-1pm and 2pm-5pm). Summer also open most weekdays as before, can be closed if warden on site. Toilets at entrance tunnel and in resort area only. Hide open at all times – best around high tide.
Public transport: Train station at site, also regular bus service operated by Stagecoach.
Habitat: High tide roost site for wildfowl and waders of Exe estuary on mudflats and shore. Dunes, dune grassland, woodland, scrub, ponds.
Key birds: *Winter*: Waders and wildfowl – large numbers. Also good for divers and Slavonian Grebe off shore. *Summer*: Particularly good for terns. Excellent variety of birds all year, especially on migration.
Contact: Andrea Buckley/Philip Chambers, Countryside Management Section, Teignbridge District Council, Forde House, Brunel Road, Newton Abbot, Devon TQ12 4XX. Visitor centre: 01626 863980. Teignbridge District Council: 01626 361101 (Ext 5754).

8. EXMINSTER MARSHES

RSPB (South West England Office).
Location: SX 954 872. Five miles S of Exeter on W bank of River Exe. Marshes lie between Exminster and the estuary.
Access: Open at all times. **Facilities:** No toilets or visitor centre. Information in RSPB car park and marked footpaths across reserve.
Public transport: Stagecoach Devon (01392 427711). Exeter to Newton Abbot/Torquay buses – stops are 400 yds from car park.
Habitat: Coastal grazing marsh with freshwater ditches, pools, reed and scrub-covered canal banks.
Key birds: *Winter*: Brent Goose, Wigeon, Water Rail, Short-eared Owl. *Spring*: Lapwing, Redshank and wildfowl breed, Cetti's Warbler on canal banks. *Summer*: Gull roosts, passage waders. *Autumn*: Peregrine, winter wildfowl increase.
Contact: RSPB, Unit 3, Lions Rest Estate, Station Road, Exminster, Exeter, Devon EX6 8DZ. 01392 824614. www.rspb.org.uk

9. HALDON WOODS/DARTMOOR VIEW BIRD OF PREY VIEWPOINT

Forest Enterprise.
Location: Five miles W of Exeter. Follow signs for the racecourse. At A38 junction take the underpass road N towards Dunchideock. Continue N until you reach an open hillside on the L with extensive views. There is a car park L signed 'Bird of Prey Viewpoint'. Park at the bottom. Follow signs to the viewing point on the adjoining hillside.
Access: Open Easter to end October.
Facilities: Viewing point with benches. Path suitable for wheelchair access.
Public transport: None.
Habitat: Plantations, clearings.
Key birds: *Spring/summer*: Wood, Grasshopper and other warblers, Redstart, Whinchat, possible Honey Buzzard, Cuckoo, Hobby, Nightjar, Turtle Dove, Tree Pipit, Woodcock. *All year*: Goshawk, Sparrowhawk, Great and Lesser Spotted Woodpecker, Stonechat, Willow Tit, Crossbill, Siskin, Redpoll.
Contact: Forest Enterprise, Bullers Hill, Kennford, Exeter, Devon, EX6 7XR. 01392 832262.

10. PLYMBRIDGE WOOD

National Trust/Forest Enterprise.
Location: At the Estover roundabout, Plymouth (near the Wrigley company factory), take the narrow, steep Plymbridge Road. Park at the bridge area at the bottom of the hill. Coming from Plympton, pick up Plymbridge Road from either Plymouth Road or Glen Road.
Access: Open all year. **Facilities:** Car park, woodland paths, picnic area.
Habitat: Mixed woodland, river, conifers.
Key birds: *Spring/summer*: Cuckoo, Wood Warbler, Redstart, Blackcap, possible Nightjar, Crossbill. *Winter*: Woodcock, Snipe, Fieldfare, Redwing, Brambling, Siskin, Redpoll, possible Crossbill. *All year*: Mandarin Duck, Sparrowhawk,

Buzzard, Kestrel, Tawny Owl, all three woodpeckers, Kingfisher, Grey Wagtail, Dipper, Goldcrest, common woodland passerines, Marsh Tit, Raven.
Contact: National Trust, Lanhydrock House, Lanhydrock, Cornwall, PL30 4DE. 01208 432691.

11. STOVER LAKE AND WOODS

Devon County Council. Rangers Office, Devon County Council, Stover Country Park, Stover, Newton Abbot, Devon, TQ12 6QG. 01626 835236.

12. YARNER WOOD

English Nature.
Location: SX 778 787. Part of East Dartmoor Woods and Heaths NNR. Two miles out of Bovey Tracey on the road to Becky Falls and Manaton.
Access: Open from 8.30am-7pm or dusk if earlier. Dogs must be on leads.
Facilities: Information/interpretation display and self-guided trails available. Hide.
Public transport: Nearest bus stops are in Bovey Tracey. Buses from here to Exeter/ Plymouth (every two hours off-peak, one hour peak) and Newton Abbot (hourly).
Habitat: Upland Western oakwood and lowland heathland.
Key birds: *All year*: Raven, Buzzard, Sparrowhawk, Lesser Spotted, Great Spotted and Green Woodpeckers. *Spring/summer*: Pied Flycatcher, Wood Warbler, Redstart, Tree Pipit, Linnet, Stonechat. *Autumn/winter*: Good range of birds with feeding at hide - Siskin, Redpoll.
Contact: Phil Page, English Nature, Yarner Wood, Bovey Tracey, Devon TW13 9LJ. 01626 832330. www.english-nature.org.uk

---

Dorset

1. ARNE

RSPB (South West England Office).
Location: SY 973 882. Four miles SE of Wareham, turn off A351 at Stoborough.
Access: Shipstal Point and hide open all year, with access from car park. Coaches and escorted parties by prior arrangement.
Facilities: Toilets in car park. Bird hide at Shipstal. Various footpaths. Reception hut (open end-May-early Sept).
Public transport: None.
Habitat: Lowland heath, woodland reedbed and saltmarsh, extensive mudflats of Poole Harbour.
Key birds: *All year*: Dartford Warbler, Little Egret, Stonechat. *Winter*: Hen Harrier, Red-breasted Merganser, Black-tailed Godwit. *Summer*: Nightjar, warblers. *Passage*: Spotted Redshank, Whimbrel, Greenshank, Osprey.
Contact: Neil Gartshore, (Senior Warden), Syldata, Arne, Wareham, Dorset BH20 5BJ. 01929 553360. www.rspb.org.uk
e-mail: neil.gartshore@rspb.org.uk

2. BROWNSEA ISLAND

Dorset Wildlife Trust.
Location: SZ 026 883. Half hour boat ride from Poole Quay. Ten minutes from Sandbanks Quay (next to Studland chain-ferry).
Access: Apr, May, Jun, Sept and Oct. Access by self-guided nature trail. Costs £2 adults, £1 children. Jul, Aug access by afternoon guided tour (2pm daily, duration 105 minutes). Costs £2 adults, £1 children.
Facilities: Toilets, information centre, five hides, nature trail.
Public transport: Poole Rail/bus station for access to Poole Quay and boats.
Habitat: Saline lagoon, reedbed, lakes, coniferous and mixed woodland.
Key birds: *Spring*: Avocet, Black-tailed Godwit, waders, gulls and wildfowl. *Summer*: Common and Sandwich Terns, Yellow-legged Gull, Little Egret, Little Grebe, Golden Pheasant. *Autumn*: Curlew Sandpiper, Little Stint.
Contact: Chris Thain, The Villa, Brownsea Island, Poole, Dorset BH13 7EE. 01202 709445.
e-mail: dorsetwtisland@cix.co.uk
www.wildlifetrust.org.uk/dorset

3. DURLSTON COUNTRY PARK

Dorset County Council.
Location: SZ 032 774. One mile S of Swanage (signposted).
Access: Visitor centre in car park open weekends and holidays during winter and daily in other seasons (phone for times).
Facilities: Guided walks, toilets, bookshop.
Public transport: 2 buses per day except Sundays and Bank Holidays.

Dorset

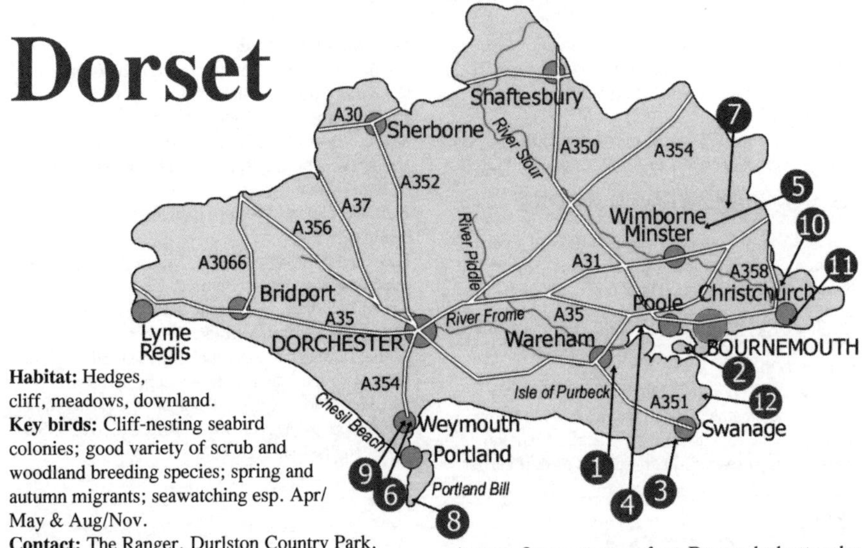

Habitat: Hedges, cliff, meadows, downland.
Key birds: Cliff-nesting seabird colonies; good variety of scrub and woodland breeding species; spring and autumn migrants; seawatching esp. Apr/May & Aug/Nov.
Contact: The Ranger, Durlston Country Park, Swanage, Dorset BH19 2JL. 01929 424443. www.durlston.co.uk

4. HAM COMMON LNR

Poole Borough Council.
Location: SY 99. W of Poole. In Hamworthy, take Blandford Road S along Lake Road, W along Lake Drive and Napier Road, leading to Rockley Park. Park in beach car park by Hamworthy Pier or Rockley Viewpoint car park, off Napier Road, opposite the entrance to Gorse Hill Central Park.
Access: Open all year. **Public transport:** None.
Habitat: Heathland, scrub, reedbeds, lake. Views over Wareham Channel and shorelines of Poole Harbour.
Key birds: *Spring/summer:* Stonechat, Dartford Warbler. *Winter*: Brent Goose, Red-breasted Merganser, occasional diver, rarer grebe, Scaup. Waders inc Whimbrel, Greenshank and Common Sandpiper. *All year*: Little Egret.
Contact: Poole Borough Council, Civic Centre, Poole BH15 2RU. 01202 633633.
e-mail: information@poole.gov.uk

5. HOLT HEATH

English Nature (Dorset Team).
Location: SU 047 036 (Whitesheet car park). Located W of Ringwood, four miles NE of Wimborne Minster. From A31, two miles E of Wimborne, take minor road N to Broomhill and Holt. After two miles, turn right at Broomhill crossroads. From there, 1.5 miles to car park.
Access: Open access on foot. Dogs to be kept under close control.
Facilities: None.
Public transport: Buses to Colehill about three miles away – Wilts & Dorset.
Habitat: Heathland, woodland.
Key birds: *Spring/summer*: Dartford Warbler, Stonechat, Nightjar, Tree Pipit. *Winter*: Hen Harrier, Merlin.
Contact: Ian Nicol, (Site Manager), English Nature, Slepe Farm, Arne, Wareham, Dorset BH20 5BN. 01202 841026.
e-mail: ian.nicol@english-nature.org.uk

6. LODMOOR

RSPB (South West England Office).
Location: SY 686 807. Adjacent Lodmoor Country Park, in Weymouth, off A353 to Wareham.
Access: Open all times.
Facilities: One viewing shelter, network of paths.
Public transport: Local bus service.
Habitat: Marsh, shallow pools, reeds and scrub, remnant saltmarsh.
Key birds: *Spring/summer*: Breeding Common Tern, warblers (including Reed, Sedge, Grasshopper and Cetti's), Bearded Tit. *Winter*: Wildfowl and waders. Passage waders and other migrants.
Contact: Keith Ballard, RSPB Visitor Centre, Swannery Car Park, Weymouth DT4 7TZ. 01305 778313. www.rspb.org.uk

7. MOORS VALLEY COUNTRY PARK AND RINGWOOD FOREST

East Dorset District Council/Forest Enterprise.
Contact: Moors Valley Country Park, Horton Road, Ashley Heath, Nr Ringwood, Dorset, BH24 2ET, 01425 470721. www.moors-valley.co.uk
e-mail: moorsvalley@eastdorset.gov.uk

8. PORTLAND BIRD OBSERVATORY

Portland Bird Observatory (registered charity).
Location: SY 681 690. Six miles S of Weymouth beside the road to Portland Bill.
Access: Open at all times. Parking only for members of Portland Bird Observatory. Self-catering accommodation for up to 20. Take own towels, sheets, sleeping bags.
Facilities: Displays and information, toilets, bookshop, equipped kitchen, laboratory.
Public transport: Bus service from Weymouth (First Dorset Transit Route 1).
Habitat: Scrub and ponds.
Key birds: *Spring/autumn*: Migrants including many rarities. *Summer*: Breeding auks, Fulmar, Kittiwake.
Contact: Martin Cade, Old Lower Light, Portland Bill, Dorset DT5 2JT. e-mail: obs@btinternet.com www.portlandbirdobs.btinternet.co.uk

9. RADIPOLE LAKE

RSPB (South West England Office).
Location: SY 677 796. In Weymouth. Enter from Swannery car park on footpaths.
Access: Visitor centre and nature trail open every day, summer (9am-5pm), winter (9am-4pm). Hide open (8.30am-4.30pm). Permit available from visitor centre required by non-RSPB members.
Facilities: Network of paths, one hide, one viewing shelter.
Public transport: Close to train station.
Habitat: Lake, reedbeds.
Key birds: *Winter*: Wildfowl. *Summer*: Breeding reedbed warblers (including Cetti's), Bearded Tit, passage waders and other migrants. Garganey regular in Spring. Good for rarer gulls.
Contact: Keith Ballard, RSPB Visitor Centre, Swannery Car Park, Weymouth DT4 7TZ. 01305 778313. www.rspb.org.uk

10. SOPLEY COMMON

Dorset Wildlife Trust.
Location: SZ 132 975. Four miles NW of Christchurch near Hurn village.
Access: Open at all times. Permits required for surveying and group visits. Dogs allowed under close control and on leads Apr to Aug. Limited disabled access. **Public transport:** None.
Habitat: Lowland heath (dry and wet) and deciduous woodland.
Key birds: *Summer*: Breeding Dartford Warbler, Nightjar, Woodlark, Stonechat. Also Hobby. *Winter*: Snipe.
Contact: Rob Brunt, Dorset Wildlife Trust, Brooklands Farm, Forston, Dorchester, Dorset DT2 7AA. 01305 264620.
e-mail: rbrunt@dorsetwt.cix.co.uk
www.wildlifetrust.org.uk/dorset

11. STANPIT MARSH SSSI, LNR

Stanpit Marsh Advisory Panel, Community Services, Christchurch Borough Council.
Location: SZ 167 924. In Christchurch.
Access: Public open space.
Facilities: Information centre.
Public transport: Wilts & Dorset bus no 123 (tel 01202 673555) Stanpit recreation ground stop. Bournemouth Yellow Buses no 20 (tel 01202 636000) Purewell Cross roundabout stop.
Habitat: Salt, fresh, brackish marsh, sand dune and scrub.
Key birds: Estuarine: Waders, winter wildfowl, migrants. Reedbed: Bearded Tit, Cetti's Warbler. Scrub: Sedge Warbler, Reed Warbler. River/streams/bankside: Kingfisher. Feeding and roosting site.
Contact: Peter Holloway, Christchurch Countryside Service, Steamer Point Nature Reserve, Highcliffe, Christchurch, Dorset BH23 4XX. 01425 272479. e-mail: countrysideservice@christchurch.gov.uk

12. STUDLAND & GODLINGSTON HEATHS

National Trust.
Location: SZ 030 846. N of Swanage. From Ferry Road N of Studland village.
Access: Open all year.
Facilities: Hides, nature trails.
Habitat: Woodland, heath, dunes, inter-tidal mudflats, saltings, freshwater lake, reedbeds, carr.
Key birds: Water Rail, Reed and Dartford Warblers, Nightjar, Stonechat. *Winter*: Wildfowl. Studland Bay, outside the reserve, has winter Black-necked and Slavonian Grebes, Scoter, Eider.
Contact: The National Trust, Countryside Office, Middle Beach Car Park, Studland, Swanage BH19 3AX.

Durham

1. CASTLE EDEN DENE

English Nature (Northumbria Team).
Location: NZ 435 397. Adjacent to Peterlee, signposted from A19 and Peterlee town centre.
Access: Open from 8am-8pm or sunset if earlier. Car park. Dogs under tight control please.
Facilities: Car parking at Oakerside Dene Lodge. 12 miles of footpath, two waymarked trails.
Public transport: Bus service to Peterlee centre.
Habitat: Yew/oak/sycamore woodland, paramaritime, limestone grassland.
Key birds: More than 170 recorded, 50 regular breeding species, typical woodland species.
Contact: Rob Lamboll, Oakerside Dene Lodge, Stanhope Chase, Peterlee, Co Durham SR8 1NJ. 0191 586 0004.

2. HAMSTERLEY FOREST

Forest Enterprise.
Location: NZ 093 315. Eight miles NW of Bishop Auckland. Main entrance is five miles from A68, S of Witton-le-Wear and signposted through Hamsterley village and Bedburn.
Access: Open all year. Toll charge. Vehicles should not be left unattended after dark.
Facilities: Visitor Centre, toilets, shop, access for disabled. Visitors should not enter fenced farmland. **Public transport:** None.
Habitat: Commercial woodland, mixed and broadleaved trees.
Key birds: *Spring/summer*: Willow Warbler, Chiffchaff, Wood Warbler, Redstart, Pied Flycatcher. *Winter*: Crossbill, Redwing, Fieldfare. *All year*: Jay, Dipper, Green Woodpecker.
Contact: Forest Enterprise, Eels Burn, Bellingham, Hexham, Northumberland, NE48 2AJ, 01434 220242.
e-mail: pippa.kirkham@forestry.gsi.gov.uk

3. JOE'S POND NATURE RESERVE

Durham Wildlife Trust.
Location: NZ 32 48. Between Durham and Sunderland on the A690. N from Durham, leave A690 S of Houghton-le-Spring on the B21284 to Fence Houses and Hetton-le-Hole. Head W towards Fence Houses and turn L at the 1st roundabout, after 800 metres, into an opencast colliery site, signed Rye Hill Site.
Access: Open all year.
Facilities: Car park.
Public transport: None.
Habitat: Scrub, pond, farmland.
Key birds: *Spring/summer*: Ruddy Duck, hirundines, Whinchat, Lesser Whitethroat, Whitethroat, Blackcap. Possible Yellow Wagtail, Redstart, Grasshopper Warbler. *Passage*: Waders, Wheatear. *Winter*: Teal, Pochard, Water Rail, Woodcock, Short-eared Owl, Kingfisher, thrushes. Chance of Merlin, Jack Snipe.
Contact: Durham Wildlife Trust, , Low Barns Nature Reserve, Witton-le-Wear, Bishop Auckland, Co Durham DL14 0AG. 01388 488 728.
e-mail: durhamwt@cix.co.uk
www.wildlifetrust.org.uk/durham/

4. MAZE PARK AND PORTRACK MARSH

Tees Valley Wildlife Trust.
Location: NZ 463 190. Located midway between Middlesbrough and Stockton. Access from A66 at Tees Barrage. Sites are located on opposite banks to the River Tees, E of the barrage.
Access: No permits required. National cycle route passes through Maze Park. Surfaced paths at both sites. Hide suitable for disabled users at Portrack Marsh. Please keep to the permissive paths and public rights of way.
Facilities: Hide at Portrack Marsh. No toilets or visitor centre.
Public transport: Regular buses between Middlesbrough and Stockton stop at the Tees Barrage (Arriva, tel 0870 6082608). Thornaby Station one mile. Frequent trains from Darlington and Middlesbrough.
Habitat: Freshwater marsh, scrub, post-industrial grassland, riverside.
Key birds: *Winter*: Ducks, passage waders, Redshank, Snipe, Lapwing, Grey Heron, Sky lark, Grey Partridge, Sand Martin, occasional Kingfisher and Grasshopper Warbler.
Contact: Bill Ashton-Wickett, Bellamy Pavilion, Kirkleatham Old Hall, Kirkleatham, Redcar TS10 5NW. 01642 759900.
e-mail: teesvalleywt@cix.co.uk
www.wildlifetrust.org.uk/teesvalley

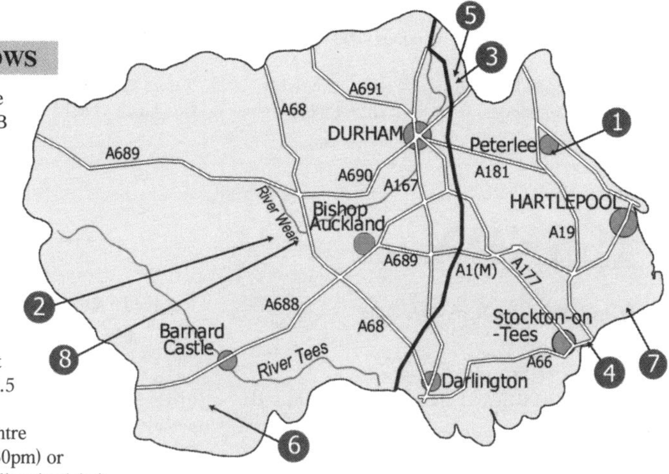

5. RAINTON MEADOWS

Durham Wildlife Trust, the City of Sunderland and RJB Mining (UK) Ltd.
Location: NZ 326 486. Located W of A690 between Durham and Sunderland. Just S of Houghton-le-Spring turn onto B1284, signposted to Fence Houses and Hetton-le-Hole. Head W towards Fence Houses and turn L at the first roundabout after 0.5 miles into Rye Hill Site.
Access: Park at Visitor Centre (entrance gate locked at 4.30pm) or Mallard Way. Paths generally wheelchair-accessible but there are some muddy areas. Main circular walk.
Facilities: Visitor Centre, toilets, café, log book, shop, wildlife display. Dogs on lead.
Public transport: Buses from Sunderland and Durham (222 and 220) stop at Mill Inn. Reserve is reached via B1284 passing under A690. Bus from Chester-le-Street (231) stops at Fencehouses Station. Walk E along B1284. Tel: Traveline 0870 608 2608.
Habitat: Reedbed, ponds, young tree plantation.
Key birds: *Spring/summer*: Great Crested Grebe, Ruddy Duck, Cuckoo, Whinchat, Reed Warbler. *Winter*: Water Rail, Kingfisher, Peregrine, Merlin, Long and Short-eared Owls. *Passage*: waders.
Contact: Trust HQ, Rainton Meadows, Chilton Moor, Houghton-le-Spring, Tyne & Wear, DH4 6PU, 0191 5843112.
e-mail: durhamwt@cix.co.uk

6. STANG FOREST AND HOPE MOOR

Forest Enterprise.01434 220242.

7. TEESMOUTH

English Nature (Northumbria).
Location: Two components, centred on NZ 535 276 and NZ 530 260, three and five miles S of Hartlepool, E of A178. Access to northern component from car park at NZ 534 282, 0.5 miles E of A178. Access to southern compartment from A178 bridge over Greatham Creek at NZ 510 254. Park in car park adjacent to A178 at NZ 508 251.
Access: Open at all times. In northern component, no restrictions over most of dunes and North Gare Sands (avoid golf course, dogs must be kept under close control). In southern component, disabled access path to public hides at NZ 516 255 and NZ 516 252 (no other access).
Facilities: Nearest toilets at Seaton Carew, one mile to the N. Disabled access path and hides (see above), interpretive panels and leaflet. Teesmouth Field Centre (Tel: 01429 264912).
Public transport: Hourly bus service operates Mon-Sat between Middlesbrough and Hartlepool, along A178 (service X9, Stagecoach Hartlepool, Tel: 01429 267082).
Habitat: Grazing marsh, dunes, intertidal flats.
Key birds: Passage and winter wildfowl and waders. Passage terns and skuas in late summer. Scarce passerine migrants and rarities. *Winter*: Merlin, Peregrine, Snow Bunting, Twite, divers, grebes.
Contact: Mike Leakey, English Nature, c/o British Energy, Tees Road, Hartlepool TS25 2BZ. 01429 853325.
e-mail: northumbria@english-nature.org.uk
www.english-nature.org.uk

8. WITTON-LE-WEAR (Low Barns)

Durham Wildlife Trust.
Location: NZ 160 315. SW of Bishop Auckland, off unclassified road between Witton-le-Wear (signposted on A68) and High Grange.
Access: Open all year.
Facilities: Three hides two with disabled access), observation tower above visitor centre (manned), nature trail.
Public transport: None.

Habitat: Former gravel workings, lake, ponds, riverbank.
Key birds: *All Year*: Greylag Geese, Kingfisher. *Summer*: Goosander, Grey Wagtail, Redpoll have bred. *Winter*: Wildfowl (inc. Goldeneye, Shoveler).
Contact: Visitor Centre Manager, Low Barns Nature Reserve, Witton-le-Wear, Bishop Auckland, Co Durham DL14 0AG. 01388 488728.

Essex

1. ABBERTON RESERVOIR

Essex Wildlife Trust.
Location: TL 963 185. Six miles SW of Colchester on B1026. Follow signs from Layer-de-la-Haye.
Access: Open Tue-Sun (9am-5pm) except Christmas Day and Boxing Day.
Facilities: Visitor centre, toilets, nature trail, five hides (disabled access). Also good viewing where roads cross reservoir.
Public transport: Phone Trust for advice.
Habitat: Nine acres on edge of 1200a reservoir.
Key birds: Nationally important for Mallard, Teal, Wigeon, Shoveler, Gadwall, Pochard, Tufted Duck, Goldeneye (most important inland site in Britain). Smew regular. Passage waders, terns, birds of prey. Tree-nesting Cormorants (largest colony in Britain); raft-nesting Common Tern. *Summer*: Yellow Wagtail, warblers, Nightingale, Corn Bunting; *Autumn*: Red-crested Pochard, Water Rail; *Winter*: Goosander.
Contact: Centre Manager, Essex Wildlife Trust, Abberton Reservoir Visitor Centre, Layer-de-la-Haye, Colchester CO2 0EU. 01206 738172. e-mail: abberton@essexwt.org.uk

2. BLUE HOUSE FARM

Essex Wildlife Trust.
Location: GR 856 976. Take B1012 E from S Woodham Ferrers. After approx three miles turn R to North Fambridge. Access is via track on left off Fambridge Road 200m S of North Fambridge station.
Access: Accessible at all times via public footpath along the seawall. Permissive footpath giving access to bird hides overlooking the fleets is open from Apr 1 - Oct 31. Please close gates as this is a working farm as well as a nature reserve.
Facilities: Car park.
Public transport: An hourly train service runs to North Fambridge via Wickford.
Habitat: Working farm, coastal grazing marsh.
Key birds: *Spring/summer*: waders, wildfowl. *Winter*: geese, wildfowl.
Contact: Essex Wildlife Trust, Abbotts Hall Farm, Great Wigborough, Colchester, Essex CO5 7R2. 01621 862960. www.essexwt.org.uk
e-mail: admin@essexwt.org.uk

3. BRADWELL BIRD OBSERVATORY

Essex Birdwatching Society
Location: 100 yards S of St Peter's Chapel, Bradwell-on-Sea. Mouth of Blackwater estuary, between Maldon and Foulness.
Access: Open all year.
Facilities: Accommodation for eight in hut; two rooms each with four bunks; blankets, cutlery, etc. supplied. **Public transport:** None.
Habitat: Mudflats, saltmarsh.
Key birds: *Winter*: Wildfowl (inc. Brent Geese, Red-throated Diver, Red-breasted Merganser), large numbers of waders; small numbers of Twite, Snow Bunting and occasional Shore Lark on beaches, also Hen Harrier, Merlin and Peregrine. Good passage of migrants usual in spring and autumn. *Summer*: Small breeding population of terns and other estuarine species.
Contact: Graham Smith, 48 The Meads, Ingatestone, Essex CM4 0AE. 01277 354034.

4. CHIGBOROUGH LAKES

Essex Wildlife Trust.
Location: GR 877 086. Lies NE of Maldon, about one mile from Heybridge on the B1026 towards Tolleshunt d'Arcy, turn N into Chigborough Road. Continue past fishery entrance and Chigborough Farm buildings until you see an entrance gate to Chigborough Quarry. The reserve entrance is just beyond this point on the L.
Access: Open all year. Do not obstruct the gravel pit entrance. **Facilities:** Car park.
Public transport: Bus: Colchester to Maldon Leisure Centre along the B1026.
Habitat: Flooded gravel pits, small ponds, willow carr, grassland, scrub.

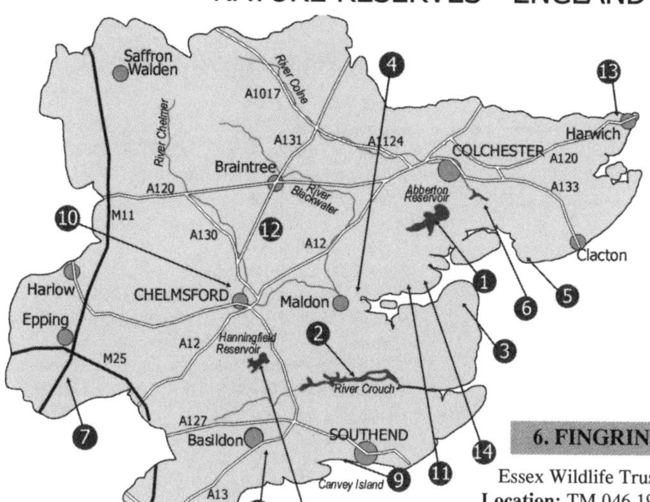

Key birds: *Spring/summer*: Sedge and Reed Warblers, Whitethroat, Reed Bunting, Willow Warbler, Great Crested and Little Grebes, Kingfisher, Water Rail. *Passage*: Waders including Greenshank. Grass snakes and common lizards have been seen, good numbers of common blue, small copper and ringlet butterflies and dragonflies.
Contact: Trust HQ, Abbotts Hall Farm, Great Wigborough, Colchester, Essex, CO5 7RZ, 01621 862960. www.essexwt.org.uk
e-mail: admin@essexwt.org.uk

5. COLNE POINT

Essex Wildlife Trust.
Location: TM 108 125. W of Clacton, via B1027 to St Osyth then Lee Wick Lane. Car park before reserve (liable to flood at very high tides).
Access: Day permit for non-Trust members.
Facilities: None.
Public transport: Phone Trust for advice.
Habitat: Mudflats, shingle pools.
Key birds: On major migration route for finches and chats. *Spring/autumn*: Birds of prey. *Summer*: Breeding Little Tern, Ringed Plover, Oystercatcher, Redshank. *Winter*: Divers, grebes, ducks, and feeding ground for Brent Geese.
Contact: The Warden, Essex Wildlife Trust, Abbotts Hall Farm, Great Wigborough, Colchester, CO5 7RZ.
e-mail: admin@essexwt.org.uk
www.essexwt.org.uk

6. FINGRINGHOE WICK

Essex Wildlife Trust.
Location: TM 046 197. Colchester five miles. The reserve is signposted from B1025 to Mersea Island, S of Colchester.
Access: Open six days per week (not Mon or Christmas or Boxing Day). No permits needed. Donations invited. Centre/reserve open (9am-5pm). Dogs must be on a lead.
Facilities: Visitor centre - toilets, shop, light refreshments, car park, displays. Reserve - seven bird hides, two nature trails, plus one that wheelchair users could use with assistance.
Public transport: None.
Habitat: Old gravel pit, large lake, many ponds, sallow/birch thickets, young scrub, reedbeds, saltmarsh, gorse heathland.
Key birds: *Autumn/winter*: Brent Goose, waders, Hen Harriers, Little Egrets. *Spring*: 40 male Nightingales. Good variety of warblers in scrub, thickets, reedbeds and Turtle Doves, Green/Great Spotted Woodpeckers. *Winter*: Dabchicks, Mute Swans, Teal, Wigeon, Shoveler, Gadwall on lake.
Contact: Laurie Forsyth, Wick Farm, South Green Road, Fingringhoe, Colchester, Essex CO5 7DN. 01206 729678. www.essexwt.org.uk
e-mail: admin@essexwt.org.uk

7. HAINAULT FOREST

Redbridge Council. Hainault Forest Country Park, 0208 500 7353.

8. HANNINGFIELD RESERVOIR

Essex Wildlife Trust. Hanningfield Reservoir Visitor Centre, Hawkswood Road, Downham, Billericay CM11 1WT. 01268 711001.
www.essexwt.org.uk

9. LEIGH

Essex Wildlife Trust.
Location: TQ 824 852. Two Tree Island, approached from Leigh on Sea.
Access: Important to keep to marked footpaths.
Facilities: Screen, nature trail, joint car park with Country Park, adjacent to reserve (height restriction barriers).
Public transport: Phone Trust for advice.
Habitat: Intertidal mudflats, saltmarshes.
Key birds: *Autumn*: Dark-bellied Brent Geese.
Contact: Trust HQ, Abbotts Hall Farm, Great Wigborough, Colchester, Essex, CO5 7RZ
e-mail: admin@essexwt.org.uk
www.essexwt.org.uk

10. LITTLE WALTHAM MEADOWS

Essex Wildlife Trust. 01621 862960.
e-mail: admin@essexwt.org.uk
www.essexwt.org.uk

11. OLD HALL MARSHES

RSPB (East Anglia Office).
Location: TL 97 51 25. Approx eight miles S of Colchester. From A12 take B1023, via Tiptree, to Tolleshunt D'Arcy. Then take Chapel Road (back road to Tollesbury), after one mile turn left into Old Hall Lane. Continue up Old Hall Lane, over speed ramp and through iron gates to cattle grid, then follow signs to car park.
Access: By permit only in advance from Warden, write to address below. Open 9am-9pm or dusk, closed Tue.
Facilities: Two trails - one of three miles and one of 6.5 miles. Two viewing screens overlooking saline lagoon area at E end of reserve. No visitor centre or toilets.
Public transport: None.
Habitat: Coastal grazing marsh, reedbed, saline lagoon, saltmarsh and mudflat
Key birds: *Summer*: Breeding Avocet, Redshank, Lapwing, Pochard, Shoveler, Gadwall, Garganey, Barn Owl. *Winter*: Brent Goose, Wigeon, Teal Shoveler, Goldeneye, Red-breasted Merganser, all the expected waders, Hen Harrier, Merlin, Short-eared Owl and Twite. *Passage*: All expected waders (particularly Spotted Redshank, Green Sandpiper and Whimbrel), Yellow Wagtail, Whinchat and Wheatear.
Contact: Paul Charlton, Site Manager c/o 1 Old Hall Lane, Tolleshunt D'Arcy, Maldon, Essex CM9 8TP. 01621 869015.
e-mail: paul.charlton@rspb.org.uk

12. PHYLLIS CURRIE RESERVE

Essex Wildlife Trust.
Location: GR: 723 182. S of Braintree. Entrance in Dumney Lane, Great Leighs. Take the road to Felsted from A131 at St Anne's Castle pub. Dumney Lane is the 1st R turn.
Access: Open all year. Dogs on lead at all times. Suitable for disabled.
Facilities: Car park, track.
Public transport: Eastern National buses run to St Anne's Castle PH from Braintree and Chelmsford.
Habitat: Pool, scrub, reedbed, wood.
Key birds: *Spring/summer*: warblers, hirundines.
Contact: Essex Wildlife Trust, Abbotts Hall Farm, Great Wigborough, Colchester, Essex CO5 7R2. 01621 862960.
e-mail: admin@essexwt.org.uk
www.essexwt.org.uk

13. STOUR ESTUARY

RSPB (East Anglia Office). 01255 886043.
e-mail: rick.vonk@RSPB.org.uk
www.RSPB.org.uk

14. TOLLESBURY WICK RESERVE

Essex Wildlife Trust.
Location: GR 970 104. On Blackwater Estuary eight miles E of Maldon. Follow B1023 to Tollesbury via Tiptree, leaving A12 at Kelvedon. Then follow Woodrolfe Road S towards the marina. Use car park at Woodrolfe Green.
Access: Open all times along public footpath on top of sea wall.
Facilities: Public toilets at Woodrolfe Green car park. **Public transport:** Bus services run to Tollesbury from Maldon, Colchester and Witham.
Habitat: Estuary with fringing saltmarsh and mudflats with some shingle. Extensive freshwater grazing marsh, brackish borrowdyke and small reedbeds.
Key birds: *Winter*: Wildfowl and waders, Short-eared Owl, Hen Harrier. *Summer*: Breeding Avocet, Redshank, Lapwing, occasional Little Tern, Reed and Sedge Warblers, Barn Owl. *Passage*: Whimbrel, Spotted Redshank.
Contact: Jonathan Smith, Tollesbury, Maldon, Essex CM9 8RJ. 01621 868628.
e-mail: jonathans@essexwt.org.uk

15. WAT TYLER COUNTRY PARK

Basildon Council.
Location: GR 739 867. Overlooks Holehaven

Creek S of Basildon. From roundabout in Pitsea where A132 joins A13 follow Wat Tyler Way S across railway and into country park.
Access: Open all year 9am-dusk.
Facilities: Visitor Centre, museum, shops, six hides, toilets for the disabled, picnic tables, wildlife garden.
Public transport: Train: nearest station Pitsea (Fenchurch St line), then walk S down Wat Tyler Way.
Habitat: Scrub, saltmarsh, mudflats, ponds, grassland, mature woodland of mostly hawthorn.
Key birds: *Spring/autumn/winter*: Wildfowl, waders. *All year*: Woodland birds.
Contact: Wat Tyler Country Park, 01268 550088.

Gloucestershire

1. COKES PIT

Cotswold Water Park Society.
Location: SU 028 953. Lake 34 of Cotswold Water Park, see location details below.
Access: Open at all times. **Facilities:** Paths are flat but there are stiles and footbridges.
Public transport: Buses from Kemble, Cheltenham, Cirencester and Swindon. Tel: 08457 090 899. Train: nearest station is four miles away at Kemble. Tel: 08457 484 950.
Habitat: Gravel extraction which has created 130 lakes, set to become one of the largest man-made wetland sites in Europe.
Key birds: *Winter*: Common wildfowl, Smew, Red-crested Pochard. *Summer*: warblers, Nightingale, Hobby, Common Tern, Reed Bunting, hirundines.
Contact: Cotswold Water Park Society, See details below.

2. COOMBE HILL MEADOWS

Gloucestershire Wildlife Trust. 01452 383333.

3. COTSWOLD WATER PARK

Cotswold Water Park Society.
Location: SU 028 953. From Cirencester, take the A419 SE towards Swindon. At Spine Road roundabouts turn onto B4696 towards Ashton Keynes. Take the fourth turning on the R to Keynes Country Park (Spratsgate Lane). The Nature Reserve car park is first on the R.
Access: Open all year.
Facilities: Paths are flat but there are stiles and footbridges. **Public transport:** Buses from Kemble, Cheltenham, Cirencester and Swindon. Tel: 08457 090 899. Train: nearest station is four miles away at Kemble. Tel: 08457 484 950.
Habitat: Gravel extraction which has created 130 lakes.
Key birds: *Winter*: Common wildfowl, Smew, Red-crested Pochard. *Summer*: Warblers, Nightingale, Hobby, Common Tern, Reed Bunting, hirundines.
Contact: Cotswold Water Park Society, Keynes Country Park, Spratsgate Lane, Shorncote, Cirencester, Glos GL7 6DF. 01285 861459;(Fax).01285 860186.
e-mail: info@waterpark.org

4. HIGHNAM WOODS

RSPB (Central England Office).
Location: SO 778 190. Signed on A40 three miles W of Gloucester.
Access: Open at all times, no permit required. Disabled access to a hide 120 yards from car park. The nature trails can be very muddy. Dogs allowed on leads.
Facilities: One nature trail (approx 1.5 miles), one birdwatching hide with winter bird-feeding programme. **Public transport:** Contact Glos. County Council public transport information line. Tel: 01452 425543.
Habitat: Ancient woodland in the Severn Vale with areas of coppice and scrub.
Key birds: *Spring/summer*: The reserve has Gloucestershire's main concentration of Nightingales - about 20 pairs. Resident birds include all three woodpeckers, Buzzard and Sparrowhawk. Ravens are frequently seen.
Contact: Ivan Proctor, The Puffins, Parkend, Lydney, Glos GL15 4JA. 01594 562852.
e-mail: ivan.proctor@rspb.org.uk
www.rspb.org.uk

5. LITTLETON BRICK PITS.

Avon Wildlife Trust.
Location: ST 590 912. From J1 on M48, take B4461 and minor road to Littleton-upon-Severn. Turn R to Littleton Warth. Park outside industrial

Gloucestershire

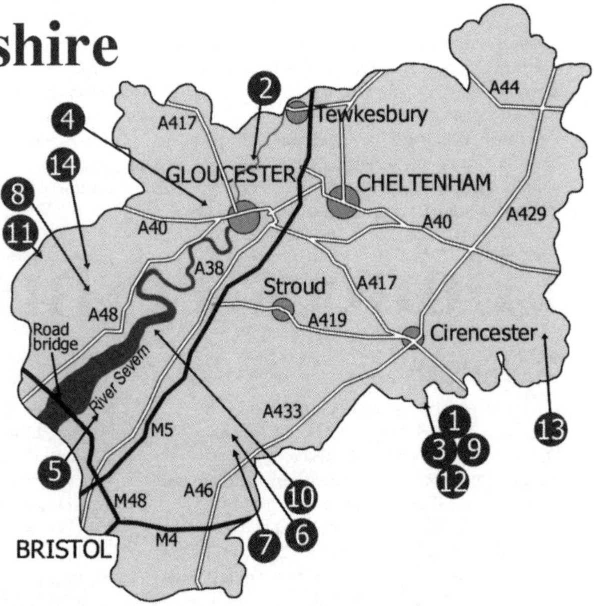

estate and then follow path through estate to the L.
Access: Limited to special events because of disturbance to the birds. **Facilities:** None.
Public transport: None.
Habitat: Reedbed, scrub, willow, near estuary.
Key birds: *Spring/summer*: Reed Bunting, Sedge Warbler, Reed Warbler. *Autumn*: Blackcap, Willow Warbler, Chiffchaff, Whitethroat.
Contact: Avon Wildlife Trust, The Wildlife Centre, 32 Jacob's Wells Road, Bristol BS8 1DR. 0117 917 7270. www.avonwildlifetrust.org.uk/ e-mail: mail@avonwildlifetrust.org.uk

6. LOWER POOLS

Gloucestershire Wildlife Trust
Location: ST743876. About a mile E of Wickwar, N of Yate.
Access: Open access.
Facilities: Car park, public footpaths.
Public transport: None.
Habitat: Mixed woodland, grassland, river.
Key birds: *Summer*: Nightingale. *All year*: Usual woodland species.
Contact: Gloucestershire Wildlife Trust, Dulverton Building, Robinswood Hill Country Park, Reservoir Road, Gloucester GL4 6SX. 01452 383333.
e-mail: info@gloucestershirewildlifetrust.co.uk
www.wildlifetrust.org.uk/gloucswt/

7. LOWER WOODS

Gloucestershire Wildlife Trust.
Location: Reserve is about one mile E of Wickwar. Main parking is at Lower Woods Lodge, via a track off the Wickwar-Hawkesbury road. Public footpaths and bridleways cross the reserve.
Access: Open all year.
Facilities: Footpaths and bridleways.
Public transport: None.
Habitat: Mixed woodland, mildly acidic or slightly calcareous clay, grassland, river, springs.
Key birds: *Spring/summer*: Nightingale. *All year*: usual woodland species.
Contact: Gloucestershire Wildlife Trust, Dulverton Building, Robinswood Hill Country Park, Reservoir Road, Gloucester GL4 6SX. 01452 383333.
e-mail: info@gloucestershirewildlifetrust.co.uk

8. NAGSHEAD

RSPB (Central England Office).
Location: SO 097 085. In Forest of Dean, N of Lydney. Signed immediately W of Parkend village on the road to Coleford.
Access: Open at all times, no permit required. The reserve is hilly and there are some stiles on nature trails. Dogs must be kept under close control.
Facilities: There are two nature trails (one mile and 2.25 miles). Information centre open at weekends mid-Apr to end Aug.
Public transport: Contact Glos. County Council public transport information line, 01452 425543.
Habitat: Much of the reserve is 200-year-old oak plantations, grazed in some areas by sheep. The rest of the reserve is a mixture of open areas and conifer/mixed woodland.
Key birds: *Spring*: Pied Flycatcher, Wood Warbler, Redstart, warblers. *Winter*: Siskin, Crossbill in some years. *All year*: Buzzard, Raven, all three woodpeckers.
Contact: see Highham Woods.

9. SHORNCOTE REEDBED

Cotswold Water Park Society.
Location: SU 034 968. S of Cirencester. Follow instructions for Cotswold Water Park to Keynes CP (third turning on the R in Spratsgate Lane). Park in car park, and follow footpath to Shorncote Reedbed.
Access: Open at all times.
Facilities: Flat paths with footbridges. Toilets, beach, swimming, Café, visitor centre, boat and cycle hire at Keynes CP. Two hides at reedbed.
Public transport: As for Cotswold Water Park.
Habitat: As for Cotswold Water Park.
Key birds: *Winter*: Common wildfowl, (large numbers of Shoveler), Smew, Peregrine, Merlin, Little Egret. *Passage*: Waders, Snipe.
Contact: Cotswold Water Park Society.

10. SLIMBRIDGE

The Wildfowl & Wetlands Trust.
Location: SO 723 048. S of Gloucester. Signposted from M5 (exit 13 or 14).
Access: Open daily except Christmas Day, (9am-5.30pm, 5pm in winter).
Facilities: Hides, observatory, observation tower, Hanson Discovery Centre, wildlife art gallery, tropical house, facilities for disabled, worldwide collection of wildfowl species.
Public transport: None.
Habitat: Reedbed, saltmarsh, freshwater pools, mudflats.
Key birds: Kingfisher, waders, raptors. *Winter*; Wildfowl esp. Bewick's Swans, White-fronted Geese, Wigeon, Teal.
Contact: Jane Allen, Marketing Manager, The Wildfowl & Wetlands Trust, Slimbridge, Gloucester GL2 7BT. 01453 891900;(Fax)01453 890927. e-mail: info.slimbridge@wwt.org.uk

11. SYMOND'S YAT

RSPB/Forest Enterprise.
Location: Hill-top site on the edge of Forest of Dean, three miles N of Coleford on the B4432 signposted from the Forest Enterprise car park. Also signposted from A40 S of Ross-on-Wye.
Access: Daily Apr-Aug only.
Facilities: Car park, toilets with adapted facilities for disabled visitors, picnic area, drinks and light snacks. Environmental education programmes available, enquire at reserve for details.
Public transport: None.
Habitat: Cliff above the River Wye and woodland.
Key birds: *Summer*: Peregrine, Nuthatch and other woodland species. Telescope is set up daily to watch the Peregrines.
Contact: The Puffins, Parkend, Lydney, Gloucestershire, GL15 4JA, 01594 562852.

12. WATERHAY

Cotswold Water Park Society.
Location: SU 060 933. See Cotswold Water Park instructions to B4696. Take third turning on R for Fridays Ham Lane, follow signs for Waterhay car park. Turn L at junction and continue for 0.5 miles. Car park is on L just before Waterhay bridge.
Access: Open at all times.
Facilities: Footpaths and bridleways are flat and generally good in summer. Often flood in winter so check weather conditions.
Public transport: Bus: Check on 08457 090 899.
Habitat: Series of restored, mature gravel pits and silt lagoons. Large reed bed, willow carr, silt lagoon, open water and hedgerows.
Key birds: *Winter*: Common wildfowl, Teal, Goldeneye, Pintail, Hen Harrier, Marsh Harrier, Merlin, Peregrine, Little Egret, Wter Rail, Cetti's Warbler, Reed Bunting, Bittern, gull roost, Lapwing, Curlew, Golden Plover. *Passage*: Waders.
Contact: Cotswold Water Park Society.

13. WHELFORD POOLS

Gloucestershire Wildlife Trust.
Location: SU 174 995. E of Cirencester. SE of Fairford. Leave Fairford E on A417, turn towards Whelford and reserve is on left (just before Whelford sign).
Access: Open at all times.
Facilities: Two hides, one with wheelchair access.
Public transport: None.
Habitat: Flooded gravel pits in eastern section of Cotswold Water Park.
Key birds: On main passage flight route (Yellow Wagtail, Black Tern, Osprey, waders). *Summer:* Breeding Common Tern, Heron, Hobby. W*inter*: Wildfowl.
Contact: Trust HQ, 01452 383333.

14. WOORGREENS LAKE AND MARSH

Gloucestershire Wildlife Trust.
Contact: Trust HQ, 01452 383333.

Hampshire

1. ALICE HOLT FOREST

Forest Enterprise.
Location: SU 73. Bisected by A325 Petersfield-Farnham road. From Bucks Horn Oak, take minor road SE for 0.3km. Turn E into road to car park.
Access: Open all year. Car parks closed dusk-8am.
Facilities: Visitor centre, car parks, trails, footpaths.
Public transport: None.
Habitat: Forestry, broadleaved woodland, pools, streams.
Key birds: *Spring/summer*: Woodcock, Turtle Dove, Nightjar, Lesser Spotted Woodpecker, Tree Pipit. Possible Mandarin, Wood Lark. *Winter*: Flocks of Siskin, Redpoll, Woodcock. *All year*: Possible Willow Tit, Woodcock, Grey Heron.
Contact: Forest Enterprise, 340 Bristol Business Park, Coldharbour Lane, Bristol BS16 1EJ. 0117 906 6000.

2. FARLINGTON MARSHES

Hampshire Wildlife Trust.
Location: SU 685 045. E side of Portsmouth. Entrance of roundabout at junction of A2030 (Eastern Road) and A27, or from Harts Farm Way, Broadmarsh, Havant (S side of A27).
Access: Open at all times, no charge or permits, but donations welcome. Dogs on leads only. Not suitable for disabled. Groups please book.
Facilities: Information at entrance and in shelter area of building. No toilets.
Public transport: None.
Habitat: Coastal grazing marsh with pools and reedbed within reserve. Views over intertidal mudflats/saltmarshes of Langstone Harbour.
Key birds: *Autumn to spring*: Waders and wildfowl. *Winter*: Brent Goose, Wigeon, Pintail etc and waders (Dunlin, Grey Plover etc). On migration wide range of waders including rarities. Reedbeds with Bearded Tit, Water Rail etc, scrub areas attract small migrants (Redstart, Wryneck, warblers etc).
Contact: Bob Chapman, c/o Hampshire Wildlife Trust, Woodside House, Woodside Road, Eastleigh, Hants SO50 4ET. 023 8061 3636. www.hwt.org.uk

3. FLEET POND LNR

Hart District Council.
Location: SY 85. Located in Fleet. From the B3013, head to Fleet Station. Park in the long-stay car park at Fleet Station. Parking also available in Chestnut Grove and Westover Road.
Access: Open all year. **Facilities:** None.
Public transport: None.
Habitat: Lake, reedbed, willow scrub.
Key birds: *Spring/autumn*: migrant waders inc Little Ringed Plover, Dunlin, Greenshank, Little Gull, occasional Kittiwake, terns, Wood Lark, Sky Lark, occasional Ring Ouzel, Firecrest, Pied Flycatcher. *Summer*: Hobby, Common Tern, Tree Pipit. *Winter*: Bittern, wildfowl, occasional Smew, Snipe, occasional Jack Snipe, Siskin, Redpoll.
Contact: Hart District Council, Civic Office, Harlington Way, Fleet, Hampshire GU51 4AE. 01252 622122.

4. HAMBLE COMMON AND COPSE

Countryside Service of Eastleigh Borough Council.
Location: SU 48 09. Hamble Common is reached via Copse Lane from B3397 Hamble Lane, which links with A27 and M27 at Windhover roundabout near Bursledon.
Access: Open all year. **Facilities:** Car parks and site linked with good network of footpaths. Paths good in summer, but very wet after rain.

Public transport: None.
Habitat: Wet heathland, scrub, woodland, meadow, grassland.
Key birds: *Winter*: Wildfowl and waders. On Southampton Water shore, Oystercatchers, Grey Plovers, Ringed Plovers, Dunlin, Turnstone, Curlew and Brent Geese common. In the creek wader numbers lower, with Redshank, Lapwing and Dunlin, occasional Greenshank, Teal, Mallard, Shelduck, Grey Heron, Kingfisher most years.
Contact: Eastleigh Borough Council, Civic Office, Leigh Road, Eastleigh, Hampshire SO50 9YN. 0238 068 8000.

5. HOOK-WITH-WARSASH LNR

Hampshire County Council. 01329 662145.

6. LANGSTONE HARBOUR

RSPB (South East England Office).
Location: SU 695 035. Harbour lies E of Portsmouth, one mile S of Havant. Car parks at Broadmarsh (SE of A27/A3(M) junction) and West Hayling LNR (first R on A2030 after Esso garage).
Access: Restricted access. Good views from West Hayling LNR, Broadmarsh and Farlington Marshes LNR (qv). Winter boat trips may be booked from nearby Portsmouth Outdoor Centre.
Facilities: None.
Public transport: Mainline trains all stop at Havant. Local bus service to W Hayling LNR.
Habitat: Intertidal mud, saltmarsh, shingle islands.
Key birds: *Summer*: Breeding waders and seabirds inc. Mediterranean Gull and Little Tern. *Passage/ winter:* Waterfowl, (inc. Black-necked Grebes, c5000 dark-bellied Brent Geese, Shelduck, Shoveler, Goldeneye and red-breasted Merganser). Waders inc. (Oystercatcher, Ringed and Grey Plover, Dunlin, Black and Bar-tailed Godwit and Greenshank). Peregrine, Merlin and Short-eared Owl.
Contact: Chris Cockburn (Warden), C/O 20 Childe Square, Stamshaw, Portsmouth, Hants PO2 8PL. 023 9265 0672.
e-mail: chris.cockburn@rspb.org.uk

7. LOWER TEST

Hampshire Wildlife Trust.
Location: SU 364 150. M271 S to Redbridge, three miles from Southampton city centre.
Access: Open at all times, guide dogs only.
Facilities: Three hides, one suitable for disabled (access by arrangement with the warden).
Public transport: Totton train station and bus stops within easy walking distance.
Habitat: Saltmarsh, brackish grassland, wet meadows, reedbed, scrapes and meres.
Key birds: *Summer*: Breeding Little, Sandwich and Common Terns, Black-headed and Mediterranean Gulls, waders. *Passage/winter*: Waders. *Autumn/ winter:* Waders (inc. Black-tailed and Bar-tailed Godwits, Oystercatcher, Ringed and Grey Plover, Dunlin). Wildfowl (inc. Shelduck Shoveler, Goldeneye, red-breasted Merganser, c7000 dark-bellied Brent Geese). Black-necked Grebe, Short-eared Owl, Peregrine.
Contact: Jess Pain, Hampshire Wildlife Trust, Woodside House, Woodside Road, Eastleigh, Hants SO50 4ET. 023 8066 7919.
e-mail: jessp@hwt.org.uk www.hwt.org.uk

8. LYMINGTON REEDBEDS

Hampshire Wildlife Trust.
Location: SZ 324 965. From Lyndhurst in New Forest take A337 to Lymington. Turn L afterrailway bridge into Marsh Lane. Park in the lay-by next to allotments. The reserve entrance is on opposite side, to R of the house and over railway crossing. The footpath exits the reserve near the Old Ampress Works, leading to a minor road between the A337 and Boldre.
Access: Open all year. The best viewpoint over the reedbeds is from Bridge Road or from the Undershore leading from the B3054.
Facilities: None. **Public transport:** Bus: at either end of the footpath, Marsh Lane and on the A337 (route 112). Five minutes walk from train station.
Habitat: One of largest reedbeds on S coast, fringed by alder and willow woodland.
Key birds: One of highest concentrations of Water Rail in the country; resident but most evident in winter. *Spring/summer*: Cetti's Warbler, Bearded Tit, Yellow Wagtail, Swallows, martins, Reed Warbler. *Passage*: Snipe, ducks. Otters in the area.
Contact: Michael Boxall, Hampshire and Isle of Wight Wildlife Trust, Woodside House, Woodside House, Woodside Road, Eastleigh, Hants SO50 4ET. 023 8066 7919.
e-mail: feedback@hwt.org.uk www.hwt.org.uk

9. LYMINGTON-KEYHAVEN NNR

Hampshire County Council.
Location: SZ 315 920. S of Lymington along seawall footpath; car parks at Bath Road, Lymington and at Keyhaven Harbour.
Access: Open all year
Facilities: None. **Public transport:** None.
Habitat: Coastal marshland and lagoons.

Key birds: *Spring*: Passage waders (inc. Knot, Sanderling, Bar-tailed and Black-tailed Godwits, Whimbrel, Spotted Redshank), Pomarine and Great Skuas. Breeding Oystercatcher, Ringed Plover and Sandwich, Common and Little Terns. *Autumn*: Passage raptors, waders and passerines. *Winter*: Wildfowl (inc. Brent Goose, Wigeon, Pintail, Red-breasted Merganser), waders (inc. Golden Plover), Little Egret, gulls.
Contact: Hampshire County Council, Mottisfont Court, High Street, Winchester, Hants SO23 8ZF.

10. MARTIN DOWN

English Nature (Wiltshire Team).
Location: SY 05 19. Nine miles SW of\Salisbury, car park on A354.
Access: Open access, organised groups should book in advance.
Facilities: Two car parks, interpretative boards.
Public transport: One bus Salisbury/Blandford.
Habitat: Chalk downland.
Key birds: *Spring/summer*: Grey Partridge, warblers, Nightingale, Stone Curlew. *Winter*: Merlin, Hen Harrier.
Contact: David Burton, Parsonage Down NNR, Cherry Lodge, Shrewton, Nr Salisbury, Wilts, 01980 620485.
e-mail: david.burton@english-nature.org.uk

11. NORTH SOLENT

English Nature (Hampshire and Isle of Wight Team).
Location: 1. Beaulieu Estate. SZ 420 975. Fifteen miles Southampton - minor roads from Beaulieu.
2. Cadland Estate. SU 460 015. Minor roads from Hythe/Fawley.
Access: 1. Permits available from Beaulieu Estate (tel 01590 614621). No dogs, designated parts only. No public right of way at Needs Ore. Public footpath along river (Beaulieu-Bucklers Hard).
2. Public rights of way only.
Facilities: 1. Hides (one with disabled access).
2. None.
Public transport: 1. None.
2. Southampton to Blackfield/Fawley bus.
Habitat: 1. Coastal - saltmarsh/estuary, grazing marsh, reedbed.
2. Heathland, river valleys.
Key birds: 1. Coastal-seabirds/waders all year and woodland species.
2. Heathland/woodland species.
Contact: Bob Lord, Sites Manager, English Nature, 1 Southampton Road, Lyndhurst SO43 7BU. 023802 86428.
e-mail: bob.lord@english-nature.org.uk
www.english-nature.org.uk

12. ROYDON WOODS

Hampshire & Isle of Wight Wildlife Trust.
Location: SU 315 009. Roydon is one mile SE of Brockenhurst. For N Roydon, head S on A337 from Brockenhurst. Take the second L after the level crossing. Go past church and park in Church Lane. Take the track S leading to the reserve. For S Roydon, head S on the A337 and turn L after the Filly Inn. There are two parking areas down the road.
Access: Open all year.
Facilities: Car park. Several bridlepaths are surfaced but the smaller ones are not and can get muddy.
Public transport: Bus: From Brockenhurst to Setley, routes 56 and 56A, past the Filly Inn.
Habitat: Ancient woodland, pastures, ponds, heath, river.
Key birds: *Spring/summer*: Redstart, warblers, Nightjar. *All year*: Usual woodland species, all three woodpeckers.
Contact: Trust HQ, Woodside Road, Eastleigh, Hampshire, SO50 4ET, 0238 0613636.
e-mail: feedback@hwt.org.uk www.hwt.org.uk

13. TITCHFIELD HAVEN

Hampshire County Council.
Location: SU 535 025. From A27 W of Fareham; public footpath follows derelict canal along W of reserve and road skirts S edge.
Access: Open Wed-Sun all year, plus Bank Hols, except Christmas and Boxing days.
Facilities: Centre has information desk, toilets, tea room and shop. Guided tours (book in advance). Hides.
Public transport: None.
Habitat: Reedbeds, freshwater scrapes, wet grazing meadows.
Key birds: *Spring/summer*: Bearded Tit, waders (inc. Black-tailed Godwit, Ruff), wildfowl, Common Tern, breeding Cetti's Warbler, Water Rail. *Winter*: Bittern.
Contact: Barry Duffin, Haven House Visitor Centre, Cliff Road, Hill Head, Fareham, Hants PO14 3JT. 01329 662145; fax 01329 667113.

Hertfordshire

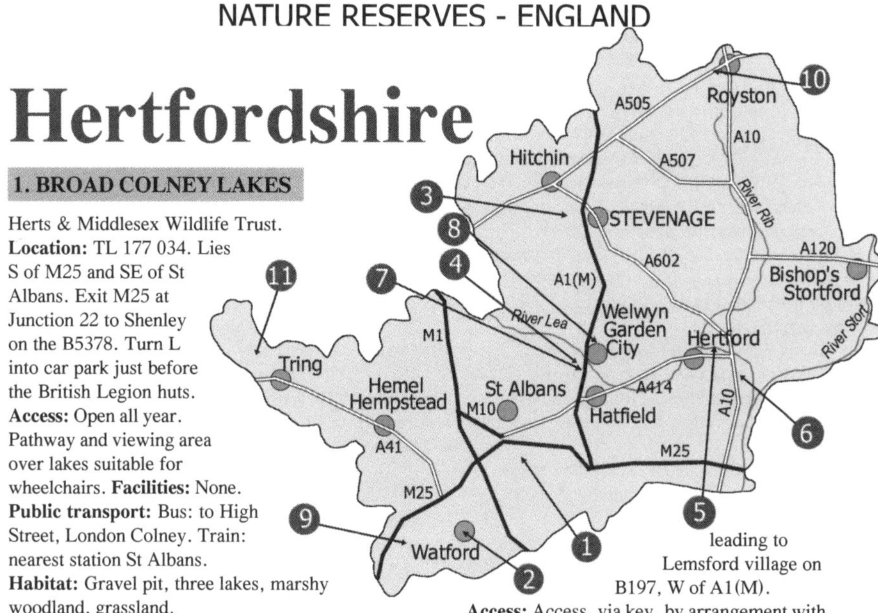

1. BROAD COLNEY LAKES

Herts & Middlesex Wildlife Trust.
Location: TL 177 034. Lies S of M25 and SE of St Albans. Exit M25 at Junction 22 to Shenley on the B5378. Turn L into car park just before the British Legion huts.
Access: Open all year. Pathway and viewing area over lakes suitable for wheelchairs. **Facilities:** None.
Public transport: Bus: to High Street, London Colney. Train: nearest station St Albans.
Habitat: Gravel pit, three lakes, marshy woodland, grassland.
Key birds: *Winter*: Siskin and Redpoll in alders, tits including Willow Tit, common water birds.
Contact: Herts & Middlesex Wildlife Trust, Herts & Middlesex Wildlife Trust, Grebe House, St Michael's Street, St Albans, Herts AL3 4SN. 01727 858 901. e-mail: info@hmwt.org

2. CASSIOBURY PARK

Welwyn & Hatfield Council.
Location: TL 090 970. Close to Watford town centre. **Access:** Open all year.
Facilities: Car park, footpaths.
Public transport: Watford Metropolitan Underground station.
Habitat: Municipal park, wetland, river, alder/ willow wood.
Key birds: *Spring/summer*: Kingfisher, Grey Wagtail. *Winter*: Snipe, Water Rail, occasional Bearded Tit.
Contact: Welwyn & Hatfield Council, Council Offices, The Campus, Welwyn Garden City, Herts AL8 6AE. 01707 357000.
e-mail: council.services@welhat.gov.uk

3. HILL END PIT

Herts & Middlesex Wildlife Trust.01727 858901.

4. LEMSFORD SPRINGS

Herts & Middlesex Wildlife Trust.
Location: TL 223 123. Lies 1.5 miles W of Welwyn Garden City town centre, off roundabout leading to Lemsford village on B197, W of A1(M).
Access: Access, via key, by arrangement with warden. Open at all times, unless work parties or group visits in progress. Keep to paths. No dogs. Not ideal for disabled due to steps up to hides.
Facilities: Two hides, chemical toilet, paths.
Public transport: Bus service to Valley Road, WGC No 366 (Sovereign Bus & Coach Co Ltd, tel 01438 726688). Nearest railway station Welwyn Garden City.
Habitat: Former water-cress beds, open shallow lagoons. Stretch of the River Lea, marsh, hedgerows.
Key birds: *Spring/summer*: Breeding warblers, Grey Wagtail, Kestrel. *Autumn/winter*: Green Sandpiper, Water Rail, Snipe, Siskin, occasional Jack Snipe. *All Year*: Kingfisher, Grey Heron, Sparrowhawk.
Contact: Barry Trevis, 11 Lemsford Village, Welwyn Garden City, Herts AL8 7TN. 01707 335517. e-mail: info@hmwt.org

5. MEADS, THE

Herts & Middlesex Wildlife Trust/Thames Water/ Smith Kline Wellcome/East Herts District Council/ Environment Agency. 01727 858901. e-mail: info@hmwt.org www.wildlifetrust.org.uk/herts

6. RYE MEADS

RSPB (Central England Region)/Hertfordshire & Middlesex Wildlife Trust.
Location: TL 387 099. E of Hoddesdon, signed from A10, near Rye House railway station.

Access: Open every day 10am-5pm (or dusk if earlier), except Christmas Day and Boxing Day.
Facilities: Disabled access and toilets. Drinks machine, staffed reception, classrooms, picnic area, car park, bird feeding area. Nature trails, hides. RSPB reserve has close circuit TV on Kingfisher and Common Terns in summer.
Public transport: Rail (Rye House) 55 metres, bus (310) stops 600 metres from entrance.
Habitat: Marsh, willow scrub, pools, scrapes, lagoons and reedbed.
Key birds: *Summer*: Breeding Tufted Duck, Gadwall, Common Tern, Kestrel, Kingfisher, nine species of warblers. *Winter*: Bittern, Shoveler, Water Rail, Teal, Snipe, Jack Snipe, Redpoll and Siskin.
Contact: The Site Manager, RSPB Rye Meads Visitor Centre, Rye Road, Stanstead Abbotts, Herts SG12 8JS. 01992 708383.

7. SHERRARDS PARK WOOD

Welwyn & Hatfield Council.
Location: TL 230 137. W of Welwyn Garden City. J6 of A1m, take A1000 S. Turn R onto Bridge road.
Access: Open all year.
Facilities: Car park, footpaths.
Public transport: None.
Habitat: Ancient woodland, mostly oak.
Key birds: *Summer*: Spotted Flycatcher. *All year*: Usual woodland species - possibly all six tits, Treecreeper, Nuthatch.
Contact: Welwyn & Hatfield Council, Council Offices, The Campus, Welwyn Garden City, Herts AL8 6AE. 01707 357000.
e-mail: council.services@welhat.gov.uk

8. STANBOROUGH REED MARSH

Herts & Middlesex Wildlife Trust.
Location: TL 230 105. Leave the A1M at J4 on A6129 Stanborough Road. At next roundabout, turn R to Welwyn Garden City town centre. Continue past lakes to next roundabout. Take a U turn and then turn L into reserve car park. Follow path between river and lake into reserve.
Access: Open all year. No access into reedbed. Circular walk. **Facilities:** None.
Public transport: Bus: stops on Stanborough Road. Train: nearest station Welwyn Garden City.
Habitat: Willow woodland, river, reed marsh.
Key birds: *Summer*: good numbers of Reed and Sedge Warblers. *Winter*: Water Rail and Corn Bunting roost.
Contact: Trust HQ. 01727 858901.

9. STOCKER'S LAKE

Herts & Middlesex Wildlife Trust. 01727 858901.

10. THERFIELD HEATH LNR

Hertfordshire & Middlesex Wildlife Trust.
Location: TL 335 400. Near Royston on A505.
Access: Open all year. **Facilities:** Car park.
Public transport: None.
Habitat: Chalk downland, arable land.
Key birds: *Summer*: Skylark, Corn Bunting. *Passage*: chats. *Winter*: Short-eared Owl, Golden Plover, Hen Harrier possible.
Contact: Trust HQ. 01727 858901. e-mail: hertswt@cix.org.uk www.wildlifetrust.org.uk/herts

11. TRING RESERVOIRS

Wilstone Reservoir - Herts & Middlesex Wildlife Trust/British Waterways; other reservoirs - British Waterways/Friends of Tring Reservoirs.
Location: Wilstone Reservoir SP90 51 34. Other reservoirs SP 92 01 35. WTW Lagoon SP 92 31 34 adjacent to Marsworth Reservoir. Reservoirs 1.5 miles due N of Tring, all accessible from B489 which leaves A41 at Aston Clinton.
Access: Reservoirs - open at all times. WTW Lagoon: open at all times by permit from FOTR. All group visits need to be cleared with British Waterways.
Facilities: Café and public house adjacent to Startops Reservoir car park, safe parking for cycles. Disabled trail from here. Pub also in Wilstone village about 800 mtrs from reservoir. Hides with disabled access at Startops/Marsworth Reservoir & WTW Lagoon.Other hides.
Public transport: Buses to and from Aylesbury & Tring including a weekend service, tel. 0870 6082608. Tring Station is 2.5 miles away via canal towpath.
Habitat: Four reservoirs with surrounding woodland, scrub and meadows. Two of the reservoirs with extensive reedbeds. WTW Lagoon with islands, surrounding hedgerows and scrub.
Key birds: *Spring/summer*: Breeding warblers, regular Hobby, occasional Black Tern, Marsh Harrier, Osprey. *Autumn*: Passage waders and wildfowl. *Winter*: Gull roost, large wildfowl flocks, bunting roosts, Bittern.
Contact: Herts & Middsx Wildlife Trust: see Directory entry, FOTR: see Peter Hearn in Bucks BTO entry, British Waterways, Watery Lane, Marsworth, Tring HP23 4LZ. 01442 825938, www.tringreservoirs.btinternet.co.uk

Kent

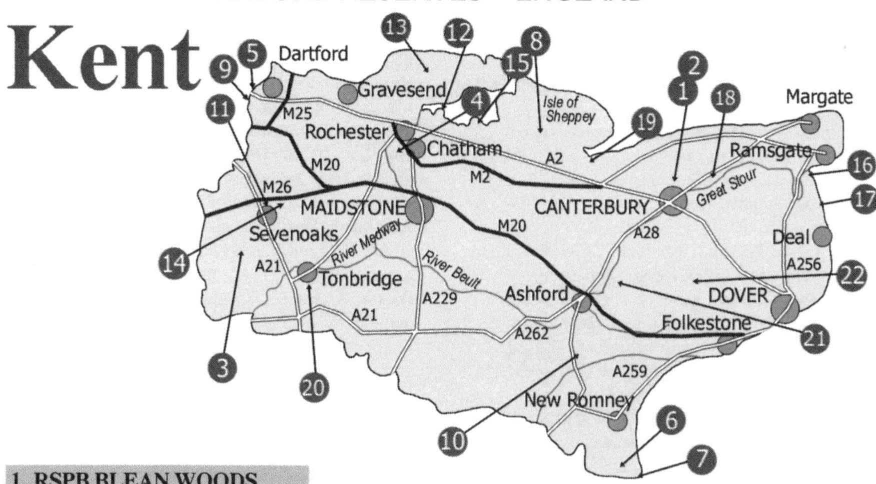

1. RSPB BLEAN WOODS

RSPB (South East England Office).
Location: TR 126 592. From Rough Common (off A290, 1.5 miles NW of Canterbury).
Access: Open 8am-9pm.
Facilities: Public footpaths and five waymarked trails.
Public transport: 24 and 24a buses from Canterbury to Rough Common.
Habitat: Woodland (mainly oak and sweet chestnut), relics of heath.
Key birds: Nightingale, Nightjar in summer, three species of woodpecker.
Contact: Michael Walter, 11 Garden Close, Rough Common, Canterbury, Kent CT2 9BP. 01227 455972.

2. BLEAN WOODS

English Nature (Kent Team).
Location: TR 120 609. NW of Canterbury on A290. Road opposite Chapel Lane at Blean.
Access: Keep to paths. **Facilities:** None.
Public transport: Buses every 15mins (between Canterbury and Whitstable) pass close to reserve.
Habitat: Mixed coppice with standard sessile oak, glades, rides.
Key birds: *Summer:* Sone 70 breeding species, inc. Woodcock, all three woodpeckers, Tree Pipit, Redstart, Nightingale, Wood Warbler, Hawfinch.
Contact: David Maylam, Colharbour Farm, Wye, Ashford, Kent TN25 5DB, 01233 812525.

3. BOUGH BEECH RESERVOIR

Kent Wildlife Trust. 01622 662012.
e-mail: kentwildlife@cix.co.uk
www.kentwildlife.co.uk

4. BURHAM MARSHES

Kent Wildlife Trust. 01622 662012.
e-mail: kentwildlife@cix.co.uk

5. DANSON PARK LNR

Bexley Council.
Location: TQ 471 753. From A2 take A221 at Danson Interchange towards Bexleyheath. From A207, Park View Road/Crook Log turn into Danson Road. **Access:** Open all year.
Facilities: Car park, display boards, toilets. Danson Stables pub/restaurant opens noon daily. Some hard surface paths. Unsuitable for wheelchairs unless weather has been dry.
Public transport: Bexleyheath rail station 15 mins' walk. Buses B13, 89, 96, B16 and B14. Tel: 020 7222 1234.
Habitat: Mixed woodland, bog garden, lake.
Key birds: *Spring*: Wheatear, Sand Martin, House Martin, flycatchers. *Summer*: Blackcap, Chiffchaff, Whitethroat, Garden and Will Warblers. *All year*: Kingfisher, Ring-necked Parakeet, Great Spotted and Green Woodpeckers, Grey Wagtail, Jay.
Contact: Bexley Council, Broadway, Bexleyheath, Kent DA6 7LB. 0208 3037777 ext 5562.
e-mail: worksdirect@bexley.gov.uk
www.bexley.gov.uk

6. DUNGENESS

RSPB (South East England Office).
Location: TR 063 196. SE of Lydd.
Access: Open daily 9am-9pm or sunset when earlier. Visitor centre open (10am-5pm, 4pm Nov-Feb). Parties over 20 by prior arrangement.

Facilities: Visitor centre, toilets (including disabled access), five hides, nature trail, wheelchair access to visitor centre and four hides.
Public transport: Service 12 from Lydd or Folkestone stops at reserve entrance on request - one mile walk to visitor centre.
Habitat: Shingle, flooded gravel pits, sallow scrub, reedbed, wet grassland.
Key birds: *Resident*: Bearded Tit. *Winter*: Bittern, Wildfowl (including Wigeon, Goldeneye, Goosander, Smew), divers and grebes. Migrant waders, landfall for passerines. *Summer*: Breeding Lapwing, Redshank, wildfowl, terns and gulls.
Contact: Christine Hawkins/Bob Gomes, Boulderwall Farm, Dungeness Road, Lydd, Romney Marsh, Kent TN29 9PN. 01797 320588/ fax 01797 321962. www.rspb.org.uk
e-mail: dungeness@rspb.org.uk

7. DUNGENESS BIRD OBSERVATORY

Dungeness Bird Observatory Trust.
Location: TR 085 173. Three miles SE of Lydd. Turn south off Dungeness Road at TR 087 185 and continue to end of road.
Access: Observatory open throughout the year.
Facilities: Accommodation available. Bring own sleeping bag/sheets and toiletries. Shared facilities including fully-equipped kitchen.
Public transport: Bus service between Rye and Folkestone, numbers 11, 12, 711, 712. Alight at the Pilot Inn, Lydd-on-Sea. Tel 01227 472082.
Habitat: Shingle promontory with scrub and gravel pits. RSPB reserve nearby.
Key birds: Breeding birds include Wheatear and Black Redstart and seabirds on RSPB Reserve. Important migration site.
Contact: David Walker, Dungeness Bird Observatory, 11 RNSSS, Dungeness, Kent TN29 9NA. 01797 321309.
e-mail dungeness.obs@tinyonline.co.uk
www.dungenessbirdobs.org.uk

8. ELMLEY MARSHES

RSPB (South East England Office).
Location: TQ 93 86 80. Isle-of-Sheppey signposted from A249, one mile beyond Kingsferry Bridge. Reserve car park is two miles from the main road.
Access: Open every day except Tue, Christmas and Boxing days. 9am-9pm or dusk if earlier. No charge to RSPB members. No dogs. Less able may drive closer to hides with Warden's permission.
Facilities: Five hides, no provision at present for disabled visitors but one hide with disabled access is planned. No visitor centre. Toilets located in car park 1.25 miles from hides.
Public transport: Swale Halt, request stop is nearest railway station on Sittingbourne to Sheerness line. Three mile walk to reserve.
Habitat: Coastal grazing marsh, ditches and pools alongside the Swale Estuary with extensive intertidal mudflats and saltmarsh
Key birds: *Spring/summer*: Breeding waders - Redshank, Lapwing, Avocet, Yellow Wagtail, passage waders, Hobby. *Autumn*: Passage waders. *Winter*: Spectacular numbers of wildfowl especially Wigeon and White-fronted Goose. Waders. Hunting raptors - Peregrine, Merlin, Hen Harrier and Short-eared Owl.
Contact: Alan Johnson, Elmley RSPB Reserve, Kingshill Farm, Elmley, Sheerness, Kent ME12 3RW. 01795 665969.

9. FOOTS CRAY MEADOWS LNR

Kent Wildlife Trust.
Location: TQ 475 717. Take the A2 W from Dartford to Bexley and pick up the A223 S to Foots Cray. Take the A211 to Sidcup. Turn R into Rectory Lane to the main car park.
Access: Open all year.
Facilities: Car parks, display boards.
Public transport: Train: Albany Park or Bexley. Bus: 492 passes along North Cray Road.
Habitat: River, wood scrub.
Key birds: *Spring*: warblers, possible Lesser Spotted Woodpecker, flycatcher. *Winter*: Water Rail, Green Sandpiper, Siskin, Redpoll, thrushes. *All year*: Kingfisher, Ring-necked Parakeet, Green and Great Spotted Woodpeckers, woodland species.
Contact: Bexley Council, Broadway, Bexleyheath, Kent DA6 7LB. 0208 3037777 ext 5562. e-mail: worksdirect@bexley.gov.uk www.bexley.gov.uk

10. HAMSTREET WOODS

English Nature (Kent Team). 01233 812525.

11. JEFFERY HARRISON RESERVE, SEVENOAKS

J
effery Harrison Memorial Trust.
Location: TQ 519 568. From A25 immediately N of Sevenoaks.
Access: Wed, Sat, Sun 10am-5pm (or dusk).
Facilities: Visitor centre, nature trail, hides.
Public transport: 15 minutes walk from Bat & Ball station, 20 minutes from Sevenoaks station.
Habitat: Flooded gravel pits.
Key birds: Wintering wildfowl, waders, woodland birds.

Contact: John Tyler, Tadorna, Bradbourne Vale Road, Sevenoaks, Kent TN13 3DH. 01732 456407. e-mail: sevenoakswildfowl@kentwildlife.org.uk

12. NOR MARSH

RSPB (South East England Office). 01634 222480.

13. NORTHWARD HILL

RSPB (South East England Office).
Location: TQ 780 765. Adjacent to village of High Halstow, off A228, approx six miles N of Rochester.
Access: Open all year, free access, trails in public area of wood joining Saxon Shoreway link adjacent to grazing marsh. Sanctuary area accessible by permit only - write to warden. Dogs allowed in public area on leads. Trails often steep and not suitable for wheelchair users.
Facilities: Three nature trails in the wood and one joining with long distance footpath. Toilets at village hall, small car park adjacent to wood.
Public transport: Buses to village of High Halstow. Contact Arriva buses for timetable.
Habitat: Ancient and scrub woodland (approximately 130 acres), grazing marsh (approximately 350 acres).
Key birds: *Spring/summer*: Wood holds UK's largest heronry (155 pairs in 2001), breeding Nightingale, Turtle Dove, scrub warblers and woodpeckers. Marshes - breeding Lapwing, Redshank, Avocet (most years), Marsh Harrier, Shoveler, Pochard. *Winter*: Wigeon, Teal Shoveler. Passage waders (ie Black-tailed Godwit). Long-eared Owl roost.
Contact: Michael Ellison, Bromhey Farm, Eastborough, Cooling, Rochester, Kent ME3 8DS. 01634 222480.

14. OARE MARSHES LNR

Kent Wildlife Trust.
Location: TR 01 36 48 (car park). Two miles N of Faversham. From A2 follow signs to Oare and Harty Ferry.
Access: Open at all times. Access along marked paths only. Dogs under strict control to avoid disturbance to birds and livestock.
Facilities: Information centre, open weekends, Bank Holidays. Two hides.
Public transport: Bus to Oare Village one mile from reserve. Train: Faversham (two miles)
Habitat: Grazing marsh, mudflats/estuary.
Key birds: *All year*: Waders and wildfowl. *Winter*: Hen Harrier, Merlin, Peregrine; divers, grebes and sea ducks on Swale. *Spring/summer*: Avocet, Garganey, Green and Wood Sandpipers, Little Stint, Black-tailed Godwit etc. Black Tern.
Contact: Trust HQ. 01622 662012. e-mail: kentwildlife@cix.co.uk www.kentwildlife.co.uk

15. OLDBURY HILL & STYANT'S WOOD

National Trust/Kent County Council. 01372 453401. www.nationaltrust.org.uk

16. RIVERSIDE COUNTRY PARK

Medway County Council.
Location: TQ 808 683. From Rochester, takeA2 E into Gillingham and turn L onto A289. After one mile, turn R onto B2004 at Grange. After one mile, the visitor centre is on the L.
Access: Open all year, free access 8.30am-4.30pm (winter) or 8.30am-8.30pm or dusk (summer).
Facilities: Visitor Centre with restaurant and toilets open every day except Christmas, Boxing and New Year's days (no parking on these days either) from 10am-5pm summer (4pm winter). Large car park and smaller one at Rainham Dock.
Public transport: Bus: contact Arriva tel: 08706 082 608. Train: nearest stations at Rainham and Gillingham. Cycle racks at visitor centre and a Sustrans cycle route.
Habitat: Mudflats, saltmarsh, ponds, reedbeds, grassland and scrub.
Key birds: *Winter*: Dunlin, Redshank, Grey Plover, Avocet, Brent Goose, Teal, Pintail, Goldeneye, Wigeon, Shelduck, Peregrine, Hen Harrier, thrushes, Short-eared Owl, Mediterranean Gull, Water Rail, Rock Pipit, Little Egret and Red-breasted Merganser.
Contact: Riverside Country Park, Lower Rainham Road, Gillingham, Kent, ME7 2XH, 01634 378987. e-mail: riversidecp@medway.gov.uk

17. SANDWICH & PEGWELL BAY LNR

Kent Wildlife Trust.
Location: TR 34 26 35. Main carpark is off A256 Sandwich - Ramsgate road at Pegwell Bay.
Access: Open 8am-8pm or dusk.
Facilities: Toilets, hide, car parking and trails.
Public transport: Bus stop within 400m (Stagecoach). Sustrans National Bike Route passes along the edge of the reserve.
Habitat: Saltmarsh, mudflats, sand dunes and coastal scrub.
Key birds: Good range of wetland birds throughout the year.
Contact: Trust HQ. 01622 662012. e-mail: kentwildlife@cix.co.uk www.kentwildlife.co.uk

18. SANDWICH BAY BIRD OBSERVATORY

Sandwich Bay Bird Observatory Trust.
Location: TR 355 575. 2.5 miles from Sandwich, five miles from Deal, 15 miles from Canterbury. A256 to Sandwich from Dover or Ramsgate. Follow signs to Sandwich Station and then Sandwich Bay.
Access: Open daily. Disabled access.
Facilities: New Field Study Centre. Visitor centre, toilets, refreshments, hostel-type accommodation.
Public transport: Sandwich train station two miles from Observatory. No buses, but within walking distance.
Habitat: Coastal, dune land, farmland, marsh, small scrape.
Key birds: *Spring/autumn passage*: Good variety of migrants and waders, specially Corn Bunting. Annual Golden Oriole. *Winter*: Golden Plover.
Contact: Kevin Thornton, Sandwich Bay Bird Observatory, Guildford Road, Sandwich Bay, Sandwich, Kent CT13 9PF. 01304 617341.
e-mail: sbbot@talk21.com

19. STODMARSH NNR

English Nature (Kent Team).
Location: TR 222 618. Lies alongside River Stour and A28, five miles NE of Canterbury.
Access: Open at all times. Keep to reserve paths and keep dogs under control.
Facilities: Fully accessible toilets available at the Stodmarsh entrance car park. Four hides (one fully accessible), easy access nature trail, footpaths and information panels. Car park, picnic area and toilets adjoining Grove Ferry entrance with easily accessible path, viewing mound and two hides.
Public transport: There is a regular bus service from Canterbury to Margate/Ramsgate. Alight at Upstreet for Grove Ferry. Hourly on Sun.
Habitat: Open water, reedbeds, wet meadows, dry meadows, woodland.
Key birds: *Spring/summer*: Breeding Bearded Tit, Cetti's Warbler, Garganey, Reed, Sedge and Willow Warblers, Nightingale. Migrant Black Tern, Hobby, Osprey, Little Egret. *Winter*: Wildfowl. Hen Harrier, Bittern.
Contact: David Feast, English Nature, Coldharbour Farm, Wye, Ashford, Kent TN25 5DB. 01233 812525 or 07767 321058 (mobile).

20. TUDELEY WOODS

RSPB (South East England Office).
Location: TQ 618 434. Beside A21, one mile S of Tonbridge. Take minor road to Capel on left immediately before Fairthorne Garage. Car park 0.25 miles on left.
Access: Open every day except Christmas Day. No dogs. No disabled facilities.
Facilities: Leaflet, three nature trails.
Habitat: Semi-natural ancient woodland, lowland heathland (restored), pasture.
Key birds: *Spring/summer*: Willow Warbler, Garden Warbler, Blackcap, Turtle Dove, Spotted Flycatcher, Nightingale, Tree Pipit, Nightjar, Hobby, Whitethroat. *All year*: Marsh Tit, Willow Tit, Nuthatch, three woodpecker species, Yellowhammer, Treecreeper.
Contact: Martin Allison, 12 The Grove, Crowborough, East Sussex TN6 1NY. 01273 775333 (South East Regional Office).
e-mail: martin/allison@rspb.org.uk
www.rspb.org.uk

21. WYE

English Nature (Kent Team).
Location: TR 079 454. NE of Ashford. From Wye up hill towards Hastingleigh, car park at roadside.
Access: Open daily except Christmas Day. No dogs. Keep to paths. **Facilities:** One nature trail.
Public transport: None.
Habitat: Downland, scrub, woodlands, grazing meadows.
Key birds: *Summer*: Breeding Sparrowhawk, Tawny Owl, Nightingale, Spotted Flycatcher, Lesser Whitethroat, Hawfinch.
Contact: David Maylam, Coldharbour Farm, Wye, Ashford, Kent TN25 5DB. 01233 812525.

22. YOCKLETTS BANK SSSI

Kent Wildlife Trust.
Location: TR 125 477. Two miles S of Petham, one mile W of the Canterbury-Hythe road (B2068). Park at the side of the road at the bottom of the hill, near Yockletts Farm.
Access: Open all year. Please keep to the paths. The reserve car park is normally open only at weekends during the main orchid-flowering period for parties booked in advance.
Facilities: None. **Public transport:** None.
Habitat: Mixed woodland, grassland.
Key birds: *Spring/summer*: Nightingale, warblers. *All year*: usual woodland species, Green and Great Spotted Woodpeckers. Good for plants.
Contact: Trust HQ. 01622 662012.
e-mail: kentwildlife@cix.co.uk
www.wildlifetrust.org.uk/kent

Lancashire

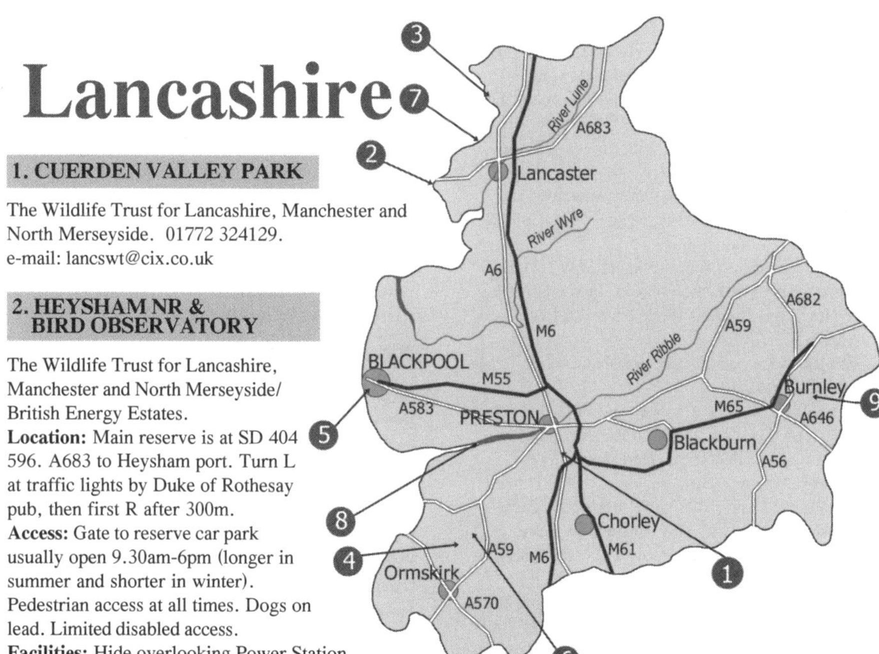

1. CUERDEN VALLEY PARK

The Wildlife Trust for Lancashire, Manchester and North Merseyside. 01772 324129.
e-mail: lancswt@cix.co.uk

2. HEYSHAM NR & BIRD OBSERVATORY

The Wildlife Trust for Lancashire, Manchester and North Merseyside/ British Energy Estates.
Location: Main reserve is at SD 404 596. A683 to Heysham port. Turn L at traffic lights by Duke of Rothesay pub, then first R after 300m.
Access: Gate to reserve car park usually open 9.30am-6pm (longer in summer and shorter in winter). Pedestrian access at all times. Dogs on lead. Limited disabled access.
Facilities: Hide overlooking Power Station outfalls. Map giving access details at the reserve car park. No manned visitor centre or toilet access but someone usually in reserve office, next to main car park, in the morning. Latest sightings board can be viewed through window if office closed.
Public transport: Train services connect with nearby Isle of Man ferry. Plenty of buses from various Heysham sites within walking distance to Lancaster (ask for nearest stop to the harbour).
Habitat: Varied: wetland, acid grassland, alkaline grassland, foreshore.
Key birds: Passerine migrants in the correct conditions. Good passage of seabirds in Spring, especially Arctic Tern. Storm Petrel and Leach's Petrel during strong onshore (SW-WWNW) winds in midsummer and autumn respectively. Good variety of breeding birds (e.g. eight species of warbler on the reserve itself). Two-three scarce land-birds each year, most frequent being Yellow-browed Warbler. Notable area for dragonflies, including scarce migrants.
Contact: Morag Angus, Reserve Warden, The Wildlife Trust for Lancashire, Manchester and N. Merseyside, The Bark, Berkeley Drive, Bamber Bridge, Preston, PR5 6BY. 07979 652138.
e-mail: woodlandview@supanet.com. Annual report from Leighton Moss RSPB reserve shop.

3. LEIGHTON MOSS

RSPB (North West England Office).
Location: SD 478 750. Four miles NW of Carnforth. Signposted from A6 N of Carnforth.
Access: Reserve open daily 9am-dusk. Visitor centre open daily 10am-5pm (except Christmas Day). No dogs. No charge to RSPB members.
Facilities: Visitor centre, shop, tea-room and toilets. Nature trails and five hides (four have wheelchair access).
Public transport: Silverdale Train Station 150 metres from reserve. Tel: 08457 484950.
Habitat: Reedbed, shallow meres and woodland.
Key birds: *All year*: Bittern, Bearded Tit, Water Rail, Pochard and Shoveler. *Summer*: Marsh Harrier, Reed and Sedge Warblers.
Contact: Robin Horner, Leighton Moss RSPB Nature Reserve, Myers Farm, Silverdale, Carnforth, Lancashire LA 0SW. 01524 701601.

4. MARTIN MERE

The Wildfowl & Wetlands Trust.
Location: SD 428 145. Six miles N of Ormskirk via Burscough Bridge (A59), 20 miles from Liverpool and Preston.
Access: Opening times: 9.30am-5.00pm (Nov-Feb),

9.30am-5.30pm (rest of year). Special dawn and evening events. Guide dogs only allowed. Admission charge. No charge for members. Fully accessible to disabled.
Facilities: Visitor centre with toilets, gift shop, restaurant, education centre, play area, nature reserve and nature trails, hides, waterfowl collection and sustainable garden. Provision for disabled visitors.
Public transport: Bus service to WWT Martin Mere from Ormskirk. Train to Burscough Bridge or New Lane Stations (both 1.5 miles from reserve).
Habitat: Open water, wet grassland, moss, copses, reedbed, parkland.
Key birds: *Winter*: Whooper and Bewick's Swans, Pink-footed Goose, various duck, Ruff, Black-tailed Godwit, Peregrine, Hen Harrier, Tree Sparrow. *Spring*: Ruff, Shelduck, Little Ringed and Ringed Plover, Lapwing, Redshank. *Summer*: Marsh Harrier, Garganey, hirundines, Tree Sparrow. *Autumn*: Pink-footed Goose, waders on passage.
Contact: Patrick Wisniewski, WWT Martin Mere, Fish Lane, Burscough, Lancs L40 0TA. 01704 895181. e-mail: info.martinmere@wwt.org.uk

5. MARTON MERE

Blackpool Borough Council. David McGrath, Community & Tourism Services, c/o Blackpool Zoo, East Park Drive, Blackpool FY3 8PP.

6. MERE SANDS WOOD

Wildlife Trust for Lancashire, Manchester and North Merseyside.
Location: SD 44 71 57. Four miles inland of Southport, 0.5 miles off A59 Preston - Liverpool road, in Rufford along B5246 (Holmeswood Road).
Access: Visitor centre open 9am-5pm daily except Christmas Day. Car park open until 8pm in summer. 750m of wheelchair-accessible path, leading to two hides and viewpoint.
Facilities: Visitor centre with toilets (disabled), seven hides, two trails, exhibition room, latest sightings board. Feeding stations
Public transport: Bus: Southport-Chorley 347 stops in Rufford, ½ mile walk. Train: Preston-Ormskirk train stops at Rufford station, one mile walk.
Habitat: Freshwater lakes, mixed woodland, sandy grassland/heath. 105h.
Key birds: *Winter*: Nationally important for Teal and Gadwall, good range of waterfowl, Kingfisher. Feeding stations attract Tree Sparrow, Bullfinch, Reed Bunting. Woodland: Treecreeper. *Summer*: Little Ringed Plover, Kingfisher, Lesser Spotted Woodpecker. *Passage*: Most years, Osprey, Crossbill, Green Sandpiper, Greenshank, Wood Warbler, Turtle Dove.
Contact: Dominic Rigby, Warden, Mere Sands Wood Nature Reserve, Holmeswood Road, Rufford, Ormskirk, Lancs L40 1TG. 01704 821809. e-mail: lancswtmsw@cix.co.uk www.wildlifetrust.org/lancashire

7. MORECAMBE BAY

RSPB (North West England Office).
Location: SD 468 667. Two miles N of Morecambe at Hest Bank.
Access: Open at all times. Do not venture onto saltmarsh or intertidal area, there are dangerous channels and quicksands.
Facilities: Viewpoint at car park.
Public transport: No 5 bus runs between Carnforth and Morecambe. Tel: 0870 608 2608.
Habitat: Saltmarsh, estuary.
Key birds: *Winter*: Wildfowl (Pintail, Shelduck, Wigeon) and waders - important high tide roost for Oystercatcher, Curlew, Redshank, Dunlin, Bar-tailed Godwit.
Contact: Robin Horner, Leighton Moss & Morecambe Bay RSPB Reserves, Myers Farm, Silverdale, Carnforth, Lancashire LA5 0SW. 01524 701601. www.rspb.org.uk

8. RIBBLE ESTUARY

English Nature (Cheshire to Lancashire team).
Location: SD 380 240.
Access: Open at all times.
Facilities: No formal visiting facilities.
Public transport: None.
Habitat: Saltmarsh, mudflats.
Key birds: High water wader roosts (of Knot, Dunlin, Black-tailed Godwit, Oystercatcher and Grey Plover) are best viewed from Southport, Marshside, Lytham and St Annes. Pink-footed Geese and wintering swans are present in large numbers from Oct-Feb on Banks Marsh and along River Douglas respectively. The large flocks of Wigeon, for which the site is renowned, can be seen on high tides from Marshside but feed on saltmarsh areas at night. Good numbers of raptors also present in winter.
Contact: Site Manager, Old Hollow, Marsh Road, Banks, Southport PR9 8EA. 01704 225624.

9. UPPER COLDWELL RESERVOIR

The Wildlife Trust for Lancashire, Manchester and North Merseyside
Location: SD 905 360. Three miles SE of Nelson. Enter from junction 13 of M65, then take minor road towards Hebden Bridge.
Access: Public footpath along N perimeter wall. Access to reserve area by permit.
Facilities: None.
Public transport: None.
Habitat: Upland reservoir, coniferous woodland, moorland.
Key birds: Breeding Tufted Duck, Little Ringed Plover, Whinchat; moors have Twite, Short-eared Owl, Golden Plover.
Contact: Trust HQ, 01772 324129.

Leicestershire and Rutland

1. BEACON HILL COUNTRY PARK

Leicestershire County Council.
Location: SK 522 149. From Loughborough, take the A512 SW for 2.5 miles. Turn L onto Breakback Road and follow it for 2.5 miles through Nanpantan. Park in the car park on the left in Woodhouse Lane.
Access: Open all year from 8am-dusk. If opening times are different, these will be clearly displayed at the park. A permissive path from Deans Lane to Woodhouse Lane is occasionally closed during the year. Please check first.
Facilities: Two pay and display car parks, easy to follow, well waymarked tracks and woodland paths. Several climbs to hill tops. Rocky outcrops slippy after rain. Information boards. Toilets at lower car park, The Outwoods car park and Woodhouse Eves. Wheelchair access along park paths but no access to summit. Refreshments at Bull's Head, Woodhouse Eaves.
Public transport: Bus: No 123 Leicester to Shepshed calls at Woodhouse Eaves. Tel: 0870 608 2608. Train: from Loughborough and Leicester.
Habitat: Forest, one of the oldest geological outcrops in England and the second highest point in Leicestershire.
Key birds: *All year*: Treecreeper, Nuthatch, Lesser Spotted and Green Woodpeckers, Great and Coal Tits, Little Owl, wagtails. *Summer*: Pied Flycatcher, Whitethroat, Blackcap, Whinchat, Garden Warbler, Stonechat.
Contact: Beacon Hill Country Park, Beacon Hill Estate Office, Broombriggs Farm, Beacon Road, Woodhouse Eaves, Loughborough, Leics., LE12 8SR, 01509 890048.

2. BURBAGE COMMON AND WOOD

Hinckley and Bosworth Borough Council.
Location: SK 447 954. NE of Hinckley. From Leicester, take A47 SW to roundabout near Barwell. Turn L onto the B4668. After about 0.25 miles, turn L onto Burbage Common Road.
Access: Open access to all areas. Dogs on lead. No wheelchair access.
Facilities: Visitor Centre open all week (not all day). Toilets, picnic areas. For information tel: 01455 633 712. Small hide in Burbage Wood. Refreshments at Wood House Farm, large parties should book. Tel: 01455 634 459.
Public transport: Bus: Arriva buses pass frequently from Hinckley and Leicester. Tel: 0870 608 2608. Train: Good train service to Hinckley from Leicester and Nuneaton. Tel: 0845 748 4950.
Habitat: Woodland, scrub and grassland.
Key birds: *Spring/summer*: Peregrine, Cuckoo, Lesser Whitethroat, Whitethroat, Garden and Willow Warblers, occasional Grasshopper Warbler. *Winter*: Lapwing, Brambling, Siskin, Twite, Redpoll, Redwing, Fieldfare and occasional Merlin and Firecrest.
Contact: Hinckley & Bosworth Borough Council, Argents Mead, Hinckley, Leicestershire, LE10 1BZ, 01455 238141.

3. EYEBROOK RESERVOIR

Corby & District Water Co.
Location: SP 853 964. Reservoir built 1940. S of Uppingham, from unclassified road W of A6003 at Stoke Dry.
Access: Access to 150 acres private grounds granted to members of Leics and Rutland Ornithological Society and Rutland Nat Hist Soc.

Organised groups with written permission (from Corby Water Co, PO Box 101, Weldon Road, Corby NN17 5UA). Tel. Fishing lodge 01536 770264.
Facilities: SSSI since 1955. Good viewing from public roads. Trout fishery season Apr-Oct.
Public transport: None.
Habitat: Open water, plantations and pasture.
Key birds: *Summer*: Good populations of breeding birds, sightings of Ospreys and Red Kite. Passage waders and Black Tern. *Winter*: Wildfowl (inc. Goldeneye, Goosander, Bewick's Swan) and waders.
Contact: Corby Water Co. www.eyebrook.org.uk

4. RUTLAND WATER

Leics and Rutland Wildlife Trust.
Location: SK 866 6760 72. 1. Egleton Reserve: from Egleton village off A6003 S of Oakham. 2. Lyndon Reserve: south shore E of Manton village off A6003 S of Oakham.
Access: 1. Open daily 9am-5pm, (4pm Nov to Jan). 2. Open winter (Sat, Sun 10am-5pm), summer daily (10am-5pm). Day permits available for both.
Facilities: 1: Anglian Water Birdwatching Centre, now enlarged. Toilets and disabled access to 11 hides, electric buggies, conference facilities. 2: Interpretive centre. Marked nature trail leaflet.
Public transport: None.
Habitat: Reservoir, lagoons, scrapes, woods, meadows, plantations.
Key birds: *Spring/autumn*: Outstanding wader passage. Also harriers, owls, passerine flocks, terns (Black, Arctic, breeding Common, occasional Little and Sandwich). *Winter*: Wildfowl (inc Goldeneye, Smew, Goosander, rare grebes, all divers), Ruff. *Summer:* Breeding Ospreys.
Contact: Tim Appleton, Fishponds Cottage, Stamford Road, Oakham, Rutland LE15 8AB. 01572 770651; fax 01572 755931; e-mail awbc@rutlandwater.org.uk; www.rutlandwater.org.uk www.ospreys.org.uk www.birdfair.org.uk.

5. SENCE VALLEY FOREST PARK

Forest Enterprise.
Location: SK 400 115. Ten miles NW of Leicester and two miles SW of Coalville, between Ibstock and Ravenstone. The car park is signed from the A447 N of Ibstock. Do not leave valuables in cars as there have been some break-ins.
Access: Open all year.
Facilities: Car park, information and recent sightings boards, hide, paths.
Public transport: None.
Habitat: Forest, rough grassland, pools, wader scrape.
Key birds: *Spring/summer*: Wheatear, Whinchat, Redstart, Common and Green Sandpiper, Ringed and Little Ringed Plovers, Redshank. Dunlin and Greenshank frequent, possible Wood Sandpiper. Reed Bunting, Meadow Pipit, Sky Lark, Linnet, Yellow Wagtail. Possible Quail. *Winter*: Stonechat, Redpoll, Short-eared Owl. Merlin, Peregrine, occasional Buzzard. Goosander and Wigeon possible.
Contact: Forest Enterprise, 340 Bristol Business Park, Coldharbour Lane, Bristol BS16 1EJ. 0117 906 6000.

Lincolnshire

1. DONNA NOOK-SALTFLEETBY

Lincolnshire Wildlife Trust.
Location: TF 422 998. Near North Somercotes, off A1031 coast road, S of Grimsby.
Access: Donna Nook beach is frequently closed as this is an active bombing range, but dunes remain open. Dogs on leads. Some disabled access.
Facilities: No toilets or visitor centre. Interpretation boards and paths.
Public transport: None.
Habitat: Dunes, slacks and intertidal areas, seashore, mudflats, sandflats.
Key birds: *Summer*: Little Tern, Ringed Plover, Oystercatcher. *Winter*: Brent Goose, Shelduck, Twite, Lapland Bunting, Shore Lark, Linnet.
Contact: Lincolnshire Wildlife Trust, Banavallum House, Manor House Street, Horncastle, Lincs LN9 5HF. 01507 526667. www.lincstrust.co.uk e-mail: lincstrust@cix.co.uk

2. FAR INGS

Lincolnshire Wildlife Trust.
Location: TA 011 229 and TA 023 230. Off Far Ings Lane, W of Barton-on-Humber, the last turn off before the Humber Bridge.
Access: Open all year. No dogs. Limited disabled access.

Facilities: Toilets, visitor centre open some weekends and weekdays - not all week. Hides and paths. **Public transport:** None.
Habitat: Chain of flooded clay pits and reedbeds.
Key birds: *Summer*: Marsh Harrier, Bittern, Bearded Tit, Water Rail. *Winter*: Wildfowl (Mallard, Teal, Gadwall, Pochard, Tufted and Ruddy Ducks).
Contact: Lionel Grooby, Far Ings Visitor Centre, Far Ings Road, Barton on Humber DN18 5RG. 01652 634507. e-mail: farings@lincstrust.co.uk www.lincstrust.co.uk

3. FRAMPTON MARSH

RSPB (East Anglia Office).
Location: TR 36 43 85. Four miles SE of Boston. From A16 follow signs to Frampton then Frampton Marsh.
Access: Open at all times. Free.
Facilities: Footpaths, bench, car park, Free information leaflets available (please contact the office), guided walks programme.
Public transport: None.
Habitat: Saltmarsh.
Key birds: *Summer*: Breeding Redshank, passage waders (inc Greenshank, Ruff and Black-tailed Godwit) and Hobby. *Winter*: Hen Harrier, Short-eared Owl, Merlin, dark-bellied Brent Goose, Twite, Golden Plover.
Contact: John Badley, RSPB Lincolnshire Wash Office, 61 Horseshoe Lane, Kirton, Kirton, Boston, Lincs PE20 1LW. 01205 724678. e-mail: john.badley@rspb.org.uk www.rspb.org.uk

4. FREISTON SHORE

RSPB (East Anglia Office).
Location: TF 39 74 24. Four miles E of Boston. From A52 at Haltoft End follow signs to Freiston Shore. **Access:** Open at all times, free.
Facilities: Footpaths, two car parks, bird hide. Free information leaflets available on site, guided walks programme. Bicycle rack.
Public transport: None.
Habitat: Saltmarsh, saline lagoon, mudflats.
Key birds: *Summer*: Breeding waders including Avocets, Little Ringed Plovers and Oystercatchers, Corn Bunting and Tree Sparrow. *Winter*: Lapland Bunting, Twite, dark-bellied Brent Goose, wildfowl, waders, birds of prey including Short-eared Owl and Hen Harrier. *Passage*: Waders, including Curlew Sandpiper and Little Stint. *Autumn:* Occasional seabirds including Arctic and Great Skuas.
Contact: John Badley, RSPB Lincolnshire Wash Office, 61 Horseshoe Lane, Kirton, Boston, Lincs PE20 1LW. 01205 724678. www.rspb.org.uk e-mail: john.badley@rspb.org.uk

5. GIBRALTAR POINT

Lincolnshire Wildlife Trust.
Location: TF 556 580. Three miles S of Skegness on the N edge of The Wash. Signposted from Skegness town centre.
Access: Reserve is open dawn-dusk all year. Seasonal charges for car parking. Free admission to reserve, visitor centre and toilets. Some access restrictions to sensitive sites at S end, open access to N. Dogs on leads at all times - no dogs on beach during summer. Visitor centre and toilets suitable for wheelchairs, as well as network of surfaced foot paths. Bird observatory and four hides suitable for wheelchairs. Day visit groups must be booked in advance. Contact Gibraltar Point Field Station for residential or day visits.
Facilities: Site also location of Wash Study Centre and Bird Observatory. Field centre is an ideal base for birdwatching/natural history groups in spring, summer and autumn. Visitor centre and gift shop open daily (May-Oct) and weekends for remainder of the year. Toilets open daily. Network of foot paths bisect all major habitats. Public hides overlook freshwater and brackish lagoons. Wash viewpoint overlooks saltmarsh and mudflats.
Public transport: Bus service from Skegness runs in occasional years but summer service only. Otherwise taxi/car from Skegness. Cycle route from Skegness.
Habitat: Sand dune grassland and scrub, saltmarshes and mudflats, freshwater marsh and lagoons.
Key birds: Large migration visible during spring and autumn passage - hirundines, chats, pipits, larks, thrushes and occasional rarities. Large numbers of waterfowl including internationally important populations of non-breeding waders. Sept-May impressive wader roosts on high tides. *Summer*: Little Tern and good assemblage of breeding warblers. *Winter*: Shore Lark, raptors, waders and wildfowl.
Contact: Kev Wilson, (Site Manager), Gibraltar Point Field Centre, Gibraltar Road, Skegness, Lincs PE24 4SU. 01754 762677.

6. RIGSBY WOOD

Lincolnshire Wildlife Trust.
Location: TF 421 762. On the A1104 between Ulceby Cross and Alford turn L to South

Lincolnshire

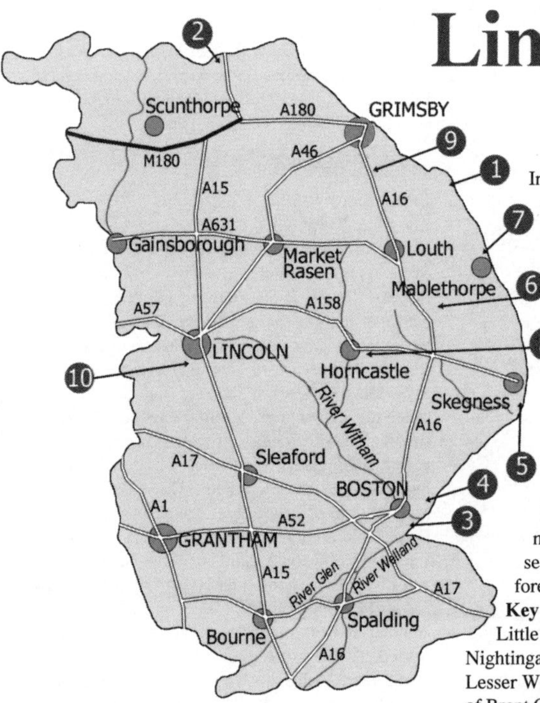

Thoresby. Wood is about two miles on the L. Park on the road. Entrance is down a track from the road.
Access: Open all year.
Facilities: Waymarked route.
Public transport: None.
Habitat: Ancient woodland.
Key birds: *Spring/summer*: Chiffchaff, Garden Warbler, Blackcap, Whitethroat, Cuckoo, Great-spotted Woodpecker, Treecreeper, Tawny Owl. *Autumn/winter*: Woodcock, Redpoll.
Contact: Trust HQ. 01507 526 667.

7. SALTFLEETBY-THEDDLETHORPE DUNES

English Nature (East Midlands Team).
Location: TF 46 59 24-TF 49 08 83. Approx two miles N of Mablethorpe. All the following car parks may be accessed from the A1031: Crook Bank, Brickyard Lane, Churchill Lane, Rimac, Sea View
Access: Open all year at all times. Dogs on leads. A purpose-built easy access trail suitable for wheelchair users starts adjacent to Rimac car park, just over 0.5 miles long meanders past ponds. Includes pond-viewing platform and saltmarsh-viewing platform.
Facilities: Toilets, including wheelchair suitability at Rimac car park (next to trail) May to end of Sept.
Public transport: Grayscroft coaches (01507 473236) and Lincolnshire Roadcar (01522 532424). Both run services past Rimac entrance (Louth to Mablethorpe service). Lincs Roadcar can connect with trains at Lincoln. Applebys Coaches (01507 357900). Grimsby to Saltfleet bus connects with Grimsby train service.
Habitat: 13th Century dunes, freshwater marsh, new dune ridge with large areas of sea blackthorn, saltmarsh, shingle ridge and foreshore.
Key birds: *Summer*: Small breeding colony of Little Terns. Breeding birds in scrub include Nightingale, Grasshopper Warbler, Whitethroat, Lesser Whitethroat, Redpoll. *Winter*: Large flocks of Brent Goose, Shelduck, Teal and Wigeon. Wintering Short-eared Owl, Hen Harrier.
Contact: Simon Cooter, English Nature, 78 High Street, Boston, Lincs PE21 8SX. 01205 311674. e-mail: simon.cooter@english-nature.org.uk

8. SNIPE DALES NATURE RESERVE

Lincolnshire Wildlife Trust.
Location: TF 319 683 (nature reserve) and TF 330 682 (country park). Well signposted off the A158 Skegness-Lincoln Road and from the B1195 Horncastle-Spilsby road.
Access: Open all year. Dogs on leads allowed in country park but not in the nature reserve. Car park charge. Some disabled access.
Facilities: Toilets, interpretation boards, one small hide, footpaths.
Public transport: Restricted bus service.
Habitat: Nature reserve – steep-sided valleys fretted by streams. Unspoilt wet-valley system. Country park – attractive walks through coniferous woodland, new plantings of broad-leaved trees, plus ponds.
Key birds: *Spring/summer*: Chaffinch, Redpoll, Willow Warbler, Willow Tit, Long-tailed Tit, Siskin, Tawny Owl, Barn Owl, Grasshopper Warbler. *Winter*: Woodcock.

Contact: Peter Graves, Snipe Dales Country Park, Lusby, Spilsby PE23 4JB. 01507 588401. www.lincstrust.co.uk

9. TETNEY MARSHES

RSPB (North of England Office).0191 281 3366.

10. WHISBY NATURE PARK

Lincolnshire Wildlife Trust.
Location: SK 914 661. W of Lincoln off A46 southern end of Lincoln relief road. Brown tourist signs.
Access: Nature Park open dawn to dusk. Consult notice board at entrance. Car park closed out of hours. Free entry. Natural World Visitor Centre open (10am-5pm), free entry. Some special exhibitions will have a charge. Disabled access. Dogs on leads.
Facilities: Toilets, visitor centre, café, education centre, waymarked routes, interpretation signs, leaflets.
Public transport: No. 65 bus Mon-Sat from Lincoln to Thorpe-on-the-Hill (1/4 mile away).
Habitat: Flooded sand and gravel pits.
Key birds: *Summer*: Common Tern on specially-built rafts, Nightingale, Whitethroat, Lesser Whitethroat, Tree Sparrow. *Winter*: Wigeon, Teal, Pochard, Tufted Duck, Goldeneye.
Contact: Phil Porter, Whisby Nature Park, Moor Lane, Thorpe-on-the-Hill, Lincoln LN6 9BW. 01522 500676. www.lincstrust.co.uk
e-mail: whisby@cix.co.uk

London, Greater

1. BATTERSEA PARK NR

London Wildlife Trust.
Location: TQ 284 775. Two entrances on Queenstown Road.
Access: Open daily when park is open.
Facilities: None.
Public transport: Battersea Park or Queenstown Road stations.
Habitat: Woodland, parkland, scrub.
Key birds: *All year*: usual woodland species.
Contact: London Wildlife Trust, Harling House, 47-51 Great Suffolk Street, London SE1 0BS. 0207 261 0447. e-mail: enquiries@wildlondon.org.uk www.wildlondon.org.uk

2. BEDFONT LAKES COUNTRY PARK

Ecology and Countryside Parks Service.
Location: TQ 080 728. OS map sheet 176 (west London). 0.5 miles from Ashford, Middx, 0.5 miles S of A30, Clockhouse Roundabout, on B3003 (Clockhouse Lane).
Access: Open 7.30am-9pm or dusk whichever is earlier, all days except Christmas Day. Disabled friendly. Dogs on leads. Main nature reserve area only open Sun (2pm-4pm).
Facilities: Toilets, information centre, several hides, nature trail, free parking, up-to-date information.
Public transport: Train to Feltham and Ashford. Bus - H26 and 116 from Hounslow.
Habitat: Lakes, wildflower meadows, woodland, scrub.
Key birds: *Winter*: Water Rail, Bittern, Smew and other wildfowl, Meadow Pipit. *Summer*: Common Tern, Willow, Garden, Reed and Sedge Warblers, Whitethroat, Lesser Whitethroat, hirundines, Hobby, Blackcap, Chiffchaff, Skylark. *Passage*: Wheatear, Wood Warbler, Spotted Flycatcher, Ring Ouzel, Redstart, Yellow Wagtail.
Contact: Paul Morgan (Ecology Ranger), BLCP, Clockhouse Lane, Bedfont, Middx TW14 8QA. 01784 423556; Fax: 01784 423451.
e-mail: bedfont-lakes@cip.org.uk

3. BRAMLEY PARK

London Wildlife Trust.
Location: TQ 352 634. Entrance off Riesco Drive, or off Broadcombe, Croydon.
Access: Open all year.
Facilities: None.
Public transport: South Croydon British Rail.
Habitat: Oak/sycamore woodland, large pond, acidic grassland and heath.
Key birds: *All year:* Usual woodland species.
Contact: London Wildlife Trust, Harling House, 47-51 Great Suffolk Street, London SE1 0BS. 0207 261 0447. e-mail: enquiries@wildlondon.org.uk www.wildlondon.org.uk

4. CAMLEY STREET NATURAL PARK

London Wildlife Trust.
Location: From Kings Cross Station drive or walk up Pancras Road between Kings Cross and St Pancras Stations. At the junction under a railway bridge turn R into Goods Way. Turn L into Camley Street and follow the telegraph pole fence to the large wrought-iron gates.
Access: Weekdays (9am-5pm), weekends (11am-5pm). Closed Fri. **Facilities:** Path.
Public transport: Nearest train/tube: Kings Cross, St Pancras.
Habitat: Woodland scrub, reedbeds, meadow, pond.
Key birds: *Spring/summer*: Warblers. *All year*: Mallard, Tufted Duck, Moorhen, Grey Heron. *Winter*: Siskin, Reed Warbler. *All year*: Sparrowhawk. Good for dragonflies.
Contact: London Wildlife Trust, Harling House, 47-51 Great Suffolk Street, London, SE1 0BS, 0207 2610447. www.wildlondon.org.uk e-mail: enquiries@wildlondon.org.uk

5. CHASE (THE) LNR

London Wildlife Trust.
Location: TQ 515 860. Lies in the Dagenham Corridor, an area of green belt between the London Boroughs of Barking & Dagenham and Havering.
Access: Open throughout the year and at all times. Reserve not suitable for wheelchair access. Eastbrookend Country Park which borders The Chase LNR has surfaced footpaths for wheelchairs.
Facilities: Millennium visitor centre, toilets, ample car parking, Timberland Trail walk.
Public transport: Rail Dagenham East (District Line) 15 minute walk. Bus 174 from Romford five minute walk.
Habitat: Shallow wetlands, reedbeds, horse-grazed pasture, scrub and wetland. These harbour an impressive range of animals and plants including the nationally rare black poplar tree. This site is a haven for birds, with approx 190 different species recorded here over the years.
Key birds: *Summer*: Breeding Reed Warbler, Lapwing, Water Rail, Lesser Whitethroat and Little Ringed Plover, Kingfisher, Reed Bunting. *Winter*: Significant numbers of Teal, Shoveler, Redwing, Fieldfare and Snipe dominate the scene. *Spring/autumn migration*: Yellow Wagtail, Wheatear, Ruff, Wood Sandpiper, Sand Martin, Ring Ouzel, Black Redstart and Hobby regular.
Contact: Gareth Winn/Tom Clarke, Project Manager/Project Officer, The Millennium Centre, The Chase, Off Dagenham Road, Rush Green, Romford, Essex RM7 0SS. 020 8593 8096. e-mail: lwtchase@cix.co.uk www.wildlifetrust.org.uk/london/

6. RIPPLE NATURE RESERVE

London Wildlife Trust/Thames Water.
Location: TQ 167 757. About eight miles from the centre of London, next to Thamesmead Park City Farm on the Thames Road/Renwick.
Access: Open all year. **Facilities:** None
Public transport: Bus: to the end of route in Thames View Estate. Tube: Barking/District Line.
Habitat: Meadow, roughland, reeds, copse, water.
Key birds: *Spring/summer*: Warblers inc Reed Warbler, migrants. *All year*: Kingfisher, Chaffinch, woodpeckers, usual woodland species.
Contact: London Wildlife Trust, Harling House, 47-51 Great Suffolk Street, London, SE1 0BS, 0207 2610447. www.wildlondon.org.uk e-mail: enquiries@wildlondon.org.uk

7. SYDENHAM HILL WOOD

London Wildlife Trust.
Location: TQ 335 722. SE London, SE26, between Forest Hill and Crystal Palace, just off South Circular (A205).
Access: Open at all times, no permits required. Some slopes make disabled access limited
Facilities: Nature trail, no toilets.
Public transport: Train - Sydenham Hill, Forest Hill. Bus - 63, 202, 356, 185, 312, 176.
Habitat: Oak and hornbeam woodland, small pond, meadow and glades.
Key birds: *Resident*: Kestrel, Sparrowhawk, Tawny Owl, all three woodpeckers, Treecreeper, Nuthatch, Song Thrush. *Summer*: Chiffchaff, Blackcap. *Winter*: Redwing, Fieldfare.
Contact: The Warden, London Wildlife Trust, Horniman Museum, 100 London Road, London SE23 3PQ. 020 8699 5698. e-mail: lwtsydenham@cix.co.uk www.wildlifetrust.org.uk/london

8. LONDON WETLAND CENTRE

The Wildfowl & Wetlands Trust.
Location: TQ 228 770. In London, Zone 2, one mile from Hammersmith.
Access: Winter (9.30am-5pm: last admission 4pm), summer (9.30am-6pm: last admission 5pm). Charge for admission.
Facilities: Visitor centre, hides, nature trails, art gallery, discovery restaurant (hot and cold food),

cinema, shop, observatory centre, seven hides (one with a lift for wheelchair access), three interpretative buildings.
Public transport: Train: Barnes. Tube: hammersmith then Duckbus 283 (comes into centre). Bus from Hammersmith - 283, 33, 72, 209. Bus from Richmond 33, 72.
Habitat: Main lake, reedbeds, wader scrape, mudflats, open water lakes, grazing marsh.
Key birds: Nationally important numbers of wintering waterfowl including Gadwall and Shoveler. Important numbers of wetland breeding birds including grebes, swans, a range of duck species, such as Pochard, plus Lapwing, Little Ringed Plover, Redshank, warblers and Reed Bunting.
Contact: John Arbon (Grounds and Facilities Manager), Stephanie Fudge (Manager), London Wetland Centre, Queen Elizabeth Walk, Barnes, London SW13 9WT. 0208 409 4400.
e-mail: info.london@wwt.org.uk
www.wwt.org.uk

Manchester, Greater

1. ASTLEY MOSS

The Wildlife Trust for Lancashire, Manchester and North Merseyside
Location: Lancs WT SJ692975. S of A580 at Astley; follow Higher Green Lane to Rindle Farm.
Access: Permit from Trust required.
Facilities: None. **Public transport:** None.
Habitat: Remnant peat bog, scrub, oak/birch woodland.
Key birds: *Spring/summer*: Breeding Tree Pipit. *Winter*: Raptors (inc. Merlin, Hen Harrier), finch flocks, thrush flocks; Long- and Short-eared Owls.
Contact: Dave Woodward, 54 Windermere Road, Leigh, Lancs WN7 1UZ.

2. AUDENSHAW RESERVOIRS

United Utilities, Bottoms Office.
Location: NW Water SJ915965. Access and parking on Audenshaw Road B6390 at N of site.
Access: No disabled access.
Facilities: Hide (contact R Travis on 0161 330 2607). Permit (free) from D Tomes, UU Bottoms Office, Woodhead Road, Tintwistle, Glossop SK13 1HS. **Public transport:** None.
Habitat: Reservoir.
Key birds: Major migration point. *Winter*: Notable gull roost inc. regular Mediterranean Gull; large Goosander roost; many rarities.

3. DOVESTONES RESERVOIR.

Location: E of Oldham. From A635, look for sign on R having passed through Greenfield. Park at bottom of dam.
Access: Open all year.
Facilities: Several easy uphill paths. Toilets at Peak District NP office. Limited access for disabled. **Public transport:** None.
Habitat: Reservoir, moorland.
Key birds: *Spring/summer*: Ring Ouzel, Twite, Peregrine, Raven, Stonechat, Whinchat, Wheatear, Dipper, Common Sandpiper. Possibility of Redstart and Crossbill. *All year*: Wildfowl.

4. ETHEROW COUNTRY PARK

Stockport Metropolitan Borough Council.
Location: SJ 965 908. B6104 into Compstall near Romiley, Stockport.
Access: Open at all times; permit required for conservation area. Keep to paths.
Facilities: Reserve area has SSSI status. Hide, nature trail, visitor centre, scooters for disabled.
Public transport: None.
Habitat: River Etherow, woodlands, marshy area.
Key birds: Sparrowhawk, Buzzard, Dipper, all three woodpeckers, Pied Flycatcher, warblers. *Winter*: Brambling, Siskin, Water Rail. Frequent sightings of Merlin and Raven over hills.
Contact: John Rowland, Etherow Country Park, Compstall, Stockport, Cheshire SK6 5JD. 0161 427 6937; fax 0161 427 3643.

5. HOLLINGWORTH LAKE

Hollingworth Lake Country Park - Rochdale MBC.
Location: SD 939 153 (visitor centre). Four miles NE of Rochdale, signed from A58 Halifax Road. Near J21 of M62 - B6225 to Littleborough.
Access: Access open to lake and surroundings at all times.
Facilities: Cafes, hide, trails and education service, car parks. Visitor centre open 10.30am-6pm (Mon-Fri), 10.30am-7pm (Sat & Sun) in summer, 11am-4pm (Mon-Fri), 10.30am-5pm (Sat & Sun) in winter.
Public transport: Bus Nos 452, 450. Train to

Manchester, Greater

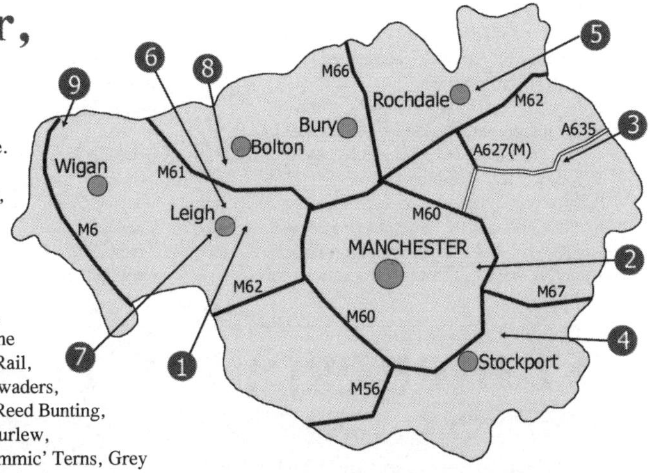

Littleborough or Smithy Bridge.
Habitat: Lake (116 acres includes 20 acre nature reserve), woodland, streams, marsh, willow scrub.
Key birds: *All year*: Great Crested Grebe, Kingfisher, Lapwing, Little Owl, Bullfinch, Cormorant. Occasional Peregrine Falcon, Sedge Warbler, Water Rail, Snipe. *Spring/autumn*: Passage waders, wildfowl, Kittiwake. *Summer*: Reed Bunting, Dipper, Common Sandpiper, Curlew, Oystercatcher, Black Tern, 'Commic' Terns, Grey Partridge, Blackcap. *Winter*: Goosander, Goldeneye, Siskin, Redpoll, Golden Plover.
Contact: The Ranger, Hollingworth Lake Visitor Centre, Rakewood Road, Littleborough, OL15 0AQ01706 373421.
e-mail: holl.lakecp@rochdale.gov.uk

6. HOPE CARR NATURE RESERVE

NW Water.
Location: SJ 664 986. In Leigh, W of Salford. From A580 E Lancs Road turn N at Greyhound Motel roundabout, L at first lights, first L at mini roundabout. **Access:** Open all year.
Facilities: Free parking, disabled access. Hide (access by prior arrangement).
Public transport: Not known.
Habitat: Purpose-built scrapes and lake adjoining sludge lagoons of Leigh ETW.
Key birds: Wide variety of breeding and wintering wildfowl; excellent for passage waders; wintering Water Pipit, Green Sandpiper.
Contact: Joe Grima, Leigh Environmental, Education Centre, Hope Carr, Hope Carr Lane, Leigh WN7 3XB. 01942 269027; fax 01942 269028; mobile 0790 9996272.

7. PENNINGTON FLASH CP

Wigan Leisure and Culture Trust
Location: SJ 640 990. One mile from Leigh town centre. Main entrance on A572 (St Helens Road).
Access: Park is signposted from A580 (East Lancs Road) and is permanently open. Four largest hides, toilets and information point open 9am-dusk (except Christmas Day). Main paths flat and suitable for disabled.
Facilities: Toilets including disabled toilet and information point. Total of seven bird hides. Site leaflet available and Rangers based on site. Group visits welcome, guided tours or a site introduction can be arranged subject to staff availability.
Public transport: Only 1 mile from Leigh bus station. Several services stop on St Helens Road near entrance to park. Contact GMPTE 0161 228 7811.
Habitat: Lake, ponds and scrapes, fringed with reeds, rough grassland, scrub and woodland.
Key birds: Waterfowl all year, waders mainly passage spring and autumn (14-plus species). Breeding Common Tern and Little Ringed Plover. Feeding station attracts Willow Tit and Bullfinch all year.
Contact: Peter Alker, Pennington Flash Country Park, St Helens Road, Leigh WN7 3PA. 01942 605253 (Also fax number).

8. RUMWORTH LODGE.

The Wildlife Trust for Lancashire, Manchester and North Merseyside
Location: SD 685 074. From J5 of M61, take A58 towards Bolton. Head N on ring road, (Beaumont Road with ample parking). Lodge is over not-too-obvious stile on the crown of the slight hill, on S side of lights. **Access:** Open all year.
Facilities: None. Not suitable for the disabled.
Public transport: None.
Habitat: Shallow reservoir, farmland.
Key birds: *Summer*: Oystercatcher, Little Ringed Plover. *All year*: wildfowl. *Passage*: Possible recent rarities inc Avocet, Little Egret and Purple Sandpiper.

Contact: Trust HQ. 01772 324129. e-mail: lancswt@cix.co.uk www.wildlifetrust.org.uk/

9. WIGAN FLASHES

Lancashire Wildlife Trust/Wigan Council/RSPB.
Location: SD 580 035. One mile from J25 of M6.
Access: Free access, open at all times. Areas suitable for disabled but some motor cycle barriers with gates. Paths being upgraded.
Facilities: None.
Public transport: 610 bus (Hawkley Hall Circular).
Habitat: Wetland with reedbed.
Key birds: Black Tern on migration. *Summer*: Nationally important for Reed Warbler and breeding Common Tern. Willow Tit, Grasshopper Warbler, Kingfisher. *Winter*: Wildfowl especially diving duck and Gadwall. Bittern (especially winter).
Contact: Mark Champion, 225 Poolstock Lane, Wigan, Lancs WN3 5JE. 01942 236337. e-mail: mark@championx.freeserve.co.uk

Merseyside

1. AINSDALE & BIRKDALE LNR

Sefton Council.
Location: SD 300 115. SD 310 138. Leave the A565 just N of Formby. Car parking areas are off the coastal road.
Access: Track from Ainsdale or Southport along the shore. Wheelchair access across boardwalks at Ainsdale Sands Lake Nature Trail and the Queen's Jubilee Nature Trail, opposite Weld Road.
Facilities: Ainsdale Visitor Centre open summer. Toilets (Easter-Oct).
Public transport: Ainsdale and Southport stations 20 minute walk. Hillside Station is a 30 minute walk across the Birkdale Sandhills to beach.
Habitat: Foreshore, dune scrub and pines .
Key birds: *Spring/summer*: Grasshopper Warbler, Chiffchaff, waders. *Winter*: Blackcap, Stonechat, Redwing, Fieldfare, waders and wildfowl. *All year*: Skylark, Grey Partridge.
Contact: Sefton Council, Southport Town Hall, Lord Street, Southport, PR8 1DA, www.sefton.gov.uk

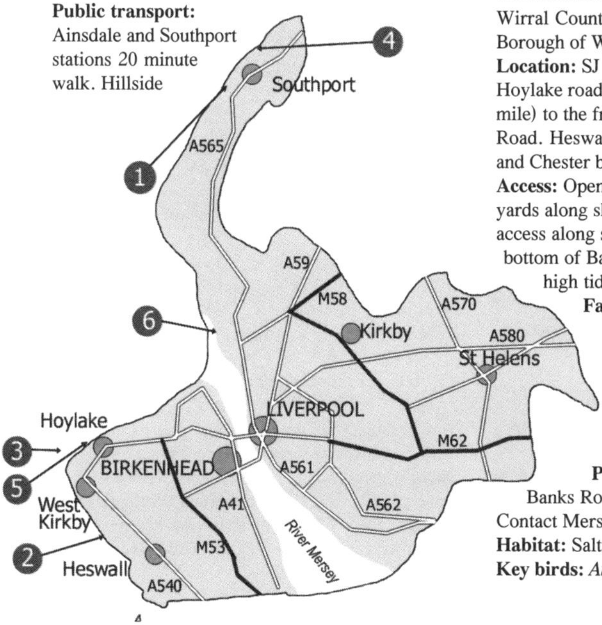

2. DEE ESTUARY

Wirral Country Park Centre (Metropolitan Borough of Wirral).
Location: SJ 255 815. Leave A540 Chester to Hoylake road at Heswall and head downhill (one mile) to the free car park at the shore end of Banks Road. Heswall is 30 minutes from South Liverpool and Chester by car.
Access: Open at all times. Best viewpoint 600 yards along shore N of Banks Road. No disabled access along shore, but good birdwatching from bottom of Banks Road. Arrive 2.5 hours before high tide.
Facilities: Toilets in car park and information board. Wirral Country Park Centre three miles N off A540 has toilets, hide, café, kiosk (all accessible to wheelchairs). Birdwatching events programme available from visitor centre.
Public transport: Bus service to Banks Road car park from Heswall bus station. Contact Mersey Travel (tel 0151 236 7676).
Habitat: Saltmarsh and mudflats.
Key birds: *Autumn/winter*: Large passage and

winter wader roosts - Redshank, Curlew, Black-tailed Godwit, Oystercatcher, Golden Plover, Knot, Shelduck, Teal, Red-breasted Merganser, Peregrine, Merlin, Hen Harrier, Short-eared Owl. Smaller numbers of Pintail, Wigeon, Bar-tailed Godwit, Greenshank, Spotted Redshank, Grey and Ringed Plovers, Whimbrel, Curlew Sandpiper, Little Stint, occasional Scaup and Little Egret.
Contact: Martyn Jamieson, Head Ranger, Wirral Country Park Centre, Station Road, Thustaston, Wirral, Merseyside CH61 0HN. 0151 648 4371/ 3884. e-mail: wirralcountrypark@wirral.gov.uk www.wirral.gov.uk/leisure/ranger

3. HILBRE ISLANDS LNR

Wirral Country Park Centre (Metropolitan Borough of Wirral).
Location: SJ 184 880. Three tidal islands in the mouth of the Dee Estuary. Park in West Kirby which is on the A540 Chester-to-Hoylake road - 30 minutes from Liverpool, 45 minutes from Chester. Follow the brown Marine Lake signs to Dee Lane pay and display car park.
Access: Two mile walk across the sands from Dee Lane slipway. No disabled access. Do not cross either way within 3.5 hours of high water - tide times and suggested safe route on noticeboard at slipway. Prior booking and permit needed for parties of six or more - max. of 50. Book early.
Facilities: Toilets at Marine Lake and Hilbre (primitive!). Permits, leaflets and tide times from Wirral Country Park Centre. Hilbre Bird Observatory (details as before).
Public transport: Bus and train station (from Liverpool) within 0.5 mile of Dee Lane slipway. Contact Mersey Travel, tel 0151 236 7676.
Habitat: Sandflats, rocky shore and open sea.
Key birds: *Late summer/autumn*: Seabird passage - Gannets, terns, skuas, shearwaters and after NW gales good numbers of Leach's Petrel. *Winter*: Wader roosts at high tide, Purple Sandpiper, Turnstone, sea ducks, divers, grebes. Passage migrants.
Contact: Martyn Jamieson, Head Ranger, Wirral Country Park Centre, Station Road, Thustaston, Wirral, Merseyside CH61 0HN. 0151 648 4371/ 3884. e-mail: wirralcountrypark@wirral.gov.uk

4. MARSHSIDE

RSPB (North West England Office).
Location: SD 355 202. On south shore of Ribble Estuary, one mile north of Southport centre on Marine Drive.
Access: Open 8.30am-5pm all year. No toilets. No dogs please. Coach parties please book in advance. No charges but donations welcomed.
Facilities: Two hides and trails accessible to wheelchairs.
Public transport: Bus service to Elswick Road/ Marshside Road half-hourly, bus No 44. Contact Southport Buses (01704 536137).
Habitat: Coastal grazing marsh and lagoons.
Key birds: *Winter*: Pink-footed Goose, wildfowl, waders, raptors. *Spring*: Breeding waders and wildfowl, Garganey, migrants. *Autumn*: Migrants. *All year*: Black-tailed Godwit.
Contact: Tony Baker, RSPB, Beechwood, Cat Tail Lane, Scarisbrick, Southport PR8 5LW. 01704 233003. e-mail: tony.baker@rspb.org.uk

5. RED ROCKS MARSH

Cheshire Wildlife Trust.
Location: SJ 206 880. Six miles W of Birkenhead immediately W of Hoylake and adjacent to the Dee estuary.
Access: Open all year.**Facilities:** Car park, hide.
Public transport: None.
Habitat: Sand dune, reedbed.
Key birds: *Spring/summer*: wildfowl, warblers. *Passage*: finches, Snow Bunting, thrushes.
Contact: Cheshire Wildlife Trust, Grebe House, Reaseheath, Nantwich, Cheshire CW5 6DG01270 610 180. e-mail: cheshirewt@cix.co.uk www.wildlifetrust.org.uk/cheshire/

6. SEAFORTH NATURE RESERVE

The Wildlife Trust for Lancashire, Manchester and North Merseyside
Location: SJ 315 970. Five miles from Liverpool city centre. From M57/M58 take A5036 to docks.
Access: Open dawn-dusk daily. £1 donation expected. No dogs. Difficult for wheelchairs.
Facilities: Toilets when visitor centre open, three hides.
Public transport: Train to Waterloo or Seaforth stations from Liverpool. Buses to dock gates from Liverpool.
Habitat: Saltwater and freshwater lagoons, scrub grassland.
Key birds: Little Gull on passage (Apr) plus Roseate, Little and Black Terns. Breeding and passage Common Tern (Apr-Sept) plus Roseate, Little and Black Terns on passage. Passage and winter waders and gulls. Passage passerines, especially White Wagtail, pipits and Wheatear.
Contact: Steve White, Seaforth Nature Reserve, Port of Liverpool, L21 1JD0151 9203769. e-mail: lwildlife@cix.co.uk

Norfolk

1. NWT CLEY MARSHES

Norfolk Wildlife Trust.
Location: TG 054 441. NWT Cley Marshes is situated three miles N of Holt on A149 coast road, half a mile E of Cley-next-the-Sea. Visitor centre and car park on inland side of the road.
Access: Open all year round. Visitor centre open Apr-Oct (10am-5pm daily), Nov-mid Dec (10am-4pm Wed-Sun). Cost: adults £3.75, children under 16 free. NWT members free.
Facilities: Visitor centre, birdwatching hides, wildlife gift shop, refreshments, toilets, coach parking, car park, disabled access to centre, boardwalk and hides and toilets, groups welcome.
Public transport: Bus service from Norwich, Fakenham and Holt Mon-Sat. The Coasthopper service stops outside daily. Connections for train and bus services at Sheringham. Special discounts to visitors arriving by bus.
Habitat: Reedbeds, salt and freshwater marshes, scrapes and shingle ridge. One of the finest birdwatching sites in Britain.
Key birds: *Feb:* Brent Goose, warblers, Wigeon, Teal, Mallard, Shoveler, Pintail. *Spring*: Chiffchaff, Wheatear, Sandwich Tern, Reed and Sedge Warblers, Ruff, Black-tailed Godwit. *Jun*: Spoonbill, Avocet, Bittern, Bearded Tit. *Autumn*: Green and Wood Sandpiper, Greenshank, Whimbrel, Little Ringed Plover.
Contact: Dick Bagnall, Oakeley Centre, NWT Cley Marshes, Cley, Holt, Norfolk NR25 7RZ. 01263 740008. e-mail BernardB@nwt.cix.co.uk www.wildlifetrust.org.uk.Norfolk

2. NWT COCKSHOOT BROAD

Norfolk Wildlife Trust.
Location: TG 344 165. Eight miles NE of Norwich. From B1140 Acle-Wroxham road, follow signs for Woodbastwick. Head E to Ranworth. On a sharp R bend, go straight down a narrow road signed 'River Only'. There is a small car park at the bottom.
Access: Open all year. **Facilities:** Car park, paths.
Public transport: None.
Habitat: Part of Bure Marshes NNR. Marshes, woodland, river.
Key birds: *Spring/summer*: Reed Warbler, possible Cetti's Warbler, Blackcap, Garden Warbler, Marsh Tit, hirundines Common Tern, Cuckoo, hirundines. *All year*: Wildfowl, common woodland birds.
Contact: Norfolk Wildlife Trust, Bewick House, 22 Thorpe Road, Norwich NR1 1UD. 01603 625 540. e-mail: admin@nwt.cix.co.uk www.wildlifetrust.org.uk/norfolk

3. NWT EAST WRETHAM HEATH

Norfolk Wildlife Trust.
Location: TL 913 887. Site lies in the centre of Breckland N of Thetford. From A11 take turning for A1075 to Watton and travel for about two miles over the level crossing and pass the lay-by to the left. Car park and entrance to reserve are by the first house on the left.
Access: Open all year dawn to dusk.
Facilities: Car park. Trail, hide.
Public transport: None.
Habitat: Breckland grass heath and meres, scrub and woodland.
Key birds: Wildfowl, wading birds, Redstart, Wood Lark.
Contact: Bev Nichols, Norfolk Wildlife Trust, Bewick house, 22 Thorpe Road, Norwich. NR1 1RY. 01603 625540.
e-mail BevN@norfolkwildlifetrust.co.uk

4. NWT HICKLING BROAD

Norfolk Wildlife Trust.
Contact: John Blackburn, Hickling Broad Visitor Centre, Stubb Road, Hickling NR12 0BN.
e-mail johnb@norfolkwildlifetrust.co.uk
www.wildlifetrust.org.uk/norfolk

5. NWT FOXLEY WOOD

Norfolk Wildlife Trust. 01603 625540.

6. HOLKHAM

English Nature (Norfolk Team). 01328 711183; fax 01328 711893.

7. HOLME BIRD OBSERVATORY

Norfolk Ornithologist's Association (NOA).
Location: TF 717 450. E of Hunstanton, signposted from A149. Access from Broadwater Road.
Access: Reserve open daily to members dawn to dusk; non-members (9am-5pm) by permit from the Observatory. Please keep dogs on leads in the reserve. Parties by prior arrangement.
Facilities: Visitor centre, car park and several

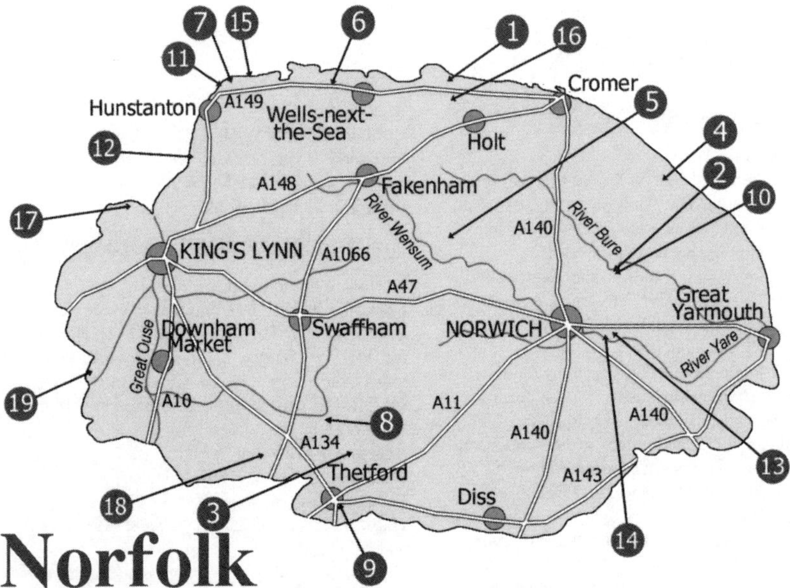

Norfolk

hides (seawatch hide reserved for NOA members) together with access to beach and coastal path.
Public transport: Coastal bus service runs from Hunstanton to Sheringham roughly every 30mins but is seasonal and times may vary. Phone Norfolk Green Bus, 01553 776 980.
Habitat: In 10 acres of diverse habitat: sand dunes, Corsican pines, scrub and reed-fringed lagoon making this a migration hotspot.
Key birds: Species list over 320. Ringed species over 150. Recent rarities include Common Crane, Red-footed Falcon, Barred Warbler, Red-breasted Flycatcher, Red-backed and Great Grey Shrikes.
Contact: Jed Andrews, Holme Bird Observatory, Broadwater Road, Holme, Hunstanton, Norfolk PE36 6LQ. 01485 525406. www.noa.org.uk
e-mail: jedandrews@shrike4.freeserve.co.uk

8. LYNFORD ARBORETUM

Forest Enterprise.
Location: TL 821 943, TL 818 935. On Downham Market-Thetford road on A134. At Mundford roundabout, follow signs to Swaffham. Take first R to Lynford Hall. Follow road past hall to car park on L. Disabled drivers can turn R. Alternatively, from roundabout head S towards Thetford. Take minor road signed L almost immediately to Lynford Lakes.
Access: Open all year. **Facilities:** Two car parks. Suitable for wheelchairs.
Habitat: Plantations, arboretum, lake.
Key birds: *Spring/summer*: Possible Wood Lark, Tree Pipit, possible Nightjar, Kingfisher, waterfowl. *Winter*: Crossbill, possible Hawfinch. *All year*: usual woodland species, woodpeckers.
Contact: Forest Enterprise, Santon Downham. Brandon, Suffolk IP27 0TJ. 01832 810 271.

9. NUNNERY LAKES

British Trust for Ornithology.
Location: TL 873 815. On S edge of Thetford, adjacent to BTO's headquarters at The Nunnery, off Nun's Bridges Road. Main access point is about 60 yards upriver of Nun's Bridges car park (TL 874 825) on the opposite side of the River Little Ouse.
Access: Open during daylight hours. BTO authorisation required for access to other parts of the reserve. Dogs on leads at all times.
Facilities: Waymarked paths with information panels, bird hide. No toilets or visitors centre.
Public transport: Various bus services to Thetford Bus Terminal, off Bridge Street (about a ten minute walk to site alongside river).
Key birds: *Spring*: Passage waders, Little Ringed Plover, Wheatear. *Summer*: Hobby, breeding Oystercatcher and Lapwing, Sky Lark, warblers. *Winter*: Water Rail, Snipe, Goosander, Gadwall, Siskin, Lesser Redpoll, Hawfinch.
Contact: 01842 750050. www.bto.org
e-mail: chris.gregory@bto.org

10. NWT RANWORTH BROAD

Norfolk Wildlife Trust. 01603 625540.

11. REDWELL MARSH

Norfolk Ornithologist's Association (NOA).
Location: TF 702 436. In Holme, off A149, E of Hunstanton. Access from Broadwater road.
Access: View from public footpath from centre of Holme village to Broadwater Road. Open at all times. **Facilities:** Member's hide, offering wheelchair access, (access from Broadwater road).
Public transport: As for Holme Bird Obs.
Habitat: Wet grazing marsh with ditches, pond and two large wader scrapes.
Key birds: Wildfowl and waders, inc. Curlew/Green/Wood and Pectoral Sandpipers, Greenshank, Spotted Redshank, Avocet and Black-tailed Godwit. Recent sightings include Little Egret, Arctic Skua, Temminck's Stint, Ring Ouzel and Grasshopper Warbler and Nightjar. Also a raptor flight path.
Contact: Jed Andrews, Holme Bird Observatory, Broadwater Road, Holme, Hunstanton, Norfolk PE36 6LQ. 01485 525406. www.noa.org.uk
e-mail: jedandrews@shrike4.freeserve.co.uk

12. SNETTISHAM

RSPB (East Anglia Office).
Location: TF 630 310. Car park two miles along Beach road, signposted off A149 King's Lynn to Hunstanton, opposite Snettisham village.
Access: Open at all times. £2 car parking fee for non-members. Dogs to be kept on leads. Two hides are suitable for wheelchairs. Disabled access is across a private road. Please phone office number for permission and directions.
Facilities: Four birdwatching hides, connected by reserve footpath. No toilets on site.
Public transport: Nearest over two miles away.
Habitat: Intertidal mudflats, saltmarsh, shingle beach, brackish lagoons, and unimproved grassland/scrub. Best visited on a high tide.
Key birds: *Autumn/winter/spring*: Waders (particularly Knot, Bar and Black-tailed Godwits, Dunlin, Grey Plover), wildfowl (particularly Pink-footed and Brent Geese, Wigeon, Gadwall, Goldeneye), Peregrine, Hen Harrier, Merlin, owls. Migrants in season. *Summer*: Breeding Ringed Plover, Redshank, Avocet, Common Tern. Marsh Harrier regular.
Contact: Jim Scott, RSPB, 43 Lynn Road, Snettisham, King's Lynn,Norfolk PE31 7LR. 01485 542689.

13. STRUMPSHAW FEN

RSPB (East Anglia Office).
Location: TG 33 06. Seven miles ESE of Norwich. Follow signposts. Entrance across level-crossing from car park, reached by turning sharp right and right again into Low Road from Brundall, off A47 to Great Yarmouth.
Access: Open dawn-dusk. Non RSPB adults £2.50, children 50p, family £5. Guide dogs only. Viewing platform for wheelchair users.
Facilities: Toilets, reception hide and two other hides, two walks, five miles of trails.
Public transport: Brundall train station one mile. Bus stop 0.5 mile – NORBIC (0845 300 6116).
Habitat: Reedbed, wet grassland and woodland.
Key birds: *Summer*: Bittern, Bearded Tit, Marsh Harrier, Cetti's Warbler and other reedbed birds. *Winter*: Bittern, wildfowl, Marsh and Hen Harrier. Swallowtails in Jun.
Contact: Tim Strudwick, Staithe Cottage, Low Road, Strumpshaw, Norwich, Norfolk NR13 4HS. 01603 715191. www.rspb.org.uk
e-mail: strumpshaw@rspb.org.uk

14. SURLINGHAM CHURCH MARSH

RSPB (East Anglia Office). 01603 715191.
e-mail: strumpshaw@rspb.org.uk

15. TITCHWELL MARSH

RSPB (East Anglia Office).
Location: TF 749 436. Near Hunstanton. Footpath along sea wall from A149 between Thornham and Titchwell.
Access: Fen and meadow trails are new additions allowing further access to the reserve. Reserve and hides open at all times.
Facilities: Visitor centre, shop with large selection of binoculars, telescopes and books, open every day 9.30am to 5pm (Nov 15 - Feb 16 2005, 9.30 to 4pm). Our new tearoom is open from 9.30am to 4.30pm every date (Nov 15 - Feb 16 2005, 9.30am to 4pm). Visitor centre and tearoom closed on Christmas day and Boxing day.
Public transport: Norfolk Green Bus 01553 776980.
Habitat: Reedbed, brackish & freshwater pools, saltmarsh, dunes, shingle.
Key birds: *Spring/summer*: Nesting Avocet, Bearded Tit, Water Rail, Marsh Harrier, Reed and Sedge Warblers. *Autumn*: Knot. *Winter*: Brent Geese, Goldeneye, Scoter, Eider, Hen Harrier roost, Snow Bunting and Shore Lark on beach.

Contact: Centre Manager, Titchwell Marsh Reserve, King's Lynn, Norfolk PE31 8BB. Tel/fax 01485 210779.

16. WALSEY HILLS

Norfolk Ornithologist's Association (NOA).
Location: TG 062 441. Up footpath and steps from A149 at Cley.
Access: Open daily throughout year.
Facilities: Visitor centre providing up-to-date birding information. Short walk through scrub. Excellent views across adjoining reserves between Cley and Salthouse. Migration watch point.
Public transport: Phone Norfolk Green Bus 01553 776980. **Habitat:** Scrub.
Key birds: Recent sightings include Cetti's Warbler, Long-eared Owl, Osprey and Common Crane. **Contact:** Tom Fletcher, 01263 740875.

17. THE WASH NNR

English Nature East Midlands Team.
Location: TR 49 22 57. 7.5 miles West of King's Lynn. From A17, follow road along East bank of River Nene at Sutton Bridge.
Access: Open access, though remain on public footpaths along seabank and keep dogs under control. **Facilities:** Car park.
Public transport: None.
Habitat: Saltmarsh and mudflats.
Key birds: *Summer*: Breeding Redshank and Oystercatcher. Massive numbers of passage and wintering waterfowl including Brent Goose, Knot, Oystercatcher, Lapwing, Redshank, Shelduck and raptors.
Contact: Simon Cooter, English Nature, 78 High Street, Boston, Lincs NG31 6BH. 01205 311674. e-mail: simon.cooter@english-nature.org.uk

18. NWT WEETING HEATH

Norfolk Wildlife Trust.
Location: TL 756 881. Weeting Heath is signposted from the Weeting-Hockwold road, two miles W of Weeting near to Brandon in Suffolk. Nature reserve can be reached via B1112 at Hockwold or B1106 at Weeting.
Access: Open daily from Apr-Sep. Cost: adults £2.00, children free. NWT members free. Disabled access to visitor centre only.
Facilities: Visitor centre, birdwatching hides, wildlife gift shop, refreshments, toilets, coach parking, car park, groups welcome (book first).
Public transport: Train services to Brandon and bus connections from Brandon High Street.
Habitat: Breckland, grass heath.
Key birds: Stone Curlew, migrant passerines, Wood Lark.
Contact: Bev Nichols, Norfolk Wildlife Trust, Bewick house, 22 Thorpe Road, NorwichNR1 1RY. 01603 625540.
e-mail BevN@norfolkwildlifetrust.co.uk

19. WELNEY

The Wildfowl & Wetlands Trust.
Location: TL 546 944. Ten miles N of Ely, signposted from A10 and A1101.
Contact: The Warden, WWT, Hundred Foot Bank, Welney, Nr Wisbech PE14 9TN. 01353 860711.
e-mail: welney@wwt.org.uk

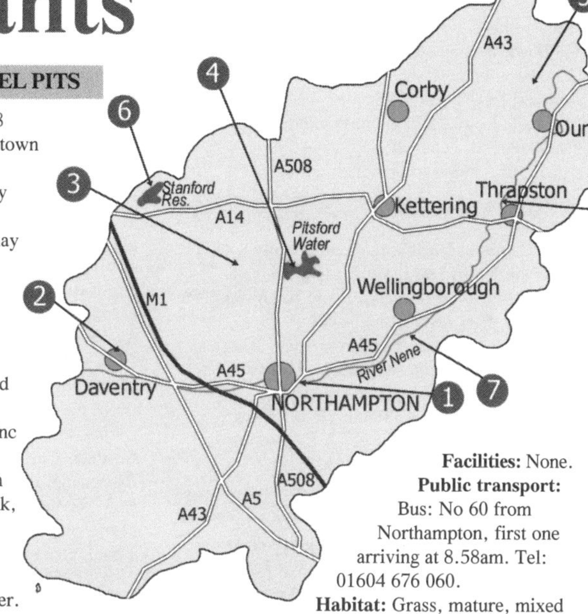

1. CLIFFORD HILL GRAVEL PITS

Location: SP 781 595. Take A428 Bedford Road from Northampton town centre E to A45 roundabout. Go straight over and turn L to park by Courtyard Hotel.
Access: Open all year. Shooting may take place Tues.
Facilities: Car park, toilets.
Public transport: None.
Habitat: Reservoir, river, grassland.
Key birds: *Spring*: Wheatear, Sand Martin, Yellow Wagtail. *Winter*: Excellent for wintering wildfowl inc Goosander, Pintail, Red-crested Pochard and Smew. Geese, Golden Plover, Green Sandpiper, Redshank, Meadow Pipit, Reed Bunting, thrushes. *All year*: Meadow Pipit, Reed Bunting, Grey Wagtail, Redpoll, Linnet, Green Woodpecker.

2. DAVENTRY RESERVOIR

Daventry District Council.
Location: SP 577 642. Country Park signposted from B4036 Daventry to Welton road.
Access: Open at all times. **Facilities:** One hide open all year, cafe, visitor centre.
Public transport: None.
Habitat: Open water, wetlands, reeds, meadows, woodland.
Key birds: *Autumn*: Passage waders inc. Dunlin, Ruff, Greenshank, Green Sandpiper; nesting Common Tern, Arctic and sometimes Black Tern on passage; gull roost; rare species inc. Pacific Swift, Baird's Sandpiper, Wilson's Phalarope, Sabine's Gull Honey Buzzard. Over 180 species recorded; 60 have bred.
Contact: Dewi Morris, Daventry Country Park, Reservoir Cottage, Northern Way, Daventry, Northants NN11 5JB. 01327 877193; e-mail countrysideservices@daventrydc.gov.uk.

3. HOLLOWELL RESERVOIR

Anglian Water.
Location: SP 683 738. From Northampton, take the A5199 NW. After eight miles, turn L. The car park is on the L. **Access:** Open all year. Permit required. Keep dogs on lead.
Facilities: None.
Public transport: Bus: No 60 from Northampton, first one arriving at 8.58am. Tel: 01604 676 060.
Habitat: Grass, mature, mixed and conifer plantations.
Key birds: *Autumn/winter*: Dunlin, Greenshank, Redshank, Green Sandpiper, Mediterranean Gull, ducks. Crossbill occurs in invasion years. Bearded Tit and Dartford Warbler occasional.
Contact: Anglian Water, Anglian House, Ambury Road, Huntingdon, Cambs, PE29 3NZ, 01480 323000.

4. PITSFORD RESERVOIR

Beds, Cambs & Northants Wildlife Trust.
Location: SP 787 702. Five miles N of Northampton. On A43 take turn to Holcot and Brixworth. On A508 take turn to Brixworth and Holcot.
Access: Lodge open mid-Mar to mid-Nov from 8am-dusk. Winter opening times variable, check in advance. Permits for reserve available from Lodge on daily or annual basis. Reserve open to permit holders 365 days a year. No dogs. Not suitable for disabled at present.
Facilities: Toilets available in Lodge, 15 miles of paths, eight bird hides, car parking.
Public transport: None.
Habitat: Open water (up to 120 ha), marginal vegetation and reed grasses, wet woodland, grassland and mixed woodland (40 ha).
Key birds: 174 species in 2000. *Summer*: Breeding

warblers, terns, Hobby, Tree Sparrow. *Autumn*: Waders only if water levels suitable. *Winter*: Wildfowl, feeding station with Tree Sparrow and Corn Bunting.
Contact: Dave Francis, Pitsford Water Lodge, Brixworth Road, Holcot, Northampton NN6 9SJ. 01604 780148.
e-mail: pitsford@cix.compulink.co.uk

5. SHORT WOOD

Beds, Cambs & Northants Wildlife Trust.
Location: TL 015 913. Via bridle path from minor road between Glapthorn and Southwick, NW of Oundle. Park on roadside verge.
Access: Open all year. **Facilities:** None.
Habitat: Primary and secondary mixed woodland (oak, ash, field maple, hazel), coppiced.
Key birds: Woodcock, Marsh Tit, warblers, Redpoll.
Contact: Trust HQ, 01604 405285.

6. STANFORD RESERVOIR

Severn Trent Water/Northants Wildlife Trust.
Location: SP 600 805. One mile SW of South Kilworth off Kilworth/Stanford-on-Avon road.
Access: Daytime, permits from Northants Wildlife Trust. No dogs. Limited access for disabled.
Facilities: Toilets (inc disabled). Two hides, perimeter track. Disabled parking. **Habitat:** Reservoir with willow, reed and hedgerow edges.
Key birds: *Winter*: Wildfowl, especially Ruddy Duck. *Spring*: Migratory terns and warblers. *Late summer*: Terns, Hobby, waders.
Contact: Northants Wildlife Trust, Ling House, Billing Lings, Northampton NN3 8BE. 01604 405285.

7. SUMMER LEYS LNR

Northamptonshire County Council.
Location: SP 886 634. Three miles from Wellingborough, accessible from A45 and A509, situated on Great Doddington to Wollaston Road.
Access: Open 24 hours a day, 365 days a year, no permits required. Dogs welcome but must be kept on leads at all times. 40 space car park, small tarmaced circular route suitable for wheelchairs.
Facilities: Three hides, one feeding station. No toilets, nearest are at Irchester Country Park on A509 towards Wellingborough.
Public transport: Nearest main station is Wellingborough. Buses run regularly to Great Doddington and Wollaston, both about a mile away. Tel: 01604 236712 (24 hrs) for timetables.
Habitat: Scrape, two ponds, lake, scrub, grassland, hedgerow.
Key birds: Hobby, Lapwing, Golden Plover, Ruff, Gadwall, Garganey, Pintail, Shelduck, Shoveler, Little Ringed Plover, Tree Sparrow, Redshank, Green Sandpiper, Oystercatcher, Black-headed Gull colony, terns.
Contact: Chris Haines, Countryside and Tourism Northamptonshire Council, PO Box 163, County Hall, Northampton NN1 1AX. 01604 237227 – please ring for a leaflet about the reserve.
e-mail: countryside@northamptonshire.gov.uk

8. THRAPSTON GRAVEL PITS & TITCHMARSH LNR

Beds, Cambs & Northants Wildlife Trust.
Location: TL 008 804.
Access: Public footpath from layby on A605 N of Thrapston.
Facilities: Two hides.
Public transport: Bus service to Thrapston.
Habitat: Alder/birch/willow wood; old duck decoy, series of water-filled gravel pits.
Key birds: *Summer*: Breeding Grey Heron (no access to Heronry), Common Tern, Little Ringed Plover; warblers. Migrants, inc. Red-necked and Slavonian Grebes, Bittern and Marsh Harrier recorded.
Contact: Trust HQ, 01604 405285

Northumberland

1. ARNOLD RESERVE, CRASTER

Northumberland Wildlife Trust.
Location: NU255197. Lies NE of Alnwick and SW of Craster village.
Access: Public footpath from car park in disused quarry. **Facilities:** Interpretation boards, information centre open in Summer. Toilets (incl disabled) and picnic site in quarry car park.
Public transport: Ariva Northumberland nos. 501 and 401.
Habitat: Semi-natural coastal woodland and scrub.
Key birds: Good site for migrant passerines to rest and feed. Interesting visitors can inc.

Bluethroat, Red-breasted Flycatcher, Barred and Icterine Warblers, Wryneck; moulting site for Lesser Redpoll. Breeding warblers in *Summer*.
Contact: Trust HQ, 0191 284 6884

2. BOLAM LAKE COUNTRY PARK

Northumberland County Council.
Location: NZ 08 81. 4.8km N of main Jedburgh Road (A696), 27km NW of Newcastle. Signed along a minor road from Belsay.
Access: Open all year, small parking fee.
Facilities: Car parks, leaflets from warden's house in the main car park.
Public transport: None.
Habitat: Parkland, lake, carr, conifers, woodland.
Key birds: *Spring/summer*: Ruddy Duck, Woodcock, Common Sandpiper, Sand Martin, House Martin, Redstart, warblers inc Grasshopper, Garden, Wood and Willow, possible flycatchers, waders. *Winter*: Whooper Swan, Greylag and Canada Geese, Wigeon, Pintail, Goosander, Water Rail, Woodcock, thrushes, Siskin, Redpoll. *All year*: Possible Grey Partridge, Green and Great Spotted Woodpeckers, Goldcrest, tits, Treecreeper, Nuthatch, Bullfinch.
Contact: Northumberland County Council, County Hall, Morpeth NE61 2EF. 01670 533100.

3. BRIARWOOD BANKS

Northumberland Wildlife Trust.
Location: NY 791 620. From Haydon Bridge, take minor road from A686 to Plankey Mill, three miles away at junction of Kingswood Burn and River Allen.
Access: Footpaths open to public. One steep route may be impassable after heavy rain.
Facilities: Parking at Plankey Mill. Picnic site and toilets at NT carpark at Allenbanks.
Public transport: None.
Habitat: Ancient woodland along steep valley.
Key birds: Pied Flycatcher, Wood Warbler, Redstart, Dipper, Woodcock, Treecreeper, Nuthatch. **Contact:** Trust HQ, 0191 284 6884.

4. COQUET ISLAND

RSPB (North of England Office). 0191 281 3366,

5. DRURIDGE BAY RESERVES

Northumberland Wildlife Trust.
Location: 1. NU 285 023. S of Amble. Hauxley (67a) approached by track from road midway

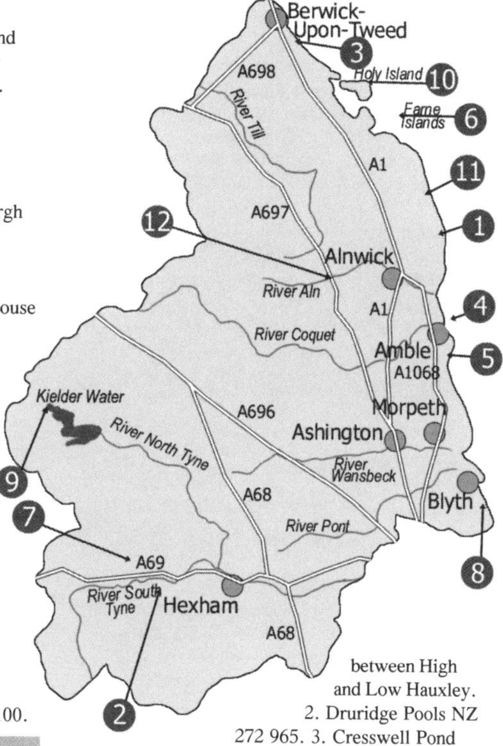

between High and Low Hauxley. 2. Druridge Pools NZ 272 965. 3. Cresswell Pond NZ 283 945. Half mile N of Cresswell.
Access: Day permits for all three reserves.
Facilities: 1. Visitor centre, five hides (one suitable for disabled). Disabled toilet. Lake with islands behind dunes. 2. Three hides. 3. Hide.
Habitat: 2. Deep lake and wet meadows with pools behind dunes. 3. Shallow brackish lagoon behind dunes fringed by saltmarsh and reedbed, mudflats.
Key birds: 1. *Spring and autumn*: Good for passage birds (inc. divers, skuas). *Summer*: Coastal birds, esp. terns (inc. Roseate). 2. Especially good in spring. Winter and breeding wildfowl; passage and breeding waders. 3. Good for waders, esp. on passage.
Contact: Jim Martin, Hauxley Nature Reserve, Low Hauxley, Amble, Morpeth, Northumberland. 01665 711578.

6. FARNE ISLANDS

The National Trust.
Location: NU 230 370. Access by boat from Seahouses Harbour. Access from A1.
Access: Apr, Aug-Sept: Inner Farne and Staple 10.30am-6pm (majority of boats land at Inner

Farne). May-Jul: Staple Island 10.30am-1.30pm, Inner Farne: 1.30pm-5pm. Disabled access possible on Inner Farne, telephone Property Manager for details. Dogs allowed on boats – not on islands.
Facilities: Toilets on Inner Farne.
Public transport: Nearest rail stations at Alnmouth and Berwick. **Habitat:** Maritime islands, 15-28 depending on state of tide.
Key birds: 18 species of seabirds/waders, four species of tern (including Roseate), 34,000-plus pairs of Puffin, Rock Pipit, Pied Wagtail, Starling, 1,200 Eider etc.
Contact: John Walton, 8 St Aidans, Seahouses, NorthumberlandNE68 7SR. 01665 720651.

7. GRINDON LOUGH

Northumberland Wildlife Trust. 0191 284 6884.

8. HOLYWELL POND

Northumberland Wildlife Trust. 0191 284 6884.

9. KIELDER FOREST

Forest Enterprise.
Location: NY 632 934. Kielder Castle is situated at N end of Kielder Water, NW of Bellingham.
Access: Forest open all year. Toll charge on 12 mile forest drive. Visitor centre has limited opening in winter.
Facilities: Visitor centre, exhibition, toilets, shop, access for disabled, licensed café. Local facilities include Youth Hostel, camp site, pub and garage.
Public transport: Bus: 814, 815, 816 from Hexham and seasonal service 714 from Newcastle.
Habitat: Commercial woodland, mixed and broadleaved trees.
Key birds: *Spring/summer*: Goshawk, Chiffchaff, Willow Warbler, Redstart, Siskin. *Winter*: Crossbill. *Resident*: Jay, Dipper, Great Spotted Woodpecker, Tawny Owl, Song Thrush, Goldcrest.
Contact: Forest Enterprise, Eels Burn, Bellingham, Hexham, Northumberland, NE48 2AJ, 01434 220242.
e-mail: pippa.kirkham@forestry.gsi.gov.uk

9. LINDISFARNE NNR

English Nature (Northumbria Team).
Location: NU 090 430. Island access lies two miles E of A1 at Beal, eight miles S of Berwick-on-Tweed. **Access:** Open all hours. Some restricted access (refuges).
Facilities: Toilets, visitor centre in village. Hide on island (new hide with disabled access at Fenham-le-Moor). Self-guided trail on island.
Public transport: Irregular bus service to Holy Island, mainly in summer. Bus route follows mainland boundary of site north-south.
Habitat: Dunes, sand and mudflats.
Key birds: *Passage and winter*: Wildfowl and waders, including pale-bellied Brent Goose, Long-tailed Duck and Whooper Swan. Rare migrants.
Contact: Phil Davey, Site Manager, Beal Station, Berwick-on-Tweed, TD15 2PB01289 381470

11. NEWTON POOL NR

National Trust (North East).
Location: NU 243 240. Follow signs to High Newton N of Embleton at junction of B1339 and B1340. In village, follow signs to Low Newton.Use car park just before village as no public parking available further on. National Trust sign in village square shows way to bird hide along Craster footpath (about a five minute walk).
Access: Open all year. From May to mid-August nest areas on beach may be cordoned off.
Facilities: Car park, hide.
Public transport: None.
Habitat: Dunes, tidal flats, beach, freshwater pool with artificial islands, scrub.
Key birds: *Spring/summer*: Grasshopper Warbler, Water Rail, Little Grebe, Whitethroat, Yellow Wagtail, Whinchat, Stonechat, Corn Bunting, terns, gulls. *Winter*: Waders, gulls.
Contact: National Trust (North East), Scots' Gap, Morpeth, Northumberland, NE61 4EG, 01670 774691.

12. THRUNTON WOOD

Forest Enterprise.
Location: NU 08 09. On A697 Morpeth-Wooler road, take minor road after New Moor crossroad (Rothbury/Alnwick junction) or Thrunton village junction to N, both signed to Thrunton Wood.
Access: Open all year. **Facilities:** Car park, trails.
Public transport: None.
Habitat: Spruce and pine plantation, crags, mature woodland, scrub.
Key birds: *Spring/summer*: Swallow, Tree Pipit, Redstart, Whinchat, Wheatear, Whitethroat, Garden Warbler, Spotted and Pied Flycatcher. *All year*: Red Grouse, Grey Partridge, Pheasant, Snipe, possible Woodcock, Great Spotted Woodpecker, usual woodland species.
Contact: Forest Enterprise, 9 Clifton Moor Business Village, James Nicolson Link, Clifton Moor, York YO30 4XG. 01904 696300.

Nottinghamshire

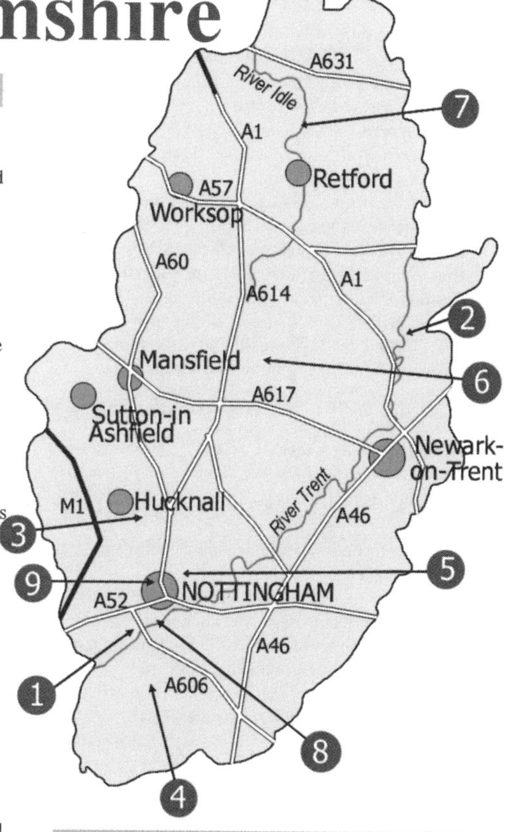

1. ATTENBOROUGH GRAVEL PITS

Nottinghamshire Wildlife Trust.
Location: SK 523 343. On A6005, seven miles SW of Nottingham alongside River Trent. Signed from main road.
Access: Open at all times. Dogs on leads. Paths suitable for disabled access.
Facilities: Nature trail (leaflet from Notts WT), one hide (key £2.50 from Notts WT).
Public transport: Railway station at Attenborough, several buses pass close to reserve (Rainbow 525A from Nottingham every ten minutes).
Habitat: Disused, flooded gravel workings with associated marginal and wetland vegetation.
Key birds: *Spring/summer*: Breeding Common Tern (40-plus pairs), Reed Warbler, Black Tern regular (bred once). *Winter*: Wildfowl (Bittern has wintered for last two years), Grey Heron colony, adjacent Cormorant roost.
Contact: Notts WT Office, The Old Ragged School, Brook Street, Nottingham NG1 1EA. 0115 958 8242. e-mail: nottswt@cix.co.uk www.wildlifetrust.org.uk/nottinghamshire

2. BESTHORPE NATURE RESERVE

Nottinghamshire Wildlife Trust.
Location: SK 817 640 and SK813 646 (access points). Take A1133 N of Newark. Turn into Trent Lane S of Besthorpe village, reserve entrances second turn on left and right turn at end of lane (at River Trent).
Access: Open access to two hides (one with disabled access from car park at present) and SSSI meadows. Dogs on leads.
Facilities: No toilets (pubs etc in Besthorpe village), two hides, paths, nature trail).
Public transport: Buses (numbers 22, 67, 68, 6, S7L) along A1133 to Besthorpe village (0.75 mile away). Tel: 0115 924 0000 or 01777 710550.
Habitat: Gravel pit with islands, SSSI neutral grasslands, hedges, reedbed, etc.
Key birds: *Spring/summer:* Breeding Grey Heron, Cormorant, Little Ringed Plover, Kingfisher, Grasshopper Warbler. *Winter:* Large numbers of ducks (Pochard, Tufted Duck, Pintail, Wigeon) and Peregrine.
Contact: Contact Notts WT Office, 0115 958 9242. e-mail: nottswt@cix.co.uk

3. BESTWOOD COUNTRY PARK

Nottingham County Council.
Location: From Nottingham, take the A611 to Hucknall. After passing Bulwell Forest Golf Course on the L, turn R down the B683 to Bestwood Village. Take the first R and the car park is on the R after the road bends L.
Access: Open all year. **Facilities:** Car parks, trails.
Public transport: None.
Habitat: Parkland, wood, lakes.
Key birds: *Spring/summer*: Turtle Dove, Cuckoo, warblers, hirundines. *Winter*: Finches, tits, thrushes. *All year*: Kingfisher, tits, Treecreeper, Green Woodpecker.
Contact: Nottingham County Council, County Hall, West Bridgford, Nottingham NG2 7QP. 0115 982 3823. e-mail: enquiries@nottscc.gov.uk

4. BUNNY OLD WOODS WEST

Nottinghamshire Wildlife Trust.
Location: SK 579 283. S of Nottingham. From city centre take A52 then A60. Limited parking off the A60. Please do not obstruct access. Further footpath access is at SK 584 293 off Wysall Lane.
Access: Open all year. **Facilities:** None
Habitat: Mixed woodland.
Key birds: *All year*: Usual woodland species, three woodpeckers, Tawny and Little Owls. *Spring/summer*: Spotted Flycatcher, Blackcap. Possible Brambling and Hawfinch. Good for butterflies.
Contact: Nottinghamshire Wildlife Trust, The Old Ragged School, Brook Street, Nottingham NG1 1EA. 0115 958 8242. e-mail: nottswt@cix.co.uk www.wildlifetrust.org.uk/nottinghamshire/

5. COLWICK COUNTRY PARK

Nottingham City Council. 0115 987 0785.
www.colwick2000.freeserve.co.uk

6. DUKE'S WOOD NATURE RESERVE

Nottinghamshire Wildlife Trust/BP Petroleum Development Ltd.
Location: 675 603. From Mansfield head E on A617. Reserve entrance is off the minor road to Eakring, which leaves the A617 near Kirklington.
Access: Open all year. School parties are particularly welcome. Please contact Trust office.
Facilities: None. **Public transport:** None.
Habitat: Mixed deciduous woodland, industrial archaeological site.
Key birds: *Spring/summer*: Blackcap, Garden Warbler, Spotted Flycatcher. *All year*: Great Spotted Woodpecker, Jay, usual woodland species. Hawfinch possible.
Contact: Nottinghamshire Wildlife Trust, The Old Ragged School, Brook Street, Nottingham, NG1 1EA, 0115 958 8242. e-mail: nottswt@cix.co.uk

7. LOUND WATERFOWL RESERVE

Tarmac/ARC/Nottinghamshire Wildlife Trust.
Location: SK 690 856. Two miles N of Retford off A638 adjacent to Sutton and Lound villages.
Access: Open at all times, use public rights of way.
Facilities: Public viewing platform/screen off chainbridge lane.
Public transport: Buses from Bawtry (Church Street), Retford bus station and Worksop (Hardy Street) on services 27/27A/83/83A/84 to Lound Village crossroads (Chainbridge Lane).
Habitat: Working gravel quarries, fish ponds, river valley, infilled and disused fly ash tanks, farmland, scrub, open water.
Key birds: *Summer*: Gulls and terns. Passage waders and raptors. *Winter*: Wildfowl, rarities inc. Ring-billed Gull, Caspian and White-winged Black Terns, Lesser Scaup, Richard's Pipit, Baird's Sandpiper. Long-billed Dowitcher, Buff-breasted Sandpiper, Pectoral Sandpiper, White Stork, Red-footed Falcon, Blue-winged Teal, Great Skua.
Contact: Lound Bird Club, Paul Hobson (Secretary), 6 St Mary's Crescent, Tickhill, Doncaster. 0794 0428326 (after 4pm).

8. WILWELL FARM NATURE RESERVE

Nottinghamshire Wildlife Trust/Rushcliffe Borough Council.
Location: Situated on the SE outskirts of Nottingham between Ruddington and Wilford.
Access: Open all year. **Facilities:** None.
Public transport: None.
Habitat: Abandoned railway cutting, neutral grassland, limestone, track bed, acid fen and scrub woodland.
Key birds: *All year*: Green Woodpecker, Sparrowhawk, usual woodland species, Tawny Owl. 91 species have been recorded on the reserve.
Contact: Nottinghamshire Wildlife Trust, The Old Ragged School, Brook Street, Nottingham, NG1 1EA, 0115 958 8242. e-mail: nottswt@cix.co.uk

9. WOLLATON PARK

Wollaton Hall.
Location: Situated approx 5 miles from Nottingham City Centre.
Access: Open all year from dawn-dusk.
Facilities: Pay/display car parks. Some restricted access (deer), leaflets.
Public transport: Trent Buses: no 22, and Nottingham City Transport: no's 31, and 28 running at about every 15 mins.
Habitat: Lake, small reedbed, woodland.
Key birds: *All year:* Main woodland species present, with good numbers of Nuthatch, Treecreeper and all three woodpeckers. *Summer*: Commoner warblers, incl Reed Warbler, all four hirundine species, Spotted Flycatcher. *Winter*: Pochard, Gadwall, Wigeon, Ruddy Duck, Goosander, occasional Smew and Goldeneye. Flocks of Siskin and Redpoll, often feeding by the lake, Redwing and occasional Fieldfare.
Contact: Wollaton Hall & Park, Wollaton, Nottingham NG8 2AE. 0115 915 3920.
e-mail: wollaton@ncmg.demon.co.uk

Oxfordshire

1. ASTON ROWANT NNR

English Nature (Thames & Chiltern Team).
Location: SU 731 966. From M40 at J6, travel NE for a short distance and turn R onto A40. After 1.5 miles at top of hill, turn R and R again into narrow lane. Drive to the end of road to car park.
Access: Open all year. Some wheelchair access, please contact site manager for more information.
Facilities: On-site parking, easy access path to viewpoint, seats, interpretation panels.
Public transport: Bus stops near reserve (Stokenchurch, Lewknor and Oxford to London).
Habitat: Chalk land, chalk scrub, beech woodland.
Key birds: *Spring/summer*: Blackcap, warblers, Turtle Dove, Tree Pipit. *Winter*: Possible Short-eared Owl, Brambling, Siskin, winter thrushes. *Passage*: Whinchat, Wheatear, Ring Ouzel. *All year:* Red Kite, Buzzard, Sparrowhawk, Woodcock, Little and Tawny Owls, Green and Great Spotted Woodpeckers, Sky Lark, Marsh Tit.
Contact: English Nature, 01844 351833. www.english-nature.org.uk

2. BLENHEIM PARK

Blenheim Palace.
Location: SP 440 160. 9.5km from Oxford at Woodstock on the A34. Various entrances available for cars and pedestrians.
Access: Open all year.
Facilities: Car parks, toilets, footpaths. Dogs on leads. **Public transport:** None.
Habitat: Lakes, woodland, pastureland.
Key birds: *Spring/summer*: Spotted Flycatcher, Blackcap, Garden Warbler, migrating Garganey. *Winter*: Wildfowl, possible Smew, Bittern, Water Rail. *All year*: Gadwall, Barn Owl, Tawny Owl, Little Owl, Kingfisher, Great Spotted and Green Woodpeckers, Jay, other usual woodland species.
Contact: Blenheim Palace, Woodstock, Oxford,

3. CHIMNEY MEADOWS NNR

Berks, Bucks & Oxon Wildlife Trust/English Nature.01865 775476. e-mail: bbowt@cix.co.uk www.wildlifetrust.org.uk/berksbucksoxon

4. FOXHOLES RESERVE

Berks, Bucks & Oxon Wildlife Trust.
Location: SP 254 206. Head N out of Burford on A424 towards Stow-on-theWold. Take third on R. Head NE on unclassified road to Bruern for 3.5km. Just before reaching Bruern, turn L along track following Cocksmoor Copse. After 750m, park in the car park on R just before some farm buildings.
Access: Open all year. Please keep to the paths.
Facilities: Car park, footpaths. Muddy in winter.
Public transport: None.
Habitat: River, woodland, wet meadow.
Key birds: *Spring/summer*: Nightingale, Yellow Wagtail, possible Redstart, Wood Warbler, Spotted Flycatcher. *Winter*: Redwing, Fieldfare, Woodcock. *All year*: Little Owl, all three woodpeckers, possible Hawfinch.
Contact: Trust HQ. 01865 775476.

5. OTMOOR NATURE RESERVE

RSPB (Central England).
Location: SP 570 126. Car park seven miles NE of Oxford city centre. From B4027, take turn to Horton-cum-Studley, then first left to Beckley. After 0.67 miles at bottom of short hill turn R (before the Abingdon Arms public house). After 200 yards, turn left into Otmoor Lane. Reserve car park is at the end of the lane (approx one mile).
Access: Open dawn-dusk. No permits or fees. No dogs allowed on the reserve visitor trail (except public rights of way). In wet conditions, some parts need wellington boots.
Facilities: Limited. Small car park with cycle racks, visitor trail (4.5km round trip) and two screened viewpoints. The reserve is not accessible by coach and is unsuitable for large groups.
Habitat: Wet grassland and open water lagoons. The lagoons are being converted into a reedbed.
Key birds: *Summer*: Breeding birds include Lapwing, Redshank, Curlew, Snipe, Yellow Wagtail, Shoveler, Gadwall, Pochard, Tufted Duck, Little Grebe, Great Crested Grebe. Hobby breeds locally. *Winter*: Wigeon, Teal, Shoveler, Pintail, Gadwall, Pochard, Tufted Duck, Lapwing, Golden Plover, Hen Harrier, Peregrine, Merlin. *Autumn/ spring passage*: Marsh Harrier, Short-eared Owl, Greenshank, Green and Common Sandpiper, Spotted Redshank and occasional Black Tern.
Contact: Neil Lambert, 01865 848385. www.rspb.org.uk

6. SHOTOVER COUNTRY PARK

Oxford City Council.
Location: SP 565 055. E of Oxford, off A40. Approach from Wheatley or Old Road, Headington.

Access: Open all year, best early morning or late in the evening.
Facilities: Car park, toilets, nature trails, booklets.
Public transport: None. **Habitat:** Woodland, farmland, heathland, grassland, scrub.
Key birds: *Spring/summer*: Willow Warbler, Blackcap, Garden Warbler, Spotted Flycatcher, Whitethroat, Lesser Whitethroat, Pied Flycatcher, Redstart, Tree Pipit. *Autumn*: Crossbill, Redpoll, Siskin, thrushes. *All year*: Sparrowhawk, Jay, tits, finches, woodpeckers, Corn Bunting.
Contact: Oxford City Council, PO Box 10, Oxford OX1 1EN. 01865 249811.

7. WARBURG RESERVE, THE

Berkshire, Buckinghamshire & Oxfordshire Wildlife Trust.
Location: SU 720 879. Leave Henley-on-Thames NW on the A4130. Turn R at the end of the Fair Mile onto the B480. L fork in Middle Assendon. After 1 mile, follow road round to R at grassy triangle, then on for 1 mile. Car park is on R.
Access: Open all year. Please keep dogs on a lead. In some areas, only guide dogs allowed.
Facilities: Visitor Centre, car park, hide with disabled access, nature trail, leaflets. Visitors with disabilities and groups should contact the warden.
Public transport: None.
Habitat: Scrub, mixed woodland, grassland, ponds.
Key birds: *Spring/summer*: Whitethroat, Lesser Whitethroat, Woodcock. *All year*: Sparrowhawk, all three woodpeckers, Red Kite, Treecreeper, Nuthatch, Tawny Owl. Good for butterflies and mammals.
Contact: Warburg Reserve, Bix Bottom, Henley-on-Thames, Oxfordshire, 01491 642001.
e-mail: bbowtwarburg@cix.co.uk

Shropshire

1. CHELMARSH RESERVOIR

South Staffordshire Water/Shropshire Wildlife Trust.
Location: SO 726 881. 6km south of Bridgnorth, off the B4555. From Chelmarsh village head S towards Highley. Turn L at Sutton and L at the T junction. From the car park, walk to the other end of the reservoir to the hides.
Access: Open all year. **Facilities:** Car park.
Public transport: None.
Habitat: Reservoir, reedbed.
Key birds: *Winter*: Wildfowl inc Pintail, Smew, geese, swans, Water Rail. *Spring/summer*: Reed and Sedge Warblers, Reed Bunting. *Passage*: possible Osprey.
Contact: Shropshire Wildlife Trust, 193 Abbey Foregate, Shrewsbury SY2 6AH. 01743 284 280 Fax 01743 284 281.

2. CLUNTON COPPICE

Shropshire Wildlife Trust.
Location: SO 343 806. Take B4385 S from Bishop's Castle. After two miles take road to Brockton, Lower Down and Clunton. Park in Clunton village and walk S into the woodland.
Access: Open at all times. Access along road and public rights of way only.
Facilities: Limited parking in small quarry entrance on R, or opposite The Crown pub.
Habitat: Oak coppice. Good for ferns, mosses and fungi.
Key birds: Buzzard and Raven regular. *Spring/summer*: Wide range of woodland birds, inc. Redstart, Wood Warbler and Pied Flycatcher, Woodcock.
Contact: Shropshire Wildlife Trust, 193 Abbey Foregate, Shrewsbury, Shropshire SY2 6AH. 01743 284280.

3. FENN'S WHIXALL AND BETTISFIELD MOSSES NNR

English Nature (North Mercia Team).
Location: Four miles SW of Whitchurch, ten miles SW of Wrexham. To S of A495 between Fenn's bank, Whixall and Bettisfield. Roadside parking at entrances, car parks at Morris's Bridge, Roundthorn Bridge, World's End and large car park at Manor House. Disabled access by prior arrangement along the railway line.
Access: Permit required except on Mosses trail routes.
Facilities: Panels at all main entrances to site, and leaflets are available when permits are applied for. Three interlinking Mosses trails explore the NNR and canal from Morris's and Roundthorn bridges.
Public transport: Bus passes nearby. Railway two miles away. **Habitat:** Peatland meres and mosses.

Key birds: *Spring/summer*: Nightjar, Hobby, Curlew, Tree Sparrow. *All year*: Sky Lark, Linnet. Water vole, brown hare. *Winter:* Short-eared Owl.
Contact: English Nature, Manor House, Mosshore, Wixhall, Shropshire SY13 2PD. 01948 880362.
e-mail: jean.daniels@english-nature.org.uk

4. GRANVILLE NATURE RESERVE

Shropshire Wildlife Trust.
Location: The reserve is located in Granville Country Park near Telford. From the M54 at J4, join the A5 to Priorslee. Go straight over at the Limekiln Bank roundabout on the B5060. Turn R at the next roundabout and the park is on the L.
Access: Open all year.
Facilities: None. **Public transport:** None.
Habitat: Open water, meadow, scrub, woodland, wetland.
Key birds: *Spring/summer*: Warblers, passage waders. *All year*: Good variety of woodland birds.
Contact: Trust HQ. 01743 284280
www.swt-granville.org.uk.

5. LLYNCLYS HILL

Shropshire Wildlife Trust.
Location: SJ 273 237. SSW of Oswestry. Park in layby on A495 at SJ277242 and walk up Turner's Lane. **Access:** Open at all times.
Facilities: None.
Public transport: None.
Habitat: Old mixed limestone sward with some woodland and scrub, small pond.
Key birds: Sparrowhawk, Green Woodpecker, Goldcrest, large warbler population. Occasional Peregrine, Buzzard. Eight species of orchid.
Contact: Trust HQ. 01743 284280.

6. MONKMOOR POOL

Severn Trent Water/Shropshire Wildlife Trust.
Location: SJ 524 136. Take the Whitchurch road out of Shrewsbury to the Heathgates roundabout. Follow Telford Way to the Monkmoor roundabout by the police station. Turn L up the no-through road. The reserve is just before the track turns under the by-pass. Park here.
Access: Open all year. Permit required.
Facilities: Car park, hide.
Habitat: Lagoon, trees, scrub.
Key birds: *Spring/summer*: Swallow, Sand Martin, House Martin, Kingfisher. *Winter*:

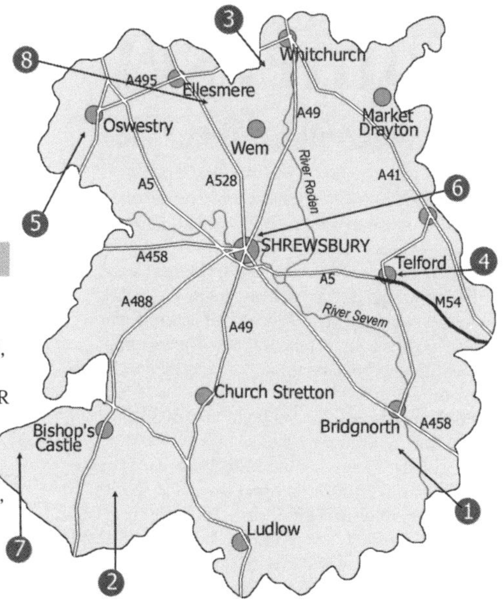

Snipe, Water Rail, wildfowl, geese.
Contact: Trust HQ. 01743 284 280.

7. RHOS FIDDLE

Shropshire Wildlife Trust.
Location: SO 206 857. NE of Knighton. Reserve is on unclassified county road between Newcastle-on-Clun and Crossways. Take B4368 Crossways road W out of Newcastle on Clun. Turn L at Caldy Bank. Continue for 2.15 miles. Cross over cattle grid and park on grassland on L.
Access: Open all year. **Facilities:** Car park.
Habitat: Heathland, agricultural land, wetland.
Key birds: *Spring/summer*: Curlew, Snipe, Sky Lark.
Contact: Trust HQ, 01743 284 280.

8. WOOD LANE

Shropshire Wildlife Trust.
Location: SJ 421 331. Turn off A528 at Spurnhill near Ellesmere.
Access: Open at all times.
Facilities: Car parks. Hides (access by permit).
Public transport: None.
Habitat: Gravel pit.
Key birds: *Summer*: Breeding Sand Martins. Popular staging post for waders (inc. Redshank, Greenshank, Ruff, Dunlin, Little Stint, Green and Wood Sandpiper). *Winter*: Lapwing and Curlew.
Contact: Trust HQ. 01743 284280

Somerset

1. BRANDON HILL NATURE PARK

Bristol City Council/Avon Wildlife Trust.
Location: 578 728. The reserve in centre of Bristol, in SW corner of Brandon Hill Park which overlooks Jacobs Wells Road. Metered parking available in nearby roads - Great George Street, Berkeley Square, car park on Jacobs Wells Road.
Access: Open all year. Wheelchair access from Great George Street and Berkeley Square only.
Facilities: Woodland walk, butterfly garden, picnic area.
Public transport: Travel line, 0870 6082608.
Habitat: Wildflower meadow, woodland.
Key birds: *Spring/summer*: Blackcap, warblers. *All year*: Jay, Bullfinch, usual woodland species.
Contact: Avon Wildlife Trust, The Wildlife Centre, 32 Jacob's Wells Road, Bristol, BS8 1DR, 0117 917 7270. www.avonwildlifetrust.co.uk

2. BREAN DOWN

National Trust (North Somerset).
Location: ST 290 590. 182 map. Five miles N of Burnham on Sea. J22 of M5, head for Weston Super Mare on A370 and then head for Brean at Lympsham. **Access:** Open all year. Dogs on lead. Steep slope - not suitable for wheelchair-users.
Facilities: Toilets one mile before property, not NT.
Public transport: Call Tourist Information Centre for details 01934 888800 (different in winter/ summer).
Habitat: Limestone and neutral grassland, scrub and steep cliffs.
Key birds: *Summer*: Blackcap, Garden Warbler, Whitethroat, Stonechat. *Winter*: Curlew, Shelduck, Dunlin on mudflat. Migrants.
Contact: The National Trust, Barton Rocks, Barton, Winscombe, North Somerset BS25 1DU. 01934 844518. e-mail: somersetoffice@ nationaltrust.org.uk

3. BRIDGWATER BAY NNR

English Nature (Somerset & Glouc Team).
Location: ST 270 470. Nine miles N of Bridgwater. Take J23 or 24 off M5. Turn N off A39 at Cannington.
Access: Hides open every day except Christmas Day. Permits needed for Steart Island (by boat only). Dogs on leads - grazing animals/nesting birds. Disabled access to hides by arrangement, other areas accessible.
Facilities: Car park at Steart. Footpath approx 0.5 miles to tower and hides.
Habitat: Estuary, intertidal mudflats, saltmarsh.
Key birds: *Winter:* Wildfowl and waders, birds of prey. *Spring/autumn:* Passage migrants.
Contact: Robin Prowse, Dowells Farm, Steart, Bridgwater, Somerset TA5 2PX. 01278 652426. www.english-nature.org.uk

4. CATCOTT LOWS

Somerset Wildlife Trust. 01823 451587.

5. CHEW VALLEY LAKE

Avon Wildlife Trust, Bristol Water Plc.
Location: ST 570 600. Reservoir (partly a Trust reserve) between Chew Stoke and West Harptree, crossed by A368 and B3114, nine miles S of Bristol.
Access: Permit for access to hides (five at Chew, two at Blagdon). Best roadside viewing from causeways at Herriott's Bridge (nature reserve) and Herons Green Bay. Day, half-year and year permits from Bristol Water, Recreation Department, Woodford Lodge, Chew Stoke, Bristol BS18 8SH. Tel/fax 01275 332339.

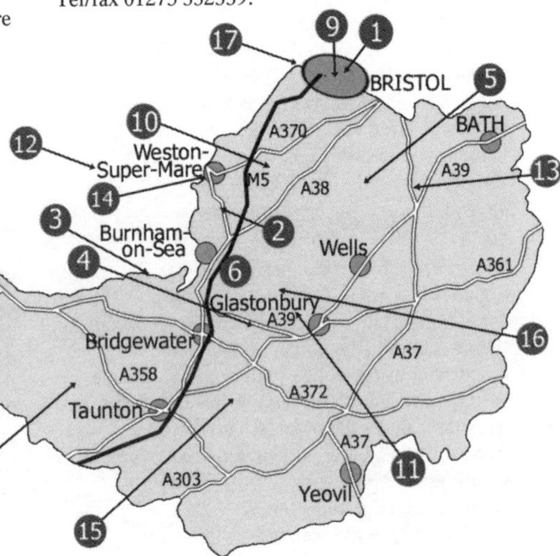

Facilities: Hides.
Public transport: Travel line, 0870 6082608.
Habitat: Reservoir.
Key birds: *Autumn/winter*: Concentrations of wildfowl (inc. Bewick's Swan, Goldeneye, Smew, Ruddy Duck), gull roost (inc. regular Mediterranean, occasional Ring-billed). Migrant waders and terns (inc. Black). Recent rarities inc. Blue-winged Teal, Spoonbill, Alpine Swift, Citrine Wagtail, Little Bunting, Ring-necked Duck, Kumlien's Gull.
Contact: Trust HQ, 0117 9177270 www.avonwildlifetrust.co.uk

6. HANKRIDGE FARM

Somerset Wildlife Trust.
Location: ST 255 255. Within Taunton. Take J5 of M5, then A38. Free parking near Hankridge entertainment/eating complexes or main access roads. Cross stile on to A38 by Bathpool Bridge and walk L at Creech Castle traffic lights, returning to the lakeside behind Italian restaurant.
Access: Open all year. **Facilities:** None.
Public transport: None.
Habitat: Lake, reedbed, scrub.
Key birds: *Spring/summer*: Reed and Sedge Warblers, Whitethroat, Blackcap, hirundines, possible Hobby. *Passage*: Waders such as Greenshank, Green and Common Sandpipers possible. **Contact:** Trust HQ. 01823 451587.

7. HORNER WOOD

Somerset Wildlife Trust.
Location: From Minehead, take A39 W to a minor road 0.8km E of Porlock signed to Horner. Park in village car park.
Access: Open all year. **Facilities:** None.
Public transport: Bus: Porlock.
Habitat: Oak woodland, moorland.
Key birds: *Spring/summer*: Wood Warbler, Pied Flycatcher, Redstart, Stonechat, Whinchat, Tree Pipit, Dartford Warbler possible. *All year*: Dipper, Grey Wagtail, woodpeckers, Buzzard, Sparrowhawk.
Contact: Trust HQ. 01823 451587.

8. LANGFORD HEATHFIELD

Somerset Wildlife Trust. 01823 451587.

9. LEIGH WOODS

National Trust (Bristol).
Location: ST 560 736. Two miles W from centre of Bristol. Pedestrian access from North Road, Leigh Woods or via Forestry Commission car park at end of Coronation Avenue, Abbots Leigh. Access to both roads is from A369 which goes from Bristol to J19 of M5.
Access: Open all year. A good network of paths around the plateau. The paths down to the towpath are steep and uneven.
Facilities: Two trails from Forestry Commission car park: purple trail (1.75 miles) on level ground, red trail (2.5 miles) more undulating.
Public transport: Bristol-Portishead. Bus service (358/658 and 359/659) goes along A369. Leaves Bristol generally at 20 and 50 minutes past the hour. First Badgerline. Tel: 0117 955 3231.
Habitat: Ancient woodland, former wood pasture, two grassland areas, calcareous grassland and scree by towpath.
Key birds: *Summer:* Peregrine, Blackcap, Chiffchaff, Spotted Flycatcher. *Winter:* Great Spotted and Green Woodpeckers, Song Thrush, Long-tailed, Marsh Tit and common tits.
Contact: Bill Morris, Reserve Office, Valley Road, Leigh Woods, Bristol, 01936 429336. e-mail: wlwbgm@smtp.ntrust.org.uk

10. PUXTON MOOR

Avon Wildlife Trust. 0117 932 6885.

11. SHAPWICK HEATH NNR

English Nature (Somerset & Gloucester Team).
Location: Situated between Shapwick and Westhay, near Glastonbury. The nearest car park to the site is at the Willows garden centre, in Westhay.
Access: Open all year. Disabled access to displays, hides. **Facilities:** Network of paths, hides. Toilets, leaflets and refreshments available at the garden centre. **Public transport:** None.
Habitat: Traditionally managed herb-rich grassland, ferny wet woodland, fen, scrub, ditches, open water, reedswamp and reedbed.
Key birds: *All year*: Ducks, waders.
Contact: English Nature (Somerset and Gloucestershire Team), Roughmoor, Bishop's Hull, Taunton, Somerset, TA1 5AA, 01823 283211. e-mail: somerset@english-nature.org.uk

12. STEEP HOLM ISLAND

Kenneth Allsop Memorial Trust.
Location: ST 229 607. Small island in Severn River, five miles from Weston-super-Mare harbour.
Access: Scheduled service depending on tides, via ferry. Advance booking advisable to ensure a place.

No animals allowed. Not suitable for disabled.
Facilities: Visitor centre, toilets, trails, basic refreshments and sales counter, postal service.
Habitat: Limestone grassland, scrub, rare flora, small sycamore wood.
Key birds: Important breeding station for Greater and Lesser Black-backed and Herring Gulls, largest colony of Cormorants in south-west of England. On migration routes.
Contact: Mrs Joan Rendell, Stonedale, 11 Fairfield Close, Milton, Weston-super-Mare BS22 8EA. 01934 632307. www.steepholm.org.uk

13. STEPHEN'S VALE

Avon Wildlife Trust/Cam Valley Wildlife Group.
Location: ST 637 578. SW of Bath. Take A368 W the A37 S. From minor road between Hallatrow and Clutton, walk to reserve via public footpath heading SE along S edge of wood on Highbury Hill. **Access:** Open access.
Facilities: Not suitable for the infirm.
Public transport: Bus from Bristol to Clutton, one mile from reserve.
Habitat: Small wooded valley, stream.
Key birds: *All year*: usual woodland birds, Dipper, Grey Wagtail.
Contact: Avon Wildlife Trust, The Wildlife Centre, 32 Jacob's Wells Road, Bristol BS8 1DR. 0117 917 7270. www.avonwildlifetrust.org.uk/ e-mail: mail@avonwildlifetrust.org.uk

14. WALBOROUGH

Avon Wildlife Trust.
Location: ST 315 579. On S edge of Weston-super-Mare at mouth of River Axe.
Access: Access from Uphill boatyard. Special access trail suitable for less able visitors.
Facilities: None.
Public transport: Travel line, 0870 6082608.
Habitat: Limestone grassland, scrub, saltmarsh, estuary.
Key birds: The Axe Estuary holds good numbers of migrant and wintering wildfowl (inc. Teal, Shelduck) and waders (inc. Black-tailed Godwit, Lapwing, Golden Plover, Dunlin, Redshank). Other migrants inc. Little Stint, Curlew Sandpiper, Ruff. Little Egret occurs each year, late summer.
Contact: Trust HQ, 0117 932 6885.

15. WEST SEDGEMOOR

RSPB (South West England Office).
Location: ST 361 238. Entrance down by-road off A378 Taunton-Langport road, one mile E of Fivehead.
Access: Access at all times to woodland car park and both hides. **Facilities:** Heronry hide, nature trail and moorland hide.
Public transport: Bus from Taunton to Fivehead.
Habitat: Semi-natural ancient oak woodland and wet grassland. Part of the Somerset Levels and Moors.
Key birds: *Spring/summer*: Breeding Grey Heron, Curlew, Lapwing, Redshank, Snipe, Buzzard, Sedge Warbler, Nightingale. Passage Whimbrel and Hobby. *Winter*: Large flocks of waders and wildfowl (including Lapwing, Golden Plover, Shoveler, Teal and Wigeon).
Contact: The Warden, Dewlands Farm, Redhill, Curry Rivel, Langport, Somerset TA10 0PH. 01458 252805, fax 01458 252184. e-mail: sally.brown@rspb.org.uk

16. WESTHAY MOOR NNR

Somerset Wildlife Trust.
Location: ST 458 438. From Glastonbury, take B3151 to site approx one mile NW of Westhay village on minor road to Godney.
Access: Open at all times.
Facilities: Hides and viewing screens, no toilets. Hides have disabled access.
Habitat: Open water and reedbeds.
Key birds: *Winter*: Bittern and wildfowl, Red-breasted Merganser, Water Rail, Goosander. *Summer*: Hobby, Reed, Sedge and Cetti's Warblers, Whitethroat.
Contact: David Reid, SWT, Fyne Court, Broomfield, Bridgwater, Somerset TA5 2EQ. 01823 451587.

17. WILLSBRIDGE MILL

Avon Wildlife Trust.
Location: ST 665 708. In SE part of Bristol. Turn N off A431 at Longwell Green along Long Beach Road, park after quarter mile in car park overlooking valley.
Access: Unrestricted access.
Facilities: Heritage sculpture trail, owl prowls and bird ID days. Ring for details.
Public transport: 332 bus, hourly service Bristol/ Bath. 45 bus Bristol/Park Estate every 20 mins.
Habitat: Broadleaved woodland, grassland, scrub, stream, pond.
Key birds: High densities of birds of woodland and scrub. *Winter*: Kingfisher and Dipper regular.
Contact: Ruth Worsley, Willsbridge Mill, Willsbridge Hill, Bristol BS30 6EX. 0117 932 6885. www.avonwildlifetrust.co.uk
e-mail: mail@avonwildlifetrust.co.uk

Staffordshire

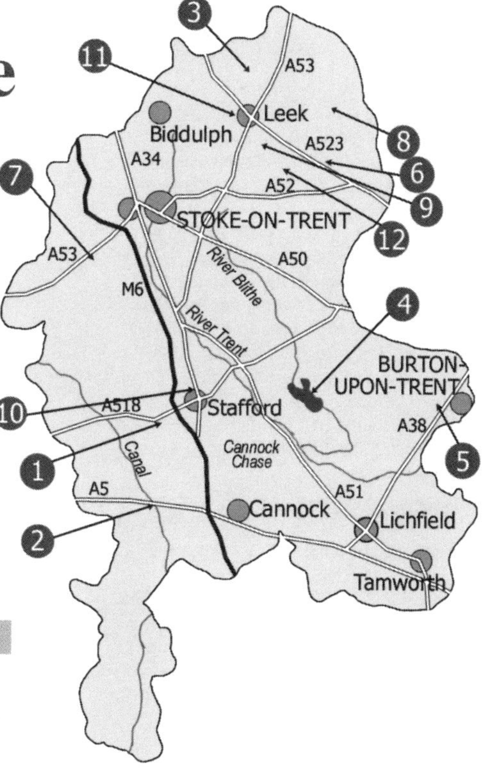

1. ALLIMORE GREEN COMMON

Staffordshire Wildlife Trust.

Location: SJ 858 193. From A518 Stafford/ Newport road in Haughton take a minor road S to Church Eaton. Reserve is one mile on L, just before Allimore Green. Roadside parking only. Please park with care and consideration.

Access: Open all year. Access is via a stile at the N end of the Common by the road. Groups of more than eight people require a Trust permit. **Facilities:** Interpretation board.

Public transport: None.

Habitat: Woodland, scrub, wet pasture, ditch.

Key birds: *Spring/summer*: Whitethroat, Willow Tit, Willow Warbler. *Winter*: Siskin,.

Contact: Trust HQ, Coutts House, Sandon, Stafford, ST18 0DN, 01889 508534.
e-mail: staffswt@cix.co.uk
www.wildlifetrust.org.uk/staffs

2. BELVIDE RESERVOIR

British Waterways Board/West Midland Bird Club.

Location: SJ865102. Near Brewood, 7 miles NW of Wolverhampton.

Access: Access only by permit from the West Midland Bird Club. **Facilities:** Hides.

Public transport: Not known.

Habitat: Canal feeder reservoir with marshy margins and gravel islands.

Key birds: Important breeding, moulting and wintering ground for wildfowl, (including Ruddy Duck, Goldeneye and Goosander), passage terns and waders. Night roost for gulls.

Contact: Miss M Surman, 6 Lloyd Square, 12 Niall Close, Edgbaston, Birmingham B15 3LX.

3. BLACK BROOK

Staffordshire Wildlife Trust.

Location: SK 020 645. N of Leek, W of A53. West of road from Royal Cottage to Gib Tor.

Access: Access is via public footpath from Gib Tor to Newstone Farm; this first passes through a conifer plantation which is outside the reserve.

Facilities: None. **Public transport:** None.

Habitat: Heather and bilberry moorland, and upland acidic grassland.

Key birds: Merlin, Kestrel, Red Grouse, Golden Plover, Snipe, Curlew, Dipper, Wheatear, Whinchat, Twite.

Contact: Trust HQ, 01889 508534.
e-mail: staffswt@cix.co.uk
www.wildlifetrust.org.uk/staffs

4. BLITHFIELD RESERVOIR

South Staffs Waterworks Co.

Location: SK 058 237. View from causeway on B5013 (Rugeley/Uttoxeter).

Access: Access to reservoir and hides by permit from West Midland Bird Club.

Facilities: None.

Public transport: None.

Habitat: Large reservoir.

Key birds: *Winter*: Good populations of wildfowl (inc. Bewick's Swan, Goosander, Goldeneye, Ruddy Duck), large gull roost (can inc. Glaucous, Iceland). Passage terns (Common, Arctic, Black) and waders, esp. in autumn (Little Stint, Curlew Sandpiper, Spotted Redshank regular).

Contact: Miss M Surman, 6 Lloyd Square, 12 Niall Close, Edgbaston, Birmingham B15 3LX.

5. BRANSTON WATER PARK

Staffordshire Wildlife Trust.
Location: SK 217 207. Follow the brown tourist sign from the A38 N. No access from the S - head to the Barton-under-Needwood exit and return N. The park is 0.5 miles S of the A5121 Burton-upon-Trent exit.
Access: Open all year. Paths flat and generally dry.
Facilities: Toilets, picnic benches.
Public transport: None.
Habitat: Reedbed, willow carr woodland, scrub.
Key birds: *Spring/summer*: Reed Warbler, Cuckoo, Reed Bunting. Important roost for Swallow and Sand Martin. *Winter*: waders, Little Ringed Plover occasionally, Pied Wagtail roost.
Contact: Trust HQ, Coutts House, Sandon, Stafford, ST18 0DN, 01889 508534.
e-mail: staffswt@cix.co.uk

6. BROWN END QUARRY NR

Staffordshire Wildlife Trust/North Staffordshire Group of the Geologists' Association.
Location: SK 090 502. Reserve is at E end of Waterhouses on the A523 Leek-Ashbourne road. The Quarry is on the N side of the road just W of the Manifold Cycle Track. Access to the parking area is over a bridge shared with a cycle hire company. **Access:** Open all year.
Facilities: Interpretation board.
Public transport: None.
Habitat: Scrub, limestone.
Key birds: *Spring/summer*: Warblers.
Contact: Staffordshire Wildlife Trust, Coutts House, Sandon, Stafford, ST18 0DN, 01889 508534. e-mail: staffswt@cix.co.uk

7. BURNT WOOD

Staffordshire Wildlife Trust.
Location: SJ 736 355. From Newcastle on the A53 to Market Drayton. When the main road crosses the B5026 turn into Kestrel Drive and then Pheasant Drive. Access also possible from the B5026 Eccleshall Road 0.3 miles from the A53. Parking is difficult for this reserve.
Access: Open all year. **Facilities:** None.
Public transport: None.
Habitat: Ancient oak woodland, pond.
Key birds: *All year*: Goshawk, Raven, Woodcock, all three woodpeckers. Good for butterflies and moths, adder, grass snake, slow worm and common lizard.
Contact: Trust HQ, Coutts House, Sandon, Stafford, ST18 0DN, 01889 508534.

8. CASTERN WOOD

Staffordshire Wildlife Trust.
Location: SK 119 537. E of Leek. Unclassified road SE of Wetton, seven miles NW of Ashbourne.
Access: Use parking area at end of minor road running due SE from Wetton.
Facilities: None. **Public transport:** None.
Habitat: Limestone grassland and woodland, spoil heaps from former lead mines.
Key birds: All three woodpeckers, warblers, Pied Flycatcher, Redstart, Sparrowhawk, Tawny Owl.
Contact: Trust HQ, Coutts House, Sandon, Stafford, ST18 0DN 01889 508534.
e-mail: staffswt@cix.co.uk

9. COOMBES VALLEY

RSPB (North West England Office).
Location: SK 005 530. Four miles from Leek along A523 between Leek and Ashbourne and 0.5 miles down unclassified road – signposted.
Access: No dogs allowed. Most of the trails are unsuitable for disabled. Open daily – no charge.
Facilities: Visitor centre, toilets, two miles of nature trail, one hide. Events and guided walks.
Public transport: None.
Habitat: Sessile oak woodland, unimproved pasture and meadow.
Key birds: *Spring:* Pied Flycatcher, Redstart, Wood Warbler. *Jan-Mar*: Displaying birds of prey.
Contact: Nick Chambers, Six Oaks Farm, Bradnop, Leek, Staffs ST13 7EU. 01438 384017.
e-mail: nick.chambers@RSPB.org.uk

10. DOXEY MARSHES

Staffordshire Wildlife Trust.
Location: SJ 903 250. In Stafford. Parking 0.25 miles off M6 J14/A5013 or walk from town centre.
Access: Open at all times. Dogs on leads. Disabled access being improved 2001.
Facilities: Two hides – accessible to wheelchairs.
Public transport: Walk from town centre via Sainsbury's.
Habitat: Marsh, pools, reedbeds, hedgerows, reed sweet-grass swamp.
Key birds: *Spring/summer*: Breeding Snipe, Lapwing, Redshank, warblers, buntings, Sky Lark, Water Rail. *Winter*: Snipe, wildfowl, thrushes, Short-eared Owl. Passage waders, vagrants.
Contact: Trust HQ, Coutts House, Sandon, Stafford, ST18 0DN01889 508534.
e-mail: staffswt@cix.co.uk
www.wildlifetrust.org.uk/staffs

11. LONGSDON WOODS

Staffordshire Wildlife Trust.
Location: SK 965 555. Reserve lies off A53 Leek road. Can be approached from Ladderedge near Leek; City Lane, Longsdon; or Rudyard Station.
Access: Public rights of way only.
Facilities: None.
Public transport: None.
Habitat: Woodland and wet grassland.
Key birds: Heronry, Sparrowhawk, Curlew, Snipe, Jack Snipe, Woodcock, Little and Tawny Owls, all three woodpeckers, Redstart, Blackcap, Garden Warbler.
Contact: Trust HQ, 01889 508534.

12. SWINEHOLES WOOD

Staffordshire Wildlife Trust.
Location: SK 046 503. From Stoke on Trent, head E on A52 to Froghall. Turn N to Ipstones and then B5053 N for 0.75 miles to a crossroads. Turn R up a minor road for 1.25 miles to a radio mast park in small lay-by on the R opposite the reserve.
Access: Open all year. Tussocky ground so walking can be difficult.
Facilities: None. **Public transport:** None.
Habitat: Lowland heath, upland moorland, woodland.
Key birds: *Spring/summer*: Roding Woodcock at dawn and dusk. *All year*: good range of woodland birds.
Contact: Trust HQ, Coutts House, Sandon, Stafford, ST18 0DN, 01889 508534.

Suffolk

1. BONNY WOOD

Suffolk Wildlife Trust.
Location: TM 076 520. The reserve is about 0.5 miles from Barking Tye and is an SSSI. From Needham Market take the B1078 to Barking.
Access: Open all year. Dogs on leads at all times. Park at the village hall.
Facilities: Nature trail. **Public transport:** None.
Habitat: Ancient, semi-natural woodland.
Key birds: *Spring/summer*: Nightingale, Blackcap, Willow warbler, Woodcock. *All year*: all three woodpeckers, Treecreeper, Tawny Owl, usual woodland birds.
Contact: Suffolk Wildlife Trust, Brooke House, Ashbocking, Ipswich IP6 9JY. 01473 890089.
e-mail: suffolkwildlife@cix.co.uk
www.wildlifetrust.org.uk/suffolk

2. CARLTON MARSHES

Suffolk Wildlife Trust.
Location: TM 508 920. SW of Lowestoft, at W end of Oulton Broad. Take A146 towards Beceles and turn R after Tesco garage.
Access: Open during daylight hours. Keep to marked paths. Dogs only allowed in some areas, on leads at all times. Car park shuts at 5.30pm
Facilities: Information centre and shop. Snacks available. **Public transport:** None.
Habitat: 100 acres of grazing marsh, peat pools and fen.
Key birds: Wide range of wetland and Broadland birds, including Marsh Harrier.
Contact: Catriona Finlayson, Suffolk Broads Wildlife Centre, Carlton Colville, Lowestoft, Suffolk NR33 8HU. 01502 564250.

3. CASTLE MARSHES

Suffolk Wildlife Trust.
Location: TM 471 904. Head E on the A146 from Beccles to Lowestoft. Take the first L turn after Three Horseshoes pub. Continue on the minor road which bends round to the R. Carry straight on - the road bends to the R again. The car park is on the L just after White Gables house.
Access: Public right of way. Unsuitable for wheelchairs. Stiles where path leaves the reserve. Unmanned level crossing is gated.
Facilities: None.
Public transport: Bus: nearest bus route is on the A146 Lowestoft to Beccles road. Tel: 0845 958 3358. Train: Beccles and Oulton Broad South on the Ipswich to Lowestoft line.
Habitat: Grazing marshes, riverbank.
Key birds: *Spring/summer*: Marsh Harrier, Cetti's Warbler, occasional Grasshopper Warbler. *Winter*: Hen Harrier, wildfowl, Snipe.
Contact: Trust HQ. 01473 890089.

Suffolk

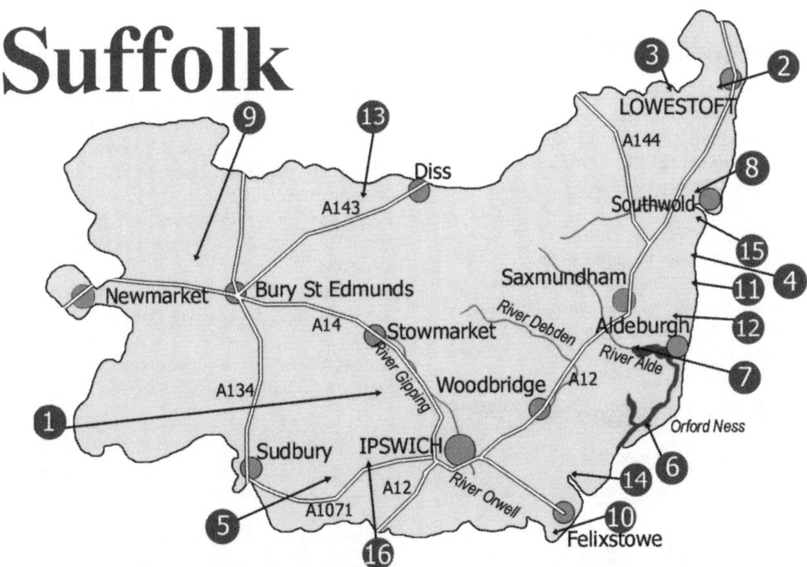

4. DINGLE MARSHES, DUNWICH

Suffolk Wildlife Trust/RSPB. The reserve forms part of the Suffolk Coast NNR.
Location: TM 48 07 20. Eight miles from Saxmundham. Follow brown signs from A12 to Minsmere and continue to Dunwich. Forest carpark (hide) - TM 46 77 10. Beach car park - TM 479 707. **Access:** Open at all times. Access via public rights of way and permissive path along beach. Dogs on lead please.
Facilities: Toilets at beach car park, Dunwich. Hide in Dunwich Forest overlooking reedbed, accessed via Forest car park. Circular trail waymarked from car park.
Public transport: None.
Habitat: Grazing marsh, reedbed, shingle beach and saline lagoons
Key birds: Reedbed: Bittern, Marsh Harrier, Bearded Tit (*all year*), Hobby (*Summer*), Hen Harrier (*Winter*). Grazing marsh: Lapwing, Avocet, Snipe, Black-tailed Godwit *(Summer)* White-fronted Goose, Wigeon, Teal, Snipe (*Winter*). Good for passage waders.
Contact: Alan Miller, Suffolk Wildlife Trust, 9 Valley Terrace, Valley Road, Leiston, Suffolk IP16 4AP. 01728 833405.
e-mail: alanm@suffolkwildife.cix.co.uk

5. GROTON WOOD LNR

Suffolk Wildlife Trust.
Location: TL 976 428. From Sudbury take A134 SE then A1071 towards Hadleigh. Turn L to Groton. Turn R at start of village then L at crossroads. Turn R at end of road. Reserve is along on L.
Access: Open all year.
Facilities: None.
Public transport: None.
Habitat: Woodland.
Key birds: *Spring/summer*: Warblers, Nightingale. *All year*: All three woodpeckers, Nuthatch, tits.
Contact: Trust HQ. 01473 890089.
e-mail: suffolkwt@cix.co.uk

6. HAVERGATE ISLAND

RSPB (East Anglia Office).
Location: TM 425 496. Part of the Orfordness NNR at the mouth of the River Alde.
Access: Open Apr-Aug (1st & 3rd weekends and every Thu), Sep-Mar (1st Sat every month). Book in advance, in writing. Park in Orford.
Facilities: None. **Public transport:** Boat trips from Orford (one mile).
Habitat: Shallow brackish water, lagoons with islands, saltmarsh, shingle beaches.
Key birds: *Summer*: Breeding Arctic, Common and Sandwich Terns, migrants. Leading site for Avocet. *Winter*: Wildfowl.
Contact: John Partridge, Manager, 30 Mundays Lane, Orford, Woodbridge, Suffolk IP12 2LX. 01394 450732.

7. HAZELWOOD MARSHES

Suffolk Wildlife Trust.
Location: TM 435 575. Four miles W of Aldeburgh. Small car park on A1094. Mile walk down sandy track.
Access: Open dawn to dusk. **Facilities:** Hide.
Public transport: Call Trust for advice.
Habitat: Estuary, marshes.
Key birds: Marshland and estuary birds; spring and autumn migrants.
Contact: Rodney West, Flint Cottage, Stone Common, Blaxhall, Woodbridge, Suffolk IP12 2DP. Tel/fax: 01728 689171;
e-mail rodwest@ndirect.co.uk.

8. HEN REEDBED NNR

Suffolk Wildlife Trust.
Location: TM 470 770. On the A1095 from Southwold to Lowestoft. Park in the lay-by on the A1095.
Access: Open all year. Dogs on leads, but not allowed in the hide. Not suitable for wheelchair use. **Facilities:** Hide, viewing platform, trail.
Public transport: None.
Habitat: Reedbed,dykes, fens, pools.
Key birds: *Spring/summer*: Marsh Harrier, Bearded Tit, Hobby, waders, ducks.
Contact: Suffolk Wildlife Trust, Brooke House, Ashbocking, Ipswich, IP6 9JY, 01473 890089.
e-mail: suffolkwildlife@cix.co.uk
www.wildlifetrust.org.uk/suffolk

9. LACKFORD LAKES

Suffolk Wildlife Trust.
Location: TL 803 708. Via track off N side of A1101 (Bury St Edmunds to Mildenhall road), between Lackford and Flempton. Five miles from Bury. **Access:** New reserve centre open 10am to 4pm Wed to Sun, (closed Mon and Tues).
Facilities: New visitor centre. Tea and coffee facilities, toilets. Eight hides.
Public transport: None.
Habitat: Restored gravel pit with open water, lagoons, islands, willow scrub.
Key birds: *Winter*: Large gull roost. Wide range of waders and wildfowl (inc. Goosander, Pochard, Tufted Duck, Shoveler. No1 hide excellent for Kingfisher). *Spring/autumn*: Migrants, inc. raptors. Breeding Shelduck, Little Ringed Plover and reedbed warblers.
Contact: Joe Davis, Lackford Lakes Visitor Centre, Lackford Lakes, Lackford, Bury St Edmunds, Suffolk IP28 6HX. 01284 728706.

10. LANDGUARD BIRD OBSERVATORY

Location: TM 283 317. Road S of Felixstowe to Landguard Nature Reserve and Fort.
Access: Visiting by appointment.
Facilities: Migration watch point and ringing station.
Public transport: Call for advice.
Habitat: Close grazed turf, raised banks with holm oak, tamarisk, etc.
Key birds: Unusual species and common migrants. Seabirds offshore.
Contact: Paul Holmes, Landguard Bird Observatory, View Point Road, Felixstowe, Suffolk IP11 8TW. Ms J Cawston 01473 748463.

11. MINSMERE

RSPB (East Anglia Office).
Location: TM 452 680. Six miles NE of Samundham. From A12 head for Westleton, N of Yoxford. Access from Westleton (follow the brown tourist signs).
Access: Open every day, except Tues, Christmas Day and Boxing Day (9am-9pm or dusk if earlier). Visitor centre open 9am-5pm (9am-4pm Nov-Jan). Tea-room 10.30am-4.30pm (10am-4pm Nov-Jan). Free to RSPB members, otherwise £5 adults, £1.50 children, £3 concession.
Facilities: Toilets, visitor centre, hides, trails.
Public transport: Train to Saxmundham then taxi.
Habitat: Woodland, wetland - reedbed and grazing marsh, heathland, dunes and beach, farmland - arable conversion to heath, coastal lagoons, 'the scrape'.
Key birds: *Summer*: Avocet, Bittern, Marsh Harrier, Bearded Tit, Redstart, Nightingale, Nightjar. *Winter*: Wigeon, White-fronted Goose, Bewick's Swan. *Autumn/spring*: Passage migrants, waders etc.
Contact: Geoff Welch, Minsmere RSPB Reserve, Westleton, Saxmundham, Suffolk IP17 3BY. 01728 648281. e-mail: minsmere@rspb.org.uk
www.rspb.org.uk

12. NORTH WARREN AND ALDRINGHAM WALKS

RSPB (East Anglia Office).
Location: TM 468 575. Directly N of Aldeburgh on Suffolk coast. Use signposted car park on beach.
Access: Open at all times. Please keep dogs under close control. Beach area suitable for disabled.
Facilities: Three nature trails, leaflet available from TIC Aldeburgh or Minsmere RSPB. Toilets

in Aldeburgh and Thorpeness.
Public transport: Bus service to Aldeburgh. First Eastern Counties (08456 020121).
Habitat: Grazing marsh, lowland heath, reedbed, woodland.
Key birds: *Winter*: White-fronted Goose, Tundra Bean Goose, Wigeon, Shoveler, Teal, Gadwall, Pintail, Snow Bunting. *Spring/summer*: Breeding Bittern, Garganey, Marsh Harrier, Hobby, Nightjar, Wood Lark, Nightingale, Dartford Warbler.
Contact: Rob Macklin, Racewalk, Priory Road, Snape, Suffolk IP17 1SD. 01728 688481.
e-mail: rob.macklin@tesco.net

13. REDGRAVE AND LOPHAM FENS

Suffolk Wildlife Trust.
Location: TM 05 07 97. Five miles from Diss, signposted and easily accessed from A1066 and A143 roads.
Access: Open all year, dogs strictly on leads only. Visitor centre open all year at weekends, call for details on 01379 688333
Facilities: Visitor centre with coffee shop, toilets, including disabled toilets, disabled/wheelchair accessible boardwalk and viewing platform. Other general circular trails (not wheelchair access).
Public transport: Buses and trains to Diss town – Simonds coaches to local villages of Redgrave and South Lopham from Diss.
Habitat: Calcareous fen, wet acid heath, scrub and woodland.
Key birds: *All year*: Water Rail, Snipe, Teal, Woodcock, Sparrowhawk, Kestrel, all three woodpeckers, Tawny and Little Owls, Shelduck. *Summer*: Reed, Sedge and Grasshopper Warblers, other leaf and *Sylvia* warblers, Hobby plus large Swallow and Starling roosts. *Winter/ occasionals on passage*: Bearded Tit, Marsh Harrier, Greenshank, Green Sandpiper, Shoveler, Gadwall, Pintail, Garganey.
Contact: Andrew Excell, Redgrave and Lopham Fens, Low Common Road, South Lopham, Diss, Norfolk IP22 2HX. 01379 687618.
e-mail: redgrave@suffolkwildlife.cix.co.uk
www.wildlifetrust.org.uk/suffolk

14. TRIMLEY MARSHES

Suffolk Wildlife Trust.
Location: TM 260 352. Main Road A14 – Felixstowe two miles – Ipswich ten miles. Parking at top of Cordy's Lane, Trimley St Mary one mile from reserve.
Access: Reserve open at all times. Visitor centre open at weekends. Dogs on lead. Best time to visit – all year.
Facilities: Visitor centre, toilets (open at weekends), five hides.
Public transport: Train station at Trimley (Station Road/Cordy's Lane).
Habitat: Wetland (84 hectares).
Key birds: *Summer:* Avocet, Marsh Harrier, Redshank, Garganey, etc. *Passage*: Curlew Sandpiper, Wood Sandpiper. *Winter:* Wildfowl.
Contact: Mick Wright, 15 Avondale Road, Ipswich, Suffolk IP3 9JT. 01473 710032.
e-mail: micktwright@btinternet.com
www.wildlifetrust.org.uk/suffolk

15. WALBERSWICK

English Nature (Suffolk Team).
Location: TM 475 733. Good views from B1387 and from lane running W from Walberswick towards Westwood Lodge; elsewhere keep to public footpaths or shingle beach.
Access: Parties and coach parking by prior arrangement.
Facilities: Hide on S side of Blyth estuary, E of A12. **Public transport:** Call for advice.
Habitat: Tidal estuary, fen, freshwater marsh and reedbeds, heath, mixed woodland, carr.
Key birds: *Spring/summer*: Marsh Harrier, Bearded Tit, Water Rail, Bittern, Nightjar. *Passage/winter*: Wildfowl, waders and raptors.
Contact: Adam Burrows, English Nature, Regent House, 110 Northgate Street, Bury St Edmunds IP33 1HP. 01502 676171.

16. WOLVES WOOD RSPB RESERVE

RSPB (East Anglia Office).
Location: Two miles E of Hadleigh on the A1071 to Ipswich.
Access: Open all year. Wellington boots advisable between Sept-May. Charge for non-members.
Facilities: Car park for fifteen cars (no coaches), group bookings, guided walks and special events, no dogs except guide dogs.
Public transport: Bus: Hadleigh (two miles). Train: nearest station Ipswich.
Habitat: Ancient woodland.
Key birds: *Spring/summer*: Nightingale, usual woodland species.
Contact: Mark Nowers, Tel/fax: 01255 886043.
e-mail: mark.nowers@rspb.org.uk
www.rspb.org.uk

Surrey

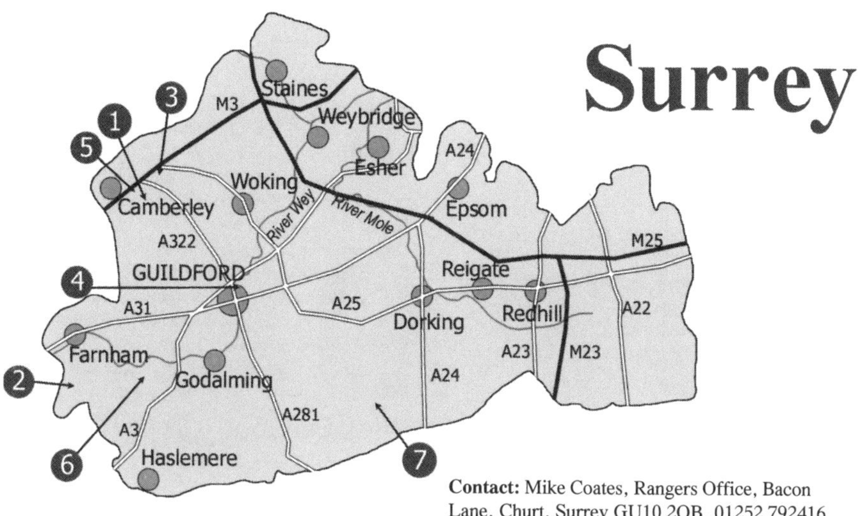

1. BRENTMOOR HEATH LNR

Surrey Wildlife Trust.
Location: SU 936 612. The reserve runs along the A322 Guildford to Bagshot road, at the intersection with the A319/B311 between Chobham and Camberley. Best access is by Brentmoor Road, which runs W from West End past Donkey Town.
Access: Open all year.
Facilities: Local buses, nos 34, 590 and 591 stop under 0.5 miles away. **Public transport:** None.
Habitat: Heathland, woodland, grassland, ponds.
Key birds: *Spring/summer*: Stonechat, Nightjar, Hobby. *All year*: usual woodland birds.
Contact: Surrey Wildlife Trust, School Lane, Pirbright, Woking, Surrey, GU24 0JN, 01483 488055. e-mail: surreywt@cix.co.uk

2. FRENSHAM COMMON

Waverley BC and National Trust.
Location: SU 855 405. Common lies on either side of A287 between Farnham and Hindhead.
Access: Open at all times. Car park (locked 9pm-9am). Keep to paths.
Facilities: Information rooms, toilets and refreshment kiosk at Great Pond.
Public transport: Call Trust for advice.
Habitat: Dry and humid heath, woodland, two large ponds, reedbeds.
Key birds: *Summer*: Dartford Warbler, Wood Lark, Hobby, Nightjar, Stonechat. *Winter*: Wildfowl (inc. occasional Smew), Bittern, Great Grey Shrike.
Contact: Mike Coates, Rangers Office, Bacon Lane, Churt, Surrey GU10 2QB. 01252 792416.

3. LIGHTWATER COUNTRY PARK

Surrey County Council.
Location: SU 921 622. From J3 of M3, take the A322 and follow brown Country Park signs. From the Guildford Road in Lightwater, turn into The Avenue. Entrance to the park is at the bottom of the road.
Access: Open all year dawn-dusk.
Facilities: Car park, visitor centre open most days during summer, toilets, leaflets.
Public transport: Train: Bagshot two miles. Tel 08457 484950. Bus: No 34 from Woking, Guildford and Camberley. Tel: 08706 082608.
Habitat: Reclaimed gravel quarries. Heath, woodland, bog.
Key birds: *Summer:* Dartford Warbler, Stonechat, Wood Lark, Tree Pipit, Hobby, Nightjar, all three woodpeckers. *Autumn*: Ring Ouzel, Crossbill, Siskin, Fieldfare, Redwing, possible Woodcock.
Contact: Surrey County Council, County Hall, Penrhyn Road, Kingston-upon-Thames, Surrey KT1 2DN. 08456 009 009.
www.surreycc.gov.uk

4. RIVERSIDE PARK, GUILDFORD

Guildford Borough Council.
Location: TQ 005515 (Guildford BC). From car park at Bowers Lane, Burpham (TQ 011 527). Three miles from town centre.
Access: Open at all times. Follow marked paths. Access to far side of lake and marshland area via boardwalk.

Facilities: Boardwalk.
Public transport: Guildford town centre to Burpham (Sainsburys) No 36 Bus (Arriva timetable information. Tel 0870 608 2608).
Habitat: Wetland, lake, meadow, woodland.
Key birds: *Summer*: Sedge, Reed and Garden Warblers, Common Tern, Lesser Whitethroat, Hobby. *Winter*: Jack Snipe, Chiffchaff, Water Rail. *Passage*: Common Sandpiper, Whinchat, Water Pipit (up to 12 most years).
Contact: Parks Helpdesk, Guildford Borough Council, Millmead House, Millmead, Guildford, Surrey GO2 5BB. 01483 444715.
e-mail: parks@guildford.gov.uk
www.guildfordborough.co.uk

5. ROWHILL COPSE LNR

Rushmoor Borough Council/Rowhill Nature Reserve Society.
Location: SU 853 497. In either direction from Farnham or Farnborough along the A325 towards Aldershot, until you come to a mini- roundabout which will be the junction with Cranmore Lane. Turn down Cranmore Lane and take the 1st R after the central bollards. Park in the car park.
Access: Open all year. **Public transport:** None.
Habitat: Heathland, alder carr, ponds.
Key birds: *All year*: all three woodpeckers, Grey Heron, Kingfisher.
Contact: Blackwater Valley Countryside Service, Ash Lock Cottage, Government Road, Aldershot, Hampshire GU11 2PS. 01252 331353 .
blackwater.valley@hants.gov.uk

6. THURSLEY COMMON

English Nature (Sussex & Surrey Team).
Location: SU 900 417. From Guildford, take A3 SW to B3001 (Elstead/Churt road). Use the Moat car park.
Access: Open access. Parties must obtain prior permission. **Facilities:** Boardwalk in wetter areas.
Public transport: None.
Habitat: Wet and dry heathland, woodland, bog.
Key birds: *Winter*: Hen Harrier and Great Grey Shrike. *Summer*: Hobby, Woodlark, Dartford Warbler, Stonechat, Curlew, Snipe, Nightjar.
Contact: Simon Nobes, English Nature, Uplands Stud, Brook, Godalming, Surrey GU8 5LA. 01428 685878.

7. WALLIS WOOD LNR

Surrey Wildlife Trust.
Location: TQ 121 388. Wallis Wood Village is about 5 miles NW of Horsham. The reserve is 0.5 miles N of the village, on the E side of Walliswood Green Road to Forest Green.
Access: Open all year.
Facilities: None. **Public transport:** None.
Habitat: Oak/hazel coppice woodland, stream, small pond.
Key birds: *All year*: usual woodland species.
Contact: Surrey Wildlife Trust, School Lane, Pirbright, Woking, Surrey, GU24 0JN, 01483 488055. e-mail: surreywt@cix.co.uk
www.surreywildlifetrust.org.uk

Sussex, East

1. BEWL WATER

Sussex Wildlife Trust/Southern Water.
Location: TQ 674 320. On the B2099 coming from Tilehurst to Wadhurst.
Access: Open all year.
Facilities: Car park, hide. Footpath round reservoir. Southern Water have a Visitor Centre on the N side but the reserve cannot be viewed from there. Call 01892 890661.
Public transport: None.
Habitat: Reservoir, woodland, plantation.
Key birds: *Spring/summer*: Chiffchaff, other warblers, terns. *Passage*: Osprey, Common Sandpiper, Green Sandpiper, Greenshank, stints. *All year*: Pochard, Wigeon, Teal, Gadwall.
Contact: Sussex Wildlife Trust, Woods Mill, Shoreham Road, Henfield, West Sussex, BN5 9SD, 01273 492630. e-mail: enquiries@sussexwt.co.uk
www.sussexwt.co.uk

2. ERIDGE ROCKS RESERVE

Sussex Wildlife Trust.
Location: Near Tunbridge Wells. Entrance to the private road is off the A26, next to a church and small printing works.
Access: Open all year. **Facilities:** Car park.
Public transport: None.
Habitat: Sandstone rock outcrop, mixed woodland.
Key birds: *Spring/summer*: Warblers. *All year*:

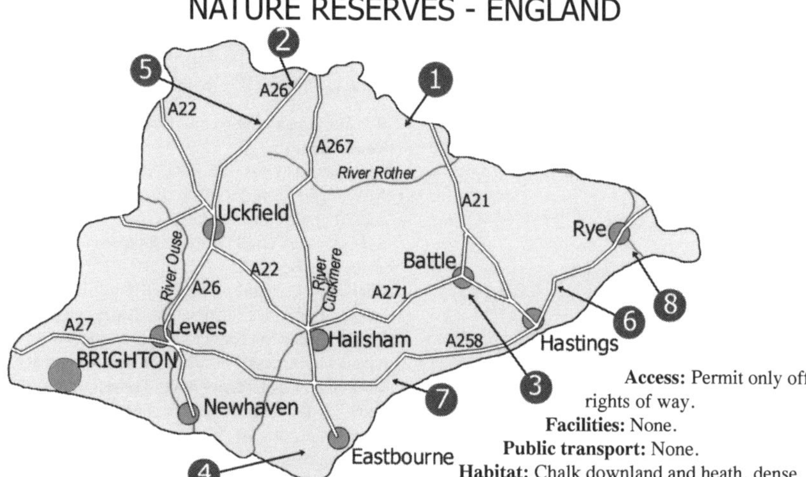

Tits, Nuthatch, Green and Great Spotted Woodpecker, finches.
Contact: Sussex Wildlife Trust, Woods Mill, Shoreham Road, Henfield, West Sussex BN5 9SD. 01273 482630. e-mail: enquiries@sussexwt.org.uk www.wildlifetrust.org.uk/sussex

3. FORE WOOD

RSPB (South East England Office).
Location: TQ 758 123. From the A2100 (Battle to Hastings) take lane to Crowhurst at Crowhurst Park Caravan Park. Park at village hall and walk back up Forwood Lane for 0.5 miles. Entrance to reserve on left at top of hill.
Access: Open all year. Closed Christmas Day. No disabled facilities. No dogs.
Facilities: Two nature trails.
Public transport: Station at Crowhurst, about 0.5 mile walk. Charing Cross/Hastings line.
Habitat: Semi-natural ancient woodland.
Key birds: Three species woodpecker, Nuthatch, Treecreeper, Sparrowhawk, Marsh Tit. *Spring/ Summer*: Blackcap, Nightingale, Spotted Flycatcher.
Contact: Martin Allison, 12 The Grove, Crowborough, East Sussex TN6 1NY. 01273 775333 (South East Regional Office).
e-mail: martin.allison@rspb.org.uk

4. LULLINGTON HEATH

English Nature (Sussex & Surrey Team).
Location: TQ 525 026. W of Eastbourne, after six miles on A259 turn N on minor road to Lullington Court for parking, then one mile up hill (bridleway).
Access: Permit only off rights of way.
Facilities: None.
Public transport: None.
Habitat: Chalk downland and heath, dense woodland scrub and areas of gorse.
Key birds: *Summer*: Breeding Nightingale, Nightjar and Grasshopper Warbler, Turtle Dove. *Winter*: Raptors (inc. Hen Harrier), Woodcock.
Contact: Malcolm Emery, English Nature, Phoenix House, 32-33 North Street, Lewes, E Sussex BN7 2PH. 01273 476595; fax 01273 483063; e-mail sussex.surrey@english-nature.org.uk; www.english-nature.org.uk.

5. OLD LODGE RESERVE

Sussex Wildlife Trust.
Location: Near Crowborough. Part of Ashdown Forest.
Access: Open all year.
Facilities: Car park, public footpaths, nature trails. No dogs. **Public transport:** None.
Habitat: Heather, pine woodland.
Key birds: *Spring/summer*: Nightjar, Redstart, Woodcock, Tree Pipit, Stonechat.
Contact: Sussex Wildlife Trust, Woods Mill, Shoreham Road, Henfield, West Sussex BN5 9SD. 01273 482630. e-mail: enquiries@sussexwt.org.uk www.wildlifetrust.org.uk/sussex

6. PETT POOLS

Sussex Wildlife Trust.
Location: TQ 903 145. NE of Hastings on A259.
Access: Good views from Rye/Hastings coast road.
Facilities: None.
Public transport: Call Trust for advice.
Habitat: Man-made shallow pools.
Key birds: *Autumn*: Good wader passage. *Winter*: Bearded Tit.
Contact: Trust HQ, 01273 492630.
e-mail: enquiries@sussexwt.co.uk

7. PEVENSEY LEVELS

English Nature (Sussex & Surrey Team).
Location: TQ 665 054. NE of Eastbourne. S of A259, one mile along minor road from Pevensey E to Norman's Bay.
Access: Good views from road.
Facilities: None.
Public transport: Call for advice.
Habitat: Freshwater grazing marsh, subject to light flooding after rains.
Key birds: *Summer*: Breeding Reed and Sedge Warblers, Yellow Wagtail, Snipe, Redshank, Lapwing. *Winter*: Large numbers of wildfowl (inc. some Bewick's and Whooper Swans) and waders (inc. Golden Plover). Birds of prey (inc. Merlin, Peregrine, Hobby, Short-eared Owl).
Contact: Malcolm Emery, English Nature, Phoenix House, 32-33 North Street, Lewes, E Sussex BN7 2PH. 01273 476595; fax 01273 483063; e-mail sussex.surrey@english-nature.org.uk; www.english-nature.org.uk.

8. RYE HARBOUR

Rye Harbour Local Nature Reserve Management Committee.
Location: TQ 941 188. One mile from Rye off A259 signed Rye Harbour. From J10 of M20 take A2070 until it joins A259.
Access: Open at all times by footpaths. Organised groups please book.
Facilities: Car park in Rye Harbour village. Information kiosk in car park. Toilets and disabled facilities near car park, four hides (one with wheelchair access), information centre open at weekends. **Public transport:** Train (tel: 08457 484950), bus (tel: 0870 608 2608), Rye tourist information (tel: 01797 226696).
Habitat: Sea, sand, shingle, pits and grassland.
Key birds: *Spring*: Passage waders, especially roosting Whimbrel. *Summer*: Breeding terns, waders, Wheatear, Yellow Wagtail. *Winter*: Wildfowl, Water Rail, Bittern.
Contact: Barry Yates, (Manager), 2 Watch Cottages, Winchelsea, East Sussex TN36 4LU. 01797 223862. e-mail: yates@clara.net www.natureserve.ryeharbour.org

Sussex, West

1. ADUR ESTUARY

RSPB (South East England Office), 01273 775333.

2. ARUNDEL

The Wildfowl & Wetlands Trust.
Location: TQ 020 081. Clearly signposted from Arundel, just N of A27.
Access: Summer (9.30am-5.30pm) winter (9.30am-4.30pm). Closed Christmas Day. Approx 1.5 miles of level footpaths, suitable for wheelchairs. No dogs except guide dogs.
Facilities: Visitor centre, restaurant, shop, hides, picnic area, seasonal nature trails. Eye of The Wind Wildlife Gallery. Corporate hire facilities.
Public transport: Arundel station, 15-20 minute walk. Tel: 01903 882131.
Habitat: Lakes, wader scrapes, reedbed.
Key birds: *Summer*: Nesting Redshank, Lapwing, Oystercatcher, Common Tern, Sedge, Reed and Cetti's Warblers, Peregrine, Hobby. *Winter*: Teal, Wigeon, Reed Bunting, Water Rail, Cetti's Warbler and occasionally roosting Bewick's Swan.
Contact: James Sharpe, Mill Road, Arundel, West Sussex BN18 9PB. 01903 883355.
e-mail: info.arundel@wwt.org.uk

3. IPING AND STEDHAM COMMONS

Sussex Wildlife Trust/Sussex Downs Conservation Board.
Location: 2.5 miles W of Midhurst on the A272. The car park is 0.5 miles down the road to Elsted on the R. There is a height barrier to prevent tall vehicles entering.
Access: Open all year.
Facilities: Car park, paths.
Public transport: None.
Habitat: Heathland, coniferous plantations, woodland.
Key birds: *Spring/summer*: Willow Warbler, Tree Pipit Whitethroat, Yellowhammer, Turtle Dove, Nightjar, Woodcock. *Winter*: Stonechat, possible Hen Harrier, finches, Siskin, Redpoll. *All year*: Sparrowhawk, Green and Great Spotted Woodpeckers, Goldcrest, Marsh Tit.
Contact: Sussex Wildlife Trust, Woods Mill,

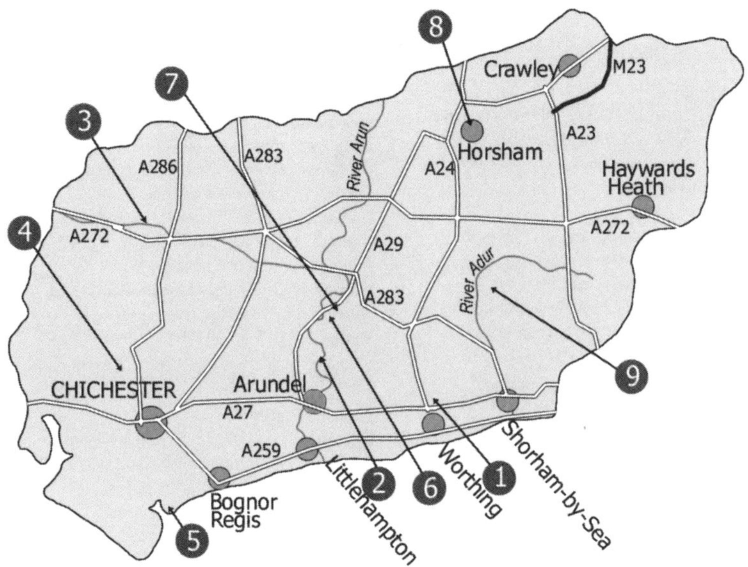

Shoreham Road, Henfield, West Sussex, BN5 9SD, 01273 492630. e-mail: sussexwt@cix.co.uk www.wildlifetrust.org.uk/sussex

4. KINGLEY VALE

English Nature (Sussex & Surrey Team). 01243 575353.

5. PAGHAM HARBOUR

West Sussex County Council.
Location: SZ 857 966. Five miles S of Chichester on B2145 towards Selsey.
Access: Open at all times, dogs must be on leads, disabled trail with accessible hide.
Facilities: Visitor centre open at weekends (10am-4pm), toilets (including disabled), three hides, one nature trail. **Public transport:** Bus stop by visitor centre. **Habitat:** Intertidal saltmarsh, shingle beaches, lagoons and farmland.
Key birds: *Spring*: Passage migrants. *Autumn*: Passage waders, other migrants. *Winter*: Brent Goose, Slavonian Grebe, wildfowl. *All year*: Little Egret.
Contact: Sarah Patton, Pagham Harbour LNR, Selsey Road, Sidlesham, Chichester, West Sussex PO20 7NE. 01243 641508.
e-mail: pagham.nr@westsussex.gov.uk

6. PULBOROUGH BROOKS

RSPB (South East England Office).
Location: TQ 054 170. Signposted on A283 between Pulborough (via A29) and Storrington (via A24). Two miles SE of Pulborough.
Access: Open daily. Visitor centre 10am-5pm (Tea-room 4.45pm, 4pm Mon-Fri in winter), closed Christmas and Boxing Days. Nature trail and hides (9am-9pm or sunset), closed Christmas Day. Admission fee for nature trail (free to RSPB members). No dogs. All hides accessible to wheelchair users, although strong help is needed.
Facilities: Visitor centre (incl RSPB shop, tea room with terrace, displays, toilets). Nature trail and four hides and two viewpoints. Large car park. Play and picnic areas. A mobility buggy is available for free hire.
Public transport: Two miles from Pulborough train station. Connecting bus service regularly passes reserve entrance (not Suns). Compass Travel (01903 233767). Cycle stands.
Habitat: Lowland wet grassland (wet meadows and ditches). Hedgerows and woodland.
Key birds: *Winter*: Wintering waterbirds, Bewick's Swan. *Spring*: Breeding wading birds and songbirds (incl Lapwing and Nightingale). *Summer*: Butterflies and dragonflies, warblers. *Autumn*: Passage wading birds, Redstart, Whinchat.
Contact: Tim Callaway, Site Manager, Upperton's Barn, Wiggonholt, Pulborough, West Sussex RH20 2EL. 01798 875851.
e-mail: pulborough.brooks@rspb.org.uk

7. WALTHAM BROOKS

Sussex Wildlife Trust.
Location: TQ 026 159. SW of Pulborough. On S side of minor road E of Coldwaltham on A29.
Access: Park at Greatham Bridge car park, not on roadside. **Facilities:** None.
Public transport: None.
Habitat: Wet grassland with muddy pools in spring, flooded meadows in winter.
Key birds: *Winter:* Waders, wildfowl (inc. Bewick's Swan, Shoveler, Teal, Wigeon). *Spring/ summer:* Redshank, Lapwing, Gadwall and Shelduck. **Contact:** Trust HQ, 01273 492630.

8. WARNHAM NATURE RESERVE

Horsham District Council.
Location: TQ 167 324. One mile from Horsham Town Centre. Reserve located off A24 at the 'Robin Hood' roundabout, on B2237.
Access: Open Thu-Sun throughout the year and Bank Holidays (10am-6pm or dusk). Free access over part of reserve, permits required for some areas (small charge day or annual permits). No dogs allowed. Good disabled access over whole reserve, with boardwalks and hardstanding paths.
Facilities: Visitor centre and café open Sat and Sun in summer, Sun only in winter. Toilets (including disabled) available, two hides, nature reserve leaflets available to lead you round.
Public transport: From Horsham Railway Station it is a mile walk along Hurst Road, with a right turn onto Warnham Road. A bus from the 'Carfax' in Horsham Centre can take you to within 150 yards of the reserve. Travel line, 0870 608 2608.
Habitat: Millpond with reedbeds, marsh, meadow and woodland (broadleaf and coniferous).
Key birds: Heronry, Great Crested Grebe, Kingfisher three woodpeckers, Willow Tit, Goldcrest. *Summer*: Hirundines, Cuckoo, Spotted Flycatcher, warblers. *Winter*: Cormorant, gulls, Water Rail, Siskin, Lesser Redpoll, Fieldfare, Redwing, Meadow Pipit. *Passage:* Waders, Wheatear, Whinchat.
Contact: Sam Bayley, Leisure Services, Park House Lodge, North Street , Horsham, W Sussex RH12 1RL. 01403 256890.

9. WOODS MILL

Sussex Wildlife Trust.
Location: TQ 218 138. Located NW of Brighton, one mile S of Henfield on A2037.
Access: Nature trail – every day except Christmas week (9am-5pm). Muddy in winter, access by wheelchair in summer. Headquarters of Sussex Wildlife Trust.
Facilities: Toilets, hide, nature trail, car park. Events programme.
Public transport: From Henfield hourly. Compass Travel 01903 233767.
Habitat: Woodland, reedbeds, wet meadow, lake.
Key birds: General woodland birds and Kingfisher all year. *Summer*: Warblers (Reed, Blackcap, Garden, Whitethroat, Lesser Whitethroat) and Nightingale.
Contact: Steve Tillman, Woods Mill, Henfield, West Sussex BN5 9SD. 01273 492630.

Tyne & Wear

1 BIG WATERS

Northumberland Wildlife Trust.
Location: NZ 227 734. Off A1, N of Newcastle. Head N along track off Wide Open/Dinnington road.
Access: View from public hide (suitable for disabled) at E end of recreation area; permit for further access from NWT. **Facilities:** Public hide.
Public transport: No information available.
Habitat: Pond, fen/wet grassland.
Key birds: Breeding & winter wildfowl; Swallow roost. **Contact:** Trust HQ, 0191 284 6884.

2 BOLDON FLATS

South Tyneside Metropolitan Council.
Location: NZ 377 614. Take A184 N from Sunderland to Boldon.
Access: View from Moor Lane on minor road NE of East Boldon station towards Whitburn.
Facilities: None. **Public transport:** None.
Habitat: Meadows, part SSSI, managed flood in winter, pond, ditches.
Key birds: *Passage/winter*: Wildfowl and waders. Gull roost may inc. Mediterranean, Glaucous, Iceland; Merlin fairly regular.

3 DERWENT WALK COUNTRY PARK

Gateshead Council.
Location: NZ 178 604. Along River Derwent, four miles SW of Newcastle and Gateshead. Several car parks along A694.
Access: Site open all times. Thornley visitor centre open weekends and Bank Holidays (12-5pm). Keys for hides available from Thornley Woodlands Centre (£2).
Facilities: Toilets at Thornley and Swalwell visitor centres. Hides at Far Pasture Ponds and Thornley feeding station.
Public transport: 45, 46, 46A, M20 and 611 buses from Newcastle/Gateshead to Swalwell/ Rowlands Gill. Bus stop Thornley Woodlands Centre. (Regular bus service from Newcastle). Information from News Travel Line. Tel: 0191 2325325.
Habitat: Mixed woodland, river, ponds, meadows.
Key birds: *Summer*: Wood Warbler, Pied Flycatcher, Green Sandpiper, Kingfisher, Dipper, Great Spotted and Green Woodpeckers, Blackcap, Garden Warbler, Nuthatch. *Winter*: Brambling, Marsh Tit, Bullfinch, Great Spotted Woodpecker, Nuthatch, Goosander, Kingfisher.
Contact: Stephen Westerberg, Thornley Woodlands Centre, Rowlands Gill, Tyne & Wear NE39 1AU. 01207 545212.
e-mail:countryside@gateshead.gov.uk
www.gateshead.gov.uk

4. MARSDEN BAY/ROCK

National Trust.
Location: NZ 404 648. Off A183 Sunderland - South Shields road.
Facilities: Popular Grotto pub built into foot of mainland cliffs opposite Marsden Rock. Also cafe and shop at Souter Lighthouse.
Habitat: Cliffs and rocks.
Key birds: Significant seabird colony with nesting Fulmars, Cormorants, Herring Gulls and Kittiwakes the most numerous. Also 25-30 pairs of Razorbills.
Contact: National Trust, Souter Lighthouse Information Centre, 0191 529 3161.

5.RYTON WILLOWS

Gateshead Council.
Location: NZ 15 65. Five miles W of Gateshead adjacent Ryton village. Driving W on A1, take the 2nd exit past Metro Centre on to A695 to Newcastle and Beydon. Turn R at roundabout W of Blaydon, on to the B6317. Turn R just past Hedgefield Inn, signed to Old Ryton Village. Take the 1st R past Jolly Fellows pub and park at bottom by railway. **Access:** Open all year.
Facilities: Car park, nature trail and free leaflet.
Public transport: Regular service to Ryton from Newcastle/Gateshead. Information from Nexus Travelline on 0191 232 5325.
Habitat: The reserve hugs S bank of River Tyne, which is tidal. At low tide,steep muddy banks. Scrub, mixed woodland, ponds.
Key birds: *Spring/summer*: Cuckoo, hirundines, Lesser Whitethroat, Whitethroat, Garden Warbler. *Passage*: Waders inc Golden Plover, possible Greenshank, Whimbrel, Green Sandpiper. *Winter*: Wildfowl, Grey Partridge, Water Rail, gulls, Grey Wagtail, Merlin,

Brambling. *All year*: Woodcock, Tawny Owl, Green and Great Spotted Woodpeckers, tits inc possible Willow and Marsh Tits, Hawfinch, Yellowhammer.
Contact: Gateshead Council, Gateshead Civic Centre, Regent Street, Gateshead NE8 1HH. 0191 433 3000.

6. ST MARY'S WETLAND AND ISLAND

Location: Wetland at NZ 345 750. Off A193 at N end of Whitley Bay sea front. Island off nearby shore. **Access:** Island accessible by causeway at low tide. **Habitat:** Coastal, rocks.
Key birds: Wildfowl and waders, good for passerine migants in spring and especially autumn. Island notable for shorebirds and observing sea passage.
Contact: Tyneside Bird Club Recorder, Ian Fisher, 74 Benton Park Road, Newcastle upon Tyne NE7 7NB.

7. SHIBDON POND

Gateshead Council.
Location: NZ 192 628. E of Blaydon, S of Scotswood Bridge, close to A1. Car park at Blaydon swimming baths. Open access from B6317 (Shibdon Road).
Access: Open at all times. Disabled access to hide. Key for hide available from Thornley Woodlands Centre (£2). **Facilities:** Hide in SW corner of pond. Free leaflet available.
Public transport: At least six buses per hour from Newcastle/Gateshead to Blaydon (bus stop Shibdon Road). Information from Nexus Travel Line (0191 232 5325).
Habitat: Pond, marsh, scrub and damp grassland.
Key birds: *Winter*: Wildfowl, Water Rail, white-winged gulls. *Summer*: Reed Warbler, Sedge Warbler, Lesser Whitethroat, Grasshopper Warbler, Water Rail. *Autumn*: Passage waders and wildfowl, Kingfisher.
Contact: Brian Pollinger, Thornley Woodlands Centre, Rowlands Gill, Tyne & Wear NE39 1AU. 1209 545212.
e-mail: thornleywoodlandscentre@unisonFree.net

8. TYNE RIVERSIDE COUNTRY PARK AND THROCKLEY POND NR

Newcastle City Council/Northumberland Wildlife Trust.
Location: NZ 158 658. From the Newcastle to Carlisle by-pass on A69(T) take A6085 into Newburn. The park is signposted along the road to Blaydon. 0.25 miles after this junction. Turn due W (the Newburn Hotel is on the corner) and after 0.5 miles the parking and information area is signed just beyond the Newburn Leisure Centre.
Access: Open all year.
Facilities: Car park. Leaflets and walk details available.
Public transport: None.
Habitat: River, pond with reed and willow stands, mixed woodland, open grassland.
Key birds: *Spring/summer*: Swift, Swallow, Whitethroat, Lesser Whitethroat. *Winter*: Sparrowhawk, Kingfisher, Little Grebe, finches, Siskin, Fieldfare, Redwing, duck, Goosander. *All year*: Grey Partridge, Green and Great Spotted Woodpecker, Bullfinch, Yellowhammer.
Contact: Northumberland Wildlife Trust, The Garden House, St Nicholas Park, Jubilee Road, Newcastle upon Tyne, NE3 3XT, 0191 2846884.
e-mail: northwildlife@cix.co.uk

9. WALLSEND SWALLOW POND

Northumberland Wildlife Trust.
Location: NZ 301 693. Halfway between Whitley Bay and Gosforth in the Rising Sun Country Park. S off A191 by garden centre.
Access: View from public hide on bridleway.
Facilities: Parking, toilets and picnic area at Rising Sun Centre. Two hides, one adapted for wheelchairs. Pond-dipping platforms.
Public transport: None.
Habitat: Shallow pool created by mining subsidence, mixed woodland.
Key birds: Breeding & winter wildfowl including Teal and Whooper Swan. Passage waders include Redshank, Greenshank.
Contact: Trust HQ, 0191 284 6884.

10. WASHINGTON

The Wildfowl & Wetlands Trust.
Location: NZ 331 566. In Washington. On N bank of River Wear, W of Sunderland. Signposted from A195, A19, A1231 and A182.
Access: Open 9.30am-5pm (summer), 9.30am-4pm (winter). Free to WWT members. Admission charge for non-members. No dogs except guide dogs. Good access for people with disabilities.
Facilities: Visitor centre, toilets, parent and baby room, range of hides. Shop and café.
Public transport: Buses to Waterview Park (250 yards walk) from Washington, from Sunderland, Newcastle-upon-Tyne, Durham and South Shields. Tel: 0845 6060260 for details.
Habitat: Wetlands and woodland.

Tyne & Wear

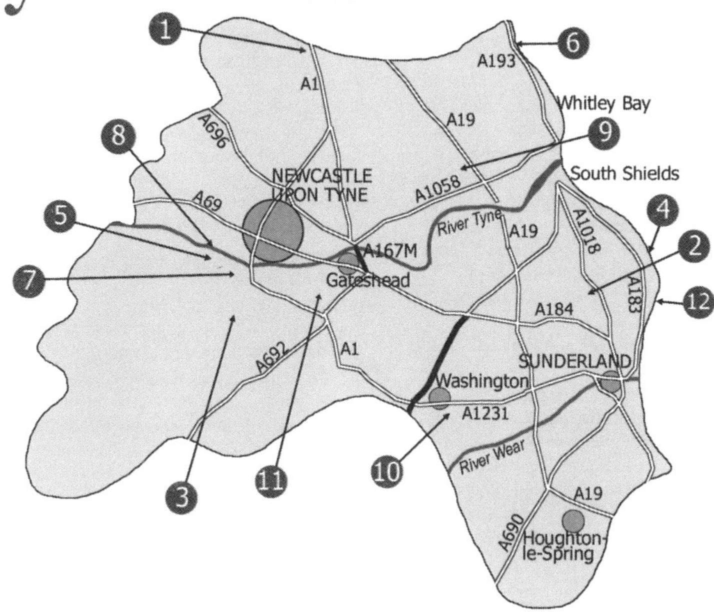

Key birds: *Spring/summer*: Nesting colony of Grey Heron, other breeders include Common Tern, Oystercatcher, Lapwing. *Winter*: Bird-feeding station visited by Great Spotted Woodpecker, Bullfinch, Jay and Sparrowhawk. Wild Goldeneye and other ducks.
Contact: Andrew Donnison, (Grounds Manager), Wildfowl & Wetlands Trust, District 15, Washington NE38 8LE. 0191 4165454 ext 222. e-mail: andrew.donnison@wwt.org.uk www.wwt.org.uk

11. WATERGATE FOREST PARK/ WASHINGWELL WOOD

Gateshead Council.
Location: NZ 229 606. Two miles SW of Newcastle.
Access: Open at all times. Access for all on several paths.
Facilities: Nature trails.
Public transport: Regular bus service to Lobley Hill from Newcastle/Gateshead. Information from Nexus Travel Line 0191 232 5325.
Habitat: Lake, conifer wood, grassland (young tree planting areas).
Key birds: *Winter*: Wildfowl, Siskin, finches. *Summer*: Wildfowl, Common Sandpiper, Sky Lark, Linnet.
Contact: Melanie Bowden, Thornley Woodlands Centre, Rowlands Gill, Tyne & Wear NE39 1AU. 01207 545212.
e-mail: thornleywoodlandscentre@unisonFree.net www.gateshead.gov.uk

12. WHITBURN BIRD OBSERVATORY

National Trust/Durham Bird Club.
Location: NZ 414 633.
Access: Access details from Recorder.
Facilities: None.
Public transport: Regular bus service along coast road between Sunderland and South Sheilds.
Habitat: Cliff top location.
Key birds: Esp. seawatching but also passerine migrants inc. rarities.
Contact: Tony Armstrong,39 Western Hill, Durham City, DH1 4RJ. 0191 386 1519;
e-mail: ope@globalnet.co.uk.

Warwickshire

1. ALVECOTE POOLS

Warwickshire Wildlife Trust.
Location: SK 253 034. Located alongside River Anker E of Tamworth. Access via Robey's Lane (off B5000) just past Alvecote Priory car park. Also along towpath via Pooley Hall visitor centre, also number of points along towpath.
Access: Some parts of extensive path system is accessible to disabled. Parking Alvecote Priory car park. Nature trail. **Facilities:** Nature trail.
Public transport: Within walking distance of the Avecote village bus stop.
Habitat: Marsh, pools (open and reedbeds) and woodland.
Key birds: *Spring/summer*: Breeding Oystercatcher, Common Tern and Little Ringed Plover. Common species include Great Crested Grebe, Tufted Duck and Snipe. Important for wintering, passage and breeding wetland birds.
Contact: Reserves Team, Brandon Marsh Nature Centre, Brandon Lane, Brandon, Coventry CV3 3GW. 02476 308993.
e-mail: reserves@warkswt.cix.co.uk
www.warwickshire-wildlife-trust.org.uk

2. BRANDON MARSH

Warwickshire Wildlife Trust.
Location: SP 386 762. Three miles SE of Coventry, 200 yards SE of A45/A46 junction (Tollbar End). Turn E off A45 into Brandon Lane. Reserve entrance 1.25 miles on right.
Access: Open weekdays (9am-5pm), weekends (10am-4.30pm). Entrance charge currently £2.50 (free to Wildlife Trust members). Wheelchair access to nature trail and Wright hide. No dogs.
Facilities: Visitor centre, toilets, tea-room (open at above times), nature trail, six hides.
Public transport: Bus service from Coventry to Tollbar End then 1.25 mile walk. Tel Travel West Midlands 02476 817032 for bus times.
Habitat: Ten pools, together with marsh, reedbeds, willow carr, scrub and small mixed woodland in 260 acres, designated SSSI in 1972.
Key birds: *Spring/summer*: Garden Warbler, Grasshopper Warbler, Whitethroat, Lesser Whitethroat, Hobby, Little Ringed Plover, Whinchat, Wheatear. *Autumn/winter*: Dunlin, Ruff, Snipe, Greenshank, Green and Common Sandpipers, Wigeon, Shoveler, Pochard, Goldeneye, Siskin, Redpoll. *All year*: Cetti's Warbler, Kingfisher, Water Rail, Gadwall, Little Grebe.
Contact: Ken Bond, Hon. Sec. Brandon Marsh Voluntary Conservation Team, 54 Wiclif Way, Stockingford, Nuneaton, Warwickshire CV10 8NF. 02476 308993.
e-mail: reserves@warkswt.cix.co.uk
www.warwickshire-wildlife-trust.org.uk

3. HARTSHILL HAYES

Warwickshire County Council.
Location: SP 317 943. Signposted as 'Country Park' from B4114 W of Nuneaton.
Access: Open all year. Closed Christmas Day.
Facilities: Three waymarked walks (one easy-going). Visitor centre, play area, toilets with facilities for disabled.
Public transport: None.
Habitat: Mixed woodland, grassland hillside.
Key birds: Warblers, woodpeckers, tits, Goldcrest.
Contact: Country Park Manager's Office, Kingsbury Water Park,

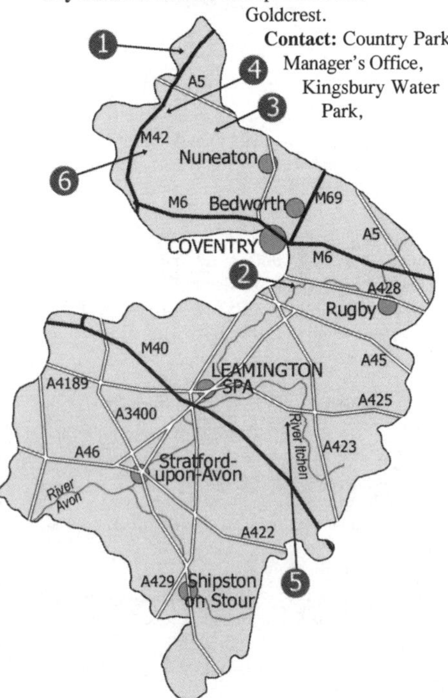

Bodymoor Heath Lane, Sutton Coldfield, West Midlands B76 0DY. 01827 872660; e-mail parks@warwickshire.gov.uk www.warwickshire.gov.uk/countryside.

4. KINGSBURY WATER PARK

Warwickshire County Council.
Location: SP 203 960. Signposted 'Water Park' from J9 M42, A4097 NE of Birmingham.
Access: Open all year except Christmas Day.
Facilities: Four hides, one with wheelchair access. Miles of flat surfaced footpaths, free loan scheme for mobility scooters. Cafes, information centre with gift shop.
Public transport: Call for advice.
Habitat: Open water; numerous small pools, some with gravel islands; gravel pits; silt beds with reedmace, reed, willow and alder; rough areas and grassland.
Key birds: *Summer*: Breeding warblers (nine species), Little Ringed Plover, Great Crested and Little Grebes. Shoveler, Shelduck and a thriving Common Tern colony. Passage waders (esp. spring). *Winter*: Wildfowl, Short-eared Owl.
Contact: Country Park Manager's Office, Kingsbury Water Park, Bodymoor Heath Lane, Sutton Coldfield, West Midlands B76 0DY. 01827 872660; e-mail parks@warwickshire.gov.uk www.warwickshire.gov.uk/countryside.

5. UFTON FIELDS

Warwickshire Wildlife Trust. 02476 308993.

6. WHITACRE HEATH

Warwickshire Wildlife Trust.
Location: SP 209 931. Three miles N of Coleshill, just W of Whitacre Heath village.
Access: Trust members only.
Facilities: Five hides.
Public transport: Within walking distance of Lea Marston village bus stop.
Habitat: Pools, wet woodland and grassland.
Key birds: *Summer*: Sedge, Garden and Willow Warbler, Reed Warbler, Lesser Whitethroat, Whitethroat and Blackcap. Migrant Curlew, Whinchat. Also Snipe, Water Rail and Kingfisher.
Contact: Reserves Team, Brandon Marsh Nature Centre, Brandon Lane, Brandon, Coventry CV3 3GW. 02476 308993.
e-mail: reserves@warkswt.cix.co.uk
www.warwickshire-wildlife-trust.org.uk

West Midlands

1. LICKEY HILLS COUNTRY PARK

Birmingham County Council.
Location: Eleven miles SW of Birmingham City Centre.
Access: Open all year.
Facilities: Car park, visitor centre with wheelchair pathway with viewing gallery, picnic site, toilets, café, shop.
Public transport: Bus: West Midlands 62 Rednal (20 mins walk to visitor centre. Rail: Barnt Green (25 mins walk through woods to the centre).
Habitat: Hills covered with mixed deciduous woodland, conifer plantations and heathland.
Key birds: *Spring/summer*: Warblers, Tree Pipit, Redstart. *Winter*: Redwing, Fieldfare. *All year*: Common woodland species.
Contact: The Visitor Centre, Lickey Hills Country Park, Warren Lane, Rednal, Birmingham, B45 8ER, 0121 4477106.
e-mail: visitorcentre@lickeyhills.fsnet.co.uk

2. MARSH LANE NATURE RESERVE

Packington Estate Enterprises Limited.
Location: SP 217 804. Equidistant between Birmingham and Coventry, both approx 7-8 miles away. Off A452 between A45 and Balsall Common. Turn right into Marsh Lane and immediately right onto Old Kenilworth Road (now a public footpath), to locked gate. Key required.
Access: Only guide dogs allowed. Site suitable for disabled. Access is by day or year permit only. Membership rates: annual - adult £20, OAP £15, children (under 16) £10 husband/wife £36, OAP husband/wife £27.50. Contact address below (9am-5.15pm). Regular newsletter provided to annual permit holders; day adult £3, OAP £2.75, children (under 16) £2 obtained from Golf Professional Shop, Stonebridge Golf Centre, Somers Road, off Hampton Lane, Meriden, nr Coventry CV7 7PL (tel 01676 522442) only three to four minutes car journey from site. Open Mon-Sun (7am-7pm).

Stonebridge Golf Centre open to non-members. Visitors can obtain drinks and meals at Stonebridge Golf Centre. £26.75 deposit required for key.
Facilities: No toilets or visitor centre. Four hides and hard tracks between hides. Car park behind locked gates.
Public transport: Hampton-in-Arden railway station within walking distance on footpath loop. Bus no 194 stops at N end of Old Kenilworth Road one mile from reserve gate.
Habitat: Two large pools with islands, three small areas of woodland, large field set aside for arable growth for finches and buntings as winter feed.
Key birds: 152 species. *Summer*: Breeding birds include Little Ringed Plover, Common Tern, most species of warbler including Grasshopper. Good passage of waders in Apr, May, Aug and Sept. Hobby and Buzzard breed locally.
Contact: Nicholas P Barlow, Packington Hall, Packington Park, Meriden, Nr Coventry CV7 7HF. 01676 522020. www.packingtonestate.net

3. ROUGH WOOD CHASE

Walsall Metropolitan Borough Council
Location: SJ 987 012. NW of Walsall town centre. From J10 of M6 travelling N, turn L on A454 then R on A462. Turn first R onto Bloxwich Road North then R into Hunts Lane. Car park is on R.
Access: Open at all times.
Facilities: Car park, footpaths, nature trail.
Public transport: WMT bus no 341 from Walsall, Park street and Willenhall.
Habitat: Mature oak and mixed woodland, grassland, open water.
Key birds: Common woodland and water species.
Contact: Countryside Services, Walsall Metropolitan Borough Council, Dept of Leisure & Community Services, PO box 42, The Civic Centre, Darwall Street, WalsallWS1 1TZ. 01922 650000;(Fax)01922 721862. www.walsall.gov.uk

4. SANDWELL VALLEY 1

Metropolitan Borough Council.
Location: SP 012 918 & SP 028 992.
Access: Access and car park from Dagger Lane or Forge Lane, West Bromwich.
Facilities: Mainly public open space. **Habitat:** Nature reserve, lakes, woods and farmland.
Key birds: *Summer*: Breeding Lapwing, Little Ringed Plover, Sparrowhawk. All three woodpeckers, Tawny Owl, Reed Warbler. Passage waders.
Contact: Senior Ranger, Sandwell Valley Country Park, Salters Lane, West Bromwich, W Midlands B71 4BG. 0121 553 0220 or 2147.

5. SANDWELL VALLEY 2

RSPB
Location: SP 035 928. Great Barr, Birmingham. Follow signs S from M6 J7 via A34. Take right at 1st junction onto A4041. Take 4th left onto Hamstead Road (B4167), then right at 1st mini roundabout onto Tanhouse Avenue.
Access: 800 metres of wheelchair accessible paths around reserve, centre fully accessible.
Facilities: Visitor Centre and car park (open Tue-Sun 9.30am-5pm) with viewing area, small shop and hot drinks, four viewing screens.
Public transport: Bus: 16 from Colmore Row, Birmingham City Centre (ask for Tanhouse Avenue). Train: Hamstead Station, then 16 bus for one mile towards West Bromwich from Hamstead (ask for Tanhouse Avenue).
Habitat: Open water, wet grassland, reedbed, dry grassland and scrub.
Key birds: *Summer*: Lapwing, Reed Warbler, Willow Tit. *Passage*: Sandpipers, Yellow Wagtail, chats, Common Tern. *Winter*: Water Rail, Snipe, Jack Snipe, Goosander, Bullfinch, woodpeckers and wildfowl.
Contact: Colin Horne, 20 Tanhouse Avenue, Great Barr, Birmingham B43 5AG. 0121 3577395.

6. SMESTOW VALLEY LNR

Contact: Mr T Weatherstone, (Leisure Services), Wolverhampton Council, Civic Centres, St Peter's Square, Wolverhampton WV1 1SJ.

7. SWAN POOL AND THE SWAG

Walsall Metropolitan Borough Council
Location: SK 040 019. Located NE of Walsall centre. Take Walsall ring road A34/A4148 N, turn R onto A461 then R onto A454 towards Aldridge. Turn L on B4154 (Stubbers Green Road), ponds are either side of this road.
Access: Ponds only viewable from road.
Habitat: Open water, reedbed.
Key birds: Common water birds, Little Grebe, Reed Bunting, Ruddy Duck, Sand and House Martins. Important hirundine roost in Autumn.
Contact: Countryside Services, Walsall Metropolitan Borough Council, Dept of Leisure & Community Services, PO box 42, The Civic Centre, Darwall Street, WalsallWS1 1TZ. 01922 650000;(Fax)01922 721862.
www.walsall.gov.uk

Wiltshire

1. FYFIELD DOWNS NNR

Wiltshire Wildlife Trust.
Location: On the Marlborough Downs. From the A345 at the N end of Marlborough a minor road signed Broad Hinton, bisects the downs, dropping steeply at Hackpen Hill to the A361 just before Broad Hinton. From Hackpen Hill walk S to Fyfield Down.
Access: Open all year but avoid the racing gallops. Keep dogs on leads.
Facilities: Car park.
Public transport: None.
Habitat: Downs.
Key birds: *Spring*: Ring Ouzel possible passage, Wheatear, Cuckoo, Redstart, common warblers. *Summer*: Possible Quail. *Winter*: Occasional Hen Harrier, possible Merlin, Golden Plover, Short-eared Owl, thrushes. *All year*: Sparrowhawk, Buzzard, Kestrel, partridges, Green and Great Spotted Woodpeckers, Goldfinch, Corn Bunting.
Contact: Wiltshire Wildlife Trust, Elm Tree Court, Long Street, Devizes, Wiltshire, SN10 1NJ, 01380 725670.
e-mail: admin@wiltshirewildlife.org
www.wiltshirewildlife.org

2. JONES'S MILL NATURE RESERVE

Wiltshire Wildlife Trust.
Location: SU 170 611. From Pewsey, follow the B3087 for 0.5 miles toward Burbage. Turn L at the crossroads into Dursden Lane. Continue along the lane and over a railway bridge. Parking is limited on the left-hand verge. Walk a short distance along the lane to the reserve entrance, a sunken track just before the 1st house on the L.
Access: Open all year as long as the habitat is not damaged.
Facilities: None.
Public transport: None.
Habitat: River, former water meadows, fen carr, pond.
Key birds: *Spring/summer*: Warblers. *All year*: Kingfisher, Little Grebe, Bullfinch, Snipe, other common species.
Contact: Wiltshire Wildlife Trust, Elm Tree Court, Long Street, Devizes, Wiltshire, SN10 1NJ, 01380 725670.
e-mail: admin@wiltshirewildlife.org
www.wiltshirewildlife.org

3. SAVERNAKE FOREST

Forest Enterprise.
Location: From Marlborough A4 Hungerford road runs along N side of the forst. Two pillars mark the Forest Hill entrance 1.5 miles E of A346/A4 junction. The Grand Avenue leads straight through middle of woodland to join a minor road from Stibb Gree on A346 N of Burbage to A4 W of Froxfield.
Access: Open all year.
Facilities: Car park, picnic site at NW end by A346. Fenced-off areas should not be entered unless there is a footpath.
Public transport: None.
Habitat: Ancient woodland, with one of the largest collections of veteran trees in Britain.
Key birds: *Spring/summer*: Garden Warbler, Blackcap, Willow Warbler, Chiffchaff, Wood Warbler, Redstart, occasional Nightingale, Tree Pipit, Spotted Flycatcher. *Winter*:Finch flocks possibly inc Siskin, Redpoll, Brambling. *All year*: Sparrowhawk, Buzzard, Woodcock, owls, all three woodpeckers, Marsh Tit, Willow Tit, Jay and other woodland birds.
Contact: Forest Enterprise, Postern Hill, Marlborough, 01672 512520

4. SWILLBROOK LAKES

Wiltshire Wildlife Trust.
Location: SU 018 934. NW of Swindon, one mile S of Somerford Keynes on Cotswold Water Park spine road; turn off down Minety Lane (parking).
Access: Open at all times.
Facilities: Footpath along N and E sides of lakes.
Public transport: None.
Habitat: Gravel pits with shallow pools, rough grassland and scrub around edges.
Key birds: *Winter*:Wildfowl (inc. Gadwall, Pochard, Smew, Goosander). *Summer*: Breeding Reed and Sedge Warblers; best site for Hobby in Cotswold WP.
Contact: Trust HQ, 01380 725670

Worcestershire

1. KNAPP AND PAPERMILL

Worcestershire Wildlife Trust.
Location: SO 749 522. Take A4103 SW from Worcester; R at Bransford roundabout then L towards Suckley, reserve is approx three miles (do not turn off for Alfrick). Park at Bridges Stone layby (SO 751 522), cross road and follow path to the Knapp House.
Access: Open daily exc Christmas Day. Large parties should contact Warden
Facilities: Hide, nature trail, small visitor centre, wildlife garden. **Public transport:** None.
Habitat: Broadleaved woodland, unimproved grassland, fast stream, old orchard in Leigh Brook Valley.
Key birds: *Summer*: Breeding Grey Wagtail, Kingfisher, Pied Flycatcher, all three woodpeckers. Buzzard, Sparrowhawk and Redstart also occur. Also otter.
Contact: The Warden, Knapp and Papermill reserve, The Knapp, Alfrick, Worcester WR6 5HR. 01886 832065.

2. MONKWOOD NATURE RESERVE

Worcestershire Wildlife Trust.
Location: SO 804 607. The reserve is about five miles NW of Worcester. On the A443 Worcester to Holt Heath road, take any of the minor roads N of Hallow to Sinton Green. At village green, take road to Monkwood by the side of the New Inn pub. About a mile down the road there is a car park on the R.
Access: Open all year.
Facilities: Two nature trails.
Public transport: None.
Habitat: Ancient woodland.
Key birds: *Spring/summer*: Garden Warbler, Lesser Whitethroat, Cuckoo, Blackcap, Woodcock. *All year*: Tawny Owl, Sparrowhawk, Jay. Good for butterflies.
Contact: Worcestershire Wildlife Trust, Lower Smite Farm, Smite Hill, Gwynedd, WR3 8SZ, 01905 754919. e-mail: worcswt@cix.co.uk www.worcswildlifetrust.co.uk

3. TIDDESLEY WOOD

Worcestershire Wildlife Trust.
Location: SO 929 462. Take the A44 from Pershore to Worcester. Turn L near town boundary just before the summit of the hill towards Besford and Croome. The entrance to the reserve is on the L after about 0.75 miles.
Access: Open all year except Christmas Day. Cycles and horses only allowed on the bridleway. Please keep dogs fully under control. Military firing range at the SW corner of the wood, do not enter the area marked by red flags. The NE plot is private property. Not suitable for the disabled.
Facilities: Information board.
Public transport: None.
Habitat: Ancient woodland, conifers.
Key birds: *Spring*: Chiffchaff, Blackcap, Cuckoo, occasional Nightingale. *All year*: Crossbill, Coal Tit, Goldcrest, Sparrowhawk, Willow Tit, Marsh Tit. *Winter*: Redwing, Fieldfare.
Contact: Worcestershire Wildlife Trust, Lower Smite Farm, Smite Hill, Hindlip, Worcester, WR3 8SZ, 01905 754919. e-mail: worcswt@cix.co.uk www.worcswildlifetrust.co.uk

4. TRENCH WOOD

Worcestershire Wildlife Trust.
Location: SO 931 585. NE of Worcester.
Access: Open daily exc Christmas Day. Mature trees to SW and SE of wood are not part of reserve
Facilities: Car park. **Public transport:** None.
Habitat: Young broadleaved woodland, mixed scrub.

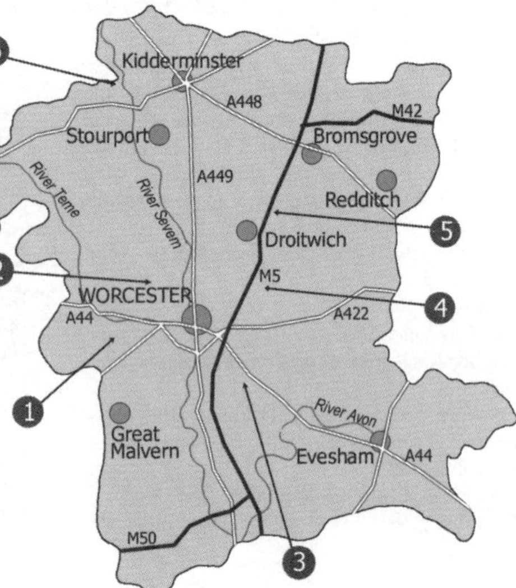

Key birds: Very good for warblers; Woodcock.
Contact: Trust HQ, 01905 754919.

5. UPTON WARREN

Worcestershire Wildlife Trust.
Location: SO 936 675. Two miles S of Bromsgrove on A38.
Access: Always open except Christmas Day. Trust membership gives access, or day permit from sailing centre. Disabled access to west hide at moors only. Dogs on leads.
Facilities: Seven hides, maps at entrances, can be very muddy.
Public transport: Birmingham/Worcester bus passes reserve entrance.
Habitat: Fresh and saline pools with muddy islands, some woodland and scrub.
Key birds: *Winter*: Wildfowl. *Spring/autumn*: Passage waders, Common Tern, Cetti's Warbler, Oystercatcher and Little Ringed Plover, many breeding warblers.
Contact: A F Jacobs, 3 The Beeches, Upton Warren, Bromsgrove, Worcs B61 7EL. 01527 861370.

6. WYRE FOREST

English Nature/Worcs Wildlife Trust.
Location: SO 750 760. A456 out of Bewdley.
Access: Observe reserve signs and keep to paths. Forestry Commission visitor centre at Callow Hill. Fred Dale Reserve is reached by footpath W of B4194 (parking at SO776763).
Facilities: Facilities for disabled (entry by car) if Warden telephoned in advance.
Public transport: None.
Habitat: Oak forest, conifer areas, birch heath, stream.
Key birds: Buzzard, Pied Flycatcher, Wood Warbler, Redstart, all three woodpeckers, Woodcock, Crossbill, Siskin, Hawfinch, Kingfisher, Dipper, Grey Wagtail, Tree Pipit.
Contact: Tim Dixon, 01531 638500.

Yorkshire, East

1. BEMPTON CLIFFS

RSPB (North of England Office).
Location: TA 197 738. Near Bridlington. Take cliff road N from Bempton Village off B1229 to car park and visitor centre
Access: Visitor centre open Mar-Nov and weekends in Dec and Feb. Public footpath along cliff top with observation points. Four miles of chalk cliffs, highest in the county. **Facilities:** Visitor centre, toilets. Viewing platforms.Picnic area.
Public transport: Railway 1.5 miles - irregular bus service to village 1.25 miles.
Habitat: Seabird nesting cliffs, farmland, scrub.
Key birds: Best to visit May to mid-July for Puffin, Gannet (only colony on English mainland), Fulmar, Kittiwake; also nesting Tree Sparrow, Corn Bunting; good migration watchpoint for skuas, shearwaters and terns.
Contact: Site Manager, RSPB Visitor Centre, Cliff Lane, Bempton, Bridlington, E Yorks YO15 1JF. 01262 851179.

2. BLACKTOFT SANDS

RSPB (North of England Office).
Location: SE 843 232. Eight miles E of Goole on minor road between Ousefleet and Adlingfleet.
Access: Open 9am-9pm or dusk if earlier. RSPB members free, £3 permit for non-members, £2 concessionary, £1 children, £6 family.
Facilities: Car park, toilets, visitor centre, six hides, footpaths suitable for wheelchairs.
Public transport: Goole/Scunthorpe bus (Sweynes' Coaches stops outside reserve entrance).
Habitat: Reedbed, saline lagoons, lowland wet grassland, willow scrub.
Key birds: *Summer*: Breeding Avocet, Marsh Harrier, Bearded Tit, passage waders (exceptional list inc many rarities). *Winter*: Hen Harrier, Merlin, Peregrine, wildfowl.
Contact: Pete Short (Warden) & Simon Wellock (Asst Warden), Hillcrest, Whitgift, Nr Goole, E Yorks DN14 8HL. 01405 704665.
e-mail: simonwellock@RSPB.org
peteshort@RSPB.org.uk www.RSPB.org

3. SPURN NATIONAL NNR

Yorkshire Wildlife Trust.
Location: Entrance Gate TA 417 151. 26 miles from Hull. Take A1033 from Hull to Patrington (via Hedon) then B1445 from Patrington to Easington and unclassed roads on to Kilnsea and Spurn Head.
Access: Normally open at all times. Vehicle

Yorkshire, East

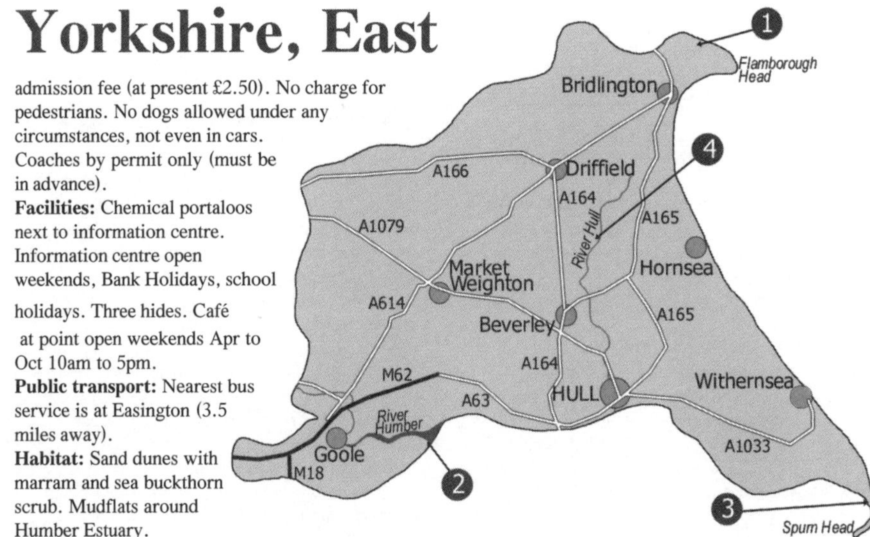

admission fee (at present £2.50). No charge for pedestrians. No dogs allowed under any circumstances, not even in cars. Coaches by permit only (must be in advance).
Facilities: Chemical portaloos next to information centre. Information centre open weekends, Bank Holidays, school holidays. Three hides. Café at point open weekends Apr to Oct 10am to 5pm.
Public transport: Nearest bus service is at Easington (3.5 miles away).
Habitat: Sand dunes with marram and sea buckthorn scrub. Mudflats around Humber Estuary.
Key birds: *Spring*: Many migrants on passage and often rare birds such as Red-backed Shrike, Bluethroat etc. *Autumn*: Passage migrants and rarities like Wryneck, Pallas's Warbler. *Winter*: Waders and Brent Goose.
Contact: Spurn Reserves Officer, Spurn NNR, Blue Bell Flat, Kilnsea, HullHU12 0UG. e-mail: spurnywt@ukonline.co.uk

4. TOPHILL LOW NATURE RESERVE

Yorkshire Water.
Location: TA 071 482. Nine miles SE of Driffield and ten miles NE of Beverley. Signposted from village of Watton on A164.
Access: Open Wed-Sun and Bank Holiday Mon. Apr-Oct (9am-6pm). Nov-Mar (9am-4pm). Charges: £2.50 per person. £1 concessions. No dogs allowed. Provision for disabled visitors (paths, ramps, hides, toilet etc).
Facilities: Visitor Centre with toilets. 13 hides (five with access for wheelchairs). Nature trails.
Habitat: Open water (two reservoirs), marshes, wader scrapes, woodland and thorn scrub.
Key birds: *Winter*: Wildfowl, gulls, Water Rail, Kingfisher. *Spring/early summer*: Passage Black-necked Grebe and Black Tern. Breeding Pochard, Kingfisher and Grasshopper Warbler. *Late Summer/autumn:* up to 20 species of passage wader.
Contact: Peter Izzard, Tophill Low Nature Reserve, Watton Carrs, Driffield, East Yorkshire YO25 9RH. 01377 270690.

Yorkshire, North

1. BOLTON ON SWALE LAKE

Yorkshire Wildlife Trust. 01904 659570.

2. BURTON RIGGS LNR

Yorkshire Wildlife Trust.
Location: 032 832. The reserve is at E end of Vale of Pickering, close to Seamer on outskirts of Scarborough. Car park the roundabout on A64, opposite Morrisons supermarket.
Access: Open all year. **Facilities:** Car park, trails.
Public transport: None.
Habitat: Old gravel pits, freshwater lakes, shingle, scrub, woodland.
Key birds: *Spring/summer*: Little Grebe, possible Little Ringed Plover. Yellow Wagtail, Whitethroat, Lesser Whitethroat, Kingfisher, Sand Martin.
Contact: Yorkshire Wildlife Trust, 10 Toft Green, York, YO1 6JT, 01904 659579.
e-mail: yorkshirewt.@cix.co.uk

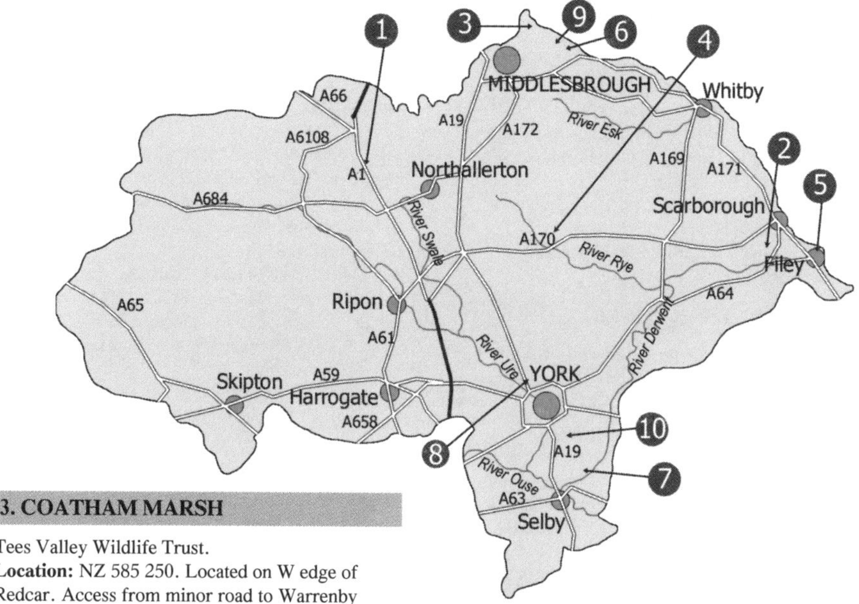

3. COATHAM MARSH

Tees Valley Wildlife Trust.

Location: NZ 585 250. Located on W edge of Redcar. Access from minor road to Warrenby from A1085/A1042.

Access: Reserve is open throughout daylight hours. Please keep to permissive footpaths only.

Facilities: Two hides. Key required for one of these – available to Tees Valley Wildlife Trust members for £10 deposit. No toilets or visitor centre.

Public transport: Very frequent bus service between Middlesbrough and Redcar. Nearest stops are in Coatham 0.25 mile from reserve (Arriva tel 0870 6082608). Redcar Central Station one mile from site. Frequent trains from Middlesbrough and Darlington.

Habitat: Freshwater wetlands, lakes, reedbeds.

Key birds: *Spring/autumn*: Wader passage (including Wood Sandpiper and Greenshank). *Summer:* Passerines (including Sedge Warbler, Yellow Wagtail). *Winter:* Ducks (including Smew). Occasional rarities, Water Rail, Great White Egret, Avocet.

Contact: Mark Fishpool, Tees Valley Wildlife Trust, Bellamy Pavilion, Kirkleatham, Redcar TS50 5NW. 01642 759900.
e-mail: teesvalleywt@cix.co.uk
www.wildlifetrust.org.uk/teesvalley

4. DUNCOMBE PARK NNR

Duncombe Park Estate.

Contact: Duncombe Park Estate, Helmsley, North Yorkshire, 01439 770213.

5. FILEY BRIGG ORNITHOLOGICAL GROUP BIRD OBSERVATORY

FBOG and Yorkshire Wildlife Trust (The Dams).

Location: TA 10 68 07. Two access roads into Filey from A165 (Scarborough to Bridlington road). Filey is ten miles N of Bridlington and eight miles S of Scarborough.

Access: Opening times – no restrictions. Dogs only in Parish Wood and The Old Tip (on lead).

Facilities: No provisions for disabled at present. Two hides at The Dams, one on The Brigg (open most weekends from late Jul-Oct, key can be hired from Country Park café). Toilets in Country Park (Apr-Nov 1) and town centre. Nature trails at The Dams, Parish Wood/Old Tip. Cliff top walk for seabirds along Cleveland Way.

Public transport: All areas within a mile of Filey railway station. Trains into Filey tel. 08457 484950; buses into Filey tel. 01723 503020

Habitat: The Dams – two freshwater lakes, fringed with some tree cover and small reedbeds. Parish Wood – a newly built wood which leads to the Old Tip, the latter has been fenced (for stock and crop strips) though there is a public trail. Carr Naze has a pond and can produce newly arrived migrants.

Key birds: *The Dams*: Breeding and wintering water birds, breeding Sedge Warbler, Reed Warbler and Tree Sparrow. *The Tip*: Important for breeding Sky Lark, Meadow Pipit, common

warblers and Grey Partridge. *Winter:* Area for buntings including Lapland. *Seawatch Hide*:Jul-Oct. All four Skuas, shearwaters, terns. *Winter*: Divers and grebes. *Totem Pole Field:* A new project should encourage breeding species and wintering larks, buntings etc. Many sub-rare/rare migrants possible at all sites.
Contact: Lez Gillard, Recorder, 12 Sycamore Avenue, Filey, N Yorks YO14 9NU. 01723 516383. e-mail: lez.gillard@talk21.com www.fbog.co.uk

6. HUNTCLIFF

Tees Valley Wildlife Trust. 01642 759900.

7. LOWER DERWENT VALLEY

English Nature (North & East Yorks).
Location: SE 691 447. Six miles SE of York, stretching 12 miles S along the River Derwent from Newton-on-Derwent to Wressle and along the Pocklington Canal. Visitor facilities at Bank Island, Wheldrake Ings YWT (SE 691 444), Thorganby (SE 693 422) and North Duffield Carrs (SE 698 366).
Access: Open all year. No dogs. Disabled access at North Duffield Carrs (two hides and car park). 600 yard path.
Facilities: North Duffield Carrs - two hides, wheelchair access. Wheldrake Ings (YWT) - five hides. Bank Island - two hides, viewing tower. Thorganby - viewing platform.
Public transport: Bus from York/Selby - contact First (01904 622992). Bicycle stands provided in car parks at Bank Island and North Duffield Carrs.
Habitat: Hay meadow and pasture, swamp, open water and alder carr woodland.
Key birds: *Spring/summer:* Breeding wildfowl and waders including Garganey and Ruff. Barn Owl and warblers. *Winter:* 20,000-plus waterfowl including Whooper Swan, Bewick's Swan, wild geese and Wigeon. Large gull roost including white-winged gulls. Also passage waders including Whimbrel.
Contact: Site Manager, English Nature, Genesis 1, Heslington Road, York YO10 5ZQ. 01904 435500. e-mail: york@english-nature.org.uk Leaflet available SAE please or check website www.english-nature.org.uk

8. MOORLANDS WOOD RESERVE

Yorkshire Wildlife Trust.
Location: From York ring road, take A19 Thirsk/ Northallerton road. After 1.6km turn R at The Blacksmith's Arms pub for Skelton. Go through the village. After 3.2km, look for an open parking area at a wide verge on the L alongside the wood and just before the entrance gate.
Access: Open all year. Entry free except May-Jun when a small charge is made.
Facilities: Car park, woodland paths. Suitable for wheelchairs. **Public transport:** None.
Habitat: Mature mixed woodland, ponds, agricultural land.
Key birds: *Spring/summer*: Cuckoo, Curlew, Garden Warbler, Blackcap, Spotted Flycatcher. *Winter*: thrushes, Siskin. *All year*: Tawny Owl, Great Spotted Woodpecker, tits inc Marsh Tit, Jay, Treecreeper, Redpoll.
Contact: Yorkshire Wildlife Trust, 10 Toft Green, York YO1 6JT. 01904 659570.
e-mail: yorkshirewt@cix.co.uk

9. SALTBURN GILL

Tees Valley Wildlife Trust. 01642 759900.
e-mail: teesvalleywt@cix.co.uk
www.wildlifetrust.org.uk/teesvalley

10. WHELDRAKE INGS LOWER DERWENT VALLEY NNR

Yorkshire Wildlife Trust.
Location: From York take A19 Selby road. After one mile turn L to Wheldrake signed Wheldrake 4 and Thorganby 6.5. After 3.5 miles pass through Wheldrake and continue towards Thorganby. After a sharp R bend turn L after 0.5 miles onto an unsigned tarmac track. Look for two old stone gateposts with pointed tops. The car park is about 0.25 miles down the track. To reach the reserve, cross the bridge and turn R over a stile.
Access: Open all year. Please keep to the riverside path. From Apr-Sep.
Facilities: Car park, four hides.
Public transport: None.
Habitat: Water meadows, river, scrub, open water.
Key birds: *Spring/summer*: Duck, Grey Partridge, Turtle Dove, some waders, Spotted Flycatcher, warblers. *Winter*: Occasional divers and scarce grebes. wildfowl inc. Pintail, Pochard, Goshawk, Hen Harrier, Water Rail, Short-eared Owl, thrushes, good mix of other birds.
Contact: Yorkshire Wildlife Trust, 10 Toft Green, York, YO1 6JT, 01904 659579.
e-mail: yorkshirewt.@cix.co.uk

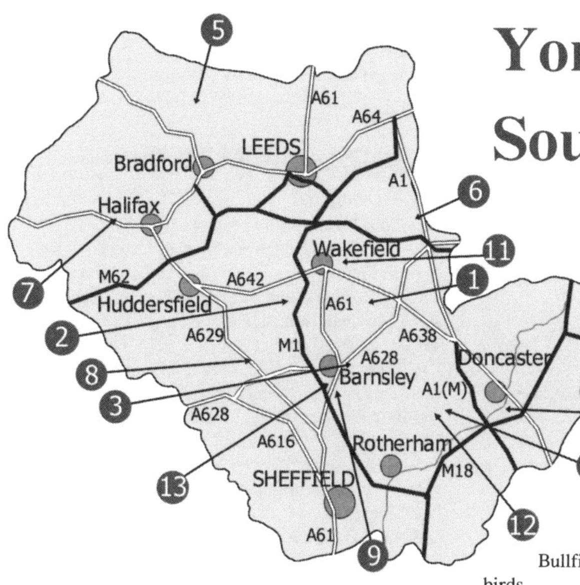

Yorkshire, South & West

1. ANGLERS COUNTRY PARK

Wakefield Metropolitan Borough Council.
Location: SE380160. SE of Wakefield. Leave A638 at signpost for Crofton. Turn left in village on road to Ryhill, turning just past Anglers pub in Wintersett hamlet.
Access: Open at all times. **Facilities:** Two hides.
Public transport: Bus service from Wakefield no 197 to Newstead. **Habitat:** Three lakes.
Key birds: *Winter*: Black-necked and Slavonian Grebes, wildfowl (inc. Wigeon, Goosander), large gull roost with regular Iceland, Glaucous, Mediterranean. Passage waders and passerines. *Spring/summer*: Breeding Little Ringed Plover, Lapwing, and warblers (inc. Grasshopper and Lesser Whitethroat).
Contact: Leisure Services, Wakefield Metropolitan Borough Council, 01924 302600.

2. BRETTON COUNTRY PARK AND OXLEY BANK WOOD

Yorkshire Wildlife Trust/Wakefield MDC.
Location: SE 295 125. Fifteen miles S of L and N of Sheffield. Leave the motorway at J38. Take the A637 Huddersfield road to the N. After 0.5 miles the entrance to the Park is on the L. Can also park in Sculpture Park's car park
Access: Open all year. Permit required for the Yorkshire Wildlife Trust area.
Facilities: Car park, visitor centre, information leaflets.
Public transport: None.
Habitat: Landscaped park, mature woodland, two lakes.
Key birds: *Spring/summer*: Cuckoo, warblers, Spotted Flycatcher, Sand Martin, Swallow. *Winter*: Fieldfare, Redwing, Brambling, Redpoll, Siskin, Hawfinch. *All year*: Kingfisher, all three woodpeckers, Little and Tawny Owls, Linnet, Bullfinch, Yellowhammer, usual woodland birds.
Contact: Yorkshire Wildlife Trust, 10 Toft Green, York, YO1 6JT, 01904 659570.
e-mail: yorkshirewt@cix.co.uk

3. CARLTON MARSH

Barnsley MBC Countryside Unit. 01226 772142.

4. DENABY INGS NATURE RESERVE

Yorkshire Wildlife Trust.
Location: The reserve is on A6023 E from Mexborough. Look for L fork signed Denaby Ings Nature Reserve. Proceed along Pastures Road for 0.5 miles and watch for second sign on R marking the entrance to car park. From car park, walk back to road to set of concrete steps on R which lead up to a small visitor centre and a hide.
Access: Open all year. **Facilities:** Car park, visitor centre, hide, trail. **Public transport:** None.
Habitat: Water, deciduous woodland, marsh, willows.
Key birds: *Spring/summer*: waterfowl, Little Ringed Plover, Turtle Dove, Cuckoo, Little Owl, Tawny Owl, Sand Martin, Swallow, Whinchat, possible Grasshopper Warbler, Lesser Whitethroat, Whitethroat, other warblers, Spotted Flycatcher, Red-legged and Grey Partridges, Kingfisher. *Passage*: Waders, Common, Arctic and Black Terns, Redstart, Wheatear. *Winter*: Whooper Swan, wildfowl, Jack Snipe, waders, Grey Wagtail, Short-eared Owl, Stonechat, Fieldfare, Redwing,

Brambling, Siskin. *All year*: Corn Bunting, Yellowhammer, all three woodpeckers possible, Willow Tit, common woodland birds.
Contact: Trust HQ. 01904 659570.
e-mail: yorkshirewt@cix.co.uk

5. DENSO MARSTON

Denso Marston.
Location: SE 167 389. Two miles from Shipley on Otley Road. Entrance through kissing gate past end of factory. **Access:** Open at all times.
Facilities: None.
Public transport: Bus from Bradford and Leeds 655, 652, 755.
Habitat: Two pools, woodland areas, meadow areas, site next to River Aire.
Key birds: *Summer*: Garden Warbler, Blackcap, Whitethroat. Insects such as common blue and brimstone butterflies and common hawker, migrant hawker, four-spotted chaser dragonflies. *Winter*: Lesser Redpoll, Siskin, Water Rail.
Contact: Andrew Clarke, Denso Marston, Otley Road, Baildon, Shipley, West Yorkshire BD17 7UR. 01274 582266.

6. FAIRBURN INGS

RSPB (North West England Office).
Location: SE 452 277. 12.5 miles from Leeds, six miles from Pontefract, 3.5 miles from Castleford situated next to A1 at Fairburn turn-off.
Access: Reserve and hides open every day (9am-dusk). Centre with shop open weekdays (11am-4pm) and weekends (10am-5pm) and Bank Holidays. Hot and cold drinks available. Dogs on leads at all times. Wheelchair-friendly boardwalk leading to Pickup Pool.
Facilities: Reserve hides include three open at all times with one locked at dusk. Toilets open when centre open or 9am-5pm. Disabled access to toilets. All nature trails are open at all times.
Public transport: Nearest train stations are Castleford or Pontefract. Buses approx every hour from Pontefract and Tadcaster. Infrequent from Castleford and Selby.
Habitat: Open water due to mining subsidence, wet grassland, marsh and willow scrub, reclaimed colliery spoil heaps.
Key birds: *Winter*: A herd of Whooper Swan usually roost. Normally up to five Smew including male, Wigeon, Gadwall, Goosander, Goldeney. Spring: Osprey, Wheatear, Little Gull and five species of tern pass through. *Summer*: Breeding birds include Reed and Sedge Warblers, Shoveler, Gadwall, Cormorant.
Contact: Chris Drake, Information Warden, Fairburn Ings Visitor Centre, Newton Lane, Fairburn, Castleford WF10 2BH. 01977 603796.

7. HARDCASTLE CRAGS

National Trust.
Location: From Halifax, follow A646 W for five miles to Hebden Bridge and pick up National Trust signs in town centre. Follow these to A6033 Kighley Road. Follow this for 0.75 miles. Turn L at the National Trust sign to the car parks.
Access: Open all year.
Facilities: Two car parks, trails.
Public transport: None.
Habitat: Wooded valley, ravines, streams.
Key birds: *Spring/summer*: Cuckoo, Redstart, Lesser Whitethroat, Garden Warbler, Blackcap, Wood Warbler, Chiffchaff, Spotted Flycatcher, Pied Flycatcher. *All year*: Sparrowhawk, Kestrel, Green and Great Spotted Woodpeckers, Tawny Owl, Jay, Marsh Tit and other woodland species.
Contact: National Trust, 27 Tadcaster Road, Dringhouses, York YO2 2QG.

8. INGBIRCHWORTH RESERVOIR

Yorkshire Water.
Location: Leave the M1 at J37 and take the A628 to Manchester and Penistone. After five miles you reach a roundabout. Turn R onto the A629 Huddersfield road. After 2.5 miles you reach Ingbirchworth. At a sign for The Fountain Inn, turn L. Pass a pub. The road bears L to cross the dam, proceed straight forward onto the track leading to the car park. From the car park, follow the footpath round the reservoir.
Access: Open all year. One of the few reservoirs in the area with access.
Facilities: Car park, picnic tables.
Public transport: None.
Habitat: Reservoir, small strip of deciduous woodland.
Key birds: *Spring/summer*: Whinchat, warblers, woodland birds, House Martin. *Spring/autumn passage*: Little Ringed Plover, Ringed Plover, Dotterel, waders, Common Tern, Arctic Tern, Black Tern, Yellow Wagtail, Wheatear. *Winter*: wildfowl, Golden Plover, waders, occasional rare gull such as Iceland or Glaucous, Grey Wagtail, Fieldfare, Redwing, Brambling, Redpoll.
Contact: Yorkshire Water, PO Box 52, Bradford BD3 7YD.

9. OLD MOOR WETLAND CENTRE

Barnsley MBC Countryside Unit.
Location: SE 422 011. From M1 J36, then A6195. From A1 J37, then A635 and A6195 – follow brown signs.
Access: Open Apr 1-Oct 31 (Wed-Sun 9am-5pm), Nov 1-Mar 31 (Wed/Thu-Sat/Sun 10am-4pm). Entry fee with Annual Membership available.
Facilities: Toilets (including disabled), large visitor centre and shop, five superb hides. All sites including hides fully accessible for disabled.
Public transport: Buses – information from South Yorkshire Passenger Transport 01709 589200.
Habitat: Lakes and flood meadows, wader scrape and reedbeds.
Key birds: *Winter*: Large numbers of wildfowl. *Summer*: Breeding waders and wildfowl. Rare vagrants recorded annually.
Contact: Debra Bushby, Old Moor Wetland Centre, Off Manvers Way, Broomhill, Wombwell, Barnsley, South Yorkshire S73 0YF. 01226 751593 Fax: 01226 751617. www.barnsley.gov.uk e-mail: oldmoor@barnsley.gov.uk

10. POTTERIC CARR

Yorkshire Wildlife Trust.
Location: SE 589 007. From M18 junction 3 take A6182 (Doncaster) and at first roundabout take third exit; entrance and car park on R after 50m.
Access: Access by permit only (01302 364152, answerphone). Parties need prior permission.
Facilities: Field Centre (light refreshments, toilet) open (10am-3pm Sun) all year. Eight hides (three for disabled). **Public transport:** None.
Habitat: Reed fen, subsidence ponds, artificial pools, grassland, woodland.
Key birds: Nesting waterfowl (inc. Shoveler, Gadwall, Pochard), Water Rail, Little Ringed Plover, Snipe, Kingfisher, all three woodpeckers, Lesser Whitethroat, Reed and Sedge Warblers also breed. *Passage/winter*: wildfowl, Bittern, Marsh Harrier, Black Tern, waders.
Contact: Trust HQ, 01904 659570.

11. PUGNEYS COUNTRY PARK

Wakefield Metropolitan Borough Council.
Location: SE 330 180. Leave M1 at J29 towards Wakefield; reserve signposted from first roundabout.
Access: Open daily 9am to one hour before sunset.
Facilities: Car parks, hide, footpaths.
Public transport: Bus from Wakefield no 443.
Habitat: The park is a restored sand and gravel working. Three lakes, open fields, small wood.
Key birds: *Spring/summer*: migrants inc Little Ringed Plover. Hirundines, Whitethroat, Lesser Whitethroat, Garden Warbler, Blackcap, Chiffchaff, Willow Warbler. *Winter*: occasional divers, rarer grebes, Whooper Swan, waders, gulls. *All year*: Water Rail, Kingfisher, Great Spotted Woodpecker, Little Owl, tits, Siskin.
Contact: Wakefield Metropolitan Borough Council, County Hall, Bond Street, Wakefield, West Yorkshire WF1 2QL. 01924 306090.

12. SPROTBOROUGH FLASH RESERVE AND THE DON GORGE

Yorkshire Wildlife Trust.
Location: From the A1, follow the A630 to Rotherham 4.8km W of Doncaster. After 0.8km, turn R at the traffic lights to Sprotborough. After approx 1.6km the road drops down the slopes of the Gorse. Cross a bridge over the river. After crossing another bridge over a canal, turn immediately L. Park 45m in a small roadside parking area on the L beside the canal. Walk along the canal bank, past The Boat Inn. The entrance to the reserve is approx 90m further on.
Access: Open all year. **Facilities:** Three hides, footpaths. **Habitat:** River, reed, gorge, woodland.
Key birds: *Summer*: Turtle Dove, Cuckoo, hirundines, Lesser Whitethroat, Whitethroat, Garden Warbler, Blackcap, Chiffchaff, Willow Warbler, Spotted Flycatcher. *Spring/autumn passage*: Little Ringed Plover, Dunlin, Greenshank, Green Sandpiper, waders, Yellow Wagtail. *Winter/all year*: wildfowl, Water Rail, Snipe, Little Owl, Tawny Owl, all three woodpeckers, thrushes, Siskin, possible Corn Bunting.
Contact: Yorkshire Wildlife Trust, 10 Toft Green, York YO1 1JT. 01904 659570.

13. WORSBROUGH COUNTRY PARK

Barnsley MBC Countryside Unit.
Location: SE 345 034. South of Barnsley, N of Junction 36 of M1. CP car park is off A61.
Access: Open access at all times.
Facilities: Hide, toilets. **Public transport:** None.
Habitat: Open water, willow carr, phragmites and typha reedbed, deciduous wood and meadow land.
Key birds: *Summer*: Breeding Ruddy Duck, Sparrowhawk, Sedge and Reed Warblers, Kingfisher, Common Tern. *Autumn*: Swallow roost. *Winter*: Gulls.
Contact: Cultural Services, Worsborough Mill, Barnsley, S Yorks S70 5LJ. 01226 774527.

SCOTLAND

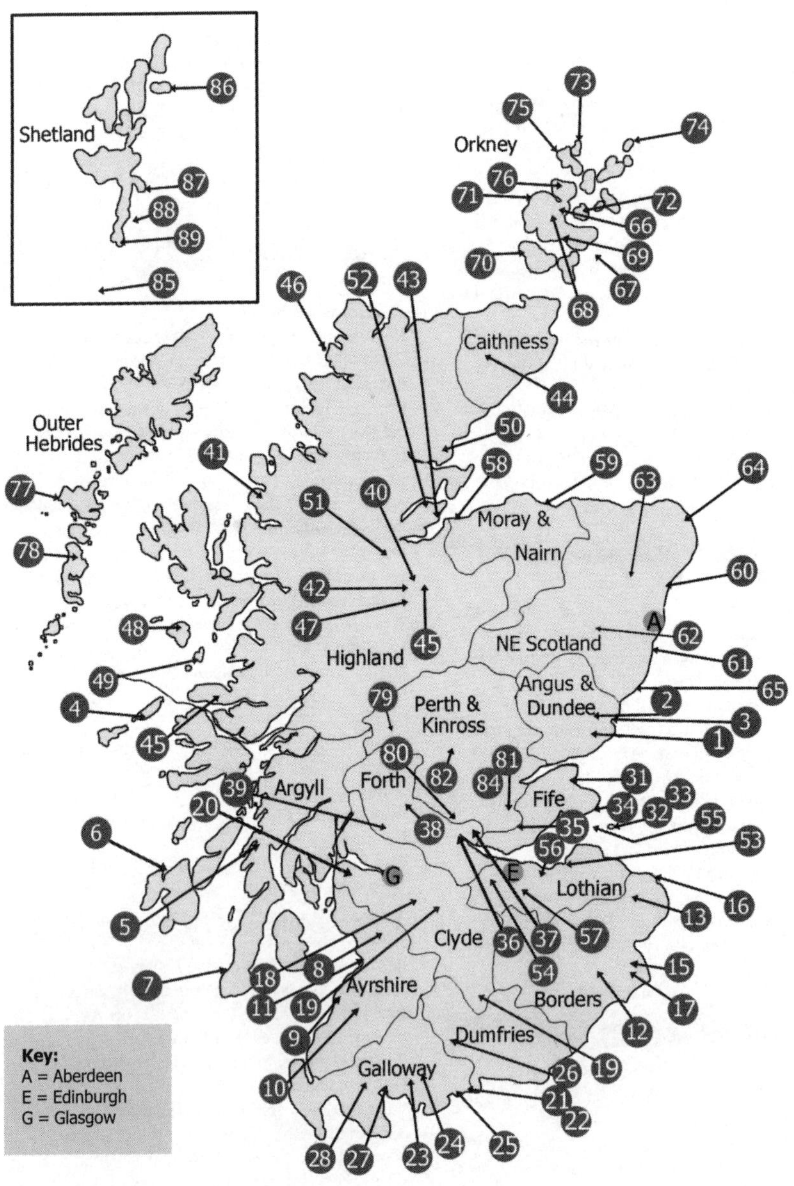

NB: Reserves in Scotland have been listed alphabetically by region (following the arrangement of the Scottish recording areas as set out by the Scottish Ornithologist's Club).

Angus & Dundee

1. BALGAVIES LOCH

Scottish Wildlife Trust. Montrose Basin Wildlife Centre, 01674 676336.

2. LOCH OF KINNORDY

RSPB (East Scotland).
Location: NO 351 539. Car park on B951 one mile W of Kirriemuir. Perth 45 minutes drive, Dundee 30 minutes drive, Aberdeen one hour.
Access: Open dawn-dusk. Disabled access to two hides via short trails.
Facilities: Three birdwatching hides.
Public transport: Nearest centre is Kirriemuir.
Habitat: Freshwater loch, fen, carr, marsh.
Key birds: *Spring/summer*: Osprey, Black-necked Grebe, Blacked-headed Gull. *Winter*: Wildfowl including Goosander, Goldeneye and Whooper Swan.
Contact: Alan Leitch, RSPB, 1 Atholl Crescent, Perth PH1 5NG. 01738 639783.
e-mail: alan.leitch@rspb.org www.rspb.org

3. MONTROSE BASIN

Scottish Wildlife Trust for Angus Council.
Location: NO 690 580 Centre of Basin. NO 702 565 Wildlife SWT Centre on A92. 1.5 miles from centre of Montrose.
Access: Apr 1-Oct 31 (10.30am-5pm). Nov 1-Mar 31, (10.30am-4pm). Will be closed for interpretive refurbishment Jan to Mar 2004.
Facilities: Visitor centre, shop, vending machine, toilets, disabled access to centre, two hides on western half of reserve.
Public transport: Train 1.5 miles in Montrose. Buses same as above.
Habitat: Estuary, saltmarsh, reedbeds, farmland.
Key birds: Pink-footed Goose - up to 35,000 arrive Oct. Wintering wildfowl and waders. Breeding Eider Ducks.
Contact: Scottish Wildlife Trust, Montrose Basin Wildlife Centre, Rossie Braes, Montrose DD10 9TJ. 01674 676336.
www.swt.org.uk
e-mail: montrosebasin@swt.org.uk

Argyll

4. COLL RSPB RESERVE

RSPB (South and West Scotland Office).
Location: NM 168 561. By ferry from Oban. Take the B8070 W from Arinagour for five miles. Turn R at Arileod. Continue for about one mile. Park at end of the road. Reception point at Totronald.
Access: Open all year. Please avoid walking through fields and crops.
Facilities: Car park, information bothy at Totronald, guided walks in summer. Corn Crake viewing bench. **Public transport:** None.
Habitat: Sand dunes, beaches, machair grassland, moorland, farmland.
Key birds: *Spring/summer*: Corn Crake, Redshank, Lapwing, Snipe. *Winter*: Barnacle and Greenland White-fronted Geese.
Contact: RSPB Coll Nature Reserve, Totronald, Isle of Coll, Argyll, PA78 6TB, 01879 230301.

5. KNAPDALE RESERVE

Scottish Wildlife Trust.
Location: NR 766 884. From the Crinan Canal at Bellanoch take the B8025 Tayvallich road. Park in the Forestry car park at the Barnluasgan Interpretation Centre.
Access: Open all year.
Facilities: Car park, forest tracks, cycle trails, leaflet.
Public transport: Not known.
Habitat: Freshwater and sea lochs, woodland, rocky coast.
Key birds: *Spring/summer*: Redstart, Tree Pipit, Willow and Wood Warblers. *All year*: Buzzard, Raven, Great Spotted Woodpecker, tits, finches.
Contact: Scottish Wildlife Trust (West Region), 71 Houldsworth Street, Finnieston, Glasgow G3 8EH. 0141 248 4647.
e-mail: westernenquiries@swt.org.uk

6. LOCH GRUINART, ISLAY

RSPB (South and West Scotland Office).
Location: Sea loch on N coast, seven miles NW from Bridgend.
Access: Hide open all hours, no dogs, visitor centre open (10am-5pm), disabled access to hide, toilets.
Facilities: Toilets, visitor centre, hide, trail.
Public transport: None.
Habitat: Low wet grasslands, moorland.

Key birds: *Sept-Apr*: Barnacle and Greenland White-fronted Goose. *May-Aug*: Corn Crake. *Sept-Nov*: Migrating wading birds.
Contact: Yvonne Brown, RSPB, Bushmills Cottage, Gruinart, Isle of Islay PH44 7PR. 01496 850505. e-mail yvonne.brown@rspb.org.uk www.rspb.org.uk

7. MACHRIHANISH SEABIRD OBSERVATORY

Eddie Maguire and John McGlynn.
Location: NR 628 209. Southwest Kintyre, Argyll. Six miles W of Campbeltown on A83, then B843.
Access: Daily May-Oct. Wheelchair access. Dogs welcome. Parking for three cars.
Facilities: Seawatching hide, toilets in nearby village. **Public transport:** Regular buses from Campbeltown (West Coast Motors, tel 01586 552319).
Habitat: Marine, rocky shore and upland habitats.
Key birds: *Summer:* Golden Eagle, Peregrine and Twite. *Autumn:* Passage seabirds and waders. Gales often produce inshore movements of Leach's Petrel and other scarce seabirds including Balearic Shearwater and Grey Phalarope. *Winter:* Great Northern Diver.
Contact: Eddie Maguire, 25B Albyn Avenue, Campbeltown, Argyll PA28 6LX. 07919 660292. www.mso.1c24.net

Ayrshire

8. AYR GORGE WOODLANDS

Scottish Wildlife Trust.
Location: NS 457 249. From Ayr take the A719 NE for about three miles to the A77. Go straight over the roundabout onto the B473 and continue to Failford. Park in the lay-by in the village.
Access: Open all year.Access by well-maintained path along west bank of River Ayr.
Facilities: Footpaths, interpretation boards, leaflets.
Public transport: None.
Habitat: Woodland.
Key birds: Woodland and riverside birds.
Contact: Scottish Wildlife Trust, Cramond House, Kirk Cramond, Cramond Glebe Road, Edinburgh, EH4 6NS, 0131 3127765.
e-mail: scottishwt@cix.co.uk

9. CULZEAN CASTLE AND COUNTY PARK

National Trust for Scotland.
Location: NS 234 103. From Ayr, head S on A719 coast road.
Access: Open all year.
Facilities: Car park, visitor centre.
Public transport: None.
Habitat: Shoreline, parkland, woodland, streams, ponds.
Key birds: *Spring/summer*: Blackcap, warblers. *Winter*: Waders, wildfowl. *All year*: Tits, finches.
Contact: National Trust for Scotland, Wemyss House, 28 Charlotte Street, Edinburgh EH2 4ET. 0131 243 9300.

10. DALMELLINGTON MOSS

Scottish Wildlife Trust.
Location: NS 460 060. From Ayr head SE on A713 to Dallmellington.
Access: Open all year. **Facilities:** Car park.
Public transport: None.
Habitat: Wet moss, willow scrub.
Key birds: *Spring/summer*: Sedge, Grasshopper and Garden Warblers. *Winter*: Thrushes, Brambling, swans.
Contact: Scottish Wildlife Trust, Cramond House, Kirk Cramond, Gramond Glebe Road, Edinburgh EH4 6NS. 0131 312 7765.
e-mail: scottishwt@cix.co.uk www.swt.org.uk

11. GARNOCK FLOODS

Scottish Wildlife Trust.
Location: NS 305 418. N of Irvine. From A78 N, take the one-way road to Bogside, just beyond A737 interchange. Park on roadside. Best viewed from cycle track along E boundary.
Access: Open all year.
Facilities: None.
Public transport: Bus service on A737, 1-2km distant.
Habitat: River, ponds, fields, wood.
Key birds: *Spring/summer*: Sedge and Willow Warblers, Lesser Whitethroat, Sand Martin. *Winter*: Wildfowl inc Goldeneye, Mute Swan, occasional Garganey, waders inc Ruff, Redshank and Snipe. Winter thrushes. *All year*: Kestrel, Sparrowhawk, Buzzard.
Contact: Scottish Wildlife Trust, Cramond House, Kirk Cramond, Gramond Glebe Road, Edinburgh EH4 6NS. 0131 312 7765.
e-mail: scottishwt@cix.co.uk www.swt.org.uk

Borders

12. BEMERSYDE MOSS

Scottish Wildlife Trust.
Location: NT 614 340. Four miles E of Melrose on minor road. Between Melrose and Smailholm.
Access: Permit required.**Facilities:** Hide with parking nearby. **Public transport:** None.
Habitat: Shallow Loch and marsh.
Key birds: *Summer*: Large Black-headed Gull colony, Black-necked Grebe, Grasshopper Warbler. *Winter:* Wildfowl, waders on migration, raptors.
Contact: Trust HQ, 0131 312 7765

13. DUNS CASTLE

Scottish Wildlife Trust. 0131 312 7765

14. GUNKNOWE LOCH AND PARK

Borders Council.
Location: NT 523 51. 3.2km from Galashiels on the A6091. Park at Gunknowe Loch.
Access: Open all year. **Facilities:** Car park, paths.
Public transport: None.
Habitat: River, parkland, scrub, woodland.
Key birds: *Spring/summer*: Grey Wagtail, Kingfisher, Sand Martin, Blackcap, Sedge and Grasshopper Warblers. *Passage*: Yellow Wagtail, Whinchat, Wheatear. *Winter*: Thrushes, Brambling, Wigeon, Tufted Duck, Pochard, Goldeneye. *All year*: Great Spotted and Green Woodpeckers, Redpoll, Goosander, possible Marsh Tit.
Contact: Borders Council,

15. THE HIRSEL

The Estate Office, The Hirsel.
Location: NT 827 403. Signed off the A698 Kelso-Coldstream road on the outskirts of Coldstream.
Access: Open all year. Private estate so please stick to the public paths.
Facilities: Car parks, visitor centre, leaflets, trails.
Public transport: Bus: Coldstream, Kelso, Berwick-upon-Tweed, Edinburgh.
Habitat: Freshwater loch, reeds, woods.
Key birds: *Spring/summer*: Redstart, Garden Warbler, Blackcap, flycatchers, possible Water Rail, wildfowl. *Autumn*: Wildfowl, Goosander, possible Green Sandpiper. *Winter*: Whooper Swan, Pink-footed Goose, Wigeon, Goldeneye, Pochard, occasional Smew, Scaup, Slavonian Grebe.
Contact: The Estate Office, The Hirsel, Coldstream TD12 4LF. 01890 882834.

16. ST ABB'S HEAD

National Trust for Scotland.
Location: NT 914 693. Lies five miles N of Eyemouth. Follow A1107 from A1.
Access: Reserve open all year. Keep dogs on lead. Cliff path is not suitable for disabled visitors.
Facilities: Visitor centre and toilets open Apr-Oct.
Public transport: Nearest rail station is Berwick-upon-Tweed. Bus service from Berwick, tel 018907 81533.
Habitat: Cliffs, coastal grasslands and loch.
Key birds: *Apr-Aug*: Seabird colonies with large numbers of Kittiwake, auks, Shag, Fulmar, migrants. *Apr-May and Sept-Oct*: Good autumn seawatching.
Contact: Kevin Rideout, Rangers Cottage, Northfield, St Abbs, Borders TD14 5QF. 018907 71443. e-mail: krideout@nts.org.uk www.nts.org.uk

17. YETHOLM LOCH

Scottish Wildlife Trust.
Location: NT 803 279. Six miles SE of Kelso. Off B6352, turning to Lochtower (unmetalled road).
Access: None to marsh during breeding season.
Facilities: Hide. Car park along rough track.
Public transport: None.
Habitat: Marshland and loch.
Key birds: *Summer:* Breeding wildfowl (including Great Crested Grebe, Shoveler and Teal). *Winter:* Whooper Swan, Pink-footed Goose and wide range of ducks.
Contact: Trust HQ, 0131 312 7765

Clyde

18. BARONS HAUGH

RSPB (South & West Scotland Office).
Contact: RSPB office, Lochwinnoch,

19. FALLS OF CLYDE

Scottish Wildlife Trust.
Location: NS 88 34 14. Approx one mile S of Lanark. Directions from Glasgow - travel S on M74 until J7 then along A72, following signs for Lanark and New Lanark.

Access: Open daylight hours all year. Partial disabled access.
Facilities: Visitor centre open 11am-5pm all year. Toilets and cafeteria on site. Seasonal viewing facility for Peregrines. Numerous walkways and ranger service offers guided walks programme.
Public transport: Scotrail trains run to Lanark (0845 7484950). Local bus service from Lanark to New Lanark.
Habitat: River Clyde gorge, waterfalls, mixed riparian/conifer woodlands, meadow, pond.
Key birds: More than 100 species of bird recorded on the reserve including unrivalled views of breeding Peregrine. Others include Goshawk, Barn Owl, Kingfisher, Dipper, Lapwing, Pied Flycatcher and Sky Lark.
Contact: Dr Stuart Glen, The Scottish Wildlife Trust Visitor Centre, The Falls of Clyde Reserve, New Lanark, South Lanark ML11 9DB. 01555 665262. e-mail: fallsofclyde@cix.co.uk

20. LOCHWINNOCH

RSPB (South & West Scotland Office).
Location: NS 358 582. 18 miles SW of Glasgow, adjacent to A760.
Access: Open every day except Christmas and Boxing Day, Jan 1 and Jan 2. (10am-5pm).
Facilities: Special facilities for schools and disabled. Refreshments. Visitor centre, hides.
Public transport: Rail station adjacent, bus services nearby.
Habitat: Shallow lochs, marsh, mixed woodland.
Key birds: *Winter*: Wildfowl (esp. Whooper Swan, Greylag, Goosander, Goldeneye). Occasional passage migrants inc. Whimbrel, Greenshank. *Summer*: Breeding Great Crested Grebe, Water Rail, Sedge and Grasshopper Warblers.
Contact: RSPB Nature Centre, Largs Road, Lochwinnoch, Renfrewshire PA12 4JF. 01505 842663; fax 01505 843026;
e-mail lochwinnoch@rspb.org.uk.

Dumfries & Galloway

21. CAERLAVEROCK

SNH (Dumfries & Galloway Area Office).
Location: NY 040 645. From Dumfries take B725 towards Caerlaverock Castle.
Access: Open all year. Visitors may enter most of the reserve, except sanctuary area. The saltmarsh (local: merse) can be dangerous at high tides; visitors should consult the Reserve Manager for advice. No permit, but organised groups should apply to Reserve Manager well in advance. Research and surveys require approval of SNH Area Manager. **Facilities:** Woodland walks.
Public transport: Buses from Dumfries.
Habitat: Saltmarsh, grassland.
Key birds: *Winter*: Barnacle, Pink-footed and Greylag Geese, Whooper and Bewick's Swans, ducks, waders and raptors.
Contact: Wally Wright, SNH Reserve Office, Hollands Farm Road, Caerlaverock, Dumfries DG1 4RS. 01387 770275.

22. CAERLAVEROCK

The Wildfowl & Wetlands Trust.
Location: NY 051 656. From Dumfries take B725 towards Bankend.
Access: Open daily except Christmas Day.
Facilities: 20 hides, heated observatory, three towers, sheltered picnic area. Self-catering accommodation and camping facilities. Nature trails in summer.
Public transport: Buses from Dumfries.
Habitat: Saltmarsh, grassland.
Key birds: *Winter*: Wildfowl esp. Barnacle Geese (max 13,700), Whooper and Bewick's Swans.
Contact: John Doherty, Centre Manager, The Wildfowl & Wetlands Trust, Eastpark Farm, Caerlaverock, Dumfries DG1 4RS. 01387 770200.

23. CARSTRAMON WOOD

Scottish Wildlife Trust.
Location: NT 592 605. Take A75 from Castle Douglas. Reserve is two miles N of Gatehouse of Fleet on minor road off B796.
Access: Open all year.
Facilities: Car parking alongside road. Network of paths. Information boards. Leaflet from tourist office in gatehouse. **Public transport:** None.
Habitat: Ancient deciduous oak woodland.
Key birds: Typical woodland birds (inc. Pied Flycatcher, Redstart, Green Woodpecker, Wood Warbler and Tree Pipit).
Contact: Trust HQ.

24. KEN/DEE MARSHES

RSPB (South and West Scotland Office).
Location: NX 699 684. Six miles from Castle Douglas – good views from A762 and A713 roads to New Galloway.

Access: From car park at entrance to farm Mains of Duchrae. Open during daylight hours. No dogs.
Facilities: Hides, nature trails. Three mile walk to hide and back, nearer parking for elderly and disabled, but phone warden first.
Public transport: None.
Habitat: Marshes, woodlands, open water.
Key birds: *All year:* Mallard, Grey Heron, Buzzard. *Spring/summer*: Pied Flycatcher, Redstart, Tree Pipit, Sedge Warbler. *Winter*: Greenland White-fronted and Greylag Geese, birds of prey (Hen Harrier, Peregrine, Merlin).
Contact: Paul Collin, Gairland, Old Edinburgh Road, Minnigaff, Newton Stewart DG8 6PL. 01671 402861.

25. MERSEHEAD

RSPB (South & West Scotland Office).
Location: NX 925 560. From Dalbeattie, take B793 or A710 to Caulkerbush.
Access: Open at all times.
Facilities: Hide, nature trails, information centre and toilets. **Public transport:** None.
Habitat: Wet grassland, arable farmland, saltmarsh, inter-tidal mudflats.
Key birds: *Winter*: Up to 9,500 Barnacle Geese, 4,000 Teal, 2,000 Wigeon, 1,000 Pintail, waders (inc. Dunlin, Knot, Oystercatcher). *Summer:* Breeding birds include Lapwing, Redshank, Sky Lark.
Contact: Eric Nielson, Mersehead, Southwick, Mersehead, Dumfries DG2 8AH. 01387 780298.

26. STENHOUSE WOOD

Scottish Wildlife Trust.
Location: NX 795 930. NE of Dumfries, on A702 Penpont-Moniaive road, near Tynron. Once in Tynron, cross the river. Turn R at the war memorial. After 0.5km, turn R into a no-through road. The reserve is on the L about 0.8km. It is not marked and you should park with care.
Access: Open all year but take not to disturb nesting birds. **Facilities:** None.
Public transport: None.
Habitat: Mixed woodland.
Key birds: *Spring/summer*: Redstart, Chiffchaff and warblers, inc Wood and Garden. *All year*: Buzzard, Great Spotted and Green Woodpeckers, tits, Siskin.
Contact: Scottish Wildlife Trust, Cramond House, Cramond House, Kirk Cramond, Cramond Glebe Road, Edinburgh EH4 6NS. 0131 3127765.
e-mail: enquiries@swt.org.uk www.swt.org.uk

27. WIGTOWN BAY LNR

Dumfries & Galloway Council.
Location: NX 465 545. Between Wigtown and Creetown. It is the largest LNR in Britain at 2845 ha. The A75 runs along the east side, with the A714 S to Wigtown and B7004 providing superb views of the LNR.
Access: Open at all times. The hides are disabled friendly. Main accesses: Roadside lay-bys on A75 near Creetown and parking at Martyr's Stake and Wigtown Harbour.
Facilities: A hide at Wigtown Harbour with views over the River Bladnoch, saltmarsh and fresh water wetland has disabled access from harbour car park. There is also a small hide at the Martyr's Stake car park and walks and interpretation in this area.
Public transport: Travel Information Line 08457 090510 (local rate 9am-5pm Mon-Fri). Bus No 415 for Wigtown and west side. Bus No 431 or 500 X75 for Creetown and E side.
Habitat: Estuary with extensive saltmarsh/merse and mudflats with newly developed fresh water wetland at Wigtown Harbour.
Key birds: *Winter*: Internationally important for Pink-footed Goose, nationally important for Curlew, Whooper Swan and Pintail, with major gull roost and other migratory coastal birds. *Summer*: Breeding waders and duck.
Contact: Elizabeth Tindal, County Buildings, Wigtown, DG8 9JH01988 402 401, mobile 07702 212 728.
e-mail: Elizabeth.Tindal@dumgal.gov.uk

28. WOOD OF CREE

RSPB (South and West Scotland Office).
Location: NX 382 708. Four miles N of Newton Stewart on minor road from Minnigaff, parallel to A714.
Access: Open during daylight hours. Dogs on lead. Not suitable for disabled.
Facilities: Nature trails.
Public transport: None.
Habitat: Oak woodland, marshes, river.
Key birds: *Spring/summer*: Pied Flycatcher, Wood Warbler, Tree Pipit, Redstart, Buzzard, Great Spotted Woodpecker, red squirrel, otter.
Contact: Paul Collin, Gairland, Old Edinburgh Road, Minnigaff, Newton Stewart DG8 6PL. 01671 402861.

Fife

29. CAMERON RESERVOIR

Scottish Wildlife Trust.
Location: NO 478 115. Four miles SSW of St Andrews. Off A915.
Access: Open access to walk round reservoir. Path liable to flooding on south side. Wellington boots advised. Dogs on leads only. Car park at NE corner of reservoir.
Facilities: SWT hide. Key available from Ian Cumming, 11 Canongate, St Andrews. Tel 01334 473773. **Public transport:** None.
Habitat: Decaying pinewoods round shore of reservoir and drowning willows.
Key birds: *Winter*: Pink-footed and Greylag Goose, Wigeon, Tufted Duck, Pochard, Mallard. Also Whooper Swan, Mute Swan, Gadwall, Pintail, Shoveler, Red-breasted Merganser, Great Crested Grebe.
Contact: Ian Cumming, 11 Canongate, St Andrews, Fife, 01334 473773.

30. CULLALOE NATURE RESERVE

Fife Council/Scottish Wildlife Trust.
Location: NT 188 877. The reserve is signposted off the B9157 N of Aberdour. Park below old dam.
Access: Open all year. Please keep dogs on leads.
Facilities: Car park, information board, viewpoint, hide, disabled access. **Public transport:** None.
Habitat: Reservoir, willow carr, grassland.
Key birds: *Spring/summer*: Whitethroat, Sedge Warbler, Lapwing. *Passage*: Waders, inc Black-tailed Godwit and Spotted Redshank. *Winter*: Wildfowl, Snipe, waders.
Contact: Scottish Wildlife Trust, Cramond House, Kirk Cramond, Cramond Glebe Road, Edinburgh EH4 6NS. 0131 3127765.
e-mail: enquiries@swt.org.uk www.swt.org.uk

31. EDEN ESTUARY

Fife Council.
Location: NO 470 195. The reserve can be accessed from Guardbridge, St Andrews (one mile) on A91, and from Leuchars via Tentsmuir Forest off A919 (four miles).
Access: The Eden Estuary Centre is open (9am-5pm) every day except Christmas Day, New Year's Day and the day of the Leuchars airshow. Reserve is open all year but a permit (from Ranger service) is required to access the N shore.
Facilities: Visitor centre at Guardbridge. Information panels. Hide at Balgove Bay (key from Ranger Service).
Public transport: Leuchars train station. Regular buses Cupar-Dundee-St Andrews. Tel: 01334 474238.
Habitat: Saltmarsh, river, tidal flats, sand dunes.
Key birds: *Winter*: Main interest is wildfowl and waders, best place in Scotland to see Black-tailed Godwit. Other species include Grey Plover, Shelduck, Bar-tailed Godwit. Offshore Common and Velvet Scoter occur and Surf Scoter is regularly seen. Peregrine, Merlin and Short-eared Owl occur in winter.
Contact: Les Hatton, Fife Ranger Service, Craigtown Country Park, St Andrews, Fife KY16 8NX. 01333 473047/07939 169291 (mobile).
e-mail: refrs@craigtoun.freserve.co.uk

32. ISLE OF MAY NNR

Scottish Natural Heritage.
Location: NT 655 995. This small island lying six miles off Fife Ness in the Firth of Forth is a National Nature Reserve.
Access: Contact boatman for day trips: J Reaper, tel 01333 310103. Keep to paths. Fishing boat from Anstruther, arranged by the Observatory. Rock landings mean that delays are possible, both arriving and leaving, because of weather.
Facilities: No dogs; no camping; no fires. Prior permission required if scientific work is to be carried out.
Public transport: None.
Habitat: Sea cliffs, rocky shoreline.
Key birds: *Summer*: Breeding auks and terns, Kittiwake, Shag, Eider, Fulmar. *Autumn/spring:* Weather-related migrations include rarities each year.
Contact: David Thorne, Craigurd House, Blyth Bridge, West Linton, Peeblesshire EH46 7AH.

33. ISLE OF MAY BIRD OBSERVATORY

Facilities: Hostel accommodation in ex-lighthouse (the Low Light) for up to six, Apr-Oct; usual stay is one week. No supplies on island; visitors must take own food and sleeping bag. Five Heligoland traps used for ringing migrants when qualified personnel present. SNH Warden usually resident Apr-Sep.
Contact: Bookings: Mike Martin, 2 Manse Park, Uphall, W Lothian EH52 6NX. 01506 855285;
e-mail: mwa.martin@virgin.net,

34. KILMINNING COAST

Scottish Wildlife Trust. 0131 312 7765.

35. LOCHORE MEADOWS

Fife Ranger Service.
Location: NT165 958. Exit the M90 at J4. Drive E past Kelty on the A909. Turn L onto the B996 Cowdenbeath-Kinross road after one mile and take the 1st R to a car park. **Access:** Open all year.
Facilities: Car park, hide. Suitable for wheelchairs.
Public transport: Bus: from Cowdenbeath/ Dunfermline to Kelty.
Habitat: Loch, meadows and woodland.
Key birds: *Spring/summer*: Pintail, other ducks, Green Woodpecker, Grasshopper Warbler, Wood Warbler, Whinchat, Common Sandpiper, Redshank, hirundines. *Winter*: Whooper Swan, Redwing, Fieldfare, Redpoll, Siskin.
Contact: Fife Ranger Service, Lochore Meadows Country Park, Crosshill, Lochgelly, Fife, 01592 414300.

Forth

36. CAMBUS POOLS

Scottish Wildlife Trust.
Location: NS 846 937. ENE of Alloa on A907. Park by river in Cambus village.
Access: Cross River Devon by bridge at NS853940 and walk down stream on R bank past bonded warehouses. Open all year.
Facilities: None. **Public transport:** None.
Habitat: Wet grassland and pools.
Key birds: Used extensively by migrants, inc. wildfowl and waders.
Contact: Trust HQ, Regional Reserves Manager, 0131 312 7765.

37. GARTMORN DAM

Clackmannanshire Council.
Location: NS 912 940. Approx one mile NE of Alloa, signposted from A908 in Sauchie.
Access: Open at all times. No charge.
Facilities: Visitor centre with toilets. Open 8.30am-8.00pm daily (Apr-Sept inclusive) and 1pm-4pm (weekends only Oct-Mar). One hide, key obtainable from visitor centre. Provision for disabled.
Public transport: Bus service to Sauchie. First Bus, 01324 613777. Stirling Bus Station, 01786 446 474.
Habitat: Open water (with island), woodland – deciduous and coniferous, farmland.
Key birds: *Summer*: Great Crested Grebe, breeding Sedge and Reed Warblers. *Autumn*: Migrant waders. *Winter*: Wildfowl (regionally important site), Kingfisher, Water Rail.
Contact: Clackmannanshire Ranger Service, Lime Tree House, Alloa, Clackmannanshire FK10 1EX. 01259 450000. e-mail: rangers@clacks.gov.uk www.clacksweb.org.uk

38. INVERSNAID

RSPB (South & West Scotland Office).
Location: NN 337 088. On E side of Loch Lomond. Via B829 W from Aberfoyle, then along minor road to car park by Inversnaid Hotel.
Access: Open all year. **Facilities:** None.
Public transport: None.
Habitat: Deciduous woodland rises to craggy ridge and moorland.
Key birds: *Summer*: Breeding Buzzard, Blackcock, Grey Wagtail, Dipper, Wood Warbler, Redstart, Pied Flycatcher, Tree Pipit. The loch is on a migration route, especially for wildfowl and waders.
Contact: RSPB, 0141 576 4100.

39. QUEEN ELIZABETH FOREST PARK

Forestry Commission (Forest Enterprise).
Contact: Forest Enterprise, 231 Corstorphine Road, Edinburgh, EH12 7AT, 0131 3340303.

Highland & Caithness

40. ABERNETHY FOREST RESERVE – LOCH GARTEN

RSPB (North Scotland Office).
Location: NH 981 184. 2.5 miles from Boat of Garten, eight miles from Aviemore. Off B970, follow 'RSPB Ospreys' road signs (Apr - Aug).
Access: Osprey Centre open daily 10am-6pm (Apr to end Aug). Disabled access. No dogs (guide dogs only). No charge to RSPB members. Non-members: adults £2.50, senior citizens £1.50, children 50p.
Facilities: Osprey Centre overlooking nesting Ospreys, toilets, optics and CCTV live pictures.
Public transport: Bus service to Boat of Garten from Aviemore, 2.5 mile footpath to Osprey

Centre. Steam railway to Boat of Garten from Aviemore.
Habitat: Caledonian pine wood.
Key birds: Ospreys nesting from Apr to Aug, Crested Tit, Crossbill, red squirrel. In 2002 hide provided views of lekking Capercaillies Apr to mid-May.
Contact: R W Thaxton, RSPB, Forest Lodge, Nethybridge, Inverness-shire PH25 3EF. 01479 821894.

41. BEINN EIGHE

Scottish Natural Heritage.
Location: NG 990 620. By Kinlochewe, Wester Ross, 50 miles from Inverness and 20 miles from Gairloch on A832.
Access: Reserve open at all times, no charge. Visitor centre open Easter-Oct (10am-5pm).
Facilities: Visitor centre, toilets, woodland trail and mountain trail - self-guided with leaflets from visitor centre. Trails suitable for all abilities.
Public transport: Very limited.
Habitat: Caledonian pine forest, dwarf shrub heath, mountain tops, freshwater loch shore.
Key birds: Golden Eagle, Scottish Crossbill, Ptarmigan, Red Grouse, Siskin. *Summer*: Black-throated Diver, Redwing, Snow Bunting.
Contact: David Miller, Reserve Manager, Scottish Natural Heritage, Anancaun, Kinlochewe, Ross-shire IV22 2PD. 01445 760254. e-mail: david.miller@snh.gov.uk

42. CAIRNGORM NNR

SNH (East Highland Area).
Location: NJ 010 010. Largest National Nature Reserve in Britain, SE of Aviemore.
Access: Unrestricted but certain areas out of bounds during deer cull season.
Facilities: Visitor centre open all year.
Public transport: Call tourist office for advice.
Habitat: Mountain, moorland, pine woodland and lochs.
Key birds: Goosander, Crested Tit, Siskin, Redstart, Crossbill, Capercaillie, Black Grouse, Ptarmigan, Dotterel, Golden Eagle.
Contact: SNH, Achantoul, Aviemore, Inverness-shire PH22 1QD. 01479 810477; fax 01479 811363.

43. FAIRY GLEN RSPB RESERVE

RSPB North Scotland Office.
Location: On the Black Isle, by Rosemarkie on the A832. **Access:** Open all year.
Facilities: Car park, nature trail.
Public transport: No 26 bus stops in Rosemarkie (approx 5 min walk to reserve).
Habitat: Broadleaved woodland in a steep-sided valley, stream, waterfalls.
Key birds: *All year*: Dipper, Buzzard, Grey Wagtail, usual woodland species.
Contact: RSPB North Scotland Office. 01463 715000.

44. FORSINARD

RSPB (North Scotland Office).
Location: NC 89 04 25. 30 miles SW of Thurso on A897. Turn off A9 at Helmsdale from the South (24 miles) or A836 at Melvich from the N coast road (14 miles).
Access: Open at all times. Contact visitor centre during breeding season (mid-Apr to end Jun) and during deerstalking season (Jul 1-Feb 15) for advice. Self-guided trail open all year, no dogs, not suitable for wheelchairs.
Facilities: Visitor centre open Apr 1-Oct (9am-6pm), seven days per week. Static and AV displays, live CCTV and webcam link to Hen Harrier nest in breeding season. Wheelchair access to centre and toilet. Guided walks Tue and Thu, May-Aug. Tea-room nearby.
Public transport: Train from Inverness and Thurso (0845 484950) visitor centre in Forsinard Station building.
Habitat: Blanket bog, upland hill farm.
Key birds: Golden Plover, Greenshank, Dunlin, Hen Harrier, Merlin, Short-eared Owl.
Contact: Norrie Russell, RSPB Forsinard, Forsinard, Sutherland KW13 6YT. 01641 571225. e-mail: forsinard@rspb.org.uk www.rspb.org.uk

45. GLENBORRODALE RSPB RESERVE

RSPB
Location: One mile W of Glenborrodale on the B8007 on the Adrnamurchan peninsula.
Access: Open all year. **Facilities:** Nature trail.
Public transport: None.
Habitat: Ancient oak wood, loch.
Key birds: *Spring/summer*: Wood Warbler, Redstart, Spotted Flycatcher. *All year*: Usual woodland species. Seals, possible otter.
Contact: RSPB, Beechwood Park, Inverness-shire, IV2 3BW, 01463 715000.

46. HANDA

Scottish Wildlife Trust.
Location: NC 138 480. Accessible by boat from

Tarbet, near Scourie–follow A894 N from Ullapool 40 miles. Continue another three miles, turn left down single track road another three miles to Tarbet.
Access: Open April-Sept. Boats leave 9.30am-2pm (last boat back 5pm). Dogs not allowed. Visitors are asked for a contribution of £2 towards costs. Not suitable for disabled due to uneven terrain.
Facilities: Three mile circular path, shelter (no toilets on island - use those in Tarbet car park). Visitors are given introductory talk and a leaflet with map on arrival.
Public transport: Post bus to Scourie (tel 01549 402357 Lairg Post Office). Train to Lairg (tel 0845 484950 National Train enquiries). No connecting public transport between Scourie and Tarbet.
Habitat: Sea cliffs, blanket bog.
Key birds: *Spring/summer*: Biggest Guillemot and Razorbill colony in Britain and Ireland. Also nationally important for Kittiwakes, Arctic and Great Skuas. Puffin, Shag, Fulmar and Common and Arctic Terns also present.
Contact: Mark Foxwell, Conservation Manager Unit, 4A, 3 Carsegate Road North, Inverness IV3 8PU. 01463 714746.
e-mail: mfoxwell@swt.org.uk www.swt.org.uk.
Charles Thomson (Boatman) 01971 502347.

47. INSH MARSHES

RSPB (North Scotland Office).
Location: NN 775 999. In Spey Valley, two miles NE of Kingussie on B970 minor road.
Access: Open at all times. No disabled access.
Facilities: Information viewpoint, two hides, three nature trails. Not suitable for disabled. No toilets.
Public transport: Nearest rail station Kingussie (two miles).
Habitat: Marshes, woodland, river, open water.
Key birds: *Spring/summer*: Waders (Lapwing, Curlew, Redshank, Snipe), wildfowl (including Goldeneye and Wigeon), Spotted Crake, Wood Warbler, Redstart, Tree Pipit. *Winter*: Hen Harrier, Whooper Swan, other wildfowl.
Contact: Pete Moore, Ivy Cottage, Insh, Kingussie, Inverness-shire PH21 1NT. 01540 661518. e-mail: pete.moore@rspb.org.uk www.kincraig.com/rspb.htn

48. ISLE OF EIGG

Scottish Wildlife Trust.
Location: NM 38 48. Small island S of Skye, reached by ferry from Maillaig or Arisaig (approx 12 miles).
Access: Ferries seven days per week (weather permitting) during summer. Four days per week (weather permitting) Sept-Apr.
Facilities: Pier centre – shops/Post Office, tea-room, craftshop, toilets.
Public transport: Caledonian MacBrayne Ferries NE from Mallaig (tel: 01687 462403), *MV Shearwater* from Arisaig (tel: 01678 450 224).
Habitat: Moorland (leading to sgurr pitchstone ridge), wood and scrub, hay fields, shoreline. Marsh and bog.
Key birds: Red-throated Diver, Golden Eagle, Buzzard, Raven. *Summer*: Manx Shearwater, Arctic Tern, various warblers, Twite, etc.
Contact: John Chester, Millers Cottage, Isle of Eigg, Small Isles PH42 4RL. 01687 482477. www.isleofeigg.org

49. ISLE OF RUM

SNH (North West Region).
Location: NM 370 970. Island lying S of Skye. Passenger ferry from Mallaig, take A830 from Fort William.
Access: Contact Reserve Office for details of special access arrangements relating to breeding birds, deer stalking and deer research.
Facilities: Kinloch Castle Hostel, 01687 462037, Bayview Guest House, 01687 462023. General store and post office, guided walks in summer.
Public transport: Caledonian MacBrayne ferry from Mallaig, 01687 450224, www.arisaig.co.uk
Habitat: Coast, moorland, woodland restoration, montane.
Key birds: *Summer:* Large Manx Shearwater colonies on hill tops; breeding auks (inc. Black Guillemot), Kittiwake, Fulmar, Eider, Golden Plover, Merlin, Red-throated Diver, Golden Eagle.
Contact: SNH Reserve Office, Isle of Rum PH43 4RR, 01687 462026; fax 01687 462805.

50. LOCH FLEET

Scottish Wildlife Trust.
Location: NH 794 965. Site lies two miles S of Golspie on the A9 and five miles N of Dornoch. View across tidal basin from A9 or unclassified road to Skelbo.
Access: Park at Little Ferry or in lay-bys around the basin.
Facilities: Guided walks in summer. Interpretive centre. **Public transport:** None.
Habitat: Tidal basin, sand dunes, shingle, woodland, marshes.
Key birds: *Winter*: Important feeding place for ducks and waders. The sea off the mouth of Loch Fleet is a major wintering area for Long-tailed

Duck, Common and Velvet Scoters, Eider Duck. Pinewood off minor road S from Golspie to Little Ferry has Crossbill, occasional Crested Tit.
Contact: Trust HQ, 0131 312 7765.

51. LOCH RUTHVEN

RSPB (North Scotland Office).
Location: H 638 281. From Inverness, take A9 SE to junction with B851. Head SW until the minor road NE at Croachy; car park one mile.
Access: Open at all times.
Facilities: None. **Public transport:** None.
Habitat: Freshwater loch and woodland.
Key birds: Best breeding site in Britain for Slavonian Grebe. Teal, Wigeon and other wildfowl breed. Peregrine, Hen Harrier and Osprey often seen.
Contact: RSPB North Scotland Office.,

52. UDALE BAY RSPB RESERVE

RSPB North Scotland Office.
Location: One mile W of Jemimaville on B9163.
Access: Open all year. **Facilities:** Hide, lay-by.
Public transport: No 26 bus stops in Jemimaville six times a day (approx 5 min walk to reserve).
Habitat: Mudflat, saltmarsh and wet grassland.
Key birds: *Spring/summer*: wildfowl, Oystercatcher, Redshank, waders. Possible Osprey fishing. *Autumn/winter*: Large flocks of wildfowl, geese, waders.
Contact: RSPB North Scotland Office, Etive House, Beechwood Park, Inverness IV2 3BW. 01463 715000.

Lothian

53. ABERLADY BAY

East Lothian Council (LNR).
Location: NT 472 806. From Edinburgh take A198 E to Aberlady. Reserve is 1.5 miles E of Aberlady village.
Access: Open at all times. Please stay on footpaths to avoid disturbance. Disabled access from reserve car park. No dogs.
Facilities: Small car park and toilets. Notice board with recent sightings at end of footbridge.
Public transport: Edinburgh to N Berwick bus service stops at reserve (request), service no 124. Railway 4 miles away at Longniddry.
Habitat: Tidal mudflats, saltmarsh, freshwater marsh, dune grassland, scrub, open sea.
Key birds: *Summer*: Breeding birds include Shelduck, Eider, Reed Bunting and up to eight species of warbler. Passage waders inc. Green, Wood and Curlew Sandpipers, Little Stint, Greenshank, Whimbrel, Black-tailed Godwit. *Winter*: Divers (esp. Red-throated), Red-necked and Slavonian grebes and geese (large numbers of Pink-footed roost); sea-ducks, waders.
Contact: Ian Thomson, 4 Craigielaw, Longniddry, East Lothian EH32 0PY. 01875 870588.

54. ALMONDELL AND CALDERWOOD

West Lothian Council.
Location: NT 077 670. Several entrances but this is closest to the visitor centre - signposted off the A89, two miles S of Broxburn.
Access: Open all year. Parking available off Bank Street in Mid Calder. Walk down the footpath beside the Masonic Hall or park in the Oakbank car park on the A71 between the two shale bings, then along the roadside to the crash barrier and in.
Facilities: Car park, café, picnic area, toilets, pushchair access, partial access for wheelchairs, visitor centre (open Sat-Thu), shop, countryside ranger service. **Public transport:** None.
Habitat: Woodland, marshland.
Key birds: *Spring/summer*: Woodcock, Tawny Owl, Grasshopper Warbler, Yellowhammer, Blackcap, Garden Warbler. *Winter*: Goldcrest, Redpoll, Willow Tit. *All year*: Dipper, Grey Wagtail, Sparrowhawk.
Contact: Almondell and Calderwood Country Park, Visitor Centre, Broxburn, West Lothian, EH52 5PE, 01506 882254.

55. BASS ROCK

Location: NT602873. Island in Firth of Forth, lying E of North Berwick.
Access: Private property. Regular daily sailings from N Berwick around Rock; local boatman has owner's permission to land individuals or parties by prior arrangement.
Facilities: None. **Public transport:** None.
Habitat: Sea cliffs.
Key birds: The spectacular cliffs hold a large Gannet colony, (up to 9000 pairs), plus auks, Kittiwake, Shag and Fulmer.
For boat details contact: Fred Marr, N Berwick on 01620 892838.

56. DUDDINGSTON LOCH

Scottish Wildlife Trust.
Location: NT 284 725. At the S end of Holyrood

Park, Edinburgh. Take the A1 along Old Church Lane, off Duddingston Road West.
Access: Open all year.
Facilities: Permit and key for hide available at visitor centre (deposit required). Centre open daily (10am-5.45pm Jun-Sep, weekends only, 10am-4pm Apr-May and Oct-Dec). **Public transport:** None.
Habitat: Loch, marshland, reedbed, woodland.
Key birds: *Spring/summer*: Fulmar, Sedge Warbler, Sky Lark, Linnet. *All year*: Grey Heron, Sparrowhawk. *Passage*: Wheatear, possible Ring Ouzel.
Contact: Scottish Wildlife Trust, Cramond House, Kirk Cramond, Gramond Glebe Road, Edinburgh EH4 6NS. 0131 312 7765.
e-mail: scottishwt@cix.co.uk www.swt.org.uk

57. GLADHOUSE RESERVOIR LNR

Scottish Water.
Location: NT 295 535. S of Edinburgh off the A703.
Access: Open all year, although there is no access to the reservoir itself. Most viewing can be done from the road (telescope required).
Facilities: Small car park on north side.
Public transport: None.
Habitat: Reservoir, grassland, farmland.
Key birds: *Spring/summer*: Oystercatcher, Lapwing, Curlew. Possible Black Grouse. *Winter*: Geese, including Pinkfeet, Twite, Brambling, Hen Harrier.
Contact: Scottish Water, PO Box 8855, Edinburgh, EH10 6YQ, 0131 4456462.
e-mail: customer.service@scottishwater.co.uk
www.esw.co.uk

Moray & Nairn

58. CULBIN SANDS

RSPB (North Scotland Office).
Location: NH 900 580. Approx ½ mile from Nairn. Access to parking at East Beach car park, signed off A96.
Access: Open at all times. Not suitable for wheelchairs. **Facilities:** Toilets at car park. Track along dunes and saltmarsh.
Public transport: Buses stop in Nairn, half mile W of site. Train station in Nairn three-quarters mile W of reserve.
Habitat: Saltmarsh, sandflats, dunes.
Key birds: *Winter*: Flocks of Common Scoter, Long-tailed Duck, Knot, Bar-tailed Godwit, Red-breasted Merganser. Rapters such as Peregrine, Merlin and Hen Harrier attracted by wader flocks. Roosting geese. *Summer*: Breeding Ringed Plover, Oystercatcher and Common Tern.
Contact: RSPB North Scotland Office., Etive House, Beechwood Park, Inverness IV2 3BW. 01463 715000.
e-mail: nsro@rspb.org.uk www.rspb.org.uk

59. SPEY BAY LEIN (THE)

Scottish Wildlife Trust.
Location: NJ 325 657. Eight miles NE of Elgin. From Elgin take A96 and B9015 to Kingston. Reserve is immediately E of village. Car parks at Kingston and Tugnet.
Access: Open all year. **Facilities:** Wildlife centre.
Public transport: None.
Habitat: Shingle, rivermouth and coastal habitats.
Key birds: *Summer*: Osprey, waders, wildfowl. *Winter*: Seaduck and divers offshore (esp. Long-tailed Duck, Common and Velvet Scoters, Red-throated Diver).
Contact: Trust HQ, 0131 312 7765.

NE Scotland

60. FORVIE

Scottish Natural Heritage.
Location: NK 034 289.
Access: Dogs on leads only. Reserve open at all times but ternery closed Apr 1 to end of Aug annually. Stevenson Forvie Centre open every day (Apr-Sept) and when staff are available outside those months.
Facilities: Interpretive display and toilets in Stevenson Forvie Centre. Bird hide, waymarked trail.
Public transport: Bluebird No 263 to Cruden Bay. Ask for the Newburgh or Collieston Crossroads stop. Tel: 01224 591381.
Habitat: Estuary, dunes, coastal heath.
Key birds: *Spring/summer*: Eider and terns nesting. *Winter*: Waders and wildfowl on estuary.
Contact: Alison Matheson (Area Officer), Scottish Natural Heritage, Stevenson Forvie Centre, Little Collieston Croft, Collieston, Aberdeenshire AB41 8RU. 01358 751330. www.snh.org.uk

61. FOWLSHEUGH

RSPB (East Scotland).
Location: NO 879 80. Cliff top path N from

Crawton, signposted from A92, three miles S of Stonehaven.
Access: Unrestricted. Boat trips (May-Jul) from Stonehaven Harbour. Booking essential. Contact East Scotland regional office. Tel: 01224 624824.
Facilities: New car park (council) with limited number of spaces 200 yards from reserve (replaced following the storm damage of 1999).
Public transport: None. **Habitat:** Sea cliffs.
Key birds: Spectacular seabird colony, mainly Kittiwake and auks.
Contact: The Warden, Starnafin, Crimond, Fraserburgh AB43 8QN. 01346 532017.
e-mail: strathbeg@rspb.org.uk www.rspb.org.uk

62. GLEN TANAR NNR

Glen Tanar Estate.
Location: 47 96. On the A93 Banchory-Braemar road. From Aboyne turn S across the river, then W on the B976. At Bridge o'Ess, turn L to Braeloine to the car park. **Access:** Open all year.
Facilities: Car parks, visitor centre (open Apr-Sep), trails. Do not attempt the summits unless you are properly prepared.
Public transport: None.
Habitat: Remnant of old Caledonian forest, heather moorland, mountains.
Key birds: *All year*: Black Grouse, Woodcock, Siskin, Grey Wagtail, Dipper. *Winter*: possible Golden Eagle.
Contact: Ranger, Glen Tanar Estate, Brooks House, Glen Tanar, Aboyne, Aberdeenshire AB34 5EU. 01339 880047.
e-mail: office@glentanar.co.uk

63. HADDO COUNTRY PARK

Haddo House.
Location: NJ 875 345. From Aberdeen head N on A90 to Ellon, then take B9005 NW to Haddo House (signposted).
Access: Open all year.
Facilities: Car parks, display boards.
Public transport: Bus: Aberdeen-Tarves stop 3.2km from house.
Habitat: Parkland, woodland, wetland, loch, ponds.
Key birds: *Spring/summer*: Sedge Warbler, Blackcap, Chiffchaff, Lapwing. *Winter*: Geese, Teal, Wigeon, Goldeneye, Goosander, Brambling. *All year*: Buzzard, Sparrowhawk, Grey Partridge, Great Spotted Woodpecker, Grey Wagtail.
Contact: Aberdeenshire Ranger Service, 01651 851489.

64. LOCH OF STRATHBEG

RSPB (East Scotland).
Location: NK 057 581. Near Crimond on the A90, nine miles S of Fraserburgh.
Access: Starnafin visitor centre and Tower Pool open at all times dawn-dusk. Loch hides, access restricted to between 8am and 4pm daily. No dogs except guide dogs please. Visitor centre not fully accessible to wheelchairs and disabled visitors.
Facilities: Visitor centre and observation room at Starnafin, four hides, Tower Pool hide, accessible via 1000 metre footpath from Starnafin, three hides overlooking loch accessed via MOD airfield. Toilets (with disabled access), car parking.
Public transport: Access to whole site is difficult without a car. Bus service between Fraserburgh and Peterhead, stops at Crimond, just over one mile from visitor centre.
Habitat: Dune loch with surrounding marshes, reedbeds, grasslands, dunes and farmland.
Key birds: *Winter*: Internationally important numbers of Whooper Swan, Pink-footed and Barnacle Geese, large numbers of winter duck including Smew. *Spring/summer*: Waders, Black-headed Gulls, Common Terns, Water Rail, farmland birds including Corn Bunting. *Spring/autumn*: Spoonbill, Little Egret, Marsh Harrier, passage waders including Black-tailed Godwit.
Contact: RSPB Warden, RSPB Loch of Strathbeg, Starnafin, Crimond, Fraserburgh, AB43 8QN. 01346 532017. www.rspb.org.uk
e-mail: strathbeg@rspb.org.uk

65. ST CYRUS

Scottish Natural Heritage.
Location: NO 764 650. Three miles N of Montrose, follow the sign saying 'Beach' from the main coast road.
Access: The whole reserve is accessible from Sept-Mar. From Apr-Aug the south of the reserve is closed for breeding birds. Disabled access limited to visitor centre and boardwalk. Dogs on leads during the breeding season, but can be let off on the beach.
Facilities: Visitor centre and toilets.
Public transport: None to reserve. Buses to the village of St Cyrus. Walk down the cliff path from there.
Habitat: Narrow dune system, calcareous grassland and cliffs.

Key birds: *Summer*: Grasshopper Warbler, Whitethroat, Willow Warbler. Terns feeding and roosting by river mouth. Nesting Peregrine.
Contact: Andrew Turner, Scottish Natural Heritage, Old Lifeboat Station, Nether, Warberton, St Cyrus DD10 0Dg. 01674 830736. www.snh.org.uk

Orkney

66. BIRSAY MOORS

RSPB (East Scotland).
Location: Access to hide at Burgar Hill, signposted from A966 at Evie (HY 346 247). Birsay Moors viewed from B9057 NW of Dounby.
Access: Open access all year round.
Facilities: Burgar Hill hide very good for watching breeding Red-throated Divers Apr to Aug.
Public transport: Orkney Coaches. Service within 0.5 mile of reserve. Tel: 01856 877500.
Habitat: Diverse example of Orkney moorland - wet and dry heath, bog, mire, scrub and some farmland.
Key birds: *Spring/summer*: Nesting Hen Harrier, Merlin, Great and Arctic Skuas, Short-eared Owl, Golden Plover, Curlew, Red-throated Diver. *Winter*: Hen Harrier roost.
Contact: The Warden, 12/14 North End Road, Stromness, Orkney KW16 3HG. 01856 850176. e-mail: orkney@rspb.org.uk www.rspb.co.uk

67. COPINSAY

RSPB (East Scotland).
Location: HY 610 010. Access by private boat or hire boat from mainland Orkney.
Access: Open all year round.
Facilities: House on island open to visitors, but no facilities. No toilets or hides.
Public transport: None.
Habitat: Sea cliffs, farmland.
Key birds: *Summer*: Stunning seabird-cliffs with breeding Kittiwake, Guillemot, Black Guillemot, Puffin, Razorbill, Shag, Fulmar, Rock Dove, Eider, Twite, Raven and Greater Black-backed Gull. Passage migrants esp. during periods of E winds.
Contact: The Warden, 12/14 North End Road, Stromness, Orkney KW16 3AG. 01856 850176. e-mail: orkney@rspb.org.uk
S Foubisher (boatman) 01856 741252 - cannot sail if wind is in the east.

68. COTTASCARTH AND RENDALL MOSS

RSPB (East Scotland).
Location: HY 360 200. Orkney reserve off A966, three miles N of Finstown. **Access:** Open all year. Hide open all year. Not suitable for dogs.
Facilities: Hide (ideal for watching raptors in the Spring) and car park.
Public transport: Orkney Coaches. Tel: 01856 877500.
Habitat: Heather moorland, areas of rushes and wet grassland.
Key birds: *Summer*: Breeding Hen Harrier, Merlin, Redshank, Oystercatcher, Curlew, Reed Bunting.
Contact: The Warden, 12/14 North End Road, Stromness, Orkney KW16 3AG. 01856 850176. e-mail: orkney@rspb.org.uk www.rspb.co.uk

69. HOBBISTER

RSPB (East Scotland).
Location: HY 396 070 or HY 381 068. Near Kirkwall.
Access: Open access between A964 and the sea. Dogs on leads please.
Facilities: A council maintained footpath to Waulkmill Bay, two car parks, walks along peat-cutters' tracks.
Public transport: Orkney Coaches. Tel: 01856 877500.
Habitat: Orkney moorland, bog, fen, saltmarsh, coastal cliffs, scrub.
Key birds: *Summer*: Breeding Hen Harrier, Merlin, Short-eared Owl, Red Grouse, Red-throated Diver, Eider, Merganser, Black Guillemot. Wildfowl and waders at Waulkmill Bay.
Contact: The Warden, 12/14 North End Road, Stromness, Orkney KW16 3AG. 01856 850176. e-mail: orkney@rspb.org.uk www.rspb.co.uk

70. HOY

RSPB (East Scotland).
Location: HY 210 025. Located in NW of Hoy, a large island S of mainland Orkney. Car ferry from Houten to Lyness.
Access: Open all year round. Keep dogs on lead. Unsuitable for disabled people – rough terrain.
Facilities: Toilet facilities at Moaness Pier and at Rackwick. Nature trail – circular route from Moaness Pier to Old Man of Hoy via Old Rackwick Post Road. Leaflets available from 2003.

Public transport: Foot passenger ferry service from Stromness to Moaness Pier. Minibus taxis
Habitat: Coastal heath, moorland, fellfield, woodland and cliffs.
Key birds: *Spring/summer:* Red-throated Diver, Merlin, Peregrine, Golden Plover, Dunlin, Great Skua, Arctic Skua, Short-eared Owl, Guillemot, Razorbill, Puffin, Fulmar, Kittiwake, Stonechat, Wheatear. *Autumn/winter*: Redwing, Fieldfare, Snow Bunting. *Migration species:* Whimbrel, Brambling plus almost anything is possible.
Contact: 1. The Warden, 01856 791298. 2. Ley House, Hoy, Orkney KW16 3NJ.

71. MARWICK HEAD

RSPB (East Scotland).
Location: HY 229 242. On W coast of mainland Orkney, near Dounby. Path N from Marwick Bay, or from car park at Cumlaquoy at HY 232 252.
Access: Open all year. Rough terrain not suitable for wheelchairs. **Facilities:** Cliff top path.
Public transport: Orkney Coaches (01856 877500).
Habitat: Rocky bay, sandstone cliffs. Beach path good place for great yellow bumble bee in Aug.
Key birds: May-Jul best. Huge numbers of Kittiwakes and auks, inc. Puffins, also nesting Fulmar, Rock Dove, Raven, Rock Pipit.
Contact: The Warden, 12/14 North End Road, Stromness, Orkney KW16 3AG. 01856 850176. e-mail: orkney@rspb.org.uk www.rspb.co.uk

72. MILL DAM

RSPB (East Scotland).
Location: HY 483 178.
Access: Hide open all year. **Facilities:** None.
Public transport: Vehicular ferry from Kirkwall to Shapinsay, 1/2 hour walk from ferry. (Orkney Ferries 01856 872044).
Habitat: Wetland. A little gem affording great views from the hide of ducks and waders in Spring, Autumn and Winter.
Key birds: *All year:* Shoveler, Pintail, Gadwall, Ruddy Duck, gulls. *Winter:* Whooper Swans, Wigeon, Teal, Shoveler.
Contact: The Warden, 12/14 North End Road, Stromness, Orkney KW16 3AG. 01856 850176. e-mail: orkney@rspb.org.uk www.rspb.co.uk

73. NORTH HILL, PAPA WESTRAY

RSPB (East Scotland).
Location: HY 496 538. Small island lying NE of Westray, reserve at N end of island's main road.
Access: Access at all times. During breeding season report to summer warden at Rose Cottage, 650 yards S of reserve entrance (Tel 01857 644240.) or use trail guide.
Facilities: Nature trails, hide/info hut.
Public transport: Orkney Ferries (01856 872044), Loganair Ferries (01856 872494).
Habitat: Sea cliffs, maritime heath.
Key birds: *Summer*: Close views of colony of Puffin, Guillemot, Razorbill and Kittiwake. Black Guillemot nest under flagstones around reserve's coastline. One of UK's largest colonies of Arctic Tern, also Arctic Skua.
Contact: Apr-Aug, The Warden at Rose Cottage, Papay Westray DW17 2BU. 01857 644240., 2. RSPB Orkney Office 12/14 North End Road, Stromness, Orkney KW16 3AG. 01856 850176. e-mail: orkney@rspb.org.uk www.rspb.co.uk

74. NORTH RONALDSAY BIRD OBSERVATORY

Location: HY 64 52. 35 miles from Kirkwall, Orkney mainland
Access: Open all year except Christmas.
Facilities: Accommodation, display room, meals, snacks etc for non-residents, fully licenced, toilets, croft walk.
Public transport: Twice daily (Mon-Sat) subsidised flights from Kirkwall (Loganair 01856 872494). Sunday flights in Summer. Once weekly ferry from Kirkwall (Fri or Sat), some Sun sailings in summer (Orkney Ferries Ltd 01856 872044).
Habitat: Crofting island with a number of eutrophic and oligotrophic wetlands. Coastline has both sandy bays and rocky shore. Walled gardens concentrate passerines.
Key birds: Prime migration site in Spring/ Autumn including regular BBRC species. Wide variety of breeding seabirds, wildfowl and waders. *Winter:* Waders and wildfowl include Whooper Swan and hard weather movements occur.
Contact: Alison Duncan, North Ronaldsay Bird Observatory, Twingness, North Ronaldsay, Orkney KW17 2BE. 01857 633200. e-mail: alison@nrbo.prestel.co.uk www.nrbo.f2s.com

75. NOUP CLIFFS, WESTRAY

RSPB (East Scotland).
Location: HY 392 500. Westray lies NE of Mainland and Rousay. Take minor road to Pierowall and Noup Farm then track NW to lighthouse.

Access: No dogs, even on a lead.
Facilities: Trail guide.
Public transport: Flights from Kirkwall daily (Loganair 01856 872494). Daily ferry (Orkney Ferries 01856 872044).
Habitat: 1.5 miles of sandstone cliffs.
Key birds: *Summer*: May-Jul best. Huge seabird colony, breeding Rock Dove, Raven, Shag, auks, Rock Pipit.
Contact: RSPB Orkney Office, 12/14 North End Road, Stromness, Orkney KW16 3AG. 01856 850176. e-mail: orkney@rspb.org.uk

76. TRUMLAND, ROUSAY

RSPB (East Scotland).
Location: HY 427 276. Ferry from Tingwall in NE Mainland to Rousay.
Access: Reserve and nature trail (access at all times) from entrance to Taversoe Tuick Cairn.
Facilities: Nature trail.
Public transport: Orkney Ferries to Rousay from Tingwall Pier Tel: 01856 751360.
Habitat: Moorland.
Key birds: *Summer*: Breeding Hen Harrier, Merlin, Short-eared Owl, Red-throated Diver, Golden Plover, Great and Arctic Skuas, Common Gull.
Contact: Egilsay Warden,.01856 821395.
e-mail: orkney@rspb.org.uk www.rspb.co.uk

Outer Hebrides

77. BALRANALD

RSPB (North Scotland Office).
Location: NF 705 707. From Skye take ferry to Lochmaddy, North Uist. Drive W on A867 for 20 miles to reserve. Turn off main road three miles NW of Bayhead at signpost to Houghharry.
Access: Open at all times, no charge. Dogs on leads. Disabled access. **Facilities:** Visitor Centre and toilets - disabled access. Marked nature trail.
Public transport: Bus service (tel 01876 560244).
Habitat: Freshwater loch, machair, coast and croft lands.
Key birds: *Summer*: Corn Crake, Corn Bunting, Lapwing, Oystercatcher, Dunlin, Ringed Plover, Redshank, Snipe. *Winter*: Twite, Greylag Goose, Wigeon, Teal, Shoveler. *Passage*: Barnacle Goose, Pomarine Skua, Long-tailed Skua.
Contact: Jamie Boyle, 9 Grenitote, Isle of North Uist, H56 5BP01876 560287.
e-mail: james.boyle3@btinternet.com

78. LOCH DRUIDIBEG

SNH (North West Region).
Location: NF 782 378. South Uist.
Access: Restricted access during breeding season.
Facilities: None.
Public transport: Regular bus service passes reserve.
Habitat: Loch, machair, coast, moorland.
Key birds: *Summer*: Breeding Greylag, waders, Corn Crake, wildfowl.
Contact: SNH Area Officer, Stilligarry, South Uist, HS8 5RS. 01870 620238; fax 01870 620350.

Perth & Kinross

79. BEN LAWYERS

National Trust for Scotland.
Location: Off A827, 1.5 miles NE of Killin, N of Loch Tay. **Access:** Open all year.
Facilities: Car park, visitor centre daily 10am-5pm (25 Mar-29 Sep) may close for 30 mins for lunch between 1pm-2pm. Toilets (one suitable for disabled), information.
Public transport: None.
Habitat: Perthshire's highest mountain.
Key birds: *Spring/summer*: Ring Ouzel, warblers, Curlew. *All year*: Raven, Red Grouse, Ptarmigan, Dipper.
Contact: Ranger's Office, National Trust for Scotland, Lynedoch, Main Street, Killin FK21 8UW. Visitor Centre (01567) 820397 or office (01567) 820988. www.nts.org.uk

80. DOUNE PONDS

Stirling Council.
Location: NN 726 019. Take the A820 Dunblane road E from the junction with the A84 Callander-Stirling road. Turn L onto Moray Street just before Doune Church. **Access:** Open all year.
Facilities: Information board, nature trail, hides. Wheelchair access to E hide. Leaflet from local tourist information offices, local library.
Public transport: Bus from Stirling and Callander to Doune.
Habitat: Pools, scrape, plantations, birch woodlands.
Key birds: *All year*: Grey Heron, Buzzard, Snipe, Goldcrest, Siskin, Red Kite. *Spring/summer*: Common Sandpiper, Whitethroat, warblers.
Contact: Stirling Council Countryside Ranger Service, Viewforth, Stirling FK8 2ET.

81. LOCH LEVEN

SNH, Loch Leven Laboratory.
Location: NO 150 010. Head S from Perth and leave M90 at exit 6, S of Kinross.
Access: Public access restricted to three short stretches of shoreline. Most birdwatchers visiting the reserve go to the RSPB nature centre at Vane Farm (qv) overlooking the loch.
Facilities: Extensive ornithological research programme.
Public transport: Bus from Perth or Edinburgh to Kinross section of shoreline.
Habitat: Lowland loch with islands.
Key birds: *Winter*: Flocks of geese (over 20,000 Pinkfeet), ducks, Whooper Swan. *Summer*: Greatest concentration of breeding ducks in Britain (10 species) and grebes. *Passage*: Waders (Golden Plover flocks up to 500).
Contact: Paul Brooks, SNH, Loch Leven Laboratory, The Pier, Kinross KY13 8UF. 01577 864439.

82. LOCH OF THE LOWES

Scottish Wildlife Trust.
Location: NO 042 435. Sixteen miles N of Perth, two miles NE of Dunkeld - just off A923 (signposted).
Access: Visitor centre open Apr-Sept inclusive (10am-5pm), mid-Jul to mid-Aug (10am-6pm). Observation hide open all year - daylight hours. No dogs allowed. Partial access for wheelchairs.
Facilities: Visitor centre with toilets, hide.
Public transport: Railway station - Birnam/ Dunkeld - three miles from reserve. Bus from Dunkeld - two miles from reserve.
Habitat: Freshwater loch with fringing woodland.
Key birds: Breeding Ospreys (Apr-end Aug). Nest in view, 200 metres from hide. Wildfowl and woodland birds. Greylag roost (Oct-Mar).
Contact: Mr Uwe Stoneman, (Manager), Scottish Wildlife Trust, Loch of the Lowes, Visitor Centre, Dunkeld, Perthshire PH8 0HH. 01350 727337.

83. QUARRYMILL WOODLAND PARK

Gannochy Trust.
Location: NO 121 253. From Perth on the A93, cross the River Tay. Follow it on the Isla Road to Blairgowrie. The Park is signposted on the R, opposite the Upper Springland building.
Access: Open all year. **Facilities:** Visitor centre, coffee shop with disabled facilities. Dogs on leads.
Public transport: Bus: Perth to Blairgowrie stops at Quarrymill. Tel: 0870 550 5050.
Habitat: Wood, stream.
Key birds: *Spring/summer*: Blackcap, Willow and Garden Warblers, Spotted Flycatcher, Chiffchaff. *All year*: Buzzard, Great Spotted Woodpecker, Jay, Goldcrest. Possible Mandarin.
Contact: Isle Road, Perth, Perthshire, 01738 633 890.

84. VANE FARM NNR

RSPB (East Scotland).
Location: NT 160 993. By Loch Leven. Take exit 5 from M90 onto B9097.
Access: Open daily (10am-5pm) except Christmas Day, Boxing Day, Jan 1 and Jan 2. Cost £3 adults, £2 concessions, 50p children, £6 family. Free to members. No dogs except guide dogs.
Facilities: Shop, coffee shop and observation room overlooking Loch Leven and the reserve all wheelchair accessible. There is a 1.25 mile hill trail through woodland and moorland. Wetland trail with three observation hides. Toilets, including disabled.
Public transport: Nearest train station Cowdenbeath (nine miles away). Nearest bus station Kinross at Green Hotel (five miles away).
Habitat: Wet grassland and flooded areas by Loch Leven. Arable farmland. Native woodland and heath moorland.
Key birds: *Spring/summer*: Breeding and passage waders (including Lapwing, Redshank, Snipe, Curlew). Farmland birds (including Sky Lark and Yellowhammer). *Winter*: Whooper Swan, Bewick's Swan, Pink-footed Goose.
Contact: Ken Shaw, Senior Site Manager, Vane Farm Nature Centre, Kinross, Tayside KY13 9LX. 01577 862355. e-mail: vanefarm@rspb.co.uk

Shetland

85. FAIR ISLE BIRD OBSERVATORY

Fair Isle Bird Observatory.
Location: HZ 2172.
Access: Open from end Apr-end Oct. Free to roam everywhere except one croft (Lower Leogh).
Facilities: Public toilets at Airstrip and Stackhoull Stores (shop). Accommodation at Fair Isle Bird Observatory (phone/e-mail: for brochure/details). Guests can be involved in observatory work and get to see birds in the hand. Slide shows, guided walks through Ranger Service.
Public transport: Tue, Thurs, Sat - ferry (12

passengers) from Grutness, Shetland. Tel: Jimmy or Florrie Stout 01595 760222. Mon, Wed, Fri, Sat – air (7 seater) from Tingwall, Shetland. Tel: Loganair 01595 840246.
Habitat: Heather moor and lowland pasture/ crofting land. Cliffs.
Key birds: Large breeding seabird colonies (auks, Gannet, Arctic Tern, Kittiwake, Shag, Arctic Skua and Great Skua). Many common and rare migrants Apr/May/early Jun, late Aug-Nov.
Contact: Deryk Shaw (Warden), Hollie Shaw (Administrator), Fair Isle Bird Observatory, Fair Isle, Shetland ZE2 9JU. 01595 760258.
e-mail: fairisle.birdobs@zetnet.co.uk
www.fairislebirdobs.co.uk

86. FETLAR

RSPB (East Scotland).
Location: HU 603 917. Lies E of Yell. Take car ferry from Gutcher, N Yell. Booking advised. Tel: 01957 722259.
Access: Part of RSPB reserve (Vord Hill) closed mid-May-end Jul. Entry during this period is only by arrangement with warden.
Facilities: Hide at Mires of Funzie. Displays etc at interpretive centre, Houbie. Toilets at ferry terminal, shop and interpretive centre.
Public transport: None.
Habitat: Serpentine heath, rough hill lane, upland mire.
Key birds: *Summer*: Breeding Red-throated Diver, Eider, Shag, Whimbrel, Golden Plover, Dunlin, skuas, Manx Shearwater, Storm Petrel. Red-necked Phalarope on Loch of Funzie (HU 655 899) viewed from road or RSPB hide overlooking Mires of Funzie.
Contact: RSPB North Isles Officer, Bealance, Fetlar, Shetland ZE2 9DJ. Tel/Fax: 01957 733246.
e-mail: malcolm.smith@rspb.org.uk

87. ISLE OF NOSS NNR

Scottish Natural Heritage (Shetland Office).
Location: HU 531 410. Four miles by car ferry and road to the E of Lerwick. Take ferry to Bressay and follow signs for Noss. Park at end of road and walk to shore (600 yards) where ferry to island will collect you (if red flag is flying, island is closed due to sea conditions).
Access: Access (Tue, Wed, Fri, Sat, Sun) 10am-5pm, late May-late Aug. Access by zodiac inflatable, unsuitable for disabled. No dogs allowed on ferry.
Facilities: Visitor centre, toilets.
Public transport: None. Post car available, phone Royal Mail on 01595 820200. Cycle hire in Lerwick.
Habitat: Dune grassland, moorland, blanket bog, sea cliffs.
Key birds: *Spring/summer:* Fulmar, Shag, Gannet, Arctic Tern, Kittiwake, Great Black-backed Gull, Great Skua, Arctic Skua, Guillemot, Razorbill, Puffin, Black Guillemot, Eider.
Contact: Simon Smith, Scottish Natural Heritage, Stewart Building, Alexandra Wharf, Lerwick, Shetland ZE1 0LL. 01595 693345.
e-mail: simon.smith@snh.gov.uk

88. MOUSA

RSPB (Shetland Office).
Location: HU 460240. Small uninhabited island east of Sandwick in South Mainland of Shetland.
Access: By ferry from Leebitton Pier, Sandwick, Shetland – mid-Apr–mid-Sept.
Facilities: The Mousa Broch is the best preserved Iron Age tower in the world (World Heritage Site).
Public transport: Buses run to Sandwick from Lerwick. Details of ferry available from Tom Jamieson (01950 431367) or his web site (www.mousaboattrips.co.uk.).
Habitat: A small uninhabited island with maritime grassland and a small area of shell sand.
Key birds: *Summer*: Storm Petrels can be seen on the special night trips run by Tom Jamieson. Arctic Tern, Arctic and Great Skuas, Black Guillemot and Puffin.
Contact: Tom Jamieson, RSPB Shetland Office, East House, Sumburgh Head Lighthouse, Virkie, Shetland ZE3 9JN. 01950 460800.

89. SUMBURGH HEAD

RSPB (Shetland Office).
Location: HU 407 079. S tip of mainland Shetland.
Access: Open all year, but seabirds best May-mid Aug.
Facilities: View points.
Public transport: None.
Habitat: Sea cliffs.
Key birds: Breeding Puffin, Guillemot, Razorbill, Kittiwake, Shag, also minke and killer whales. Humpback whale seen occasionally.
Contact: RSPB Shetland Office, East House, Sumburgh Head Lighthouse, Virkie, Shetland ZE3 9JN. 01950 460 800.

East Wales

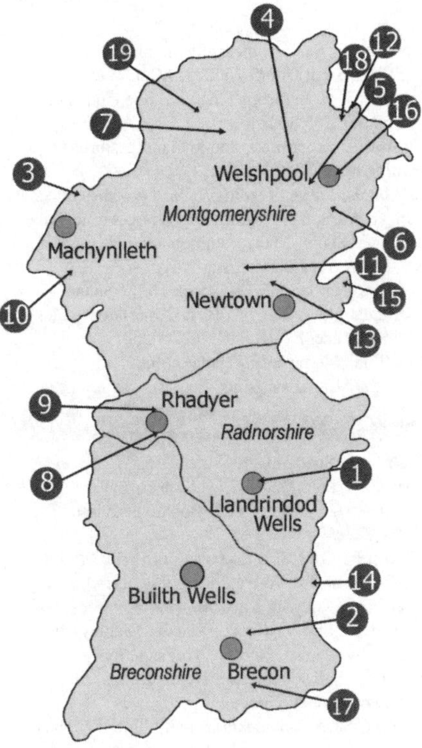

1. BAILEY EINON

Radnorshire Wildlife Trust.
Location: SO 083 613. From Llandrindod Wells, take the Craig Road leading to Cefnllys Lane. Down this road is Shaky Bridge with a car park and picnic site. A kissing-gate downstream from the picnic site marks the reserve entrance. Please do not park in front of the kissing-gate.
Access: Open all year.
Facilities: Car park, picnic site, waymarked trail.
Public transport: None.
Habitat: Woodland, river.
Key birds: *Spring/summer*: Pied Flycatcher, Redstart, Wood Warbler. *All year*: Great Spotted Woodpecker, Buzzard, usual woodland birds.
Contact: Radnorshire Wildlife Trust, Warwick House, High Street, Llandrindod Wells, Powys, LD1 6AG, 01597 823298.
e-mail: radnorshirewt@cix.co.uk
www.waleswildlife.co.uk

2. BRECHFA POOL

Brecknock Wildlife Trust.
Location: SO 118 377. Travelling NE from Brecon look for lane off A470, 1.5 miles SW of Llyswen; on Brechfa Common, pool is on right after cattle grid.
Access: Open dawn to dusk. **Facilities:** None.
Public transport: None.
Habitat: Marshy grassland, large shallow pool.
Key birds: Teal, Wigeon, Bewick's Swan, Redshank, Lapwing, Dunlin
Contact: Trust HQ, 01874 625708.

3. BWLCHCOEDIOG

W K and Mrs J Evans.
Location: SH 878 149. From Machynlleth take A489 NE for 14 miles. Half mile east of Mallwyd, turn left into Cwm Cewydd, then 1.25 miles up the valley. Park at Bwlchcoediog House.
Access: Open all year round. No dogs, in fenced areas, please keep to paths.
Facilities: None.
Public transport: None.
Habitat: Farmland, woodland, streams, two ponds, lake.
Key birds: *Summer:* Breeding Tree Pipit, Redstart, Garden and Wood Warblers, Pied and Spotted Flycatchers. *Winter:* Woodcock, Brambling, Raven, Buzzard, Sparrowhawk. *All Year*: Siskin, occasional Peregrine, Red Kite, Dipper.
Contact: W K and Mrs J Evans, Bwlchcoediog Isaf, Cwm Cewydd, Mallwyd, Machynlleth, Powys SY20 9EE. 01650 531243.

4. COED PENGUGWM

Montgomeryshire Wildlife Trust.
Location: SJ 103 142. On a minor road one mile N of Pontrobert towards Llanfihangel. Park on the reserve cark park down a short but steep track opposite Pendugwm Farm.
Access: Open all year.
Facilities: Footpaths.
Public transport: None.
Habitat: Broadleaved woodland, stream.
Key birds: *Spring/summer*: Pied Flycatcher, Redstart. *All year*: Buzzard, Sparrowhawk, woodpeckers, usual woodland species. Good for mammals.
Contact: Montgomeryshire Wildlife Trust, Collot

House, 20 Severn Street, Welshpool, Powys, SY21 7AD, 01938 555654. e-mail: montwt@cix.co.uk www.wildlifetrust.org.uk/montgomeryshire

5. CWM-Y-WYDDEN

Montgomeryshire Wildlife Trust.
Location: SJ 136 025. The reserve is about four miles W of Berriew and two miles E of Manafon, S of the B4390. Park by the crossroads at the lane to Dinnant. Walk down the lane and cross the river. Turn L in front of the farmhouse and follow the footpath to the stile into the wood.
Access: Open all year. **Facilities:** None.
Public transport: None.
Habitat: Sessile oak woodland.
Key birds: *Spring/summer*: Redstart, usual woodland species.
Contact: Montgomeryshire Wildlife Trust, Collot House, 20 Severn Street, Welshpool, Powys, SY21 7AD, 01938 555654. e-mail: montwt@cix.co.uk www.wildlifetrust.org.uk/montgomeryshire

6. DOLYDD HAFREN

Montgomeryshire Wildlife Trust.
Location: SJ 208 005. W of B4388. Go through Forden village and on about 1.5 miles. Turn right at sharp left bend at Gaer Farm and down farm track to car park at the other end.
Access: Open at all times - dogs to be kept on lead at all times. **Facilities:** Two bird hides.
Public transport: None.
Habitat: Riverside flood meadow - bare shingle, permanent grassland, ox-bow lakes and new pools.
Key birds: Goosander, Redshank, Lapwing, Snipe, Oystercatcher, Little Ringed Plover. *Winter*: Curlew.
Contact: Al Parrot, c/o Montgomeryshire Wildlife Trust, Collot House, 20 Severn Street, Welshpool, Powys SY21 7AD. 01938 555654.
e-mail: montwt@cixcompulink.co.uk
www.wildlifetrust.org.uk/montwt

7. ELAN VALLEY

Dwr Cymru Welsh Water & Elan Valley Trust.
Location: SN 928 646 (visitor centre). Three miles SW of Rhayader, off B4518.
Access: Mostly open access.
Facilities: Visitor centre and toilets (open mid Mar-end Oct), nature trails all year and hide at SN 905 617.
Public transport: Post bus from Rhayader and Llandrindod Wells.
Habitat: 45,000 acres of moorland, woodland, river and reservoir.
Key birds: *Spring/summer*: Birds of prey, upland birds including Golden Plover and Dunlin. Woodland birds include Redstart and Pied Flycatcher.
Contact: Pete Jennings, Rangers Office, Elan Valley Visitor Centre, Rhayader, Powys LD6 5HP. 01597 810880.
e-mail: pete@elanvalley.org.uk
www.elanvalley.org.uk

8. GILFACH

Radnorshire Wildlife Trust.
Location: SN 952 714. Two miles NW from Rhayader/Rhaeadr-Gwy. Take minor road to St Harmon from A470 at Marteg Bridge.
Access: Centre Easter-Sept 31 (10am-5pm). Apr (every day). May/Jun (Fri-Mon). Jul/Aug (every day). Sept (Fri-Mon). Reserve open every day all year. Dogs on leads only. Disabled access and trail.
Facilities: Visitor centre - open as above. Way-marked trails. **Public transport:** None.
Habitat: Upland hill farm, river, oak woods, meadows, hill-land.
Key birds: *Spring/summer*: Pied Flycatcher, Redstart. *All year*: Dipper, Red Kite.
Contact: Tim Thompson, Gilfach, St Harmon, Rhaeadr-Gwy, Powys LD6 5LF. 01597 870 301.
e-mail: tim@ratgilfoelfisnet.co.uk http//westwales.co.uk/gilfach.htm

9. GLASLYN, PLYNLIMON

Montgomeryshire Wildlife Trust.
Location: SN 826 941. Nine miles SE of Machynlleth. Off minor road between the B4518 near Staylittle and the A489 at Machynlleth. Go down the track for about a mile.
Access: Open at all times - dogs on a lead at all times. **Facilities:** Footpath.
Public transport: None.
Habitat: Heather moorland and upland lake.
Key birds: Red Grouse, Short-eared Owl, Meadow Pipit, Sky Lark, Wheatear and Ring Ouzel, Red Kite, Merlin, Peregrine. Goldeneye - occasional. *Winter*: Greenland White-fronted Goose.
Contact: Montgomeryshire Wildlife Trust, Collot House, 20 Severn Street, Welshpool, Powys SY21 7AD. 01938 555654.
e-mail: montwt@cix.compulink.co.uk

10. LLANGORSE LAKE

Privately owned.
Location: Head NW on the A40 between Brecon

and Crickhowell, turn off at Bwlich onto the B4560. A minor road from Cathedine leads to S shore. Access to N shore is at Llangorse village.
Access: Open all year. A footpath from the parking area near Llangorse only goes along the W and S shore to Llagasty-Talyllyn. **Facilities:** None.
Public transport: Train from Cardiff to Merthyr Tydfil then bus to Brecon. Only one post bus per day to Llangorse.
Habitat: The second largest natural lake in Wales.
Key birds: *Winter*: Wildfowl, Cormorant, Snipe, Jack Snipe, occasional Bittern. *Passage*: Oystercatcher, Ringed Plover, Dunlin, Black-tailed Godwit, Whimbrel, Greenshank, Green Sandpiper, Little Gull, terns.

11. LLYN MAWR

Montgomeryshire Wildlife Trust.
Location: SO 009 971. From Newtown, head NW on A470 and then take minor 'no through' road N of Clatter. Stay close to shore.
Access: Permit required. **Facilities:** None.
Public transport: None.
Habitat: Upland lake, wetland, scrub.
Key birds: *Summer*: Breeding Great Crested Grebe, Black-headed Gull, Snipe, Curlew, Whinchat. *Winter*: Occasional Goldeneye, Goosander, Whooper Swan.
Contact: Trust HQ, 01938 555654.

12. LLANYMYNECH ROCKS

Montgomeryshire Wildlife Trust/Shropshire Wildlife Trust.
Location: SJ 267 218. To the W of the A483 between Pant and Llanymynech. Park in the small car park at the end of the cul-de-sac called Pant Underhill Lane.
Access: Open all year. Please keep to the clearly marked paths. Do not go near the edges of cliffs of stand beneath rock faces.
Facilities: Marked paths. **Public transport:** None.
Habitat: Abandoned limestone quarries, grassland, woodland.
Key birds: *Spring/summer*: Jackdaw, Peregrine.
Contact: Montgomeryshire Wildlife Trust, Collot House, 20 Severn Street, Welshpool, Powys SY21 7AD. 01738 555654.

13. PWLL PENARTH

Montgomeryshire Wildlife Trust.
Location: SO 137 926. Take B4568 from Newtown to Llanllwchaiarn, turn down by church and follow lane for a mile to sewage works gates.
Access: Open at all times. Disabled access via Severn Trent sewage works between 9am-4pm, Mon-Fri only. Dogs to be kept on lead at all times.
Facilities: Two hides. **Public transport:** None.
Habitat: Lake, Sand Martin bank, arable crops.
Key birds: *Late spring/summer*: Sand Martin, Lapwing, Sky Lark, Grey Wagtail. *Winter*: Buntings, finches. *All year*: Kingfisher, Mallard, Coot, Canada Goose, Ruddy Duck.
Contact: Mike Green, Montgomeryshire Wildlife Trust, Collot House, 20 Severn Street, Welshpool, Powys SY21 7AD. 01938 555654.
e-mail: montwt@cix.compulink.co.uk
www.wildlifetrust.org.uk/montwt

14. PWLL-Y-WRACH

Brecknock Wildlife Trust.
Location: SO 165 327. Between Hay-on-Wye and Brecon at foot of Black Mountains. Half mile SE of Talgarth, access is from minor road. In Talgarth town centre, turn off main road opposite to Bell Hotel. Carry straight on past entrance to the old hospital site now the Pryn Centre and after 250m, reserve is on right.
Access: Limited car parking. **Facilities:** Keep to public footpaths (inc. one for disabled).
Public transport: None.
Habitat: Steep valley woodland, stream and waterfall.
Key birds: Dipper, Grey Wagtail, woodland species (inc. Pied Flycatcher, Wood Warbler). Dormouse colony.
Contact: Trust HQ, 01874 625708.

15. ROUNDTON HILL

Montgomeryshire Wildlife Trust.
Location: SO 293 947. SE of Montgomery. From Churchstoke on A489, take minor road to Old Churchstoke, R at phone box, then first R.
Access: Open access. Tracks rough in places.
Facilities: Car park. Waymarked trails.
Public transport: None.
Habitat: Ancient hill grassland, woodland, streamside wet flushes, scree, rock outcrops.
Key birds: Buzzard, Raven, Wheatear, all three woodpeckers, Tawny Owl, Redstart, Linnet, Goldfinch.
Contact: Trust HQ, 01938 555654.

16. SEVERN FARM POND

Montgomeryshire Wildlife Trust.
Location: SJ 228 068. From the centre of Welshpool take the B4381 (Leighton road) over the

railway. Reserve is signposted from there. Reserve is between the railway and the factories on the Severn Farm Industrial Estate.
Access: Open all year. This is the Trust's first urban educational reserve.
Facilities: Footpath suitable for wheelchair, hide, dipping pond, picnic tables.
Public transport: None. **Habitat:** Meadow, pond.
Key birds: *Spring/summer*: Swallow, House Martin. *All year*: Reed Bunting, Mute Swan, Moorhen, Coot, Ruddy Duck.
Contact: Montgomeryshire Wildlife Trust, Collot House, 20 Severn Street, Welshpool, Powys, SY21 7AD, 01938 555654. e-mail: montwt@cix.co.uk www.wildlifetrust.org.uk/montgomeryshire

17. TALYBONT RESERVOIR

Dur Cymn Welsh Water
Location: SO 100 190. Take minor road off B4558 S of Talybont, SE of Brecon.
Access: No access to reservoir area, view from road. **Facilities:** Displays at the Glyn Collwm information centre at Aber, between the reservoir and Talybont. Bird hide.
Public transport: None.
Habitat: Reservoir, woodland.
Key birds: *Winter*: Wildfowl (inc. Goldeneye, Goosander, Whooper Swan), Redpoll, Siskin. Migrant waders.

18. TY BRITH MEADOWS

Montgomeryshire Wildlife Trust.
Location: SJ 244 178. The reserve is about two miles W of Four Crosses, adjacent to a minor road that runs W off the B4393. Reserve is accessed through the signed field gate off a metalled road.
Access: Open all year.
Facilities: Public footpath.
Habitat: Meadows, stream.
Key birds: *Spring/summer*: Lapwing. Excellent for flora. Best in early summer.
Contact: Montgomeryshire Wildlife Trust, Collot House, 20 Severn Street, Welshpool, Powys, SY21 7AD, 01938 555654. e-mail: montwt@cix.co.uk www.wildlifetrust.org.uk/montgomeryshire

19. VYRNWY (LAKE)

RSPB (North Wales Office).
Location: SJ 020 193. Located WSW of Oswestry. Nearest village is Llanfyllin on A490. Take B4393 to lake.
Access: Reserve open all year. Visitor centre open Apr-Dec (10.30am-4.30pm), Dec-Apr weekends only (10.30am-4.30pm).
Facilities: Toilets, visitor centre, hides, nature trails, coffee shop, RSPB shop, craft workshops.
Public transport: Train and bus Welshpool (25 miles away).
Habitat: Heather moorland, woodland, meadows, rocky streams and large reservoir.
Key birds: Dipper, Kingfisher, Pied Flycatcher, Wood Warbler, Redstart, Peregrine and Buzzard.
Contact: Jo Morris, Centre Manager, RSPB Lake Vyrnwy Reserve, Bryn Awel, Llanwddyn, Oswestry, Shropshire SY10 0LZ. 01691 870278.
e-mail: lake.vyrnwy@rspb.org.uk

North Wales

1. BARDSEY BIRD OBSERVATORY

Bardsey Bird Observatory.
Location: SH 11 21. Private 444 acre island. One hour boat journey from Pwllheli (18 miles SW of Bangor).
Access: Mar-Nov. No dogs. Visitor accommodation in 150-year-old farmhouse (two single, two double, two x four dorms). To stay at the Observatory contact Alicia Normand (tel 01758 760667, e-mail bob&lis@solfach.freeserve.co.uk). Day visitors by Bardsey Island Trust (tel Mike Wynn 01758 730326).
Facilities: Public toilets available for day visitors. Three hides, one on small bay, two seawatching.
Public transport: Trains from Birmingham to Pwllheli. Tel: 0345 484950. Arriva bus from Bangor to Pwllheli. Tel: 0870 6082608.
Habitat: Sea-birds cliffs viewable from boat only. Farm and scrubland, Spruce plantation, willow copses and gorse-covered hillside.
Key birds: *All Year*: Chough, Peregrine. *Spring/ summer*: Manx Shearwaters 16,000 pairs, other seabirds. Migrant warblers, chats, Redstart, thrushes. *Autumn*: Many rarities including Eye-browed Thrush, Lanceolated Warbler, Iberian

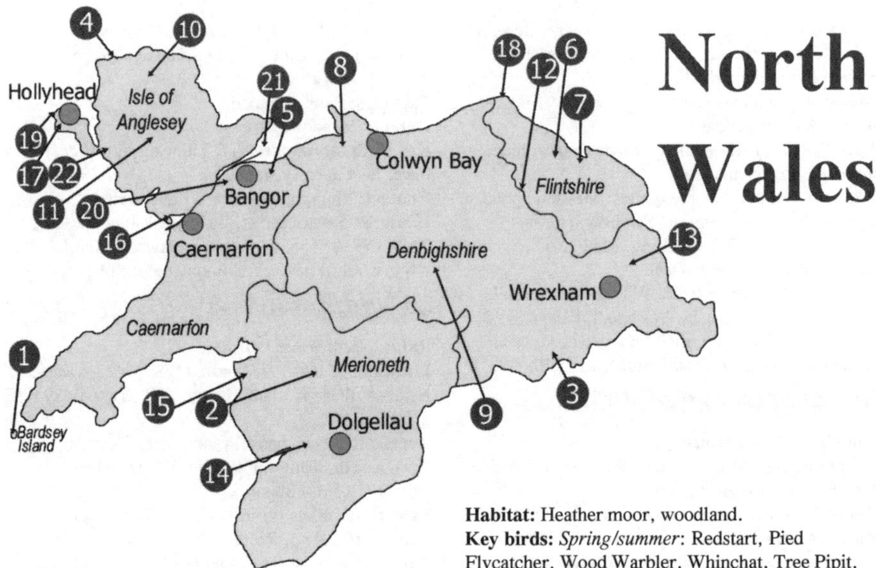

Chiffchaff, Collared Flycatcher, etc.
Contact: Steven Stansfield, Cristin, Ynys Enlli (Bardsey), off Aberaron, via Pwllheil, Gwynedd LL53 8DE. 07855 264151.
e-mail: steve@bbfo.freeserve.co.uk
www.bbfo.org.uk

2. CADAIR IDRIS

CCW (North West Area).
Location: SH 728 116. Three miles SW of Dolgellau. Take A487 SE to junction with B4405.
Access: Permit for enclosed woodland. Footpath to lake of Llyn Cau, a superb upland cwm.
Facilities: Leaflet. **Public transport:** None.
Habitat: Cliffs, heath.
Key birds: *Summer*: Breeding Raven, Wheatear, Ring Ouzel, Pied Flycatcher.
Contact: Cyngor Cefn Gwlad Cymru/CCW, Hen Ysgol, Llanfair, Harlech, Gwynedd LL46 2TA. 01766 781803.

3. CEIRIOG FOREST

Forest Enterprise.
Location: SJ 166 384. From Glyn Ceiriog take the road to Nantyr. Turn R at white cottage called Bryn Awel, through a gate marked Glyndyfrdwy into forest. Park at the picnic site.
Access: Open all year. Long walk on metalled path.
Facilities: None. **Public transport:** None.
Habitat: Heather moor, woodland.
Key birds: *Spring/summer*: Redstart, Pied Flycatcher, Wood Warbler, Whinchat, Tree Pipit, Ring Ouzel, Wheatear. *All year*: Black Grouse, Dipper, Grey wagtail, Red Grouse, Raven, Chaffinch, Redpoll, Siskin, Crossbill, all three woodpeckers, Sparrowhawk, Buzzard.
Contact: Forest Enterprise Wales, Victoria Terrace, Aberystwyth, Ceredigion, SY23 2DQ, 01970 612367.

4. CEMLYN

North Wales Wildlife Trust.
Location: SH 337 932. Ten miles from Holyhead, Anglesey, minor roads from A5025 at Tregele.
Access: Open all the time. Dogs on leads. Disabled viewing from adjacent road. During summer months walk on seaward side of ridge and follow signs. **Facilities:** None.
Public transport: None.
Habitat: Brackish lagoon, shingle, ridge.
Key birds: *Summer*: Breeding terns. *Winter*: Waders/ducks (including Little Grebe, Goldeneye and Shoveler).
Contact: Chris Wynne, North Wales Wildlife Trust, 376 High Street, Bangor, Gwynedd LL57 1YE. 01248 351541. e-mail: nwwt@cix.co.uk
www.wildlifetrust.org.uk/northwales

5. COEDYDD ABER NNR

CCW (North West Area).
Location: SH 660 710. E of Bangor.
Access: From car park at Bont Newydd, N of Aber

Falls. Permit required for places away from designated routes.
Facilities: Small visitor centre. Leaflets.
Public transport: Buses from Bangor and Conwy to Abergwyngregyn Village
Habitat: Upland valley, deciduous woodland, river and spectacular waterfall.
Key birds: *All year:* Dipper, Grey Wagtail, Buzzard, Raven, woodland birds. *Summer:* Warblers and Ring Ouzel.
Contact: Duncan Brown (Summer Warden), 01286 672500.

6. COED-Y-FELIN LNR

Wimpey Asphalt/North Wales Wildlife Trust.
Location: SJ 192 677. The reserve is situated four miles NW of Mold at Hendre, on the A541. There is a small car park at the W end with disabled access and a large car park at the E end.
Access: Open all year.
Facilities: Car parks. **Public transport:** None.
Habitat: Ancient woodland.
Key birds: *Spring/summer*: Warblers. *All year*: Usual woodland species.
Contact: North Wales Wildlife Trust, 376 High Street, Bangor, Gwynedd LL57 1YE. 01248 351541. e-mail: nwwt@cix.co.uk www.wildlifetrust.org.uk/northumberland/

7. CONNAHS QUAY

Deeside Naturalists' Society.
Location: SJ 275 715. NW of Chester. Take B5129 from Queensferry towards Flint, two miles.
Access: Advance permit required.
Facilities: Field studies centre, four hides.
Public transport: None.
Habitat: Saltmarsh, mudflats, grassland scrub, open water, wetland meadow.
Key birds: High water roosts of waders, inc. Black-tailed Godwit, Oystercatcher, Redshank, Spotted Redshank. Passage waders. *Winter*: Wildfowl (inc. Teal, Pintail, Goldeneye), Merlin, Peregrine.
Contact: R A Roberts, 38 Kelsterton Road, Connahs Quay, Flints CH5 4BJ.

8. CONWY

RSPB (North Wales Office).
Location: SH 799 771. On E bank of Conwy Estuary. Access from A55 at exit signed to Conwy and Deganwy.
Access: Open daily (10am-5pm) or dusk if earlier. Closed for Christmas Day.
Facilities: Visitor centre, toilets including disabled. Two hides, accessible to wheelchairs. Trails firm and level, though a little rough in places. Two further hides accessible to pedestrians.
Public transport: Train service to Llandudno Junction. Bus service to Tesco supermarket, Llandudno Junction. Tel: 08706 082 608.
Habitat: Open water, islands, reedbeds, grassland, estuary.
Key birds: *Spring/summer*: Breeding Reed and Sedge Warblers, Lapwing, Redshank, Sky Lark, Reed Bunting and rarities. *Autumn*: Passage waders and rarities. *Winter*: Kingfisher, Goldeneye, Red-breasted Merganser, wildfowl.
Contact: Ian Higginson, Conwy RSPB Nature Reserve, Llandudno Junction, Conwy, North Wales LL33 9XZ. 01492 584091.

9. GORS MAEN LLWYD

North Wales Wildlife Trust.
Location: SH 975 580. Follow A5 to Cerrigydrudion (seven miles S of site), then take B4501 and go past the Llyn Brennig Visitor Centre. Approx two miles beyond centre, turn right (still on B4501). First car park on right approx 300 yards after the cattle grid.
Access: Open all the time. Dogs on leads. Keep to the paths. Rare breeding birds on the heather so keep to paths.
Facilities: In second car park by lake shore there are toilets and short walk to bird hide. Paths are waymarked, but can be very wet and muddy in poor weather. **Public transport:** None.
Habitat: Heathland. Heather and grass overlooking large lake.
Key birds: *Summer*: Red and Black Grouse, Hen Harrier, Merlin, Sky Lark, Curlew. *Winter*: Wildfowl on lake.
Contact: Neil Griffiths, Reserves Officer, NWWT, 376 High Street, Bangor, Gwynedd LL57 1YE. 01248 351541. e-mail: nwwt@cix.co.uk www.wildlifetrust.org.uk/northwales

10. LLYN ALAW

Welsh Water/United Utilities.
Location: SH 390 865. Large lake five miles from Amlwch in northern part of Anglesey. Signposted from A55/A5/B5112/B5111/B5109.
Access: Open all year. No dogs to hides or sanctuary area but dogs allowed (maximum two per adult) other areas.
Facilities: Toilets (including disabled), two hides, two nature trails, information centre, car parks,

network of mapped walks, picnic sites, information boards.
Public transport: Not to within a mile.
Habitat: Large area of standing water, shallow reedy bays, hedges, scrub, woodland, marsh, grassland.
Key birds: *Summer*: Lesser Whitethroat, Sedge and Grasshopper Warblers, Little and Great Crested Grebes, Tawny Owl, Barn Owl, Buzzard. *Winter*: Whooper Swan, Goldeneye, Hen Harrier, Short-eared Owl, Redwing, Fieldfare, Peregrine, Raven. *All year*: Bullfinch, Siskin, Redpoll, Goldfinch, Stonechat. *Passage waders*: Spotted Redshank, Curlew and Green Sandpiper, Ruff.
Contact: Jim Clark, Llyn Alaw, Llantrisant, Holyhead LL65 4TW. 01407 730762.
e-mail: llynalaw@amserve.net

11. LLYN CEFNI

Welsh Water/United Utilities.
Location: SH 440 775. A reservoir located two miles NW of Llangefni, in central Anglesey. Follow B5111 or B5109 from the village.
Access: Open at all times. Dogs allowed except in sanctuary area. **Facilities:** Toilets (near waterworks), picnic site, hide, information boards.
Public transport: Bus 32, 4 (45 Sat only, 52 Tue and Thu only). Tel 0870 6082608 for information.
Habitat: Large area of open water, reedy bays, coniferous woodland, carr, scrub.
Key birds: *Summer*: Sedge, Whitethroat and Grasshopper Warblers, Buzzard, Tawny Owl, Little Grebe, Gadwall, Shoveler. *Winter*: Waterfowl (Whooper Swan, Goldeneye), Crossbill, Redpoll, Siskin, Redwing. *All year*: Stonechat, Treecreeper, Song Thrush.
Contact: Jim Clark, Llyn Alaw, Llantrisant, Holyhead LL65 4TW. 01407 730762.
e-mail: llynalaw@amserve.net

12. LOGGERHEADS COUNTRY PARK

Location: Off A494. W of Mold. Take minor road after Cadole. **Access:** Open all year.
Facilities: Large car park, visitor centre, café, leaflet. **Public transport:** None.
Habitat: Limestone woodland, river.
Key birds: *Spring/summer*: Pied and Spotted Flycatchers, Redstart, Garden Warbler, Blackcap, Wood Warbler, Chiffchaff. *All year*: All three woodpeckers, Tawny Owl, Sparrowhawk, Nuthatch, Treecreeper, Goldcrest, Redpoll, Hawfinch. Occasional Crossbill.
Contact: Loggerheads Country Park, Loggerheads, Mold, Denbighshire, CH5 5LH,

13. MARFORD LNR

North Wales Wildlife Trust.
Location: SJ 357 560. From Wrexham follow signs for the A483 to Chester. Just past a roundabout turn R onto the B5445 to Gresford and Marford. At Marford turn L into Springfield Lane, just past the Trevor Arms Hotel. The reserve entrance is on the L just before the railway bridge. Park either side of the bridge.
Access: Open all year.
Facilities: Path. **Public transport:** None.
Habitat: Disused sand and gravel pit, cliff face, grassland, scrub, woodland, pool.
Key birds: *Spring/summer*: Spotted Flycatcher, Wood Warbler, good range of migrant birds. *All year*: Woodpeckers inc. Lesser Spotted, Linnet, Yellowhammer, woodland birds.
Contact: Adrian Lloyd, NWWT, Loggerheads Country Park, Nr Mold, Denbighshire CH7 5LH. 01248 351541. e-mail: nwwt@cix.co.uk
www.wildlifetrust.org.uk/northwales

14. MAWDDACH VALLEY

RSPB (North Wales Office).
Location: SH 696 185 (information centre). Two miles W of Dolgellau on A493. Next to toll bridge at Penmaenpool.
Access: Reserve open at all times. Information centre open daily during Easter week and from Whitsun to first weekend of Sept (11am-5pm). Between Easter week and Whitsun, weekends only (noon-4pm). **Facilities:** Toilets and car park at information centre.
Public transport: Buses run along A493. Morfa Mawddach railway halt four miles from information centre.
Habitat: Oak woodlands of Coed Garth Gell and willow/alder scrub at Arthog Bog SSSI.
Key birds: *Spring/summer*: Pied Flycatcher, Redstart and Tree Pipit. *Winter*: Raven, roving flocks of Siskin, Redpoll with Goosander and Goldeneye on the estuary.
Contact: The Warden, Mawddach Valley Nature Reserves, Abergwynant Lodge, Penmaenpool, Dolgellau, Gwynedd LL40 1YF. 01341 422071.
e-mail: mawddach@rspb.org.uk www.rspb.org.uk

15. MORFA HARLECH NNR

Countryside Council for Wales.
Location: SH 574 317. On the A496 Harlech road.
Access: Open all year. **Facilities:** Car park.
Public transport: None.
Habitat: Shingle, coast, marsh, dunes.

Key birds: *Spring/summer*: Whitethroat, Spotted Flycatcher, Grasshopper Warbler, migrants. *Passage*: waders, Manx Shearwater, ducks. *Winter*: Divers, Whooper Swan, Wigeon, Teal, Pintail, Scaup, Common Scoter, Hen Harrier, Merlin, Peregrine, Short-eared Owl, Little Egret, Water Pipit, Snow Bunting, Twite. *All year/breeding*: Redshank, Lapwing, Ringed Plover, Snipe, Curlew, Shelduck, Oystercatcher, Stonechat, Whinchat, Wheatear, Linnet, Reed Bunting, Sedge Warbler. Also - Red-breasted Merganser, Kestrel, gulls.
Contact: Countryside Council for Wales North West Wales, Maes y Ffynnon, Ffordd, Bangor, Gwynedd, LL57 2DN, 0845 1306229.
e-mail: enquiries@ccw.gov.uk www.ccw.gov.uk

16. NEWBOROUGH WARREN

CCW (North West Area).
Location: SH 406 670/430 630. In Se corner of Anglesey. From Menai Bridge head Sw on A4080 to Niwbwrch or Malltraeth.
Access: Permit required for places away from designated routes. **Facilities:** None.
Public transport: None.
Habitat: Sandhills, estuaries, saltmarshes, dune grasslands, rocky headlands.
Key birds: Wildfowl and waders at Malltraeth Pool (visible from road), Braint and Cefni estuaries (licensed winter shoot on marked areas of Cefni estuary administered by CCW); waterfowl at Llyn Rhosddu (public hide).
Contact: W Sandison, CCW North West Area, Tel/fax 01248 716422; mobile 0468 918572.

17. PEHNROS COASTAL PARK

Location: SH 275 805. Signposted from A55, J2. Take A5 to Holyhead and follow signs to Park.
Access: Five mile walk of good, easy-to-follow paths with some inclines but nothing steep. Wheelchair access with good views from car park.
Facilities: Café, information board and toilets.
Public transport: Bus: contact Arriva 0870 608 2608. Train: Holyhead within walking distance from Morawelon.
Habitat: Woodland, farmland, rocky coast, beaches, mudflats.
Key birds: *Spring*: Winter waders, duck and geese. Wimbrel, Whitethroat and Lesser Whitethroat, Sedge Warbler, Shelduck, Oystercatcher. Treecreeper, Goldcrest, Redpoll, Sparrowhawk and Buzzard.

18. POINT OF AIR

RSPB (North Wales Office).
Location: SJ 140 840. At mouth of the Dee Estuary. Three miles E of Prestatyn. Access from A548 coast road to Talacre village. Park at end of Station Road. **Access:** Open at all times.
Facilities: Car park, public hide overlooking saltmarsh and mudflats, accessible to wheelchairs. No visitor centre. Toilets in Talacre village. Group bookings, guided walks and events.
Public transport: Rail – Prestatyn.
Habitat: Intertidal mud/sand, saltmarsh, shingle.
Key birds: *Spring/summer*: Breeding Sky Lark, Meadow Pipit, Reed Bunting. *Late summer*: Pre-migratory roost of Sandwich and Common Terns. *Autumn*: Passage waders. *Winter*: Roosting waterfowl (eg Shelduck, Pintail), Oystercatcher, Curlew, Redshank, Merlin, Peregrine, Short-eared Owl. Rarities have occurred.
Contact: John Harrison, Burton Point Farm, Station Road, Burton, Nr Neston, Cheshire CH64 5SB. 0151 3367681.
e-mail: john.harrison@rspb.org.uk

19. SOUTH STACK CLIFFS

RSPB (North Wales Office).
Location: SH 205 823. W of Holyhead, Anglesey. Take A5 to Holyhead and follow bron tourist signs to South Stack **Access:** No restrictions.
Facilities: Car parks. Information centre (Ellin's Tower) with windows overlooking main auk colony open daily (11am-5pm Easter-Sep), with live CCTV of the seabirds. Public footpaths.
Public transport: Mainline station Holyhead. Infrequent bus service, Holyhead-South Stack. Tel. 0870 608 2608.
Habitat: Sea cliffs, maritime heath.
Key birds: Peregrine, Chough, Fulmar, Puffin, Guillemot, Razorbill, Kittiwake, Shag, migrant warblers. Seabirds on passage.
Contact: Alastair Moralee, Plas Nico, South Stack, Holyhead, Anglesey LL65 1YH. 01407 764973.

20. SPINNIES

North Wales Wildlife Trust.
Location: SH 613 721. Three miles from Bangor, Gwynedd. Use minor roads from A5122 or A55.
Access: Open all the time. Dogs on leads. Main path suitable for wheelchair users.
Facilities: Two hides, one suitable for wheelchair users. **Public transport:** None.
Habitat: Woodland, tidal pool.

Key birds: Waders and passage species, woodland birds, Kingfisher, Little Egret.
Contact: Chris Wynne, North Wales Wildlife Trust, 376 High Street, Bangor, Gwynedd LL57 1YE. 01248 351541. e-mail: nwwt@cix.co.uk www.wildlifetrust.org.uk/northwales

21. TRAETH LAFAN

Gwynedd Council.
Location: NE of Bangor, stretching to Penmaenmawr. 1) Minor road from old A55 near Tal-y-Bont (SH 610 710) to Aber Ogwen car park by coast (SH 614 723). 2) Also access from minor road from Aber village to Morfa Aber LNR (SH 646 731) 3) track to Morfa Madryn LNR (SH 667 743), and 4) Llanfairfechan promenade (SH 679 754). **Access:** Open access from 1,2, 3 and 4.
Facilities: Public paths. 2) Car park and hide. 3) Hides. 4) Toilets and cafés.
Public transport: Call council for advice.
Habitat: Intertidal sands and mudflats, wetlands, streams. SPA and SSSI.
Key birds: Third most important area in Wales for wintering waders; of national importance for moulting Great Crested Grebe and Red-breasted Merganser; internationally important for Oystercatcher and Curlew; passage waders; winter concentrations of Goldeneye and Greenshank, and of regional significance for wintering populations of Black-throated, Red-throated & Great Northern Divers and Black-necked & Slavonian Grebes.
Contact: Planning and Economic Development Dept, Gwynedd Council, Council Offices, Caernarfon LL55 1SH. 01286 679381; fax 01286 673324; e-mail ruralservices@gwynedd.gov.uk.

22. VALLEY LAKES

RSPB (North Wales Office).
Location: Two miles S of Caergeilliog.
Access: Open all year.
Facilities: Nature trail.
Public transport: Bus: Meas Awyr/RAF Valley daily from Bangor and Holyhead. Train: Valley (four miles)/Rhosneigr (seven miles).
Habitat: Reed-fringed lakes, small rocky outcrops.
Key birds: *Summer*: Cetti's Warbler. *All year*: ducks, waterfowl.
Contact: RSPB (Welsh Region), Maes Y Ffynnon, Penrhosgarnedd, Bangor, Gwynedd, 01248 363800.

South Wales

1. ABERTHAW SALTMARSH

The Wildlife Trust of South and West Wales.
Location: ST 037 661. E of Aberthaw Power Station, W of Barry.
Access: Open access. Park in East Aberthaw village.
Facilities: None.
Public transport: Call Trust for advice.
Habitat: Lias limestone cliffs, saltmarsh, pebble beach, saline lagoon, coastal scrub.
Key birds: *All year:* Stonechat, Black Redstart is regular. *Spring:* Migrants. *Autumn*: Migrant waders and passerines. *Winter*: Peregrine in winter. Good seawatching.
Contact: Trust HQ, 01656 724100.
e-mail: wtsww@cix.co.uk

2. COSMESTON LAKES

Vale of Glamorgan Council.
Location: ST 179 692. From J33 on M4, head S on A4243 and A4231 towards Barry. Head E on B4267 through Sully. The park is on the L, west of Cosmeston, signposted from the road.
Access: Open all year. Most of the footpath system suitable for wheelchairs.
Facilities: Visitor Centre open daily (not 25 Dec), summer (10am-6pm), winter (10am-4pm). Café, shop and toilets.
Public transport: Bus: regular from Penarth to Barry stops outside the main entrance. Train: main line train to Cardiff, then to Penarth (1.5 miles from the lakes). Public transport information, tel: 08706 082 608.
Habitat: Former limestone quarry workings, ponds, paddock.
Key birds: *Spring/summer*: Buzzard, Tawny Owl, Sedge and Reed Warblers, Lesser Whitethroat, Garden Warbler, Marsh Tit. *Winter*: Little Grebe, Wigeon, Gadwall, Pochard, Water Rail, Kingfisher.
Contact: Cosmeston Lakes Country Park, Sully, Penarth, Glamorgan, 02920 701678.
e-mail: cosmestonlakes@valeofglamorgan.gov.uk

3. CROES ROBERT RESERVE

Gwent Wildlife Trust.
Location: SO 475 060. Leave Monmouth on the B4293 towards Trellech. Turn R past Trellech School to Cwmcarvan. After 1.25 miles turn R and the reserve and car park will be on the R.
Access: Open all year.
Facilities: None. **Public transport:** None.
Habitat: Broadleaved woodland, springs, wet flushes.
Key birds: *Spring/summer*: Nightingale, Grasshopper Warbler, warblers, Woodcock. *All year*: Great Spotted Woodpecker, Bullfinch, Long-tailed Tit.
Contact: Gwent Wildlife Trust, 16 White Swan Court, Church Street, Monmouth, Gwent, NP25 3NY, 01600 715501.
e-mail: gwentwildlife@cix.co.uk
www.wildlifetrust.org.uk/gwent

4. CWM CLYDACH

RSPB (South Wales Office).
Location: SN 584 026. Three miles N of J45 on M4, through the village of Clydach on B4291.
Access: Open at all times along public footpaths and waymarked trails.
Facilities: Nature trails, car park, information boards.
Public transport: Buses from Swansea stop at reserve entrance. Nearest railway station is eight miles away in Swansea.
Habitat: Oak woodland on steep slopes lining the banks of the fast-flowing Lower Clydach River.
Key birds: *Spring/summer*: Nesting Buzzard, Sparrowhawk and Raven. Nestboxes are used by Pied Flycatcher, Redstart and tits while Wood Warbler, all three species of woodpecker, Nuthatch, Treecreeper and Tawny Owl also nest. Dipper and Grey Wagtail frequent the river.
Contact: Martin Humphreys, 2 Tyn y Berllan, Craig Cefn Par, Clydach, Swansea SA6 5TL. 01792 842927.

5. CWM COL-HUW

The Wildlife Trust of South and West Wales.
Location: SS 957 674. Site includes Iron Age fort, overlooking Bristol Channel. From Bridgeend take B4265 S to Llanwit Major. Follow beach road from village.
Access: Park in seafront car park. Climb steps. Open all year.
Facilities: All year toilets and café. Information boards. **Public transport:** None.
Habitat: Unimproved grassland, woodland, scrub and Jurassic blue lias cliff.
Key birds: Cliff-nesting House Martin colony, breeding Fulmar, Grasshopper Warbler. Large autumn passerine passage. Peregrine. Seawatching vantage point. Occasional Chough.
Contact: Trust HQ, 01656 724100.
e-mail: wtsww@cix.co.uk

6. KENFIG NNR

Bridgend County Borough Council.
Location: SS 802 811. Seven miles W of Bridgend. From J37 on M4, drive towards Porthcawl, then North Cornelly, then follow signs.
Access: Open at all times.
Facilities: Toilets, hides, free car parking and nature trail for visually impaired. Visitor centre open weekends and holidays (10am-4.30pm), weekdays (2pm-4.30pm).
Public transport: None.
Habitat: Sand dunes, dune slacks, Kenfig Pool, Sker Beach.
Key birds: *Summer*: Warblers including Cetti's, Grasshopper, Sedge, Reed, Willow and Whitethroat. One of the UK's best sites for orchids. *Winter*: Wildfowl, Water Rail, Bittern, grebes.
Contact: David Carrington, Ton Kenfig, Bridgend, CF33 4PT01656 743386.
e-mail: carridg@bridgend.gov.uk

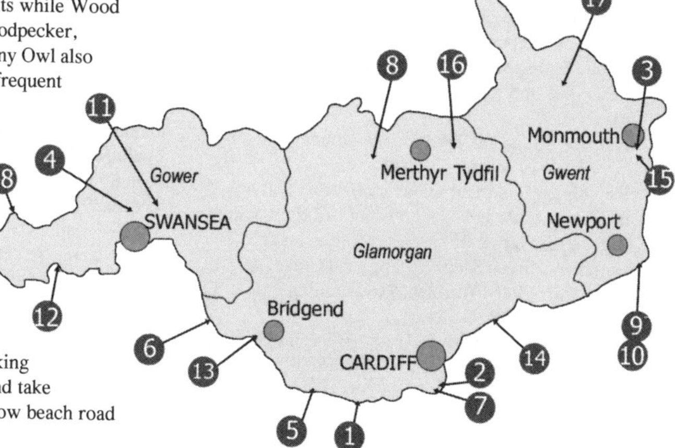

7. LAVERNOCK POINT

The Wildlife Trust of South and West Wales.
Location: ST 182 680. Public footpaths S of B4267 between Barry & Penarth.
Access: No restrictions. **Facilities:** None.
Public transport: Call Trust for advice.
Habitat: Cliff top, unimproved grassland, scrub.
Key birds: Seawatching in late summer; Glamorgan's best migration hotspot in autumn.
Contact: Trust HQ, 01656 724100.
e-mail: wtsww@cix.co.uk

8. LLYN FACH

The Wildlife Trust of South and West Wales.
Location: SN 905 038. From Merthyr Tydfil take A465 W to Hirwaun, then head S on A4061 to car park 1.8 miles away.
Access: Open dawn to dusk. **Facilities:** None.
Public transport: None.
Habitat: Lake, bog, cliff and scree, surrounded by plantations.
Key birds: Nesting Raven, Ring Ouzel also Buzzard, Sparrowhawk. Chance of Peregrine and Goshawk.
Contact: Trust HQ, 01656 724100.
e-mail: wtsww@cix.co.uk

9. MAGOR MARSH

Gwent Wildlife Trust.
Location: ST 427 867. S of Magor. Leave M4 at exit 23, turning R onto B4245. S of Magor village, look for gate on Whitewall Common on E side of reserve.
Access: Open all year. Keep to path. Parties give advance notice.
Facilities: Hide, information centre, car park, footpaths and boardwalks.
Public transport: Bus service to Magor village. Reserve is approx 10 mins walk along Redwick road.
Habitat: Sedge fen, reedswamp, willow carr, damp hay meadows and open water.
Key birds: Important for overwintering and migratory birds and as a breeding site for marsh and wetland birds. 85 species recorded including Garganey, Green Sandpiper, Spotted Crake. *All year:* Snipe, Reed Warbler, Reed Bunting, Lapwing.
Contact: Gwent Wildlife Trust, 16 Swan Court, Church Street, Monmouth NP25 3NY. 01600 715501. e-mail: gwentwildlife@cix.co.uk
www.wildlifetrust.org.uk/gwent

10. MAGOR PILL TO COLDHARBOUR PILL

Gwent Wildlife Trust.
Location: ST 437 847. Overlooks River Severn, E of Newport. **Access:** Access from Magor Pill Farm track down to sea wall.
Facilities: None.
Public transport: None.
Habitat: Foreshore, intertidal mudflats.
Key birds: Passage and winter waders.
Contact: Derek Upton, 14 Westfield, Caldicot, Newport, Gwent NP6 4HE. 01291 420137.

11. MELINCWRT WATERFALLS

The Wildlife Trust of South and West Wales.
Location: SN 825 017. The reserve is signposted from the A465(T) road, five miles NE of Neath. The car park is on the W side of the B4434 S of Resolven. The reserve entrance is on the opposite side of the road via a public footpath.
Access: Open all year.
Facilities: Car park, path.
Public transport: None.
Habitat: Narrow gorge with oak woodland, 80 foot high waterfall.
Key birds: *Spring/summer*: Pied Flycatcher, Redstart, warblers. *All year*: Dipper, Grey Wagtail, usual woodland birds.
Contact: The Wildlife Trust for South and West Wales, Nature Centre, Fountain Road, Tondu, Mid Glamorgan, CF32 0EH, 01656 724100.
e-mail: information@wtsww.cix.co.uk
www.wildlifetrust.org.uk/wtsww

12. OXWICH

CCW (Swansea Office).
Location: SS 872 773. 12 miles from Swansea, off A4118.
Access: NNR open at all times. No permit required for access to foreshore. Dunes, woodlands and facilities.
Facilities: Private car park, summer only. Toilets summer only. Marsh boardwalk and marsh lookout. No visitor centre, no facilities for disabled visitors.
Public transport: Bus service Swansea/Oxwich. First Cymru, tel 01792 580580.
Habitat: Freshwater marsh, saltmarsh, foreshore, dunes, woodlands.
Key birds: *Summer*: Breeding Reed, Sedge and Cetti's Warblers, Treecreeper, Nuthatch, woodpeckers. *Winter*: Wildfowl.
Contact: Countryside Council for Wales, RVB

House, Llys Felin Newydd, Phoenix Way, Swansea SA7 9FG. 01792 763500.

13. PARC SLIP NATURE PARK

The Wildlife Trust of South and West Wales.
Location: SS 880 840. Tondu, half mile W of Aberkenfig. From Bridgend take A4063 N, turning L onto B4281 after passing M4. Reserve is signposted from this road.
Access: Open dawn to dusk.
Facilities: Three hides, nature trail, interpretation centre.
Public transport: None.
Habitat: Restored opencast mining site, wader scrape, lagoons.
Key birds: *Summer*: Breeding Tufted Duck, Lapwing, Sky Lark. Migrant waders (inc. Little Ringed Plover, Green Sandpiper), Little Gull. Kingfisher, Green Woodpecker.
Contact: Trust HQ, 01656 724100.
e-mail: wtsww@cix.co.uk

14. PETERSTONE WENTLOOGE

Gwent Wildlife Trust.
Location: ST 269 800. Reserve over looks River Severn, between Newport and Cardiff.
Access: Public footpaths to sea wall, use B4239.
Facilities: None.
Public transport: None.
Habitat: Foreshore, inter-tidal mudflats, grazing.
Key birds: Passage waders and winter wildfowl.
Contact: Trust HQ, 01600 715501.

15. PRIORY WOOD SSSI

Gwent Wildlife Trust.
Location: SO 352 058. N of the Usk near Chain Bridge.
Access: Open all year. Very limited parking.
Facilities: None. **Public transport:** None.
Habitat: Varied broadleaved woodland with cherry trees.
Key birds: *Spring/summer*: Pied Flycatcher, warblers. *All year*: Great Spotted Woodpecker, usual woodland species. *Winter*: Hawfinch.
Contact: Gwent Wildlife Trust, 16 White Swan Court, Church Street, Monmouth, Gwent, NP25 3NY, 01600 715501.
e-mail: gwentwildlife@cix.co.uk
www.wildlifetrust.org.uk/gwent

16. SILENT VALLEY RESERVE

Gwent Wildlife Trust.
Location: SO 187 062. On the A4046 2.5 miles S of Ebbw Vale is a one-way system in Cwm. Come out of this on the N side and take the 2nd R by a corner shop. Park in the car park about 0.3 miles by Cwm Cemetery. Walk N across a flat grass playing area and along a path to the reserve entrance.
Access: Open all year.
Facilities: None.
Public transport: None.
Habitat: One of the most westerly and highest natural beech woods in Britain.
Key birds: *Spring/summer*: Pied Flycatcher, Redstart. *Winter*: Siskin, Redpoll, tits. *All year*: Usual woodland species, Great Spotted Woodpecker.
Contact: Gwent Wildlife Trust HQ. 101600 715501. www.wildlifetrust.org.uk/gwente

17. STRAWBERRY COTTAGE WOOD

Gwent Wildlife Trust.
Location: SO 315 214. N of Abergavenny. Leave A465 at Llanvihangel Crucorney on minor road to Llanthony, about 1.25 miles.
Access: Open at all times. Keep to waymarked trail.
Facilities: None.
Public transport: None.
Habitat: Mixed woodland on valley side.
Key birds: Buzzard, Redstart, Pied Flycatcher, Wood Warbler.
Contact: Jerry Lewis, Y Bwthyn Gwyn, Coldbrook, Abergavenny, Monmouthshire NP7 9TD. 01873 855091;(W)01633 644856.

18. WHITEFORD NNR

Location: SS 450 960. Pass through Llanmadoc village, downhill, turn R at church to Cwm Ivy. Lane leads from here downhill to Whiteford Plantation. Follow footpath through Plantation, across Burrows to hide on Berges Island.
Access: Free access. Best to get to hide before a.m. high water for waders and wildfowl.
Facilities: None. Area not recommended for those with restricted mobility but excellent view of Whiteford Marsh from hillside road above Britannia Inn at Cheriton.
Public transport: None.
Habitat: Conifer plantation, marsh, mudflats.
Key birds: *Autumn/winter*: Divers, Red-necked, Slavonian and Black-necked Grebes, Brent Goose, Wigeon, Teal, Pintail and Eider. Common and Jack Snipe occur, with Whimbrel and Spotted Redshank on passage. Turnstone and Purple Sandpiper at Whiteford Point.

West Wales

1. CASTLE WOODS

The Wildlife Trust of South and West Wales.
Location: SN 615 217. About 60 acres of wodland overlooking River Tywi, W of Llandeilo town centre. **Access:** Open all year by footpath from Tywi Bridge, Llandeilo (SN 627 221).
Facilities: Call for advice.
Public transport: None.
Habitat: Old mixed deciduous woodlands.
Key birds: All three woodpeckers, Buzzard, Raven, Sparrowhawk. *Summer:* Pied and Spotted Flycatchers, Redstart, Wood Warbler. *Winter:* On water meadows below, look for Teal, Wigeon, Goosander, Shoveler, Tufted Duck and Pochard.
Contact: Steve Lucas, Area Officer, 35 Maesquarre Road, Betws, Ammanford, Carmarthenshire SA18 2LF. 01269 594293.
e-mail: information@wtsww.cix.co.uk
www.wildlifetrust.org.uk/wtsww

2. CORS CARON

CCW (West Wales Area).
Location: SN 697 632 (car park). Reached from B4343 N of Tregaron.
Access: Open access to S of car park along the railway to boardwalk, out to SE bog. Access to rest of the reserve by permit. Dogs on lead.
Facilities: None at present.
Public transport: None.
Habitat: Raised bog, river, fen, wet grassland, willow woodland, reedbed.
Key birds: *Summer*: Lapwing, Redshank, Curlew, Red Kite, Grasshopper Warbler, Whinchat. *Winter:* Teal, Wigeon, Whooper Swan, Hen Harrier, Red Kite.
Contact: Paul Culyer, CCW, Neuaddlas, Tregaron, Ceredigion. 01974 298480.
www.ccw.gov.uk
e-mail:
p.culyer@ccw.gov.uk

3. DINAS & GWENFFRWD

RSPB (South Wales Office).
Location: SN 788 472. Dinas car park off B road to Llyn Brianne Reservoir.
Access: Public nature trail at Dinas open at all times. **Facilities:** None
Public transport: Nearest station at Llandovery.
Habitat: Hillside oakwoods, streams, bracken slopes and moorland.
Key birds: Buzzard, Pied Flycatcher, Redstart, Wood Warbler, Tree Pipit, Red Kite and Peregrine in area. Dipper, Goosander, Raven.
Contact: M Humphreys, 2 Tyn y Berllan, Craig Cefn Par, Craig Cefn Parc, Clydach, SwanseaSA6 5TL. 01792 842927. www.rspb.org.uk

4. DYFI

CCW (West Wales Area).
Location: SN 610 942. Large estuary area W of Machyalleth. Public footpaths off A493 E of Aberdyfi, and off B4353 (S of river); minor road

from B4353 at Ynyslas to dunes and parking area. **Access:** Ynyslas dunes and the estuary have unrestricted access. No access to Cors Fochno (raised bog) for casual birdwatching; permit required for study and research purposes. Good views over the bog and Aberleri marshes from W bank of Afon Leri.
Facilities: Public hide overlooking marshes beside footpath at SN 611 911. **Public transport:** None.
Habitat: Sandflats, mudflats, saltmarsh, creeks, dunes, raised bog, grazing marsh.
Key birds: *Winter:* Greenland White-fronted Goose, wildfowl, waders and raptors. *Summer*: Breeding wildfowl and waders (inc. Teal, Shoveler, Merganser, Lapwing, Curlew, Redshank).
Contact: Mike Bailey, CCW Warden, Plas Gogerddan, Aberystwyth, Ceredigion SY23 3EE. 01970 821100.

5. THE NATIONAL WETLANDS CENTRE, LLANELLI

The Wildfowl & Wetlands Trust.
Location: SS 533 984. Leave M4 at junction 47. Signposted from A484, E of Llanelli.
Access: Open daily (9.30am-5.30am summer, earlier in winter) except Chirstmas Eve and Christmas Day.
Facilities: Visitor centre, restaurant, hides, education facilities, disabled access. Overlooks Burry Inlet. **Public transport:** None.
Habitat: Inter-tidal mudflats, reedbeds, pools, marsh, waterfowl collection.
Key birds: Large flocks of Curlew, Oystercatcher, Redshank on saltmarsh. *Winter*: Pintail, Wigeon, Teal. Also Little Egret, Short-eared Owl, Peregrine.
Contact: Nigel Williams, Centre Manager, The National Wetlands Centre, Penclacwydd, Llwynhendy, Llanelli SA14 9SH. 01554 741087; (Fax)01554 744101. www.wwt.org.uk
e-mail: info.llanelli@wwt.org.uk

6. PENGELLI FOREST

The Wildlife Trust of South and West Wales.
Location: SN 123 396. Between Fishguard and Cardigan. Take minor road off A487 from Felindre Farchog/Eglwyswrw.
Access: Open all year. No permit, but keep to trails. **Facilities:** Trails.
Public transport: None.
Habitat: 40 acre sessile oak wood, 120 acre mixed oak/ash wood (inc. scrub, rides).
Key birds: *Summer:* Pied Flycatcher, Redstart, Wood Warbler. *All year:* Buzzard, Raven, woodpeckers.
Contact: Welsh Wildlife Centre, Cilgerran, Cardigan SA43 2TB. 01239 621212.

7. RAMSEY ISLAND

RSPB (South Wales Office).
Location: SM 706237. One mile offshore St Justinians, slipway, two miles W of St Davids.
Access: Open every day, Apr 1-Oct 31.
Facilities: Toilets, small RSPB shop, tuck shop, hot drinks and snacks, self-guiding trail.
Public transport: Trains to Haverfordwest Station. Hourly buses to St Davids, taxi to St Justinians.
Habitat: Acid grassland, maritime heath, seacliffs.
Key birds: *Spring/summer*: Cliff-nesting auks (Guillemot, Razorbill). Kittiwake, Lesser, Great Black-backed, Herring Gulls, Shag, Peregrine, Raven, Chough, Lapwing, Wheatear, Stonechat.
Contact: RSPB, Southerland House, Castle Bridge, Cowbridge Rd East, Cardiff CF11 9AB. 07836 535733. www.rspb.org.uk

8. SKOKHOLM ISLAND

The Wildlife Trust of South and West Wales.
Location: SM 738 037. Island lying S of Skomer.
Access: Day visits, Mon only Jun-Aug from Martinshaven. Weekly accomm. Apr-Sep, tel 01239 621212 for details and booking.
Facilities: Call for details.
Public transport: None.
Habitat: Cliffs, bays and inlets.
Key birds: *Summer*: Large colonies of Razorbill, Puffin, Guillemot, Manx Shearwater, Storm Petrel, Lesser Black-backed Gull. Migrants inc. rare species.
Contact: Trust HQ, 01239 621212.

9. SKOMER ISLAND

The Wildlife Trust of South and West Wales.
Location: SM 725 095. Fifteen miles from Haverfordwest. Take B4327 turn-off for Marloes, embarkation point at Martin's Haven, two miles past village.
Access: Apr 1-Oct 31. Boats sail at 10am, 11am and noon every day except Mon (Bank Holidays excluded). Closed four days beginning of Jun for seabird counts. Not suitable for infirm (steep landing steps and rough ground).
Facilities: Information centre, toilets, two hides, wardens, booklets, guides, nature trails.
Public transport: None.

Habitat: Maritime cliff, bracken, bluebells and red campion, heathland, freshwater ponds.
Key birds: Largest colony of Manx Shearwater in the world (overnight). Puffin, Guillemot, Razorbill (Apr-end Jul). Kittiwake (until end Aug), Fulmar (absent Oct), Short-eared Owl (during day Jun and Jul), Chough, Peregrine, Buzzard (all year), migrants.
Contact: Juan Brown, Skomer Island, Marloes, Pembs SA62 2BJ. 07971 114302.
e-mail: skomer@wtww.co.uk

10. WELSH WILDLIFE CENTRE

The Wildlife Trust of South and West Wales.
Location: SN 188 451. Two miles SE of Cardigan. River Teifi is N boundary. Sign posted from Cardigan to Fishguard Road.
Access: Open 10am-5pm all year. Free parking for WTWW members, £5 non-members. Dogs welcome - on a lead. Disabled access to visitor centre, paths, four hides.
Facilities: Visitor centre, restaurant, network of paths and seven hides.
Public transport: Train station, Haverfordwest (23 miles). Bus station in Cardigan. Access on foot from Cardigan centre, ten mins.
Habitat: Wetlands, marsh, swamp, reedbed, open water, creek (tidal), river, saltmarsh, woodland.
Key birds: Cetti's Warbler, Kingfisher, Water Rail, Greater Spotted Woodpecker, Dipper, gulls, Marsh Harrier, Sand Martin, Hobby, Redstart, occasional Bittern.
Contact: Chris Lawrence, The Welsh Wildlife Centre, Cillgerran, Cardigan SA43 2TB. 01239 621212.
e-mail: information@wtsww.cix.co.uk
www.wildlifetrust.org.uk/wtsww

11. WESTFIELD PILLS

The Wildlife Trust of South and West Wales.
Location: SM 958 073.
Access: Open all year.
Facilities: Car park, cycle track.
Public transport: None.
Habitat: Freshwater lagoons, disused railway embankment, scrub, woodland margins.
Key birds: *Spring/summer*: Hirundines, Whitethroat, Blackcap, Spotted Flycatcher. *Passage*: waders. *Winter*: Little Grebe, Peregrine, Water Rail, Woodcock, Fieldfare, Redwing, Siskin, Redpoll. *All year*: Sparrowhawk, Kingfisher, Tawny Owl, Grey Wagtail, Dunnock, Raven, Bullfinch.
Contact: The Wildlife Trust of South and West Wales, Nature Centre, Fountain Road, Tondu, Mid Glamorgan, CF32 0EH, 01239 621212.

12. YNYS-HIR

RSPB (CYMRU).
Location: SN 68 29 63. Off A487 Aberystwyth - Machynlleth road in Eglwys-fach village. Six miles SW of Machynlleth.
Access: Open every day (9am-9pm or dusk if earlier). Visitor centre open daily Apr-Oct (10am-5pm), weekends only Nov-Mar (10am-4pm).
Facilities: Visitor centre and toilets, both with disabled access. Numerous trails and seven hides.
Public transport: Bus service to Eglwys-fach from either Machynlleth or Aberystwyth, tel. 01970 617951. Rail service to Machynlleth.
Habitat: Estuary, freshwater pools, woodland and wet grassland.
Key birds: *Winter*: Greenland White-fronted Goose, Wigeon, Hen Harrier, Barnacle Goose. *Spring/summer*: Wood Warbler, Redstart, Pied Flycatcher. *All year*: Peregrine, Red Kite, Buzzard, Goshawk
Contact: Frances Hazell, Ynys-Hir RSPB Nature Reserve, Eglwys-fach, Machynlleth, Powys SY20 8TA. 01654 700222.
e-mail: Frances.hazell@rspb.org.uk

Channel Islands

COLIN McCATHIE RESERVE (VALE POND)

La Société Guernesiaise.
Location: Perry's Island Guide (page 6 B5).
Access: Open at all times.
Facilities: Hide on road to Vale Church must be used. **Public transport:** Hourly bus service 7/7A (island circular)., tel: 01481 720210.
Habitat: Brackish tidal pond, reed fringes.
Key birds: Passage waders. *Summer*: Breeding Reed Warbler, Moorhen, Coot. *Winter*: Wildfowl, Water Rail, Little Egret, Snipe, Kingfisher.
Contact: Vic Froome (Section Secretary), La Cloture, Courtil de Bas Lane, St Sampson's, Guernsey GY2 4XJ. 01481 254841.

LA CLAIRE MARE

La Société Guernesiaise.
Location: Perry's Island Guide (page 12 C5).
Access: Open at all times.
Facilities: Hide down concrete track off the Rue de la Rocque Road then boardwalk to second hide.
Public transport: Hourly bus service 7/7A (island circular), tel: 01481 720210.
Habitat: Reedbeds, pasture, willow thickets, scrape.
Key birds: Passage waders and passerines. *Summer*: Breeding Reed Warbler, Moorhen, Coot, Kestrel. *Winter*: Wildfowl, Water Rail, Snipe, Kingfisher.
Contact: Vic Froome, 01481 254841.

PLEINMONT

La Société Guernesiaise.
Location: Perry's Island Guide Page 32 B3.
Access: Open at all times.
Facilities: Public footpath around reserve.
Public transport: Hourly bus service 7/7A (island circular) 0.5 miles from Imperial Hotel, tel 01481 720210.
Habitat: Cliff-top headland of scrub, remnant heathland and small fields.
Key birds: Passage passerines. *Summer*: Breeding Dartford Warbler, Whitethroat, Stonechat and Linnet.
Contact: Vic Froome, 01481 254841.

Isle of Man

BALLALOUGH REEDBEDS RESERVE

Manx Wildlife Trust.
Location: SC 258 682. Accessible from the Castletown by-pass on the A5, which forms part of the S boundary of the reserve.
Access: Open all year. **Facilities:** Car park.
Public transport: None.
Habitat: Meadow, reedbed.
Key birds: *Spring/summer*: Willow Warbler, Sedge Bunting, Reed Bunting.
Contact: Manx Wildlife Trust, Tynwald Mills, St Johns, Isle of Man IM4 3AE. 01624 801985.
e-mail: manxwt@cix.org.uk
www.wildlifetrust.org.uk/manxwt

BREAGLE GLEN

Manx Wildlife Trust/Castletown Town Commissioners Habitats.
Location: SC 196 688. In Port Erin from St Georges Crescent, which forms the whole N and W boundary.
Access: Open all year. **Facilities:** None.
Public transport: Regular bus service from Douglas to Port Erin and then short walk.
Habitat: Small woodland area, shrubs.
Key birds: *Passage*: Yellow-browed Warbler, Barred Warbler, Firecrest, Red-breasted Flycatcher have been recorded.
Contact: Tricia Sayle, Reserves Officer, Manx Wildlife Trust, Tynwald Mills, St John's, Isle of Man IM4 3AE. 01624 801985.
e-mail: manxwt@cix.co.uk
www.wildlifetrust.org.uk/manxwt

CALF OF MAN BIRD OBSERVATORY

Administration Department, Manx National Heritage.
Location: SC 15 65. Small island off the SW tip of the Isle of Man. Local boat from Port Erin or Port St Mary.
Access: Apr-Oct. No dogs, fires or camping.
Facilities: Accommodation for eight people in

three bedrooms at Observatory Apr-Oct. Bookings: Administration Department (address below).
Public transport: Local boat from Port Erin or Port St Mary.
Habitat: Heather/bracken moor and seabird cliffs.
Key birds: *All year*: Hen Harrier, Peregrine and Chough. *Summer*: Breeding seabirds (nine species including Storm Petrel, Manx Shearwater). Excellent spring and autumn migration, seabird migration best in autumn.
Contact: Tim Bagworth, (Warden), Manx National Heritage, Manx Museum, Douglas, Isle of Man IM1 3LY.

CLOSE SARTFIELD

Manx Wildlife Trust.
Location: SC 361 956. From Ramsey drive W on A3. Turn on to B9, take third right and follow this road for nearly a mile. Reserve entrance is on right.
Access: Open all year round. No dogs. Path and boardwalk suitable for wheelchairs from car park through wildflower meadow and willow scrub to hide.
Facilities: Car park, hide, reserve leaflet (50p, available from office) outlines circular walk.
Public transport: None.
Habitat: Wildflower-rich hay meadow, marshy grassland, willow scrub/developing birch woodland, bog.
Key birds: *Winter*: Large roost of Hen Harrier. *Summer*: Corncrake (breeding 1999 and 2000 after 11 years' absence), Curlew, warblers.
Contact: Tricia Sayle, Reserves Officer, Manx Wildlife Trust, Tynwald Mills, St John's, Isle of Man IM4 3AE. 01624 801985.
e-mail: tricia@manxwt.cix.co.uk

COOILDARRY

Manx Wildlife Trust.
Location: SC 319 896. Entrance approximately one mile S of Kirk Michael village, left of A3.
Access: Open all year round. Not suitable for disabled. Dogs to be kept on a lead.
Facilities: Well-maintained paths throughout. Leaflet (50p) available from office. Nearest toilets in Kirk Michael village.
Public transport: Buses run regularly past the lower entrance off A4.
Habitat: Woodland.
Key birds: Raven, Sparrowhawk.
Contact: Manx Wildlife Trust, 01624 801985.
e-mail: tricia@manxwt.cix.co.uk

CURRAGH KIONDROGHAD

Manx Wildlife Trust.
Location: Turn into Church Road from the A2 near Onchan. Park on the L as the road dips. To reach the reserve cross a piece of land on the L owned by Onchan Commissioners.
Access: Open all year. **Facilities:** None.
Public transport: Regular bus service from Douglas to Onchan and then short walk.
Habitat: Wetland, trees, neutral grassland, swamp.
Key birds: *Spring/summer*: Woodcock, Grey Wagtail, Chiffchaff. *Winter*: Hen Harrier.
Contact: Tricia Sayle, Reserves Officer, Manx Wildlife Trust, Tynwald Mills, St John's, Isle of Man IM4 3AE. 01624 801985.
e-mail: manxwt@cix.co.uk
www.wildlifetrust.org.uk/manxwt

CRONK Y BING

Manx Wildlife Trust.
Location: NX 381 017. Take A10 coast road N from Jurby. Approx two miles along there is a sharp right hand turn over a bridge. Before the bridge there is a track to the left. A parking area is available at the end of the track.
Access: Open all year round. Dogs to be kept on a lead. Not suitable for the disabled.
Facilities: None. **Public transport:** None.
Habitat: Open dune and dune grassland.
Key birds: *Summer*: Terns. *Winter*: Divers, grebes, skuas, gulls.
Contact: Tricia Sayle, Reserves Officer, Manx Wildlife Trust, Tynwald Mills, St John's, Isle of Man IM4 3AE. 01624 801985.
e-mail: tricia@manxwt.cix.co.uk

DALBY MOUNTAIN

Manx Wildlife Trust.
Location: SC 233769. Approx two miles S of Dalby village, lying adjacent to the A27.
Access: Open all year round. Dogs to be kept on a lead. Not suitable for wheelchairs.
Facilities: None.
Public transport: None.
Habitat: Heathland.
Key birds: Hen Harrier, Red Grouse.
Contact: Tricia Sayle, Reserves Officer, Manx Wildlife Trust, Tynwald Mills, St John's, Isle of Man IM4 3AE. 01624 801985.
e-mail: tricia@manxwt.cix.co.uk

COUNTY DIRECTORY

Lapwing by Richard Johnson

ENGLAND

THE INFORMATION in the directory has been obtained either from the persons listed or from the appropriate national or other bodies. In some cases, where it has not proved possible to verify the details directly, alternative responsible sources have been relied upon. When no satisfactory record was available, previously included entries have sometimes had to be deleted. Readers are requested to advise the editor of any errors or omissions.

BEDFORDSHIRE

Bird Atlas/Avifauna
An Atlas of the Breeding Birds of Bedfordshire 1988-92 by R A Dazley and P Trodd (Bedfordshire Natural History Society, 1994).

Bird Recorders
Dave Odell, The Hobby, 74 The Links, Kempston, Bedford, MK42 7LT. 01234 857149; e-mail: davehobby@onetel.net.uk

Bedfordshire Bird Club Records & Research Committee, Phil Cannings, 30 Graham Gardens, Luton, LU3 1NQ. H:01582 400394; W:01234 842220; e-mail: philcannings@btopenworld.com

Bird Report
BEDFORDSHIRE BIRD REPORT (1946-), from Mrs Mary Sheridan, 28 Chestnut Hill, Linslade, Leighton Buzzard, Beds LU7 2TR.

BTO Regional Representative & Regional Development Officer
RR, Phil Cannings, 30 Graham Gardens, Luton, Beds, LU3 1NQ. H:01582 400394; W:01234 842220; e-mail: philcannings@btopenworld.com

RDO, Judith Knight, 381 Bideford Green, Linslade, Leighton Buzzard, Beds, LU7 2TY. Home 01525 378161; e-mail: judy.knight@tinyonline.co.uk

Club
BEDFORDSHIRE BIRD CLUB, (1992; 242). Miss Sheila Alliez, Flat 61 Adamson Court, Hillgrounds Road, Kempston, Bedford, MK42 8QZ. e-mail: alliezsec@peewit.freeserve.co.uk www.bedsbirdclub.org.uk

Ringing Groups
IVEL RG, Errol Newman, 29 Norse Road, Goldington, Bedford, MK41 0NR. 01234 343119; e-mail: lew.n@virgin.net

RSPB, Dr A D Evans, 6 Jennings Close, Potton, Sandy, Beds, SG19 2SE.

RSPB Local Groups
BEDFORD, (1970; 80). Barrie Mason, 6 Landseer Walk, Bedford, MK41 7LZ. 01234 262280.

SOUTH BEDFORDSHIRE, (1973; 150). Mick Price, 120 Common Road, Kensworth, Beds LU6 3RG. 01582 873268.

Wildlife Trust
See Cambridgeshire.

BERKSHIRE

Bird Atlas/Avifauna
The Birds of Berkshire by P E Standley et al (Berkshire Atlas Group/Reading Ornithological Club, 1996).

Bird Recorder
Peter Standley, Siskins, 7 Llanvair Drive, South Ascot, Berks, SL5 9HS. 01344 623502.

Bird Reports
BERKSHIRE BIRD BULLETIN (Monthly, 1986-), from Brian Clews, 118 Broomhill, Cookham, Berks, SL6 9LQ. 01628 525314.

BIRDS OF BERKSHIRE (1974-) from Recorder.

BIRDS OF THE THEALE AREA (1988-), from Secretary, Theale Area Bird Conservation Group.

NEWBURY DISTRICT BIRD REPORT (1959-), from Secretary, Newbury District Ornithological Club.

BTO Regional Representative & Regional Development Officer
RR, Chris Robinson, 2 Beckfords, Upper Basildon, Reading, RG8 8PB. 01491 671420; e-mail: chris.robinson@hp.com

Clubs
BERKSHIRE BIRD BULLETIN GROUP, (1986;

100). Berkshire Bird Bulletin Group, PO Box 680, Maidenhead, Berks, SL6 9ST. 01628 525314.

NEWBURY DISTRICT ORNITHOLOGICAL CLUB, (1959; 110). Trevor Maynard, 15 Kempton Close, Newbury, Berks, RG14 7RS. 01635 36752; e-mail: info@ndoc.org.uk www.ndoc.org.uk.

READING ORNITHOLOGICAL CLUB, (1945; 200). Renton Righelato, 63 Hamilton Road, Reading RG1 5RA. 0787 981 2564; e-mail: renton@righelato.net www.roc.care4free.net

THEALE AREA BIRD CONSERVATION GROUP, (1988; 75). Brian Uttley, 60 Omers Rise, Burghfield Common, Reading RG7 3HH. 0118 983 2894. www.bramblingphotos.com

Ringing Groups

NEWBURY RG, J Legg, 1 Malvern Court, Old Newtown Road, Newbury, Berks, RG14 7DR. e-mail: janlegg@talk21.com

RUNNYMEDE RG, D G Harris, 22 Blossom Waye, Hounslow, TW5 9HD. e-mail: daveharris@tinyonline.co.uk

RSPB Local Groups

EAST BERKSHIRE, (1974; 200). Ken Panchen, 7 Knottocks End, Beaconsfield, Bucks, HP9 2AN. 01494 675779; e-mail: ken.panchen@care4free.net.

READING, (1986; 80). Carl Feltham, 39 Moriston Close, Reading, RG30 2PW. 0118 941 1713.

WOKINGHAM & BRACKNELL, (1979; 200). Patrick Crowley, 56 Ellis Road, Crowthorne, Berks, RG45 6PT. 01344 776473; e-mail: patrick.crowley@btinternet.com www.wbrspb.btinternet.co.uk

Wildlife Hospitals

KESTREL LODGE, D J Chandler, 101 Sheridan Avenue, Caversham, Reading, RG4 7QB. 01189 477107. Birds of prey, ground feeding birds, waterbirds, seabirds. Temporary homes for all except large birds of prey. Veterinary support. Small charge.

LIFELINE, Wendy Hermon, Treatment Centre Co-ordinator, Swan Lifeline, Cuckoo Weir Island, South Meadow Lane, Eton, Windsor, Berks, SL4 6SS. 01753 859397; (fax) 01753 622709; www.swanlifeline.org.uk
Registered charity. Thames Valley 24-hour swan rescue and treatment service. Veterinary support and hospital unit. Operates membership scheme.

Wildlife Trust

Director see Oxfordshire.

BUCKINGHAMSHIRE

Bird Atlas/Avifauna

The Birds of Buckinghamshire ed by P Lack and D Ferguson (Buckinghamshire Bird Club, 1993).

Bird Recorder

Andy Harding, 15 Jubilee Terrace, Stony Stratford, Milton Keynes, MK11 1DU. H:01908 565896; W:01908 653328; e-mail: a.v.harding@open.ac.uk.

Bird Reports

AMERSHAM BIRDWATCHING CLUB ANNUAL REPORT (1975-), from Secretary.

BUCKINGHAMSHIRE BIRD REPORT (1980-), from Rosie Hamilton, 56 Church Hill, Cheddington, Leighton Buzzard, Beds, LU7 0SY.

NORTH BUCKS BIRD REPORT (10 pa), from Recorder.

BTO Regional Representative & Regional Development Officer

RR, Mick A'Court, 6 Chalkshire Cottages, Chalkshire road, Butlers Cross, Bucks, HP17 0TW. (H)01296 623610; (W)01494 462246; e-mail: a.arundinaceous@virgin.net mick@focusrite.com

RDO, Peter Hearn, 160 High Street, Aylesbury, Bucks, HP20 1RE. (Home & (fax)) 01296 581520; (work) 01296 424145.

Clubs

AMERSHAM BIRDWATCHING CLUB, (1973; 70). Mary Mackay, 26A Highfield Close, Amersham, Bucks, HP6 3HG. 07980 503879.

BUCKINGHAMSHIRE BIRD CLUB, (1981; 300). Roger S Warren, Bakery Lodge, Skirmett, Henley on Thames, Oxon, RG9 6TD. 01491 638544.

NORTH BUCKS BIRDERS, (1977; 50). Andy Harding, 15 Jubilee Terrace, Stony Stratford, Milton Keynes, MK11 1DU. (H)01908 565896; (W)01908 653328.

Ringing Groups

HUGHENDEN RG, Peter Edwards, 8 The Brackens, Warren Wood, High Wycombe, Bucks, HP11 1EB. 01494 535125.

RSPB Local Groups

See also Herts: Chorleywood,
AYLESBURY, (1981; 220). Barry Oxley, 3 Swan

Close, Station Road, Blackthorn, Bicester, Oxon, OX25 1TU. 01869 247780.

NORTH BUCKINGHAMSHIRE, (1976; 400). Jim Parsons, 8 The Mount, Aspley Guise, Milton Keynes, MK17 8EA. 01908 582450.

Wildlife Hospitals
MILTON KEYNES WILDLIFE HOSPITAL, Mr & Mrs V Seaton, 150 Bradwell Common Boulevard, Milton KeynesMK13 8BE. 01908 604198;
www-tec.open,ac.uk/staff/robert/robert.html
Registered charity. All species of British birds and mammals. Veterinary support.

WILDLIFE HOSPITAL TRUST, St Tiggywinkles, Aston Road, Haddenham, Aylesbury, Bucks, HP17 8AF. 01844 292292; (fax) 01844 292640;
e-mail: mail@sttiggywinkles.org.uk
www.sttiggywinkles.org.uk
Registered charity. All species. Veterinary referrals and helpline for vets and others on wild bird treatments. Full veterinary unit and staff.
Pub: *Bright Eyes* (free to members - sae).

Wildlife Trust
Director see Oxfordshire.

CAMBRIDGESHIRE

Bird Atlas/Avifauna
An Atlas of the Breeding Birds of Cambridgeshire (VC 29) P M M Bircham et al (Cambridge Bird Club, 1994).

The Birds of Cambridgeshire: checklist 2000 (Cambridge Bird Club).

Bird Recorders
CAMBRIDGESHIRE, John Oates, 7 Fassage Close, Lode, Cambridge, CB5 9Eh. 01223 812546, (M)07860 132708. e-mail: joates9151@aol.com

HUNTINGDON & PETERBOROUGH, John Clark, 7 Westbrook, Hilton, Huntingdon, Cambs, PE28 9NW. 01480 830472.

Bird Reports
CAMBRIDGESHIRE BIRD REPORT (1925-), from Secretary, Cambridgeshire Bird Club.

PAXTON PITS BIRD REPORT (1994-), from Trevor Gunton, 15 St James Road, Little Paxton, Cambs, PE19 6QW. ((tel/fax))01480 473562.

PETERBOROUGH BIRD CLUB REPORT (1999-), from Secretary, Peterborough Bird Club.

BTO Regional Representatives
CAMBRIDGESHIRE, John Le Gassick, 17 Acacia Avenue, St Ives, Cambs, PE27 6TN. 01480 391991; e-mail: john.legassick@ntlworld.com

HUNTINGDON & PETERBOROUGH, Philip Todd, 01733 810832.
e-mail: huntspbororr@yahoo.co.uk

Clubs
CAMBRIDGESHIRE BIRD CLUB, (1925; 290). Bruce Martin, 178 Nuns Way, Cambridge, CB4 2NS. 01223 700656;
e-mail: bruce.s.martin@ntlworld.com
www.cambridgeshirebirdclub.org.uk

GREATER PETERBOROUGH ORNITHOLOGICAL GROUP, (1983; 20). Martin Coates, 63 Primrose Way, Stamford, PE9 4BU. 01780 755016;
e-mail: martin.shelagh@virgin.net

PETERBOROUGH BIRD CLUB, (1999; 190) Chris Hamlett, 21 Carisbrook Court, Longthorpe, Peterborough PE3 6DJ. 01733 331814;
e-mail: gordon.hamlett@btinternet.com

ST NEOTS BIRD & WILDLIFE CLUB, (1993; 150). Tim Watling, 39 Shakespeare Road, Eaton Socon, St Neots, Cambs, PE19 8HG. 01480 212763; e-mail: tim@watling2000.fsnet.co.uk
www.paxton-pits.org.uk

Ringing Group
WICKEN FEN RG, Dr C J R Thorne, Norden House, 17 The Footpath, Coton, Cambs, CB3 7PX. 01954 210566; e-mail: cjrt@cam.ac.uk

RSPB Local Groups
CAMBRIDGE, (1977; 150). Colin Kirtland, 22 Montgomery Road, Cambridge, CB4 2EQ. 01223 363092.

HUNTINGDONSHIRE, (1982; 200). Pam Peacock, Old Post Office, Warboys Road, Pidley, Huntingdon, Cambs, PE28 3DA. 01487 840615;
e-mail: pam.peacock@care4free.net
www.huntsrspb.co.uk

Wildlife Trust
BEDS, CAMBS, NORTHANTS & PETERBOROUGH WILDLIFE TRUST, (1990; 12,000). 3B Langford Arch, London Road, Sawston, Cambridge, CB2 4EE. 01223 712400; (fax) 01223 712412; e-mail: cambswt@cix.co.uk

CHESHIRE

Bird Atlas/Avifauna
The Birds of Sandbach Flashes 1935-1999 by Andrew Goodwin and Colin Lythgoe (The Printing House, Crewe, 2000).

Bird Recorder (inc Wirral)
Tony Broome, 4 Larchwood Drive, Wilmslow, Cheshire, SK9 2NU. 01625 540434.

Bird Report
CHESHIRE & WIRRAL BIRD REPORT (1969-), from David Cogger, 113 Nantwich Road, Middlewich, Cheshire, CW10 9HD. 01606 832517; e-mail: memsec@cawos.org www.cawos.org

SOUTH EAST CHESHIRE ORNITHOLOGICAL SOCIETY BIRD REPORT (1985-), from secretary, South East Cheshire Ornithol Soc. 01270 582642.

BTO Regional Representatives & Regional Development Officer
MID RR, Paul Miller. 01928 787535; e-mail: huntershill@worldline.co.uk

NORTH & EAST RR, position vacant.

SOUTH RR & RDO, Charles Hull, Edleston Cottage, Edleston Hall Lane, Nantwich, Cheshire, CW5 8PL. 01270 628194; e-mail: edleston@yahoo.co.uk

Clubs
CHESHIRE & WIRRAL ORNITHOLOGICAL SOCIETY, (1988; 355). David Cogger, 113 Nantwich Road, Middlewich, Cheshire, CW10 9HD. 01606 832517; e-mail: memsec@cawos.org www.cawos.org

CHESTER & DISTRICT ORNITHOLOGICAL SOCIETY, (1967; 50). David King, 13 Bennett Close, Willaston, South Wirral, CH64 2XF. 0151 327 7212.

KNUTSFORD ORNITHOLOGICAL SOCIETY, (1974; 45). Roy Bircumshaw, 267 Longridge, Knutsford, Cheshire, WA16 8PH. 01565 634193. www.10x50.com

LANCASHIRE & CHESHIRE FAUNA SOCIETY, (1914; 140). Dave Bickerton, 64 Petre Crescent, Rishton, Lancs, BB1 4RB. 01254 886257; e-mail: bickertond@aol.com www.lacfs.org.uk

LYMM ORNITHOLOGY GROUP, (1975; 65). Mrs Ann Ledden, 4 Hill View, Widnes, WA8 9AL. 0151 424 0441.

MID-CHESHIRE ORNITHOLOGICAL SOCIETY, (1963; 80). Les Goulding, 7 Summerville Gardens, Stockton Heath, WarringtonWA4 2EG. 01925 265578; e-mail: les@goulding7.fsnet.co.uk http://myweb.tiscali.co.uk/barnowl/MCOS

NANTWICH NATURAL HISTORY SOCIETY, (1979; 40). Mike Holmes, 4 Tenchers Field, Stapeley, Nantwich, Cheshire CW5 7GR. 01270 611577; e-mail: mike@mimprove.com www.nantnats.fsnet.co.uk

SOUTH EAST CHESHIRE ORNITHOLOGICAL SOCIETY, (1964; 110). Colin Lythgoe, 11 Waterloo Road, Haslington, Crewe, CW1 5TF. 01270 582642.

WILMSLOW GUILD BIRDWATCHING GROUP, (1965; 55). Tom Gibbons, Chestnut Cottage, 37 Strawberry Lane, Wilmslow, Cheshire, SK9 6AQ. 01625 520317.

Ringing Groups
MERSEYSIDE RG, P Slater, 45 Greenway Road, Speke, Liverpool, L24 7RY.

SOUTH MANCHESTER RG, C M Richards, Fairhaven, 13 The Green, Handforth, Wilmslow, Cheshire, SK9 3AG. 01625 524527; e-mail: cliveandkay.richards@care4free.net

RSPB Local Groups
CHESTER, (1987; 350). Bernard Wright, Carden Smithy, Clutton, Chester, CH3 9EP. 01829 782243; e-mail: knoydart@globalnet.co.uk

MACCLESFIELD, (1979; 394). Peter Kirk, Field Rise, Dumbah Lane, West Bollington, Macclesfield, Cheshire, SK10 5AB. 01625 829119; e-mail peter@kirk199.freeserve.co.uk www.macclesfieldrspb.org.uk

NORTH CHESHIRE, (1976; 100). Not known at time of going to press. Please contact RSPB for further details. 01484 861148; www.rspb.org.uk

Wildlife Hospitals
RSPCA STAPELEY GRANGE WILDLIFE HOSPITAL, London Road, Stapeley, Nantwich, Cheshire, CW5 7JW. 0870 442 7102.
All wild birds. Oiled bird wash facilities and pools. Veterinary support.

SWAN SANCTUARY, Mrs C Clements, 24 St

David's Drive, Callands, Warrington, WA5 5SB. 01925 636245.
Veterinary support.

Wildlife Trust
CHESHIRE WILDLIFE TRUST, (1962; 3600). Grebe House, Reaseheath, Nantwich, Cheshire, CW5 6DG. 01270 610180; (fax) 01270 610430; e-mail: cheshirewt@cix.co.uk
www.wildlifetrust.org.uk/cheshire

CORNWALL

Bird Recorders
CORNWALL, K Wilson, No.1 Tol-pedn House, School Hill Road, St Levan, Penzance, Cornwall, TR19 6LP. 01736 871800;
e-mail: kesteraw@yahoo.co.uk

ISLES OF SCILLY, Paul Stancliffe, 1 Longstones Terrace, St Mary's, Isles of Scilly, TR21 0NW.
e-mail: paulnabby@supanet.com

Bird Reports
BIRDS IN CORNWALL (1931-), from the County Recorder.

ISLES OF SCILLY BIRD REPORT and NATURAL HISTORY REVIEW 2000 (1969-), from Club Secretary, Isles of Scilly Bird Group.

BTO Regional Representatives & Regional Development Officers
CORNWALL RR Terry Hasdell. 01209 710 683;
e-mail: terryhasdell@aol.com

ISLES OF SCILLY RR & RDO, Will Wagstaff, 42 Sally Port, St Mary's, Isles of Scilly, TR21 0JE. 01720 422212;
e-mail: william.wagstaff@virgin.net

Clubs
CORNWALL BIRDWATCHING & PRESERVATION SOCIETY, (1931; 990). Darrell Clegg, 55 Lower Fore Street, Saltash, CornwallPL12.

CORNWALL WILDLIFE TRUST PHOTOGRAPHIC GROUP, (40). David Chapman, 41 Bosence Road, Townshend, Nr Hayle, CornwallTR27 6AL. 01736 850287;
e-mail: david@ruralimages.freeserve.co.uk
www.ruralimages.freeserve.co.uk

ISLES OF SCILLY BIRD GROUP, (2000; 450). Nigel Hudson, Post Office Flat, St Mary's, Isles of Scilly; TR21 0LL01720 422267;
e-mail: nig_hudson@lineone.net

Ringing Group
SCILLONIA SEABIRD GROUP, Peter Robinson, 19 Pine Park Road, Honiton, Devon, EX14 2HR. 01404 549873;
e-mail: pjrobinson2@compuserve.com

RSPB Local Group
CORNWALL, (1972; 550). Michael Lord, Gue Gassel, Church Cove, The Lizard, Cornwall, TR12 7PH. 01326 290981.

Wildlife Hospital
MOUSEHOLE WILD BIRD HOSPITAL & SANCTUARY ASSOCIATION LTD, Raginnis Hill, Mousehole, Penzance, Cornwall, TR19 6SR. 01736 731386.
All species. No ringing.

Wildlife Trust
CORNWALL WILDLIFE TRUST, (1962; 6000). Five Acres, Allet, Truro, Cornwall, TR4 9DJ. 01872 273939; (fax) 01872 225476;
e-mail: cornwt@cix.co.uk

CUMBRIA

Bird Atlas/Avifauna
The Breeding Birds of Cumbria by Stoff, Callion, Kinley, Raven and Roberts (Cumbria Bird Club, 2002).

Bird Recorders
COUNTY, Colin Raven, 18 Seathwaite Road, Barrow-in-Furness, Cumbria, LA14 4LX.

NORTH EAST (Carlisle & Eden), Michael F Carrier, Lismore Cottage, 1 Front Street, Armathwaite, Cumbria, CA4 9PB. 01697 472218.

NORTH WEST (Allerdale & Copeland), J K Manson, Fell Beck, East Road, Egremont, Cumbria, CA22 2ED. 01946 822947;
e-mail: jake@jakemanson.freeserve.co.uk

SOUTH (South Lakeland & Furness), Ronnie Irving, 24 Birchwood Close, Kendal, Cumbria, LA9 5BJ. 01539 727523;
e-mail: ronald.irving@virginnet.co.uk

Bird Reports
BIRDS AND WILDLIFE IN CUMBRIA (1970-), from D Clarke, Tullie House Museum, Castle Street, Carlisle, Cumbria, CA3 8TP.
e-mail: DavidC@carlisle-city.gov.uk

WALNEY BIRD OBSERVATORY REPORT, from Warden, see Reserves.

BTO Regional Representatives
NORTH RR, Clive Hartley. 01228 576 349; e-mail: hartleyclive@aol.com

SOUTH RR, Stephen Dunstan, 29 Greenfinch Court, Herons Reach, Blackpool, FY3 8FG. 01253 301009; e-mail: stephen@greenfinch.fslife.co.uk

Clubs
ARNSIDE & DISTRICT NATURAL HISTORY SOCIETY, (1967; 221). Mrs GM Smith, West Wind, Orchard Road, Arnside, via Carnforth, Cumbria, LA5 0DP. 01524 762522.

CUMBRIA BIRD CLUB, (1989; 230). Peter Ullrich, 25 Arlecdon Parks Road, Arlecdon, Frizington, Cumbria, CA26 3XG. 01946 861376; www.cumbriabirdclub.freeserve.co.uk

CUMBRIA RAPTOR STUDY GROUP, (1992). P N Davies, Snowhill Cottage, Caldbeck, Wigton, Cumbria, CA7 8HL. 016973 712249; e-mail: pete.caldbeck@virgin.net

Ringing Groups
EDEN RG, G Longrigg, Mere Bank, Bleatarn, Warcop, Appleby, Cumbria, CA16 6PX.

MORECAMBE BAY WADER RG, J Sheldon, 415 West Shore Park, Barrow-in-Furness, Cumbria, LA14 3XZ. 01229 473102.

WALNEY BIRD OBSERVATORY, K Parkes, 176 Harrogate Street, Barrow-in-Furness, Cumbria, LA14 5NA. 01229 824219.

RSPB Local Groups
CARLISLE, (1974; 400). Alistair Leslie, 15 High Garth Meadows, Ivegill, Carlisle, CA4 0PA. 01697 473138.

SOUTH LAKELAND, (1973; 340). Ms Kathleen Atkinson, 2 Langdale Crescent, Windermere, Cumbria, LA23 2HE. 01539 444254.

WEST CUMBRIA, (1986; 230). Neil Hutchin, Orchard House, Main Street, Greysouthen, Cockermouth, Cumbria, CA13 0UG. 01900 825231; e-mail: neil@hutchin50.fsnet.co.uk

Wildlife Trust
CUMBRIA WILDLIFE TRUST, (1962; 5000). Brockhole, Windermere, Cumbria, LA23 1LJ. 01539 448280; (fax) 01539 448281; e-mail: cumbriawt@cix.co.uk

DERBYSHIRE

Bird Atlas/Avifauna
Birds of Derbyshire by RA Frost. (Moorland Publishing Co. Hartington, Derbys 1978).

Bird Recorders
1. Rare breeding records, Roy A Frost, 66 St Lawrence Road, North Wingfield, Chesterfield, Derbyshire, S42 5LL. 01246 850037.

2. Records Committee & rarity records, Rodney W Key, 3 Farningham Close, Spondon, Derby, DE21 7DZ. 01332 678571; e-mail: rod.key@talk21.com

3. Annual Report editor, Richard M R James, 10 Eastbrae Road, Littleover, Derby, DE23 1WA. 01332 771787.

Bird Reports
BENNERLEY MARSH WILDLIFE GROUP ANNUAL REPORT, from Club Secretary.

CARSINGTON BIRD CLUB ANNUAL REPORT, from Club Secretary.

DERBYSHIRE BIRD REPORT (1954-), from Bryan Barnacle, Mays, Malthouse Lane, Froggatt, Hope Valley, Derbyshire S32 3ZA. 01433 630726; e-mail: barney@mays1.demon.co.uk.

OGSTON BIRD CLUB REPORT (1970-), from Club Secretary.

BTO Regional Representatives
NORTH RR, Dave Budworth, 121 Wood Lane, Newhall, Swadlincote, Derbys, DE11 0LX. 01283 215188; e-mail: dbud01@aol.com

SOUTH RR, Dave Budworth, 121 Wood Lane, Newhall, Swadlincote, Derbys, DE11 0LX. 01283 215188; e-mail: dbud01@aol.com

Clubs
BENNERLEY MARSH WILDLIFE GROUP, (1995; 135). Mr R Davis, 3 Windrush Close, Bramcote, Nottingham, NG9 3LN. 0115 9228547.

BAKEWELL & DISTRICT BIRD STUDY GROUP, (1987; 70). Ann Wrench, Longstone Byre, Little Longstone, Nr Bakewell, Derbys, DE45 1NN. e-mail: ann.wrench@btinternet.com

BUXTON FIELD CLUB, (1946; 78). B Aries, 1 Horsefair Avenue, Chapel-en-le-Frith, High Peak, Derbys, SK23 9SQ. 01298 815291.

CARSINGTON BIRD CLUB, (1992; 257). Mrs Dorothy Evans, 41 Belvedere Avenue, Walton, Chesterfield, Derbys, S40 3HY. 01246 238421; e-mail: dmevans41@lineone.net www.carsingtonbirdclub.co.uk.

DERBYSHIRE ORNITHOLOGICAL SOCIETY, (1954; 550). Steve Shaw, 84 Moorland View Road, Walton, Chesterfield, Derbys, S40 3DF. 01246 236090;
e-mail: steveshaw@ornsoc.freeserve.co.uk
www.derbyshireOS.org.uk

OGSTON BIRD CLUB, (1969; 965). Mrs Ann Hunt, 2 Sycamore Avenue, Glapwell, Chesterfield, S44 5LH. 01623 812159
www.ogstonbirdclub.co.uk

SOUTH PEAK RAPTOR STUDY GROUP, (1998; 12). M E Taylor, 76 Hawksley Avenue, Newbold, Chesterfield, Derbys, S40 4TL. 01246 277749.

Ringing Groups
DARK PEAK RG, W M Underwood, Ivy Cottage, 15 Broadbottom Road, Mottram-in-Longdendale, Hyde, Cheshire SK14 6JB.
e-mail: w.m.underwood@talk21.com

SORBY-BRECK RG, Geoff P Mawson, Moonpenny Farm, Farwater Lane, Dronfield, Sheffield, S18 1RA. 01246 415097;
e-mail: gpmawson@hotmail.com

SOUDER RG, Dave Budworth, 121 Wood Lane, Newhall, Swadlincote, Derbys, DE11 0LX. 0121 6953384.

RSPB Local Groups
CHESTERFIELD, (1987; 274). Not known at time of going to press. Please contact the RSPB for further information. www.rspb.org.uk

DERBY, (1973; 480). Brian Myring, 74 The Bancroft, Etwall, Derby, DE65 6NF. 01283 734851.

HIGH PEAK, (1974; 200). Peter Griffiths, 17 Clifton Drive, Marple, Stockport SK6 6PP. 0161 427 5325.

Wildlife Trust
DERBYSHIRE WILDLIFE TRUST, (1962; 5000). Elvaston Castle, Derby, DE72 3EP. 01332 756610; (fax) 01332 758872;
e-mail: derbywt@cix.co.uk

DEVON

Bird Atlas/Avifauna
Tetrad Atlas of Breeding Birds of Devon by H P Sitters (Devon Birdwatching & Preservation Society, 1988).

Bird Recorder
Mike Tyler, The Acorn, Shute Road, Kilmington, Axminster, Devon EX13 7ST. 01297 34958;
e-mail: mike@mwtyler.freeserve.co.uk

Bird Reports
DEVON BIRD REPORT (1928-), from H Kendall, 33 Victoria Road, Bude, Cornwall, EX23 8RJ. 01288 353818;
e-mail: harvey.kendall@btopenworld.com.

LUNDY FIELD SOCIETY ANNUAL REPORT (1946-), from Secretary. Index to Report is on Society's website.

BTO Regional Representative & Regional Development Officer
John Woodland, Glebe Cottage, Dunsford, Exeter, EX6 7AA. (tel/fax) 01647 252494;
e-mail: jwoodland@btodv.fsnet.co.uk

Clubs
DEVON BIRDWATCHING & PRESERVATION SOCIETY, (1928; 1200). Mrs Joy Vaughan, 28 Fern Meadow, Okehampton, Devon, EX20 1PB. 01837 53360;
e-mail: joy@vaughan411.freeserve.co.uk.

KINGSBRIDGE & DISTRICT NATURAL HISTORY SOCIETY, (1989; 130). Martin Catt, Migrants Rest, East Prawle, Kingsbridge, Devon, TQ7 2DB. 01548 511443;
e-mail: martin.catt@btinternet.com

LUNDY FIELD SOCIETY, (1946; 450). Chris Webster, 38 Greenway Avenue, Taunton, Somerset, TA2 6HY. 01823 282889;
e-mail: chris@webster5.demon.co.uk
www.lundy.org.uk

TOPSHAM BIRDWATCHING & NATURALISTS' SOCIETY, (1969; 90). Mrs Janice Vining, 2 The Maltings, Fore Street, Topsham, Exeter, EX3 0HF. 01392 873514; e-mail: tbns@talk21.com

Ringing Groups
DEVON & CORNWALL WADER RG, R C Swinfen, 72 Dunraven Drive, Derriford, Plymouth, PL6 6AT. 01752 704184.

LUNDY FIELD SOCIETY, A M Taylor, 26 High Street, Spetisbury, Blandford, Dorset, DT11 9DJ. 01258 857336; e-mail: ammataylor@yahoo.co.uk.

SLAPTON BIRD OBSERVATORY, Peter Ellicott, 10 Chapel Road, Alphington, Exeter, EX2 8TB. 01392 277387.

RSPB Local Groups
EXETER & DISTRICT, (1974; 466). Allan Hancock, Pineta, Sand Down Lane, Newton St

Cyres, Exeter, EX5 5DE. 01392 851744; e-mail: allan.h@care4free.net

NORTH DEVON, (1976; 63). David Gayton, 29 Merrythorne Road, Fremington, Barnstaple, Devon, EX31 3AL. 01271 371092.

PLYMOUTH, (1974; 600). Mrs Eileen Willey, 11 Beverstone Way, Roborough, Plymouth, PL6 7DY. 01752 208996.

Wildlife Hospitals

BIRD OF PREY CASUALTY CENTRE, Mrs J E L Vinson, Crooked Meadow, Stidston Lane, South Brent, Devon, TQ10 9JS. 01364 72174.
Birds of prey, with emergency advice on other species. Aviaries, releasing pen. Veterinary support.

BONDLEIGH BIRD HOSPITAL, Manager, Samantha Hart, North Tawton, Devon, EX20 2AJ. 01837 82328.
All species. 14 aviaries, 2 aquapens. Veterinary support available, if requested, with payment of full charges.

CATT, Martin, Migrants Rest, East Prawle, Kingsbridge, Devon, TQ7 2DB. 01548 511443; e-mail: martin.catt@btinternet.com
Collects and records oiled birds and gives initial treatment before forwarding to cleaning station.

HURRELL, Dr L H
Birds of prey only. Veterinary support.
Contact: Dr Hurrell, 201 Outland Road, Peverell, Plymouth, PL2 3PF. 01752 771838.

TORBAY WILDLIFE RESCUE CENTRE, Malcolm Higgs, 6A Gerston Place, Paignton, S Devon, TQ3 3DX. 01803 557624
www.twrs.fsnet.co.uk
All wild birds, inc. oiled. Pools, aviaries, intensive care, washing facilities. Open at all times. 24-hr veterinary support. Holding areas off limits to public as all wildlife must be returned to the wild.

Wildlife Trust

DEVON WILDLIFE TRUST, (1962; 10600). Shirehampton House, 35-37 St David's Hill, Exeter, EX4 4DA. 01392 279244; (fax) 01392 433221; e-mail: devonwt@cix.co.uk

DORSET

Bird Atlas/Avifauna

Dorset Breeding Bird Atlas (working title). In preparation.

Bird Recorder

James Lidster, 35 Napier Road, Poole, Dorset BH15 4LX. 01202 672406; e-mail: dorsetbirds@btopenworld.com

Bird Reports

DORSET BIRDS (1987-), from Miss J W Adams, 16 Sherford Drive, Wareham, Dorset, BH20 4EN. 01929 552299.

THE BIRDS OF CHRISTCHURCH HARBOUR (1959-), from Ian Southworth, 1 Bodowen Road, Burton, Christchurch, Dorset BH23 7JL.

PORTLAND BIRD OBSERVATORY REPORT, from Warden, see Reserves,

BTO Regional Representatives

Catherine and Graham Whitby, 2 Helston Close, Portesham, Weymouth, Dorset, DT3 4EY. 01305 871301; e-mail: catherineandgraham@portisham2.fsnet.co.uk.

Clubs

CHRISTCHURCH HARBOUR ORNITHOLOGICAL GROUP, (1956; 150). John Hall, 15 Kingsbere Gardens, Haslemere Avenue, Highcliffe, Dorset, BH23 5BQ. 01425 275610.

DORSET BIRD CLUB, (1987; 550). Mrs Eileen Bowman, 53 Lonnen Road, Colehill, Wimborne, Dorset, BH21 7AT. 01202 884788.

DORSET NATURAL HISTORY & ARCHAEOLOGICAL SOCIETY, (1845; 2188). Dorset County Museum, High West Street, Dorchester, Dorset, DT1 1XA. 01305 262735; e-mail: dorsetcountymuseum@dor-mus.demon.co.uk
www.dorsetcountymuseum.co.uk

Ringing Groups

CHRISTCHURCH HARBOUR RS, E C Brett, 3 Whitfield Park, St Ives, Ringwood, Hants, BH24 2DX.

PORTLAND BIRD OBSERVATORY, Martin Cade, Old Lower Light, Portland Bill, Dorset, DT5 2JT. 01305 820553; e-mail: obs@btinternet.com
www.portlandbirdobs.btinternet.co.uk

STOUR RG, R Gifford, 62 Beacon Park Road, Upton, Poole, Dorset, BH16 5PE.

RSPB Local Groups

BLACKMOOR VALE, (1981; 106). Mrs Margaret Marris, 15 Burges Close, Marnhull, Sturminster Newton, Dorset, DT10 1QQ. 01258 820091.

EAST DORSET, (1974; 405). Tony Long (Group Leader: S.Cresswell), 93 Wimborne Road, Corfe Mullen, Wimborne, BH21 3DS. 01202 880508; e-mail: joan.tony@euphony.net.

POOLE, (1982; 305). John Derricott, 51 Dacombe Drive, Upton, Poole, Dorset, BH16 5JJ. 01202 776312.

SOUTH DORSET, (1976; 400). Marion Perriss, Old Barn Cottage, Affpuddle, Dorchester, Dorset, DT2 7HH. 01305 848268;
e-mail: affpuddle@btinternet.com.

Wildlife Hospital
SWAN RESCUE SANCTUARY, Ken and Judy Merriman, The Wigeon, Crooked Withies, Holt, Wimborne, Dorset, BH21 7LB. 01202 828166; mobile 0385 917457;
e-mail: ken@swan-rescue.fsnet.co.uk
www.swan-rescue.co.uk
Swans. Hospital unit with indoor ponds and recovery pens. Outdoors: 35 ponds and lakes, and recovery pens. 24-hr veterinary support. Viewing by appointment only.

Wildlife Trust
DORSET WILDLIFE TRUST, (1961; 8000). Brooklands Farm, Forston, Dorchester, Dorset, DT2 7AA. 01305 264620; (fax) 01305 251120;
e-mail: dorsetwt@cix.co.uk;
www.wildlifetrust.org.uk/dorset/

DURHAM

Bird Atlas/Avifauna
*A Summer Atlas of Breeding Birds of County Durham*by Stephen Westerberg/Kieth Bowey. (Durham Bird Club, 2000).

Bird Recorders
Tony Armstrong, 39 Western Hill, Durham City, DH1 4RJ. 0191 386 1519;
e-mail: ope@globalnet.co.uk

CLEVELAND, Rob Little, 5 Belgrave Court, Seaton Carew, Hartlepool TS25 1BF. 01429 428940. e-mail: rob.little@ntlworld.com

Bird Reports
BIRDS IN DURHAM (1971-), from D Sowerbutts, 9 Prebends Fields, Gilesgate, Durham, DH1 1HH.

CLEVELAND BIRD REPORT (1974-), from Mr J Sharp, 10 Glendale, Pinehills, Guisborough, TS14 8JF. 01287 633976.

BTO Regional Representatives
David L Sowerbutts, 9 Prebends Field, Gilesgate Moor, Durham, DH1 1HH. H:0191 386 7201; W:0191 374 3011;
e-mail: d.l.sowerbutts@durham.ac.uk

CLEVELAND RR, Russell McAndrew, 5 Thornhill Gardens, Hartlepool, TS26 0HX. 01429 277291.

Clubs
DURHAM BIRD CLUB, (1975; 263). Kevin Spindloe, 21 Comrie Road, Hartlepool, TS25 4JQ. 01429 867550; e-mail: kevinspindloe@hotmail.com

SUMMERHILL (HARTLEPOOL) BIRD CLUB, (2000; 75). Kevin Spindloe, 22 Comrie Road, Hartlepool, TS25 4JQ. 01430 867550.

TEESMOUTH BIRD CLUB, (1960; 220). Chris Sharp, 20 Auckland Way, Hartlepool, TS26 0AN. 01429 865163.

Ringing Groups
DURHAM RG, S Westerberg, 32 Manor Road, Medomsley, Consett, Co Durham, DH8 6QW. 01207 563862.

DURHAM DALES RG, J R Hawes, Fairways, 5 Raby Terrace, Willington, Crook, Durham, DL15 0HR.

RSPB Local Group
DURHAM, (1974; 125). Lo Brown, 4 Ann's Place, Langley Moor, Durham, DH7 8JY. 0191 378 2433.

Wildlife Trust
DURHAM WILDLIFE TRUST, (1971; 3500). Rainton Meadows, Chilton Moor, Houghton-le-Spring, Tyne & Wear, DH4 6PU. 0191 5843112; (fax) 0191 584 3934; e-mail: durhamwt@cix.co.uk

ESSEX

Bird Atlas/Avifauna
Birds of Essex (provisional title) by Simon Woods (Essex Birdwatching Society, date to be announced).

The Breeding Birds of Essex by M K Dennis (Essex Birdwatching Society, 1996). New county avifauna, edited by Simon Wood, to be published during 2001

Joint Bird Recorders
Peter J O'Toole. e-mail: pjotoo@essex.ac.uk

Bob Flindall, 60 Lady Lane, Chelmsford, Essex CM2 0TH. 01245-344206 (after 7pm).
e-mail: robert.flindall@btinternet.com

Howard Vaughan, 103 Darnley Road, Strood'
Rochester, KENT ME2 2EY
Tel: 01634-325864 (after 7pm).
e-mail: howardebs@blueyonder.co.uk

Bird Report
ESSEX BIRD REPORT (inc Bradwell Bird Obs records) (1950-), from Peter Dwyer, Sales Officer, 48 Churchill Avenue, Halstead, Essex, CO9 2BE. (tel/fax) 01787 476524;
e-mail: petedwyer@petedwyer.plus.com or pete@northessex.co.uk

BTO Regional Representatives & Regional Development Officer
NORTH-EAST RR & RDO, Peter Dwyer, 48 Churchill Avenue, Halstead, Essex, CO9 2BE. (tel/fax) 01787 476524;
e-mail: petedwyer@petedwyer.plus.com or pete@northessex.co.uk

NORTH-WEST RR, Roy Ledgerton, 25 Bunyan Road, Braintree, Essex, CM7 2PL. 01376 326103;
e-mail: r.ledgerton@virgin.net

SOUTH RR, position vacant.

Club
ESSEX BIRDWATCHING SOCIETY, (1949; 750). Roy Ledgerton, 25 Bunyan Road, Braintree, Essex, CM7 2PL. 01376 326103;
e-mail: r.ledgerton@virgin.net

Ringing Groups
ABBERTON RG, C P Harris, Wylandotte, Seamer Road, Southminster, Essex, CM0 7BX.

BASILDON RG, B J Manton, 72 Leighcliff Road, Leigh-on-Sea, Essex, SS9 1DN. 01702 475183;
e-mail: bjmanton@lineone.net

BRADWELL BIRD OBSERVATORY, C P Harris, Wyandotte, Seamer Road, Southminster, Essex, CM0 7BX.

RSPB Local Groups
CHELMSFORD, (1976; 5500 in catchment area). Mike Logan Wood, Highwood, Ishams Chase, Wickham Bishops, Essex, CM8 3LG. 01621 892045.

COLCHESTER, (1981; 220). Mrs V Owen, Tawnies, Hall Lane, Langenhoe, Colchester, CO5 7NA.

SOUTHEND, (1983; 200). Peter D Hirst, 61 Symons Avenue, Eastwood, Leigh on Sea, EssexSS9 5QD. 01702 527069;
e-mail: southendrspb@btconnect.com
www.southendrspb.co.uk

Wildlife Trust
ESSEX WILDLIFE TRUST, (1959; 15500). Fingringhoe Wick Nature Reserve, South Green Road, Fingringhoe, Colchester, CO5 7DN. 01206 729678; (fax) 01206 729298;
e-mail: admin@essexwt.org.uk
www.essexwt.org.uk

GLOUCESTERSHIRE

Bird Atlas/Avifauna
Atlas of Breeding Birds of the North Cotswolds. (North Cotswold Ornithological Society, 1990).

Bird Recorder
GLOUCESTERSHIRE EXCLUDING S.GLOS (AVON). Not known at time of going to press.

Bird Reports
CHELTENHAM BIRD CLUB BIRD REPORT (1998-), from Secretary.

GLOUCESTERSHIRE BIRD REPORT (1953-), from Peter Jones, 2 Beech Close, Highnam, Gloucester GL2 8EG. 01452 413561;
e-mail: peter@joneshighnam.freeserve.co.uk

NORTH COTSWOLD ORNITHOLOGICAL SOCIETY ANNUAL REPORT (1983-), from Secretary.

BTO Regional Representative
Mike Smart, 143 Cheltenham Road, Gloucester, GL2 0JH. Home/work 01452 421131;
e-mail: smartmike@smartmike.fsnet.co.uk

Clubs
CHELTENHAM BIRD CLUB, (1976; 89). Mrs Frances Meredith, 14 Greatfield Drive, Charlton Kings, Cheltenham, GL53 9BU. 01242 516393;
e-mail: chelt.birds@virgin.net
www.beehive.thisisgloucestershire.co.uk/cheltbirdclub

DURSLEY BIRDWATCHING & PRESERVATION SOCIETY, (1952; 502). Maurice Bullen, 20 South Street, Uley, Dursley, Glos, GL11 5SP. 01453 860004. email: dursleybirdwatch@hotmail.com or maurice.bullen@care4free.net
http://beehive.thisisgoloucestershire.co.uk/dbwps.

GLOUCESTERSHIRE NATURALISTS' SOCIETY, (1948; 600). Mike Smart, 143 Cheltenhem Road, Gloucester, GL2 0JH. 01452 421131; e-mail: smartmike@smartmike.fsnet.co.uk

NORTH COTSWOLD ORNITHOLOGICAL SOCIETY, (1982; 60). T Hutton, 15 Green Close,

Childswickham, Broadway, Worcs, WR12 7JJ. 01386 858511.

Ringing Groups
COTSWOLD WATER PARK RG. R Hearn, Wildfowl & Wetlands Trust, Slimbridge, Glos, GL2 7BT. 01453 891900 ext 185;
e-mail: richard.hearn@wwt.org.uk

SEVERN ESTUARY GULL GROUP, M E Durham, 6 Glebe Close, Frampton-on-Severn, Glos, GL2 7EL. 01452 741312.

SEVERN VALE RG, R Hearn, Wildfowl & Wetlands Trust, Slimbridge, Glos, GL2 7BT. 01453 891900 ext 185; e-mail: richard.hearn@wwt.org.uk

WILDFOWL & WETLANDS TRUST, R Hearn, Wildfowl & Wetlands Trust, Slimbridge, Glos, GL2 7BT. 01453 891900 ext 185;
e-mail: richard.hearn@wwt.org.uk

RSPB Local Group
GLOUCESTERSHIRE, (1972; 787). David Cramp, 2 Ellenor, Alderton, Tewkesbury, GL20 8NZ. 01242 620281.

Wildlife Hospital
GLOUCESTER WILDLIFE RESCUE CENTRE, Alan and Louise Brockbank, 2 Home Farm, Hartpury, Glos, GL19 3DE. 01452 700038;
e-mail: louise.brockbank@lineone.net
http://beehive.thisisgloucestershire.co.uk/gloswildliferescue
Intensive care, treatment and rehabilitation facilities. Vetinary support. No restrictions or conditions.

VALE WILDLIFE RESCUE - WILDLIFE HOSPITAL + REHABILITATION CENTRE, Ms Caroline Gould, Station Road, Beckford, Tewkesbury, Glos, GL20 7AN. 01386 882288; (fax)01386 882299; e-mail: info@vwr.org.uk
www.vwr.org.uk
All wild birds. Intensive care. Registered charity. Veterinary support.

Wildlife Trust
GLOUCESTERSHIRE WILDLIFE TRUST, (1961; 6200). Dulverton Building, Robinswood Hill Country Park, Reservoir Road, Gloucester, GL4 6SX. 01452 383333; (fax) 01452 383334;
e-mail: info@gloucswt.cix.co.uk
www.gloucesterwildlife.co.uk

HAMPSHIRE

Bird Atlas/Avifauna
Birds of Hampshire by J M Clark and J A Eyre (Hampshire Ornithological Society, 1993).

Bird Recorder
John Clark, 4 Cygnet Court, Old Cove Road, Fleet, Hants, GU51 2RL. (tel/fax) 01252 623397;
e-mail: johnclark@cygnetcourt.demon.co.uk

Bird Reports
HAMPSHIRE BIRD REPORT (1955-), from Mrs Margaret Boswell, 5 Clarence Road, Lyndhurst, Hants, SO43 7AL. 023 8028 2105;
e-mail: mag.bos@btinternet.com
2001 edition £9 including p&p.

HANTS/SURREY BORDER BIRD REPORT (1971-), from Recorder.

BTO Regional Representative
Glynne C Evans, Waverley, Station Road, Chilbolton, Stockbridge, Hants, SO20 6AL. H:01264 860697; W:01962 847435;
e-mail: hantsbto@hotmail.com

Clubs
HAMPSHIRE ORNITHOLOGICAL SOCIETY, (1979; 955). Peter Dudley, 3 Copsewood Road, Hythe, Southampton, SO45 5DX. 02380 847149;
e-mail: peter.dudley@lineone.net

SOUTHAMPTON & DISTRICT BIRD GROUP, (1994; 100). Les Stride, 196 Calmore Road, Calmore, Southampton, SO40 2RA. 023 8086 8058; e-mail: lestri@compuserve.com.

Ringing Groups
FARLINGTON RG, D A Bell, 38Holly Grove, Fareham, Hants, PO16 7UP.

ITCHEN RG, W F Simcox, 10 Holdaway Close, Kingsworthy, Winchester, SO23 7QH.

LOWER TEST RG, J Pain, Owlery Holt, Nations Hill, Kingsworthy, Winchester, SO23 7QY. 023 8066 7919; e-mail: jessp@hwt.org.uk

RSPB Local Groups
BASINGSTOKE, (1979; 90). Peter Hutchins, 35 Woodlands, Overton, Whitchurch, RG25 3HN. 01256 770831.

NORTH EAST HAMPSHIRE, (1976; 350). Graham Dumbleton, 28 Castle Street, Fleet, Hants, GU52 7ST. 01252 622699.

PORTSMOUTH, (1974; 205). Gordon Humby, 19 Charlesworth Gardens, Waterlooville, Hants, PO7 6AU. 02392 353949.

WINCHESTER & DISTRICT, (1974; 152).

Maurice Walker, Jesmond, 1 Compton Way, Olivers Battery, Winchester, SO22 4EY. 01962 854033.

Wildlife Hospital
NEW FOREST OWL SANCTUARY, Bruce Berry, New Forest Owl Sanctuary, Crow Lane, Crow, Ringwood, Hants, BH24 1EA. 01425 476487; e-mail: nfosowls@aol.com
www.owlsanctuary.co.uk
A selection of Owls, Hawks and Falcons from around the world with flying demonstrations at set times throughout the day. An opportunity to observe birds of prey at close range, an enjoyable day for the whole family. Open daily Feb to Nov.

Wildlife Trust
HAMPSHIRE WILDLIFE TRUST, (1960; 11,295). 8 Romsey Road, Eastleigh, Hants, SO50 9AL. 023 8061 3636; (fax) 023 8061 2233;
e-mail: hampswt@cix.co.uk

HEREFORDSHIRE

Bird Recorder
Steve Coney, 5 Springfield Road, Withington, Hereford, HR1 3RU. 01432 850068;
e-mail: coney@bluecarrots.com

Bird Report
THE YELLOWHAMMER - Herefordshire Ornithological Club annual report, (1951-), from Mr I Evans, 12 Brockington Drive, Tupsley, Hereford HR1 1TA. 01432 265509;
e-mail: iforelaine@care4free.net.

BTO Regional Representative
Steve Coney, 5 Springfield Road, Withington, Hereford, HR1 3RU. 01432 850068;
e-mail: coney@bluecarrots.com

Club
HEREFORDSHIRE ORNITHOLOGICAL CLUB, (1950; 409). TM Weale, Foxholes, Bringsty Common, Worcester, WR6 5UN. 01886 821368; e-mail weale@tinyworld.co.uk.

Ringing Group
LLANCILLO RG, Dr G R Geen, 6 The Copse, Bannister Green, Felsted, Dunmow, Essex, CM6 3NP. 01371 820189; e-mail: thegeens@aol.com

Wildlife Hospital
ATHENE BIRD SANCTUARY, B N Bayliss, 61 Chartwell Road, Hereford, HR1 2TU. 01432 273259. Birds of prey, ducks and waders, seabirds, pigeons and doves. Heated cages, small pond. Veterinary support.

Wildlife Trust
HEREFORDSHIRE NATURE TRUST, (1962; 1450). Lower House Farm, Ledbury Road, Tupsley, Hereford, HR1 1UT. 01432 356872; (fax) 01432 275489; e-mail: herefordwt@cix.co.uk
www.wildlifetrust.org.uk/hereford

HERTFORDSHIRE

Bird Atlas/Avifauna
Birds at Tring Reservoirs by R Young et al (Hertfordshire Natural History Society, 1996).

Mammals, Amphibians and Reptiles of Hertfordshire by Hertfordshire NHS in association with Training Publications Ltd, 3 Finway Court, Whippendell Road, Watford WD18 7EN, (2001).

The Breeding Birds of Hertfordshire by K W Smith et al (Herts NHS, 1993).

Bird Recorder
Mike Ilett, 14 Cowper Crescent, Bengeo, Hertford, Herts, SG14 3DY.
e-mail: michael.ilett@uk.tesco.com

Bird Report
HERTFORDSHIRE BIRD REPORT (1898-1998), from Linda Smith, 24 Mandeville Rise, Welwyn Garden City, Herts.

BTO Regional Representative & Regional Development Officer
Chris Dee, 26 Broadleaf Avenue, Thorley Park, Bishop's Stortford, Herts, CM23 4JY. H:01279 755637; e-mail: chris_w_dee@hotmail.com

Clubs
FRIENDS OF TRING RESERVOIRS, (1993; 350). Judith Knight, 381 Bideford Green, Linslade, Leighton Buzzard, Beds, LU7 2TY. 01525 378161
www.tringreservoirs.btinternet.co.uk

HERTFORDSHIRE BIRD CLUB, (1971; 290) Part of Hertfordshire NHS. Jim Terry, 46 Manor Way, Borehamwood, Herts WD6 1QY. 020 8905 1461; e-mail: jim@jayjoy.fsnet.co.uk

HERTFORDSHIRE NATURAL HISTORY SOCIETY, Christine Shepperson, 63 Station Road, Smallford, Herts AL4 0HB.
e-mail: c.m.shepperson@herts.ac.uk

Ringing Groups
AYLESBURY VALE RG (main activity at

Marsworth), S M Downhill, 12 Millfield, Berkhamsted, Herts, HP4 2PB. 01442 865821; e-mail: smdjbd@waitrose.com

MAPLE CROSS RG, P Delaloye, 34 Watford Road, Croxley Green, Herts, WD3 3BJ. 01923 442182; e-mail: pdelaloye@tiscali.co.uk

RYE MEADS RG, D G Baggott, 86 Fordwich Rise, Hertford, SG14 2DE. www.rmrg.care4free.net

TRING RG, Mick A'Court, 6 Chalkshire Cottages, Chalkshire road, Butlers Cross, Bucks ,HP17 0TW. H:01296 623610; W:01494 462246; e-mail: mick@focusrite.com or a.arundinaceous.virgin.net

RSPB Local Groups
CHORLEYWOOD & DISTRICT, (1977; 142). Sam Thomas, 36 Field Way, Rickmansworth, Herts WD3 2EJ. 01923 449917; e-mail: sam.thomas@tesco.net

HARPENDEN, (1974; 1000). Peter Thomley, 10 Lea Road, Harpenden, Herts, AL5 4PG. 01582 620755.

HEMEL HEMPSTEAD, (1973; 130). Paul Green, 207 Northridge Way, Hemel Hempstead, Herts, HP1 2AU. 01442 266637; e-mail: paul@310nrwhh.freeserve.co.uk www.hemelrspb.org.uk.

HITCHIN & LETCHWORTH, (1973; 106). Ms Jean Crystal, Amadeus House, Charlton, Hitchin, Herts, SG4 7TE. 01462 433912; e-mail: jeanlcrystal@aol.com http://uk.geocities.com/hitchin_letchworth_rspb

POTTERS BAR & BARNET, (1977; 1800 in catchment area). Stan Bailey, 23 Bowmans Close, Potters Bar, Herts, EN6 5NN. 01707 646073.

ST ALBANS, (1979; 1550 in catchment area). John Maxfield, 46 Gladeside, Jersey Farm, St Albans, Herts, AL4 9JA. 01727 832688; e-mail: peterantram@antram.demon.co.uk www.antram.demon.co.uk/

SOUTH EAST HERTS, (1971; 150). Phil Blatcher, 3 Churchfields, Broxbourne, Herts, EN10 7JU. 01992 441024; e-mail: SE_Herts_RSPB@hotmail.com

STEVENAGE, (1982; 1300 in catchment area). Mrs Ann collis, 16 Stevenage Road, Walkern, Herts, 01483 861547.

WATFORD, (1974; 610). John Britten, Harlestone, 98 Sheepcot Lane, Garston, Watford, WD25 0EB. 01923 673205; e-mail: john.britten@btinternet.com

Wildlife Hospital
SWAN CARE, Secretary, Swan Care, 14 Moorland Road, Boxmoor, Hemel Hempstead, Herts, HP1 1NH. 01442 251961. Swans. Sanctuary and treatment centre. Veterinary support.

Wildlife Trust
HERTS & MIDDLESEX WILDLIFE TRUST, (1964; 8500). Grebe House, St Michael's Street, St Albans, Herts, AL3 4SN. 01727 858901; (fax) 01727 854542; e-mail: hertswt@cix.co.uk

ISLE OF WIGHT

Bird Recorder
G Sparshott, Leopards Farm, Main Road, Havenstreet, Isle of Wight, PO33 4DR. 01983 882549.

Bird Reports
ISLE OF WIGHT BIRD REPORT (1986-) (Pre-1986 not available), from Mr DJ Hunnybun, 40 Churchill Road, Cowes, Isle of Wight, PO31 8HH. 01983 292880.

BTO Regional Representative
James C Gloyn, 3 School Close, Newchurch, Isle of Wight, PO36 0NL. 01983 865567; e-mail: gloynjc@yahoo.com

Clubs
ISLE OF WIGHT NATURAL HISTORY & ARCHAEOLOGICAL SOCIETY, (1919; 500). Dr Margaret Jackson, The Fruitery, Brook Hill, Brook, Newport, Isle of Wight, PO30 6EP. 01983 740015.

ISLE OF WIGHT ORNITHOLOGICAL GROUP, (1986; 135). Mr DJ Hunnybun, 40 Churchill Road, Cowes, Isle of Wight, PO31 8HH. 01983 292880.

RSPB Local Group
ISLE OF WIGHT, (1979; 206). Not known at time of going to press. For further information please contact RSPB, 01273 775333. www.rspb.org.uk

Wildlife Trust
Director, See Hampshire,

KENT

Bird Atlas/Avifauna
Birdwatching in Kent by DW Taylor. Meresborough Books 1985.

The Birds of Kent by D W Taylor et al (Kent Ornithological Society, 1981).

Kent Ornithological Society Winter Bird Survey by N Tardivel (KOS, 1984).

Bird Recorder
Don Taylor, 1 Rose Cottages, Old Loose Hill, Loose, Maidstone, Kent, ME15 0BN. 01622 745641; e-mail: Don.Taylor@care4free.net

Bird Reports
DUNGENESS BIRD OBSERVATORY REPORT (1989-), from Warden, see Reserves,

KENT BIRD REPORT (1952-), from Dave Sutton, 61 Alpha Road, Birchington, Kent, CT7 9ED. 01843 842541;
e-mail: dave@suttond8.freeserve.co.uk

SANDWICH BAY BIRD OBSERVATORY REPORT, from Warden, see Reserves.

BTO Regional Representative
RR, Martin Coath, 77 Oakhill Road, Sevenoaks, Kent, TN13 1NU. 01732 460710;
e-mail: mcoath@waitrose.com

Club
KENT ORNITHOLOGICAL SOCIETY, (1952; 720). Mrs Ann Abrams, 4 Laxton Way, Faversham, Kent ME13 8LJ. e-mail: chrisabrams@eurobell.co.uk

Ringing Groups
DARTFORD RG, R Taylor, 21 Dallin Road, Plumstead, London SE18 3NY.

DUNGENESS BIRD OBSERVATORY, David Walker, Dungeness Bird Observatory, Dungeness, Romney Marsh, Kent, TN29 9NA. 01797 321309;
e-mail: dungeness.obs@tinyonline.co.uk
www.dungenessbirdobs.org.uk

RECULVER RG, Chris Hindle, 42 Glenbervie Drive, Herne Bay, Kent, CT6 6QL. 01227 373070;
e-mail: christopherhindle@hotmail.com

SANDWICH BAY BIRD OBSERVATORY, K J Webb, Sandwich Bay Bird Observatory, Guilford Road, Sandwich, Kent, CT13 9PF. 01304 617341;
e-mail: kevwebb88@hotmail.com

SWALE WADER GROUP, Rod Smith, 67 York Avenue, Chatham, Kent, ME5 9ES. 01634 865863; e-mail: rod.Smith@care4free.net

RSPB Local Groups
CANTERBURY, (1973; 235). Jean Bomber, St Heliers, 30a Castle Road, Tankerton, Whitstable, Kent, CT5 2DY. 01227 277725.

GRAVESEND & DISTRICT, (1977; 260). Peter Heathcote, 9 Greenfinches, New Barn, Kent, DA3 7ND. 01474 704298:
e-mail: peter@heathcote100.freeserve.co.uk
www.gravesend-rspb.freeserve.co.uk

MAIDSTONE, (1973; 250). Dick Marchese, 11 Bathurst Road, Staplehurst, Tonbridge, Kent, TN12 0LG. 01580 892458.

MEDWAY, (1974; 230). Sue Carter, 31 Ufton Lane, Sittingbourne, ME10 1JB. 01795 427854
www.medway-rspb.pwp.blueyonder.co.uk

SEVENOAKS, (1974; 300). Bernard Morris, New House, Kilkhampton, Bude, Cornwall, EX23 9RZ. 01288 321727; or 07967 564699;(fax)01288 321838;
e-mail: bernard@amorris32.freeserve.co.uk

SOUTH EAST KENT, (1981; 220). Keith Shepherd, 23 Barton Road, Dover, Kent, CT16 9NF. 01304 225757.

THANET, (1976; 200). Paul Hale, 2 Shutler Road, Broadstairs, Kent, CT10 1HD. 01843 601482;
e-mail: paul.hale@care4free.net

TONBRIDGE, (1975; 120 reg attendees/1700 in catchment). Ms Gabrielle Sutcliffe, 1 Postern Heath Cottages, Postern Lane, Tonbridge, Kent, TN11 0QU. 01732 365583.

Wildlife Hospital
RAPTOR CENTRE, Eddie Hare, Ivy Cottage, Groombridge Place, Groombridge, Tunbridge Wells, Kent, TN3 9QG. 01892 861175; (fax) 01892 863761. www.raptorcentre.co.uk
Birds of prey. Veterinary support.

Wildlife Trust
KENT WILDLIFE TRUST, (1958; 10500). Tyland Barn, Sandling, Maidstone, Kent, ME14 3BD. 01622 662012; (fax) 01622 671390;
e-mail: kentwildlife@cix.co.uk
www.wildlifetrust.org.uk/kent

LANCASHIRE

Bird Atlas/Avifauna
An Atlas of Breeding Birds of Lancaster and District by Ken Harrison (Lancaster & District Birdwatching Society, 1995).

Breeding Birds of Lancashire and North Merseyside (2001), sponsored by North West Water. Contact: Bob Pyefinch, 12 Bannistre Court, Tarleton, Preston PR4 6HA.

Bird Recorder
(See also Manchester),
Lancashire and North Merseyside, Steve White,

102 Minster Court, Crown Street, Liverpool, L7 3QD. 0151 707 2744; e-mail: lwildlife@cix.co.uk

Bird Reports

BIRDS OF LANCASTER & DISTRICT (1959-), from Secretary, Lancaster & District BWS.
EAST LANCASHIRE ORNITHOLOGISTS' CLUB BIRD REPORT (1982-), from Secretary, £3.50.

BLACKBURN & DISTRICT BIRD CLUB ANNUAL REPORT (1992-), from Doreen Bonner, 6 Winston Road, Blackburn, BB1 8BJ. (tel/fax)01254 261480; www.blackburnbirds.freeuk.com.

FYLDE BIRD REPORT (1983-), from Paul Ellis, 18 Staining Rise, Staining, Blackpool FT3 0BU.

LANCASHIRE BIRD REPORT (1914-), from Secretary, Lancs & Cheshire Fauna Soc.

BTO Regional Representatives & Regional Development Officer

EAST RR, Tony Cooper, 28 Peel Park Avenue, Clitheroe, Lancs, BB7 1ET. 01200 424577; e-mail: tonycooper@beeb.net

NORTH & WEST RR, Keith Woods, 01524 811478.

SOUTH RR, Philip Shearwood, Netherside, Green Lane, Whitestake, Preston, PR4 4AH. 01772 745488; e-mail: phil.shearwood@virgin.net

Clubs

BLACKBURN & DISTRICT BIRD CLUB, (1991; 134). Jim Bonner, 6 Winston Road, Blackburn, BB1 8BJ. (tel/fax)01254 261480.

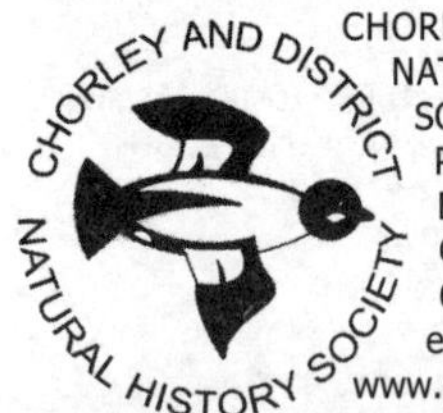

CHORLEY & DISTRICT NATURAL HISTORY SOCIETY, (1979; 170). Phil Kirk, Millend, Dawbers Lane, Euxton, Chorley, Lancs, PR7 6EB. 01257 266783; e-mail: philkirk@clara.net www.philkirk.clara.net/cdnhs/

EAST LANCASHIRE ORNITHOLOGISTS' CLUB, (1955; 45). Doug Windle, 39 Stone Edge Road, Barrowford, Nelson, Lancs, BB9 6BB. 01282 617401; e-mail: doug.windle@care4free.net

FYLDE BIRD CLUB, (1982; 60). Paul Ellis, 18 Staining Rise, Blackpool, FY3 0BU. 01253 891281; e-mail: paulellis@fyldebirdclub.freeuk.com or kinta.beaver@man.ac.uk www.fyldebirdclub.org

FYLDE NATURALISTS' SOCIETY, (1946; 120). Gerry Stephen, 10 Birch Way, Poulton-le-Fylde, Blackpool, FY6 7SF. 01253 895195.

LANCASHIRE & CHESHIRE FAUNA SOCIETY, (1914; 140). Dave Bickerton, 64 Petre Crescent, Rishton, Lancs, BB1 4RB. 01254 886257; e-mail: bickertond@aol.com www.lacfs.org.uk

LANCASHIRE BIRD CLUB, (1996). Dave Bickerton, 64 Petre Crescent, Rishton, Lancs, BB1 4RB. 01254 886257; e-mail: bickertond@aol.com www.lacfs.org.uk

LANCASTER & DISTRICT BIRD WATCHING SOCIETY, (1959; 200). Andrew Cadman, 57 Greenways, Over Kellet, Carnforth, Lancs, LA6 1DE. 01524 734462; e-mail: ldbws@yahoo.co.uk http://libweb.lancs.ac.uk/ldbws.htm.

ROSSENDALE ORNITHOLOGISTS' CLUB, (1976; 35). Ian Brady, 25 Church St, Newchurch, Rossendale, Lancs, BB4 9EX. 01706 222120.

Ringing Groups

FYLDE RG, G Barnes, 17 Lomond Avenue, Marton, Blackpool, FY3 9QL.

MORECAMBE BAY WADER RG, J Sheldon, 415 West Shore Park, Barrow-in-Furness, Cumbria, LA14 3XZ. 01229 473102.

NORTH LANCS RG, John Wilson BEM, 40 Church Hill Avenue, Warton, Carnforth, Lancs, LA5 9NU.

SOUTH WEST LANCASHIRE RG, J D Fletcher, 4 Hawksworth Drive, Freshfield, Formby, Merseyside, L37 7EZ. 01704 877837.

RSPB Local Groups

BLACKPOOL, (1983; 170). Alan Stamford, 6 Kensington Road, Cleveleys, FY5 1EP. 01253 859662.

LANCASTER, (1972; 210). John Wilson BEM, 40 Church Hill Avenue, Warton, Carnforth, Lancs, LA5 9NU.

Wildlife Trust

LANCASHIRE WILDLIFE TRUST, (1962; 3500). Cuerden Park Wildlife Centre, Shady Lane, Bamber Bridge, Preston, PR5 6AU. 01772 324129; (fax): 01772 628849; e-mail: lancswt@cix.co.uk www.wildlifetrust.org.uk/lancashire

LEICESTERSHIRE & RUTLAND

Bird Recorder

Rob Fray, 5 New Park Road, Aylestone, Leicester, LE2 8AW. 0116 223 8491; e-mail: robfray@fray-r.freeserve.co.uk

Bird Reports
LEICESTERSHIRE & RUTLAND BIRD REPORT (1941-), from Mrs S Graham, 5 Brading Road, Leicester, LE3 9BG. 0116 262 5505; e-mail: jsgraham83@aol.com

RUTLAND NAT HIST SOC ANNUAL REPORT (1965-), from Club Secretary.

BTO Regional Representative
LEICESTER & RUTLAND, Tim Grove, 35 Clumber Street, Melton Mowbray, Leicestershire LE13 0ND. 01664 850766.

Clubs
BIRSTALL BIRDWATCHING CLUB, (1976; 50). Ken J Goodrich, 6 Riversdale Close, Birstall, Leicester, LE4 4EH. 0116 267 4813.

LEICESTERSHIRE & RUTLAND ORNITHOLOGICAL SOCIETY, (1941; 462). Mrs Marion Vincent, 48 Templar Way, Rothley, Leicester, LE7 7RB. 0116 230 3405 www.lros.org.uk

MARKET HARBOROUGH & DISTRICT NATURAL HISTORY SOCIETY, (1971; 40). Mrs Marion Mills, 36 Nelson Street, Market Harborough, Leics LE16 9AY. 01858 462346.

RUTLAND NATURAL HISTORY SOCIETY, (1964; 256). Mrs L Worrall, 6 Redland Close, Barrowden, Oakham, Rutland, LE15 8ES. 01572 747302.

Ringing Groups
RUTLAND WATER RG, D Roizer, 38 Kestrel Road, Oakham, Rutland, LE15 6BU.

STANFORD RG, M J Townsend, 87 Dunton Road, Broughton Astley, Leics, LE9 6NA.

RSPB Local Groups
LEICESTER, (1969; 1600 in catchment area). Chris Woolass, 136 Braunstone Lane, Leicester, LE3 2RW. 0116 2990078; e-mail: chris@jclwoolass.freeserve.co.uk

LOUGHBOROUGH, (1970; 300). Robert Orton, 12 Avon Road, Barrow-on-Soar, Leics, LE12 8LE. 1509 413936.

Wildlife Trust
LEICESTERSHIRE & RUTLAND WILDLIFE TRUST, (1956; 3000). Longfellow Road, Knighton Fields, Leicester, LE2 6BT. 0116 270 2999; (fax) 0116 270 9555; e-mail: leicswt@cix.co.uk

LINCOLNSHIRE

Bird Recorders
NORTH, see below.

SOUTH, Steve Keightley (also acting as caretaker for North Lincolnshire). e-mail: s.keightley@tesco.net

Bird Reports
LINCOLNSHIRE BIRD REPORT inc GibraltarPointBirdObs(1979-), from R K Watson, 8 High Street, Skegness, Lincs, PE25 3NW. 01754 763481.

SCUNTHORPE & NORTH WEST LINCOLNSHIRE BIRD REPORT (1973-), from Secretary, Scunthorpe Museum Society, Ornithological Section,

BTO Regional Representatives & Regional Development Officer
EAST RR, Position vacant.

NORTH RR, Position vacant.

SOUTH RR, Richard & Kay Heath, 56 Pennytoft Lane, Pinchbeck, Spalding, Lincs, PE11 3PQ. 01775 767055; e-mail: heathsrk@ukonline.co.uk

WEST RR, Peter Overton, Hilltop Farm, Welbourn, Lincoln, LN5 0QH. Work 01400 273323; e-mail: nyika@biosearch.org.uk

RDO, Nicholas Watts, Vine House Farm, Deeping St Nicholas, Spalding, Lincs, PE11 3DG. 01775 630208.

Club
LINCOLNSHIRE BIRD CLUB, (1979; 220). M Harrison, Sherbrooke, Holme Road, Kirton Holme, Boston, Lincs, PE20 1SY. 01205 290575.

SCUNTHORPE MUSEUM SOCIETY (Ornithological Section), (1973; 50). Craig Nimick, 115 Grange Lane South, Scunthorpe, N Lincs, DN16 3BW. 01724 339659.

Ringing Groups
GIBRALTAR POINT BIRD OBSERVATORY, Mark Grantham, 12 Sybill Wheeler Close, Thetford, Norfolk, IP24 1TG. 01842 750050; (M)07818 497470.

MID LINCOLNSHIRE RG, J Mawer, 18 Standish Lane, Immingham, Lincs, DN40 2HA. 01469 518549.

WASH WADER RG, P L Ireland, 27 Hainfield

Drive, Solihull, W Midlands, B91 2PL. 0121 704 1168; e-mail: enquiries@wwrg.org.uk

RSPB Local Groups
GRIMSBY AND CLEETHORPES DISTRICT, (1986; 2200). Brian Sykes, 93 Humberstone Road, Grimsby, Lincs, 01472 320418.
e-mail: brian.sykes3@ntlworld.com
www.rspb.members.easyspace.com

LINCOLN, (1974; 250). Peter Skelson, 26 Parksgate Avenue, Lincoln, LN6 7HP. 01522 695747; e-mail: peterskelson@hotmail.com
www.lincoln.rspb.care4free.net

SOUTH LINCOLNSHIRE, (1987; 350). Barry Hancock, The Limes, Meer Booth Road, Antons Gowt, Boston, Lincs, PE22 7BG. 01205 280057.

Wildlife Hospital
FEATHERED FRIENDS WILD BIRD RESCUE, Colin Riches, 5 Blacksmith Lane, Thorpe-on-the-Hill, Lincoln, LN6 9BQ. 01522 684874.
All species. Purpose-built hospital unit. Heated cages, etc. Membership and adoption scheme available. Quarterly newsletter. Veterinary support.

Wildlife Trust
LINCOLNSHIRE WILDLIFE TRUST, (1948; 10800). Banovallum House, Manor House Street, Horncastle, Lincs, LN9 5HF. 01507 526667; (fax) 01507 525732; e-mail: info@lincstrust.co.uk
www.lincstrust.co.uk

LONDON, GREATER

Bird Atlas/Avifauna
New Atlas of Breeding Birds of the London Area by Keith Betton (London Natural History Society, in preparation).

Bird Recorder see also Surrey
Andrew Self, 16 Harp Island Close, Neasden, London, NW10 0DF.
e-mail: andrewself@lineone.net
www.users.globalnet.co.uk/~lnhsweb

Bird Report
CROYDON BIRD SURVEY (1995), from Secretary, Croydon RSPB Group, 020 8777 9370.

LONDON BIRD REPORT (20-mile radius of St Paul's Cath) (1936-), from Catherine Schmitt, 4 Falkland Avenue, London, N3 1QR.

BTO Regional Representative
LONDON & MIDDLESEX RR, Derek Coleman, 23c Park Hill, Carshalton, Surrey, SM5 3SA. 020 8669 7421.

Clubs
LONDON NATURAL HISTORY SOCIETY (Ornithology Section), (1858; 1145). Ms N Duckworth, 9 Abbey Court, Cerne Abbas, Dorchester, Dorset, DT2 7JH. 01300 341 195.

MARYLEBONE BIRDWATCHING SOCIETY, (1981; 88). Judy Powell, 7 Rochester Terrace, London, NW1 9JN. 020 7485 0863; e-mail: birdsmbs@yahoo.com
www.geocities.com/birdsmbs

Ringing Groups
LONDON GULL STUDY GROUP - (SE including Hampshire, Surrey, Susex, Berkshire and Oxfordshire). Mark Fletcher, 24 The Gowans, Sutton-on-the-Forest, York, YO61 1DJ.
e-mail: m.fletcher@csl.gov.uk

RUNNYMEDE RG, D G Harris, 22 Blossom Waye, Hounslow, TW5 9HD.
e-mail: daveharris@tinyonline.co.uk

RSPB Local Groups
BEXLEY, (1979; 100). David James, 78 Colney Road, Dartford, DA1 1UH. 01322 274791;
e-mail: dartdiva56@hotmail.com

BROMLEY, (1972; 285). Bob Francis, 2 Perry Rise, Forest Hill, London, SE23 2QL. 020 8669 9325. www.bromleyrspb.org.uk

CENTRAL LONDON, (1970; 350). Miss Annette Warrick, 12 Tredegar Sq, London, E3 5AD. 020 8981 9624; www.janja@dircon.co.uk/rspb
e-mail: annette@warricka.freeserve.co.uk

CROYDON, (1973; 4000 in catchment area). Sheila Mason, 5 Freshfields, Shirley, Croydon, CR0 7QS. 020 8777 9370.
www.croydon-rspb.org.uk

ENFIELD, (1971; 2700). Norman G Hudson, 125 Morley Hill, Enfield, Middx, EN2 0BQ. 020 8363 1431.

HAVERING, (1972; 270). David Coe, 8 The Fairway, Upminster, Essex, RM14 1BS. 01708 220710.

NORTH LONDON, (1974; 3000). John Parsons, 65 Rutland Gardens, Harringay, London, N4 1JW. 020 8802 9537.

NORTH WEST LONDON, (1983; 800). Bob Husband, The Firs, 49 Carson Road, Cockfosters, Barnet, Herts, EN4 9EN. 020 8441 8742.

PINNER & DISTRICT, (1972; 300). Dennis Bristow, 118 Crofts Road, Harrow, Middx, HA1 2PJ. 020 8863 5026.

RICHMOND & TWICKENHAM, (1979; 375). Steve Harrington, 93 Shaftesbury Way, Twickenham, TW2 5RW. 020 8898 4539.

WEST LONDON, (1973; 400). Alan Bender, 6 Allenby Road, Southall, Middx, UB1 2HQ. 020 8571 0285.

Wildlife Hospitals
WILDLIFE RESCUE & AMBULANCE SERVICE, Barry and June Smitherman, 19 Chesterfield Road, Enfield, Middx, EN3 6BE. 020 8292 5377. All categories of wild birds. Emergency ambulance with full rescue equipment, boats, ladders etc. Own treatment centre and aviaries. Veterinary support. Essential to telephone first.

Wildlife Trust
LONDON WILDLIFE TRUST, (1981; 7500). Harling House, 47-51 Great Suffolk Street, London, SE1 0BS. 0207 261 0447; (fax) 0207 261 0538; e-mail: londonwt@cix.co.uk
www.wildlifetrust.org.uk/london

MANCHESTER, GREATER

Bird Atlas/Avifauna
Breeding Birds in Greater Manchester by Philip Holland et al (1984).

Bird Recorder
Mrs A Judith Smith, 12 Edge Green Street, Ashton-in-Makerfield, Wigan, WN4 8SL. 01942 712615; e-mail: judith@gmbirds.freeserve.co.uk
www.gmbirds.freeserve.co.uk

Bird Reports
BIRDS IN GREATER MANCHESTER (1976-), from Mrs M McCormick, 91 Sinderland Road, Altrincham WA14 5JJ (only editions up to year 2000. Year 2001 onwards from County Recorder).

LEIGH ORNITHOLOGICAL SOCIETY BIRD REPORT (1971-), from J Critchley, 2 Albany Grove, Tyldesley, Manchester, M29 7NE. 01942 884644.

BTO Regional Representative & Regional Development Officer
RR, position vacant.

RDO, Jim Jeffery, 20 Church Lane, Romiley, Stockport, Cheshire, SK6 4AA. H:0161 494 5367; W:01625 522107 ext 112;
e-mail: j.jeffery@kudos-idd.com

Clubs
GREATER MANCHESTER BIRD CLUB, (1954; 70). Dr R Sandling, Maths Dept, The University, Manchester M13 9PL.
e-mail: rsandling@man.ac.uk

GREATER MANCHESTER BIRD RECORDING GROUP, (2002: 40) Restricted to contributors of the county bird report. Mrs A Judith Smith, 01942 712615; e-mail: judith@gmbirds.freeserve.co.uk
www.gmbirds.freeserve.co.uk

HALE ORNITHOLOGISTS, (1968; 58). Ms Diana Grellier, 8 Apsley Grove, Bowdon, Altrincham, Cheshire, WA14 3AH. 0161 928 9165.

LEIGH ORNITHOLOGICAL SOCIETY, (1971; 150). Mr D Shallcross, 10 Holden Brook Close, Leigh, Lancs, WN7 2HL. 01942 260161
www.leighos.org.uk

ROCHDALE FIELD NATURALISTS' SOCIETY, (1970; 90). Mrs J P Wood, 196 Castleton Road, Thornham, Royton, Oldham, OL2 6UP. 0161 345 2012; www.rochdaleonline.org (listed under societies and events).

STOCKPORT BIRDWATCHING SOCIETY, (1972; 80). Dave Evans, 36 Tatton Road South, Stockport, Cheshire, SK4 4LU. 0161 432 9513;
e-mail: Dave.36tatton@ntlworld.com

Ringing Groups
LEIGH RG, A J Gramauskas, 21 Elliot Avenue, Golborne, Warrington, WA3 3DU. 0151 929215.

SOUTH MANCHESTER RG, C M Richards, Fairhaven, 13 The Green, Handforth, Wilmslow, Cheshire, SK9 3AG. 01625 524527;
e-mail: cliveandray.richards@care4free.net

RSPB Local Groups
BOLTON, (1978; 550). Mrs Alma Scholfield, 29 Redcar Road, Little Lever, Bolton, BL3 1EW. 01204 791745.

MANCHESTER, (1972; 3600 in catchment area). Peter Wolstenholme, 31 South Park Road, Gatley, Cheshire, SK8 4AL. 0161 428 2175.

STOCKPORT, (1979; 250). Brian Hallworth, 69 Talbot Street, Hazel Grove, Stockport, SK7 4BJ. 0161 456 5328;
e-mail: bwh.hgsmgm@freeserve.co.uk

WIGAN, (1973; 80). Graham Tonge, 29 St Andrew's Drive, Wigan, Lancs. 01942 248238.

Wildlife Hospital
THREE OWLS BIRD SANCTUARY AND

RESERVE, Trustee, Nigel Fowler, Wolstenholme Fold, Norden, Rochdale, OL11 5UD. 01706 642162; 24-hr helpline 07973 819389; e-mail: info@threeowls.co.uk www.threeowls.co.uk
Registered charity. All species of wild bird. Rehabilitation and release on Sanctuary Reserve. Open every Sunday 1200-1700, otherwise visitors welcome by appointment. Bi-monthly newsletter. Veterinary support.

Wildlife Trust
Director, see Lancashire.

MERSEYSIDE & WIRRAL

Bird Atlas see Cheshire.

Bird Recorders see Cheshire, Lancashire.

Bird Reports see also Cheshire
HILBRE BIRD OBSERVATORY REPORT, from Warden, see Reserves.

NORTHWESTERN BIRD REPORT (1938-irregular), from Secretaries, Merseyside Naturalists' Assoc.

BTO Regional Representatives
MERSEYSIDE RR and RDO, Bob Harris, 2 Dulas Road, Wavertree Green, Liverpool, L15 6UA. (Work) 0151 706 4311; e-mail: harris@liv.ac.uk

WIRRAL RR, position vacant.

Clubs
LIVERPOOL ORNITHOLOGISTS' CLUB (membership by invitation), (1953; 40). Mrs V McFarland, The Cedars, Quakers Lane, Heswall, Wirral, CH60 6RD.

MERSEYSIDE NATURALISTS' ASSOCIATION, (1938; 260). Steven Cross, 58 Kingswood Avenue, Waterloo, Liverpool, L22 4RL.

WIRRAL BIRD CLUB, (1977; 150). Mrs Hilda Truesdale, Cader, 8 Park Road, Meols, Wirral, CH47 7BG. 0151 632 2705; www.wirralbirdclub.com.

Ringing Groups
MERSEYSIDE RG, P Slater, 45 Greenway Road, Speke, Liverpool, L24 7RY.

SOUTH WEST LANCASHIRE RG, J D Fletcher, 4 Hawksworth Drive, Freshfield, Formby, Merseyside, L37 7EZ. 01704 877837.

RSPB Local Groups
LIVERPOOL, (1966; 162). Chris Tynan, 10 Barker Close, Huyton, Liverpool, L36 0XU. 0151 480 7938; e-mail: christtynan@aol.com www.livbird.pwp.blueyonder.co.uk

SEFTON COAST, (1980; 150). Peter Taylor, 26 Tilston Road, Walton, Liverpool, L9 6AJ. 0151 524 1905; e-mail: ptaylor@liv.ac.uk www.scmg.freeserve.co.uk.

SOUTHPORT, (1974; 250). Brenda Nicholl, 01704 872421.

WIRRAL, (1982; 120). Steve Woolfall, 85 Ridgemere Road, Pensby, Wirral, Merseyside, CH61 8RR. 0151 648 6007; e-mail: swoolfall@btinternet.com http://website.lineone.net/~dave.jowitt/

Wildlife Trust
Director, See Lancashire.

NORFOLK

Bird Atlas/Avifauna
The Birds of Norfolk by Moss Taylor, Michael Seago, Peter Allard & Don Dorling (Pica Press, 1999).

Bird Recorder
Giles Dunmore, 49 NelsonRoad, Sheringham, Norfolk, NR26 8DA. 01263 822550.

Bird Reports
CLEY BIRD CLUB 10-KM SQUARE BIRD REPORT (1987-), from Secretary.

NAR VALLEY ORNITHOLOGICAL SOCIETY ANNUAL REPORT (1976-), from Secretary.

NORFOLK BIRD & MAMMAL REPORT (1953-), from Secretary, Norfolk and Norwich Naturalists Society, Castle Museum, Norwich, NR1 3JU.

NORFOLK ORNITHOLOGISTS' ASSOCN ANNUAL REPORT (1961-), from Secretary.

BTO Regional Representatives
NORTH-EAST RR, Chris Hudson, Cornerstones, Ringland Road, Taverham, Norwich, NR8 6TG. 01603 868805; e-mail: chris.hudson@osb.uk.net.

NORTH-WEST RR, Nick Gallichan, Walnut Cottage, High Road, Tilney cum Islington, King's Lynn, PE34 3BN. 01553 617310; e-mail: nick@strange-brew.freeserve.co.uk

SOUTH-EAST RR, position vacant.

SOUTH-WEST RR, Vince Matthews, Rose's Cottage, The Green, Merton, Thetford, Norfolk, IP25 6QU. 01953 884125;
e-mail: yam@yamatthews.u-net.com.

Clubs

CLEY BIRD CLUB, (1986; 300). Peter Gooden, 45 Charles Road, Holt, Norfolk, NR25 6DA. 01263 712368.

GREAT YARMOUTH BIRD CLUB, (1989; 70). Keith R Dye, 104 Wolseley Road, Great Yarmouth, Norfolk, NR31 0EJ. 01493 600705.

NAR VALLEY ORNITHOLOGICAL SOCIETY, (1976; 125). Ian Black, Three Chimneys, Tumbler Hill, Swaffham, Norfolk, PE37 7JG. 01760 724092; e-mail: ian_a_black@hotmail.com

NORFOLK & NORWICH NATURALISTS' SOCIETY, (1869; 490). Dr Tony Leech, 3 Eccles Road, Holt, Norfolk, NR25 6HJ. 01263 712282;
e-mail: leecha@dialstart.net
www.nnns.org.uk

NORFOLK BIRD CLUB, (1992; 350). Vernon Eve, Pebble House, The Street, Syderstone, King's Lynn, Norfolk, PE31 8SD. 01485 578121.

NORFOLK ORNITHOLOGISTS' ASSOCIATION, (1962; 1100). Jed Andrews, Broadwater Road, Holme-next-Sea, Hunstanton, Norfolk, PE36 6LQ. 01485 525406.

Ringing Groups

BTO NUNNERY RG, Dawn Balmer, 39 Station Road, Thetford, Norfolk, IP24 1AW.
e-mail: dawn.balmer@bto.org
www.nunnery-ringing.org.uk

HOLME BIRD OBSERVATORY, J M Reed, 21 Hardings, Panshanger, Welwyn Garden City, Herts, AL7 2EQ. 01707 336351.

NORTH WEST NORFOLK RG, J M Reed, 21 Hardings, Panshanger, Welwyn Garden City, Herts, AL7 2EQ. 01707 336351.

SHERINGHAM RG, D Sadler, Denver House, 25 Holt Road, Sheringham, Norfolk, NR26 8NB. 01263 821904; e-mail: dhsadler@onetel.net.uk

UEA RG, D Thomas, 15 Grant Street, Norwich, NR2 4HA.

WASH WADER RG, P L Ireland, 27 Hainfield Drive, Solihull, W Midlands, B91 2PL. 0121 704 1168; e-mail: enquiries@wwrg.org.uk

WISSEY RG, Dr S J Browne, End Cottage, 24 Westgate Street, Hilborough, Norfolk, IP26 5BN.
e-mail: sjbathome@aol.com

RSPB Local Groups

NORWICH, (1971; 330). Charles Seagrave, 2 Riverside Cottages, Barford, Norwich, NR9 4BE. 01603 759752;
e-mail:seagrave@connectfree.co.uk
www.NorwichRSPB.org.uk

WEST NORFOLK, (1977; 247). Mr R Gordon, 3 Rectory Close, King's Lynn, Norfolk, PE32 1AS. 01485 600937;
e-mail: robanngordon@btopenworld.com.

Wildlife Trust

NORFOLK WILDLIFE TRUST, (1926; 17,500). 72 Cathedral Close, Norwich, NR1 4DF. 01603 625540; (fax) 01603 630593;
e-mail: admin@nwt.cix.co.uk

NORTHAMPTONSHIRE

Bird Recorder

Paul Gosling, 23 Newtown Road, Little Irchester, Northants, NN8 2DX. 01933 227709;
e-mail: paul_gosling@lineone.net

Bird Report

NORTHAMPTONSHIRE BIRD REPORT (1969-), from Mr A Coles, 99 Rickyard Road, The Arbours, Northampton NN3 3RR.

BTO Regional Representative & Regional Development Officer

RR, Bill Metcalfe, Blendon, Rockingham Hills, Oundle, Peterborough, PE8 4QA. 01832 274797.

RDO, Bill Metcalfe, Blendon, Rockingham Hills, Oundle, Peterborough, PE8 4QA. 01832 274797.

Clubs

DAVENTRY NATURAL HISTORY SOCIETY, (1970; 18). Leslie G Tooby, The Elms, Leamington Road, Long Itchington, Southam, Warks, CV47 9PL. 0192 681 2269.

NORTHAMPTONSHIRE BIRD CLUB, (1973; 100). Mrs Eleanor McMahon, Oriole House, 5 The Croft, Hanging Houghton, Northants, NN6 9HW. 01604 880009.

Ringing Group

NORTHANTS RG, D M Francis, 2 Brittons Drive, Billing Lane, Northampton, NN3 5DP.

RSPB Local Groups

MID NENE, (1975; 350). Michael Ridout, Melrose, 140 Northampton Road, Rushden, Northants, NN10 6AN. 01933 355544.

NORTHAMPTON, (1978; 3000). Liz Wicks, 6 Waypost Court, Lings, Northampton, NN3 8LN. 01604 513991.

Wildlife Trust
Director, See Cambridgeshire.

NORTHUMBERLAND

Bird Atlas/Avifauna
The Atlas of Breeding Birds in Northumbria edited by J C Day et al (Northumberland and Tyneside Bird Club, 1995).

Bird Recorder
Ian Fisher, 74 Benton Park Road, Newcastle upon Tyne, NE7 7NB. 0191 266 7900;
e-mail: ian@hauxley.freeserve.co.uk
www.ntbc.org.uk

Bird Reports
BIRDS IN NORTHUMBRIA (1970-), from Muriel Cadwallender, 22 South View, Lesbury, NE66 3PZ. 01665 830884;
e-mail: tmcadwallender@lineone.net

BIRDS ON THE FARNE ISLANDS (1971-), from Secretary, Natural History Society of Northumbria.

BTO Regional Representative & Regional Development Officer
RR, Tom Cadwallender, 22 South View, Lesbury, Alnwick, Northumberland, NE66 3PZ. H:01665 830884; W:01670 533039;
e-mail: tmcadwallender@lineone.net

RDO, Muriel Cadwallender, 22 South View, Lesbury, Alnwick, Northumberland, NE66 3PZ. 01665 830884;
e-mail: tmcadwallender@lineone.net

Clubs
NATURAL HISTORY SOCIETY OF NORTHUMBRIA, (1829; 850). David C Noble-Rollin, Hancock Museum, Barras Bridge, Newcastle upon Tyne, NE2 4PT. 0191 232 6386;
e-mail: nhsn@ncl.ac.uk www.NHSN.ncl.ac.uk

NORTH NORTHUMBERLAND BIRD CLUB, (1984; 210). David Welch, 26 Armstrong Cottages, Bamburgh, Northumberland, NE69 7BA. 01668 214403.

NORTHUMBERLAND & TYNESIDE BIRD CLUB, (1958; 270). Sarah Barratt, 18 Frances Ville, Scotland Gate, Northumberland, NE62 5ST. 01670 827465:
e-mail: sarah.barratt@btopenworld.com.

NTBC
Northumberland & Tyneside Bird Club

Ringing Groups
BAMBURGH RS, Mike S Hodgson, 31 Uplands, Monkseaton, Whitley Bay, Tyne & Wear, NE25 9AG. 0191 252 0511.

NATURAL HISTORY SOCIETY OF NORTHUMBRIA, Dr C P F Redfern, The Natural History Society of Northumberland, The Hancock Museum, Newcastle on Tyne NE2 4PT.

NORTHUMBRIA RG. Secretary, B Galloway, 34 West Meadows, Stamfordham Road, Westerhope, Newcastle upon Tyne, NE5 1LS. 0191 286 4850.

Wildlife Hospitals
BERWICK SWAN & WILDLIFE TRUST, The Honourable Secretary, North Road Industrial Estate, Berwick upon Tweed TD15 1UN. 01289 302882; e-mail: mail@swan-trust.org.uk
www.swan-trust.org.uk Registered charity. All categories of birds. Pools for swans and other waterfowl. Veterinary support.

WILDLIFE IN NEED SANCTUARY, Mrs Lisa Bolton, Shepherds Cottage, Chatton, Alnwick, Northumberland, NE66 5PX. 01668 215281.
All categories of birds. Number of gulls restricted. Oiled birds sent to Swan & Wildlife Trust, Berwick. Heated bird room. Aviaries. Veterinary support. Visiting strictly by appointment.

Wildlife Trust
NORTHUMBERLAND WILDLIFE TRUST, (1962; 5000). The Garden House, St Nicholas Park, Jubilee Road, Newcastle upon Tyne, NE3 3XT. 0191 284 6884; (fax) 0191 284 6794;
e-mail: mail@northwt.org.uk

NOTTINGHAMSHIRE

Bird Recorders
Steve Keller, 17 Suffolk Avenue, Beeston Rylands, Notts, NG9 1NN. 0115 917 1452;
e-mail: s.keller@ntlworld.com

Bird Reports
LOUND BIRD REPORT (1990-), from Mr G Hobson, 11 Sherwood Road, Harworth, Doncaster, DN11 8HY. 01302 743654.

BIRDS OF NOTTINGHAMSHIRE (1943-), from Davis, 3 Windrush Close, Bramcote View, Nottingham, NG9 3LN. 0115 922 8547;
e-mail: prlg@talk21.com

NETHERFIELD WILDLIFE GROUP ANNUAL REPORT (1999-), from Neil Matthews, 4 Shellbourne Close, Heronridge, Nottingham NG5 9LL. £4 inc postage.

BTO Regional Representative
RR, Mrs Lynda Milner, 6 Kirton Park, Kirton,

Newark, Notts, NG22 9LR. 01623 862025; e-mail: lyndamilner@hotmail.com

Clubs

COLWICK PARK WILDLIFE GROUP, (1994; 150). Michael Walker, 14 Ramblers Close, Colwick, Nottingham, NG4 2DN. 0115 961 5494 www.colwick2000.freeserve.co.uk

LOUND BIRD CLUB, (1991; 50). P Hobson, 6 St Mary's Crescent, Tickhill, Doncaster, DN11 9JW. 07940 428326; e-mail: tichodroma@btinternet.com

NETHERFIELD WILDLIFE GROUP, (1999; 130). Philip Burnham, 57 Tilford Road, Newstead Village, Nottingham, NG15 0BU.

NOTTINGHAMSHIRE BIRDWATCHERS, (1935; 420). Ms Jenny Swindels, 21 Chatsworth Road, West Bridgeford, Nottingham. 0115 9812432. www.nottm.birds.care4free.net

WOLLATON NATURAL HISTORY SOCIETY, (1976; 99). Mrs P Price, 33 Coatsby Road, Hollycroft, Kimberley, Nottingham, NG16 2TH. 0115 938 4965.

Ringing Groups

BIRKLANDS RG, A D Lowe, 12 Midhurst Way, Clifton Estate, Nottingham, NG11 8DY. e-mail: birklandsringinggroup@tiscali.co.uk

NORTH NOTTS RG, Adrian Blackburn, Suleska, 1 Richmond Road, Retford, Notts, DN22 6SJ. 01777 706516; (M)07718 766873: e-mail: blackburns@suleska.freeserve.co.uk.

SOUTH WEST NOTTINGHAMSHIRE RG, K J Hemsley, 8 Grange Farm Close, Toton, Beeston, Notts, NG9 6EB. e-mail: k.hemsley@ntlworld.com

TRESWELL WOOD INTEGRATED POPULATION MONITORING GROUP, Chris du Feu, 66 High Street, Beckingham, Notts, DN10 4PF. e-mail: chris@beckingham0.demon.co.uk

RSPB Local Groups

MANSFIELD AND DISTRICT, (1986; 200). Chris Watkinson, 9 Ashford Rise, Sutton-in-Ashfield, Notts, NG17 2BB. 01623 403669.

NOTTINGHAM, (1974; 514). Andrew Griffin, Hawthorn Cottage, Thoroton, Notts, NG13 9DS. 01949 851426; www.notts-rspb.org.uk e-mail: andrew@thoroton.fsworld.co.uk

Wildlife Trust

NOTTINGHAMSHIRE WILDLIFE TRUST, (1963; 4300). The Old Ragged School, Brook Street, Nottingham, NG1 1EA. 0115 958 8242; (fax) 0115 924 3175; e-mail: nottswt@cix.co.uk www.wildlifetrust.org.uk/nottinghamshire

OXFORDSHIRE

Bird Atlas/Avifauna

Birds of Oxfordshire by J W Brucker et al (Oxford, Pisces, 1992).

The New Birds of the Banbury Area by T G Easterbrook (Banbury OS, 1995).

Bird Recorder

Ian Lewington, 119 Brasenose Road, Didcot, Oxon, OX11 7BP. 01235 819792; e-mail: ian@recorder.fsnet.co.uk

Bird Reports

BIRDS OF OXFORDSHIRE (1921-), from Roy Overall, 30 Hunsdon Road, Iffley, Oxford, OX4 4JE. 01865 775632.

BANBURY ORNITHOLOGICAL SOCIETY ANNUAL REPORT (1952-), from A Turner, 33 Newcombe Close, Milcombe, Nr Banbury, Oxon, OX15 4RN. 01295 720938.

BTO Regional Representatives & Regional Development Officer

NORTH, Frances Marks, 15 Insall Road, Chipping Norton, Oxon, OX7 5LF. 01608 644425.

SOUTH RR & RDO, Dr John Melling, 17 Lime Grove, Southmoor, Nr Abingdon, Oxon OX13 5DN. 01865 820867; e-mail: john@melling17lg.freeserve.co.uk.

Clubs

BANBURY ORNITHOLOGICAL SOCIETY, (1952; 100). Tony Clark, 11 Rye Close, Banbury, Oxon, OX16 7XG. 01295 268900.

OXFORD ORNITHOLOGICAL SOCIETY, (1921; 320). David Hawkins, The Long House, Park Lane, Long Hanborough, Oxon, OX29 8RD. 01993 880027; e-mail: dhawkins@dircon.co.uk www.oos.org.uk

Ringing Group

EDWARD GREY INSTITUTE, Dr A G Gosler, c/o Edward Grey Institute, Department of Zoology, South Parks Road, Oxford, OX1 3PS. 01865 271158.

RSPB Local Groups

OXFORD, (1977; 100). Ian Kilshaw, 6 Queens Court, Bicester, Oxon, OX26 6JX. Tel 01869 601901; (fax) 01869 600565; e-mail: ian.kilshaw@ntlworld.com www.rspb-oxford.org.uk

VALE OF WHITE HORSE, (1977; 275). David Lovegrove, 17 Chiltern Crescent, Wallingford, Oxon, OX10 0PE. 01491 835692.

Wildlife Trust
BBOWT, (1959; 11,000). The Lodge, 1 Armstrong Road, Littlemore, Oxford, OX4 4XT. 01865 775476;(fax) 01865 711301;
e-mail: bbowt@cix.co.uk

SHROPSHIRE

Bird Atlas/Avifauna
Atlas of the Breeding Birds of Shropshire (Shropshire Ornithological Society, 1995).

Bird Recorder
Geoff Holmes, 22 Tenbury Drive, Telford Estate, Shrewsbury, SY2 5YF. 01743 364621.

Bird Report
SHROPSHIRE BIRD REPORT (1956-) Annual, from Secretary, Shropshire, Ornithological Society.

BTO Regional Representative
Allan Dawes, Rosedale, Chapel Lane, Trefonen, Oswestry, Shrops, SY10 9DX. 01691 654245;
e-mail: dawes.rosedale@talk21.com

Club
SHROPSHIRE ORNITHOLOGICAL SOCIETY, (1955; 800). John Turner, 1 Brookside Gardens, Yockleton, Shrewsbury, SY5 9PR. 01743 821678;
e-mail: peregrineleada@aol.com
www.shropshirebirds.com

RSPB Local Group
SHROPSHIRE, (1992; 240). Roger M Evans, 31 The Wheatlands, Bridgnorth, WV16 5BD.

Wildlife Trust
SHROPSHIRE WILDLIFE TRUST, (1962; 2000). 167 Frankwell, Shrewsbury, SY3 8LG. 01743 241691; (fax) 01743 366671;
e-mail: shropshirewt@cix.co.uk
www.shropshirewildlifetrust.org.uk

SOMERSET & BRISTOL

Bird Atlas/Avifauna
Atlas of Breeding Birds in Avon 1988-91 by R L Bland and John Tully (John Tully, 6 Falcondale Walk, Westbury-on-Trym, Bristol BS9 3JG, 1992).

The Birds of Exmoor and Dartmoor by DK Ballance and BD Gibbs. (Isabelline Books, 2 Highbury House, 8 Woodland Crescent, Falmouth TR11 4QS. 2003)

Bird Recorders
Brian D Gibbs, 23 Lyngford Road, Taunton, Somerset, TA2 7EE. 01823 274887;
e-mail: brian.gibbs@virgin.net
www.somornithosoc.freeserve.co.uk

BATH, NE SOMERSET, BRISTOL, S GLOS, Harvey Rose, 12 Birbeck Road, Bristol, BS9 1BD. H:0117 968 1638; W:0117 928 7992;
e-mail: h.e.rose@bris.ac.uk

Bird Reports
AVON BIRD REPORT (1977-), from Dr HE Rose, 12 Birbeck Road, Bristol BS9 1BD.

EXMOOR NATURALIST (1974-), from Secretary, Exmoor Natural History Society.

SOMERSET BIRDS (1913-), from David Ballance, Flat 2, Dunboyne, Bratton Lane, Minehead, Somerset, TA24 8SQ. 01643 706820.

BTO Regional Representatives & Secretary
AVON RR, Richard L Bland, 11 Percival Road, Bristol, BS8 3LN. 01179 734828;
e-mail: richardbland@blueyonder.co.uk

AVON REGIONAL SECRETARY, John Tully, 6 Falcondale Walk, Westbury-on-Trym, Bristol, BS9 3JG. 0117 950 0992; e-mail: johntully4@aol.com

SOMERSET RR, Eve Tigwell, Hawthorne Cottage, 3 Friggle Street, Frome, Somerset, BA11 5LP. 01373 451630;
e-mail: evetigwell@aol.com

Clubs
BRISTOL NATURALISTS' SOCIETY (Ornithological Section), (1862; 550). Dr Mary Hill, 15 Montrose Avenue, Redland, Bristol, BS6 6EH. 0117 942 2193; e-mail: terry@jhill15.fsnet.co.uk
www.bristolnats.org.uk

BRISTOL ORNITHOLOGICAL CLUB, (1966; 690). Mrs Judy Copeland, 19 St George's Hill, Easton-in-Gordano, North Somerset, BS20 0PS. (tel/fax) 01275 373554;
e-mail: judy.copeland@ukgateway.net
www.boc-bristol.org.uk

CAM VALLEY WILDLIFE GROUP, (1994: 295). Helena Crouch, Bronwen, Farrington Road, Paulton, Bristol, BS39 7LP. 01761 410731.
e-mail: jim-helena@supanet.com
www.camvalleywildlifegroup.org.uk

EXMOOR NATURAL HISTORY SOCIETY, (1974; 450). Miss Caroline Giddens, 12 King George Road, Minehead, Somerset, TA24 5JD. 01643 707624; e-mail: carol.enhs@virgin.net

MID-SOMERSET NATURALISTS' SOCIETY, (1949; 20). Roy Brearly, 2 Quayside, Bridgwater, Somerset, TA6 3TA. 01278 427100.

SOMERSET ORNITHOLOGICAL SOCIETY, (1923; 350). Miss Sarah Beavis, The Old Surgery, 4 The Barton, Hatch Beauchamp, Taunton, Somerset, TA3 6SG. 01823 480948.

Ringing Groups

CHEW VALLEY RS, W R White, Church View Cottage, Mead Lane, Blagdon, N Somerset, BS40 7UA. 01761 463157 (evgs); e-mail: warwickw@architen.com

GORDANO VALLEY RG, Lyndon Roberts, 20 Glebe Road, Long Ashton, Bristol, BS41 9LH. 01275 392722; e-mail: mail@lyndonroberts.com

RSPCA, S Powell, 1 Rosemill Cottage, Rosemill Lane, Ilminster, Somerset, TA19 5PR.

STEEP HOLM RS, A J Parsons, Barnfield, Tower Hill Road, Crewkerne, Somerset, TA18 8BJ. 01460 73640.

RSPB Local Groups

BATH (NE SOMERSET), (1989; 250). Anne Workman, 6 Englishcombe Way, Bath BA2 2EU. 01225 428091.

CREWKERNE & DISTRICT, (1979; 328). Denise Chamings, Daniels Farm, Lower Stratton, South Petherton, Somerset, TA13 5LP. 01460 240740; e-mail: rspb@crewkerne.fslife.co.uk www.crewkerne.fslife.co.uk.

TAUNTON, (1975; 148). Eric Luxton, 33 Hoveland Lane, Taunton, Somerset, TA1 2EY. 01823 283033.

WESTON-SUPER-MARE (N SOMERSET), (1976; 215). Don Hurrell, Freeways, Star, Winscombe, BS25 1PS. 01934 842717.

Wildlife Trusts

AVON WILDLIFE TRUST, (1980; 4500). Wildlife Centre, 32 Jacobs Wells Road, Bristol, BS8 1DR. 0117 926 8018; (fax) 0117 929 7273; e-mail: avonwt@cix.co.uk

SOMERSET WILDLIFE TRUST, (1964; 8000). Fyne Court, Broomfield, Bridgwater, Somerset, TA5 2EQ. 01823 451587; (fax) 01823 451671; e-mail: somwt@cix.co.uk www.wildlifetrust.org.uk/somerset

STAFFORDSHIRE

Bird Recorder

Mrs Gilly Jones, 4 The Poplars, Lichfield Road, Abbots Bromley, Rugeley, Staffs, WS15 3AA. 01283 840555.

Bird Report

See West Midlands.

BTO Regional Representatives

NORTH EAST, John Cameron. 01889 564568; e-mail: John.Cameron3@tesco.net

SOUTH & CENTRAL, Liz Palmer, 58 Fontenaye Road, Coton Green, Tamworth, Staffs, B79 8JU. 01827 52715; e-mail: LIZPALMER5@aol.com

WEST, Martin Godfrey. 01785 229 713; e-mail: MartinandRosie@aol.com

Clubs

WEST MIDLAND BIRD CLUB (STAFFORD BRANCH), Andy Lawrence, 14 Jack Haye Lane, Light Oaks, Stoke-on-Trent, ST2 7NG. 01782 253502.

WEST MIDLAND BIRD CLUB (TAMWORTH BRANCH), (1992). Barbara Stubbs, 19 Alfred Street, Tamworth, Staffs, B79 7RL. 01827 57865.

RSPB Local Groups

BURTON-ON-TRENT, (1973; 50). Dave Lummis, 121 Wilmot Road, Swadlincote, Derbys, DE11 9EN. 01283 219902. www.basd-rspb.co.uk.

LICHFIELD & DISTRICT, (1977; 1150). Ray Jennett, 12 St Margarets Road, Lichfield, Staffs, WS13 7RA. 01543 255195.

NORTH STAFFORDSHIRE, (1982; 176). John Booth, 32 St Margaret Drive, Sneyd Green, Stoke-on-Trent, ST1 6EW. 01782 262082; www.geocities.com/nsrspb.

SOUTH WEST STAFFORDSHIRE, (1972; 190). Mrs Theresa Dorrance, 39 Wilkes Road, Codsall, Wolverhampton, WV8 1RZ. 01902 847041.

Wildlife Hospitals

BRITISH WILDLIFE RESCUE CENTRE, Alfred Hardy, Amerton Working Farm, Stowe-by-Chartley, Stafford, ST18 0LA. 01889 271308. On A518 Stafford/Uttoxeter road. All species, including imprints and permanently injured. Hospital, large aviaries and caging. Open to the public every day. Veterinary support.

GENTLESHAW BIRD OF PREY HOSPITAL, Robert A Smith, 5 Chestall Road, Cannock Wood, Rugeley, Staffs, WS15 4RB. 01543 676372 www.gentleshawwildlife.co.uk
Registered charity. All birds of prey (inc. owls). Hospital cages and aviaries; release sites. Veterinary support. Also GENTLESHAW BIRD OF PREY AND WILDLIFE CENTRE, Fletchers Country Garden Centre, Stone Road, Eccleshall, Stafford. 01785 850379 (1000-1700).

RAPTOR RESCUE, BIRD OF PREY REHABILITATION, J M Cunningham, 8 Harvey Road, Handsacre, Rugeley, Staffs, WS15 4HF. 01543 491712; (Nat. advice line) 0870 241 0609; e-mail: mickcunningham@btinternet.com www.raptorrescue.org.uk
Birds of prey only. Heated hospital units. Indoor flights, secluded aviaries, hacking sites, rehabilitation aviaries/flights. Falconry rehabilitation techniques, foster birds for rearing young to avoid imprinting. Veterinary support. Reg charity no. 283733

Wildlife Trust
STAFFORDSHIRE WILDLIFE TRUST, (1969; 4000). Coutts House, Sandon, Stafford, ST18 0DN. 01889 508534; (fax) 01889 508422; e-mail: staffswt@cix.co.uk

SUFFOLK

Bird Atlas/Avifauna
Birds of Suffolk by S H Piotrowski (February 2003).

Bird Recorders
NORTH EAST, Richard Walden, 21 Kilbrack, Beccles, Suffolk, NR34 9SH. 01502 713521; e-mail: walden1@supanet.com

SOUTH EAST (inc. coastal region from Slaughden Quay southwards), Brian Thompson, e-mail: brianhilli@aol.com

WEST (whole of Suffolk W of Stowmarket, inc. Breckland), Colin Jakes, 7 Maltward Avenue, Bury St Edmunds, Suffolk, IP33 3XN. 01284 702215; e-mail: cjjakes@supanet.com

Bird Report
SUFFOLK BIRDS (inc Landguard Bird Observatory Report) (1950-), from Ipswich Museum, High Street, Ipswich, Suffolk.

BTO Regional Representative
Mick T Wright, 15 Avondale Road, Ipswich, IP3 9JT. 01473 710032; e-mail: micktwright@btinternet.com

Clubs
LAVENHAM BIRD CLUB, (1972; 54). Richard Michette, 7 Clopton Drive, Long Melford, Sudbury, Suffolk, CO10 9LJ. 01787 377741 (day).

SUFFOLK ORNITHOLOGISTS' GROUP, (1973; 650). Andrew M Gregory, 1 Holly Road, Ipswich, IP1 3QN. 01473 253816.

Ringing Groups
DINGLE BIRD CLUB, Dr D Pearson, 4 Lupin Close, Reydon, Southwold, Suffolk, IP18 6NW. 01502 722348.

LACKFORD RG, Dr Peter Lack, 11 Holden Road, Lackford, Bury St Edmunds, Suffolk, IP28 6HZ. e-mail: peter.diane@tinyworld.co.uk

LANDGUARD RG, Mr SH Piotrowski, 29 Churchfields Road, Long Stratton, Norfolk, NR15 2WH. 01508 531115.

MARKET WESTON RG, Dr R H W Langston, Walnut Tree Farm, Thorpe Street, Hinderclay, Diss, Norfolk, IP22 1HT. e-mail: rlangston@wntfarm.demon.co.uk

RSPB Local Groups
BURY ST EDMUNDS, (1982; 150). Trevor Hart, 7 Westgart Gardens, Bury St Edmunds, Suffolk, IP33 3LB. 01284 705165.

IPSWICH, (1975; 200). PL Wright, 116 Bucklesham Rd, Ipswich, Suffolk, IP3 8TU. 01473 273737; e-mail: plwright@compuserve.com

LOWESTOFT & DISTRICT, (1976; 130). Mr E Beaumont, 52 Squires Walk, Lowestoft, Suffolk, NR32 4LA. 01502 560126.

WOODBRIDGE, (1986; 350). Colin Coates, 42A Bredfield Road, Woodbridge, Suffolk, IP12 1JE. 01394 385209.

Wildlife Trust
SUFFOLK WILDLIFE TRUST, (1961; 15,000). Brooke House, The Green, Ashbocking, Ipswich, IP6 9JY. 01473 890089; (fax) 01473 890165; e-mail: suffolkwildlife@cix.co.uk www.wildlifetrust.org.uk/suffolk

SURREY

Bird Atlas/Avifauna
Birds of Surrey (avifauna). Due 2004.

Bird Recorder
SURREY (includes Greater London south of the Thames and east to the Surrey Docks). Jeffery Wheatley, 9 Copse Edge, Elstead, Godalming, Surrey, GU8 6DJ. 01252 702450;(fax) 01252 703650.

Bird Report
SURBITON AND DISTRICT BIRD WATCHING SOCIETY (1972-), from Thelma Caine, 21 More Lane, Esher, Surrey KT10 8AJ.

SURREY BIRD REPORT (1952-), from J Gates, 90 The Street, Wrecclesham, Farnham, Surrey, GU10 4QR.

BTO Regional Representative
Hugh Evans, 31 Crescent Road, Shepperton, Middx, TW17 8BL. 01932 227781;
e-mail: hugh_w_evans@lineone.net

Clubs
SURBITON & DISTRICT BIRDWATCHING SOCIETY, (1954; 200). Gary Caine, 21 More Lane, Esher, Surrey KT10 8AJ. 01372 468432;
e-mail: birds@sdbws.ndo.co.uk
www.sdbws.ndo.co.uk

SURREY BIRD CLUB, (1957; 420). Mrs Jill Cook, Moorings, Vale Wood Drive, Lower Bourne, Farnham, Surrey, GU10 3HW. 01252 792876;
e-mail: jilck@aol.com
www.surreybirdclub.org.uk

Ringing Groups
HERSHAM RG, A J Beasley, 29 Selbourne Avenue, New Haw, Weybridge, Surrey, KT15 3RB. e-mail: abeasley00@hotmail.com

RUNNYMEDE RG, D G Harris, 22 Blossom Waye, Hounslow, TW5 9HD.
e-mail: daveharris@tinyonline.co.uk

RSPB Local Groups
DORKING & DISTRICT, (1982; 310). Alan Clark, 11 Maplehurst, Fetcham, Surrey, KT22 9NB. 01372 450607.

EAST SURREY, (1984; 3000 in catchment area). Brian Hobley, 26 Alexandra Road, Warlingham, Surrey, CR6 9DU. 01883 625404.

EPSOM & EWELL, (1974; 168). Janet Gilbert, 78 Fair(fax) Avenue, Ewell, Epsom, Surrey, KT17 2QQ. 0208 394 0405.

GUILDFORD AND DISTRICT, (1974; 550). Alan Bowen, Newlands, 13 Mountside, Guildford, Surrey, GU2 4JD. 01483 567041.

NORTH WEST SURREY, (1973; 140). Ms Mary Braddock, 20 Meadway Drive, New Haw, Surrey, KT15 2DT. 01932 858692;
e-mail: mary.braddock@virgin.net
www.nwsurreyrspb.org.uk

Wildlife Hospitals
THE SWAN SANCTUARY, See National Directory

WILDLIFE AID, Simon Cowell, Randalls Farm House, Randalls Road, Leatherhead, Surrey, KT22 0AL. 01372 377332; 24-hr emergline 09061 800 132 (50p/min); (fax) 01372 375183;
e-mail: wildlife@pncl.co.uk
www.wildlife-aid.org.uk/wildlife
Registered charity. Wildlife hospital and rehabilitation centre helping all native British species. Special housing for birds of prey. Membership scheme and fund raising activities. Veterinary support.

Wildlife Trust
SURREY WILDLIFE TRUST, (1959; 7500). School Lane, Pirbright, Woking, Surrey, GU24 0JN. 01483 488055; (fax) 01483 486505;
e-mail: surreywt@cix.co.uk
www.surreywildlifetrust.co.uk

SUSSEX

Bird Atlas/Avifauna
The Birds of Selsey Bill and the Selsey Peninsular (a checklist to year 2000), from: Mr O Mitchell, 4 Lodge Close, Middleton-on-Sea, West Sussex PO22 6NF.

The Birds of Selsey and Pagham 2003 from: Mr O Mitchell, (see above).

Birds of Sussex ed by Paul James (Sussex Ornithological Society, 1996).

Fifty years of Birdwatching 1953-2003 Shoreham District Ornithological Society 2003. From 50th Anniversary Book, SDOS, 7 Berberis Court, Shoreham by Sea, West Sussex.

Henfield Birdwatch 2000 Mike Russell (Editor), Henfield Birdwatch.

Bird Recorder
John A Hobson, 23 Hillside Road, Storrington, W Sussex, RH20 3 LZ. 01903 740155;
e-mail: janthobson@aol.com

Bird Reports
BIRDS OF RYE HARBOUR NR ANNUAL REPORT (1977- published every 5 years), from Dr Barry Yates, see Clubs.

PAGHAM HARBOUR LOCAL NATURE RESERVE ANNUAL REPORT, from Warden, see Reserves.

SHOREHAM DISTRICT ORNITHOLOGICAL SOCIETY ANNUAL REPORT (1952-), from Secretary.

SUSSEX BIRD REPORT (1963-), from J E Trowell, Lorrimer, Main Road, Icklesham, Winchelsea, E Sussex, TN36 4BS.
e-mail: membership@susos.org.uk
www.susos.org.uk

BTO Regional Representative
Dr A Barrie Watson, 83 Buckingham Road, Shoreham-by-Sea, W Sussex, BN43 5UD. 01273 452472; e-mail: abwatson@mistral.co.uk

Clubs
FRIENDS OF RYE HARBOUR NATURE RESERVE, (1973; 1500). Dr Barry Yates, 2 Watch Cottages, Nook Beach, Winchelsea, E Sussex, TN36 4LU. 01797 223862; e-mail: yates@clara.net www.naturereserve.ryeharbour.org

HENFIELD BIRDWATCH, (1999; 110). Mike Russell, 31 Downsview, Small Dole, Henfield, West Sussex, BN5 9YB. 01273 494311; e-mail: mikerussell@sussexwt.org.uk.

SHOREHAM DISTRICT ORNITHOLOGICAL

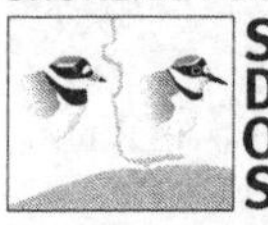

SOCIETY, (1953; 120). Mrs B Reeve, The Old Rectory, Coombes, Lancing, W Sussex, BN15 0RS. 01273 452497.

SUSSEX ORNITHOLOGICAL SOCIETY, (1962; 1500). Mr Richard Cowser, Beavers Brook, The Thatchway, Angmering, BN16 4HJ. 01903 770259; e-mail: cowser@btinternet.com www.susos.org.uk

Ringing Groups
BEACHY HEAD RS, R D M Edgar, 32 Hartfield Road, Seaford, E Sussex BN25 4PW.

CUCKMERE RG, Tim Parmenter, 22 The Kiln, Burgess Hill, W Sussex, RH15 0LU. 01444 236526.

RYE BAY RG, AJ Martin, Elms Farm, Pett Lane, Icklesham, Winchelsea, E Sussex, TN36 4AH. 01797 226374; e-mail: alan@wetlandtrust.org

STEYNING RINGING GROUP, B R Clay, 30 The Drive, Worthing, W Sussex, BN11 5LL. e-mail: brian.clay@ntlworld.com

RSPB Local Groups
BATTLE, (1973; 100). Miss Lynn Jenkins, 61 Austen Way, Guestling, Hastings, E Sussex, TN35 4JH. 01424 432076; e-mail: battlerspb@freewire.co.uk www.battlerspb.freewire.co.uk

BRIGHTON & DISTRICT, (1974; 450). Marion Couldery, 81 Hove Park Road, Hove, East Sussex BN3 6LN. 01273 555750; e-mail: MarionCouldery@aol.com

CHICHESTER & SW SUSSEX, (1979; 245). Robin Storkey, 219 Goring Road, Worthing, West Sussex, BN12 4PQ. 01903 700125.

CRAWLEY & HORSHAM, (1978; 148). Andrea Saxton, 104 Heath Way, Horsham, W Sussex, RH12 5XS.

EAST GRINSTEAD, (1998; 218). Nick Walker, 14 York Avenue, East Grinstead, W Sussex, RH19 4TL. 01342 315825.

EASTBOURNE & DISTRICT, (1993; 520). AM Squires, 5 Hyperion Avenue, Polegate, E Sussex, BN25 5HT. 01323 487392

HASTINGS & ST LEONARDS, (1983; 145). Richard Prebble, 1 Wayside, 490 Sedlescombe Road North, St Leonards-on-Sea, E Sussex, TN37 7PH. 01424 751790.

HEATHFIELD, (1979; 75). Mrs Dorothy Cull, 33 Horam Park Close, Horam, E Sussex, TN21 0HW. 01435 812093.

Wildlife Hospital
BRENT LODGE BIRD & WILDLIFE TRUST, Penny Cooper, Brent Lodge, Cow Lane, Sidlesham, Chichester, West Sussex, PO20 7LN. 01243 641672. All species of wild birds and small mammals. Full surgical and medical facilities (inc. X-ray). Purpose-built oiled bird washing unit. Veterinary support.

Wildlife Trust
SUSSEX WILDLIFE TRUST, (1961; 11000). Woods Mill, Shoreham Road, Henfield, W Sussex, BN5 9SD. 01273 492630; (fax) 01273 494500; e-mail: sussexwt@cix.co.uk

TYNE & WEAR

Bird Recorders
See Durham, Northumberland.

Bird Report See Durham, Northumberland.

Clubs
NATURAL HISTORY SOCIETY OF NORTHUMBRIA, (1829; 900). David C Noble-Rollin, Hancock Museum, Barras Bridge, Newcastle upon Tyne, NE2 4PT. 0191 232 6386; e-mail: david.noble-rollin@ncl.ac.uk

NORTHUMBERLAND & TYNESIDE BIRD CLUB, (1958; 270). Sarah Barratt, 3 Haydon Close, Red House Farm, Gosforth, Newcastle upon Tyne, NE3 2BY. 0191 213 6665.

RSPB Local Groups
NEWCASTLE UPON TYNE, (1969; 250). John Evans, 21 Beacon Drive, Brunswick Green, Wideopen, Newcastle upon Tyne, NE13 7HB. 0191 236 2369.

SUNDERLAND & SOUTH TYNESIDE, (1982; 25). Paul Metters, Almonte, 1 Bloomfield Drive, Elemore View, East Rainton, Houghton-le-Spring, Tyne & Wear, DH5 9SF. 0191 5120083.

WARWICKSHIRE

Bird Recorder
Jonathan Bowley, 17 Meadow Way, Fenny Compton, Southam, Warks, CV47 2WD. 01295 770069; e-mail: bowley@tesco.net

Bird Report
See West Midlands.

BTO Regional Representatives
WARWICKSHIRE, position vacant.

RUGBY, Barrington Jackson, 5 Harris Drive, Rugby, Warks, CV22 6DX. 01788 814466; e-mail: jacksonbj2@aol.com

Clubs
NUNEATON & DISTRICT BIRDWATCHERS' CLUB, (1950; 82). Alvin K Burton, 23 Redruth Close, Horeston Grange, Nuneaton, Warwicks, CV11 6FG. 024 7664 1591.

WEST MIDLAND BIRD CLUB (SOLIHULL BRANCH), George Morley, 64 Cambridge Avenue, Solihull, West Midlands, B91 1QF.

Ringing Groups
ARDEN RG, Roger J Juckes, 24 Croft Lane, Temple Grafton, Alcester, Warks B49 6PA. 01789 778748.

BRANDON RG, David Stone, Overbury, Wolverton, Stratford-on-Avon, Warks, CV37 0HG. 01789 731488.

RSPB Local Group
See West Midlands.

Wildlife Trust
WARWICKSHIRE WILDLIFE TRUST, (1970; 7000). Brandon Marsh Nature Centre, Brandon Lane, Coventry, CV3 3GW. 024 7630 2912; (fax) 024 7663 9556; e-mail: admin@warkswt.cix.co.uk www.wildlifetrust.org.uk

WEST MIDLANDS

Bird Atlas/Avifauna
The Birds of the West Midlands edited by Graham Harrison et al (West Midland Bird Club, 1982). Under revision.

Bird Recorder
Tim Hextell, 39 Windermere Road, Handsworth, Birmingham, B21 9RQ. 0121 551 9997; www.westmidlandbirdclub.com

Bird Reports
THE BIRDS OF SMESTOW VALLEY AND DUNSTALL PARK (1988-), from Secretary, Smestow Valley Bird Group.

WEST MIDLAND BIRD REPORT (inc Staffs, Warks, Worcs and W Midlands) (1934-), from Mr J Reeves, 9 Hintons Coppice, Knowle, Solihull, B93 9RF.

BTO Regional Representative
BIRMINGHAM & WEST MIDLANDS, vacant.

Clubs
SMESTOW VALLEY BIRD GROUP, (1988; 56). Frank Dickson, 11 Bow Street, Bilston, Wolverhampton, WV14 7NB. 01902 493733.

WEST MIDLAND BIRD CLUB, (1929; 2000). Mr MJ West, 6 Woodend Road, Walsall, WS5 3BG. 01922 639931; e-mail: westwoodend@care4free.net

WEST MIDLAND BIRD CLUB (BIRMINGHAM BRANCH), (1995; 800). John N Sears, 14 Ingram Street, Malmesbury, Wilts, SN16 9BX. 01666 824417.

Ringing Groups
MERCIAN RG (Sutton Coldfield), R L Castle, 91 Maney Hill Road, Sutton Coldfield, West Midlands, B72 1JT. 0121 686 7568.

RSPB Local Groups
BIRMINGHAM, (1975; 100). John Bailey, 52 Gresham Road, Hall Green, Birmingham, B28 0HY. 0121 777 4389. www.rspb-birmingham.org.uk

COVENTRY & WARWICKSHIRE, (1969; 130). Alan King, 69 Westmorland Road, Coventry, CV2 5BO. 024 7672 7348.

SOLIHULL, (1983; 2600 in catchment area). John Roberts, 115 Dovehouse Lane, Solihull, West Midlands, B91 2EQ. 0121 707 3101; e-mail: d.john.roberts@care4free.net

STOURBRIDGE, (1978; 150). Paul Banks, 4 Sandpiper Close, Wollescote, Stourbridge, DY9 8TD. 01384 898948; e-mail: picapica@tinyworld.co.uk.

SUTTON COLDFIELD, (1986; 250). Joanna Bazen, 66 Station Road, Wylde Green, Sutton Coldfield, B73 5LA. 0121 354 5626.

WALSALL, (1970). Mike Pittaway, 2 Kedleston Close, Bloxwich, Walsall WS3 3TW. 01922 710568; e-mail: chair@rspb-walsall.org.uk www.rspb-walsall.org.uk

WOLVERHAMPTON, (1974; 110). Ian Wiltshire, 25 Oakridge Drive, Willenhall, WV12 4EN. 01902 630418.

Wildlife Hospitals
KIDD, D J, 20 Parry Road, Ashmore Park, Wednesfield, Wolverhampton, WV11 2PS. 01902 863971. All birds of prey, esp. owls. Aviaries, isolation pens. Veterinary support.

WEDNESFIELD ANIMAL SANCTUARY, Jimmy Wick, 92 Vicarage Road, Nordley, Wednesfield, Wolverhampton, WV11 1SF. 01902 823064. Birds of prey, softbills, seed-eaters. Brooders, incubators, outdoor aviaries, heated accomm. Telephone first. Veterinary support.

Wildlife Trust
BIRMINGHAM AND BLACK COUNTRY WILDLIFE TRUST, (1980; 900). 28 Harborne Road, Edgbaston, Birmingham, B15 3AA. 0121 454 1199; (fax) 0121 454 6556; e-mail: urbanwt@cix.co.uk

WILTSHIRE

Bird Atlas/Avifauna
Birds of Wiltshire by J Ferguson-Lees and P Castle et al. Due early 2004.

Bird Recorder
Rob Turner, 14 Ethendun, Bratton, Westbury, Wilts, BA13 4RX. 01380 830862; e-mail: robt14@btopenworld.com.

Bird Report
Published in Hobby (journal of the Wiltshire OS) (1975-), from John Osbourne, 4 Fairdown Avenue, Westbury, Wilts BA13 3HS. 01373 864593.

BTO Regional Representatives
NORTH, Mark Lang, 1 Sherington Mead, Pewsham, Wilts, SN15 3TU. e-mail: mark@marknsams.fsnet.co.uk

SOUTH, Andrew Carter, Standlynch Farm, Downton, Salisbury, SP5 3QR. 01722 710382; e-mail: standlynch@aol.com

Clubs
SALISBURY & DISTRICT NATURAL HISTORY SOCIETY, (1952; 181). J Pitman, 10 The Hardings, Devizes Road, Salisbury, SP2 9LZ. 01722 327395.

WILTSHIRE ORNITHOLOGICAL SOCIETY, (1974; 504). Phil Deacon, 12 Rawston Close, Nythe, Swindon, Wilts SN3 3PW. 01793 528930.

Ringing Group
WEST WILTSHIRE RG, Mr M.J. Hamzij, 13 Halfway Close, Trowbridge, Wilts, BA14 7HQ.

RSPB Local Groups
NORTH WILTSHIRE, (1973; 104). Derek Lyford, 9 Devon Road, Swindon, SN2 1PQ. 01793 520997; e-mail: derek.lyford@the-tp.net

SOUTH WILTSHIRE, (1986; 800). Tony Goddard, Clovelly, Lower Road, Charlton All Saints, Salisbury, SP5 4HQ. 01725 510309.

Wildlife Hospital
CALNE WILD BIRD AND ANIMAL RESCUE CENTRE, Tom and Caroline Baker, 2 North Cote, Calne, Wilts, SN11 9DL. 01249 817893. All species of birds. Large natural aviaries (all with ponds), release areas, incubators, heated cages. Day and night collection. Veterinary support.

Wildlife Trust
WILTSHIRE WILDLIFE TRUST, (1962; 10,000). Elm Tree Court, Long Street, Devizes, Wilts, SN10 1NJ. 01380 725670; (fax) 01380 729017; e-mail: admin@wiltshirewildlife.org www.wiltshire-web.co.uk/wildlife

WORCESTERSHIRE

Bird Recorder
Andy Warr. 14 Bromsgrove St, Worcester WR3 8AR, 01905 28281. e-mail: worcs-recorder@westmidlandbirdclub.com

Bird Report See West Midlands.

BTO Regional Representative
G Harry Green MBE, Windy Ridge, Pershore Road, Little Comberton, Pershore, Worcs, WR10 3EW. 01386 710377; e-mail: harrygreen@britishlibrary.net

Ringing Group
WYCHAVON RG, J R Hodson, 15 High Green, Severn Stoke, Worcester, WR8 9JS. 01905 754919(day), 01905 371333(eve); e-mail: john.hodson@tesco.net.

Club
WEST MIDLAND BIRD CLUB (KIDDERMINSTER BRANCH). Celia Barton, 28A Albert Street, Wall Heath, KingswinfordDY6 0NA. 01384 839838;
e-mail: kidderminster@westmidlandbirdclub.com

RSPB Local Group
WORCESTER & MALVERN, (1980; 300). Garth Lowe, Sunnymead, Old Storridge, Alfrick, Worcester, WR6 5HT. 01886 833362.

Wildlife Trust
WORCESTERSHIRE WILDLIFE TRUST, (1968; 8000). Lower Smite Farm, Smite Hill, Hindlip, Worcester, WR3 8SZ. 01905 754919; (fax) 01905 755868; e-mail: worcswt@cix.co.uk
www.worcswildlifetrust.co.uk

YORKSHIRE

Bird Atlas/Avifauna
Atlas of Breeding Birds in the Leeds Area 1987-1991 by Richard Fuller et al (Leeds Birdwatchers' Club, 1994).

The Birds of Halifax by Nick Dawtrey (only 20 left), 14 Moorend Gardens, Pellon, Halifax, W Yorks, HX2 0SD.

Birds of The Harrogate District by John Mather (Harrogate and District Naturalists' Society 2001).

The Birds of Yorkshire by John Mather (Croom Helm, 1986).

*An Atlas of the Breeding Birds of the Huddersfield Area, 1987-1992.*by Brian Armitage et al (2000) - very few copies left.

Birds of Barnsley by Nick Addey (Pub by author, 114 Everill Gate Lane, Broomhill, Barnsley S73 0YJ, 1998).

Bird Recorders
VC61 (East Yorkshire), Geoff Dobbs, 12 Park Avenue, Hull, HU5 3ER. 01482 341524;
e-mail: geoffdobbs@aol.com

VC62 (North Yorkshire East), Russell Slack, 64 Sundew Gardens, High Green, Sheffield, S35 4DU. 01142 845300.

VC63 (South & West Yorkshire), Lance Degnan, 14 Fiddlers Drive, Armthorpe, Doncaster, DN3 4TT. 01302 835094; e-mail: lance.degnan@lineone.net

VC64 (West Yorkshire)/HARROGATE & CRAVEN, Jim Pewtress, 31 Piercy End, Kirbymoorside, York, YO62 6DQ. 01751 431001;
e-mail: jim@pewtress.co.uk

VC65 (North Yorkshire West), Nick Morgan, Linden, Church View, Ainderby Steeple, Northallerton, N Yorks, DL7 9PU. 01609 770168;
e-mail: nick.morgan1@virgin.net

Bird Reports
BARNSLEY & DISTRICT BIRD STUDY GROUP REPORT (1971-), from Secretary.

BRADFORD NATURALISTS' SOCIETY ANNUAL REPORT, from Mr I Hogg, 23 St Matthews Road, Bankfoot, Bradford, BD5 9AB.

BRADFORD ORNITHOLOGICAL GROUP REPORT (1987-), from Jenny Barker, 3 Chapel Fold, Slack Lane, Oakworth, Keighley, BD22 0RQ.

DONCASTER BIRD REPORT (1955-), from Mr M Roberts, 30 St Cecillia's Road, Belle Vue, Doncaster, DN4 5EG. 01302 361731.

FILEY BRIGG BIRD REPORT (1976-), from Mr C Court, 12 Pinewood Avenue, Filey, YO14 9NS.

FIVE TOWNS BIRD REPORT (1995-), from Secretary, Five Towns Bird Group.

HALIFAX BIRDWATCHERS' CLUB ANNUAL REPORT (1991-), from Nick C Dawtrey, 14 Moorend Gardens, Pellon, Halifax, W Yorks, HX2 0SD. 01422 364228.

HARROGATE & DISTRICT NATURALISTS' ORNITHOLOGY REPORT (1996-), from Secretary.

BIRDS IN HUDDERSFIELD (1966-), from Mr Brian Armitage, 106 Forest Road, Dalton, Huddersfield HD5 8ET.

LEEDS BIRDWATCHERS' CLUB ANNUAL REPORT (1949-), from Secretary.

BIRDS OF ROTHERHAM (1975-), from Secretary, Rotherham Orn Soc. Only back-issues available, £2 inc postage.

SCARBOROUGH AND DISTRICT BIRD REPORT (1996-), from Robin Hopper, 10A Ramshill Road, Scarborough, N Yorkshire YO11 2QE.

BIRDS IN THE SHEFFIELD AREA (1973-), from Tony Morris, 4A Raven Road, Sheffield, S7 1SB.
e-mail: tonyjmorris@blueyonder.co.uk
www.sbsg.org

THE BIRDS OF SK58 (1993-), from Secretary, SK58 Birders.

SPURN BIRD OBSERVATORY ANNUAL REPORT, from Warden, see Reserves.

NEW SWILLINGTON INGS BIRD REPORT (1989-), GL Haigh, 79 Whitehouse Avenue, Great Preston, Leeds LS26 8BN.

TOPHILL LOW BIRD REPORT (1996-), from Recorder for VC61.

WINTERSETT AREA ANNUAL REPORT (1988-), from Steve Denny, 13 Rutland Drive, Crofton, Wakefield, WF4 1SA. 01924 864487.

YORK ORNITHOLOGICAL CLUB ANNUAL REPORT (1970-), from Mr P Watson, 1 Oak Villa, Hodgson Lane, Upper Poppleton, York YO26 6EA.

YORKSHIRE NATURALISTS' UNION: BIRD REPORT (1940-) and *RARE AND SCARCE BIRDS REPORT 2000*, from club Secretary.

BTO Regional Representatives & Regional Development Officers

NORTH-EAST RR, Michael Carroll. 01751 476550.

NORTH-WEST RR, Gerald Light. 01756 753720.

SOUTH-EAST AND SOUTH-WEST RR, Chris Falshaw, 6 Den Bank Crescent, Sheffield, S10 5PD. 0114 230 3857; e-mail: chris.falsh@virgin.net

EAST RR, F X Moffatt, 102 Norwood, Beverley, E Yorks, HU17 9HL. 01482 882791; e-mail: frankie@xmofatt.freeserve.co.uk.

BRADFORD RR & RDO, Mike L Denton, 77 Hawthorne Terrace, Crosland Moor, Huddersfield, HD4 5RP. 01484 646990.

HARROGATE RR, Mike Brown, 48 Pannal Ash Drive, Harrogate, N Yorks, HG2 0HU. H:01423 567382; W:01423 507237; e-mail: mike@ppcmail.co.uk

LEEDS & WAKEFIELD RR & RDO, Peter Smale, 2A Hillcrest Rise, Leeds, LS16 7DL. 0113 226 9526; e-mail: petersmale@ntlworld.com

RICHMOND RR, John Edwards, 7 Church Garth, Great Smeaton, Northallerton, N Yorks, DL6 2HW. (H)01609 881476; (W)01609 780780 extn 2452; e-mail: john@garthwards.fsnet.co.uk

YORK RR, Rob Chapman, 12 Moorland Road, York, YO10 4HF. 01904 633558; e-mail: robert.chapman@tinyworld.co.uk

Clubs

BARNSLEY & DISTRICT BIRD STUDY GROUP, (1970; 35). Graham Speight, 58 Locke Avenue, Kingstone, Barnsley, South Yorkshire S70 1QH. 01226 321300.

BRADFORD NATURALISTS' SOCIETY, (1875; 30). D R Grant, 19 The Wheatings, Ossett, W Yorks, WF5 0QQ. 01924 273628.

BRADFORD ORNITHOLOGICAL GROUP, (1987; 200). Shaun Radcliffe, 8 Longwood Avenue, Bingley, W Yorks, BD16 2RX. 01274 770960; www.bradfordbirders.co.uk.

CASTLEFORD & DISTRICT NATURALISTS' SOCIETY, (1956; 25). Michael J Warrington, 31 Mount Avenue, Hemsworth, Pontefract, W Yorks, WF9 4QE. 01977 614954; e-mail: michael@warrington31mount.freeserve.co.uk.

DONCASTER & DISTRICT ORNITHOLOGICAL SOCIETY, (1955; 40). Mrs C McKee, 14 Poplar Close, Branton, Doncaster, DN3 3QA. 01302 532454.

FILEY BRIGG ORNITHOLOGICAL GROUP, (1977; 70). Jack Whitehead, 15 The Beach, Filey, N Yorkshire, YO14 9LA. 01723 514565.

FIVE TOWNS BIRD GROUP, (1994; 20). Robert Knight, 2 Milnes Grove, Airedale, Castleford, W Yorkshire, WF10 3EZ. 01977 510761; e-mail: f.t.b.g@lineone.net

HALIFAX BIRDWATCHERS' CLUB, (1992). Nick C Dawtrey, 14 Moorend Gardens, Pellon, Halifax, W Yorks, HX2 0SD. 01422 364228.

HARROGATE & DISTRICT NATURALISTS' SOCIETY, (1947; 400). Mrs J McClean, 6 Rossett Park Road, Harrogate, N Yorks, HG2 9NP. 01423 879095; e-mail: joan_mcclean@hotmail.com

HORNSEA BIRD CLUB, (1967; 35). John Eldret, 44 Rolston Road, Hornsea, HU18 1UH. 01964 532854.

HUDDERSFIELD BIRDWATCHERS' CLUB, (1966; 80). David Butterfield, 15 Dene Road, Skelmanthorpe, Huddersfield, HD8 9BU. 01484 862006; e-mail: dbutt52@hotmail.com

HULL VALLEY WILDLIFE GROUP, (1997; 175). The Secretary, Roy Lyon, 560 Hotham Road South, Hull HU5 5LE.

LEEDS BIRDWATCHERS' CLUB, (1949; 60). Mrs Shirley Carson, 2 Woodhall Park Gardens, Stanningley, Pudsey, W Yorks, LS28 7XQ. 0113 255 2145; e-mail: shirley.carson@care4free.net

NEW SWILLINGTON INGS BIRD GROUP, (1989; 20). Nick Smith, 40 Holmsley Lane, Woodlesford, Leeds, LS26 8RN. 0113 282 6154.

PUDSEY ORNITHOLOGY CLUB, (1989; 23). Alan Patchett, 102 Half Mile Lane, Leeds, LS13 1DB. 0113 2299038.

ROTHERHAM & DISTRICT ORNITHOLOGICAL SOCIETY, (1974; 90). Malcolm Taylor, 18 Maple Place, Chapeltown, Sheffield, S35 1QW. 0114 246 1848. http://members.lycos.co.uk/RDOS.

SCALBY NABS ORNITHOLOGICAL GROUP, (1993; 15). Ian Glaves, Halleykeld House, Chapel Lane, Sawdon, Scarborough, N Yorkshire, YO13 9DZ. 01723 859766.

SHEFFIELD BIRD STUDY GROUP, (1972; 160). Margaret Miller, 14 Worcester Close, Sheffield, S10 4JF. 0114 230 4110;
e-mail: margaret@margaret6.fsnet.co.uk

SK58 BIRDERS, (1993; 60). Andy Hirst, 15 Hunters Drive, Dinnington, Sheffield, S25 2TG. 01909 560310; www.sk58.freeserve.co.uk
e-mail: sk58birders@sk58.freeserve.co.uk

SORBY NHS (ORNITHOLOGICAL SECTION), (1918; 40). Derek Bateson, 41 Westbourne Road, Sheffield, S10 2QT. 0114 268 1575;
e-mail: president@sorby.org.uk

WAKEFIELD NATURALISTS' SOCIETY, (1851; 40). Philip Harrison, 392 Dewsbury Road, Wakefield, W Yorks, WF2 9DS. 01924 373604.

YORK ORNITHOLOGICAL CLUB, (1967; 80). Ian Traynor, The Owl House, 137 Osbaldwick Lane, York, YO10 3AY. www.yorkbirding.org.uk
e-mail: info@yorkbirding.org.uk

YORKSHIRE NATURALISTS' UNION (Ornithological Section), (1940; 500). W F Curtis, Farm Cottage, Atwick, Driffield, YO25 8DH. 01964 532477.

Ringing Groups

BARNSLEY RG, M C Wells, 715 Manchester Road, Stocksbridge, Sheffield, S36 1DQ. 0114 288 4211.

DONCASTER RG, D Hazard, 41 Jossey Lane, Scawthorpe, Doncaster, S Yorks, DN5 9DB. 01302 788044; e-mail: davehazard@netscapeonline.co.uk

EAST DALES RG, S P Worwood, 18 Coltsgate Hill, Ripon, N Yorks, HG4 2AB.

EAST YORKS RG, Peter J Dunn, 43 West Garth Gardens, Cayton, Scarborough, N Yorks, YO11 3SF. 01723 583149;
e-mail: pjd@fbog.co.uk; www.eyrg.org

SORBY-BRECK RG, Geoff P Mawson, Moonpenny Farm, Farwater Lane, Dronfield, Sheffield, S18 1RA. 01246 415097;
e-mail: gpmawson@hotmail.com

SOUTH CLEVELAND RG, W Norman, 2 Station Cottages, Grosmont, Whitby, N Yorks, YO22 5PB. 01947 895226; e-mail: wilfgros@lineone.net

SPURN BIRD OBSERVATORY, I D Walker, 31 Walton Park, Pannal, Harrogate, N Yorks, HG3 1EJ. 01423 879408.

TEES RG, E Wood, Southfields, 16 Marton Moor Road, Nunthorpe, Middlesbrough, Cleveland, TS7 0BH. 01642 323563;
e-mail; redshank@ntlworld.co.uk

WINTERSETT RG, P Smith, 16 Templar Street, Wakefield, W Yorks, WF1 5HB. 01924 375082.

RSPB Local Groups

AIREDALE AND BRADFORD, (1972; 3500 in catchment area). Peter Sutcliffe, 10 Southfield Mount, Riddlesden, Keighley, W Yorks, BD20 5HS. 01535 600937.

CLEVELAND, (1974; 200). Mark Stokeld, 38 Ash Grove, Kirklevington, Cleveland, TS15 9NQ. 01642 783819; e-mail: mark@stokeld.demon.co.uk www.stokeld.demon.uk

CRAVEN & PENDLE, (1986; 250). Ian Cresswell, Dove House, Skyreholme, Skipton, N Yorks, BD23 6DE. 01756 720355;
e-mail: ian@cravenandpendlerspb.org
www.cravenandpendlerspb.org

DONCASTER, (1984; 100). Sue Clifton, West Lodge, Wadworth Hall Lane, Wadworth, Doncaster, DN11 9BH. (tel/fax) 01302 854956;
e-mail: sue@westlodge53.freeserve.co.uk

EAST YORKSHIRE, (1986;110). Trevor Malkin, 49 Taylors Field, Driffield, E Yorks, YO25 6FQ. 01377 257325.

HUDDERSFIELD & HALIFAX, (1981; 200). David Hemingway, 267 Long Lane, Dalton, Huddersfield, HD5 9SH. 01484 301920.

HULL & DISTRICT, (1983; 334). Derek Spencer, The Old Brewhouse, Main Road, Burton Pidsea, Hull, HU12 9AX. 01964 670024.

LEEDS, (1975; 450). Linda Jenkinson, 112 Eden Crescent, Burley, Leeds, LS4 2TR. 0113 230 4595 www.rspb-leeds.ndo.co.uk.

SHEFFIELD, (1981; 475). John Badger, 24 Athersley Gardens, Owlthorpe, Sheffield, S20 6RW. 0114 247 6622; www.rspb-sheffield.org.uk.

WAKEFIELD, (1987; 150). Paul Disken, 6 Northfield Road, Dewsbury, W Yorks, WF13 2JX. 01924 456352.

WHITBY, (1977; 120). Fred Payne, 16 Hermitage Way, Sleights, Whitby, N Yorks, YO22 5HG. 01947 810022.

YORK, (1973; 600). Chris Lloyd, 7 School Lane, Upper Poppleton, York, YO26 6JS. 01904 794865;
e-mail: chris.a.lloyd@care4free.net
www.yorkrspb.org.uk.

Wildlife Hospital
ANIMAL HOUSE WILDLIFE WELFARE, Mrs C Buckroyd, 14 Victoria Street, Scarborough, YO12 7SS. 01723 371256; shop 01723 375162. All species of wild birds. Prior telephone call requested. Collection if required. Veterinary support.

Wildlife Trusts
TEES VALLEY WILDLIFE TRUST, (1979; 4000). Bellamy Pavilion, Kirkleatham Old Hall, Kirkleatham, Redcar, Cleveland, TS10 5NW. 01642 759900; (fax) 01642 480401; e-mail: teesvalleywt@cix.co.uk

SHEFFIELD WILDLIFE TRUST, (1985; 250). Norfolk House, Stafford Lane, Sheffield, S2 5HR. 0114 272 2377; (fax) 0114 279 6458; e-mail: sheffieldwt@cix.co.uk

YORKSHIRE WILDLIFE TRUST, (1946; 8000). 10 Toft Green, York, YO1 6JT. 01904 659570; (fax) 01904 613467; e-mail: yorkshirewt@cix.co.uk

SCOTLAND

For this section we are following the arrangement of the Scottish recording areas as set out by the Scottish Ornithologists' Club.

Bird Report
See Scottish Ornithologists' Club in National Directory.

Club
See Scottish Ornithologists' Club in National Directory.

ANGUS & DUNDEE

Bird Recorder
ANGUS & DUNDEE, Dan A Carmichael, 2a Reres Road, Broughty Ferry, Dundee, DD5 2QA. 01382 779981;
e-mail: dan@carmichael2a.fsworld.co.uk

Bird Report
ANGUS & DUNDEE BIRD REPORT (1974-), From Secretary, SOC Tayside Branch.

BTO Regional Representatives & Regional Development Officer
ANGUS RR & RDO, Ken Slater, Braedownie Farmhouse, Glen Clova, Kirriemuir, Angus, DD8 4RD. 01575 550233.

Clubs
ANGUS & DUNDEE BIRD CLUB, (1997; 166). Bob McCurley, 22 Kinnordy Terrace, Dundee, DD4 7NW. 01382 462944;
e-mail: megmccurley@onetel.com

SOC TAYSIDE BRANCH, (145). James Whitelaw, 36 Burn Street, Dundee, DD3 0LB. 01382 819391

Ringing Group
TAY RG, Ms S Millar, Edenvale Cottage, 1 Lydox Cottages, Dairsie, Fife, KY15 4RN.

RSPB Local Group
DUNDEE, (1972;110). Ron Downing, 3 Lynnewood Place, Dundee,DD4 7HB. 01382 451987.

ARGYLL

Bird Recorder
ARGYLL, Paul Daw, Tigh-na-Tulloch, Tullochgorm, Minard, Argyll, PA32 8YQ.
e-mail: monedula@globalnet.co.uk

Bird Reports
ARGYLL BIRD REPORT (1984-), from Dr Bob Furness, The Cnoc, Tarbet, Argyll G83 7DG. 01301 702603.

MACHRIHANISH SEABIRD OBSERVATORY REPORT (1992-), From Observatory, see Reserves & Observatories.

BTO Regional Representatives
ARGYLL (MULL, COLL, TIREE AND MORVERN), position vacant.

ARGYLL MAINLAND, BUTE, GIGHA AND ARRAN, David Wood, Drover's House, Bellanoch, Lochgilphead, Argyll, PA31 8SN.
e-mail: puffinus@stormie.idps.co.uk

ISLAY, JURA, COLONSAY RR, Dr Malcolm Ogilvie, Glencairn, Bruichladdich, Isle of Islay, PA49 7UN.
e-mail: maogilvie@indaal.demon.co.uk

Club

ARGYLL BIRD CLUB, (1983;170). Bill Staley, 16 Glengilp, Ardrishaig, Argyll, PA30 8HT.
e-mail: pabstaley@freeuk.com

ISLE OF MULL BIRD CLUB. (2001;130), Len White, Ard Dochas, Lochdon, Isle of mull, Argyll PA64 6AP. 01680 812335; e-mail: arddochas@aol.com

Ringing Group

TRESHNISH AUK RG, S W Walker, Snipe Cottage, Hamsterley, Bishop Auckland, Co Durham, DL13 3NX.
e-mail: snipe@snipe.screaming.net

AYRSHIRE

Bird Recorder

AYRSHIRE, Angus Hogg, 11 Kirkmichael Road, Crosshill, Maybole, Ayrshire, KA19 7RJ.
e-mail: recorder@ayrshire-birding.org.uk

Bird Reports

AYRSHIRE BIRD REPORT (1976-), from Dr RG Vernon, 29 Knoll Park, Ayr KA7 4RH. £4.50.

BTO Regional Representative

AYRSHIRE RR, position vacant.

Club

SOC AYRSHIRE, (1962; 135). Henry Martin, 9 Shawfield Avenue, Ayr, KA7 4RE. 01292 442086; www.ayrshire-birding.org.uk

RSPB Local Groups

CENTRAL AYRSHIRE, (1978; 50). James Thomson, Sundrum Smithy, Ayr, KA6 6LR. 01292 570351.

NORTH AYRSHIRE, (1976; 180). Isobel Passway, C/O Ardrossan Civic Centre Ardrossan, North Ayrshire. 01294 462485.

Wildlife Hospital

HESSILHEAD WILDLIFE RESCUE CENTRE, Gay & Andy Christie, Gateside, Beith, Ayrshire, KA15 1HT. 01505 502415.
All species. Releasing aviaries. Veterinary support.

BORDERS

Bird Atlas/Avifauna

The Breeding Birds of South-east Scotland, a tetrad atlas 1988-1994 by R D Murray et al. (Scottish Ornithologists' Club, 1998).

Bird Recorder

Ray Murray, 4 Bellfield Crescent, Eddleston, Peebles, EH45 8RQ. 01721 730677;
e-mail: ray.d.murray@ukgateway.net

Bird Report

BORDERS BIRD REPORT (1979-), From Malcolm Ross, The Tubs, Dingleton Road, Melrose, Borders.

BTO Regional Representative

RR, Alex Copland, Keeraun Hill, Banagher, Co Offaly, Ireland; e-mail: crex@eircom.net

Club

SOC BORDERS BRANCH, (90). Vicky McLellan, 18 Glen Crescent, Peebles, EH45 9BS. 01721 724580.

Ringing Group

BORDERS RG, (1991; 10) Dr T W Dougall, 38 Leamington Terrace, Edinburgh, EH10 4JL. (Office tel) 0131 469 5557; (Office fax) 0131 469 5599

CAITHNESS

Bird Recorders

CAITHNESS, Stan Laybourne, Old Schoolhouse, Harpsdale, Halkirk, Caithness, KW12 6UN. 01847 841244.

Bird Reports

CAITHNESS BIRD REPORT (1983-), From Julian Smith, St John's, Brough, Dunnet, Caithness;
e-mail: designsmith@madasafish.com

BTO Regional Representatives & Regional Development Officers

CAITHNESS, Hugh Clark, Bellfield, 3 Lindsay Place, Wick, Caithness, KW1 4PF. 01955 605372;
e-mail: hugh@lindsayplace.fsnet.co.uk

Clubs

SOC CAITHNESS BRANCH, (51). Stan Laybourne, Old Schoolhouse, Harpsdale, Halkirk, Caithness, KW12 6UN. 01847 841244.

CLYDE

Bird Atlas/Avifauna
A Guide to Birdwatching in the Clyde Area (2001) by Cliff Baister and Marin Osler (Scottish Ornithologists' Club, Clyde branch).

Clyde Breeding Bird Atlas (working title). In preparation.

Bird Recorder
CLYDE ISLANDS (Arran, Bute and the Cumbraes), Bernard Zonfrillo, 28 Brodie Road, Glasgow, G21 3SB. 0141 557 0791

CLYDE, Iain P Gibson, 8 Kenmure View, Howwood, Johnstone, Renfrewshire, PA9 1DR. 01505 705874.

Bird Reports
CLYDE BIRDS (1973-), from Jim & Valerie Wilson, 76 Laigh Road, Newton Mearns, Glasgow, G77 5EQ. e-mail: jim.val@btinternet.com

Club
SOC CLYDE BRANCH, (300). Alison Robertson, Flat2/3, 3 Priorwood Court,Glasgow, G13 1GE. 0141 9581747;
e-mail: alison@bogcotton.freeserve.co.uk

Ringing Groups
CLYDE RG, (1979; 18) I Livingstone, 57 Strathview Road, Bellshill, Lanarkshire, ML4 2UY.01698 749844; e-mail: iainliverg@aol.com

RSPB Local Groups
GLASGOW, (1972;141). Jim Coyle, 6 Westerlands, Anniesland, Glasgow, G12 0FB. 0141 579 7565.

HAMILTON, (1976;90). Mrs Isabel Crinean, 15A Central Avenue, Cambuslang, Glasgow, G72 8AY. 0141 641 1292; www.baronshaugh.co.uk

HELENSBURGH, (1975; 62). Alistair McIntyre, Craggan, Rosneath Road, Helensburgh, Dunbartonshire, G84 0EJ.
e-mail: almc@jameswatt.co.uk

RENFREWSHIRE, (1986; 200). Ms Alison Purssell, 2 Glencairn Place, High Street, Kilmacolm, PA13 4BT. 01505 872576.

DUMFRIES & GALLOWAY

Bird Recorders
NITHSDALE, ANNANDALE & ESKDALE, Steve Cooper, WWT Caerlaverock, Eastpark Farm, Caerlaverock, Dumfries, DG1 4RS.
e-mail: steve.cooper@wwt.org.uk
www.wwtck.free-online.co.uk

2, Paul N Collin, Gairland, Old Edinburgh Road, Minnigaff, Newton Stewart, Wigtownshire, DG8 6PL. 01671 402861;
e-mail: paul.collin@rspb.org.uk

Bird Report
DUMFRIES & GALLOWAY REGION BIRD REPORT (1985-), From Peter Norman, Low Boreland, Tongland Road, Kirkcudbright, DG6 4UU. 01557 331429.

BTO Regional Representatives
DUMFRIES RR, Duncan Irving, 12 Great Eastern Drive, Glancaple, Dumfries. 01387 770265.

KIRKCUDBRIGHT RR, Andrew Bielinski, 41 Main Street, St Johns Town of Dalry, Castle Douglas, Kirkcudbright, DG7 3UP. 01644 430418(eve); 01671 401075(day);
e-mail: andrew@bielinski.fsnet.co.uk

WIGTOWN RR, Geoff Sheppard, The Roddens, Leswalt, Stranraer, Wigtownshire, DG9 0QR.
e-mail: geoff.sheppard@tesco.net

Clubs
SOC DUMFRIES BRANCH, (1961; 105). Brian Smith, Rockiemount, Colvend, Dalbeattie, Dumfries, DG5 4QW. 01556 620617

SOC STEWARTRY BRANCH, (1976; 77). Miss Joan Howie, 60 Main Street, St Johns Town of Dalry, Castle Douglas, Kirkcudbrightshire, DG7 3UW. 01644 430226.

SOC WEST GALLOWAY BRANCH, (1975; 50). Geoff Sheppard, The Roddens, Leswalt, Stranraer, Wigtownshire, DG9 0QR.
e-mail: geoff.sheppard@tesco.net

Ringing Group
NORTH SOLWAY RG, Geoff Sheppard, The Roddens, Leswalt, Stranraer, Wigtownshire, DG9 0QR. e-mail: geoff.sheppard@tesco.net

RSPB Local Group
GALLOWAY, (1985;158). Robert M Greenshields, Nether Linkins, Gelston, Castle Douglas, DG7 1SU. 01556 680217;
e-mail: greenshields@netherlinkins.fsnet.co.uk

FIFE

Bird Recorders
FIFE REGION INC OFFSHORE ISLANDS

(NORTH FORTH), David Ogilvie, 25 Fillons Road, Kirkcaldy, Fife KY2 6LT.
e-mail: davidogilvie8@aol.com

ISLE OF MAY BIRD OBSERVATORY, Iain English, 19 Nethan Gate, Hamilton, S Lanarks, ML3 8NH. e-mail: i.english@talk21.com

Bird Reports
FIFE BIRD REPORT (1988-) (FIFE & KINROSS BR 1980-87), From Willie McBay, 41 Shamrock Street, Dunfermline, Fife, KY12 0JQ.01383 723464; e-mail: wmcbay@aol.com

ISLE OF MAY BIRD OBSERVATORY REPORT (1985-), From David Thorne, Craigurd House, Blyth Bridge, West Linton, Peeblesshire, EH46 7AH.

BTO Regional Representative
FIFE & KINROSS RR, Norman Elkins, 18 Scotstarvit View, Cupar, Fife, KY15 5DX. 01334 654348; e-mail: jandnelkins@rapidial.co.uk

Clubs
FIFE BIRD CLUB, (1985; 270). Willie McBay, 41 Shamrock Street, Dunfermline, Fife, KY12 0JQ. 01383 723464.

LOTHIANS AND FIFE MUTE SWAN STUDY GROUP, (1978), Allan & Lyndesay Brown, 61 Watts Gardens, Cupar, Fife, KY15 4UG.
e-mail: swans@allanwbrown.co.uk
www.swanscot.org.uk

SOC FIFE BRANCH, (1950; 170). Fiona Butler, 7 Marionfield Place, Cupar, Fife, KY15 5JN. 01334 654895.

Ringing Groups
ISLE OF MAY BIRD OBSERVATORY, Margaret Thorne, Craigurd House, West Linton, Peebles EH46 7AH. 01721 752612.

TAY RG, Ms S Millar, Edenvale Cottage, 1 Lydox Cottages, Dairsie, Fife, KY15 4RN.

Wildlife Hospital
SCOTTISH SPCA WILD LIFE REHABILITATION CENTRE, Middlebank Farm, Masterton Road, Dunfermline, Fife, KY11 8QN. 01383 412520
All species. Open to visitors, groups and school parties. Illustrated talk on oiled bird cleaning and other aspects of wildlife rehabilitation available. Veterinary support.

FORTH

Bird Recorder
UPPER FORTH, Dr C J Henty, Edgehill East, 7b Coneyhill Road, Bridge of Allan, Stirling, FK9 4EL. 01786 832166

Bird Report
FORTH AREA BIRD REPORT (1975-) - published in The Forth Naturalist and Historian, University of Stirling, From Dr Henty (see recorder) or Hon Sec. Lindsay Corbett, University of Stirling, Stirling FK9 4LA. 01259 215091.

BTO Regional Representative
Neil Bielby, 56 Ochiltree, Dunblane, Perthshire, FK15 0DF. e-mail: neil.bielby@ntlworld.com

Club
SOC CENTRAL SCOTLAND BRANCH, (1968; 101). Ian Wilson, 100 Causeway Head Road, Stirling FK9 5HJ. 01786 473877

RSPB Local Group
FORTH VALLEY, (1996; 150). David Redwood, 8 Strathmore Avenue, Dunblane, Perthshire FK15 9HX. 01786 825493; e-mail: d.redwood@tesco.net
http://forthrspb.p5.org.uk

HIGHLAND

Bird Atlas/Avifauna
The Birds of Sutherland by Alan Vittery (Colin Baxter Photography Ltd, 1997).

Birds of Skye by Andrew Currie. In preparation.

Bird Recorders
ROSS-SHIRE, INVERNESS-SHIRE, SUTHERLAND, Alistair McNee, Liathach, 4 Balnafettack Place, Inverness IV3 8TQ. 01463 220493; (M)07763 927814;
e-mail: aj.mcnee@care4free.net

Bird Reports
HIGHLAND BIRD REPORT (1991-), from Recorder. 2002 edition £6.50 including p&p.

SUTHERLAND BIRD REVIEW (2002-), from Alan Vittery, 164 West Clyne, Brora, Sutherland, KW9 6NH. 01408 621827.

BTO Regional Representatives & Regional Development Officers
INVERNESS & SPEYSIDE RR & RDO, Hugh Insley, 1 Drummond Place, Inverness, IV2 4JT.
e-mail: hugh.insley@freeuk.com

RUM, EIGG, CANNA & MUCK RR & RDO, Bob Swann, 14 St Vincent Road, Tain, Ross-shire, IV19 1JR. e-mail: bob.swann@freeuk.com

ROSS-SHIRE RR, position vacant.

SUTHERLAND, David Davenport. 01408 641 295.

SKYE RR, Robert McMillan. 01471 866305; e-mail: bob@skye.birds.com

Clubs
EAST SUTHERLAND BIRD GROUP, (1976; 80). Alan Vittery, 164 West Clyne, Brora, Sutherland, KW9 6NH. 01408 621827.

SOC HIGHLAND BRANCH, (1955; 136). Janet Crummy, Coalhaugh, Tomatin, Inverness, IV13 7YS. 01808 511261.

Ringing Groups
EAST ROSS RG, Ivan Brockway, Courthill, Tain, Ross-shire, IV19 1NE. 01349 852521.

HIGHLAND RG, Bob Swann, 14 St Vincent Road, Tain, Ross-shire, IV19 1JR.
e-mail: bob.swann@freeuk.com

RSPB Local Group
HIGHLAND, (1987; 198). Richard Prentice, Lingay, Lewiston, Drumnadrochit, Inverness, IV63 6UW. 01456 450526.

LOTHIAN

Bird Atlas/Avifauna
The Breeding Birds of South-east Scotland, a tetrad atlas 1988-1994 by R D Murray et al. (Scottish Ornithologists' Club, 1998).

Bird Recorder
David J Kelly, 20 Market View, Tranent, East Lothian, EH32 9AX.
e-mail: dj_kelly@btinternet.com

Bird Reports
LOTHIAN BIRD REPORT (1979-), from Recorder.

WEST LOTHIAN BIRD CLUB REPORT (1991-), From Secretary, West Lothian Bird Club.

BTO Regional Representative
Alan Heavisides, 9 Addiston Crescent, Balerno, Edinburgh, EH14 7DB.
e-mail: a.heavisides@napier.ac.uk

Clubs
EDINBURGH NATURAL HISTORY SOCIETY, (1869; 200). Mr Michael Osborne, 2 Old Woodside, Bush Estate, Penicuik, Midlothian, EH26 0PQ. 0131 445 3824.

FOULSHIELS BIRD GROUP, (1991; 5). Frazer Henderson, 2 Elizabeth Gardens, Stoneyburn, W Lothian, EH47 8BP. 01501 762972.

LOTHIANS AND FIFE MUTE SWAN STUDY GROUP, (1978; 12) Allan & Lyndesay Brown, 61 Watts Gardens, Cupar, Fife, KY15 4UG.
e-mail: swans@allanwbrown.co.uk

SOC LOTHIAN BRANCH, (1936; 440). John Hamilton, 30 Swanston Gardens, Edinburgh EH10 7DL. 0131 445 5317.

WEST LOTHIAN BIRD CLUB, (1990; 20). Alan Paterson, 17 Main Street, Winchburgh, Broxburn, W Lothian.

Ringing Group
LOTHIAN RG, Mr M Cubitt, 12 Burgh Mills Lane, Linlithgow,W est Lothian EH49 7TA.

RSPB Local Group
EDINBURGH, (1974;450). Hugh Conner, 22 Tippett Knowes, Winchburgh, West Lothian, EH52 6UW. e-mail: h.m.conner@blueyonder.co.uk
http://rspb-edinpwp.blueyonder.co.uk

MORAY & NAIRN

Bird Atlas/Avifauna *The Birds of Moray and Nairn* by Martin Cook (Mercat Press, 1992).

Bird Recorder
NAIRN, Martin J H Cook, Rowanbrae, Clochan, Buckie, Banffshire, AB56 5EQ. 01542 850296;
e-mail: martin.cook9@virgin.net

MORAY, Martin J H Cook, Rowanbrae, Clochan, Buckie, Banffshire, AB56 5EQ. 01542 850296.

Bird Reports
MORAY & NAIRN BIRD REPORT (1985-), from Moray Recorder.

BTO Regional Representatives
NAIRN RR, Bob Proctor, 94 Reid Street, Bishopmill, Elgin, Moray, IV30 4HH.
e-mail: bob.proctor@rspb.org.uk

MORAY RR, Bob Proctor, 94 Reid Street, Bishopmill, Elgin, Moray, IV30 4HH.
e-mail: bob.proctor@rspb.org.uk

NORTH EAST SCOTLAND

Bird Atlas/Avifauna
The Birds of North East Scotland by S T Buckland, M V Bell & N Picozzi (North East Scotland Bird Club, 1990).

Bird Recorder
NORTH-EAST SCOTLAND, Andrew Thorpe, 30 Monearn Gardens, Milltimber, Aberdeen, AB13 0EA. e-mail: andrewthorpe3@aol.com

Bird Reports
NORTH-EAST SCOTLAND BIRD REPORT (1974-), From Dave Gill, Drakemyre Croft, Cairnorrie, Methlick, Aberdeenshire, AB41 0JN. 01651 806252;
e-mail: dave@drakemyre.freeserve.co.uk

NORTH SEA BIRD CLUB ANNUAL REPORT (1979-), from NSBC Recorder, see below.

BTO Regional Representatives & Regional Development Officer
ABERDEEN RDO, Kath Hamper, 9 Mid Street, Inverallochy, Fraserburgh, Aberdeenshire, AB43 8YA. 01346 583015

ABERDEEN NORTH RR, Peter Walker, Westgate House, Udny, Ellon, Aberdeenshire, AB41 6SD. e-mail: pkwalkers@aol.com

KINCARDINE & DEESIDE, Graham Cooper, Westbank, Beltie Road, Torphins, Banchory, Aberdeen, AB31 4JT. H:01339 882706

Clubs
NORTH SEA BIRD CLUB, (1979; 200). Andrew Thorpe, (Recorder), Ocean Laboratory and Centre for Ecology, Aberdeen University, Newburgh, Ellon, Aberdeenshire, AB41 6AA.
e-mail: a.thorpe@abdn.ac.uk

SOC GRAMPIAN BRANCH, (1956; 110). John Wills, Bilbo, Monymusk, Inverurie, Aberdeenshire, AB51 7HA. 01467 651296;
e-mail: bilbo@monymusk.freeserve.co.uk

Ringing Groups
ABERDEEN UNIVERSITY RG, Andrew Thorpe, Ocean Laboratory and Centre for Ecology, Aberdeen University, Newburgh, Ellon, Aberdeenshire, AB41 6AA.
e-mail: a.thorpe@abdn.ac.uk

GRAMPIAN RG, R Duncan, 86 Broadfold Drive, Bridge of Don, Aberdeen, AB23 8PP.
e-mail: Raymond@waxwing.fsnet.co.uk

RSPB Local Group
ABERDEEN, (1975; 190). Dr MJ Williams, 48 Oakhill Road, Aberdeen,AB15 5ES. 01224 208046.

Wildlife Hospital
GRAMPIAN WILDLIFE REHABILITATION TRUST, 40 High Street, New Deer, Turriff, Aberdeenshire, AB53 6SX. 01771 644489. Veterinary surgeon. Access to full practice facilities. Will care for all species of birds.

ORKNEY

Bird Atlas/Avifauna
The Birds of Orkney by CJ Booth et al (The Orkney Press, 1984).

Bird Recorder
Jim Williams, Frurholm, Finstown, Orkney, KW17 2EQ. 01856 761317;
e-mail: jim@geniefea.freeserve.co.uk

Bird Report
ORKNEY BIRD REPORT (inc North Ronaldsay Bird Report) (1974-), from Mr EJ Williams, Fairholm, Finstown, Orkney, KW17 2EQ.
e-mail: jim@geniefea.freeserve.co.uk

BTO Regional Representative & Regional Development Officer
Colin Corse, Garrisdale, Lynn Park, Kirkwall, Orkney, KW15 1SL. e-mail: ccorse@aol.com

Club
SOC ORKNEY BRANCH, (1993; 15). Stuart Williams, Crafty, Firth, Orkney, KW17 2ES.
e-mail: stuart@gavia.freeserve.co.uk

Ringing Groups
NORTH RONALDSAY BIRD OBSERVATORY, Ms A E Duncan, Twingness, North Ronaldsay, Orkney, KW17 2BE.
e-mail: alison@nrbo.prestel.co.uk
www.nrbo.f2s.com

ORKNEY RG, Colin J Corse, Garrisdale, Lynn Park, Kirkwall, Orkney, KW15 1SL. H:01856 874484; W:01856 884156.

SULE SKERRY RG, Dave Budworth, 121 Wood Lane, Newhall, Swadlincote, Derbys, DE11 0LX. 0121 695 3384.

RSPB Local Group
ORKNEY, (1985; 300). Neil McCance, West End, Burray, Orkney. 01856 731260.

OUTER HEBRIDES

Bird Recorders
OUTER HEBRIDES, Andrew Stevenson, The Old Stores, Bornish, Isle of South Uist HS8 5SA; e-mail: andrewstevenson@snh.gov.uk

WESTERN ISLES, Brian Rabbitts. 01876 580328; e-mail: brian.rabbitts@virgin.net

Bird Report
OUTER HEBRIDES BIRD REPORT (1989-), from Recorder.

BTO Regional Representatives & Regional Development Officer
BENBECULA & THE UISTS RR & RDO, Brian Rabbits, 01876 580328; e-mail: brian.rabbitts@virgin.net

LEWIS & HARRIS RR. 1, Tony Pendle, 3 Linsiadar, Isle of Lewis,HS2 9DR. e-mail: ellerpendle@madasafish.com

LEWIS & HARRIS RR. 2, Chris Reynolds, 11 Reef, Isle of Lewis, HS2 9HU. e-mail: juliareynolds@btinternet.com

Ringing Group
SHIANTS AUK RG, David Steventon, Welland House, 207 Hurdsfield Road, Macclesfield, Cheshire, SK10 2PX. 01625 421936.

PERTH & KINROSS

Bird Recorder
PERTH & KINROSS, Ron Youngman, Blairchroisk Cottage, Ballinluig, Pitlochry, Perthshire, PH9 0NE. 01796 482324; e-mail: blairchroisk@aol.com

Bird Report
PERTH & KINROSS BIRD REPORT (1974-), from Recorder.

BTO Regional Representatives
PERTHSHIRE RR, Andrew Wight, 01783 710623; e-mail: perth@interramp.co.uk

Clubs
PERTHSHIRE SOCIETY OF NATURAL SCIENCE (Ornithological Section), (1964; 57). Miss Esther Taylor, 23 Verena Terrace, Perth,PH2 0BZ. 01738 621986.

RSPB Local Groups
TAYSIDE, (1988; 160). Alan Davis, 6 Grey Street, Perth,PH2 0JJ. 01738 622480.

SHETLAND

Bird Recorders
FAIR ISLE, Deryk Shaw, Bird Observatory, Fair Isle, Shetland, ZE2 9JU. e-mail: fairisle.birdobs@zetnet.co.uk

SHETLAND, Kevin Osborn, 20 Nederdale, Lerwick, Shetland, ZE1 0SA. 01595 695974; e-mail: k.o@virgin.net

Bird Reports
FAIR ISLE BIRD OBSERVATORY REPORT (1949-), from Scottish Ornithologists' Club, 21 Regent Terrace, Edinburgh, EH7 5BT. 0131 556 6042.

SHETLAND BIRD REPORT (1969-) no pre 1973 available, From Martin Heubeck, East House, Sumburgh Lighthouse, Virkie, Shetland, ZE3 9JN. e-mail: martinheubeck@btinternet.com

BTO Regional Representative
RR and RDO Dave Okill, Heilinabretta, Cauldhame, Trondra, Shetland, ZE1 0XL. (H)01595 880450; (W)01595 696926.

Club
SHETLAND BIRD CLUB, (1973; 200). Reinoud Norde, Lindale, Ireland, Bigton, Shetland, ZE2 9JA. 01950 422467: e-mail: reinoud.norde@lineone.net

Ringing Groups
FAIR ISLE BIRD OBSERVATORY, Deryk Shaw, Bird Observatory, Fair Isle, Shetland, ZE2 9JU. e-mail: fairisle.birdobs@zetnet.co.uk

SHETLAND RG, Dave Okill, Heilinabretta, Cauldhame, Trondra, Shetland, ZE1 0XL. (H)01595 880450; (W)01595 696926

WALES

Bird Report
See Welsh Ornithological Society in National Directory.

BTO Honorary Wales Officer
BTO WALES OFFICER, John Lloyd, Cynghordy, Llandovery, Cambs SA20 0LN.
e-mail: thelloyds@dial.pipex.com

Club
See Welsh Ornithological Society in National Directory.

EAST WALES

Bird Atlas/Avifauna
Birds of Radnorshire. In preparation, due spring 2001.

The Gwent Atlas of Breeding Birds by Tyler, Lewis, Venables & Walton (Gwent Ornithological Society, 1987).

Bird Recorders
BRECONSHIRE, Martin F Peers, Cyffylog, 2 Aberyscir Road, Cradoc, Brecon, Powys, LD3 9PB. 01874 623774.

GWENT, Chris Jones, 22 Walnut Drive, Caerleon, Newport, Gwent, NP6 1SB. 01633 423439.
e-mail: chris.jones@newport.gov.uk

MONTGOMERYSHIRE, Brayton Holt, Scops Cottage, Pentrebeirdd, Welshpool, Powys, SY21 9DL. 01938 500266.

RADNORSHIRE, Pete Jennings, Penbont House, Elan Valley, Rhayader, Powys, LD6 5HS. (H)01597 811522; (W)01597 810880;
e-mail: petejelanvalley@hotmail.com

Bird Reports
BRECONSHIRE BIRDS (1962-), from Brecknock Wildlife Trust.

GWENT BIRD REPORT (1964-), from Jerry Lewis, Y Bwthyn Gwyn, Coldbrook, Abergavenny, Monmouthshire, NP7 9TD. (H)01873 855091; (W)01633 644856

MONTGOMERYSHIRE BIRD REPORT (1981-82-), from Montgomeryshire Wildlife Trust.

RADNOR BIRDS (1987/92-), from Radnorshire Recorder.

BTO Regional Representatives & Regional Development Officer
BRECKNOCK RR, John Lloyd, Cynghordy, Llandovery, Carms, SA20 0LN.
e-mail; thelloyds@dial.pipex.com

GWENT RR, Jerry Lewis, Y Bwthyn Gwyn, Coldbrook, Abergavenny, Monmouthshire, NP7 9TD.(H)01873 855091;(W)01633 644856

MONTGOMERY RR, Brayton Holt (retiring end 2002), Scops Cottage, Pentrebeirdd, Welshpool, Powys, SY21 9DL. 01938 500266.

RADNORSHIRE RR & RDO, Pete Jennings, Penbont House, Elan Valley, Rhayader, Powys, LD6 5HS.(H)01597 811522;(W)01597 810880;
e-mail: petejelanvalley@hotmail.com

Clubs
GWENT ORNITHOLOGICAL SOCIETY, (1964; 350). T J Russell, The Pines, Highfield Road, Monmouth, Gwent, NP25 3HR. 01600 716266.

MONTGOMERYSHIRE FIELD SOCIETY, (1946; 170). Maureen Preen, Ivy House, Deep Cutting, Pool Quay, Welshpool, Powys, SY21 9LJ. Tel: Mary Oliver, 01686 413518.

MONTGOMERYSHIRE WILDLIFE TRUST BIRD GROUP, (1997; 104). A M Puzey, Four Seasons, Arddleen, Llanymynech, Powys, SY22 6RU. 01938 590578.

RADNOR BIRD GROUP, (1986; 60). Pete Jennings, Penbont House, Elan Valley, Rhayader, Powys, LD6 5HS. 01597 811522;
e-mail: petejelanvalley@hotmail.com

Ringing Groups
GOLDCLIFF RG, Vaughan Thomas, Gilgal Cottage, Gilfach, Llanvaches, S Wales, NP26 3AZ. 01633 817161.

LLANGORSE RG, Jerry Lewis, Y Bwthyn Gwyn, Coldbrook, Abergavenny, Monmouthshire, NP7 9TD.(H)01873 855091;(W)01633 644856

Wildlife Trusts
BRECKNOCK WILDLIFE TRUST, (1963; 893). Lion House, Bethel Square, Brecon, Powys, LD3 7AY. e-mail: brecknockwt@cix.co.uk

GWENT WILDLIFE TRUST, (1963;1200). 16 White Swan Court, Church Street, Monmouth, Gwent, NP25 3NY.
e-mail: gwentwildlife@cix.co.uk

MONTGOMERYSHIRE WILDLIFE TRUST, (1982; 1000). Collot House, 20 Severn Street, Welshpool, Powys, SY21 7AD. e-mail: montwt@cix.co.uk

RADNORSHIRE WILDLIFE TRUST, (1987; 789). Warwick House, High Street, Llandrindod Wells, Powys, LD1 6AG. e-mail: radnorshirewt@cix.co.uk

NORTH WALES

Bird Atlas/Avifauna

The Birds of Caernarfonshire by John Barnes (1998, from Lionel Pilling, 51 Brighton Close, Rhyl LL18 3HL).

Bird Recorders

ANGLESEY, Stephen Culley, Millhouse, Penmynydd Road, Menai Bridge, Anglesey, LL59 5RT. e-mail: SteCul10@aol.com

CAERNARFON, John Barnes, Fach Goch, Waunfawr, Caernarfon, LL55 4YS. 01286 650362.

DENBIGHSHIRE & FLINTSHIRE, Norman Hallas, 63 Park Avenue, Wrexham, LL12 7AW. (Tel/fax) 01978 290522; e-mail: narmanhallas@aol.com

MEIRIONNYDD, D L Smith, 3 Smithfield Lane, Dolgellau, Gwynedd, LL40 1BU. 01341 421064.

Bird Reports

BARDSEY BIRD OBSERVATORY ANNUAL REPORT, from Warden, see Reserves.

CAMBRIAN BIRD REPORT (sometime Gwynedd Bird Report) (1953-), from Mr Rhion Pritchard, Pant Afonig, Hafod Lane, Bangor, Gwynedd, LL57 4BU. e-mail: rhion@pritchardr.freeserve.co.uk

CLWYD BIRD REPORT, from Dr Anne Brenchley, Tyr Fannog, 43 Black Brook, Sychdyn, Mold, Flints, CH7 6LT. 01352 750118.

MEIRIONNYDD BIRD REPORT Published in *Cambrian Bird Report (above)*.

WREXHAM BIRDWATCHERS' SOCIETY ANNUAL REPORT (1982-), from Secretary, Wrexham Birdwatchers' Society.

BTO Regional Representatives

ANGLESEY RR, Tony White. 01407 710 137.

CAERNARFON RR, John Barnes, Fach Goch, Waunfawr, Caernarfon, LL55 4YS. 01286 650362.

CLWYD EAST RR, Anne Brenchley, Ty'r Fawnog, 43 Black Brook, Sychdyn, Mold, CH7 6LT. e-mail: ian.anne@imsab.idps.co.uk

CLWYD WEST RR, Mel ab Owain, 31 Coed Bedw, Abergele, Conwy, LL22 7EH. 01745 826528; e-mail: melabowain@cix.co.uk

MEIRIONNYDD RR, Peter Haveland, Ty Manceinion, Penmachno, Betws-y-Coed, Gwynedd, LL24 0UD. e-mail: peter.haveland@tesco.net

Clubs

BANGOR BIRD GROUP, (1947; 100). Secretary, Bangor Bird Group, 12 St Helens Street, Caernarfon, Gwynedd LL55 2HU. e-mail: n.brown@bangor.ac.uk

CAMBRIAN ORNITHOLOGICAL SOCIETY, (1952; 162). Mr Rhion Pritchard, Pant Afonig, Hafod Lane, Bangor, Gwynedd, LL57 4BU. 01248 671301; http://mysite.freeserve.com/cambrianos

CLWYD BIRD RECORDING GROUP, a representative group of the main bird/ naturalist societies of the old county of Clwd. Main responsibility to produce annual Clwyd Bird report. Contact Anne Brenchley (see BTO RR) e-mail: anne.brenchley@cbrg1.idps.co.uk

CLWYD ORNITHOLOGICAL SOCIETY, (1956; 45). Miss Lynn Davies, Preswylfa, Berthen Rd, Lixwm, Holywell, Flints, CH8 8LT. 01352 781106.

DEE ESTUARY CONSERVATION GROUP, (1973; 24 grps). N J Friswell, 8 Oaklands Crescent, Tattenhall, Chester, CH3 9QT. 01829 770463.

DEESIDE NATURALISTS' SOCIETY, (1973; 500). Roy Hamer, 13 Parc Gorsedd, Gorsedd, Holywell, Flints, CH8 8RP. 01352 716273.

WREXHAM BIRDWATCHERS' SOCIETY, (1974; 90). Miss Marian Williams, 10 Lake View, Gresford, Wrexham, Clwyd, LL12 8PU. 01978 854633.

Ringing Groups

BARDSEY BIRD OBSERVATORY, Steven Stansfield, Bardsey Island, off Aberdaron, Pwllheli, Gwynedd, LL53 8DE. 07855 204151; e-mail: steve@bbfo.freeserve.co.uk

MERSEYSIDE RG, P Slater, 45 Greenway Road, Speke, Liverpool, L24 7RY.

SCAN RG, D J Stanyard, Court Farm, Groeslon, Caernarfon, Gwynedd, LL54 7UE. 01286 881 669.

RSPB Local Group

NORTH WALES, (1986; 130). Paul Braid, 01492 516260; e-mail: p.braid@virgin.net140

Wildlife Trust
NORTH WALES WILDLIFE TRUST, (1963; 2400). 376 High Street, Bangor, Gwynedd, LL57 1YE. e-mail: nwwt@cix.co.uk

SOUTH WALES

Bird Atlas/Avifauna
An Atlas of Breeding Birds in West Glamorgan by David M Hanford et al (Gower Ornithological Society, 1992).

Birds of Glamorgan by Clive Hurford and Peter Lansdown (Published by the authors, c/o National Museum of Wales, Cardiff, 1995).

Bird Recorders
GLAMORGAN (EAST), Steve Moon, 36 Rest Bay Close, Porthcawl, Bridgend, CF36 3UN. e-mail: moonsj@bridgend.gov.uk

GOWER (WEST GLAMORGAN), Robert Taylor, 285 Llangyfelach Road, Brynhyfryd, Swansea, SA5 9LB. 01792 464780; (M)07966 880541. e-mail: rob@birding.freeserve.co.uk

Bird Reports
EAST GLAMORGAN BIRD REPORT (title varies 1963-95) 1996-2001, from Alan S Rorney, 10 Parc-y-Nant, Nantgarn, Rhondda, CF15 7JT.

GOWER BIRDS (1965-), from Audrey Jones, 24 Hazel Road, Uplands, Swansea, SA2 0LX. 01792 298859.

BTO Regional Representatives
EAST GLAMORGAN (former Mid & South Glam) RR, Rob Nottage, 32 Village Farm, Bonvilston, Cardiff, CF5 6TY. e-mail: rob@nottages.freeserve.co.uk

WEST RR, Bob Howells, Ynys Enlli, 14 Dolgoy Close, West Cross, Swansea, SA3 5LT. e-mail: bobhowells31@hotmail.com

Clubs
CARDIFF NATURALISTS' SOCIETY, (1867; 225). Stephen R Howe, Department of Geology, National Museum of Wales, Cardiff, CF10 3NP. e-mail: steve.howe@nmgw.ac.uk

GLAMORGAN BIRD CLUB, (1990; 170). Steve Moon, Kenfig National Nature Reserve, Ton Kenfig, Pyle, Bridgend, CF33 4PT. e-mail: moonsj@bridgend.gov.uk

GOWER ORNITHOLOGICAL SOCIETY, (1956; 120). Audrey Jones, 24 Hazel Road, Uplands, Swansea, SA2 0LX. 01792 298859.

Ringing Groups
FLAT HOLM RG, Brian Bailey, Tamarisk House, Wards Court, Frampton-on-Severn, Glos, GL2 7DY. e-mail: brianhbailey98@freeserve.co.uk

KENFIG RG, Mr D.G. Carrington, 25 Bryneglwys Gardens, Porthcawl, Bridgend, Mid Glamorgan, CF36 5PR.

RSPB Local Groups
CARDIFF & DISTRICT, (1973; 4500). Mrs Margaret Read, 121 Lavernock road, Penarth, South Wales, CF64 3QG. 02920 709537; e-mail: mereadcmt@aol.com

WEST GLAMORGAN, (1985; 421). Maggie Cornelius, 01792 229244. www.westglam-rspb.org.uk

Wildlife Hospitals
GOWER BIRD HOSPITAL, Karen Kingsnorth and Simon Allen, Valetta, Sandy Lane, Pennard, Swansea, SA3 2EW. 01792 371630; e-mail: gbh@valetta.u-net.com
All species of wild birds, also hedgehogs and small mammals. Prior phone call essential. Gower Bird Hospital cares for sick, injured and orphaned wild birds and animals with the sole intention of returning them to the wild. Post release radio tracking projects, ringing scheme. Contact us for more information.

LLEWELLYN, Paul, 104 Manselfield Road, Murton, Swansea, SA3 3AG. e-mail: p.j.llewellyn@swansea.ac.uk
All species of birds but specialist knowledge of raptors. Veterinary support.

Wildlife Trust
GLAMORGAN WILDLIFE TRUST, (1961; 1300). Fountain Road, Tondu, Bridgend, CF32 0EH. e-mail: glamorganwt@cix.co.uk

WEST WALES

Bird Atlas/Avifauna
Birds of Pembrokeshire by Jack Donovan and Graham Rees (Dyfed Wildlife Trust, 1994).

Bird Recorders
CARMARTHENSHIRE, Tony Forster, Ffosddu, Salem, Llandeilo, Carmarthenshire, SA19 7NS. 01558 824237; e-mail: tony-forster@supanet.com.

CEREDIGION, Hywel Roderick, 32 Prospect Street, Aberystwyth, Ceredigion, SY23 1JJ. e-mail: hywel@adar.freeserve.co.uk

PEMBROKESHIRE. 1, Jack Donovan MBE, The Burren, 5 Dingle Lane, Crundale, Haverfordwest, Pembrokeshire, SA62 4DJ. 01437 762673.

2, Graham Rees, 22 Priory Avenue, Haverfordwest, Pembrokeshire, SA61 1SQ. 01437 762877.

Bird Reports
CARMARTHENSHIRE BIRDS (1982-), from Carmarthenshire Recorder.

CEREDIGION BIRD REPORT (biennial 1982-87; annual 1988-), from Wildlife Trust of South and West Wales.

PEMBROKESHIRE BIRD REPORT (1981-), fromTJ Price, 2 Wordsworth Ave, Haverfordwest, Pembrokeshire, SA61 1SN.

BTO Regional Representatives
CARDIGAN RR, Moira Convery, 41 Danycoed, Aberystwyth,SY23 2HD.
e-mail: moira@mconvery.freeserve.co.uk

CARMARTHEN RR, David Poulter, Ty Isaf, Pentrepoeth, Idole, Carmarthen, SA32 8DH.
e-mail: d.poulter@tiscali.co.uk

PEMBROKE RR, Annie Poole and Bob Haycock, 1 Rushmoor, Martletwy, Pembrokeshire.

Clubs
LLANELLI NATURALISTS, (1971; 100). Richard Pryce, Trevethin, School Road, Pwll, Llanelli, Carmarthenshire, SA15 4AL.
e-mail: pryceeco@aol.com

PEMBROKESHIRE BIRD GROUP, (1993; 60). T J Price, 2 Wordsworth Ave, Haverfordwest, Pembs, SA61 1SN. 01437 779667.

Ringing Group
PEMBROKESHIRE RG, J Hayes, 3 Wades Close, Holyland Road, Pembroke, SA71 4BN. 01646 687036.

Wildlife Hospitals
NEW QUAY BIRD HOSPITAL, Jean Bryant, Penfoel, Cross Inn, Llandysul, Ceredigion, SA44 6NR. 01545 560462.
All species of birds. Fully equipped for cleansing oiled seabirds. Veterinary support.

WEST WILLIAMSTON OILED BIRD CENTRE, Mrs J Hains, Lower House Farm, West Williamston, Kilgetty, Pembs, SA68 0TL. 01646 651236.
Facilities for holding up to 200 Guillemots, etc. for short periods. Initial treatment is given prior to despatch to other washing centres during very large oil spills; otherwise birds are washed at the Centre with intensive care and rehabilitation facilities. Also other species. Veterinary support.

Wildlife Trust
WILDLIFE TRUST WEST WALES, (1938; 3100). Welsh Wildlife Centre, Cilgerran, Cardigan, SA43 2TB. e-mail: june@wildlife-wales.org.uk
www.wildlife-wales.org.uk

NORTHERN IRELAND

Bird Recorder
George Gordon, 2 Brooklyn Avenue, Bangor, Co Down, BT20 5RB. 028 9145 5763;
e-mail: gordon@ballyholme2.freeserve.co.uk

Bird Reports
NORTHERN IRELAND BIRD REPORT, from Secretary, Northern Ireland, Birdwatchers' Association (see, National Directory).

IRISH BIRD REPORT, Included in Irish Birds, BirdWatch Ireland in National Directory.

COPELAND BIRD OBSERVATORY REPORT, from see Reserves.

BTO Regional Representatives
BTO IRELAND OFFICER, Ken Perry, 43 Portstewart Road, Coleraine, Co Londonderry, BT52 1RW. 028 7034 2985;
e-mail: kennethwilliamperry@hotmail.com

ANTRIM & BELFAST, Position vacant,

ARMAGH, David W A Knight, 20 Mandeville Drive, Tandragee, Craigavon, Co Armagh, BT62 2DQ. 028 38 840658.

DOWN, Position vacant.

LONDONDERRY, Charles Stewart, Bravallen, 18 Duncrun Road, Bellarena, Limavady, Co Londonderry, BT49 0JD.028 77 750468;
e-mail: Charles.Stewart2@btinternet.com

TYRONE SOUTH & FERMANAGH, Philip S Grosse, 30 Tullybroom Road, Clogher, Co Tyrone, BT76 0UW. 028 8554 8606;
e-mail: phigro@aol.com

TYRONE NORTH, Mary Mooney, 20 Leckpatrick Road, Ballymagorry, Strabane, Co Tyrone, BT82 0AL. 028 7188 2442;
e-mail: memooney@foxlodge.healthnet.co.uk

Clubs
NORTHERN IRELAND BIRDWATCHERS' ASSOCIATION See National Directory.

NORTHERN IRELAND ORNITHOLOGISTS' CLUB See National Directory.

CASTLE ESPIE BIRDWATCHING CLUB, (1995; 60). Dot Blakely, 31 Clandeboye Way, Bangor, Co Down, BT19 1AD. 028 9145 0784.

Ringing Groups
ANTRIM & ARDS RG, M McNeely, 35 Balleyvalley Heights, Banbridge, Co Down, BT32 4AQ. 028 406 29823.

COPELAND BIRD OBSERVATORY, C W Acheson, 28 Church Avenue, Dunmurry, Belfast, BT17 9RS.

NORTH DOWN RINGING GROUP, Hugh Thurgate, 16 Inishmore, Killyleagh, Downpatrick, Co Down, BT30 9TP.

RSPB Local Groups
ANTRIM, (1977; 23). Agnes Byron, 59 Tirgracey Road, Mucamore, Co Antrim, BT41 4PS. 028 9446 2207.

BANGOR, (1973; 25). Michael Richardson, 10 Belgravia Road, Bangor, Co Down, BT19 6XJ. 028 9146 2705.

BELFAST, (1970; 130). Ron Houston, 7 Kingsdale Park, Belfast,BT5 7BY. 028 9079 6188.

COLERAINE, (1978; 45). Ken Perry, 43 Portstewart Road, Coleraine, Co Londonderry, BT52 1RW. 028 7034 2985;
e-mail: kennethwilliamperry@hotmail.com

FERMANAGH, (1977; 28). Doreen Morrison, 91 Derrin Road, Cornagrade, Enniskillen, Co Fermanagh, BT74 6BA. 028 6632 6654.

LARNE, (1974; 35). Jimmy Christie, 314 Coast Road, Ballygally, Co Antrim, BT40 2QZ. 028 2858 3223.

LISBURN, (1978; 30). David McCreedy, 10 Downside Avenue, Banbridge, Co Down, BT32 4BP. 028 4062 6125.

Wildlife Hospital
TACT WILDLIFE CENTRE, Mrs Patricia Nevines, 2 Crumlin Road, Crumlin, Co Antrim, BT29 4AD. Tel/fax 028 944 22900;
e-mail: t.a.c.t@care4free.net
All categories of birds treated and rehabilitated; released where practicable, otherwise given a home. Visitors (inc. school groups and organisations) welcome by prior arrangement. Veterinary support.

Wildlife Trust
ULSTER WILDLIFE TRUST, (1978; 2100). 3 New Line, Crossgar, Co Down, BT30 9EP. 028 4483 0282; fax 028 4483 0888;
e-mail: ulsterwt@cix.co.uk

REPUBLIC OF IRELAND

Bird Recorders
1, For none rarities, details of area recorders can be found from BirdWatch Ireland, Ruttledge House, 8 Longford Place, Monkstown, Co Dublin; +353 (0)1 280 4322; fax +353 (0)1 2844 407;
e-mail: info@birdwatchireland.org

2. Rarities, Paul Milne, 100 Dublin Road, Sutton, Dublin 13, +353 (0)1 8325653;
e-mail: paul.milne@oceanfree.net

Bird Reports
Contact BirdWatch Ireland for the following:
IRISH BIRD REPORT.
CAPE CLEAR BIRD OBSERVATORY ANNUAL REPORT.
CORK BIRD REPORT (1963-71; 1976-).
EAST COAST BIRD REPORT (1980-).

BTO Regional Representative
BTO IRELAND OFFICER, Ken Perry, 43 Portstewart Road, Coleraine, Co Londonderry, BT52 1RW. From Eire: (048) 7034 2985, from UK: (028) 7034 2985;
e-mail: kennethwilliamperry@hotmail.com

BirdWatch Ireland Branches
Branches may be contacted in writing via BirdWatch Ireland HQ, see contact details above.

Ringing Groups
CAPE CLEAR BIRD OBSERVATORY, S Wing, 30 Irsher Street, Appledore, Devon, EX39 1RZ.

GREAT SALTEE RS, O J Merne, 20 Cuala Road, Bray, Co Wicklow.

MUNSTER RG, K P Collins, Ballygambon, Lisronagh, Clonmel, Co Tipperary;
e-mail: kevcoll@indigo.ie

SHANNON WADER RG, P A Brennan, The Crag, Stonehall, Newmarket-on-Fergus, Co Clare.

CHANNEL ISLANDS

BTO Regional Representative
Jamie Hooper, 1 Trinity Cottages, Torteval, Guernsey, GY8 0QD. Tel/fax 01481 266924

Ringing Group
The Channel Islands ringing scheme is run by the Société Jersiaise.

ALDERNEY

Bird Recorder
Mark Atkinson, No 4, Ferndale Estate, Newtown, Alderney, BY9 3YR. 01481 823286.

Bird Report
ALDERNEY SOCIETY ORNITHOLOGY REPORT (1992-), from Recorder.

GUERNSEY

Bird Atlas/Avifauna
Birds of the Bailiwick of Guernsey (working title). In preparation.

Bird Recorder
Mark Lawlor, Pentland, 15 Clos des Pecqueries, La Passee, St Sampson's, Guernsey, GY2 4TU. 01481 258168. e-mail: mplawlor@gtonline.net

Bird Report
REPORT & TRANSACTIONS OF LA SOCIÉTÉ GUERNESIAISE (1882-), from Recorder.

Clubs
LA SOCIÉTÉ GUERNESIAISE (Ornithological Section), (1882; 30). Vic Froome, La Cloture, Coutil de Bas Lane, St Sampsons, Guernsey, GY2 4XJ. 01481 254841. www.societe.org.gg

RSPB Local Group
GUERNSEY, (1975; 350+). Michael Bairds, Le Quatre Vents, La Passee, St Sampsons, Guernsey, GY2 4TS. 01481 255524; e-mail: mikebairds@gtonline.net
www.rspbguernsey.co.uk

Wildlife Hospital
GUERNSEY. GSPCA ANIMAL SHELTER, Mrs Jayne Le Cras, Rue des Truchots, Les Fiers Moutons, St Andrews, Guernsey, Channel Islands, GY6 8UD. 01481 257261; e-mail: jaynelecras@gspca.org.gg All species. Modern cleansing unit for oiled seabirds. 24-hour emergency service. Veterinary support.

JERSEY

Bird Recorder
Tony Paintin, 16 Quennevais Gardens, St Brelade, Jersey, Channel Islands, JE3 8FQ. 01534 741928; e-mail: cavokjersey@hotmail.com

Bird Report
JERSEY BIRD REPORT, from Secretary (Publications), Société Jersiaise.

Club
SOCIÉTÉ JERSIAISE (Ornithological Section), (1948; 40). Roger Noel, 7 Pier Road, St Helier, Jersey, JE2 4XW. 01534 758314

RSPB Local Group
JERSEY, Robert Burrow, 1 Southlands, Green Road, St Clements, Jersey, JE2 6QA. 01534 32167

Wildlife Hospital
JERSEY. JSPCA ANIMALS' SHELTER, Pru Bannier, 89 St Saviour's Road, St Helier, Jersey, JE2 4GJ. 01534 724331; fax 01534 871797; e-mail: info@jspca.org.je All species. Expert outside support for owls and raptors. Oiled seabird unit. Veterinary surgeon on site. Educational Centre.

ISLE OF MAN

Bird Atlas/Avifauna
Manx Bird Atlas. 5-yr BBS and Winter Atlas research completed. Publication in preparation, available 2004. Contact: Chris Sharpe (see below BTO).

Bird Recorder
Dr Pat Cullen, Troutbeck, Cronkbourne, Braddan, Isle of Man, IM4 4QA. Home: 01624 623308; Work 01624 676774; e-mail: bridgeen@mcb.net

Bird Reports
MANX BIRD REPORT (1947-), published in *Peregrine.* From G D Craine, 8 Kissack Road, Castletown, Isle of Man, IM9 1NP.e-mail: g.craine@advsys.co.uk

CALF OF MAN BIRD OBSERVATORY ANNUAL REPORT, from Secretary, Manx National Heritage, Manx Museum, Douglas, Isle of Man, IM1 3LY.

BTO Regional Representative & Regional Development Officer
RR, Dr Pat Cullen, as above, 01624 623308.

RDO, Chris Sharpe, 33 Mines Road, Laxey, Isle of Man, IM4 7NH. 01624 861130;
e-mail: chris@manxbirdatlas.org.uk

Club
MANX ORNITHOLOGICAL SOCIETY, (1967; 150). Mrs A C Kaye, Cronk Ny Ollee, Glen Chass, Port St Mary, Isle of Man, IM9 5PL. 01624 834015.

Ringing Groups
CALF OF MAN BIRD OBSERVATORY, Tim Bagworth, Calf of Man, c/o Kionsleau, Plantation Road, Port St Mary, Isle of Man, IM9 5AY. Mobile 07624 462858

MANX RINGING GROUP. Chris Sharpe, 33 Mines Road, Laxey, Isle of Man, IM4 7NH. 01624 861130;
e-mail: chris@manxbirdatlas.org.uk

Wildlife Trust
MANX WILDLIFE TRUST, (1973; 900). Tynwald Mills, St Johns, Isle of Man, IM4 3AE. 01624 801985; fax 01624 801022;
e-mail: manxwt@cix.co.uk
www.mcb.net./mwt/

ARTICLES IN BIRD REPORTS

Avon Bird Report 2001
The Avon Common Bird Census 1962-1999 by RI Bland
Species New to Avon, Laughing Gull and Baird's Sandpiper by AH Davis and N Voaden
Abberant Grey Heron at Blagdon Lake, by KJ Hall
A Scandinavian Rock Pipit at Chew Valley Lake by JP Martin
House Sparrow Nesting Survey, Southmead, Bristol by J Tully
BBS Avon Survey and Avon Ringing Report for 2001 by J Tully and LF Roberts

Angus & Dundee Bird Report 2001
Summer and Winter Migrants in Angus
Tay Ringing Group Recoveries and Controls by L Hatton and S Millar
Status of Black-Necked Grebes in Angus by AJ Leitch
Ivory Gull by G Christer
Red-Breasted Goose by G Addison
Angus Weather by N Elkins

Ayrshire Bird Report 2002
Park Life: the Birds of an Urban Country Park by M Rugger
The Kestrel in Ayrshire in 2002 by G Riddle
Sparrowhawk Breeding Details 2002 by Ian Todd
Late Season Breeding Ravens by Dave Grant
Mute Swan Survey 2002 by K Waite
Chronological Summary by A Hogg

Breconshire Birds 2002
Tern Passage in Breconshire by Michael Shrubb
The Llangorse Ringing Report by J Lewis and B Haycock

Cambridgeshire Bird Report 2001
Red Necked Stint at Somersham GP by J Oates
American Golden Plover at Swaffham Prior Fen by J Oates
Red Brested Flycatcher at Wicken Fen by R Parslow
Dartford Warbler at Cherry Hinton – 2nd County Record by C Kelly
Arctic Redpoll at Woodwalton Fen 2nd County Record by R Patient
Also Articles on Red Rumped Swallow and Yellow Browed Warbler

Carmarthenshire Birds 2001
Explanation of Conservation Status
Notes on the Birds of Dinefwr Park Carmarthenshire
County Species List (first one) all by Tony Forster

Ceredigion Bird Report 201
Ceredigion Black-Headed Gull Colonies by H Roderick and P Davis
Ceredigion Bird Ringing Report 2001 by D Reed

Clwyd Bird Report 2001
The Population Status of the UK's Birds – the Red List Updated by A Brenchley
Bird Conservation on the Dee Estuary by C Pirie

Derbyshire Bird Report 2001
The Return of the Buzzard by M Lacey and A Messenger
Red-Spotted Bluethroat at Beeley Moor by R Carrington
Rose-Coloured Starling at Hilton by R Key
Puffin found near Chesterfield by A Hattersley
The Status and Occurrence of Yellow-Legged Gull and Caspan Gull in Derbyshire by R Key

Devon Bird Report 2001
Prey Selection of Urban Peregrine Falcons in 2001 by N Dixon and E Drewith
Observations of Visible Migrations on the SW Devon Coast by S Geary
Foot and Mouth Disease – Impact on Bird and Birding by R Hibbert
Rose-Breasted Grosbeak on Lundy by S Cooper
Black-Faced Bunting on Lundy by R Patient
Siberian Stonechat at Start Point by M Langman
Redpoll Showing Characteristics of Mealy Redpoll by M Knott
Swifts in Plymouth tower by L Hurrell
Devon Ringing Report for 2001 by R Sinfen
Breeding Birds Survey 1994-2000 – Devon Ups and Downs by P Reay
Summary of Seabird 2000 in Devon by S Geary

Dorset Bird Report 2001
Peregrine Falcons Fostering Herring Gull Chicks by R Baker
Birding Sites in Dorset – Abbotsbury Swannery by S Gomes
Report on Bird Ringing in Dorset in 2001 by S Hales

East Glamorgan Bird Report 2001
Influx of Grey Phalaropes
Kenfig Ringing Report
Flatholm Ringing Report
BTO 2001 Survey Report
Butterflies and Moths Highlights

ARTICLES IN BIRD REPORTS

Fair Isle Bird Report 2002
Update on Survey of Diseases and Causes of Death in Wild Birds on Fair Isle by J Waine
Fair Isle – Birds and Food by M Preswood
Fair Isle, one of the Last Restaurants for Northern Wheatears heading for Iceland and Greenland by J Delingest
Monthly Summary by P French and D Shaw
Earliest and Latest Migrant Dates by A Ball
Systematic List by D Shaw
Ringing Report by A Bull
A Selection of Rarities From 2002
Other Wildlife by A Bull
Fair Isle Checklist by A Bull

Fife Bird Report 2001
Fife's Best Birds at a Glance
Systematic List
Blyth's Reed Warbler – New to Mainland Fife by J Cobb
Dusky Warbler – New to Mainland Fife by J Cobb
Flava Wagtails Breeding in Fife by Prof TC Smout
Red Breasted Goose – A New Bird for the County by D Dickson
Fife Ringing Report by B Little

Forth Area Bird Report 2001 (Within forth Naturalist and Historian Vol 25)
JA Harvie-Brown (1844-1916), Ornithologist - People of the Forth (14) by Ken Mackay.

Gloucestershire Bird Report 200
Glos Ringing Report by RD Hearn
Nestbox Reports From Nagshead and Hignam RSPB Reserves by I Proctor
Glos Garden Bird Survey 2000 by M Sutcliffe
Peregrines at Symonds Yat Rock by P Jones
Severn Estuary Gull Group 2000 by M Durham
Summary of BBS Summer 2000 Results by M Smart

Hampshire Bird Report 2001
Hampshire Ringing Report 2001 by D Bell
Hampshire Fieldwork 1998-2001 by B Sharkey
A Record Breaking Year for Seabirds by R Whynn
Cory's Shearwater – 2nd record for Hants by M Moody and G Horace-Davis
Unusual Nest Fellows by J Eyre

Highland Bird Report 2002
Highland Ringing Groups by D Butterfield and B Swann
Crossbills by R Summers
A Birder's Calender by A Mcnee

The Isle of Wight Bird Report 2001
The Wetland Bird Survey 2000-2001 by J Cheverton
Roosting Little Egrets in the Isle of Wight in 2001 by K Lover and J Willmott

Kent Bird Report 2001 (50th Anniversary Edition)
Rock Pipit Survey 2001 by I Hodgson
Firecrest Survey 2001 A Henderson
Diet of Long Eared Owls on Sheppey by P Oliver
Colour Ringed Med Gulls by R Henson
Dartford Warblers in Kent by J Van Der Dol
Reminiscences from 1952 by J Braggs

Leicetershire and Rutland Bird Report 2002
Review of the Year by R Fray
Leicestershire and Rutland Wildfowl Counts by R Fray
Franklin's Gull – New to the County List by G Pullan
Records Review by R Fray and A Harrop
Ringing Report by N Judson

Bird in Greater Manchester 2001
Earliest and Latest Arrival and Departure Dates – A Comparison 1974-1990 + 1991-2000 by A Bissitt and A Smith

Norfolk Bird Report 2002 (50th Edition)
A History and Celebration of Fifty Years of the Norfolk Bird Report by P Allard
Changes in the Breeding Birds of Norfolk in the Last 50 Years by M Taylor
The Marsh Harrier in Norfolk – A Review of Its Historical and Current Status by J Williamson
The History and Development of Sheringham Bird Observatory by D Sadler
Pallid Harrier – the First Record in Norfolk by S Votier and R Johnson

North East Scotland Bird Report 2001
Grampian Ringing Group Summary 2001 by R Duncan
Grasshopper Warblers at a Regular Breeding Site in Banffshire 1990-2002 by R Leverton
Autumn Turnover of Pink Footed Geese at Meikle Loch by R Duncan
Occurrence of a European Storm Petrel in NE Scotland in Apparent First Summer Plumage by P Baxter and H Scott
Whiskered Tern at Meikle Loch - the Second Scottish Record by K Gillon and P Crockett

Birds in Northumbria 2002
Birding Sites Xi – Budle Bay by Ch Knox
Birding Sites Xii – Colt Crag and Hallington Reservoirs by R forster
Wetland Bird Survey by R Norman and S Holliday
Greenland White-Fronted Geese Wintering at Grindon Lough by M Frankis
Northumberland's first Greenland White-Fronted Goose by M Frankis
Ringing at Island Seabird Colonies in the North East – Ringing Projects and Recoveries in 2002 by C Redfern
Reed Warblers at Gosforth Park – trends and recoveries 1998-2002 by C Redfern and I Davidson
The Breeding Bird Survey Report No3 - 2000-2002, by T and M Cadwallender
Ringing Recoveries by I Fisher
Breeding Waders of Wet Meadows in Northumberland 2002 by T and M Cadwallender
Wilson's Petrel – an Addition to the County List by M Kitching
The 2002 Mute Swan Census in Northhumberland by J Coleman, A Rickeard and P Rickeard
Roseate Tern Numbers at St Mary's Island 2002 by N Dales
Great Spotted Woodpeckers in 2002 by B Galloway
'Big Day' County Bird Racing in Northumberland by M Hepple
Two Unusual Nests (Jackdaw and Black-Headed Gull) by Linsay Mcdougall
Great Black-Backed Gulls in the Mouths of the Rivers Tyne and Blythe 2001-2002 by D Turner

The Shropshire Bird Report 2001
The Goshawk in South Shropshire by Cl Mout
Peregrine Teaching Young to Hunt by J Tucker

Somerset Birds 2002
BTO National Pregrine Survey 2002 – Report for Somerset by N Williams
The Exmoor Breeding Bird Survery 2002 by D Balance
River Barle – Waterways Survey 1997-2002 by M and R Vaughan

Surrey Bird Report 2000
The Honey Buzzard influx of Autumn 2000 by J Gates
The Common Birds Census in Surrey 1995-2000 by D Griffin
Bird Ringing in Surrey 2000 by R Denyer

NATIONAL DIRECTORY

Cormorants and Great Black-backed Gull by Michael Webb

ARMY ORNITHOLOGICAL SOCIETY (1960; 250).
Open to MOD employees and civilians who have an interest in their local MOD estate. Activities include field meetings, expeditions, the preparation of checklists of birds on Ministry of Defence property, conservation advice and an annual bird count. Annual journal *The Osprey*, published with the RNBWS and RAFOS from easter 2001. Bulletins/newsletters twice a year.
Contact: Hon Secretary, Lt Col P S Bennett, AD Ops, HQ DLO, Spur 9, E Block, MOD Ensleigh, Bath, BA1 5AB, 020 7218 6750.

ASSOCIATION FOR THE PROTECTION OF RURAL SCOTLAND (1926).
Works to protect Scotland's countryside from unnecessary or inappropriate development, recognising the needs of those who live and work there and the necessity of reconciling these with the sometimes competing requirements of recreational use.
Contact: Director, Mrs Joan Geddes, Gladstone's Land, 3rd Floor, 483 Lawnmarket, Edinburgh, EH1 2NT, 0131 225 7012; (Fax)0131 225 6592; e-mail: aprs@aprs.org.uk

ASSOCIATION OF COUNTY RECORDERS AND EDITORS (1993; 120).
The basic aim of ACRE is to promote best practice in the business of producing county bird reports, in the work of Recorders and in problems arising in managing record systems and archives. Organises periodic conferences and publishes *newsACRE.*
Contact: Secretary, M J Rogers, 2 Churchtown Cottages, Towednack, St Ives, Cornwall, TR26 3AZ, 01736 796223.
e-mail: judith@gmbirds.freeserve.co.uk

BARN OWL TRUST
Registered charity. Aims to conserve the Barn Owl and its environment through conservation, education, research and information. 25 free leaflets on all aspects of Barn Owl conservation. Educational material inc. video and resource pack. Book *Barn Owls on Site*, a guide for planners and developers (priced). Works with and advises landowners, farmers, planners, countryside bodies and others to promote a brighter future for Britain's Barn Owls. Currently pursuing proactive conservation schemes in SW England, including Devon and Cornwall surveys, to secure breeding sites and form a stable basis for population expansion. Open to phone calls Mon-Fri (9.30-5.30). Send SAE for information.
Contact: Secretary, Barn Owl Trust, Waterleat, Ashburton, Devon, TQ13 7HU, 01364 653026; e-mail: info@barnowltrust.org.uk
www.barnowltrust.org.uk

BIRD OBSERVATORIES COUNCIL (1970).
Objectives are to provide a forum for establishing closer links and co-operation between individual autonomous observatories and to help co-ordinate the work carried out by them. All accredited bird observatories affiliated to the Council undertake a ringing programme and provide ringing experience to those interested, most also provide accommodation for visiting birdwatchers.
Contact: Secretary, Peter Howlett, c/o Dept of Biodiversity, National Museums & Galleries, Cardiff, CF10 3NP, 0292 057 3233; (Fax)0292 023 9009; e-mail: peter.howlett@nmgw.ac.uk
www.birdobscouncil.org.uk

BIRD STAMP SOCIETY (1986; 250).
Quarterly journal *Flight* contains philatelic and ornithological articles. Lists all new issues and identifies species. Runs a quarterly Postal Auction; number of lots range from 400 to 800 per auction.
Contact: Secretary, Graham Horsman, 9 Cowley Drive, Worthy Down, Winchester, Hants, SO21 2QW, 01962 889381; (Fax)01962 887423.

BIRDWATCH IRELAND (1968; 5000).
The trading name of the Irish Wildbird Conservancy, a voluntary body founded in 1968 by the amalgamation of the Irish Society for the Protection of Birds, the Irish Wildfowl Conservancy and the Irish Ornithologists' Club. Now the BirdLife International partner in Ireland with 21 voluntary branches. Conservation policy is based on formal research and surveys of birds and their habitats. Owns or manages an increasing number of reserves to protect threatened species and habitats. Publishes *Wings* quarterly and *Irish Birds* annually, in addition to annual project reports and survey results.
Contact: Oran O'Sullivan, Ruttledge House, 8 Longford Place, Monkstown, Co Dublin, Ireland, +353 (0)1 2804322; (Fax)+353 (0)1 2844407; e-mail: info@birdwatchireland.org
www.birdwatchireland.ie

BRITISH BIRDS RARITIES COMMITTEE (1959).
The Committee adjudicates records of species of rare occurrence in Britain (marked 'R' in the Log Charts). Its annual report, which is published in *British Birds*. The BBRC also assesses records from the Channel Islands. In the case of rarities trapped for ringing, records should be sent to the Ringing

Figures appearing in brackets following the names of organisations indicate the date of formation and, if relevant, the current membership.

Office of the British Trust for Ornithology, who will in turn forward them to the BBRC.
Contact: Hon Secretary, M J Rogers, 2 Churchtown Cottages, Towednack, St Ives, Cornwall, TR26 3AZ, 01736 796223.
www.bbrc.org.uk

BRITISH DRAGONFLY SOCIETY.
The BDS aims to promote the conservation and study of dragonflies. Members receive two issues of *Dragonfly News* and *BDS Journal* each year in spring and autumn. There are countrywide field trips, an annual members day and training is available on aspects of dragonfly ecology.
Contact: Hon Secretary, Dr WH Wain, The Haywain, Hollywater Road, Bordon, Hants GU35 0AD. www.dragonflysoc.org.uk

BRITISH FALCONERS' CLUB (1927; 1200).
Largest falconry club in Europe, with regional branches. Its aim is to encourage responsible falconers and conserve birds of prey by breeding, holding educational meetings and providing facilities, guidance and advice to those wishing to take up the sport. Publishes *The Falconer* annually and newsletter twice yearly.
Contact: Director, Ian A Timmins, Home Farm, Hints, Tamworth, Staffs, B78 2DW, Tel/(Fax)01543 481737; e-mail: falconers@zetnet.co.uk
www.users.zetnet.co.uk/bfc

THE BRITISH LIBRARY SOUND ARCHIVE WILDLIFE SECTION (1969).
(Formerly BLOWS - British Library of Wildlife Sounds). The most comprehensive collection of bird sound recordings in existence: over 130,000 recordings of more than 8000 species of birds worldwide, available for free listening. Copies or sonograms of most recordings can be supplied for private study or research and, subject to copyright clearance, for commercial uses. Contribution of new material and enquiries on all aspects of wildlife sounds and recording techniques are welcome. Publishes *Bioacoustics* journal, CD and cassette guides to bird songs. Comprehensive catalogue available on-line at http:\\cadensa.bl.uk
Contact: Curator, Richard Ranft, British Library, National Sound Archive, 96 Euston Road, London, NW1 2DB, 020 7412 7402/3;
e-mail: nsa-wildsound@bl.uk
www.bl.uk/sound-archive

BRITISH MUSEUM (NAT HIST) see Walter Rothschild Zoological Museum

BRITISH ORNITHOLOGISTS' CLUB
(1892; 600).
Membership open only to members of the British Ornithologists' Union. A registered charity, the Club's objects are 'the promotion of scientific discussion between members of the BOU, and others interested in ornithology, and to facilitate the publication of scientific information in connection with ornithology'. The Club maintains a special interest in avian systematics, taxonomy and distribution. About eight dinner meetings are held each year. Publishes the *Bulletin of the British Ornithologists' Club* quarterly, also (since 1992) a continuing series of occasional publications.
Contact: Hon Secretary, Cdr M B Casement OBE RN, Dene Cottage, West Harting, Petersfield, Hants, GU31 5PA, 01730 825280;
e-mail: mbcasement@aol.com.uk

BRITISH ORNITHOLOGISTS' UNION
(1858; 1,500).
Founded by Professor Alfred Newton FRS and one of the world's oldest and most respected ornithological societies. It aims to promote ornithology within the scientific and birdwatching communities, both in Britain and around the world. This is largely achieved by the publication of its quarterly international journal, *Ibis* (1859-), featuring work at the cutting edge of our understanding of the world's birdlife. An active programme of meetings, seminars and conferences inform birdwatchers and ornithologists about the work being undertaken around the world. This often includes research projects that have received financial assistance from the BOU's ongoing programme of Ornithological Research Grants, which includes student sponsorship. The BOU also runs the Bird Action Grant scheme to assist projects aimed at conserving or researching species on the UK's Biodiversity Action Plan (BAP) list. Part of the BOU Library is housed at the Linnean Society, whilst copies of exchange journals, books reviewed in *Ibis* and offprints are held as part of the Alexander Library in the Zoology Department of the University of Oxford (see Edward Grey Institute). The BOU Records Committee maintains the official British List) see below.
Contact: Administrator, Steve Dudley, Natural History Museum, Akeman Street, Tring, Herts, HP23 6AP, 01442 890080; (Fax)0207 942 6150;
e-mail: bou@bou.org.uk
www.bou.org.uk www.ibis.ac.uk

BRITISH ORNITHOLOGISTS' UNION RECORDS COMMITTEE
The BOURC is a standing committee of the British Ornithologists' Union. Its function is to maintain the British List, the official list of birds recorded in Great Britain. The up-to-date list can be viewed on the BOU website. Where vagrants are involved it is concerned only with those which relate to potential additions to the British List (ie first records). In this it differs from the British Birds Rarities Committee (qv). In maintaining the British List, it also differs from the BBRC in that it examines, where necessary, important pre-1950 records, monitors introduced species for possible admission to or deletion from the List, and reviews taxonomy and nomenclature generally. BOURC reports are published in *Ibis.* Decisions contained in these reports, which affect the List, are also announced via the popular birdwatching press.
Contact: Secretary, Dr Tim Melling, The Natural History Museum, Akeman Street, Tring, Herts, HP23 6AP, 01442 890080; (Fax)0207 942 6150; e-mail: bourc.sec@bou.org.uk
www.bou.org.uk

BRITISH TRUST FOR ORNITHOLOGY (1933; 12,500).

A registered charity governed by an elected Council, it has a rapidly growing membership and enjoys the support of a large number of county and local birdwatching clubs and societies through the BTO/Bird Clubs Partnership. Its aims are: 'To promote and encourage the wider understanding, appreciation and conservation of birds through scientific studies using the combined skills and enthusiasm of its members, other birdwatchers and staff.' Through the fieldwork of its members and other birdwatchers, the BTO is responsible for the majority of the monitoring of British birds, British bird population and their habitats. BTO surveys include the National Ringing Scheme, the Nest Record Scheme, the Breeding Bird Survey (in collaboration with JNCC and RSPB), and the Waterways Breeding Bird Survey - all contributing to an integrated programme of population monitoring. The BTO also runs projects on the birds of farmland and woodland, also (in collaboration with WWT, RSPB and JNCC) the Wetland Bird Survey, in particular Low Tide Counts. Garden BirdWatch, which started in 1995, now has more than 16,000 participants. The Trust has 140 voluntary regional representatives (see County Directory) who organise fieldworkers for the BTO's programme of national surveys in which members participate. The results of these co-operative efforts are communicated to government departments, local authorities, industry and conservation bodies for effective action. For details of current activities see National Projects. Members receive *BTO News* six times a year and have the option of subscribing to the thrice-yearly journal, *Bird Study* and twice yearly *Ringing & Migration*. Local meetings are held in conjunction with bird clubs and societies; there are regional and national birdwatchers' conferences, and specialist courses in bird identification and modern censusing techniques. Grants are made for research, and members have the use of a lending and reference library at Thetford and the Alexander Library at the Edward Grey Institute of Field Ornithology (qv).
Contact: Director, Professor Jeremy J D Greenwood, British Trust for Ornithology, The Nunnery, Thetford, Norfolk, IP24 2PU, 01842 750050; (fax)01842 750030; www.bto.org
e-mail: btostaff@bto.org

BRITISH WATERFOWL ASSOCIATION
The BWA is an association of enthusiasts interested in keeping, breeding and conserving all types of waterfowl, including wildfowl and domestic ducks and geese. It is a registered charity, without trade affiliations, dedicated to educating the public about waterfowl and the need for conservation as well as to raising the standards of keeping and breeding ducks, geese and swans in captivity.
Contact: Mrs Sue Schubert, PO Box 163, Oxted RH8 0WP, 01892 740212.
e-mail: info@waterfowl.org.uk
www.waterfowl.org.uk

BRITISH WILDLIFE REHABILITATION COUNCIL (1987).
Its aim is to promote the care and rehabilitation of wildlife casualties through the exchange of information between people such as rehabilitators, zoologists and veterinary surgeons who are active in this field. Organises an annual symposium or workshop. Publishes a regular newsletter. Supported by many national bodies including the Zoological Society of London, the British Veterinary Zoological Society, the RSPCA, the SSPCA, and the Vincent Wildlife Trust.
Contact: Secretary, Tim Thomas, Wildlife Department, RSPCA, Causeway, Horsham, W Sussex, RH12 1HG, 0870 010 1181.
www.nimini.demon.co.uk/bwrc

BTCV (formerly British Trust for Conservation Volunteers) (1959).
Involves people of all ages in practical conservation work, much of which directly affects

bird habitats. There are more than 2500 local conservation groups affiliated to BTCV, which also provides a service to many other bodies including the JNCC, RSPB, WWT and county wildlife trusts, national parks, water authorities, local authorities and private landowners. More than 750 training courses are run annually on the theory of management and practical techniques, for example woodland and wetland management, hedging, etc. Runs working holidays in UK and overseas. Publishes a quarterly newsletter, *The Conserver*, a series of practical handbooks and a wide range of other publications. Further information and a list of local offices is available from the above address.
Contact: Chief Executive, Tom Flood, 80 York Way, London, N1 9NG, 020 7713 5327; (Fax)020 7278 8967; e-mail: tflood@btcv.org.uk www.btcv.org.uk

BTCV SCOTLAND
Runs 7-14 day 'Action Breaks' in Scotland during which participants undertake conservation projects; weekend training courses in environmental skills; midweek projects in Edinburgh, Glasgow, Aberdeen, Stirling and Inverness.
Contact: Balallan House, 24 Allan Park, Stirling, FK8 2QG, 01786 479697; (Fax)01786 465359; e-mail: stirling@btcv.org.uk www.btcv.org.uk

CAMPAIGN FOR THE PROTECTION OF RURAL WALES
Its aims are to help the conservation and enhancement of the landscape, environment and amenities of the countryside, towns and villages of rural Wales and to form and educate opinion to ensure the promotion of its objectives. It recognises the importance of the indigenous cultures of rural Wales and gives advice and information upon matters affecting protection, conservation and improvement of the visual environment.
Contact: Director, Merfyn Williams, Ty Gwyn, 31 High Street, Welshpool, Powys, SY21 7YD, 01938 552525/556212; (Fax)552741; www.cprw.org.uk e-mail: info@cprw.org.uk

CANADA GOOSE STUDY GROUP
No longer active in ringing, the Group still functions to monitor records.
Contact: Dr C B Thomas, Dept of Chemistry, University of York, Heslington, York, YO10 5DD, 01904 432532; (Fax)01904 432516; e-mail: cbt1@york.ac.uk

CENTRE FOR ECOLOGY & HYDROLOGY (CEH)
The work of the CEH, a component body of the Natural Environment Research Council, includes a range of ornithological research, covering population studies, habitat management and work on the effects of pollution. The CEH has a long-term programme to monitor pesticide and pollutant residues in the corpses of predatory birds sent in by birdwatchers, and carries out detailed studies on affected species. The Biological Records Centre (BRC), which is part of the CEH, is responsible for the national biological data bank on plant and animal distributions (except birds).
Contact: Director, Prof Pat Nuttall, Monks Wood, Abbots Ripton, Huntingdon, PE28 2LS, 01487 772400. www.ceh.ac.uk

COUNTRY LANDOWNERS' ASSOCIATION (50,000).
The CLA is at the heart of rural life and is the voice of the countryside for England and Wales, campaigning on issues which directly affect those who live and work in rural communities. Its members together manage 60% of the countryside. CLA members range from some of the largest landowners, with interests in forest, moorland, water and agriculture, to some of the smallest with little more than a paddock or garden.
Contact: Secretary, 16 Belgrave Square, London, SW1X 8PQ, 020 7235 0511.

COUNTRYSIDE AGENCY (1999)
Is the statutory body working to make life better for people in the countryside and improve the quality of the countryside for everyone. The Countryside Agency will help to achieve the following; empowered, active and inclusive communities, high standards of rural services, vibrant local economies, all countryside managed sustainably, recreation opportunities for all, realising the potential of the urban fringe. The Countryside Agency is funded by Defra who is a major customer for their work.
Offices
North East Region. Cross House, Westgate Road, Newcastle upon Tyne NE1 4XX, 0191 269 1600; (Fax)0191 269 1601
North West Region. 7th Floor, Bridgewater House, Whitworth Street, Manchester M1 6LT. 0161 237 1061;(fax)0161 237 1062
Haweswater Road, Penrith, Cumbria CA11 7EH. 01768 865752;(fax)01768 890414.
South West Region. Bridge House, Sion Place, Clifton Down, Bristol BS8 4AS. 0117 973 9966;(fax)0117 923 8086.
Second Floor, 11-15 Dix's Field, Exeter EX1 1QA. 01392 477150;(fax)01392 477151.

Yorkshire & The Humber Region. 4th Floor Victoria Wharf, No 4 The Embankment, Sovereign Street, Leeds LS1 4BA. 0113 246 9222;(fax)0113 246 0353
East Midlands Region. 18, Market Place, Bingham, Nottingham NG13 9AP. 01949 876200;(fax)01949 876222
West Midlands Region. 1st Floor, Vincent House, Tindal Bridge, 92-93 Edward Street, Birmingham B1 2RA. 0121 233 9399:(fax)0121 233 9286
Eastern Region. 2nd Floor, City House, 126-128 Hills Road, Cambridge CB2 1PT. 01223 354462;(fax)01223 273550.
South East Region. Dacre House, Dacre Street, London SW1H 0DH, 020 7340 2900;(fax)020 7340 2911.
Sterling House, 7 Ashford Road, Maidstone ME14 5BJ. 01622 765222;(fax)01622 662102.
Contact: Chief Executive, Richard Wakeford, John Dower House, Crescent Place, Cheltenham, Glos, GL50 3RA, 01242 521381; (Fax)01242 584270.

COUNTRYSIDE COUNCIL FOR WALES
The Government's statutory adviser on wildlife, countryside and maritime conservation matters in Wales. It is the executive authority for the conservation of habitats and wildlife. Through partners, CCW promotes protection of landscape, opportunities for enjoyment, and support of those who live, work in, and manage the countryside. It enables thesepartners, including local authorities, voluntary organisations and interested individuals, to pursue countryside management projects through grant aid. CCW is accountable to the National Assembly for Wales which appoints its Council members and provides its annual grant-in-aid.
Area Offices
West Area. Plas Gogerddan, Aberystwyth, Ceredigian, SY23 3EE. 01970 821100
North West Area. Llys y bont, Ffordd y Parc, Parc Menai, Bangor, Gwynedd, LL57 4BH. 01248 672500
South Area. Unit 4, Castleton Court, Fortran Road, St Mellons, Cardiff CF3 0LT. 02920 772400
East Area. Eden House, Ithon Road, Llandrindod, Powys, LD1 6AS, 01597 827400
North East Area. Victoria House, Grosvenor Street, Mold CH7 1EJ. 01352 706600
Contact: Maes-y-Ffynnon, Penrhosgarnedd, Bangor, Gwynedd, 01248 385500; (Fax)01248 355782; (Enquiry unit)0845 1306229.
www.ccw.gov.uk

CPRE (formerly Council for the Protection of Rural England) (1926; 45,000).
Patron HM The Queen. CPRE now has 43 county branches and 200 local groups. It seeks to provide well researched and practical solutions to problems affecting the English countryside. Membership open to all.
Contact: Director, Ms K Parminter, Warwick House, 25 Buckingham Palace Road, London, SW1W 0PP, 020 7976 6433; (Fax)020 7976 6373; e-mail: info@cpre.org.uk
www.cpre.org.uk

DEPARTMENT OF THE ENVIRONMENT FOR NORTHERN IRELAND
Responsible for the declaration and management of National Nature Reserves, the declaration of Areas of Special Scientific Interest, the administration of Wildlife Refuges, the classification of Special Protection Areas under the EC Birds Directive, the designation of Special Areas of Conservation under the EC Habitats Directive and the designation of ramsar sites under the Ramsar Convention. It administers the Nature Conservation and Amenity Lands (Northern Ireland) Order 1985, the Wildlife (Northern Ireland) Order 1985, the Game Acts and the Conservation (Natural Habitats, etc) Regulations (NI) 1995.
Contact: Bob Bleakley, Environment and Heritage Service, Commonwealth House, 35 Castle Street, Belfast, BT1 1GU, 028 9054 6521. e-mail: bob.bleakley@doeni.gov.uk

DISABLED BIRDER'S ASSOCIATION (2000;250).
The DBA is a registered charity and international movement, which aims to promote access to reserves and other birding places and to a range of services, so that people with different needs can follow the birding obsession as freely as able-bodied people. Membership is currently free and open to all, either disabled or able-bodied. We are keen for new members to help give a strong voice to get our message across to those who own and manage nature reserves to ensure that they think access when they are planning and improving their facilities. We are also seeking to influence those who provide birdwatching services and equipment. The DBA runs an annual overseas trip.
Contact: DBA, 18 St Mildreds Road, Cliftonville, Margate, Kent, CT9 2LT.
e-mail: bo@fatbirder.com
www.disabledbirdersassociation.org.uk

EDWARD GREY INSTITUTE OF FIELD ORNITHOLOGY (1938).
The EGI takes its name from Edward Grey, first Viscount Grey of Fallodon, a life-long lover of birds

and former Chancellor of the University of Oxford, who gave his support to an appeal for its foundation capital. The Institute now has a permanent research staff; it usually houses some 12-15 research students, two or three senior visitors and post-doctoral research workers. The EGI also houses Prof Sir John Krebs's Ecology & Behaviour Group, which studies the ecology, demography and conservation of declining farmland birds. Field research is carried out mainly in Wytham Woods near Oxford and on the island of Skomer in West Wales. In addition there are laboratory facilities and aviary space for experimental work. The Institute houses the Alexander Library, one of the largest collections of 20th century material on birds in the world. The library is supported by the British Ornithologists Union who provides much of the material. Included in its manuscript collections are diaries, notebooks and papers of ornithologists. It also houses the British Falconers Club library. The Library is open to members of the BOU and the Oxford Ornithological Society; other bona fide ornithologists may use the library by prior arrangement.

Contact: Head, Dr BC Sheldon, Department of Zoology, South Parks Road, Oxford, OX1 3PS, 01865 271274, e-mail: lynne.bradley@zoology.oxford.ac.uk
Alexander Library 01865 271143;
e-mail: lnda.birch@zoo.ox.ac.uk
web-site, EGI: http://egiwcruzool.zoo.ox.ac.uk/EGI/egihome.htm web-site library http://users.ox.ac.uk/~zoolib/

ENGLISH NATURE (1991)
Advises Government on nature conservation in England. It promotes, directly and through others, the conservation of England's wildlife and geology within the wider setting of the UK and its international responsibilities. It selects, establishes and manages National Nature Reserves (many of which are described in Part 9: Reserves and Observatories), and identifies and notifies Sites of Special Scientific Interest. It provides advice and information about nature conservation and supports and conducts research relevant to these functions. Through the Joint Nature Conservation Committee (qv), English Nature works with sister organisations in Scotland and Wales on UK and international nature conservation issues.

Contact: Northminster House, Peterborough, PE1 1UA, 01733 455100; (Fax)01733 455103; e-mail: enquiries@english-nature.org.uk
www.english-nature.org.uk

Local Teams

Bedfordshire and Cambridgeshire. Ham Lane House, Ham Lane, Nene Park, Orton Waterville, Peterborough PE2 5UR, 01733 405850;(fax)01733 394093; e-mail: beds.cambs.nhants@english-nature.org.uk

Cheshire and Lancashire. Pier House, 1st Floor, Wallgate, Wigan WN3 4AL. 01942 820342;(fax)01942 820364;
e-mail: northwest@english-nature.org.uk

Cornwall & Isles of Scilly. Trevint House, Strangways Villas, Truro TR1 2PA. 01872 265710;(fax)01872 262551;
e-mail: cornwall@english-nature.org.uk

Cumbria. Juniper House, Murley Moss, Oxenholme Road, Kendal LA9 7RL. 01539 792800;(fax)01539 792830; e-mail; cumbria@english-nature.org.uk

Devon. Level 2, Rensdale House, Bonhay Rd, Exeter, EX4 3AW, 01392 889770;(fax)01392 437999; e-mail: devon@english-nature.org.uk

Dorset. Slepe Farm, Arne, Wareham, Dorset BH20 5BN. 01929 557450
;(fax)01929 554752; e-mail: dorset@english-nature.org.uk

Eastern Area. The Maltings, Wharf Road, Grantham, Lincs NG31 6BH. 01476 584800;(fax)01476 570927;
e-mail: eastmidlands@english-nature.org.uk

Essex, London and Hertfordshire. Harbour House, Hythe Quay, Colchester CO2 8JF. 01206 796666;(fax)01206 794466;
e-mail; essex.herts@english-nature.org.uk

Hampshire and Isle of Wight. 1 Southampton Road, Lyndhurst, Hants SO43 7BU. 02380 283944;(fax)02380 283834;
e-mail; hants.iwight@english-nature.org.uk

Hereford and Worcester. Bronsil House, Eastnor, Nr Ledbury HR8 1EP. 01531 638500;(fax)01531 638501; e-mail: Hereford and Worcester @english-nature.org.uk

Humber to Pennines. Bull Ring House, Northgate, Wakefield, W Yorks WF1 1HD. 01924 334500;(fax)01924 201507;
e-mail; humber.pennines@english-nature.org.uk

Kent. The Countryside Management Centre, Coldharbour Farm, Wye, Ashford, Kent TN25 5DB. 01233 812525;(fax)01233 812520; e-mail; kent@english-nature.org.uk

Norfolk. 60 Bracondale, Norwich NR1 2BE. 01603 598400;(fax)01603 762552;
e-mail: norfolk@english-nature.org.uk

North and East Yorkshire. Genesis 1, University Road, Heslington, York YO10 5ZQ. 01904 435500;(fax)01904 435520;
e-mail: york@english-nature.org.uk

North Mercia (Shrops, Staffs, Warks, W Mid). Attingham Park, Shrewsbury SY4 4TW. 01743 709611;(fax)01743 709303; e-mail: North Mercia @english-nature.org.uk
Northumbria. Stocksfield Hall, Stocksfield, Northumberland NE4 7TN. 01661 845500;(fax)01661 845501;
e-mail: northumbria@english-nature.org.uk
Peak District and Derbyshire. Endcliffe, Deepdale Business Park, Ashford Road, Bakewell DE45 1GT. 01629 816640;(fax)01629 816679. e-mail: peak.derbys@english-nature.org.uk
Somerset and Gloucester. Roughmoor, Bishop's Hull, Taunton, Somerset TA1 5AA. 01823 283211;(fax)01823 272978; e-mail: somerset@english-nature.org.uk
Suffolk. Regent House, 110 Northgate Street, Bury St Edmunds, Suffolk IP33 1HP. 01284 762218;(fax)01284 764318;
e-mail: suffolk@english-nature.org.uk
Sussex and Surrey. Phoenix House, 32-33 North Street, Lewes, E Sussex BN7 2PH. 01273 476595;(fax)01273 483063;
e-mail: sussex.surrey@english-nature.org.uk
Thames and Chilterns. Foxhold House, Thornford Road, Crookham Common, Thatcham, Berks RG19 8EL. 01635 268881;(fax)01635 267027;
e-mail: thames.chilterns@english-nature.org.uk
Wiltshire. Prince Maurice Court, Hambleton Avenue, Devizes, Wilts SN10 2RT. 01380 726344;(fax)01380 721411;
e-mail: wiltshire@english-nature.org.uk

ENVIRONMENT AGENCY (THE) (1996)
A non-departmental body that aims to protect and improve the environment and to contribute towards the delivery of sustainable developmentthrough the integrated management of air, land and water. Functions include pollution prevention and control, waste minimisation,management of water resources, flood defence, improvement of salmon and freshwater fisheries, conservation of aquatic species,navigation and use of inland and coastal waters for recreation. Sponsored by the Department of the Environment, Transport and the Regions, MAFF and the Welsh Office.
Regional Offices
Anglian. Kingfisher House, Goldhay Way, Orton Goldhay, Peterborough PE2 5ZR. 01733 371811; fax 01733 231840.
North East. Rivers House, 21 Park Square South, Leeds LS1 2QG. 0113 244 0191; fax 0113 246 1889.
North West. Richard Fairclough House, Knutsford Road, Warrington WA4 1HG. 01925 653999; fax 01925 415961.
Midlands. Sapphire East, 550 Streetsbrook Road, Solihull B91 1QT. 0121 711 2324; fax 0121 711 5824.
Southern. Guildbourne House, Chatsworth Road, Worthing, W Sussex BN11 1LD. 01903 832000; fax 01903 821832.
South West. Manley House, Kestrel Way, Exeter EX2 7LQ. 01392 444000; fax 01392 444238.
Thames. Kings Meadow House, Kings Meadow Road, Reading RG1 8DQ. 0118 953 5000; fax 0118 950 0388.
Wales. Rivers House, St Mellons Business Park, St Mellons, Cardiff CF3 0EY. 029 2077 0088; fax 029 2079 8555.
Contact: Rio House, Waterside Drive, Aztec West, Almondsbury, Bristol, BS32 4UD, 01454 624400; (Fax)01454 624409; www.environment-agency.gov.uk

FARMING AND WILDLIFE ADVISORY GROUP (FWAG) (1969).
An independent UK registered charity led by farmers and supported by government and leading countryside organisations. Its aim is to unite farming and forestry with wildlife and landscape conservation. Active in most UK counties. There are 85 Farm Conservation Advisers who give practical advice to farmers and landowners to help them integrate environmental objectives with commercial farming practices. Technical Director, Richard Knight.
Contact: Chief Executive, Robert Bettley-Smith, National Agricultural Centre, Stoneleigh, Kenilworth, Warwickshire, CV8 2RX, 024 7669 6699; (Fax)024 7669 6760;
e-mail: info@fwag.org.uk
www.fwag.org.uk

FIELD STUDIES COUNCIL (1943).
Cathy Preston, Preston Montford, Montford Bridge, Shrewsbury, SY4 1HW, 01743 852100; (Fax)01743 852101;
e-mail: fsc.headoffice@field-studies-council.org
www.field-studies-council.org
FSC Overseas, Preston Montford, Montford Bridge, Shrewsbury SY4 1HW. 01743 852100; (Fax)01743 852101; e-mail: fsc.overseas.ukonline.co.uk

Manages Centres where students from schools, universities and colleges of education, as well as individuals of all ages, could stay and study various aspects of the environment under expert guidance. The courses include many for birdwatchers, providing opportunities to study birdlife on coasts, estuaries, mountains and islands. There are some courses demonstrating bird ringing and others for members of the Wildlife Explorers. The length of the courses varies: from a weekend up to seven days' duration. Research workers and naturalists wishing to use the records and resources are welcome. FSC Overseas includes birdwatching in its programme of overseas courses.

Centres:
Blencathra Field Centre, Threlkeld, Keswick, Cumbria CA12 4SG, 017687 79601;
e-mail: enquiries.bl@field-studies-council.org
Castle Head Field Centre, Grange-over-Sands, Cumbria LA11 6QT, 015395 38120,
e-mail: enquiries.ch@field-studies-council.org
Dale Fort Field Centre, Haverfordwest, Pembs SA62 3RD, 01646 636205,
e-mail: enquiries.df@field-studies-council.org
Epping Forest Field Centre, High Beach, Loughton, Essex, IG10 4AF, 020 8502 8500,
e-mail: enquiries.ef@field-studies-council.org
Flatford Mill Field Centre, East Bergholt, Suffolk, CO7 6UL, 01206 298892,
e-mail: enquiries.fm@field-studies-council.org
Derrygonnelly Field Centre, Tir Navar, Creamery St, Derrygonnelly, Co Fermanagh, BT93 6HW. 028 686 41673, e-mail:
fsc.derrygonnelly@ukonline.co.uk
Juniper Hall Field Centre, Dorking, Surrey, RH5 6DA, 0845 458 3507,
e-mail: enquiries.jh@field-studies-council.org
Kindrogan Field Centre, Enochdhu, Blairgowrie, Perthshire PH10 7PG. 01250 881286, e-mail:
kindrogan@btinternet.com
Margam Park Field Centre, Port Talbot SA13 2TJ. 01639 895636, e-mail:
margam_sustainable_centre@hotmail.com
Malham Tarn Field Centre, Settle, N Yorks, BD24 9PU, 01729 830331,
e-mail: fsc.malham@ukonline.co.uk
Nettlecombe Court, The Leonard Wills Field Centre, Williton, Taunton, Somerset, TA4 4HT, 01984 640320,
e-mail: enquiries.nc@field-studies-council.org
Orielton Field Centre, Pembroke, Pembs,SA71 5EZ, 01646 623920,
e-mail: enquiries.or@field-studies-council.org
Preston Montford Field Centre, Montford Bridge, Shrewsbury, SY4 1DX, 01743 852040,
e-mail: enquiries.pm@field-studies-council.org
Rhyd-y-creuau, the Drapers' Field Centre Betws-y-coed, Conwy, LL24 0HB, 01690 710494,
e-mail: enquiries.rc@field-studies-council.org
Slapton Ley Field Centre, Slapton, Kingsbridge, Devon, TQ7 2QP, 01548 580466, e-mail:
enquiries.sl@field-studies-council.org

FLIGHTLINE
Northern Ireland's daily bird news service. Run under the auspices of the Northern Ireland Birdwatchers' Association (qv).
Contact: George Gordon, 2 Brooklyn Avenue, Bangor, Co Down, BT20 5RB, 028 9146 7408;
e-mail: gordon@ballyholm2.freeserve.co.uk

FORESTRY COMMISSION
The Forestry Commission of Great Britain is the government department responsible for the protection and expansion of Britain's forests and woodlands. The organisation is run from national offices in England, Wales and Scotland, working to targets set by Commissioners and Ministers in each of the three countries. Its objectives are to protect Britain's forests and resources, conserve and improve the biodiversity, landscape and cultural heritage of forests and woodlands, develop opportunities for woodland recreation and increase public understanding and community participation in forestry.
Contact: Forestry Commission Headquarters, Silvan House, 231 Corstorphine Road, Edinburgh, EH12 7AT, 0845 367 3787; (Fax) 0131 334 3047; Media enquiries: 0131 314 6550.
e-mail: enquiries@forestry.gsi.gov.uk
www.forestry.gov.uk
Details of wildlife viewing sites aross the country can be found on www.forestry.gov.uk/forestry/wildwoods
Forestry Commission National Offices:
England: Great Eastern House, Tenison Road, Cambridge CB1 2DU. 01223 314546; (Fax)01223 460699, e-mail: fc.nat.off.eng@forestry.gsi.gov.uk
Scotland: Address as HQ above, 0131 334 0303, (Fax)0131 314 615,
e-mail: as.nat.office@forestry.gsi.gov.uk
Wales: Victoria Terrace, Aberystwyth, Ceredigion SY23 2DQ. 01970 625866; (Fax)01970 626177.

(1971; 150,000).
The largest international network of environmental groups in the world, represented in 68 countries. It is one of the leading environmental pressure groups in the UK. It has a unique network of campaigning local groups, working in 250 communities in England, Wales and Northern Ireland. It is largely funded by supporters with more than 90% of income coming from individual donations, the rest from special fundraising events, grants and trading.
Contact: 26/28 Underwood Street, London, N1 7JQ, 020 7490 1555; (Fax)020 7490 0881;
e-mail: info@foe.co.uk www.foe.co.uk

GAME CONSERVANCY TRUST
(1933; 24,000).
A registered charity which researches the conservation of game and other wildlife in the British countryside. More than 60 scientists are engaged in detailed work on insects, pesticides, birds (30 species inc. raptors) mammals (inc. foxes), and habitats. The results are used to advise government, landowners, farmers and conservationists on practical management techniques which will benefit game species, their habitats, and wildlife. Each June an *Annual Review* of 100 pages lists about 60 papers published in the peer-reviewed scientific press.
Contact: Director General, Dr G R Potts, Fordingbridge, Hampshire, SP6 1EF, 01425 652381; (Fax)01425 651026;
e-mail: info@gct.org.uk www.gct.org.uk

GAY BIRDERS CLUB (1995; 300+).
A voluntary society for lesbian, gay and bisexual birdwatchers, their friends and supporters, over the age of consent, in the UK and worldwide. The club has 3-400 members and a network of regional contacts. It organises day trips, weekends and longer events at notable birding locations in the UK and abroad; about 200+ events in a year. Members receive a quarterly newletter with details of all events. There is a Grand Get Together every 18 months. Membership £12 waged and £5 unwaged.
Contact: GeeBeeCee, BCM-Mono, London, WC1N 3XX. e-mail: enquiries@gbc-online.org.uk www.gbc-online.org.uk

GOLDEN ORIOLE GROUP (1987). Sec.
Organises censuses of breeding Golden Orioles in parts of Cambridgeshire, Norfolk and Suffolk. Maintains contact with a network of individuals in other parts of the country where Orioles may or do breed. Studies breeding biology, habitat and food requirements of the species.
Contact: Jake Allsop, 5 Bury Lane, Haddenham, Ely, Cambs, CB6 3PR, 01353 740540;
e-mail: jakeallsop@aol.com
www.goldenoriolegroup.org.uk

HAWK AND OWL TRUST (1969).
Registered charity dedicated to the conservation and appreciation of all birds of prey including owls. Publishes a newsletter *Peregrine* and educational materials for all ages. The Trust achieves its major aim of creating and enhancing wild habitats for birds of prey through projects which involve practical research, creative conservation and education. Projects are often conducted in close partnership with landowners, farmers and others. Members are invited to take part in population studies, field surveys, etc. Studies of Barn and Little Owls, Hen Harrier, and Goshawk are in progress. The Trust's National Conservation and Education Centre at Newland Park, Gorelands Lane, Chalfont St Giles, Bucks, is now open to the public and offers schools and other groups cross-curricular environmental activities.

Contact: Membership administration: 11 St Mary's Close, Abbotskerswell, Newton Abbot, Devon, TQ12 5QF. www.hawkandowl.org
e-mail: hawkandowltrust@aol.com

IRISH RARE BIRDS COMMITTEE (1985).
Assesses records of species of rare occurrence in the Republic of Ireland. Details of records accepted and rejected are incorporated in the Irish Bird Report, published annually in Irish Birds. In the case of rarities trapped for ringing, ringers in the Republic of Ireland are required to send their schedules initially to the National Parks and Wildlife Service, 51 St Stephen's Green, Dublin 2. A copy is taken before the schedules are sent to the British Trust for Ornithology.
Contact: Hon Secretary, Paul Milne, 100 Dublin Road, Sutton, Dublin 13; +353 (0)1 8325653;
e-mail: pjmilne@hotmail.com

JOINT NATURE CONSERVATION COMMITTEE (1990).
A committee of the three country agencies (English Nature, Scottish Natural Heritage, and the Countryside Council for Wales), together with independent members and representatives from Northern Ireland and the Countryside Agency. It is supported by specialist staff. Its statutory responsibilities include the establishment of common standards for monitoring, the analysis of information and research; advising Ministers on the development and implementation of policies for or affecting nature conservation; the provision of advice and the dissemination of knowledge to any persons about nature conservation; and the undertaking and commissioning of research relevant to these functions. JNCC additionally has the UK responsibility for relevant European and wider international matters. The Species Team, located at the HQ address above, is responsible for terrestrial bird conservation.
Contact: Monkstone House, City Road, Peterborough, PE1 1JY, 01733 562626; (Fax)01733 555948; www.jncc.gov.uk
e-mail: feedback@jncc.gov.uk

LINNEAN SOCIETY OF LONDON (1788).
Named after Carl Linnaeus, the 18th century Swedish biologist, who created the modern system of scientific biological nomenclature, the Society promotes all aspects of pure and applied biology. It houses Linnaeus's collection of plants, insects and fishes, library and correspondence. The Society has a major reference library of some 100,000 volumes. Publishes the *Biological, Botanical and Zoological Journals*, and the *Synopses of the British Fauna*.
Contact: Executive Secretary, Dr J C Marsden, Burlington House, Piccadilly, London, W1J 0BF, 020 7434 4479; (Fax)020 7287 9364;
e-mail: john@linnean.org
www.linnean.org

LITTLE OWL STUDY GROUP (2002; 37).
Formed to promote the study and conservation of Little Owls (*Athene noctua*) in Britain and to develop a population monitoring network for Little Owls. The LOSG is part of the International Little Owl Working Group, a Europe wide organisation networking Little Owl Research and Conservation. The Little Owl is declining at an alarming rate across Europe and is endangered in at least three Western European countries. To combat this, a European Species Action Plan is being developed, to put in place the necessary monitors, conservation, and education measures for its long term survival. Project *Athene* is the British leg of this SAP.(See National Projects).
Contact: Roy Leigh, C/O Biota, The Old Barn, Moseley Hall Farm, Chilford Road, Knutsford, Cheshire, WA16 8RB, 0871 734 0111; (Fax)0871 734 0555; e-mail: rsl@biota.co.uk

THE MAMMAL SOCIETY (1954; 2,500).

The Mammal Society is the voice for British mammals and the only organisation solely dedicated to the study and conservation of all British mammals. They seek to raise awareness of mammals, their ecology and their conservation needs, to survey British mammals and their habitats to identify the threats they face, to promote mammal studies in the UK and overseas, to advocate conservation plans based on sound science, to provide current information on mammals through our publications, to involve people of all ages in their efforts to protect mammals, to educate people about British mammals and to monitor mammal population changes.
Contact: Enquiries, 2B Inworth Street, London SW11 3EP, 020 7350 2200; (Fax)020 7350 2211;
e-mail: enquiries@mammal.org.uk
www.mammal.org.uk

MANX ORNITHOLOGICAL SOCIETY see County Directory

MANX WILDLIFE TRUST see County Directory

NATIONAL BIRDS OF PREY CENTRE (1967).
Concerned with the conservation and captive breeding of all raptors. Approx 85 species on site. Birds flown daily. Open Feb-Nov.
Contact: Mrs J Parry-Jones MBE, Newent, Glos, GL18 1JJ, 0870 9901992; www.nbpc.co.uk
e-mail: jpj@nbpc.demon.co.uk

NATIONAL TRUST (1895; 3.1million).
Charity depending on voluntary support of its members and the public. Largest private landowner with over 603,862 acres of land and nearly 600 miles of coast. Works for the preservation of places of historic interest or natural beauty, in England, Wales and N Ireland. The Trust's coast and countryside properties are open to the public at all times, subject only to the needs offarming, forestry and the protection of wildlife. Over a quarter of the Trust's land holding is designated SSSI or ASSI (N Ireland)and about 10% of SSSIs in England and Wales are wholly or partially owned by the Trust, as are 31 NNRs (eg Blakeney Point, FarneIslands, Wicken Fen and large parts of Strangford Lough, N Ireland). Fifteen per cent of Ramsar Sites include Trust land, as do 27%of SPAs. 71 of the 117 bird species listed in the UK Red Data Book are found on Trust land.
Head of Nature Conservation: Dr H J Harvey, Estates Dept, 33 Sheep Street, Cirencester, Glos GL7 1RQ. 01285 651818. Northern Ireland Office: Rowallane House, Saintfield, Ballynahinch, Co. Down BT24 7LH. 028 975 10721.
Contact: Emily Brooks, Communications, 36 Queen Anne's Gate, London, SW1H 9AS, 020 7222 9251. www.nationaltrust.org.uk

NATIONAL TRUST FOR SCOTLAND (1931; 230,000).
An independent charity, its 90 properties open to the public are described in its annual guide.
Contact: Marketing Department, Wemyss House, 28 Charlotte Square, Edinburgh, EH2 4ET, 0131 243 9300. www.nts.org.uk

NATURE PHOTOGRAPHERS' PORTFOLIO (1944).
A society for photographers of wildlife, especially

birds. Circulates postal portfolios of prints and transparencies.
Contact: Hon Secretary, A Winspear-Cundall, 8 Gig Bridge Lane, Pershore, Worcs, WR10 1NH, 01386 552103.

NORTHERN IRELAND BIRDWATCHERS' ASSOCIATION (1991; 90).
The NIBA Records Committee, established in 1997, has full responsibility for the assessment of records in N Ireland. NIBA also publishes the *Northern Ireland Bird Report*.
Contact: Hon Secretary, William McDowell, 4 Gairloch Park, Holywood, Co Down, BT18 0LZ, 028 9059 4390;
e-mail: williamm.mcdowell@ntlworld.com

NORTHERN IRELAND ORNITHOLOGISTS' CLUB (1965; 150).
Operates two small reserves in Co Down. Operates a Barn Owl nestbox scheme and a winter feeding programme for Yellowhammers. Has a regular programme of lectures and field trips for members. Publishes *The Harrier* quarterly.
Contact: Gary Wilkinson, The Roost, 139 Windmill Road, Hillsborough, Co Down, BT26 6NP 028 9263 9254.
www.nioc.fsnet.co.uk

PEOPLE'S DISPENSARY FOR SICK ANIMALS (1917).
Registered charity. Provides free veterinary treatment for sick and injured animals whose owners qualify for this charitable service.
Contact: Director General, Mrs Marilyn Rydstrom, Whitechapel Way, Priorslee, Telford, Shrops, TF2 9PQ, 01952 290999;
e-mail: pr@pdsa.org.uk
www.pdsa.org.uk

RARE BREEDING BIRDS PANEL (1973).
An independent body funded by the JNCC and RSPB. Both bodies are represented on the panel as are BTO and ACRE. It collects all information on rare breeding birds in the United Kingdom, so that changes in status can be monitored as an aid to present-day conservation and stored for posterity. Special forms are used (obtainable free from the secretary and the website) and records should if possible be submitted via the county and regional recorders. Since 1996 the Panel also monitors breeding by scarcer non-native species and seeks records of these in the same way. Annual report is published in *British Birds*. For details of species covered by the Panel see Log Charts and the websites.
Contact: Secretary, Dr Malcolm Ogilvie, Glencairn, Bruichladdich, Isle of Islay, PA49 7UN, 01496 850218; www.rbbp.org.uk
e-mail: rbbp@indaal.demon.co.uk

ROYAL AIR FORCE ORNITHOLOGICAL SOCIETY (1965; 295).
RAFOS organises regular field meetings for members, carries out ornithological census work on MOD properties and mounts major expeditions annually to various UK and overseas locations. Publishes a Newsletter twice a year, a Journal annually, and reports on its expeditions and surveys.
Contact: General Secretary, RAFOS, MOD DE(C) Conservation, Blandford House, Farnborough Road, Aldershot, Hants, GU11 2HA, 01225 468416.

ROYAL NAVAL BIRDWATCHING SOCIETY (1946; 167 full and 93 associate members and library).
Cover all main ocean routes, the Society has developed a system for reporting the positions and identity of seabirds and landbirds at sea by means of standard sea report forms, much of the system being computerised. Members are encouraged to photograph birds while at sea and a library of photographs and slides is maintained. Publishes a Bulletin and an annual report entitled *The Sea Swallow*.
Contact: Hon Secretary, FS Ward Esq., 16 Cutlers Lane, Stubbington, Fareham, Hants, PO14 2JN.+44 1329 665931; e-mail: fsward@lineone.net

ROYAL PIGEON RACING ASSOCIATION (1897; 42,000).
Exists to promote the sport of pigeon racing and controls pigeon racing within the Association. Organises liberation sites, issues rings, calculates distances between liberation sites and home lofts, and assists in the return of strays. May be able to assist in identifying owners of ringed birds caught or found.
Contact: General Manager, RPRA, The Reddings, Cheltenham, GL51 6RN, 01452 713529;
e-mail: gm@rpra.org or strays@rpra.org
www.rpra.org

ROYAL SOCIETY FOR THE PREVENTION OF CRUELTY TO ANIMALS (1824; 43,690).
In addition to its animal homes, the Society also runs a woodland study centre and nature reserve at Mallydams Wood in East Sussex and specialist wildlife rehabilitation centres at West Hatch,

Taunton, Somerset TA3 5RT (01823 480156), at Station Road, East Winch, King's Lynn, Norfolk PE32 1NR (01553 842336), and London Road, Stapeley, Nantwich, Cheshire CW5 7JW (0870 4427102). Inspectors are contacted through their Regional Communications Centres, which can be reached via the Society's 24-hour national cruelty and advice line: 08705 555 999.
Contact: RSPCA Headquarters, Willberforce Way, Horsham, West Sussex, RH13 9RS, 0870 0101181; (Fax)0870 7530048.
www.rspca.org.uk

ROYAL SOCIETY FOR THE PROTECTION OF BIRDS (1889; 1,036,000).
UK Partner of BirdLife International and Europe's largest voluntary wildlife conservation body. The RSPB, a registered charity, is governed by an elected body (see also RSPB Phoenix and RSPB Wildlife Explorers). Its work in the conservation of wild birds and habitats covers the acquisition and management of nature reserves; research and surveys; monitoring and responding to development proposals, land use practices and pollution which threaten wild birds and biodiversity; and the provision of an advisory service on wildlife law enforcement.
Work in the education and information field includes formal education in schools and colleges, and informal activities for children through Wildlife Explorers; publications (including *Birds*, a quarterly magazine for members, *Bird Life*, a bi-monthly magazine for RSPB Wildlife Explorers, *Wild Times* for under-8s); displays and exhibitions; the distribution of moving images about birds; and the development of membership activities through Members' Groups.
The RSPB currently manages 182 nature reserves in the UK, covering more than 313,000 acres; more than 50% of this area is owned. Sites are carefully selected, mostly as being of national or international importance to wildlife conservation. The aim is to conserve a countrywide network of reserves with all examples of the main bird communities and with due regard to the conservation of plants and other animals. Visitors are generally welcome to most reserves, subject to any restrictions necessary to protect the wildlife or habitats.
Current national projects include extensive work on agriculture, and conservation and campaigning for the conservation of the marine environment and to halt the illegal persecution of birds of prey. Increasingly, there is involvement with broader environmental concerns such as climate change and transport.
The RSPB's International Dept works closely with Birdlife International and its partners in other countries and is involved with numerous projects overseas, especially in Europe and Asia.
Regional Offices
RSPB North England, 4 Benton Terrace, Sandyford Road, Newcastle upon Tyne NE2 1QU. 0191 281 3366.
RSPB North West, Westleigh Mews, Wakefield Road, Denby Dale, Huddersfield HD8 8QD. 01484 861148.
RSPB Central England, 46 The Green, South Bar, Banbury, Oxon OX16 9AB. 01295 253330.
RSPB East Anglia, Stalham House, 65 Thorpe Road, Norwich NR1 1UD. 01603 661662.
RSPB South East, 2nd Floor, Frederick House, 42 Frederick Place, Brighton BN1 4EA. 01273 775333.
RSPB South West, Keble House, Southernhay Gardens, Exeter EX1 1NT. 01392 432691.
RSPB Scotland HQ, Dunedin House, 25 Ravelston Terrace, Edinburgh EH4 3TP. 0131 311 6500.
RSPB North Scotland, Etive House, Beechwood Park, Inverness IV2 3BW. 01463 715000.
RSPB East Scotland, 10 Albyn Terrace, Aberdeen AB1 1YP. 01224 624824.
RSPB South & West Scotland, 10 Park Quadrant, Glasgow G3 6BS. 0141 331 0993.
RSPB North Wales, Maes y Ffynnon, Penrhosgarnedd, Bangor, Gwynedd LL57 2DW. 01248 363800.
RSPB South Wales, Sutherland House, Castlebridge, Cowbridge Road East, Cardiff CF11 9AB. 029 2035 3000.
RSPB Northern Ireland, Belvoir Park Forest, Belfast BT8 7QT. 028 9049 1547.
Contact: Chief Executive, Graham Wynne, The Lodge, Sandy, Beds, SG19 2DL, 01767 680551; (Fax)01767 692365;
e-mail: (firstname.name)@rspb.org.uk
www.rspb.org.uk

RSPB WILDLIFE EXPLORERS and RSPB PHOENIX (formerly YOC) (1965; 140,000).
Junior section of the RSPB. There are more than 300 groups run by 700 volunteers. Activities include projects, holidays, roadshows, competitions, and local events for children, families and teenagers. Publishes 2 bi-monthly magazines, *Bird Life* (aimed at 8-12 year olds) and *Wild Times* (aimed at under 8s) and 1 quarterly magazine *Wingbeat* (aimed at teenagers).
Contact: Principal Youth Officer, David Chandler,

RSPB Youth Unit, The Lodge, Sandy, Beds, SG19 2DL, 01767 680551;
e-mail: explorers@rspb.org.uk and phoenix@rspb.org.uk www.rspb.org.uk/youth

SCOTTISH BIRDS RECORDS COMMITTEE (1984).
Set up by the Scottish Ornithologists' Club to ensure that records of species not deemed rare enough to be considered by the British Birds Rarities Committee, but which are rare in Scotland, are fully assessed; also maintains the official list of Scottish birds.
Contact: Secretary, R W Forrester, The Gables, Eastlands Road, Rothesay, Isle of Bute, PA20 9JZ. www.the-soc.org.uk

SCOTTISH NATURAL HERITAGE (1991).
Statutory body established by the Natural Heritage (Scotland) Act 1991 and responsible to Scottish Ministers. Its aim is to promote Scotland's natural Heritage, its care and improvement, its responsible enjoyment, its greater understanding and appreciation and its sustainable use.
Contact: Chief Executive, SNH, Ian Jardine, 12 Hope Terrace, Edinburgh, EH9 2AS, 0131 447 4784; www.snh.org.uk

SCOTTISH ORNITHOLOGISTS' CLUB (1936; 2250).
The Club has 14 branches (see County Directory). Each with a programme of winter meetings and field trips throughout the year. The SOC organises an annual weekend conference in the autumn anda joint SOC/BTO one-day birdwatchers' conference in spring. Publishes quarterly newsletter *Scottish Bird News*, the bi-annual *Scottish Birds*, the annual *Scottish Bird Report* and the *Raptor Round Up*. The SOC is developing a new resource centre in Scotland, details of which can be found on the website.
Contact: Development Manager, Bill Gardner MBE, Harbout Point, Newhailes Road, Musselburgh, EH21 6SJ, 0131 653 0653; (Fax)0131 6530654; www.the-soc.org.uk
e-mail: mail@the-soc.org.uk

SCOTTISH SOCIETY FOR THE PREVENTION OF CRUELTY TO ANIMALS (1839).
Represents animal welfare interests to Government, local authorities and others. Educates young people to realise their responsibilities. Maintains an inspectorate to patrol and investigate and to advise owners about the welfare of animals and birds in their care. Maintains 13 welfare centres, two of which include oiled bird cleaning centres. Bird species, including birds of prey, are rehabilitated and where possible released back into the wild.
Contact: Chief Executive, Ian Gardiner, Braehead Mains, 603 Queensferry Road, Edinburgh, EH4 6EA, 0131 339 0222; (Fax)0131 339 4777;
e-mail: enquiries@scottishspca.org
www.scottishspca.org

SCOTTISH WILDLIFE TRUST (1964; 22,000).
Has members' groups throughout Scotland. Aims to conserve all forms of wildlife and has over 125 reserves, many of great birdwatching interest, covering some 50,000 acres. Member of The Wildlife Trusts partnership and organises Scottish Wildlife Watch. Publishes *Scottish Wildlife* three times a year.
Contact: Chief Executive, Steve Sankey, Cramond House, Off Cramond Glebe Road, Edinburgh, EH4 6NS, 0131 312 7765; (Fax)0131 312 8705;
e-mail: enquiries@swt.org.uk
www.swt.org.uk

SEABIRD GROUP (1966; 350).
Concerned with conservation issues affecting seabirds. Co-ordinates census and monitoring work on breeding seabirds; has established and maintains the Seabird Colony Register in collaboration with the JNCC; organises triennial conferences on seabird biology and conservation topics. Small grants available to assist with research and survey work on seabirds. Publishes the *Seabird Group Newsletter* every four months and the journal, *Atlantic Seabirds,* quarterly in association with the Dutch Seabird Group.
Contact: Bob Swann, 14 St Vincent Road, Tain, Ross-shire, IV19 1JR, 01862 894329;
e-mail: bob.swann@freeuk.com

SOCIETY OF WILDLIFE ARTISTS (1964; 70 Members, 10 Associates).
Registered charity. Annual exhibitions held in Sept/Oct at the Mall Galleries, London.
Contact: President, Bruce Pearson, Federation of British Artists, 17 Carlton House Terrace, London, SW1Y 5BD, 020 7930 6844.
www.swla.co.uk

SWAN SANCTUARY (THE)
Founded by Dorothy Beeson BEM. A registered charity which operates nationally, with 6 rescue centres in the UK and 1 in Ireland. Has a fully equipped swan hospital with an operating theatre, 2 treatment rooms, x-ray facilities and a veterinary

surgeon. Present site has 3 lakes and 10 rehabilitation ponds where some 3,000 swans a year are treated. 24-hour service operated, with volunteer rescuers on hand to recover victims of oil spills, vandalism etc. A planned new site will allow visitors. Provides education and training. Reg. charity number 1002582.
Contact: Secretary, Field View, Pooley Green, Egham, Surrey, TW20 8AT, 01784 431667; (Fax)01784 430122;
e-mail: swans@swanuk.org.uk
www.swanuk.org.uk

SWAN STUDY GROUP (80).
An association of both amateur and professionals, from around the UK. Most are concerned with Mute Swans, but Bewick's and Whooper Swan biologists are also active members. The aim of the Group is to provide a forum for communication and discussion, and to help co-ordinate co-operative studies. Annual meetings are held at various locations in the UK at which speakers give presentations on their own fieldwork.
Contact: Helen Chisholm, 14 Buckstone Howe, Edinburgh, EH10 6XF, 0131 445 2351;
e-mail: h.chisholm@aol.ac.uk

UK400 CLUB (1981).
Serves to monitor the nation's leading twitchers and their life lists, and to keep under review contentious species occurrences. Publishes a bi-monthly magazine *Rare Birds* and operates a website; www.uk400clubonline.co.uk. Membership open to all.
Contact: L G R Evans, 8 Sandycroft Road, Little Chalfont, Amersham, Bucks, HP6 6QL, 01494 763010; e-mail: LGREUK400@aol.com
www.uk400clubonline.co.uk

ULSTER WILDLIFE TRUST see County Directory

WADER STUDY GROUP (1970; 600).
An association of wader enthusiasts, both amateur and professional, from all parts of the world. The Group aims to maintain contact between them, to help in the organisation of co-operative studies, and to provide a vehicle for the exchange of information. Publishes the Wader Study Group Bulletin three times a year and holds annual meetings throughout Europe.
Contact: Membership Secretary, Wader Study Group, Rod West, c/o BTO, The Nunnery, Thetford, Norfolk, IP24 2PU.
e-mail: rodwest@ndirect.co.uk

WALTER ROTHSCHILD ZOOLOGICAL MUSEUM
Founded by Lionel Walter (later Lord) Rothschild, the Museum displays British and exotic birds (1500 species) including many rarities and extinct species. Galleries open all year except 24-26 Dec. Adjacent to the Bird Group of the Natural History Museum - with over a million specimens and an extensive ornithological library, an internationally important centre for bird research.
Contact: Akeman Street, Tring, Herts, HP23 6AP, 020 7942 6171.
www.nhm.ac.uk/museum/tring

WELSH KITE TRUST (1996).
A registered charity that undertakes the conservation and annual monitoring of Red Kites in Wales. It attempts to locate all the breeding birds, to compile data on population growth, productivity, range expansion etc. The Trust liaises with landowners, acts as consultant on planning issues and with regard to filming and photography, and represents Welsh interests on the UK Kite Steering Group. Provides a limited rescue service for injured kites and eggs or chicks at risk of desertion or starvation. Publishes a newsletter Boda Wennol twice a year, sent free to members of Friends of the Welsh Kite and to all landowners with nesting Kites.
Contact: Tony Cross, Samaria, Nantmel, Llandrindod Wells, Powys, LD1 6EN, 01597 860524; e-mail: tony.cross@welshkitetrust.org
www.welshkitetrust.org

WELSH ORNITHOLOGICAL SOCIETY (1988; 250).
Promotes the study, conservation and enjoyment of birds throughout Wales. Runs the Welsh Records Panel which adjudicates records of scarce species in Wales. Publishes the journal *Welsh Birds* twice a year, along with newsletters, and organises an annual conference.
Contact: Paul Kenyon, 196 Chester Road, Hartford, Northwich, CW8 1LG, 01606 77960; e-mail: pkenyon196@aol.com
www.members.aol.com/welshos/cac

WETLAND TRUST
Set up to encourage conservation of wetlands and develop study of migratory birds, and to foster international relations in these fields. Destinations for recent expeditions inc. Brazil, Senegal, The Gambia, Guinea-Bissau, Nigeria, Kuwait, Thailand, Greece and Jordan. Large numbers of birds are ringed each year in Sussex and applications are invited from individuals to train in bird ringing or extend their experience.

Contact: AJ Martin, Elms Farm, Pett Lane, Icklesham, Winchelsea, E Sussex, TN36 4AH, 01797 226374; e-mail: alan@wetlandtrust.org

WILDFOWL & WETLANDS TRUST (THE) (1946; 106,000 members and 4,700 bird adopters). Registered charity founded by the late Sir Peter Scott; its mission - to conserve wetlands and their biodiversity. WWT has nine centres with reserves (see Arundel, Caerlaverock, Castle Espie, Llanelli, Martin Mere, Slimbridge, Washington, Welney, and The London Wetland Centre in Reserves and Observatories section). The centres are nationally or internationally important for wintering wildfowl; they also aim to raise awareness of and appreciation for wetland species, the problems they face and the conservation action needed to help them. Programmes of walks and talks are available for visitors with varied interests - resources and programmes are provided for school groups. Centres, except Caerlaverock and Welney, have wildfowl from around the world, inc. endangered species. Research Department works on population dynamics, species management plans and wetland ecology. The Wetland Advisory Service (WAS) undertakes contracts, and Wetland Link International promotes the role of wetland centres for education and public awarenes
Contact: Managing Director, Tony Richardson, Slimbridge, Glos, GL2 7BT, 01453 890333; (Fax)01453 890827; www.wwt.org.uk e-mail: enquiries@wwt.org.uk

WILDLIFE SOUND RECORDING SOCIETY (1968; 327).
Works closely with the Wildlife Section of the National Sound Archive. Members carry out recording work for scientific purposes as well as for pleasure. A field weekend is held each spring, and members organise meetings locally. Four CD sound magazines of members' recordings are produced for members each year, and a journal, *Wildlife Sound*, is published twice a year.
Contact: Hon Membership Secretary, WSRS, Mike Iannantuoni, 36 Wenton Close, Cottesmore, Oakham, Rutland, LE15 7DR, 01572 812447; www.scbm.fsnet.co.uk/usrs.htm

WILDLIFE TRUSTS (THE)
A nationwide network of 46 local Wildlife Trusts and 100 urban Wildlife Groups which work to protect wildlife in town and country. The Wildlife Trusts manage more than 2300 nature reserves, undertake a wide range of other conservation and education activities, and are dedicated to the achievement of a UK richer in wildlife. Publ *Natural World*. See also Wildlife Watch.
Contact: The Kiln, Waterside, Mather Road, Newark, NG24 1WT, 01636 677711; (Fax)01636 670001; e-mail: info@wildlife-trusts.cix.co.uk www.wildlifetrusts.org

WILDLIFE WATCH (1971; 24,000+).
The junior branch of The Wildlife Trusts (see previous entry). It supports 1500 registered volunteer leaders running Watch groups across the UK. Publishes *Watchword* and *Wildlife Extra*.
Contact: Development Officer, Avril Rawson, The Wildlife Trusts, The Kiln, Waterside, Mather Road, Newark, NG24 1WT, 0870 0367711; (Fax)00870 0360101;
e-mail: watch@wildlife-trusts.cix.co.uk
www.wildlifewatch.org/watch

WWF-UK (1961).

WWF is the world's largest independent conservation organisation, comprising 27 national organisations. It works to conserve endangered species, protect endangered spaces, and address global threats to nature by seeking long-term solutions with people in government and industry, education and civil society. Publishes *WWF News* (quarterly magazine).
Contact: Chief Executive, Robert Napier, Panda House, Weyside Park, Catteshall Lane, Godalming, Surrey, GU7 1XR, 01483 426444; (Fax)01483 426409; www.wwf-uk.org

ZOOLOGICAL PHOTOGRAPHIC CLUB (1899).
Circulates black and white and colour prints of zoological interest via a series of postal portfolios.
Contact: Hon Secretary, Martin B Withers, 93 Cross Lane, Mountsorrel, Loughborough, Leics, LE12 7BX, 0116 229 6080.

ZOOLOGICAL SOCIETY OF LONDON (1826).
Carries out research, organises symposia and holds scientific meetings. Manages the Zoological Gardens in Regent's Park (first opened in 1828) and Whipsnade Wild Animal Park near Dunstable, Beds, each with extensive collections of birds. The Society's library has a large collection of ornithological books and journals. Publications include the *Journal of Zoology*, *Animal Conservation*, *The Symposia* and *The International Zoo Yearbook*.
Contact: Director General, Dr Michael Dixon, Regent's Park, London, NW1 4RY, 020 7722 3333. www.zsl.org

NATIONAL PROJECTS

NOTICE TO BIRDWATCHERS

National ornithological projects depend for their success on the active participation of amateur birdwatchers. In return they provide birdwatchers with an excellent opportunity to contribute in a positive and worthwhile way to the scientific study of birds and their habitats, which is the vital basis of all conservation programmes. The following entries provide a description of each particular project and a note of whom to contact for further information (full address details are in the previous section).

BARN OWL MONITORING PROGRAMME

A BTO project

Volunteers monitor artificial nest sites an record site occupancy, clutch size, brood size and breeding success. Qualified ringers may catch and ring adults and chicks and record measurements. Volunteers must be qualified bird ringers or nest recorders with a Schedule 1 licence for Barn Owl. Contact Peter Beaven,
e-mail: peter.beaven@bto.org

BEWICK'S SWAN RESEARCH

A WWT project

Recognition of individual Bewick's Swans by their black and yellow bill markings has been used for an extensive study of the flock wintering at Slimbridge, Gloucestershire since 1964. The swans show a high level of both site and mate fidelity; 10 to 50% of the birds identified each season have been recorded at Slimbridge in previous years. Factors affecting the life cycle of individual birds can therefore be analysed in detail.

A regular ringing programme was introduced in 1967 to identify staging sites used during migration to and from the Russian breeding grounds, and to continue monitoring individuals that transferred to other wintering sites. Bewick's Swans have also been caught and ringed at Caerlaverock (Dumfries & Galloway) and Welney (Norfolk) since 1979, and at Martin Mere (Lancashire) since 1990.

Since 1991 staff have made one or two expeditions to the Russian arctic each summer, to study the swans' breeding biology in collaboration with scientists from Russia, the Netherlands and Denmark. Sightings of marked birds are invaluable for maintaining the life-history records of individual swans.

Contact: Eileen Rees, WWT.

BREEDING BIRD SURVEY

Supported by the BTO, JNCC and the RSPB.

Begun in 1994, the BBS is designed to keep track of the changes in populations of our common breeding birds. It is dependent on volunteer birdwatchers throughout the country who can spare about five hours a year to cover a 1x1km survey square. There are just two morning visits to survey the breeding birds each year.

Survey squares are picked at random by computer to ensure that all habitats and regions are covered. Since its inception it has been a tremendous success, with more than 2,200 squares covered and more than 200 species recorded each year. Contact: Mike Raven, BTO, or your local BTO Regional Representative (see County Directory).

CORE MONITORING CENSUS (formerly COMMON BIRDS CENSUS)

This survey has officially finished. This was the main source of population monitoring in the wider countryside from 1962-2000, but has now been superseded by the Breeding Bird Survey. Nevertheless, CBC is still the best method to use at a local scale, producing maps showing the locations of bird's territories for a defined area. This is especially useful to study the relationship of breeding birds with their habitats. Although new participants are not needed currently, the method is still valuable and will be available on the BTO website.

CONCERN FOR SWIFTS

A Concern for Swifts Group project.

Endorsed by the BTO and the RSPB, the Group monitors Swift breeding colonies, especially where building restoration and maintenance are likely to cause disturbance. Practical information can be provided to owners, architects, builders and others, as well as advice on nest boxes and the use of specially adapted roof tiles. The help of interested birdwatchers is always welcome. Contact: Jake Allsop, 01353 740540; e-mail: jakeallsop@aol.com

CONSTANT EFFORT SITES SCHEME

A BTO project for bird ringers, funded by a partnership of the BTO, the JNCC, Duchas the Heritage Service - National Parks & Wildlife Service (Ireland) and the ringers themselves.

Participants in the Scheme monitor common songbird populations by mist-netting and ringing birds throughout the summer at more than 130 sites across Britain and Ireland. Changes in numbers of adults captured provide an index of population changes between years, while the ratio of juveniles to adults gives a measure of productivity. Between-year recaptures of birds are used to study variations in adult survival rates. Information from CES complements that from other long-term BTO surveys. Contact: Dawn Balmer, BTO.

CORMORANT ROOST SITE INVENTORY AND BREEDING COLONY REGISTER

R. Sellers and WWT.

Daytime counts carried out under the Wetland Bird Survey provide an index of the number of Cormorants wintering in Great Britain, but many birds are known to go uncounted on riverine and coastal habitats.

Dr Robin Sellers, in association with WWT, therefore established the Christmas Week Cormorant Survey which, through a network of volunteer counters, sought to monitor the numbers of Cormorants at about 70 of the most important night roosts in GB. In 1997, this project was extended to produce a comprehensive Cormorant Roost Site Inventory for Great Britain. Over 100 county bird recorders and local bird experts helped compile the inventory, which currently lists 291 night roosts, mostly in England.

In 1990, Robin Sellers also established the Cormorant Breeding Colony Survey to monitor numbers and breeding success of Cormorants in the UK at both coastal and inland colonies. Some 1,500 pairs of Cormorants, representing perhaps 15% of the local UK population, now breed inland. New colonies are forming every year as the population inland increases annually by 19%.

The first European-wide Cormorant survey will be undertaken in January 2003, organised in the UK by WWT. Anyone wishng to take part in either roost or breeding surveys should contact Colette Hall at WWT.

GARDEN BIRD FEEDING SURVEY

A BTO project.

The 2002/03 season completed 33 years of the GBFS. Each year 250 observers record the numbers and variety of garden birds fed by man in the 26 weeks between October and March. It is the longest running survey of its type in the world. Gardens are selected by region and type, from city flats, suburban semis and rural houses to outlying farms. Contact: David Glue, BTO.

BTO/CJ GARDEN BIRDWATCH

A BTO project, supported by C J WildBird Foods.

Started in January 1995, this project is a year-round survey that monitors the use that birds make of gardens. Approximately 16,000 participants from all over the UK and Ireland keep a weekly log of species using their gardens. The data collected are used to monitor regional, seasonal and year-to-year changes in the garden populations of our commoner birds. To cover costs there is an annual registration fee of £12. There is a quarterly colour magazine and all new joiners receive a full-colour, garden bird handbook.

Contact: Jacky Prior/Carol Povey, BTO.

GOLDEN ORIOLE CENSUS

A Golden Oriole Group project.

With support from the RSPB, the Golden Oriole Group has undertaken a systematic annual census of breeding Golden Orioles in the Fenland Basin since 1987. In recent years national censuses have been made, funded by English Nature and the RSPB, in which some 60 volunteer recorders have participated. The Group is always interested to hear of sightings of Orioles and to receive offers of help with its census work. Studies of breeding biology, habitat and food requirements are also carried out.

Contact: Jake Allsop, Golden Oriole Group.

GOOSE CENSUSES

A WWT project

Britain and Ireland support internationally important goose populations. During the day, many of these feed away from wetlands and are therefore not adequately censused by the Wetland Bird Survey. Additional surveys are therefore undertaken to provide estimates of population size. These primarily involve roost counts, supplemented by further counts of feeding birds.

Most populations are censused up to three times a year, typically during the autumn, midwinter, and spring. In addition, counts of the proportion of juveniles in goose flocks are undertaken to provide estimates of annual productivity. Further volunteers are always needed. In particular, counters in Scotland, Lancashire and Norfolk are sought. For more information contact: Richard Hearn, WWT, e-mail richard.hearn@wwt.org.uk.

HERONRIES CENSUS

A BTO project.

This survey started in 1928 and has been carried out under the auspices of the BTO since 1934. It represents the longest continuous series of population data for any European breeding bird.

Counts are made at a sample of heronries each year, chiefly in England and Wales, to provide an index of the current population level; data from Scotland and Northern Ireland are scant and more contributions from these countries would be especially welcomed. Herons may be hit hard during periods of severe weather but benefit by increased survival over mild winters. Their position at the top of a food chain makes them particularly vulnerable to pesticides and pollution. Contact: John Marchant, BTO.

BTO HOUSE SPARROW PROJECT

An eighteen month survey, commencing in March 2003, will investigate how House Sparrows use our gardens and urban areas. Volunteers will also look in detail at the species' distributions within towns and villages in different areas of the country. Volunteers wishing to take part should contact the BTO House Sparrow Officer, BTO, The Nunnery, Thetford, Norfolk, IP24 2PU, e-mail: sparrows@bto.org

IRISH WETLAND BIRD SURVEY (I-WeBS)

A joint project of BirdWatch Ireland, the National Parks & Wildlife Service of the Dept of Arts, Culture & the Gaeltacht, and WWT, and supported

by the Heritage Council and WWF-UK.
Established in 1994, I-WeBS aims to monitor the numbers and distribution of waterfowl populations wintering in Ireland in the long term, enabling the population size and spatial and temporal trends in numbers to be identified and described for each species.
Methods are compatible with existing schemes in the UK and Europe, and I-WeBS collaborates closely with the Wetland Bird Survey (WeBS) in the UK. Synchronised monthly counts are undertaken at wetland sites of all habitats during the winter. Counts are straightforward and counters receive a newsletter and full report annually. Additional help is always welcome, especially during these initial years as the scheme continues to grow. Contact: Kendrew Colhoun, BirdWatch Ireland.

LITTLE OWLS - PROJECT *ATHENE*
Little Owl Study Group
The Little Owl is declining at an alarming rate across Europe and is endangered in at least three Western European countries. To combat this, a European Species Action Plan is being developed, to put in place the necessary monitors, conservation, and education measures for its long term survival. Project *Athene* is the British leg of this plan.
It is a two-tier monitoring programme that anybody can become involved with. To monitor numbers of Little Owls a playback method is employed using standardised protocol. Nest site recording provides a more in-depth information on the population dynamics of the owls. You can join the LOSG and dependant on your time and expertise, carry out Little Owl surveys in your own patch. Contact Roy Leigh: Little Owl Study Group, C/O Biota, 71-73 Ascot Court, Middlewish Road, Northwich, Cheshire CW9 7BP. 01606 333296;
e-mail: RSL@biota.co.uk for further information

LOW TIDE COUNTS SCHEME
see Wetland Bird Survey

MANX CHOUGH PROJECT
A Manx registered charitable trust.
Established in 1990 to help the conservation of the Chough in the Isle of Man, leading to its protection and population increase. The main considerations are the maintenance of present nest sites, provision of suitable conditions for the reoccupation of abandoned sites and the expansion of the range of the species into new areas of the Island. Surveys and censuses are carried out. Raising public awareness of and interest in the Chough are further objects. Contact: Allen S Moore, Lyndale, Derby Road, Peel, Isle of Man IM5 1HH. 01624 843798.

MIGRATION WATCH
A BTO/BirdWatch Ireland project for all birdwatchers, sponsored by Northumbrian Water Ltd and in association with Bird Watching magazine.
Migration Watch, a three-year project that started in 2002, uses the latest Internet technology to record the timing and pattern of arrival for a wide range of spring migrants. You can record all the migrant birds you see (and those that you don't see!) at your birdwatching sites such as your garden, the local park or a nature reserve. The results are displayed on the website (www.bto.org/migwatch) in a variety of ways including animated maps, tables and graphs and are provided at a national and regional level. Contact: Dawn Balmer, BTO
(E-mail: migwatch.organiser@bto.org)

NEST RECORD SCHEME
A BTO Project forming part of the BTO's Integrated Population Monitoring programme carried out under contract with the JNCC.
All birdwatchers can contribute to this scheme by sending information about nesting attempts they observe into the BTO on standard Nest Record Cards or electronically via the IPMR computer package. The NRS monitors changes in the nesting success and the timing of breeding of Britain's bird species. Guidance on on how to record and visit nests safely, without disturbing breeding birds, is available in a free starter pack from the Nest Records Unit. Contact: Peter Beaven at e-mail: nest.records@bto.org

PREDATORY BIRDS MONITORING SCHEME
A Centre for Ecology and Hydrology project
Scientists at the CEH, Monks Wood have been monitoring the levels of various pollutants, including pesticides, in predatory birds for over 35 years. This work relies largely on members of the public sending in any predatory bird carcases they find. Species required include: Sparrowhawk, Kestrel, Barn Owl, Heron, Kingfisher, Great-crested Grebe, Merlin, Peregrine, Buzzard and other large birds of prey. They are interested in receiving all carcases of these birds, even if the cause of death is known, such as window collisions and roadkills. Whole specimens found dead should be packed in a sealed plastic bag, placed inside a padded envelope or small box, (mark the outside of the package 'PERISHABLE GOODS') and sent by FIRST CLASS post to; Heath Malcolm, CEH, Monks Wood, Abbots Ripton, Huntingdon, Cambs, PE28 2LS. Personal postage costs will be refunded in stamps. Please enclose the following information: Name and address of finder, date bird was found, location and circumstances in which the bird was found. A report of the cause of death and analytical results will be sent to the finder once examinations are complete. If you require additional information, please do not hesitate to get in touch, either by telephone, 01487 772498 or
e-mail: hmm@ceh.ac.uk
The success of the Centre's work depends on the contribution of volunteers.

RAPTOR AND OWL RESEARCH REGISTER
A BTO project
The Register has helped considerably over the past 27 years in encouraging and guiding research, and in the co-ordination of projects. There are currently almost 500 projects in the card index file through which the Register operates.
The owl species currently receiving most attention are Barn and Tawny. As to raptors, the most popular subjects are Kestrel, Buzzard, Sparrowhawk, Hobby and Peregrine, with researchers showing increasing interest in Red Kite, and fewer large in-depth studies of Goshawk, Osprey and harriers. Contributing is a simple process and involves all raptor enthusiasts, whether it is to describe an amateur activity or professional study. The nature of research on record varies widely – from local pellet analyses to captive breeding and rehabilitation programmes to national surveys of Peregrine, Buzzard and Golden Eagle. Birdwatchers in both Britain and abroad are encouraged to write for photocopies of cards relevant to the species or nature of their work. The effectiveness of the Register depends upon those running projects (however big or small) ensuring that their work is included. Contact: David Glue, BTO.

RED KITE RE-INTRODUCTION PROJECT
An English Nature/SNH/RSPB project supported by Forest Enterprise, Yorkshire Water and authorities in Germany and Spain
The project involves the translocation of birds from Spain, Germany and the expanding Chilterns population for release at sites in England and Scotland. Records of any wing-tagged Red Kites in England should be reported to Ian Carter at English Nature, Northminster House, Peterborough, PEI IUA (tel 01733 455281). Scottish records should be sent to Brian Etheridge at RSPB's North Scotland Regional Office, Etive House, Beechwood Park, Inverness, IV2 3BW (tel 01463 715000).

Sightings are of particular value if the letter/ number code (or colour) of wing tags can be seen or if the bird is seen flying low over (or into) woodland. Records should include an exact location, preferably with a six figure grid reference.

RETRAPPING ADULTS FOR SURVIVAL PROJECT
A BTO project for bird ringers, funded by a partnership of the BTO, the JNCC, Duchas the Heritage Service - National Parks & Wildlife Service (Ireland) and the ringers themselves.
This project started in 1998 and is an initiative of the BTO Ringing Scheme. It aims to gather re-trap information for a wide range of species, especially those of conservation concern, in a variety of breeding habitats, allowing the monitoring of survival rates.

Detailed information about survival rates from the RAS Project will help in the understanding of changing population trends. Ringers choose a target species, decide on a study area and develop suitable catching techniques. The aim then is to catch all the breeding adults of the chosen species within the study area. This is repeated each breeding season for a minimum of five years. The results will be relayed to conservation organisations who can use the information to design effective conservation action plans. Contact: Dawn Balmer, BTO.

RINGING SCHEME
A BTO project for bird ringers, funded by a partnership of the BTO, the JNCC, Duchas the Heritage Service - National Parks & Wildlife Service (Ireland) and the ringers themselves.
The purpose of the Ringing Scheme is to study mortality, survival and migration by marking birds with individually numbered metal rings which carry a return address. About 2,000 trained and licensed ringers operate in Britain and Ireland, and together they mark around 750,000 birds each year.
All birdwatchers can contribute to the scheme by reporting any ringed birds they find either via the BTO website or by letter. Anyone finding a ringed bird should note the ring number, species (if known), when and where the bird was found, and what happened to it. If the bird is dead, please remove the ring and send it to us – if writing, please flatten it out and tape it to your letter. Finders who send their name and address will be given details of where and when the bird was ringed. About 12,000 ringed birds are reported each year and an annual report is published. Contact: Jacquie Clark, BTO.

SIGHTINGS OF COLOUR-MARKED BIRDS
Various bodies.
Studies of movements of colour-marked birds depend heavily on the help of birdwatchers. On sighting a colour-marked bird full details should be recorded and sent to the appropriate contact below. The information will be passed on to the person who marked the bird, who will send details of marking to the observer. Unfortunately some birds cannot be traced, for example, if rings have been lost or are not all seen. *Waders:* Wader Study Group, c/o Rob Robinson, BTO.
Wildfowl: Richard Hearn, WWT, Slimbridge, Gloucester GL2 7BT.
Cormorant: Stuart Newson, BTO
Chough: Eric Bignal, Kindrochaid, Bruichladdich, Islay PA44 7PP.
Large gulls: Peter Rock, 59 Concorde Drive, Westbury-on-Trym, Bristol BS10 6PX.
Small gulls: K T Pedersen, Daglykkevej 7, DK-2650 Hridovre, Denmark.
All other species: Linda Milne, Ringing Unit, BTO.

THE SWALLOW FEEDING SURVEY 2004
A BTO Survey
The BTO are looking to collate important, nationally representative, data on the foraging habitat preferences of Swallows. These data are not provided by the Breeding Bird Survey and therefore a survey is being designed to provide a more detailed index of foraging activity for associated habitats (note, this will **N**OT be a population study). The survey will require two

Barn Owl Mobbed by Swallows by Michael Webb.

visits to a tetrad between late May and mid August 2004, to cover the main breeding period of Swallows. Data will be sought from about 1,000 tetrads across the UK and include additional counts of martins, Swifts and predators (birds of prey). It is likely that observers will record Swallow 'passes' (to be defined) and categorical habitat details, and the total time spent on each tetrad visit is expected to be around 2-3 hours. If you would like to take part in this survey in 2004 then please contact Dr Ian Henderson at the BTO, Thetford.

SWIFTS see Concern for Swifts

2003 UK PEREGRINE SURVEY

A joint BTO/Raptor Study Groups project, supported by JNCC/EHS/EN/CCW/SNH/SOC/ RSPB.

The survey in 2003 aims to provide solid data about the numbers of Peregrines breeding throughout the UK information that is especially important in the light of perceived conflicts between raptors and game rearing and pigeon racing interests.

The Peregrine is listed on Schedule 1 of the Wildlife and Countryside Act 1981 and a licence is required to disturb a bird at its nest. The survey is being organised on the ground through the network of Raptor Study Groups, where they exist, or through designated regional organisers. Volunteer birdwatchers, with experience of raptor survey, who wish to take part and others, who can provide information on the location of territorial Peregrines, particularly those birds located in cities, should contact the national organiser, who will put them in touch with their local raptor study group organiser. National Organiser: Humphrey Crick, BTO Scotland.

WATERWAYS BIRD SURVEY

A BTO project

From March to July each year participants survey linear waterways (rivers and canals) to map the position and activity of riparian birds. Results show both numbers and distribution of breeding territories for each waterside species at each site. An annual report on population change is published in *BTO News*. Since 1998, WBS has run parallel with the Waterways Breeding Bird Survey, which uses a transect method.

WBS maps show the habitat requirements of the birds and can be used to assess the effects of waterway management. Coverage of new plots is always required, especially in poorly covered areas such as Northern Ireland, Scotland, Wales, SW England and the North East. Contact: John Marchant, BTO.

WATERWAYS BREEDING BIRD SURVEY

A BTO project, supported by the Environment Agency

WBBS uses transect methods like those of the Breeding Bird Survey to record bird populations along randomly chosen stretches of river and canal throughout the UK. Just two survey visits are needed during April-June. WBBS began in 1998 and is currently in a development phase, in which its performance is being assessed against the long established Waterways Bird Survey. Coverage of random sites requires a further boost in 2004-05. Contact BTO Regional Representative (see County Directory) to enquire if any local stretches require coverage, otherwise John Marchant at BTO HQ.

WeBS PILOT DISPERSED WATERBIRDS SURVEY

A WeBS project funded by the BTO, WWT, RSPB and JNCC

Little is known about the numbers of dabbling ducks, Moorhen, Coot, Little Grebe, Heron etc that winter on small water bodies, streams, flooded fields, ditches and dykes, away from Wetland Bird Survey (WeBS) sites. Furthermore, there are no reliable population estimates of wintering Ruff or either species of Snipe. This survey aims to improve the population estimates of these waterbird species on all areas within lowland Britain not counted by other WeBS surveys.

Volunteers are being asked to intensively survey one-kilometre OS grid squares, which have been randomly selected from all lowland one-kilometre squares in Great Britain. Numbers of waterbirds and gulls will be recorded in different broad-scale habitats (*e.g.* river, dry woodland, arable etc). The selection has been stratified according to the proportion of urban and wet areas in the square. WeBS Local Organisers are coordinating counters in their local region, and we are hoping to cover 1,500 squares. Contacts: Michael Armitage, Steve Holloway, BTO; Mark Pollitt, WWT.

WeBS RIVERINE SURVEY

A Wetland Bird Survey project (qv)

Whilst the Wetland Bird Survey (WeBS) achieves excellent coverage of estuaries and inland still waters, rivers are poorly monitored by comparison. Consequently, WeBS undoubtedly misses a significant proportion of the UK populations of several species which use rivers, eg. Little Grebe, Mallard, Tufted Duck, Goldeneye and Goosander. The WeBS Riverine Survey in 2001/02 will be the first national survey of waterbirds on rivers during winter. It aims to estimate total numbers of birds on rivers throughout the UK and to identify particularly important river stretches for birds. Exact methods are being finalised following a pilot last winter, but in essence will involve simply counting the numbers of waterbirds (esp. ducks) on particular stretches of river and canal (sections for counts will probably be 2.5 km long). Many counters in addition to those involved in the pilot will be required. Contact: James Robinson at WWT.

WETLAND BIRD SURVEY

A joint scheme of BTO, WWT, RSPB & JNCC

The Wetland Bird Survey (WeBS) is the monitoring scheme for non-breeding waterbirds in the UK. The principal aims are:

1. to determine the population sizes of waterbirds:
2. to determine trends in numbers and distribution:
3. to identify important sites for waterbirds:
4. to conduct research which underpins waterbird conservation.

WeBS data are used to designate important waterbird sites and protect them against adverse development, for research into the causes of declines, for establishing conservation priorities and strategies and to formulate management plans for wetland sites and waterbirds.

Once monthly, synchronised Core Counts are made at as many wetland sites as possible. Low Tide Counts are made on about 20 estuaries each winter to identify important feeding areas. Counts take just a few hours and are relatively straightforward. The 3,000 participants receive regular newsletters and a comprehensive annual report. New counters are always welcome. Contacts: WeBS Secretariat, WWT (for Core Counts and general enquiries) and Andy Musgrove, BTO (Low Tide Counts).

WHOOPER SWAN RESEARCH

A WWT/Icelandic Museum of Nature History project

WNW's long-term study of Whooper Swans commenced in 1979 with the completion of swan pipes at Caerlaverock (Dumfries & Galloway) and Welney (Norfolk) and the subsequent development of a ringing programme for this species. Whooper Swans have been ringed at Martin Mere (Lancashire) from 1990 onwards. Since 1988, staff have made regular expeditions to Iceland where they collaborate with Icelandic ornithologists in monitoring clutch and brood sizes, and in catching the families and non-breeding flocks. The study aims to determine factors affecting the reproductive success of the Icelandic-breeding Whooper Swan population which winters mainly in Britain and Ireland. Relocating the families in winter is important for assessing the number of cygnets that survive autumn migration. Efforts made by birdwatchers to read Whooper Swan rings and to report the number of juveniles associated with ringed birds, are therefore particularly useful. The first and last dates on which ringed birds are seen at a site are also valuable for monitoring the movements of the swans in winter. Contact: Eileen Rees, WWT.

WILDFOWL COLOUR RINGING

A WWT project

The Wildfowl & Wetlands Trust co-ordinates all colour ringing of swans, geese and ducks on behalf of the BTO. The use of unique coloured leg-rings enables the movements and behaviour of known individuals to be observed without recapture. The rings are usually in bright colours with engraved letters and/or digits showing as black or white, and can be read with a telescope at up to 200m. Colour-marked neck collars, and plumage dyes, have also been used on geese and swans. Any records of observations should include species, location, date, ring colour and mark, and which leg the ring was on (most rings read from the foot upwards). The main study species are Mute Swan, Bewick's Swan, Whooper Swan, Pink-footed Goose, Greylag Goose, Greenland and European White-fronted Geese, Barnacle Goose, Brent Goose, Shelduck and Wigeon. Records will be forwarded to the relevant study, and when birds are traced ringing details will be sent back to the observer. All sightings should be sent to: Research Dept (Colour-ringed Wildfowl), WWT.

WINTER GULL ROOST SURVEY (WinGS) 2003/04

A BTO project, funded by JNCC, English Nature, SNH, CCW EHSNI, Northumbrian Water.

The 6th Winter Gull Roost Survey will monitor all known major sites, as well as surveying other areas using a sampling approach. The survey aims to produce total population estimates and to identify the most important gull roost sites. Contact: Michael Armitage or Steve Holloway.

WOODLAND RE-SURVEY PROJECT

A Woodland Bird Group project undertaken by the BTO and RSPB, funded by DEFRA, Forestry Commission, English Nature, RSPB, BTO and Woodland Trust.

Woodland plots originally surveyed either in the 1970's and 80's for the BTO's Common Bird Census or by the RSPB with point counts in the 1980s will be re-surveyed in 2003 and 2004. The aims are to accurately assess the changes in bird populations of a large sample of woods and to attempt to identify regional variations and specific factors (such as habitat change and fragmentation, deer and squirrel impacts) which may be responsible. Survey work will be undertaken by contract fieldworkers and volunteers. Contact: Greg Conway or Chris Hewson, BTO. (email: greg.conway@bto.org or chris.hewson@bto.org).

INTERNATIONAL DIRECTORY

Crane by Norman McCanch

FOREIGN NATIONAL ORGANISATIONS

The BirdLife Partnership

BirdLife is a Partnership of non-governmental organisations (NGOs) with a special focus on conservation and birds. Each NGO Partner represents a unique geographic territory/country.

The BirdLife Network explained

Partners: Membership-based NGOs who represent BirdLife in their own territory. Vote holders and key implementing bodies for BirdLife's Strategy and Regional Programmes in their own territories.

Partners Designate: Membership-based NGOs who represent BirdLife in their own territory, in a transition stage to becoming full Partners. Non-vote holders.

Affiliates: Usually NGOs, but also individuals, foundations or governmental institutions when appropriate. Act as a BirdLife contact with the aim of developing into, or recruiting, a BirdLife Partner in their territory.

Secretariat: The co-ordinating and servicing body of BirdLife International.

Secretariat Addresses

BirdLife Cambridge Office
BirdLife International
Wellbrook Court
Girton Road
Cambridge CB3 0NA
United Kingdom
Tel. +44 1 223 277 318
Fax +44 1 223 277200
Email birdlife@birdlife.org.uk
http://www.birdlife.net

BirdLife Americas Regional Office
Birdlife International
Vicente Cárdenas 120 y Japon,
3rd Floor
Quito
Ecuador
Postal address
BirdLife International
Casilla 17-17-717
Quito
Ecuador
Tel. +593 2 453 645
Fax +593 2 459 627
Email birdlife@birdlife.org.ec
http://www.geocities.com/RainForest/Wetlands/6203

BirdLife Asia Regional Office
Jl. Jend. Ahmad Yani No. 11
Bogor 16161
Indonesia
Postal address
PO Box 310/Boo
Bogor 16003
Indonesia
Tel. +62 251 333 234/+62 251 371 394
Fax +62 251 357 961
Email birdlife@indo.net.id
http://www.kt.rim.or.jp/~birdinfo/indonesia

BirdLife European Regional Office
Droevendaalsesteeg 3a PO Box 127, NL- 6700 AC, Wageningen
The Netherlands
Tel. +31 317 478831
Fax +31 317 478844
Email birdlife@birdlife.agro.nl

European Community Office (ECO)
BirdLife International
22 rue de Toulouse
B-1040 Brussels
Belgium
Tel. +32 2280 08 30
Fax +32 2230 38 02
Email bleco@ibm.net

BirdLife Middle East Regional Office
BirdLife International
c/o Royal Society for the Conservation of Nature (RSCN)
PO Box 6354
Amman 11183
Jordan
Tel: +962 6 535-5446
Fax: +962 6 534-7411
Email birdlife@nol.com.jo

AFRICA

PARTNERS

Burkina Faso
Fondation des Amis de la Nature (NATURAMA), 01 B.P. 6133, Ouagadougou 01.
e-mail: naturama@fasonet.bf

Ethiopia
Ethiopian Wildlife and Natural History Society, PO Box 13303, Addis Ababa, Pub: *Agazen; Ethiopian Wildl. and Nat. Hist. Newsl. (& Annual Report); Ethiopian Wildl. and Nat. Hist. Soc. Quarterly News (WATCH); Walia (WATCH) (Ethiopia).*
e-mail: ewnhs@telecom.net.et
http://ewnhs@telecom.net.et

Ghana
Ghana Wildlife Society, PO Box 13252, Accra, Pub: *Bongo News; NKO (The Parrots).*
e-mail: wildsoc@ighmail.com

Kenya
Nature Kenya, PO Box 44486, 00100 GPO. Nairobi. Pub: *Bulletin of the EANHS; Journal of East African Natural; Kenya Birds.* e-mail: eanhs@africaonline.co.ke
www.naturekenya.org

Nigeria
Nigerian Conservation Foundation, PO Box 74638, Victoria Island, Lagos. Pub: *NCF Matters/News/Newsletter; Nigerian Conservation Foundation Annual Report.*
e-mail: ncf@hyperia.com
http://ncf@hyperia.com

Vulturine Guineafowl by George Brown

Seychelles
Nature Seychelles, BirdLife Seychelles, P O Box 1310, Suite 202, Aarti Chambers, Mont Fleuri, Mahe. Pub: *Zwazo - a BirdLife Seychelles Newsletter.* e-mail: birdlife@seychelles.net

Sierra Leone
Conservation Society of Sierra Leone, PO BOX 1292, Freetown. Pub: *Rockfowl Link, The.* e-mail: cssl@sierratel.sl

South Africa
BirdLife South Africa, PO Box 515, Randburg 2125, Pub: *Newsletter of BirdLife South Africa; Ostrich.*
e-mail: info@birdlife.org.za
www.birdlife.org.za

Tanzania
Wildlife Conservation Society of Tanzania, PO Box 70919, Dar es Salaam, Pub: *Miombo.*
e-mail: wcst@africaonline.co.tz

Uganda
Nature Uganda, PO Box 27034, Kampala. Pub: *Naturalist - A Newsletter of the East Africa Nat. His. Soc.*
e-mail: eanhs@infocom.co.ug

PARTNERS DESIGNATE

Tunisia
Association "Les Amis des Oiseaux", Avenue 18 Janvier 1952, Ariana Centre, App. C209, 2080 Ariana, Tunis. Pub: *Feuille de Liaison de l'AAO; Houbara, l'.*
e-mail: aao.bird@planet.tn
http://aao.bird@planet.tn

Zimbabwe
BirdLife Zimbabwe, PO Box CY 161, Causeway, Harare. Pub: *Babbler (WATCH) (Zimbabwe); Honeyguide.*
e-mail: birds@zol.co.zw

AFFILIATES

Botswana
Botswana Bird Club, IUCN Private Bag 00300, Gaborone, Pub: *Babbler (WATCH) (Botswana).*

Burundi
Association Burundaise pour la Protection des Oiseaux, P O Box 7069, Bujumbura
e-mail: aboburundi@yahoo.fr

Cameroon
Cameroon Ornithological Club, PO Box 3055, Messa, Yaoundé.
e-mail: coc@iccnet.cm

Egypt
Sherif Baha El Din, 3 Abdala El Katib St, Dokki, Cairo.
e-mail: baha@internetegypt.com

Rwanda
Association pour la Conservation de la Nature au Rwanda, P O Box 4290, Kigali,
e-mail: acnr_@hotmail.com

Zambia
Zambian Ornithological Society, Box 33944, Lusaka 10101, Pub: *Zambian Ornithological Society Newsletter.*
e-mail: zos@zamnet.zm
www.fisheagle.org

AMERICAS

PARTNERS

Argentina
Aves Argentina / AOP, 25 de Mayo 749, 2 piso, oficina 6, 1002 Buenos Aires. Pub: *Hornero; Naturaleza & Conservacion; Nuestras Aves; Vuelo de Pajaro.*
e-mail: info@avesargentinas.org.ar
http://members.tripod.com/~HARPIA/aop.html

Belize
The Belize Audubon Society, 12 Fort Street, PO Box 1001, Belize City. Pub: *Belize Audubon Society Newsletter.*
e-mail: base@btl.net
www.belizeaudubon.org

Bolivia
Asociacion Armonia, Calle Mexico 110, esquina Ecuador, Casilla 3081, Santa Cruz de la Sierra. Pub: *Aves en Bolivia.*
e-mail: armonia@scbbs-bo.com
http://armonia@scbbs-bo.com

FOREIGN NATIONAL ORGANISATIONS

Canada
Bird Studies Canada, PO Box/ 160, Port Rowan, Ontario N0E 1M0. Pub: *Bird Studies Canada - Annual Report; Birdwatch Canada.*
e-mail: mbradstreet@bsc-eoc.org
www.bsc-eoc.org

Canada
Canadian Nature Federation (CNF), 1 Nicholas Street, Suite 606, Ottawa, Ontario, K1N 7B7. Pub: *Grass 'n Roots; IBA News Canada; Nature Canada; Nature Matters; Nature Watch News (CNF).*
e-mail: cnf@cnf.ca www.cnf.ca

Ecuador
Fundación Ornitholǒgica del Ecuador, La Tierra 203 y Av. de los Shyris, Casilla 17-17-906, Quito.
e-mail: cecia@uio.satnet.net
www.geocities.com/RainForest/Jungle/7633/ingles.html

Jamaica
BirdLife Jamaica, 2 Starlight Avenue, Kingston 6, Pub: *Broadsheet: BirdLife Jamaica; Important Bird Areas Programme Newsletter.*
e-mail: birdlifeja@yahoo.com
www.birdelifejamaica.com

Panama
Panama Audubon Society, Apartado 2026, Ancón, Balboa. Pub: *Toucan.*
e-mail: audupan@psi.net.pa
www.pananet.com/audubon

Venezuela
Sociedad Conservacionista Audubon de, Apartado 80.450, Caracas 1080-A, Venezuela. Pub: *Audubon (Venezuela) (formerly Boletin Audubon).*
e-mail: audubondevenezuela @audubondevenezuela.org

PARTNERS DESIGNATE

Mexico
CIPAMEX, Apartado Postal 22-012, D.F. 14091, Mexico. Pub: *AICA's; Cuauhtli Boletin de Cipa Mex.*
e-mail: cipamex@ campus.iztacala.unam.mx
http://coro@servidor.unam.mx

Paraguay
Guyra Paraguay,, Coronel Rafael Franco 381 c/ Leandro Prieto, Casilla de Correo 1132, Asunción. Pub: *Boletin Jara Kuera.*
e-mail: guyra@highway.com.py
www.mbertoni.org.py

United States
National Audubon Society, 700 Broadway, New York, NY, 10003. Pub: *American Birds; Audubon (USA); Audubon Field Notes; Audubon Bird Conservation Newsletter.*
e-mail: jwells@audobon.org
www.audubon.org

Chile
Union de Ornitologis de Chile (UNORCH), Casilla 13.183, Santiago 21. Pub: *Boletin Chileno de Ornitologia; Boletin Informativo (WATCH) (Chile).*
e-mail: unorch@entelchile.net
www.geocities.com/RainForest/4372

AFFILIATES

Bahamas
Bahamas National Trust, PO Box N-4105, Nassau. Pub: *Bahamas Naturalist; Currents; Grand Bahama Update.*
e-mail: bnt@bahamas.net.bs
http://bnt@bahamas.net.bs
www.bahamas.net.bs/environment

Cuba
Dr Martín Acosta, Museo Historia Natural, Facultad de Biologia, U.H., 25 e/J e I Vedado, La Habana
e-mail: poey@comuh.uh.cu

El Salvador
SalvaNATURA, 33 Avenida Sur #640, Colonia Flor Blanca, San Salvador.
e-mail: salvanatura@saltel.net

Falkland Islands
Falklands Conservation, PO Box 26, Stanley,. or Falklands Conservation, 1 Princes Avenue, Finchley, London N3 2DA, UK. Pub: *Falklands Conservation.*
e-mail: conservation@ horizon.co.fk
www. falklands-nature.demon.co.uk

Honduras
Sherry Thorne, c/o Cooperación Técnica, Apdo 30289 Toncontín, Tegucigalpa.
e-mail: pilar_birds@yahoo.com

Suriname
Foundation for Nature Preservation in Suriname, Cornelis Jongbawstraat 14, PO BOX 12252, Paramaribo
e-mail: stinasu@sr.net

Uruguay
GUPECA, Casilla de Correo 6955, Correo Central, Montevideo. Pub: *Achara.* e-mail: gupeca@ adinet.com.uy
www. uruguayos.nu/gupeca/achara.htm

ASIA

PARTNERS

Japan
Wild Bird Society of Japan (WBSJ), International Centre-WING, 2-35-2 Minamidaira, Hino City, Tokyo, 191-0041, Japan. Pub: *Strix; Wild Birds; Wing.*
e-mail: int.center@ wing-wbsj.or.jp

Malaysia
Malaysian Nature Society, PO Box 10750, 50724 Kuala Lumpur. Pub: *Enggang; Suara Enggang; Malayan Nature Journal; Malaysian Naturalist.* www.mns.org.my
e-mail: natsoc@po.jaring.my

Philippines
Haribon Foundation, Suites 401-404 Fil-Garcia Bldg, 140 Kalayaan Avenue cor. Mayaman St, Diliman, Quezon CIty 1101. Pub: *Haribon Foundation Annual Report; Haring Ibon; Philippine Biodiversity.*
e-mail: birdlife@haribon.org.ph
www.haribon.org.ph

Singapore
Nature Society (Singapore), The Sunflower, 510 Geylang Road, 02-05, The Sunflower, 398466. Pub: *Nature News; Nature Watch (Singapore).*
e-mail: natsoc@singnet.com.sg
www.post1.com/home/naturesingapore

Taiwan
Wild Bird Society of Taiwan, 1F, No. 3, Lane 36 Chinglung St., 116 Taipei, Taiwan. Pub: *Yuhina Post.*
e-mail: wbst@ms12.hinet.net
http://wildbird.hinet.net/taipei

Thailand
Bird Conservation Society of Thailand, 69/12 Soi Ramindra, 24 Jarakheebua Lardprao, Bangkok, 10230. Pub: *Bird Conservation Society of Thailand.*
e-mail: bcst@box1.a-net.net.th

PARTNER DESIGNATE

India
Bombay Natural History Society, Hornbill House, Shaheed Bhagat Singh Road, Mumbai-400 023. Pub: *Buceros; Hornbill; Journal of the Bombay Natural History Society.*
e-mail: bnhs@bom4.vsnl.net.in
www.museums.or.ke/eanhs/eanhs.html

AFFILIATES

Hong Kong
The Hong Kong Birdwatching Society, GPO BOX 12460. Pub: *Hong Kong Bird Report.*
e-mail: hkbws@hkbws.org.uk
http://hkbws@hkbws.org.uk
www.hkbws.org.hk

Nepal
Bird Conservation Nepal, GPO 12465, Kathmandu. Pub: *Bird Conservation Nepal (Danphe); Ibisbill.*
e-mail: birdlife@mos.com.np
http://birdlife@mos.com.np

Pakistan
Ornithological Society of Pakistan, PO Box 73, 109D Dera Ghazi Khan, 32200. Pub: *Pakistan Journal of Ornithology.*
e-mail: osp@mul.paknet.com.pk

Sri Lanka
Field Ornithology Group of Sri Lanka, Dept of Zoology, University of Colombo, Colombo 03. Pub: *Malkoha - Newsletter of the Field Ornithology Group of Sri Lanka.*
e-mail: fogsl@slt.lk
http://fogsl@slt.lk

EUROPE

Austria
BirdLife Austria, Museumplatz 1/10/8, AT-1070 Wien. Pub: *Egretta; Vogelschutz in Osterreich.*
e-mail: birdlife@blackbox.at

Belgium
BirdLife Belgium (BNVR-RNOB-BNVS), Kardinaal, Mercierplein 1, 2800 Mechelen, Belgium.
e-mail: wim.vandenbossche@natuurpunt.be
www.natuurreservaten.be

Bulgaria
Eesti Ornitiliigiaühing (EOÜ), PO Box 50, BG-1111, Sofia. Pub: *Neophron (& UK).*
e-mail: bspb_hq@bspb.org

Czech Republic
Czech Society for Ornithology (CSO), Hornomecholupska 34, CZ-102 00 Praha 10. Pub: *Ptaci Svet; Sylvia; Zpravy Ceske Spolecnosti Ornitologicke.*
e-mail: cso@birdlife.cz

Denmark
Dansk Ornitologisk Forening (DOF), Vesterbrogade 138-140, 1620 Kobenhavn V. Pub: *DAFIF - Dafifs Nyhedsbrev; Dansk Ornitologisk Forenings Tidsskrift; Fugle og Natur.* e-mail: dof@dof.dk
www.dof.dk

Estonia
Estonian Ornithological Society (EOU), PO Box 227, Vesti Str. 4, EE-50002 Tartu, Estonia. Pub: *Hirundo Eesti Ornitoogiauhing.*
e-mail: jaanus.elts@eoy.ee
www.loodus.ee/hirundo

Finland
BirdLife SUOMI Finland, Annankatu 29 A, PO Box 1285, FI 00101, Helsinki. Pub: *Linnuston-Suojelu; Linnut; Tiira.*
e-mail: office@birdlife.fi
www.birdlife.fi

France
Ligue pour la Protection des Oiseaux (LPO), La Corderie Royale, BP 263, FR-17305, Rochefort Cedex. Pub: *Lettre Internationale; Ligue Francaise Pour La Protection des Oiseaux; Oiseau, L' (LPO); Outarde infos.*
e-mail: lpo@lpo-birdlife.asso.fr
http://lpo@lpo-birdlife.a

Germany
Naturschutzbund Deutschland, Herbert-Rabius-Str. 26, D-53225 Bonn, Germany. Pub: *Naturschutz Heute (NABU) Naturschutzbund Deutschland.* e-mail: Naturschutz.heute@NABU.de
NABU@NABU.de

Gibraltar
Gibraltar Ornithological and Nat. History Society, Jew's Gate, Upper Rock Nature Reserve, PO Box 843, GI. Pub: *Alectoris; Gibraltar Nature News.* e-mail: gohns@gibnet.gi
www.gibraltar.gi/gonhs

Greece
Hellenic Ornithological Society (HOS), Vas. Irakleiou 24, GR-10682 Athens, Greece, GR-10681, Athens. Pub: *HOS Newsletter.*
e-mail: birdlife-gr@ath.forthnet.gr
www.ornithologiki.gr

Hungary
Hungarian Orn. and Nature Cons. Society (MME), Kolto u. 21, Pf. 391, HU-1536, Budapest. Pub: *Madartani Tajekoztato; Madartavlat; Ornis Hungarica; Tuzok.* e-mail: mme@mme.hu
www.mme.hu

Iceland
Icelandic Society for the Protection of Birds, Fuglaverndarfélag Islands, PO Box 5069, IS-125 Reykjavik, Iceland.
e-mail: fuglavernd@fuglavernd.is

Ireland
BirdWatch Ireland, Ruttledge House, 8 Longford Place, Monkstown, Co. Dublin. Pub: *Irish Birds; Wings (IWC Birdwatch Ireland).*
e-mail: bird@indigo.ie
www.birdwatchireland.ie

Israel
Society for the Protection of Nature in Israel, Hashsela 4, Tel-Aviv 66183. Pub: *SPNI News.*
e-mail: ioc@netvision.net.il
http://ioc@netvision.net.il

FOREIGN NATIONAL ORGANISATIONS

Italy
Lega Italiana Protezione Uccelli (LIPU), Via Trento 49, IT-43100, Parma. Pub: *Ali Giovani; Ali Notizie.*
e-mail: lipusede@box1.tin.it
www.lipu.it

Latvia
Latvijas Ornitologijas Biedriba (LOB), Ak 1010 Riga-50, LV 1050. Pub: *Putni Daba.*
e-mail: putni@parks.lv

Luxembourg
Letzebuerger Natur-a Vulleschutzliga (LNVL), Kraizhaff, route de Luxembourg.L-1899 Kockelscheuer. Pub: *Regulus (WATCH); Regulus Info (& Annual Report) (WATCH); Regulus Wissenschaftliche Berichte (WATCH).*
e-mail: secretary@luxnatur.lu
www.luxnatur.lu

Malta
BirdLife Malta, 57 Marina Court, Flat 28, Triq Abate Rigord, MT-Ta' Xbiex, MSD 12, MALTA. Pub: *Bird Talk (WATCH) (Malta); Bird's Eye View (WATCH) (Malta); Il-Merill.*
e-mail: info@birdlifemalta.org
www.birdlifemalta.org

Netherlands
Vogelbescherming Nederland, PO Box 925, NL-3700 AX Zeist. Pub: *Vogelniews; Vogels.*
e-mail:
birdlife@vogelbescherming.nl

Norway
Norsk Ornitologisk Forening, Sandgata 30 B, N-7012 Trondheim, Norway. Pub: *Fuglearet; Fuglefauna; Var; Ringmerkaren.*
e-mail: nof@birdlife.no
www.birdlife.no

Poland
Polish Society for the Protection of Birds (OTOP), PO Box 335, PL-80-958, Gdansk 50. Pub: *Ptaki; Ptasie Ostoje.*
e-mail: office@otop.most.org.pl

Portugal
Sociedade Portuguesa para o Estuda das, Aves (SPEA), Rua da Vitoria, 53-2 Dto, 1100-618, Lisboa. Pub: *Pardela.*
e-mail: spea@ip.pt
www.spea.pt

Romania
Romanian Ornithological Society (SOR), Str. Gheorghe Dima 49/2, RO-3400 Cluj. Pub: *Alcedo; Buletin AIA; Buletin de Informare Societatea Ornitologica Romana; Milvus (Romania).*
e-mail: sorcj@codec.ro
http://sorcj@codec.ro

Slovakia
Soc. for the Prot. of Birds in Slovakia (SOVS), PO Box 71, 093 01 Vranov nad Topl'ou. Pub: *Spravodaj SOVS; Vtacie Spravy.*
e-mail: sovs@changenet.sk
www.sovs.miesto.sk

Slovenia
BirdLife Slovenia (DOPPS), Drustvo Za Opazovanje in Proucevanje Ptic Slovenije. Pub: *Acrocephalus; Svet Ptic.*
e-mail: dopps@dopps-drustvo.si

Spain
Sociedad Espanola de Ornitologia (SEO), C/ Melquiades Biencinto 34, E-28053, Madrid. Pub: *Ardeola; Areas Importantes para las Aves.*
e-mail: seo@seo.org
www.seo.org

Sweden
Sveriges Ornitologiska Forening (SOF), Ekhagsvagen 3, SE 104-05, Stockholm. Pub: *Fagelvarld; var; Ornis Svecica.*
e-mail: birdlife@sofnet.org
www.sofnet.org

Switzerland
Schweizer Vogelschutz (SVS), BirdLife Schweiz, Postfach, 8036 Zurich. Pub: *Oiwvos Ornis; Ornis Junior; Ornithologische Beobachter; Der Ornithos; Steinadler.*
e-mail: svs@birdlife.ch
www.birdlife.ch

Turkey
Dogal Hayati Koruna Dernegi (DHKD), Buyuk Postane Caddesi No.: 43-45, Kat: 5-6 Bahcekapi 34420, Istanbul. Pub: *Kelaynak; Kuscu Bulteni.*
e-mail: kelaynak@dhkd.org
www.dhkd.org

United Kingdom
Royal Society for the Protection of Birds, The Lodge, Sandy, Bedfordshire, SG19 2DL.
e-mail: info@RSPB.org.UK

PARTNERS DESIGNATE

Albania
Albanian Society for the Protection of Birds, Museum of Natural Science, Rr. E. Kavajes 132, Tirana
e-mail: mns@albmail.com

Belarus
Bird Conservation Belarus (APB), PO Box 306, BY 220050. Pub: *Subbuteo - The Belarusian Ornithological Bulletin.*
e-mail: APB-Minsk@mail.ru

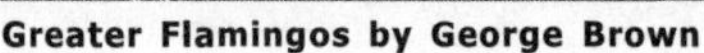

Greater Flamingos by George Brown

Iceland
Icelandic Institute of Natural History, PO Box 5320, IS-125 Reykjavik. Pub: *Bliki.*
e-mail: bliki@ni.is
http://ni.is/bliki.htm

Lithuania
Lietuvos Ornitologu Draugija (LOD), Naugarduko St. 47-3, LT-2006, Vilnius, Lithuania. Pub: *Baltasis Gandras.*
e-mail: lod@birdlife.lt
www.birdlife.lt

Russian Federation
Russian Bird Conservation Union (RBCU), Building 1, Shosse Entuziastov 60, 111123, RU-Moscow. Pub: *Newsletter of the Russian Bird Conservation Union.*
e-mail: rbcu@online.ru
http://rbcu@online.ru

Ukraine
Ukrainian Union for Bird Conservation (UTOP), PO Box 33, Kiev, 1103, UA. Pub: *Life of Birds.*
e-mail: utop@iptelecom.net.ua
http://utop@iptelecom.net.ua

AFFILIATES

Liechtenstein
Botanish-Zoologische Gesellschaft, Im Bretscha 22, FL-9494 Schaan, Liechtenstein.
e-mail: broggi@pingnet.li or renat@pingnet.li

Andorra
Associacio per a la Defensa de la Natura, Apartado de Correus Espanyols No 96, Andora La Vella, Principat d'Andorra. Pub: *Aiguerola.*
e-mail: and@andorra.ad

Croatia
Croatian Society for Bird and Nature Protection, Iiirski Trg 9, HR-10000 Zagreb, Croatia. Pub: *Troglodytes.*
e-mail: jasmina@mahazu.hazu.hr
http://jasmina@mahazu.hazu.

Cyprus
Cyprus Ornithological Society, PO Box 28076, CY-Nicosia 2090, Cyprus.
e-mail: melis@cytanet.com.cy

Georgia
Georgian Centre for the Conservation of Wildlife, 1 Mosashvili Str, 99 Tbilisi GE-380073, Georgia.
e-mail:
Ramaz_Gokhelashvili@dai.com

Switzerland
UNEP/Global Resource Information Database, International Environment House (IEH), 11 Chemin des Anemones, 1219 Chatelaine, Geneva. Pub: *GRID - Geneva Quarterly Bulletin.*
e-mail: info@grid.unep.ch
www.grid.unep.ch/

MIDDLE EAST

PARTNERS

Jordan
Royal Society of the Conservation of Nature, PO Box 6354, Jubeiha-Abu-Nusseir Circle, Amman 11183. Pub: *Al Reem.*
e-mail: adminrscn@rscn.org.jo
www.rscn.org.jo

Lebanon
Society for the Protection of Nature and Natural Resources in Lebanon, PO Box 11-8281, Beirut, Lebanon.
e-mail: r-jaradi@cyberia.net.lb

PARTNER DESIGNATE

Palestine
Wildlife Palestine Association, PO BOX 89, Beit Sahour. Pub: *Palestine Wildlife Society - Annual Report.* www.wildlife-pal.org
e-mail: wildlife@palnet.com

AFFILIATES

Bahrain
Dr Saeed A. Mohamed, PO Box 40266, Bahrain.
e-mail: sam53@batelco.com.bh

Iran, Islamic Republic of
Dr Jamshid Mansoori, Head, Ornithology Unit, Department of the Environment, PO Box: 5181, Tehran 15875, Iran.
e-mail: birdlifeiran@hotmail.com

Saudi Arabia
National Commission for Wildlife Cons & Dev, NCWDC, PO Box 61681, Riyadh 11575. Pub: *Phoenix; The.*
e-mail: ncwcd@zajil.net

PACIFIC

PARTNER

Australia
Birds Australia, 415 Riversdale Road, Hawthorn East, VIC 3123, Australia. Pub: *Australia Garcilla; Birds Australia Annual Report; Eclectus; Emu; Wingspan (WATCH) (Australia); from wingspan@birdsaustralia.com.au.*
e-mail: mail@birdsaustralia.com.au
www.birdsaustralia.com.au

AFFILIATES

Fiji
Dr Dick Watling, c/o Environment Consultants Fiji, P O Box 2041, Government Buildings, Suva, Fiji.
e-mail: watling@is.com.fj

French Polynesia
Société d'Ornithologie de Polynésie "Manu", B.P. 21 098, Papeete, Tahiti.
e-mail: sop.manu@mail.pf

Palau
Palau Conservation Society, PO BOX 1811, Koror, PW96940. Pub: *Ngerel a Biib.*
e-mail: pcs@palaunet.com

Samoa
O le Si'osi'omaga Society Incorporated, O le Si'osi'omaga Society Inc., P O Box 2282, Apia, Western Samoa. e-mail: ngo_siosiomaga@samoa.ws

New Zealand
Royal Forest & Bird Protection Society of, PO Box 631, Wellington. Pub: *Forest & Bird; Forest & Bird Annual Report; Forest & Bird Conservation News.*
e-mail:
l.bates@wn.forest-bird.org.nz
www.forest-bird.org.nz

INTERNATIONAL ORGANISATIONS

AFRICAN BIRD CLUB.
c/o Birdlife International as below.
e-mail (general): keithbetton@hotmail.com
(membership and sales):
Moira.Y.Hargreaves@btinternet.com
www.africanbirdclub.org
Pub: *Bulletin of the African Bird Club*.

BIRDLIFE INTERNATIONAL.
Wellbrook Court, Girton Road, Cambridge, CB3 ONA, +44 (0)1223 277318; fax +44 (0)1223 277200,
Pub: *World Birdwatch*. www.birdlife.net

EAST AFRICA NATURAL HISTORY SOCIETY see Kenya in preceding list.

EURING (European Union for Bird Ringing).
Euring Data Bank, NIOO Centre for Terrestrial Ecology, PO Box 40, NL-6666 ZG Heteren, Netherlands.
www.nioo.knaw.nl/euring.htm.

EUROPEAN WILDLIFE REHABILITATION ASSOCIATION (EWRA).
Les Stocker MBE, c/o Wildlife Hospital Trust, Aston Road, Haddenham, Aylesbury, Bucks, HP17 8AF, +44 (0)1844 292292; fax +44 (0)1844 292640, www.sttiggywinkles.org.uk

FAUNA AND FLORA INTERNATIONAL.
Great Eastern House, Tenison Road, Cambridge, CB1 2TT, +44 (0)1223 571000; fax +44 (0)1223 461481,
Pub: *Fauna & Flora News; Oryx*. www.ffi.org.uk

LIPU-UK
(the Italian League for the Protection of Birds).
David Lingard, Fernwood, Doddington Road, Whisby, Lincs, LN6 9BX, +44 (0)1522 689030, e-mail: david@lipu-uk.org www.lipu-uk.org Pub: *The Hoopoe*, annually, *Ali Notizie,* quarterley.

NEOTROPICAL BIRD CLUB.
As OSME below. Pub: *Cotinga*.
www.neotropicalbirdclub.org

ORIENTAL BIRD CLUB.
As OSME below. Pub: *The Forktail; Bull OBC.*
www.orientalbirdclub.org

ORNITHOLOGICAL SOCIETY OF THE MIDDLE EAST (OSME).
c/o The Lodge, Sandy, Beds, SG19 2DL.
Pub: *Sandgrouse*.
www.osme.org

TRAFFIC International (formerly Wildlife Trade Monitoring Unit).
219 Huntingdon Road, Cambridge, CB3 ODL, +44 (0)1223 277427; fax +44 (0)1223 277237.
Pub: *TRAFFIC Bulletin*.
e-mail: traffic@trafficint.org

WEST AFRICAN ORNITHOLOGICAL SOCIETY.
R E Sharland, 1 Fisher's Heron, East Mills, Hants, SP6 2JR. Pub: *Malimbus*.

WETLANDS INTERNATIONAL.
PO Box 471, 6700 AL Wageningen, Netherlands, +31 317 478854; fax +31 317 478850,
Pub: *Wetlands*.
www.wetlands.org

WORLD OWL TRUST.
The World Owl Centre, Muncaster Castle, Ravenglass, Cumbria, CA18 1RQ, +44 (0)1229 717393; fax +44 (0)1229 717107,
www.owls.org

WORLD PHEASANT ASSOCIATION.
PO Box 5, Lower Basildon, Reading, RG8 9PF, +44 (0)118 984 5140; fax +44 (0)118 984 3369,
Pub: *WPA News*. www.pheasant.org.uk

WORLD WIDE FUND FOR NATURE.
Avenue du Mont Blanc, CH-1196 Gland, Switzerland, +41 22 364 9111; fax +41 22 364 5358,
www.panda.org

QUICK REFERENCE SECTION

Female Marsh Harrier by Mark James

TIDE TABLES: USEFUL INFORMATION

BRITISH SUMMER TIME
In 2004 BST applies from 0100 on 28 March to 0100 on 31 October.

Note that all the times in the following tables are GMT.
During British Summer Time one hour should be added.

Predictions are given for the times of high water at Dover throughout the year.

The times of tides at the locations shown here may be obtained by adding or subtracting their 'tidal difference' as shown opposite (subtractions are indicated by a minus sign).

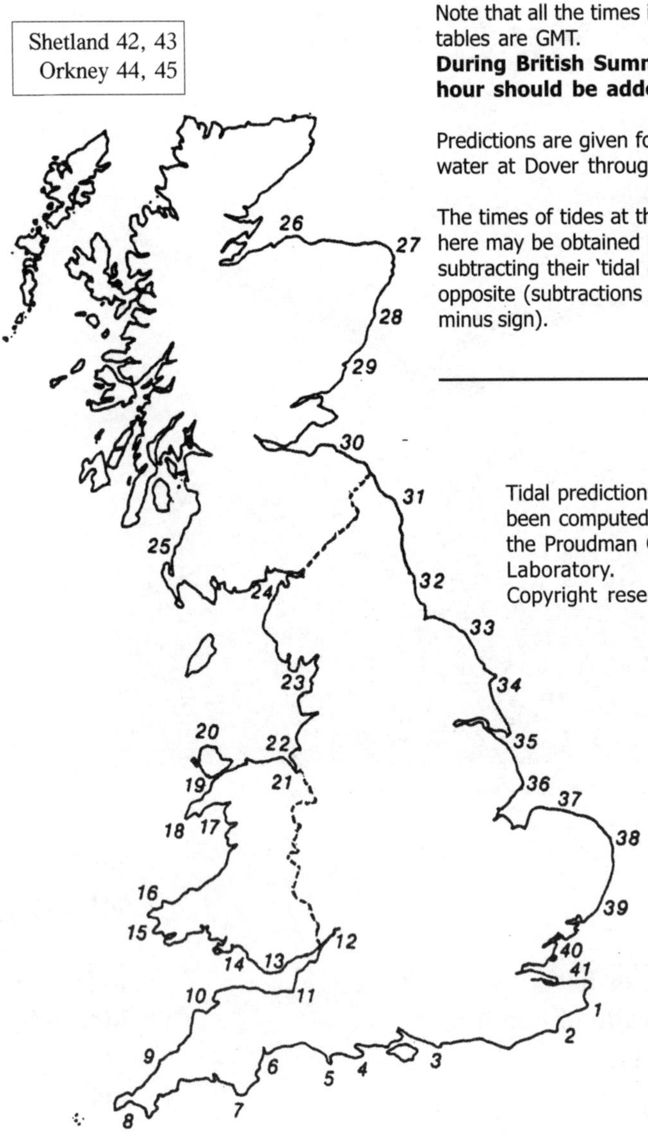

Shetland 42, 43
Orkney 44, 45

Tidal predictions for Dover have been computed by the Proudman Oceanographic Laboratory.

Map showing locations for which tidal differences are given on facing page.

TIDE TABLES 2004

Example 1
To calculate the time of first high water at Girvan on February 16

1. Look up the time at Dover (06 51)* = 06:51am
2. Add the tidal difference for Girvan = 0.54
3. Therefore the time of high water at Girvan = 07:45 am

Example 2
To calculate the time of second high water at Blakeney on June 13

1. Look up the time at Dover (20 11) = 8:11 pm
2. Add 1 hour for British Summer Time (21 11) = 9:11 pm
3. Subtract the tidal difference for Blakeney = - 4.07
4. Therefore the time of high water at Blakeney = 5:04 pm

*All Dover times are shown on the 24-hour clock.
Thus, 08 14 = 08.14 am; 14 58 = 2.58
Following the time of each high water the height of the tide is given, in metres.

(Tables for 2005 are not available at the time of going to press.)

TIDAL DIFFERENCES

1	Dover	See pp 338-340
2	Dungeness	-0 12
3	Selsey Bill	0 09
4	Swanage (lst H.W.Springs)	-2 36
5	Portland	-4 23
6	Exmouth (Approaches)	-4 48
7	Salcombe	-5 23
8	Newlyn (Penzance)	5 59
9	Padstow	-5 47
10	Bideford	-5 17
11	Bridgwater	-4 23
12	Sharpness Dock	-3 19
13	Cardiff (Penarth)	-4 16
14	Swansea	-4 52
15	Skomer Island	-5 00
16	Fishguard	-3 48
17	Barmouth	-2 45
18	Bardsey Island	-3 07
19	Caernarvon	-1 07
20	Amlwch	-0 22
21	Connahs Quay	0 20
22	Hilbre Island (Hoylake/West Kirby)	-0 05
23	Morecambe	0 20
24	Silloth	0 51
25	Girvan	0 54
26	Lossiemouth	0 48
27	Fraserburgh	1 20
28	Aberdeen	2 30
29	Montrose	3 30
30	Dunbar	3 42
31	Holy Island	3 58
32	Sunderland	4 38
33	Whitby	5 12
34	Bridlington	5 53
35	Grimsby	-5 20
36	Skegness	-5 00
37	Blakeney	-4 07
38	Gorleston	-2 08
39	Aldeburgh	-0 13
40	Bradwell Waterside	1 11
41	Herne Bay	1 28
42	Sullom Voe	-1 34
43	Lerwick	0 01
44	Kirkwall	-0 26
45	Widewall Bay	-1 30

NB. Care should be taken when making calculations at the beginning and end of British Summer Time. See worked examples above.

Time Zone **GMT** | Tidal Predictions : **HIGH WATERS 2004** | Units **METRES**

Datum of Predictions = **Chart Datum : 3.67 metres below Ordnance Datum (Newlyn)**

British Summer Time : **28th March to 31st October**

DOVER

January

DATE	DAY		Morning hr min	m	Afternoon hr min	m
1	Th		05 48	5·6	18 41	5·3
2	F		06 57	5·5	19 45	5·4
3	Sa		08 00	5·6	20 41	5·5
4	Su		08 55	5·7	21 29	5·8
5	M		09 41	5·9	22 10	6·0
6	Tu		10 22	6·0	22 48	6·1
7	W	○	10 57	6·1	23 21	6·3
8	Th		11 31	6·2	23 55	6·3
9	F		** **	* *	12 05	6·2
10	Sa		00 30	6·4	12 40	6·2
11	Su		01 05	6·4	13 17	6·2
12	M		01 42	6·4	13 55	6·1
13	Tu		02 21	6·3	14 37	6·0
14	W		03 04	6·2	15 26	5·9
15	Th	☾	03 53	6·1	16 24	5·8
16	F		04 53	6·0	17 28	5·7
17	Sa		05 59	5·9	18 37	5·6
18	Su		07 10	5·9	19 50	5·8
19	M		08 20	6·0	21 02	6·0
20	Tu		09 26	6·2	22 03	6·2
21	W	●	10 24	6·4	22 55	6·5
22	Th		11 17	6·6	23 42	6·6
23	F		** **	* *	12 05	6·6
24	Sa		00 25	6·7	12 50	6·5
25	Su		01 05	6·7	13 31	6·4
26	M		01 45	6·6	14 10	6·2
27	Tu		02 24	6·4	14 51	6·0
28	W		03 05	6·2	15 36	5·7
29	Th	☽	03 51	5·9	16 28	5·4
30	F		04 46	5·6	17 33	5·2
31	Sa		05 56	5·3	18 51	5·0

DOVER

February

DATE	DAY		Morning hr min	m	Afternoon hr min	m
1	Su		07 17	5·2	20 06	5·2
2	M		08 27	5·3	21 05	5·4
3	Tu		09 22	5·5	21 50	5·7
4	W		10 05	5·8	22 28	6·0
5	Th		10 41	6·0	23 02	6·2
6	F	○	11 13	6·2	23 35	6·4
7	Sa		11 45	6·3	** **	* *
8	Su		00 11	6·5	12 22	6·4
9	M		00 46	6·6	12 58	6·5
10	Tu		01 22	6·6	13 35	6·4
11	W		01 57	6·6	14 13	6·3
12	Th		02 35	6·5	14 55	6·1
13	F	☾	03 20	6·3	15 49	5·9
14	Sa		04 18	6·0	16 53	5·6
15	Su		05 27	5·7	18 11	5·4
16	M		06 51	5·6	19 45	5·4
17	Tu		08 21	5·7	21 05	5·8
18	W		09 32	6·0	22 01	6·1
19	Th		10 26	6·3	22 48	6·4
20	F	●	11 13	6·5	23 28	6·6
21	Sa		11 54	6·5	** **	* *
22	Su		00 08	6·7	12 30	6·5
23	M		00 43	6·8	13 05	6·5
24	Tu		01 18	6·7	13 39	6·3
25	W		01 52	6·6	14 13	6·1
26	Th		02 26	6·3	14 48	5·9
27	F		03 02	6·0	15 27	5·5
28	Sa	☽	03 46	5·6	16 21	5·2
29	Su		04 48	5·1	17 44	4·9

DOVER

March

DATE	DAY		Morning hr min	m	Afternoon hr min	m
1	M		06 25	4·9	19 24	4·9
2	Tu		07 56	5·0	20 35	5·2
3	W		08 58	5·3	21 25	5·6
4	Th		09 41	5·7	22 03	5·9
5	F		10 15	6·0	22 36	6·2
6	Sa	○	10 46	6·2	23 09	6·5
7	Su		11 20	6·5	23 44	6·7
8	M		11 56	6·6	** **	* *
9	Tu		00 19	6·8	12 33	6·7
10	W		00 56	6·8	13 11	6·6
11	Th		01 31	6·8	13 49	6·5
12	F		02 10	6·6	14 31	6·3
13	Sa	☾	02 55	6·3	15 25	5·9
14	Su		03 56	5·9	16 32	5·5
15	M		05 14	5·5	18 02	5·2
16	Tu		06 57	5·3	19 49	5·4
17	W		08 31	5·6	21 01	5·7
18	Th		09 33	6·0	21 51	6·1
19	F		10 19	6·2	22 32	6·4
20	Sa	●	10 59	6·4	23 09	6·6
21	Su		11 33	6·5	23 42	6·7
22	M		** **	* *	12 05	6·5
23	Tu		00 18	6·7	12 37	6·5
24	W		00 50	6·7	13 08	6·4
25	Th		01 19	6·5	13 36	6·2
26	F		01 48	6·3	14 06	6·0
27	Sa		02 16	6·0	14 38	5·7
28	Su	☽	02 52	5·6	15 23	5·3
29	M		03 47	5·1	16 39	4·9
30	Tu		05 30	4·8	18 27	4·8
31	W		07 14	4·9	19 50	5·1

DOVER

April

DATE	DAY		Morning hr min	m	Afternoon hr min	m
1	Th		08 20	5·2	20 45	5·5
2	F		09 05	5·6	21 26	5·9
3	Sa		09 41	6·0	22 03	6·3
4	Su		10 15	6·3	22 36	6·6
5	M	○	10 50	6·6	23 13	6·8
6	Tu		11 28	6·7	23 49	6·9
7	W		** **	* *	12 08	6·8
8	Th		00 27	6·9	12 47	6·7
9	F		01 08	6·8	13 31	6·5
10	Sa		01 52	6·6	14 19	6·3
11	Su		02 44	6·2	15 16	5·9
12	M	☾	03 51	5·7	16 26	5·5
13	Tu		05 19	5·4	18 01	5·3
14	W		07 05	5·4	19 36	5·5
15	Th		08 23	5·7	20 41	5·8
16	F		09 18	6·0	21 27	6·1
17	Sa		09 58	6·2	22 05	6·4
18	Su		10 34	6·3	22 41	6·5
19	M	●	11 04	6·4	23 16	6·6
20	Tu		11 38	6·4	23 49	6·6
21	W		** **	* *	12 11	6·4
22	Th		00 22	6·5	12 41	6·3
23	F		00 50	6·4	13 10	6·2
24	Sa		01 17	6·1	13 38	6·0
25	Su		01 45	5·9	14 10	5·8
26	M		02 20	5·6	14 54	5·4
27	Tu	☽	03 15	5·2	16 03	5·1
28	W		04 46	4·9	17 31	5·0
29	Th		06 19	5·0	18 53	5·2
30	F		07 29	5·3	19 55	5·5

Time Zone **GMT**

Tidal Predictions : **HIGH WATERS 2004**

Units **METRES**

Datum of Predictions = **Chart Datum : 3.67 metres below Ordnance Datum (Newlyn)**

British Summer Time : **28th March to 31st October**

DOVER

May

DATE	DAY		Morning hr min	m	Afternoon hr min	m
1	Sa		08 20	5·7	20 42	5·9
2	Su		09 01	6·0	21 22	6·3
3	M		09 40	6·4	22 01	6·6
4	Tu	○	10 19	6·6	22 41	6·8
5	W		11 00	6·7	23 21	6·9
6	Th		11 45	6·8	** **	* *
7	F		00 06	6·9	12 32	6·7
8	Sa		00 54	6·7	13 22	6·5
9	Su		01 46	6·4	14 16	6·3
10	M		02 45	6·1	15 13	6·0
11	Tu	☾	03 54	5·7	16 19	5·7
12	W		05 17	5·5	17 41	5·5
13	Th		06 46	5·5	19 04	5·6
14	F		07 53	5·7	20 04	5·8
15	Sa		08 45	5·9	20 54	6·0
16	Su		09 26	6·0	21 34	6·2
17	M		10 03	6·1	22 12	6·3
18	Tu		10 38	6·2	22 49	6·4
19	W	●	11 13	6·3	23 26	6·4
20	Th		11 48	6·3	23 59	6·3
21	F		** **	* *	12 22	6·3
22	Sa		00 30	6·2	12 54	6·2
23	Su		01 00	6·0	13 25	6·0
24	M		01 31	5·8	14 00	5·9
25	Tu		02 10	5·6	14 44	5·7
26	W		03 02	5·4	15 39	5·5
27	Th	☽	04 11	5·2	16 45	5·4
28	F		05 24	5·2	17 55	5·4
29	Sa		06 32	5·4	18 58	5·7
30	Su		07 29	5·7	19 53	6·0
31	M		08 19	6·0	20 41	6·3

DOVER

June

DATE	DAY		Morning hr min	m	Afternoon hr min	m
1	Tu		09 06	6·3	21 27	6·6
2	W		09 53	6·5	22 14	6·7
3	Th	○	10 42	6·6	23 03	6·8
4	F		11 33	6·7	23 55	6·7
5	Sa		** **	* *	12 26	6·6
6	Su		00 50	6·6	13 18	6·5
7	M		01 46	6·4	14 10	6·4
8	Tu		02 44	6·1	15 02	6·2
9	W	☾	03 43	5·9	15 58	5·9
10	Th		04 49	5·6	17 03	5·8
11	F		06 01	5·5	18 13	5·7
12	Sa		07 05	5·6	19 17	5·7
13	Su		08 00	5·6	20 11	5·8
14	M		08 49	5·8	21 01	6·0
15	Tu		09 33	5·9	21 46	6·0
16	W		10 14	6·0	22 26	6·1
17	Th	●	10 53	6·1	23 06	6·1
18	F		11 30	6·2	23 42	6·1
19	Sa		** **	* *	12 06	6·2
20	Su		00 16	6·1	12 40	6·2
21	M		00 50	6·0	13 15	6·2
22	Tu		01 24	5·9	13 50	6·1
23	W		02 02	5·8	14 28	6·0
24	Th		02 44	5·7	15 12	5·9
25	F	☽	03 36	5·6	16 04	5·8
26	Sa		04 35	5·6	17 03	5·8
27	Su		05 37	5·6	18 05	5·8
28	M		06 39	5·7	19 05	6·0
29	Tu		07 41	5·9	20 06	6·2
30	W		08 40	6·1	21 04	6·4

DOVER

July

DATE	DAY		Morning hr min	m	Afternoon hr min	m
1	Th		09 37	6·3	22 00	6·5
2	F	○	10 34	6·5	22 56	6·6
3	Sa		11 28	6·6	23 52	6·6
4	Su		** **	* *	12 20	6·7
5	M		00 47	6·6	13 08	6·6
6	Tu		01 39	6·4	13 55	6·5
7	W		02 27	6·2	14 40	6·4
8	Th		03 15	6·0	15 27	6·2
9	F	☾	04 05	5·8	16 19	6·0
10	Sa		05 03	5·6	17 19	5·8
11	Su		06 06	5·4	18 25	5·6
12	M		07 12	5·4	19 31	5·6
13	Tu		08 14	5·5	20 33	5·6
14	W		09 09	5·7	21 25	5·7
15	Th		09 56	5·9	22 10	5·9
16	F		10 35	6·0	22 49	6·0
17	Sa	●	11 11	6·2	23 26	6·1
18	Su		11 47	6·3	23 59	6·1
19	M		** **	* *	12 20	6·4
20	Tu		00 33	6·2	12 56	6·4
21	W		01 07	6·2	13 31	6·4
22	Th		01 42	6·1	14 04	6·3
23	F		02 19	6·0	14 41	6·2
24	Sa		02 59	5·9	15 23	6·1
25	Su	☽	03 49	5·8	16 17	6·0
26	M		04 49	5·7	17 20	5·9
27	Tu		05 58	5·6	18 30	5·8
28	W		07 12	5·6	19 45	5·9
29	Th		08 30	5·8	20 56	6·1
30	F		09 37	6·1	22 00	6·3
31	Sa	○	10 34	6·4	22 56	6·5

DOVER

August

DATE	DAY		Morning hr min	m	Afternoon hr min	m
1	Su		11 23	6·6	23 47	6·6
2	M		** **	* *	12 08	6·8
3	Tu		00 34	6·6	12 50	6·8
4	W		01 18	6·5	13 31	6·7
5	Th		01 59	6·4	14 09	6·6
6	F		02 37	6·1	14 49	6·4
7	Sa	☾	03 19	5·9	15 33	6·1
8	Su		04 08	5·6	16 25	5·7
9	M		05 07	5·3	17 31	5·4
10	Tu		06 23	5·1	18 53	5·2
11	W		07 43	5·2	20 09	5·3
12	Th		08 47	5·4	21 09	5·5
13	F		09 36	5·7	21 56	5·8
14	Sa		10 15	6·0	22 32	6·0
15	Su		10 50	6·2	23 03	6·1
16	M	●	11 23	6·4	23 34	6·3
17	Tu		11 56	6·5	** **	* *
18	W		00 06	6·4	12 29	6·6
19	Th		00 40	6·4	13 03	6·6
20	F		01 14	6·4	13 34	6·6
21	Sa		01 48	6·3	14 07	6·5
22	Su		02 26	6·2	14 47	6·3
23	M	☽	03 12	6·0	15 39	6·1
24	Tu		04 14	5·7	16 48	5·8
25	W		05 30	5·5	18 12	5·5
26	Th		07 05	5·4	19 49	5·6
27	F		08 37	5·7	21 08	6·0
28	Sa		09 39	6·1	22 04	6·3
29	Su		10 26	6·5	22 52	6·5
30	M	○	11 09	6·7	23 34	6·7
31	Tu		11 47	6·9	** **	* *

Time Zone **GMT**

Tidal Predictions : **HIGH WATERS 2004**

Units **METRES**

Datum of Predictions = **Chart Datum : 3.67 metres below Ordnance Datum (Newlyn)**

British Summer Time : **28th March to 31st October**

DOVER

September

DATE	DAY	Morning hr min	m	Afternoon hr min	m
1	W	00 12	6·7	12 25	6·9
2	Th	00 49	6·6	13 00	6·8
3	F	01 22	6·5	13 35	6·7
4	Sa	01 56	6·3	14 09	6·4
5	Su	02 33	6·0	14 45	6·1
6	M ☾	03 13	5·7	15 30	5·7
7	Tu	04 07	5·3	16 34	5·2
8	W	05 28	5·0	18 12	4·9
9	Th	07 07	5·0	19 46	5·0
10	F	08 21	5·3	20 49	5·4
11	Sa	09 12	5·7	21 34	5·7
12	Su	09 50	6·0	22 07	6·0
13	M	10 22	6·3	22 35	6·3
14	Tu ●	10 53	6·5	23 04	6·5
15	W	11 26	6·7	23 37	6·6
16	Th	11 58	6·8	** **	* *
17	F	00 11	6·6	12 30	6·8
18	Sa	00 44	6·6	13 03	6·8
19	Su	01 19	6·5	13 38	6·6
20	M	01 59	6·3	14 20	6·3
21	Tu ☽	02 48	6·0	15 15	6·0
22	W	03 53	5·6	16 34	5·5
23	Th	05 21	5·3	18 20	5·3
24	F	07 17	5·4	20 04	5·6
25	Sa	08 34	5·8	21 09	6·0
26	Su	09 27	6·2	21 57	6·3
27	M	10 10	6·5	22 36	6·5
28	Tu ○	10 46	6·8	23 11	6·6
29	W	11 21	6·9	23 44	6·7
30	Th	11 55	6·9	** **	* *

DOVER

October

DATE	DAY	Morning hr min	m	Afternoon hr min	m
1	F	00 18	6·6	12 29	6·8
2	Sa	00 49	6·5	13 00	6·6
3	Su	01 21	6·3	13 31	6·4
4	M	01 52	6·1	14 02	6·0
5	Tu	02 26	5·8	14 38	5·6
6	W ☾	03 12	5·4	15 34	5·1
7	Th	04 28	5·0	17 20	4·8
8	F	06 12	4·9	19 07	4·9
9	Sa	07 39	5·2	20 16	5·3
10	Su	08 34	5·6	20 59	5·7
11	M	09 13	6·0	21 32	6·0
12	Tu	09 47	6·3	22 01	6·3
13	W	10 18	6·6	22 32	6·6
14	Th ●	10 50	6·8	23 04	6·7
15	F	11 24	6·9	23 41	6·8
16	Sa	11 59	6·9	** **	* *
17	Su	00 19	6·8	12 37	6·8
18	M	01 00	6·6	13 18	6·6
19	Tu	01 45	6·4	14 07	6·3
20	W ☽	02 40	6·0	15 12	5·8
21	Th	03 50	5·6	16 41	5·5
22	F	05 20	5·4	18 32	5·4
23	Sa	07 04	5·5	19 55	5·7
24	Su	08 14	5·9	20 52	6·0
25	M	09 04	6·2	21 37	6·3
26	Tu	09 43	6·5	22 12	6·4
27	W	10 19	6·7	22 45	6·5
28	Th ○	10 53	6·8	23 17	6·6
29	F	11 28	6·8	23 49	6·6
30	Sa	** **	* *	12 02	6·7
31	Su	00 23	6·5	12 33	6·5

DOVER

November

DATE	DAY	Morning hr min	m	Afternoon hr min	m
1	M	00 54	6·3	13 03	6·3
2	Tu	01 25	6·1	13 34	6·0
3	W	01 59	5·9	14 09	5·6
4	Th	02 42	5·6	15 01	5·2
5	F ☾	03 44	5·3	16 25	5·0
6	Sa	05 07	5·1	18 01	4·9
7	Su	06 32	5·2	19 15	5·2
8	M	07 36	5·5	20 06	5·6
9	Tu	08 24	5·9	20 45	5·9
10	W	09 04	6·2	21 22	6·3
11	Th	09 39	6·5	21 58	6·5
12	F ●	10 17	6·8	22 36	6·7
13	Sa	10 55	6·9	23 19	6·8
14	Su	11 37	6·9	** **	* *
15	M	00 04	6·8	12 23	6·8
16	Tu	00 51	6·6	13 12	6·5
17	W	01 43	6·4	14 11	6·2
18	Th	02 41	6·1	15 19	5·9
19	F ☽	03 46	5·8	16 38	5·6
20	Sa	05 02	5·7	18 09	5·5
21	Su	06 26	5·7	19 22	5·7
22	M	07 35	5·9	20 20	5·9
23	Tu	08 28	6·1	21 05	6·0
24	W	09 12	6·3	21 43	6·2
25	Th	09 51	6·4	22 18	6·3
26	F ○	10 29	6·5	22 55	6·4
27	Sa	11 06	6·5	23 31	6·4
28	Su	11 42	6·4	** **	* *
29	M	00 06	6·4	12 16	6·3
30	Tu	00 40	6·3	12 49	6·1

DOVER

December

DATE	DAY	Morning hr min	m	Afternoon hr min	m
1	W	01 12	6·2	13 21	5·9
2	Th	01 48	6·0	13 57	5·7
3	F	02 27	5·8	14 42	5·5
4	Sa	03 15	5·6	15 40	5·3
5	Su ☾	04 14	5·4	16 50	5·2
6	M	05 21	5·4	17 59	5·3
7	Tu	06 26	5·5	19 01	5·5
8	W	07 24	5·8	19 53	5·8
9	Th	08 14	6·1	20 42	6·1
10	F	09 02	6·4	21 29	6·4
11	Sa	09 49	6·6	22 17	6·6
12	Su ●	10 36	6·8	23 06	6·7
13	M	11 27	6·8	23 58	6·7
14	Tu	** **	* *	12 19	6·7
15	W	00 50	6·7	13 15	6·5
16	Th	01 42	6·6	14 11	6·3
17	F	02 33	6·4	15 09	6·1
18	Sa ☽	03 27	6·2	16 11	5·8
19	Su	04 26	6·0	17 19	5·6
20	M	05 31	5·8	18 26	5·6
21	Tu	06 40	5·8	19 29	5·6
22	W	07 43	5·8	20 26	5·7
23	Th	08 38	5·9	21 15	5·8
24	F	09 27	6·0	21 58	6·0
25	Sa	10 11	6·1	22 38	6·2
26	Su ○	10 52	6·2	23 16	6·3
27	M	11 30	6·2	23 52	6·3
28	Tu	** **	* *	12 05	6·2
29	W	00 26	6·3	12 37	6·1
30	Th	01 00	6·3	13 10	6·0
31	F	01 34	6·2	13 43	5·9

SEA AREAS

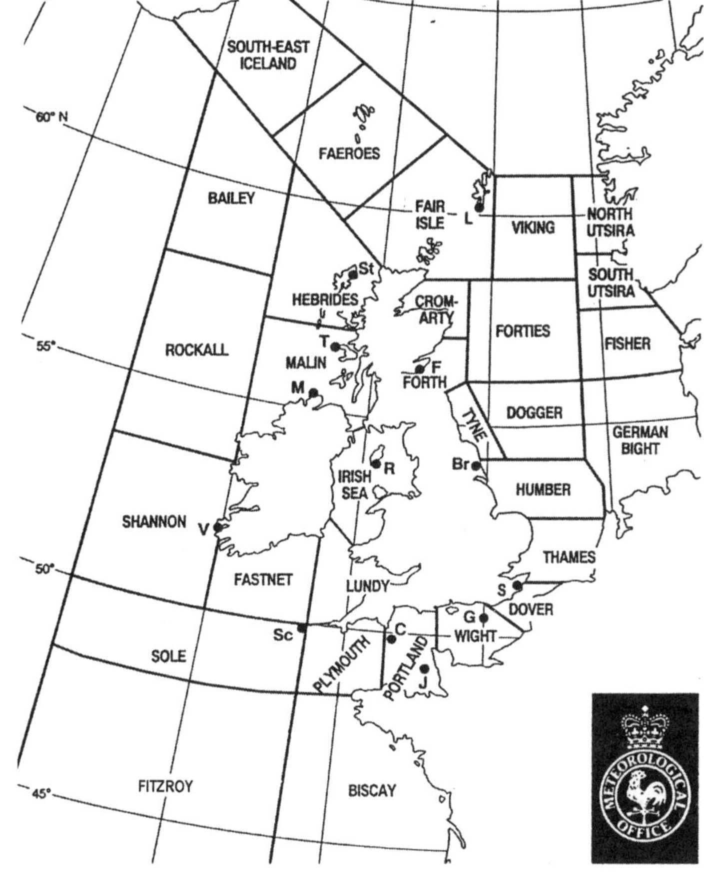

STATIONS WHOSE LATEST REPORTS ARE BROADCAST IN THE 5-MINUTE FORECASTS

Br Bridlington; C Channel Light-Vessel Automatic; F Fife Ness; G Greenwich Light-Vessel Automatic; J Jersey; L Lerwick; M Malin Head; R Ronaldsway; S Sandettie Light-Vessel Automatic; Sc Scilly Automatic; St Stornoway; T Tiree; V Valentia

From information kindly supplied by the Meteoroligical Office

REVISION OF SEA AREAS

On 4 February 2002, the southern boundary of areas Plymouth and Sole, and the northern boundary of areas Biscay and Finisterre were realigned along the Metarea I/II boundary at 48°27' North. At the same time, sea area Finisterre was renamed FitzRoy.

Did you know that the new FitzRoy shipping area is named after the founder of the Met Office?

SUNRISE AND SUNSET TIMES

Predictions are given for the times of sunrise and sunset on every Sunday throughout the year. For places on the same latitude as the following, add 4 minutes for each degree of longitude west (subtract if east).

These times are in GMT, except between 01 00 on Mar 28 and 01 00 on Oct 31, when the times are in BST (1 hour in advance of GMT).

		London		Manchester		Edinburgh	
		Rise	Set	Rise	Set	Rise	Set
Jan	4	08 06	16 05	08 25	16 03	08 43	15 52
	11	08 03	16 14	08 21	16 13	08 38	16 03
	18	07 58	16 25	08 15	16 24	08 31	16 16
	25	07 50	16 36	08 06	16 37	08 21	16 30
Feb	1	07 40	16 49	07 55	16 50	08 09	16 45
	8	07 29	17 02	07 43	17 04	07 55	17 00
	15	07 16	17 14	07 29	17 18	07 40	17 15
	22	07 02	17 27	07 14	17 32	07 23	17 31
	29	06 47	17 40	06 58	17 45	07 06	17 46
Mar	7	06 32	17 52	06 42	17 59	06 48	18 00
	14	06 16	18 04	06 25	18 12	06 30	18 15
	21	06 01	18 16	06 08	18 25	06 12	18 29
	28	06 45	19 28	06 51	19 38	06 53	19 44
Apr	4	06 29	19 39	06 35	19 50	06 35	19 58
	11	06 13	19 51	06 18	20 03	06 17	20 12
	18	05 58	20 03	06 02	20 16	05 59	20 26
	25	05 44	20 15	05 46	20 29	05 42	20 41
May	2	05 30	20 26	05 32	20 41	05 26	20 55
	9	05 18	20 37	05 18	20 54	05 11	21 08
	16	05 07	20 48	05 06	21 05	04 58	21 22
	23	04 58	20 58	04 56	21 16	04 46	21 34
	30	04 51	21 07	04 48	21 26	04 37	21 45

SUNRISE AND SUNSET TIMES

		London		Manchester		Edinburgh	
		Rise	**Set**	**Rise**	**Set**	**Rise**	**Set**
Jun	6	04 46	21 14	04 43	21 33	04 30	21 53
	13	04 43	21 19	04 40	21 39	04 27	22 00
	20	04 43	21 22	04 39	21 42	04 26	22 03
	27	04 45	21 22	04 42	21 42	04 29	22 03
Jul	4	04 50	21 20	04 47	21 39	04 35	21 59
	11	04 57	21 15	04 54	21 34	04 43	21 53
	18	05 05	21 08	05 03	21 26	04 53	21 44
	25	05 14	20 59	05 14	21 16	05 05	21 33
Aug	1	05 25	20 48	05 25	21 05	05 17	21 20
	8	05 35	20 36	05 37	20 51	05 31	21 05
	15	05 46	20 23	05 49	20 37	05 44	20 49
	22	05 58	20 08	06 01	20 21	05 58	20 32
	29	06 09	19 53	06 13	20 25	06 12	20 14
Sep	5	06 20	19 37	06 25	19 48	06 25	19 56
	12	06 31	19 21	06 38	19 31	06 39	19 38
	19	06 42	19 05	06 50	19 14	06 53	19 19
	26	06 54	18 49	07 02	18 57	07 06	19 01
Oct	3	07 05	18 33	07 15	18 40	07 20	18 42
	10	07 17	18 18	07 27	18 24	07 34	18 24
	17	07 28	18 03	07 40	18 07	07 49	18 07
	24	07 41	17 48	07 53	17 52	08 03	17 50
	31	06 53	16 35	07 07	16 38	07 18	16 34
Nov	7	07 05	16 23	07 20	16 25	07 33	16 19
	14	07 17	16 12	07 33	16 13	07 48	16 06
	21	07 29	16 04	07 46	16 03	08 02	15 55
	28	07 40	15 57	07 58	15 56	08 15	15 47
Dec	5	07 50	15 53	08 08	15 51	08 26	15 41
	12	07 57	15 52	08 16	15 49	08 35	15 38
	19	08 03	15 53	08 22	15 50	08 41	15 39
	26	08 06	15 57	08 25	15 55	08 44	15 43

GRID REFERENCES

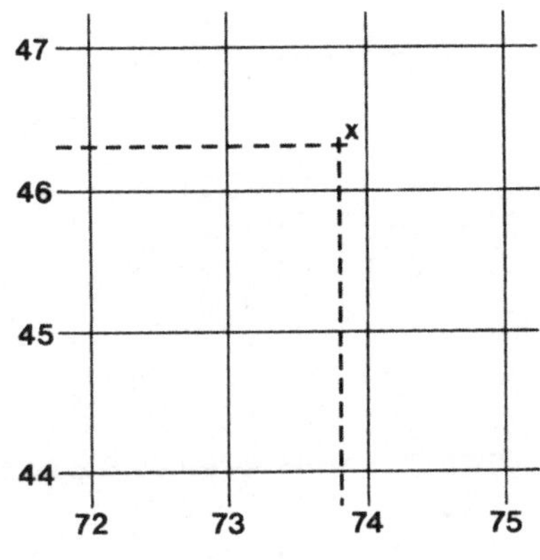

A grid reference is made up of letters and numbers. Two-letter codes are used for 100km squares on the National Grid (opposite) and single-letter codes on the Irish Grid (below).

The squares may be further subdivided into squares of 10km, 1km or 100m, allowing for increasingly specific references. On a given map the lines forming the squares are numbered in the margins, those along the top and bottom being known as 'eastings' and those along the sides as 'northings'. A reference number is made up of the relevant letter code plus two sets of figures, those representing the easting followed by the northing. According to the scale of the map they can either be read off directly or calculated by visually dividing the intervals into tenths. For most purposes three-figure eastings plus three-figure northings are adequate.

The example above, from an Ordnance Survey 'Landranger' map, illustrates how to specify a location on a map divided into lkm squares: the reference for point X is 738463. If that location lies in square SP (see map opposite), the full reference is SP738463.

LETTER CODES FOR IRISH GRID 10km SQUARES

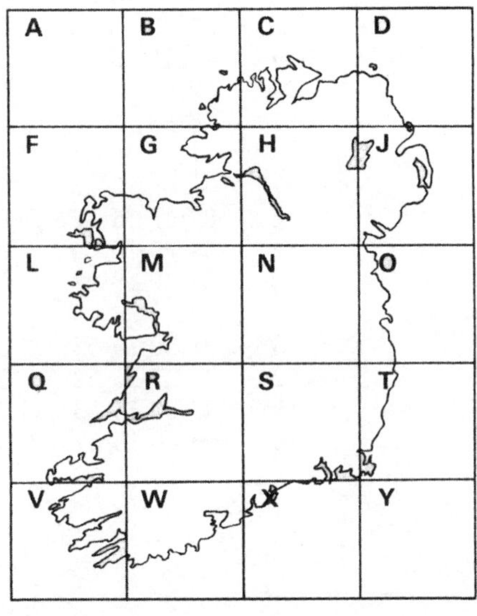

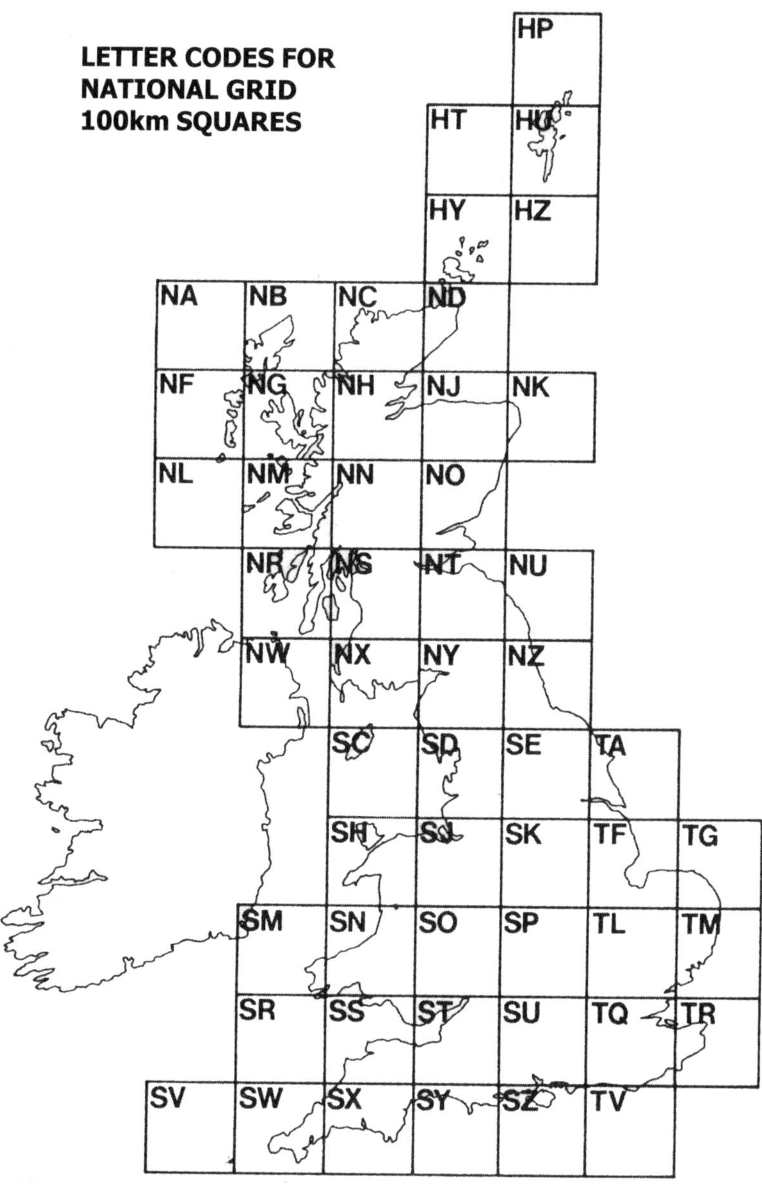
LETTER CODES FOR
NATIONAL GRID
100km SQUARES
HP
HT
HU
HY
HZ
NA
NB
NC
ND
NF
NG
NH
NJ
NK
NL
NM
NN
NO
NR
NS
NT
NU
NW
NX
NY
NZ
SC
SD
SE
TA
SH
SJ
SK
TF
TG
SM
SN
SO
SP
TL
TM
SR
SS
ST
SU
TQ
TR
SV
SW
SX
SY
SZ
TV

SCHEDULE 1 SPECIES

Under the provisions of the Wildlife and Countryside Act 1981 the following bird species (listed in Schedule 1 - Part I of the Act) are protected by special penalties at all times.

Avocet,
Bee-eater
Bittem
Bittern, Little
Bluethroat
Brambling
Bunting, Cirl
Bunting, Lapland
Bunting, Snow
Buzzard, Honey
Chough
Corncrake
Crake, Spotted
Crossbills (all species)
Curlew, Stone
Divers (all species)
Dotterel
Duck, Long-tailed
Eagle, Golden
Eagle, White-tailed
Falcon, Gyr
Fieldfare
Firecrest
Garganey
Godwit, Black-tailed
Goshawk
Grebe, Black-necked
Grebe, Slavonian
Greenshank
Gull, Little
Gull, Mediterranean
Harriers (all species)
Heron, Purple
Hobby
Hoopoe
Kingfisher
Kite, Red
Merlin
Oriole, Golden
Osprey
Owl, Barn
Owl, Snowy
Peregrine
Petrel, Leach's
Phalarope, Red-necked
Plover, Kentish
Plover, Little Ringed
Quail, Common
Redstart, Black
Redwing
Rosefinch, Scarlet
Ruff
Sandpiper, Green
Sandpiper, Purple
Sandpiper, Wood
Scaup
Scoter, Common
Scoter, Velvet
Serin
Shorelark
Shrike, Red-backed
Spoonbill
Stilt, Black-winged
Stint, Temminck's
Swan, Bewick's
Stone-curlew
Swan, Whooper
Tern, Black
Tern, Little
Tern, Roseate
Tit, Bearded
Tit, Crested
Treecreeper, Short-toed
Warbler, Cetti's
Warbler, Dartford
Warbler, Marsh
Warbler, Savi's
Whimbrel
Woodlark
Wryneck

The following birds and their eggs (listed in Schedule 1 - Part II of the Act) are protected by special penalties during the close season, which is Feb 1 to Aug 31 (Feb 21 to Aug 31 below high water mark), but may be killed outside this period - Goldeneye, Greylag Goose (in Outer Hebrides, Caithness, Sutherland, and Wester Ross only), Pintail.

THE BIRDWATCHER'S CODE OF CONDUCT

1. Welfare of birds must come first
Whether your particular interest is photography, ringing, sound recording, scientific study or just birdwatching, remember that the welfare of birds must always come first.

2. Habitat protection
A birds's habitat is vital to its survival and therefore we must ensure that our activities do not cause damage.

3. Keep disturbance to a minimum
Birds' tolerance of disturbance varies between species and seasons. Therefore, it is safer to keep all disturbance to a minimum. No birds should be disturbed from the nest in case the opportunities for predators to take eggs or young are increased. In very cold weather, disturbance to birds may cause them to use vital energy at a time when food is difficult to find. Wildfowlers impose bans during cold weather: birdwatchers should exercise similar discretion.

4. Rare breeding birds
If you discover a rare breeding bird and feel that protection is necessary, inform the appropriate RSPB Regional Officer, or the Species Protection Department at the RSPB, The Lodge,

Sandy, Beds SG19 2DL. Otherwise, it is best in almost all circumstances to keep the record strictly secret to avoid disturbance by other birdwatchers and attacks by egg-collectors. Never visit known sites of rare breeding birds unless they are adequately protected. Even your presence may give away the site to others and cause so many other visitors that the birds may fail to breed successfully. Disturbance at or near the nest of species listed on the First Schedule of the Wildlife and Countryside Act 1981 is a criminal offence.

5. Rare migrants
Rare migrants or vagrants must not be harassed. If you discover one, consider the circumstances carefully before telling anyone. Will an influx of birdwatchers disturb the bird or others in the area? Will the habitat be damaged? Will problems be caused with the landowner?

6. The law
The bird protection laws, as now embodied in the Wildlife and Countryside Act 1981, are the result of hard campaigning by previous generations of birdwatchers. As birdwatchers, we must abide by them at all times and not allow them to fall into disrepute.

7. Respect the rights of landowners
The wishes of landowners and occupiers of land must be respected. Do not enter land without permission. Comply with permit schemes. If you are leading a group, do give advance notice of the visit, even if a formal permit scheme is not in operation. Always obey the Country Code.

8. Keeping records
Much of today's knowledge about birds is the result of meticulous record keeping by our predecessors. Make sure you help to add to tomorrow's knowledge by sending records to your county bird recorder.

9. Birdwatching abroad
Behave abroad as you would at home. This code should be firmly adhered to when abroad (whatever the local laws). Well behaved birdwatchers can be important ambassadors for bird protection.

(Reprinted with permisson from the RSPB)

NATIONAL AND REGIONAL BIRDLINES

Birdline name	To obtain information	To report sightings (hotlines)
National		
Bird Information Service	09068 700222	01263 741140
www.birdingworld.co.uk		
Flightline (Northern Ireland)	028 9146 7408	
Regional		
Northern Ireland	028 9146 7408	
Scotland*	09068 700 234	01292 611 994
Wales *	09068 700 248	01492 544 588
East Anglia	09068 700 245	01603 763 388
www.birdnews.co.uk		or 08000 830 803
Midlands *	09068 700 247	01905 754 154
North East*	09068 700 246	01426 983 963
North West *	09068 700 249	0151 336 6188
South East	09068 700 240	07626 933 933
www.southeastbirdnews.co.uk		or 08000 377 240
South West	09068 700 241	01426 923 923

* www.uk-birding.co.uk

Charges
At the time of compilation, calls to 09068 numbers cost 60p per minute.

COUNTY BIRDWATCH TALLIES

The County Birdrace has become an institution in British birdwatching – providing both a personal challenge to those seeking to break records for species seen in one day, but also raising money via sponsorship for local and national conservation projects. For information on how to participate in 2003, contact *Birdwatch* magazine, Solo Publishing, 3D/F Leroy House, 436 Essex Road, Islington, London N1 3QP.

Rules

1. Teams shall comprise four members, all resident in the geographical area of the birdwatch, one of whom may be a driver and/or record-keeper.
2. Geographical areas shall generally be those used by the network of Bird Recorders.
3. A tally must be achieved on one calendar day.
4. No species shall be included in the tally unless seen or heard by at least three members of the team.
5. Team members and birds must be within the defined area at the time of recording.
6. Admitted species shall be those on the relevant official country list (eg. the British List for England, Scotland and Wales), plus Feral Pigeon; rarities must be accepted by the appropriate (county or national) Rarities Committee. Schedule D species shall be excluded.
7. Escapes, sick, injured or oiled birds shall not be admitted.
8. Attracting birds with a tape recording shall not be allowed.
9. The Birdwatchers' Code of Conduct shall be strictly observed.

Meadow Pipit by Richard Johnson

Tallies opposite are accepted and published in good faith. A listing does not imply that the above rules have been adhered to, nor that any authentication or adjudication has been made.
A county or region's best record is used in determining its position in the table. If the same total has been reached in more than one year, only the first is given.

( ) Numbers within curved brackets indicate the latest known total number of species on the county or region's list. In order to ensure consistency as to which species should be included on the list, Rule 6 should be applied.

If the same total has been reached by more than one county or region the names are listed alphabetically and a joint position indicated by an 'equals' sign (=).

COUNTY BIRDWATCH TALLIES

	County	Race total	County total	Year
1	Norfolk	162	(413)	2000
2	Dorset	158	(406)	1989
3	Yorkshire	155	(428)	1998
4	Kent	153	(402)	1999
5	Grampian	152	(352)	1999
6	Hampshire	151	(358)	1994
7	Cheshire	149	(338)	1993
8	Suffolk	148	(371)	1992
9	Highland	146	(246)	1988
10	Durham	144	(354)	2003
11=	Cleveland	142	(354)	1994
11=	Northumb	142	(394)	2000
13	Lancs & N Merseyside	141	(349)	1996
14=	Cumbria	140	(344)	1996
14=	Devon	140	(412)	2001
16=	Highland, NE Scotland	136	(?)	1993
16=	Sussex	136	(380)	1996
16=	Anglesey	136	(307)	1987
19	Gwynedd			
20	(old county)	135	(349)	1989
20=	Tayside, Angus/ Dundee	134	(306)	2003
20=	Highland, N Scotland	134	(?)	1988
22	N Ireland	133	(309)	1993
23=	Fife (excl Isle of May)	130	(305)	1996
23=	Cambs	130	(330)	2000
23=	Cambs/Hunts/ P'boro	130	(330)	2000
26	Derbyshire	129	(311)	1998
27=	Cornwall	128	(451)	1992
27=	Lincolnshire	128	(369)	1988
27=	Lothian	128	(343)	1994
30	Ayrshire	127	(292)	1991
31=	Caernarf.	126	(351)	1993
31=	Notts	126	(308)	1991
33=	Clwyd	125	(313)	1995
33=	Staffordshire	125	(293)	1993
35=	Borders	124	(310)	2003
35=	Somerset	124	(346)	2003
35=	Yorkshire,E	124	(353)	1993
38	Essex	123	(365)	1996
39=	Carmarthen	122	(294)	1991
39=	Gloucs	122	(316)	1998
41=	Berkshire	121	(309)	1990
41=	Caithness	121	(292)	1994
41=	Moray & Nairn	121	(291)	1993
44=	Eire	119	(425)	1996
44=	Wexford	119	(?)	1992
46=	Manchester	118	(303)	1992
46=	Wiltshire	118	(308)	1989
48	Merioneth	117	(263)	1989
49=	Dumfries & Galloway	115	(279)	1986
49=	Glams (Old)	115	(300)	1986
49=	Pembroke	115	(355)	1995
49=	Surrey	115	(325)	1995
53=	Northants	114	(314)	1998
53=	Oxon	114	(297)	2000
53=	Shetland	114	(419)	1992
53=	Worcs	114	(287)	1995
57=	Bucks	113	(276)	1990
57=	Isle of Wight	113	(321)	1989
57=	London	113	(352)	1994
60=	Montgomery	112	(227)	1991
60=	Rutland	112	(277)	1994
62=	Bedfordshire	111	(288)	1996
62=	Glams,East	111	(300)	1993
62=	Gwent	111	(290)	1991
62=	Warwicks	111	(297)	1993
66	Glams,West	110	(290)	1991
67	Leics	109	(308)	1998
68=	Central	108	(248)	1996
68=	Herts	108	(299)	1989
70	Ceredigion	107	(291)	1986
71=	Merseyside	105	(?)	1993
71=	Western Isles	105	(341)	1985
73	Avon	104	(320)	1993
74	Shropshire	103	(263)	1989
75	Cornwall, Scilly	102	(407)	2000
76	Radnorshire	97	(235)	1988
77	Guernsey	96	(306)	1992
78	Breconshire	95	(256)	1991
79	West Mid	92	(265)	1995
80	Hereford	90	(259)	1994

The following do not have a one-day tally but are listed for their County total. Alderney(267), Argyll (320), Clyde (287), Fife, Isle of May (273), Highland, Sutherland (268), Isle of Man (287), Jersey (303), Orkney (364), Shetland, Fair Isle (359).

INDEX TO BIRD RESERVES AND OBSERVATORIES

INDEX TO RESERVES

INDEX TO RESERVES